D1490209

WRITING PROSE

WRITING PROSE

TECHNIQUES AND PURPOSES

THIRD CANADIAN EDITION

THOMAS S. KANE • LEONARD J. PETERS • **MAURICE R. LEGRIS**

OXFORD
UNIVERSITY PRESS

OXFORD
UNIVERSITY PRESS

70 Wynford Drive, Don Mills, Ontario M3C 1J9
www.oup.com/ca

Oxford University Press is a department of the University of Oxford.
It furthers the University's objective of excellence in research, scholarship,
and education by publishing worldwide in

Oxford New York
Auckland Bangkok Buenos Aires Cape Town Chennai
Dar es Salaam Delhi Hong Kong Istanbul Karachi Kolkata
Kuala Lumpur Madrid Melbourne Mexico City Mumbai Nairobi
São Paulo Shanghai Taipei Tokyo Toronto

Oxford is a trade mark of Oxford University Press
in the UK and in certain other countries

Published in Canada
by Oxford University Press

Copyright © Oxford University Press Canada 2003

The moral rights of the author have been asserted

Database right Oxford University Press (maker)

First published 2003

All rights reserved. No part of this publication may be reproduced,
stored in a retrieval system, or transmitted, in any form or by any means,
without the prior permission in writing of Oxford University Press,
or as expressly permitted by law, or under terms agreed with the appropriate
reprographics rights organization. Enquiries concerning reproduction
outside the scope of the above should be sent to the Rights Department,
Oxford University Press, at the address above.

You must not circulate this book in any other binding or cover
and you must impose this same condition on any acquirer.

Since this page cannot accommodate all the copyright notices, pages 461–4
constitute an extension of the copyright page.

National Library of Canada Cataloguing in Publication Data

Writing prose : techniques and purposes / [edited by] Thomas S. Kane,
Leonard J. Peters, Maurice R. Legris.—3rd Canadian ed.

Includes index.
ISBN 0–19–541287–7

1. College readers.   2. English language—Rhetoric.
I. Kane, Thomas S.   II. Peters, Leonard J.   III. Legris, Maurice

PE1417.W74 2003   808'.0427   C2003–900045–1

Cover and text design: Brett Miller

1 2 3 4 – 05 04 03 02

This book is printed on permanent (acid-free) paper ∞.

Printed in Canada

CONTENTS

Easy writing's vile hard reading.

—Richard Sheridan

PREFACE

Writing Prose: Technique and Purposes was first published in 1959. Its editors, Thomas S. Kane and Leonard J. Peters, published the sixth edition of this extremely popular text in 1986. The first two Canadian editions appeared in 1981 and 1987. The present volume, although it continues to use the critical apparatus pioneered by Kane and Peters and uses a few of the essays they had published, is largely new.

In spite of the significant changes in the contents of the book, its aim and structure remain essentially the same as those of previous editions. Students will closely analyze examples of good prose by both famous writers and others who are relatively unknown. They will first consider the writer's purpose, insofar as it can be determined, and the sort of reader to whom the essay is addressed. They will then look carefully at the organization of the essay with regard to both its structural principles and, more specifically, to such matters as the use of topic sentences, transitions, organizing and concluding sentences, irony, signposts, rhetorical questions, and so on. From there students will go on to analyze individual sentences—types of sentences, length and structure, punctuation, and logic. Finally, they will look closely at specific words: at definitions, etymologies, figures of speech, connotations, allusions, etc.

Having dealt with these elements of analysis, which are found in the critical apparatus accompanying each essay, students will find three final sections: a brief list of specific points to be learned from the study of the essay; some suggestions for writing assignments which are closely related to the analysis just finished; and some directions about specific points students are to include in the compositions they will write—points also related to the essay they have just analyzed. As Professors Kane and Peters remarked in the preface to their first edition, asking students to imitate good writers 'does not mean a sterile conformity. But it does mean that any writer, if he is to be successful, must learn to use and to adapt to his own purposes the tools of others. It means that each writer must study the work of others if he is to learn to use the vast resources of the English language.'

Since the intent of this book is to acquaint students with the various techniques of good prose, our primary criterion for selecting the works to be included has been high quality. Readers will notice, however, that there is a considerable diversity among the selections. Some are undoubtedly classics, such as Swift's 'A Modest Proposal' and Thoreau's *Walden*, which have been universally admired by generations of readers. Others are occasionally affected by weaknesses of one kind or another. This is merely to say, of course, that not all the writers included here are of the same genius as a Swift or a Thoreau. Yet they are all worth reading and studying, and students will find that they can profit greatly from all of them.

The selections in this text range in length from short paragraphs (especially in the section devoted to exposition) to complete, full-length essays. Instructors may wish to begin with the shorter selections and have their students write only a paragraph or two before going on to read, and write, at greater length. The traditional categories have been used—exposition, argument, description, and narration—to which have been added two further categories: definition and writing about writing. The section on exposition has been further divided into illustration, restatement, comparison, analogy, reasons, effects, and analysis. There is also a section on persuasion, as distinct from argument, on the grounds that the aims of these two kinds of writing are often widely disparate. It is made clear that the various categories often intermingle, with, for instance, exposition often involving description and narration, and persuasion including exposition.

Instructors may, of course, take up the selections in this text in any order they wish. They may also find that some of the questions following each selection are not appropriate for their classes, and may wish to substitute their own. It should be noted that, since technical terms have frequently been used in the questions, these have been briefly explained in a glossary at the end of the book. These terms are printed in **bold** type the first time they are used in each set of questions. Because each selection and its questions are self-contained, some of the questions will prove repetitious; since we have assumed, however, that no class will read every selection, the repetition of some key points is justifiable.

However instructors wish to use this book—whether they change the order of the selections, or add or substitute questions of their own, or modify the suggestions for writing, or even have their students question the questions—they are urged, above all, to encourage their students to read more widely in the authors represented here and in many others. Instructors must, in short, constantly remind their students that the study of good writing is indispensable to the practice of good writing.

This third Canadian edition of *Writing Prose* has been thoroughly revised and updated. Of the eighty-five essays now included fifty-four are new, all but one of them complete essays. The introductions for each section have been revised, as has the critical apparatus for most of the essays retained from the previous edition. The biographical headnotes have been updated where necessary, the glossary has been rewritten and considerably enlarged, and a thematic index has been added. An author–title index is also included.

Many debts have been incurred in the preparation of this book. I am grateful to those who used either of the first two editions in their classes and made fine suggestions for the improvement of the latest edition, especially Professors Jane Flick, of the University of British Columbia, and Lahoucine Ouzgane, of the University of Alberta, as well as the anonymous reviewers of an early version of the manuscript of this edition. Sandra Bell, of the National Library of Canada, and Lorna Knight, chief of the Canadian Literature Research Service, Ottawa, helped provide information for the biographical headnotes, as did Jesse Bundon, of Oxford University Press. Several graduate research assistants in the Department of English at the University of Alberta helped me with the library footwork—Neil Scotten, Leslie Robertson, Lisa Ward, and Alison Coleman—and my son, André Legris, provided valuable computer help. Professor David Jackel and I collaborated on the first two Canadian editions of this book; ill health kept him from working on this one, although his hand is still prominent at a number of places.

Several people at Oxford University Press deserve my thanks, among them Richard Teleky, who skilfully saw the first two editions of this book through the press when he was still at Oxford, and Len Husband and Euan White, who helped in the early stages of this edition. Jane Tilley and Laura Macleod were especially helpful with their suggestions and constant encouragement. To Eric Sinkins I owe my heartfelt thanks: he went through the manuscript with extraordinary care and precision, making all kinds of corrections and suggestions, always with tact and kindness. The book is by far the better for his critical eye. Any problems or deficiencies which remain are, of course, my responsibility.

Maurice Legris

A Note to the Student

Unfortunately there is no quick and easy way of learning to write. Good writing is hard work, but when you bring it off—when you really succeed in saying what you set out to say—it is among the most rewarding of all activities. One way to acquire skill in composition is to look closely at what good writers do and to ask yourself questions about it. In this text we do just that—offer you examples of well-written prose and ask for questions which we hope will lead you to discover some of its techniques and strategies.

We have tried to make the questions specific and clear and self-contained. As much as possible we have avoided technicalities of grammar and rhetoric. Occasionally, of course, it is necessary to use a word from those disciplines—'appositive' or 'metaphor', for example. The first time such a term appears in any set of questions it is set in bold to indicate that it is briefly defined in the Glossary beginning on page 465. Generally, however, the questions will require only that you study the selection and think about it. What you learn should apply to your own compositions, following the directions which are given after each selection for a writing assignment. That, finally, is the whole point: not simply to understand what another writer has done, but to do so yourself.

T.S.K. / L.J.P.

EXPOSITION

Different kinds of writing achieve different purposes. We traditionally divide all prose into four kinds, according to its controlling purpose: *narration, description, exposition,* and *persuasion* (to which *argument* is closely related). Of these, exposition is especially important to the university student, since much of what she reads, and most of what she writes, is expository prose. The key point is that exposition is writing that explains. In general, it answers the questions *how?* and *why?* Most of the books on the shelves of any university library are examples of exposition: histories, literary essays, theories of economics, studies of government and law, the findings of sociology, the investigations of science—the purpose of all of these, however different, is to explain. Although exposition is often formal and academic, it also appears in magazines and newspapers—in any place where people look for explanations. It is the most common kind of writing, the sort with which we conduct our workaday affairs—the business letter, the doctor's case study, the lawyer's brief, the engineer's report—and the writing with which we attempt to control our world, whether our means of doing so is a complicated system of philosophy, a cook book, or a computer manual.

What, then, is not exposition? If the guiding purpose of the writer is to tell a story, to tell merely what happened, then we say the writing is *narration* rather than exposition. If the writer intends to tell us how something looks, to re-create a thing in words, we call it *description.* If the writer's intention is to convince us about something, she has used *persuasion* (by appealing to our senses) or *argument* (by appealing mainly to our reason). A narrative arranges its material in time; description most often organizes in space. We might think of narration as a stage play or motion picture in words, and of description as a verbal photograph or painting. Exposition, on the other hand, organizes its subject not in time or space but by logic. Whether she is writing about people, things, ideas, or some combination of these, the expository writer is a person thinking, interpreting, informing, and persuading. Although she may appeal to our emotions, she is more likely to appeal to our reason by using evidence and logic—although exposition is distinct from argument and persuasion because of its objective, which is to explain. In other words, exposition is less like a stage play or painting and more like a lecture, explanation, or discussion.

Seldom is any piece of writing pure exposition. Just as the lecturer tells a story or uses maps, charts, or slides to interest the audience and clinch a point, so the expository writer may turn for aid to narration or description. Often these kinds of writing become so fused as to be practically indistinguishable: a description of the structure of an atom is as much an explanation as it is a picture; the historical narrative is as much concerned with the *why* and *how* as with what actually happened. Even so, the traditional classification of prose into description, narration, exposition, and persuasion is useful as long as we are aware of its limitations. The expository writer should always remember that the primary purpose of exposition is to explain by logic and to show relationships.

The writing of exposition begins, therefore, in an understanding of the broad purpose to be achieved, which will guide and shape the writer's organization. Like all composition, it begins in the writer's head. Even before she sharpens her pencil or turns on her computer, the expository writer must ask herself four questions:

- What specific point do I intend to make?
- Is my point worth making?
- For whom am I writing?
- How can I best convey my point to my readers?

Unless the writer has carefully answered each of these questions, no amount of good grammar and correct spelling will save her, and her composition will be worthless. Determining the reader and the purpose is easily half the task of writing. Once the writer has decided what point she intends to make, her composition is already half organized, if not completely planned. The writer has already saved herself time by eliminating several false starts, and she has successfully resisted the temptation to lose herself and her reader in the thickets and bypaths of her subject. With her reader in mind she has already solved many of her problems of diction and tone as well, and, however awkwardly she has expressed herself when she has finished, she will know that she has fulfilled the first requirement of all writing—a definite point for a definite reader.

On paper, the writing of exposition begins with paragraphs. Within each paragraph the writer shapes and develops a single idea. Every expository writer therefore must understand the nature and construction of paragraphs. To begin our definition we may say that paragraphs are like humans: each is an individual, unlike any other; yet, as all humans are alike in having a head, eyes, two arms, and two legs, all paragraphs are alike in sharing, so to speak, the same anatomy. Learning to write good paragraphs must begin with an understanding of the pattern common to all. Paragraphs of exposition contain two different kinds of statements. The first—a general, rather abstract statement—is called the *topic sentence*. Here, the writer says, 'This is what I assert or believe in a general way; this is my opinion, my evaluation or conclusion about the subject of this paragraph.' For instance, Wayne Johnston, writing about the problems that Hollywood filmmakers had while trying to make a movie in Newfoundland, begins his opening paragraph on page 31 with this topic sentence: 'Word that movie versions of *The Shipping News* and *The Bird Artist* are to be filmed in the province makes one wonder if Hollywood producers have forgotten what happened the last time they discovered Newfoundland.' Sometimes the topic idea of a paragraph is so clear that it is only implied. In this case, the writer feels she will not lose her reader if she fails to state her topic idea in so many words. A second class of statements in every paragraph consists of *particular* facts, examples, illustrations, and supporting details that say, in effect, 'This is the evidence that leads me to believe or conclude what I do. You may not agree with what I say, but at least you understand now why I believe or conclude it.'

Most often the topic sentence stands first in the paragraph, unless one or two sentences of transition go before. Less frequently, the topic sentence appears at the end, in a paragraph that is developed from particular to general—a pattern useful both for variation and, building as it does to a climax, for emphasis. Sometimes, for the sake of clarity or emphasis, the writer may restate her topic idea in a second or third sentence and again in the final sentence of a paragraph. With or without restatement the expository writer usually moves from topic sentence to supporting details, from general to particular.

The particulars of exposition are patterns of logic and evidence, patterns that may shape individual paragraphs, a group of several paragraphs, or the composition in its entirety. Thus, in his opening two paragraphs on page 7, Wayne Grady tells an anecdote, followed, in the next paragraph, by a generalization. The rest of his essay shows how the problem summed up in the anecdote is related to the generalization. Again, the expository writer may throw new light upon two things by comparing and contrasting them, showing how they are alike and yet different, as J.A. Davidson does in his essay when he compares Canadian pronunciation with that of Americans. Or the writer may employ the logical pattern of cause and effect. Joan Didion's 'Los Angeles Notebook' (pp. 113–15) is organized by discussing the effects of the Santa Ana wind on human behaviour. In short, the expository writer uses common methods of logic and thinking: she uses *illustration* to develop her material by means of examples, statistics, data, facts, specific details, and other particulars; she uses *restatement* to build paragraphs by the simple device of repeating the topic idea; she uses *comparison* to examine two or more things in order to note their similarities and differences, often by means of contrast; she uses *analogy* to compare two unlike things in order to show that what is true of one may also be true of the other; she examines *reasons* to give the basis or cause for some event, fact, action, or belief; she traces *effects* to show how causes have results or consequences; and she uses *analysis* to explain the parts that make up something and how they relate, discerning subtle patterns, revealing causes and effects. The selections that follow illustrate these common types of expository development. Every student of composition should learn to use them.

BARBARA W. TUCHMAN

The distinguished American historian Barbara W. Tuchman (1912–89) twice won the Pulitzer Prize—for *The Guns of August* (1962), an account of the onset and early phases of World War I, and for *Stilwell and the American Experience in China* (1971), an analysis of the World War II experiences of the American general aptly named 'Vinegar Joe'. *The Zimmermann Telegram* (1962) and *The Proud Tower* (1966) are, respectively, an account of the causes of World War I and an account of the cultural and intellectual history in the period before that war. Tuchman's other books include *A Distant Mirror: The Calamitous 14th Century* (1978) and *Practicing History* (1982), a collection of essays.

This paragraph is taken from one of a collection of essays by various authors on the problems of contemporary higher education. Tuchman's thesis is that educators must do more to promote the values they profess to believe in and not be afraid of exercising discipline to maintain those values. The paragraph suggests that young people welcome a wise and responsible authority. It is a good instance of how to develop a topic by an illustration.

Patterns

It is human nature to want patterns and standards and a structure of behaviour. A pattern to conform to is a kind of shelter. You see it in kindergarten and primary school, at least in those schools where the children when leaving the classroom are required to fall into line. When the teacher gives the signal, they fall in with alacrity; they know where they belong and they instinctively like to *be* where they belong. 5 They like the feeling of being in line.

1967

ROGER REVELLE

Roger Revelle (1909–91) was an educator and scientist. He directed the Scripps Institute of Oceanography and taught science and public policy at the University of California at San Diego. He also founded and directed the Center for Population Studies at Harvard University and wrote extensively about pollution and population control. Among the books he co-edited are *America's Changing Environment* (1970), *The Survival Equation: Man, Resources, and His Environment* (1971), and *Population and Social Change* (1972). The selection below is taken from the essay 'Pollution and Cities', one of a collection of articles by various scholars dealing with the problems faced by modern cities. In his essay Revelle surveys the various environmental dangers threatening cities and suggests possible solutions. Like the preceding paragraph by Barbara Tuchman, this one demonstrates how to use illustrations effectively.

Our Deteriorating Environment

In many ways, the quality of our environment has deteriorated with each new advance of the gross national product. Increases in electric power production mean the burning of more coal and fuel oil, and hence the discharge of more sulphur dioxide into the air. The growth of the paper industry has brought a vast increase in trash. The production of new automobiles and the discard of old ones has resulted in 5 unsightly piles of hulks. The growth of urban automobile transportation is choking both the mobility of the city and the lungs of city dwellers.

1967

QUESTIONS
Reader and Purpose
1. Even if you knew nothing about Tuchman's larger purpose you might guess that she approves of a more patterned, disciplined mode of life than many people live today. What details in her paragraph suggest this?
2. Is Revelle trying to convince us of the truth of his assertion to the same degree that Tuchman is? If not, what is his purpose? Is this purpose still relevant today, more than thirty years after he wrote?
3. Beyond their larger aims, each writer has the immediate purpose of supporting a topic by examples, one of the easiest and most effective ways of generating an expository paragraph. Sometimes a paragraph is developed from only a single example; sometimes from several. Which of these selections uses only one illustration? Which more than one?
4. Illustrations should be pertinent and specific—genuine and particular instances of the assertion stated in the topic sentence. Being specific often means translating an **abstract** and general idea into an image, that is, something that we can see or hear (or grasp with any of our other senses). In Tuchman's paragraph the **abstraction** is 'patterns and standards and a structure of behaviour'. What is the illustration? In what sense is it an **image**? Why is it especially pertinent to the writer's point?

Organization
5. Identify the **topic sentence** in each paragraph. At what point in the paragraph is it placed?
6. A good topic statement is clear and succinct. Often, too, its key term comes at the end. ('Key term' here means the word or phrase expressing what the rest of the paragraph will be chiefly concerned with.) In light of these characteristics, are the topic sentences of these two paragraphs well or poorly written?
7. A paragraph should have unity: its sentences should hang together. Do you notice anything about sentences 2–5 of Revelle's paragraph that makes them hang together? The final two sentences of Tuchman's paragraph contain four **main clauses**. How are they unified?

Sentences

8. In prose that reads well sentences are similar enough to sound unified, yet varied enough not to bore the reader. One way of achieving such a style is to vary a basic sentence pattern. For example, each of the five sentences in Revelle's paragraph is **simple**, containing one subject–verb link. Study the final three sentences of Revelle's selection. How has he made slight changes in the simple pattern of subject-verb-object to prevent monotony?

9. Do the final two sentences of Tuchman's paragraph show a similar variation of a basic pattern?

Diction

10. Look up: (in Tuchman) *conform* (2), *alacrity* (4), *instinctively* (5); (in Revelle) *environment* (1), *deteriorated* (1), *hence* (3), *sulphur dioxide* (4–5).

11. Explain the meanings of these phrases as fully as you can: (in Tuchman) *a structure of behaviour* (1); (in Revelle) *the gross national product* (2), *in unsightly piles of hulks* (5–6), *the mobility of the city* (6).

12. **Tone** means roughly the sense of a distinct personality that a writer conveys in her writing. It reflects a writer's attitudes towards her subject, her readers, and herself; and we sense it in sentence structure and especially in diction. One important aspect of tone is the degree of formality or informality used by the writer to address the reader: whether the writer appears to be lecturing an audience, keeping a distance between them and herself; or whether she seems more relaxed, as if she were talking to friends. How would Tuchman's tone be affected if we substituted 'variety' for 'kind' and 'one' for 'you' in line 2?

13. Why would these changes be less effective? (in Tuchman): an unitalicized *be* (5); (in Revelle): 'ugly junk heaps' for 'unsightly piles of hulks' (6), 'decreasing' for 'choking' (6), 'breathing' for 'lungs' (7).

POINTS TO LEARN

1. Good illustrations are pertinent and detailed. They support a generalization with a specific case, an **abstraction** with a **concrete** example.

2. A memorable sentence style has variety within similarity.

3. Read out loud what you write. Listen. Write to please your ears.

SUGGESTIONS FOR WRITING

Use one of the following assertions as a topic sentence and support it by illustration in a paragraph of five or six sentences (about 120 words). You may develop only a single example or several, but in either case be sure your examples are specific and to the point.

Young people do not want 'patterns and standards and a structure of behaviour'; they do not like the 'feeling of being in line'.

Some of my classmates are weird.

Some teachers have very little sense of what students really think.

Life in a big city is exciting and full of surprises.

Efficient and inexpensive garbage collection makes North American homeowners less inclined to 'Reduce, Reuse, and Recycle'.

IMPROVING YOUR STYLE

1. Somewhere in your paragraph, compose three or four consecutive simple sentences with enough variation in each to keep them from sounding monotonous. As a way of testing the result, read your paragraph out loud. If the sentences seem too much alike, vary their structure a little until they do not.
2. After you have finished the paragraph rewrite it twice, altering the diction where possible to make it sound (1) less formal and (2) more formal than your original version.

WAYNE GRADY

Canadian writer Wayne Grady (1948–) has done important work as an editor and critic of Canadian short fiction and is a respected reviewer of a wide variety of books. He has been the managing editor of both *Harrowsmith* and *Books in Canada*, and has twice won a Governor General's Award for his translations of Québécois literature into English. He has edited the well-known *Penguin Book of Short Stories* (1980), the *Penguin Book of Modern Canadian Short Stories* (1982), *Intimate Strangers: New Stories from Quebec* (1986), and *Treasures of the Place: Three Centuries of Nature Writing in Canada* (1992). Among his many other books are *Toronto the Wild: Field Notes of an Urban Naturalist* (1995); *The Quebec Anthology, 1830–1990*, which he co-edited with Matt Cohen (1996); *Chasing the Chinook: On the Trail of Canadian Words and Culture* (1998); and *The Bone Museum: Travels in the Lost Worlds of Dinosaurs and Birds* (2000).

The Haunting Powers of God's Dog

1   With my finger I smear a small dab of crunchy peanut butter on the release mechanism, then pry back the spring-loaded snap bar and set the pin into the cog. Then I place the loaded trap on the floor, tight against the cabin wall. We've been having mouse problems in the cabin. A whole colony of them seems to have moved in for the winter. Every night we hear them scrabbling at the log walls and clicking 5 across the sink, and every morning there are mouse turds on the drainboard; claw and tooth marks in the soap. This morning I'd noticed, just after brushing my teeth, that the entire bristled end of my toothbrush was crosshatched with tiny incisor marks.

2   When I check my trap the next morning, it is upside down and a pair of tiny white feet are sticking out from under it. I pick it up and turn it over, noting the 10 creamy brown fur on the upper body, the delicate, almost human feet with long, thin toes and wrinkled palms like those of a newborn baby. The mouse's black eyes define beadiness—they *are* beads, like the shiny heads of tailor's pins, staring at nothing with astonished concentration. White-footed mouse, *Peromyscus leucopus*. I carry it outside by the tail and toss it into the trees. It bounces on the frozen grass as though it has no 15 weight at all.

—

3   We are all victims of our own mythologies. In all the stories we tell about ourselves, human beings are the losers. I have been struck by this during the year I've spent doing research on the coyote and its place in North America. We all know coyotes kill sheep—just as rodents carry plague, and wolves attack people. There is enough truth   20
in each of the stories to make us believe the lies. Some coyotes kill sheep, yes, and some people rob banks.

4   A friend of mine tells me about Scott Gilmore, a sheep farmer just outside Tamworth, in eastern Ontario, who says that so far this year, he's lost 45 sheep to coyotes. He has only 60 ewes left, and he says he's getting out of farming. 'Coyotes done   25
me in,' he told my friend. When I call him, he sounds robust, even cheerful.

5   'Did you really lose 45 sheep?' I ask him.

6   'Yes, I did,' he booms. 'Lambs and ewes. Actually, it's 55 now. Nobody seems to want to do anything about it, either. All those do-gooders out there trying to save coyotes, and here I am, feedin' 'em.' He laughs. He doesn't sound like someone who is   30
getting out of farming. 'Are you?' I ask.

7   'Hell, no! I'm 75 years old. What else would I do?'

8   I tell him I'd like to come out to talk to him. 'Good enough,' he says.

—

9   Where do truth and myth collide? When did they part company? In 1861,   35
Mark Twain, travelling west, saw his first coyote from the window of a train. He didn't like what he saw. 'The coyote', he wrote in *Roughing It*, 'is a long, slim, sick and sorry-looking skeleton with a grey wolf skin stretched over it, a tolerably bushy tail that forever sags down with a despairing expression of forsakenness and misery, a furtive and evil eye, and a long, sharp face with slightly lifted lip and exposed teeth. He has a general slinking expression all over. The coyote is a living, breathing allegory of Want.'   40

10   *Roughing It* was published in 1872, the same year Yellowstone National Park was established in Wyoming 'for the pleasure and enjoyment of the people'. Park officials, under the impression that pleasure and enjoyment were a matter of pastoral views of elk, immediately set about ridding the park of wolves and coyotes. Biologist Adolph Murie noted sourly in 1940 that coyote and wolf eradication began as soon   45
as hunting became so wanton as to imperil the existence of game animals. By the time Murie's book appeared, every wolf and thousands of coyotes had been trapped or poisoned, and as a result, the elk herd had declined until it was, in Murie's words, 'hovering on the brink of disaster'.

11   One day last summer, as I was hiking along a trail in Yellowstone, I sat down   50
to eat my lunch on a ridge overlooking a wide valley. My foot jangled something metallic, a length of chain that ran into a crevice between two rocks. Using a stick, I dug out a pair of rusted leg-hold traps, the kind that, until 1935, government agents used to capture coyotes. I stepped on the spring bar and opened the jaws of one of the traps, and the release pin held. I poked a stick into it, and the jaws snapped shut   55
and broke off the end of the stick. There was a large 'V' in the middle of the foot pad and, around it, the words 'Victor, Made in the USA'. I meant to turn the traps in at the ranger station in Mammoth, but I never got around to it. Now they sit on my desk,

reminders of how the mechanism of myths can linger on long after the truth that set
them in motion has died.   60

—

12   I check my mousetraps every morning—I put out two of them now—and every
morning I have two more mice, each looking eerily unharmed except for a deep crease
across the back of the neck where the snap bar is buried. The head juts up at a natural angle, and the staring eyes and the small open mouth look as though the mouse
has been caught in mid-sentence. One morning, though, one of the mice is creased 65
across the middle of its back. It must have been licking a smear of peanut butter near
the top of the trap's wooden base and inadvertently stepped on the trigger. It is no less
dead than the other mouse, but the trap is several centimetres from where I set it the
night before. I wonder whether the mouse struggled before it died or if its spinal cord
continued to send contract-and-expand signals to its legs for a while after death. As I 70
remove the body, something familiar in the design of the words stamped in red ink
on the wood catches my attention. They are arranged around a large 'V' and say
'Victor. Woodstream Corp., Lititz, Pa., USA'.

—

13   Gordon Hewitt was Canada's consulting zoologist at the end of the past century,
a century that had seen the disappearance of the bison, the grey wolf, the mountain 75
lion, the bald eagle, the osprey, and the grizzly from most of their former ranges and
of the passenger pigeon and the great auk from the face of the earth. Hewitt wrote the
revision to the Northwest Game Act in 1917 and published a book in 1921 called *The
Conservation of the Wild Life of Canada*. The chapter 'The Value of Wild Life to the
Nation' begins ominously enough from the point of view of, say, deer: 'One of the 80
most serious problems of the present day is the gradually increasing cost of food, particularly meat.'
14   Wildlife for Hewitt meant 'game animals'—ungulates, for the most part—
although he also included swans, polar bears, barren-ground grizzlies, and the rare
white kermode bear. His purpose was to show that 'wild life' could be economically 85
useful to the Dominion: he proposed schemes for the domestication of bison, caribou,
and muskox and wrote about 'the decorative value of our wild life'.
15   Wolves, cougars, and coyotes had a chapter all to themselves: it was called 'The
Enemies of Wild Life'. 'Any rational system of wild-life protection', it began, 'must
take into account the control of the predatory species of mammals and birds.' In most 90
Canadian provinces, predator control was accomplished by means of a bounty system: local authorities were required to pay $1 to anyone who brought in a coyote
'scalp'—both ears joined by an isthmus of skin. Between 1907 and 1917 in
Saskatchewan alone, this system accounted for the slaughter of 204,424 coyotes, for
which municipalities paid $232,000 in bounties. Oddly enough, in Hewitt's view, the 95
huge number of dead coyotes was proof the bounty system wasn't working. To him,
so many coyotes trapped meant that there were too many coyotes out there.
16   Hewitt wanted to replace bounties with something like the American system.
He would divide the entire country west of Ontario into districts and put an inspector
in each district to supervise a squad of full-time, salaried agents whose sole job it 100

would be to hunt coyotes. The beauty of this system, Hewitt wrote, was that the agents would have to turn their pelts over to the Crown, and coyote pelts at the time were worth $10 to $15 on the fur market. If all the coyotes killed in Saskatchewan had been taken by federal employees and sold at the annual Hudson's Bay Company fur auction, the government would have made $3 million instead of spending 105 $232,000 on bounties.

17   Fortunately for everyone, coyotes included, Hewitt's scheme went nowhere. Bounties continued and increased for the next 50 years. They were officially banned in Ontario in 1972, but at least three counties—Grey, Bruce, and Simcoe, the three primary sheep-farming regions—still pay hunters to kill coyotes. One Simcoe County 110 hunter created a sensation in 1992 when he drove into Barrie with his entire winter kill of 50 coyotes in the back of his pickup truck, parked in front of City Hall, and went in to claim his bounty. Actually, they don't call it a bounty anymore, because bounties are illegal. They call it 'reimbursement for control of predators'. As one Ministry of Natural Resources biologist told me, 'I guess that's sort of like paying 115 someone to hunt for you, which is also illegal in Ontario. But it's a big province.'

—

18   The Navajo word for coyote means 'God's dog', the ancient palindrome. When the Navajo hunted a coyote that had been preying on their sheep, they did so with great ceremony. As they trailed the coyote across the desert, they sprinkled its tracks with corn pollen, their symbol of long life and health. When they found the coyote, 120 they apologized for having to kill it and then did so with as little violence as they could manage. Then they buried it, placing a small turquoise bead in each nostril to aid the return of God's dog to its master.

19   In Native myth, the world is an imperfect place, and Coyote the Trickster was sent 'to make things right'. He accomplishes this in a bumbly sort of way. He peoples 125 the earth, gives names to the animals, places some clans here and others there, creates hills where there had been only water, islands where there once were turtles. He brings fire down from the mountains. But then things begin to go wrong. Coyote is greedy and curious. He steals tobacco from Crow. He steals Chickadee's magic arrows and then loses them. He stretches his penis across a river so that he can have inter- 130 course with the Mallard Duck girl. He is indeed an allegory of Want. He is nature incarnate. To the Navajo, there is no separation between truth and myth. To the Navajo, all history is natural history.

20   For example, the Navajo word for mouse, *na'atoosi*, means 'the one that sucks on things', and traditional teaching warns against contact with mice. They must be 135 kept out of houses and away from food, and clothing touched by a mouse must be burned. According to Ben Muneta, a Navajo doctor in New Mexico, mice were thought to be the bearers of disease, which is spread through their droppings and saliva. In a closed room, Navajo legend says, the power of the mouse would take over and destroy you if it got in your eyes or nose or mouth.   140

21   I am reading this in a magazine article about a new illness called Four Corners disease that was first diagnosed in a Navajo community in the American Southwest in 1993. The disease, which killed 25 people in two months, is caused by a previ-ously unknown species of hantavirus. It takes the form of haemorrhagic fever—first

you feel as if you're getting the flu, then your lungs fill up with blood, then you die. 145
There are 200 known species of hantaviruses, all carried by rodents. The rodent
carrying the Four Corners virus was the deer mouse—*Peromyscus maniculatus*. There
had been a population explosion of deer mice in the past year, partly, the article
points out, because a wet summer had produced bumper crops of seeds and berries.
But I also knew there had been a massive coyote-eradication program throughout the 150
Southwest. In 1992, government agents there had killed nearly 100,000 coyotes, and
100,000 coyotes could have eaten one hell of a lot of deer mice.

22   A few hours after reading the article, sitting in the cabin, I begin to feel the flu
coming on. My head aches, there is a pinched feeling in my sinuses, and when I stand
up, I feel dizzy. I remember my toothbrush, which must have been coated with mouse 155
saliva, and the dried mouse droppings in the cupboard. My forehead feels hot. Pulling
on my coat, I stumble outside to fill my lungs with fresh air, and after a while, my
pulse rate goes back down and I feel better.

23   I also feel foolish. But this night, when I set my two traps against the cabin wall,
I wear gloves.   160

---

24   We are accustomed to thinking of myths as lies. That allowing coyotes to run
with deer herds will improve the health of the herd, we say, is a myth, by which we
mean it is not true. At the same time, we know that myths are the foundation stories
of our culture. They are the basis of our beliefs. That humans have dominion over the
creatures of the earth is, we believe, true. What happens to a society when it knows 165
that everything it believes to be true is based on a lie?

25   We declare war on ourselves. In the legends of the Navajo and the Okanagan
and the Blackfoot and the Nez Percé, when Coyote is killed, he is always brought back
to life. In our world, coyotes also keep coming back. Although millions of coyotes
have been killed by ranchers, sheep farmers, and federal agents over the past century 70
and a half, there are more of them now than ever. Their range, once confined to the
flat, arid grasslands of the Great Plains, now extends south to the Panama Canal,
north to Alaska, west to Vancouver, and east to Nova Scotia. When coyotes become
victims of our myths, they just go over the hill and have more coyotes.

26   When we become victims, even of our own mythologies, we seek our own 175
forms of revenge. After World War I, we threw cyanide canisters into coyote dens, as
if the dens were bunkers. We've run them down with snowmobiles until their hearts
burst. We've sawed off their lower jaws and then let them go so that they would starve
to death. We've wrapped them in burlap bags soaked in gasoline, set torches to them,
and turned them loose in the desert. After World War II, we used new poisons. 180
Compound 1080, which works on the central nervous system, causes its victims to
age and die within a few hours. Coyotes have been found lying on their sides, slaver-
ing, their legs running at full gallop.

27   One story I heard has the quality of myth. A sheep rancher in Arizona caught
a coyote, tied a stick of dynamite to its side, lit the dynamite, and let the coyote run 185
off into the desert, hoping it would enter its den and blow up its own pups. Instead,
Coyote ran straight under the rancher's brand-new pickup truck.

---

28   At Scott Gilmore's farm, the side road veers sharply to the right. There is a small garage near the road, then a short lane to the white frame house, and beyond that, the barns. In the yard beside the house, a black and white Border collie is gnawing busily   190 on something and doesn't look up when I pass. The whole yard is strewn with bones, fresh sheep bones, some with flesh attached. Two of the skulls still have teeth in them and something in the eye sockets I don't want to look at. Two glistening spinal columns lie in an explosion of white wool and blood, as though someone has just broken open a David Cronenberg pillow.   195

29   'The dog drags them up here,' Gilmore says. He is standing in the doorway behind a screen door. 'Yesterday, she came back with a deer femur, don't know where the hell she got that.' He opens the door and steps out onto the porch, a big man: big hands, big face, big neck, barrel chest, and cavernous voice. He doesn't look anywhere near 75.

30   We go through the door into the dining room, a small wallpapered room nearly   200 taken up by a huge pedestalled table and six chairs. He starts talking about coyotes, except he doesn't call them coyotes, he calls them wolves. One of the myths coyotes suffer from is that they are really small wolves. Brush wolves. They aren't. They have their own DNA. They are older than wolves.

31   'Three years ago,' he says, 'I began losing lambs to wolves early in the spring, and   205 I tried to get the township to do something about it. I asked that they arrange to send a Natural Resources trapper in before the real damage started. Well, two months went by, and I lost eight more lambs, so I contacted the local MPP, that was on a Thursday afternoon, and he immediately called the Natural Resources offices in Tweed, and on Friday morning, the township clerk called me to tell me the trapper would be here the   210 following Tuesday. That trapper came and got 22 wolves off my land.'

32   'How do you mean, "got"?' I ask him.

33   'Trapped,' says Gilmore. 'Killed. And I never lost another lamb after that. So this year when it started up again, I just wrote straight to the Minister of Natural Resources. That was in June, and a letter came from his office saying he'd get back to   215 me at his earliest convenience. It hasn't come yet, and I've lost 55 sheep that I know of and probably more that I don't know of.'

34   'What about compensation?' I ask. 'Have you applied for that?'

35   'Oh, I put my application in to the township,' he says. 'I've been paid for maybe 32 lambs out of the 55 I've lost—the ones the wolves pick up and carry away, you've   220 got no evidence, you see—so it leaves me without much income from my sheep. I've slaughtered only 12 lambs this year. But the $3,000 the township's paid me in compensation, well, they could've trapped out every wolf in the township for that.'

36   'Have you tried trapping them out yourself?' I ask.

37   'Well, it seems to me that that's not my job, is it. There was a fella from Napanee   125 came out one day, asked me if he could set some traps. I said go ahead. He set out four or five traps, came back the next day, and he'd caught my dog and one of the neighbour's cats. You have to know what you're doing to catch a wolf.'

38   The dog is still in the yard when I leave, still gnawing on what is left of two or three sheep. I'm trying to separate the truth from the myths in what Gilmore has   230 told me. I stop, meaning to ask him what it's like to be a sheep farmer with a dog that has developed such an obvious taste for mutton, but when I turn around, the door is closed.

39   It's dark when I get back to the cabin. There are no mice in the traps because this morning I decided not to set them. It wasn't a huge decision; I'd just lost the taste 235 for it. Maybe tomorrow, I'll try to find where they get in and nail a tin-can lid over the hole. I light two kerosene lamps, put the kettle on the stove for tea, and step back outside to look at the stars.

40   The sound comes from the other side of a granite ridge that cuts across the south end of the muskrat swamp, just under Orion. Coyotes, howling. It isn't so much 240 a howling as an ululation, a talking in tongues; it rises and falls, weaves and curls, seems to hover at the edge of speech, and it brings my eyes down from the stars with a snap. Coyotes, howling.

41   As I stand here in the dark, trying to fix the sound in my memory, there comes the whistle of a train filtering through the trees, and I think, Yes, that's it exactly. 245 Coyote howls and train whistles are not so much single sounds as braids of sound, one chord made up of a whole range of notes. Coyotes and trains both speak to us of somewhere else, some distant place where we are not and may never be. Some mythical place. They convey an intelligence, a sense of longing and regret, a wistfulness, as if they know they are the voice of the unattainable. They leave us standing in the 250 frozen woods with our ears straining and our hearts burdened with an undefinable feeling of loss. And not their loss, either, but ours.

1995

QUESTIONS
Reader and Purpose
1. Although Grady's essay is included in this text under *Exposition* it also clearly has a persuasive purpose. What is that purpose? How can a piece of expository prose describing a situation or a condition also be persuasive?
2. Why does Grady not tell us where his cabin is located? What difference would it make—important or not—had he given us the precise location?
3. What is the **tone** of this essay? How is the tone related to the essay's title?

Organization
4. At the beginning of paragraph 3 Grady says, 'We are all victims of our own mythologies.' How does this statement serve as a **transition** from the preceding two paragraphs? To what extent does it serve to organize the major parts of the rest of the essay?
5. How is the question at the beginning of paragraph 9 both a summary and a transition?
6. How effective is the contrast between paragraphs 17 and 18? In your opinion is Grady being sentimental here?
7. What is Grady getting at in paragraphs 22 and 23? Do you find this passage convincing?
8. Paragraph 28 takes up where paragraph 8 left off. Is this too much of a gap? Should Grady have used a sentence or two to remind the reader who Gilmore is?

9. Outline briefly what Grady does in each of the nine sections of this essay (the divisions in the text are marked by symbols)? Do these shifts in focus make the essay choppy? Could Grady dispense with the division markers by using better transition sentences?

10. In paragraphs 11 and 12 Grady identifies the manufacturer of two kinds of traps. What point is he making? Would Grady's point be sufficiently clear if he did not identify the common manufacturer of the two traps?

11. This essay is built on two main themes. What are these themes? How has Grady kept the two themes integrated?

Sentences

12. In the fourth sentence of paragraph 3 would a comma serve as well as the dash?

13. The first sentence quoted from Twain's *Roughing It* in paragraph 9 is structured as a four-part series. Would this sentence be clearer if the first three parts were each followed by a semicolon?

14. The first sentence of paragraph 11 is introduced by a **phrase** that is followed by two **clauses**. Would this sentence be more effective if these three elements were arranged in a different combination?

Diction

15. Look up: *cog* (2), *incisor* (8), *mythology* (17), *rodents* (20), *ewes* (25), *furtive* (38), *allegory* (40), *pastoral* (43), *eradication* (45), *imperil* (46), *inadvertently* (67), *ungulates* (83), *predatory* (90), *palindrome* (117), *hantavirus* (144), *ululation* (241).

16. What does Grady mean by the expression *That humans have dominion over the creatures of the earth* (164–5)? What is the source of this statement?

POINTS TO LEARN

1. Presenting a bad situation by illustration can be a method of persuasion.

2. The writer's use of persuasion can be effective even when the reader is not directly informed that this is part of the writer's purpose.

SUGGESTIONS FOR WRITING

1. Write a short essay of 4–7 paragraphs in which you explain the relationship between myth and truth that Grady describes in paragraphs 24–27.

2. Write a paragraph of 4–6 sentences in which you present a series of points. Make clear the progression from minor to major points, as Grady does in, for example, paragraphs 12, 19, and 41.

IMPROVING YOUR STYLE

1. Include in your essay a series of at least three parts.

2. Begin at least two paragraphs with a sentence that is both a summary and a transition.

JOHN HENRY RALEIGH

John Henry Raleigh (1920–2001) was a literary critic and a scholar of nineteenth- and twentieth-century British and American literature. In the essay from which this passage is taken he is concerned with the social background of the English novel during the second half of the nineteenth century. He uses material from Henry Mayhew (1812–87), an English journalist and writer best known for his graphic and detailed study of lower-class London, *London Labour and the London Poor* (1851–64), the work Raleigh cites in his essay. Raleigh's paragraphs show again the effective use of specific details to illustrate a topic idea.

The London Poor

1   The life of the London poor in the nineteenth century was, for the most part, miserable, and no one who has read Henry Mayhew, that great sociologist, can ever forget his grim and heartbreaking peoples and scenes. If man had set out consciously to fashion a hell for his fellow men, he could not have done better than nineteenth-century English culture did with the poor who 'lived' off the streets of London. Indeed 5 Mayhew's descriptions in *London Labour and the London Poor* sometimes convey a kind of Pandemonium quality and one can almost sniff the sulphur in the air. His description of a crowd entering a 'Penny Gaff'—a kind of temporary theatre which put on salacious performances—suggests some of the horror.

> Forward they came, bringing an overpowering stench with them, laughing and 10
> yelling as they pushed their way through the waiting room. One woman carry-
> ing a sickly child with a bulging forehead, was reeling drunk, the saliva running
> down her mouth as she stared about with a heavy fixed eye. Two boys were
> pushing her from side to side, while the poor infant slept, breathing heavily, as
> if stupified, through the din. Lads jumping on girls, and girls laughing hysteri- 15
> cally from being tickled by the youths behind them, every one shouting and
> jumping, presented a mad scene of frightful enjoyment.

2   But if anything, as over against this evil of stench and noise, the lonely pathos of individual tragedies is even more frightful: the blind streetseller who had once been a tailor and had worked in a room seven feet square, with six other people, from five 20 in the morning until ten at night, the room having no chimney or window or fire, though no fire was needed even in the winter, and in the summer it was like an oven. This is what it was like in the daytime, but 'no mortal tongue', the man told Mayhew, could describe what it was like at night when the two great gaslights went on. Many times the men had to be carried out of the room fainting for air. They told the master 25 he was killing them, and they knew he had other rooms, but to no avail. The gaslights burned into the man's eyes and into his brain until, 'at last, I was seized with rheumatics in the brain, and obliged to go into St Thomas's Hospital. I was there eleven months, and *came out stone blind*'; or the crippled streetseller of nutmeg graters, who crawled, literally, out into the streets where he stayed from ten to six eking out his 30 pitiful existence, six days a week. On wet days he would lie in bed, often without

food. 'Ah,' he told Mayhew, 'It *is* very miserable indeed lying in a bed all day, and in a lonely room, without perhaps a person to come near one—helpless as I am—and hear the rain beat against your windows, all that with nothing to put to your lips.' Thus, if in what follows the life of the poor is shown to have some moments of joy,   35 these are, it is remembered, only oases in an illimitable desert of misery.

1968

QUESTIONS

Reader and Purpose

1. This passage is preliminary to Raleigh's discussion of the nineteenth-century novel. What fact does he wish to establish here?
2. A practical problem every writer faces is distinguishing between information his readers may be expected to know and special facts they probably will not be familiar with and which therefore must be explained. To define for readers what they already know is to risk insulting them; on the other hand, to fail to explain what they do not know may annoy them. Where in his first paragraph does Raleigh presume his reader's ignorance? Are his explanations necessary? Are they clear enough to tell his readers what they need to know? Are they over-elaborate?

Organization

3. The **topic sentence** of paragraph 1 contains two broad ideas: express them in your own words. Does the second sentence add a new idea or merely repeat that of the first?
4. How does the extended quotation from Mayhew support Raleigh's topics? Why is that passage not enclosed in quotation marks?
5. Why does the writer begin the second paragraph with *but*? Is there a logical contradiction here? If it is not logical, how might the 'contradiction' be described? In the opening sentence of paragraph 2 what words other than *but* help to forge the link to the first paragraph?
6. What is the topic of paragraph 2? How does it differ from that of the opening paragraph? Paragraph 2 also develops by examples. How many are there?
7. The semicolon in line 29 marks a major dividing point in this paragraph. Explain why. Might it be argued that this semicolon is a bit confusing and that the organization would be clearer if a new sentence were begun at this point?

Sentences

8. How has the writer constructed his first sentence to throw stress on the word *miserable*? Why does this word merit such emphasis?
9. Raleigh sets off the definition in lines 8–9 with dashes. What does this mark signal to the reader about how the enclosed material is related to the rest of the sentence? What other punctuation might have been used? Would commas have worked as well?
10. To an alert reader the colon in line 19 indicates something about how the material to follow relates to what has just been said. Explain.

Diction

11. Look up: *grim* (3), *salacious* (9), *stench* (10), *pathos* (18), *avail* (26), *eking* (30).
12. What do you understand by the expression *stone blind* (29)?
13. Which words or phrases in paragraph 1 repeat the idea expressed by *miserable* (2)? Which repeat the idea of *hell* (4)? What is the source of the term *Pandemonium* (7)?
14. *For the most part* (1) is a **qualifier**. What purpose does it serve? What idea does the phrase *if anything* convey in line 18?
15. Sentences sometimes begin with **connectives** that alert the reader to how the ensuing idea is related to what has just been said. For instance, *however* indicates the new thought is somehow contradictory. What relationship is suggested by *indeed* (5) and by *thus* (35)?
16. Why would the following substitutes be less effective in Raleigh's context: 'make' for 'fashion' (4), 'society' for 'culture' (5), 'smell' for 'sniff' (7), 'reveals' for 'suggests' (9)?
17. Identify the **figure of speech** found in *oases in an illimitable desert of misery* (36). Do you think it is effective?
18. The success of an illustration often depends upon its specificity. So judged, the example taken from Mayhew is successful. Examine its diction. What words are especially detailed? (A test is to consider the problem from the point of view of an artist trying to paint the scene from this description.) To how many senses does Mayhew appeal? What attitude toward the poor is implied by his diction?

POINTS TO LEARN

1. The value of an example often depends upon the detail with which it is presented.
2. When you write, think about what your readers may be presumed to know and what needs to be explained.
3. Important words may be stressed by being isolated within the sentence.

SUGGESTIONS FOR WRITING

Develop one of these topics in a short composition of one or two paragraphs, using detailed examples. If possible, include a quotation as one of your examples and try to incorporate the author and title smoothly into your text.

> For the student, schoolwork is part boredom, part desperation.

> For the poor, life is still miserable.

IMPROVING YOUR STYLE

1. Use a colon to set up a specific instance of a general idea.
2. Expand or define an important point with a phrase set off by dashes.
3. Use the connectives *however*, *indeed*, and *thus* to open sentences; be sure, of course, that the sentences are appropriately related to the preceding ideas.

J.A. DAVIDSON

The Reverend J.A. Davidson is a retired minister of the United Church of Canada. He was a chaplain in the Canadian Army, where he rose to the rank of captain while serving in such places as Fort Churchill, Manitoba. He also spent several years as Protestant chaplain at the Royal Military College in Kingston, Ontario. He later taught at the Ottawa Lay School of Theology before moving west and becoming a columnist for the Victoria *Times Colonist*. Although without formal training in linguistics, he has for many years written about Canadian English and the numerous variations in its pronunciation.

Talking 'Funny'

1   Several years ago the English comedienne Joyce Grenfell said this to a Canadian reporter: 'A Canadian accent defies copying. It's a subtle blend of too many influences.'

2   One of Irving Layton's early poems is about a native of Kingston, Ontario, who spent three years at Oxford University, and 'Now his accent / makes even Englishmen / wince, and feel / unspeakably colonial.'   5

3   A character in Kingsley Amis's novel *The Egyptologists*, Buck Remus, a Canadian television 'personality' working in London, is described as having a 'floor-of-the-mouth Canadian voice'.

4   Hugh MacLennan, who came from Nova Scotia, said in one of his essays that when he asked a pub-keeper in the Scottish Highlands how he guessed he was   10
Canadian, he was told, 'You are not English, that is certain, and you are not American. You still have some of *the* voice.'

5   During World War II I met in London, England, a relative of a relative. In almost her first words to me she expressed relief that I did not have, as she put it, 'a beastly Yankee accent'. I did sense, though, that my flat prairie speech caused her   15
some discomfort.

6   David Crystal, a British—actually Welsh—expert in language, in his little book, *The English Language* (Penguin, 1988) said this about Canadian speech: 'To British people, Canadians may sound American; to Americans they may sound British. Canadians themselves insist on not being identified with either, and certainly there is   20
a good deal of evidence in support of this view.'

7   Do we who have grown up in Canada have a distinctive way of speaking English? Can we generally be identified by others as Canadians because of the way we speak? Or is Canadian speech merely a variety of what has been conveniently called 'General American'? General American, the most widespread mode of speech in the   25
USA, prevails, generally, in New York State west of the Hudson, New Jersey, Pennsylvania, and the states of the Middle West and the Far West.

8   General American is heard everywhere in Canada. It comes at us through television and radio and film. And we know that there are many similarities between General American and what can be called 'General Canadian'—a way of speech that   30
prevails from coast to coast, with a few significant regional variants.

9   Mario Pei, of Columbia University, New York City, underscored the obvious when he wrote this: 'The English of Canada sounds far more like an American than a

British dialect.' He suggested that Canadian speech differs from the American only in a few 'Britishisms' in usage and pronunciation. I think his ear failed him. The late 35 Walter Avis, a leading Canadian authority, was, I think, much sounder when he said that Canadian English 'is neither American nor British, but a complex different in many respects from both in vocabulary, grammar, and syntax—*and pronunciation*'.

10   If you listen carefully you can, in most instances, distinguish between General American and General Canadian. There are subtle differences in intonation and 40 rhythm, and there are several not terribly subtle differences in pronunciation.

11   We native Canadians, by and large, sound every *r* that can be sounded. We do not roll them in the Scottish way, but we—most of us, anyway—sound all of them. And we are inclined to be suspicious of native Canadians who fail to sound all their *r*'s, particularly those at the ends of words. We feel that they are deliberately Englishing 45 or Harvarding their tongues to show that they are more cultured than us ordinary Canadians.

12   Some Americans sound every *r*, but most of them miss a few, either in the middles of words or at the ends. Compare the speech of Lloyd Robertson and Pamela Wallin with that of their American counterparts: listen carefully.   50

13   The distinctively Canadian mode of speech had its beginnings in the early settlements of English-speaking people in the Maritime provinces, Quebec's Eastern Townships, and old Ontario. Many of the settlers were of English background, but much of the early settlement was Scottish, and there was a notable Irish element. Scottish and Irish speech provided much of the foundation of what was to become 55 General Canadian. On the other hand, early American speech was influenced more by the English of England, with its gradual loss of *r* as a consonant, particularly at the ends of words.

14   The consistently sounded *r* prevails in Canada, and there is no indication that either the pressure of General American or the prestige of the Standard English of 60 England will shake it loose from the vast majority of English-speaking Canadians.

15   Canadian speech has sharp, short vowel sounds—on the whole, sharper and shorter than those in General American. Our *ou* diphthong is a conspicuous example of this. It is the sound that Americans seem to have in mind when they tell us that we 'sure do talk funny'; they find it a quaint, backwoodsy sort of thing.   65

16   Some years ago Walter Pidgeon told readers of a Canadian magazine that when he first went from his native New Brunswick to New York to seek fame and fortune on the stage he found that he was somewhat handicapped by his Canadian accent. He said he had difficulty with words such as *about* and *mouse*. I can see the young Walter Pidgeon standing in front of a mirror in a New York theatrical boardinghouse, saying 70 again and again, 'Not "mouse", you peasant—"mayouse".'

17   H.B. Woods, an expert in Canadian English, says that about 6 per cent of the vowel sounds in Canadian English differ from those in General American. He mentions, of course, the notorious -*ou*-, and the ways in which we say words such as 'bite' and 'nice' and 'wife' and 'point' and 'voice'. And he discusses the 'rounded' Canadian 75 vowel in 'body' and 'doctor' and 'water'.

18   There are other vowel sounds which distinguish Canadians from Americans. Many, perhaps most, Canadians say 'instityootion', whereas Americans say 'institootion'. And there are 'prodyooce'/'prodooce', 'styoopid'/'stoopid', and others of that

nature. Many Canadians, however, tend to take the American way here. Some of us 80
now refer to the Queen's husband as 'the *Dook*'—with the sound as in 'spook'. Then
there is the 'executiv'/'executeeve', 'negativ'/'negateeve' thing.

19   We Canadians tend to be a little fussier than Americans with sounding the *t*.
Many Americans give the *t* in the middle of words almost a *d*-sound. I have heard very
able American broadcasters say 'eighdy' and 'idendical' and 'congradulations'. (I won- 85
der if Mr Pidgeon came to call himself 'Walder'.)

20   In some words Americans underplay the *t* almos' to the point of extinction. Last
year I heard a political candidate in an American state say on television, 'cosly programs' ('progr'ms', that is). And with many of them the last day of the week has
become 'Sa'erday'—but then it has become that with many Canadians.   90

21   This, of course, is a rather inadequate analysis. There are Americans who sound
every *r*. And some are very fastidious with the *t*. There may even be some who say
'mouse' the way I do. And there are many Canadians whose ways of speaking seem to
refute this analysis. But consider these factors together, along with American intona-
tions and speech rhythms, and you will have to admit that a reasonable case can be 95
made for the existence of a distinctively Canadian way in speech that is not simply a
variant of General American.

22   Within General Canadian there are regional and other distinctive styles of
speech. (Newfoundland is a special case. I do not wish to discuss Newfoundland
speech here. No mainlander can discuss Newfoundland speech with impunity.)   100

23   The Maritimer can generally be identified as such by certain speech characteristics, many of Scottish origin. A friend suggested to me in a letter many years ago that
there is a General Bluenose accent, with several sub-accents within it. He wrote:
'Though the people in the south and west ends of Halifax speak my own impeccable
English, there is in the north end a particularly unpleasant accent—"hid" for head, 105
"new-erth" for north—which sounds like that of a Bronx telephone operator.'

24   He also told me that on Grand Manan Island, off the south coast of New
Brunswick, a US southern accent prevails. He once heard a man there say, 'Wot with
the dowg bahkin, an ma wife grawlin, a man don't hahdly git no wuk done no haow.'
Several years later I spent a week on Grand Manan, and I was delighted to hear the 110
soft speech of the natives, reflecting, in their relative isolation for nearly two centuries,
the speech of their ancestors who had come up from the Carolinas during the
American Revolution—speech modified by undertones of Bluenose.

25   The Maritimes are rich in regional overlays. Scots-Irish vowels are prevalent in
many parts. In Lunenberg, Nova Scotia, there is still a trace of the German. It is one of 115
the pleasing little ironies in Canadian history that, as the historian A.R.M. Lower put
it, 'These Germans, who early lost their language, are virtually the oldest English-
speaking Canadians.'

26   Ontario speech has, generally, a slight nasal tone. In southwestern Ontario
Canadian speech tends to come quite close to General American, although not in all 120
areas. It is interesting to hear a man from, say, Chatham, and of impeccable United
Empire Loyalist background, speaking in the manner of a son of the American
Revolution whose family helped open up Ohio.

27   The Ottawa Valley has a mode of speech which seems to mix dilute Irish with
a trace of Yankee twang. Just south of it, in Lanark County, some of the older people 125

have a way of speaking which I have heard described as 'Scotch-with-a-lot-of-water'.

28   Prairie people generally speak similarly to their Ontario cousins, but with less of the nasal tone and with a characteristic flatness. And they tend to enunciate more crisply.   130

29   Most Canadian-born-and-raised people in British Columbia speak like prairie people: many of them are transplants from the wide open spaces. But there are some interesting overlays of accent, such as the one of some of the natives of Vancouver Island which I have heard called, among other things, 'The Duncan Mumble' and 'The Oak Bay Blether'. These seem a strange mixture of Winnipeg and Oxford.   135

30   A few special accents have been precipitated as overlays on General Canadian. In Toronto there are two interesting sub-accents which perhaps can be labelled 'Toronto Tough' and 'Toronto Dainty'. Toronto Tough is a sort of Canadianized Brook-lynese, but it lacks the crude charm of the original. An obvious example of this is, 'Howja like Trawna?'.   140

31   Toronto Dainty is genteel: it rings of Establishment, with a capital 'E'. It is Canadian, all right, but some of its practitioners seem to be hinting in their speech that they do wish they had gone to a good school in England. A curious throatiness creeps into certain words: you hear this when a Dainty Torontonian says *Toe-rawn-teau.*

32   Dainty accents have been identified in other parts of Canada. We had a few of   145 them in North Battleford, Saskatchewan, when I was a boy there many years ago.

33   In academia a mode of speech similar to Toronto Dainty has become rather common. I have been told that this seems to be spreading, particularly among younger scholars in the humanities. Similar to it is the speech of some of our diplomats and loftier federal public servants—which an insider told me some years ago   150 may go with the hanky-up-the-sleeve gambit.

34   Most of the Canadian military speak ordinary General Canadian, but some of them cultivate 'just-ever-so British' overlays. A few of our naval officers, Canadian born and bred, have felt impelled to RN their voices a little. Some of our soldiers have been known to affect a touch of what has been called 'the Sandhurst Snarl', which,   155 when put on top of basic Manitoba, for instance, becomes rather amusing. For a few years after the war some of our airmen indulged in the 'RAF Ruffle', in which haws and huffs, strained through bushy moustaches, tended to muffle some meaningful sounds: now the trend among our flyers seems to be towards the American.

35   Observers have detected among the clergy of Canada a tendency to affect a   160 touch of pious toniness in their speech. When a Canadian parson feels that he really must improve his pulpit voice he may become a little careless with his r's and give some of his a's a genteel broadening. When excited he may utter hooting tones. Chestiness in pulpit-speech perhaps comes from the inhaling of too much of the dust of old hymnbooks.   165

36   Still relevant is a statement made many years ago by Stephen Leacock: 'I myself talk Ontario English; I don't admire it, but it's all I can do; anything is better than affectation.' (Leacock said that in Canada we use 'English for literature, Scotch for ceremony, and American for conversations'.)

37   Will a distinctively Canadian mode of speech prevail? Henry Sweet, a pioneer   170 in spoken-English studies—said to have been Bernard Shaw's model for Henry

Higgins in *Pygamalion*—pointed out that a spoken language is 'necessarily a vague and floating entity'. It is impossible to predict in which direction, or directions, General Canadian will float—but surely a little guessing is not beyond us here.

38   Will General Canadian float in the direction of General American until it is 175 absorbed by it? Some experts think that the absorption process is well underway. There can be no doubting that many features of American speech have spread into Canada and probably will continue to spread. But will this necessarily lead to absorption? Changes, of course, will take place in Canadian speech, but perhaps basic Americanization has now gone about as far as it is going to go. Our grim determina- 180 tion to sustain the Canadian identity, with a certain vagueness as to what that actually is, will have much to do with the further development and preservation of a distinctively Canadian mode of speech.

39   Mind you, there are Canadians—some of whom are competent in linguistics— who think it will be almost a miracle if the distinctively Canadian mode of speech, 185 one quite distinct from General American, survives the next fifty years. To such people I point out that if they wish to talk linguistic miracle they can do no better than consider the miracle that has already taken place, the survival of distinctive Canadian speech during the past fifty years, in which we have been subjected to the constant pressure of General American through radio and television and film. 190

40   The first generation to have been raised on television is now sliding into middle age, and there is no convincing evidence that, by and large, its tongues have been Americanized. Our three oldest children are now in their forties, and they talk funny, just like their parents.

41   Will General Canadian, then, float in the direction of the Standard English of 195 England, the so-called 'Received Pronunciation'? This is the mode of speech we conveniently, if not completely accurately, labelled Oxford or BBC English.

42   Some Canadians do seem to be trying to give it a gentle shove in that direction. I have been told that a little of that kind of shoving is done in some of our private schools. Such efforts have not been notably successful, but a few of the victims take 200 on just a touch of the British and seem to suggest by their way of speaking that although they are Canadians they rather disapprove of the ways in which most of their compatriots speak.

43   I must now confess that of all varieties of spoken English the ones I find most pleasant to listen to are those of soft-voiced, well-educated Scots and English— 205 although when they become shrill or snobbish or sarcastic they arouse in me homicidal feelings more rapidly than any other modes of speech.

44   I do not think that Canadian speech will float very far in the direction of Oxford and the BBC. This may bother the English woman who said, in a ruling-class accent, that it distressed her that Canadians do not even *try* to speak 'proper' English. 210

45   The Canadian Broadcasting Corporation, through both television and radio, and the Canadian Television Network (CTV) are primary agencies in the maintenance of General Canadian. In their news and public affairs departments they effectively present a clean, clear Canadian mode of speech, uncluttered and generally free of affectation. But those two corporations work both sides of the street: perhaps the 215 greatest threat to General Canadian is in American television, which both of them help make so readily available to us.

46   My prediction is that Canadian speech will continue to float in its own special channel and that for the foreseeable future we Canadians will continue to talk funny.

1993

QUESTIONS

Reader and Purpose

1. How is this essay an example of exposition by illustration?
2. Compare the first seven paragraphs with the final six paragraphs of this essay. What further conclusions can you draw about Davidson's purpose?
3. What does Davidson mean by his title?
4. How do paragraphs 22, 32, 34, and 35 help to define the author's **tone**?

Organization

5. This is not a very long essay, yet it has 46 paragraphs. What does this tell you about the essay's organization?
6. What do the first six paragraphs do? What is the function of paragraph 7?
7. How does paragraph 8 serve as a **transition** between the paragraph that precedes it and those that follow.
8. How is paragraph 21 a conclusion to what precedes it? How does it also serve as a transition to the paragraphs that follow?
9. What two functions does paragraph 22 have?
10. What function do illustrations play in the organization of paragraphs 23–29?
11. Compare paragraphs 7, 38, and 41. What steps in his exposition is Davidson taking?

Sentences

12. Would commas have been as effective as the dashes in paragraphs 6, 9, and 11?
13. Would a dash, or a comma, be more appropriate than the colon in paragraph 12?
14. Does the first sentence of paragraph 16 lack punctuation? Why, or why not? Compare the punctuation of this sentence with that of the last sentence in paragraph 21 and the last sentence in paragraph 24.

Diction

15. Look up: *subtle* (2), *complex* (37), *syntax* (38), *intonation* (40), *consonant* (57), *diphthong* (63), *quaint* (65), *variant* (97), *impunity* (100), *Bluenose* (103), *nasal* (119), *United Empire Loyalist* (122), *genteel* (141), *academia* (147), *affectation* (168).
16. In paragraph 11 Davidson writes 'Englishing or Harvarding'. Do you think that this kind of usage is correct? Is it appropriate? He also writes 'more cultured than us ordinary Canadians'. Is his use of *us* rather than *we* correct? acceptable? To answer this question you might refer to two or three handbooks on English usage.
17. What does Davidson mean by *hanky-up-the-sleeve gambit* in paragraph 33?
18. What is the **irony** in paragraph 32?
19. How do such expressions as *to RN [Royal Navy] their voices* and *haws and huffs* (paragraph 34) add to Davidson's comic tone?

POINTS TO LEARN

1. Short paragraphs can be effective as part of a writer's overall strategy.
2. A series of paragraphs can be governed by one concluding paragraph.
3. Humour, sparingly used but well placed, can be highly effective as illustration.

SUGGESTIONS FOR WRITING

1. Write a short essay in which you limit each paragraph to no more than four sentences, with most paragraphs being illustrations. Choose a topic such as, for example, a survey of different kinds of articles you own (camping equipment, computer apparatus, sports equipment, carpentry tools, books in your personal library, auto parts, cooking utensils, etc.).
2. Consider your own pronunciation of some of the words used as examples by Davidson. Would you consider your pronunciation, by Davidson's standards, more Canadian than American? more American? Illustrate with examples of your own pronunciation.

IMPROVING YOUR STYLE

1. In two or three paragraphs treat your topic humorously, but without exaggeration.
2. Use dashes in two or three sentences.

JAMES McCOOK

A former associate editor of the *Ottawa Journal*, James McCook was for many years interested in the history of western Canada. His numerous articles on this subject appeared in such periodicals as *The Beaver* and *Canadian Geographic*. A journalist in London during World War II, he later became a life member of the parliamentary press gallery in Ottawa. One memorable incident in his varied career occurred in the late 1940s: assigned by the Canadian Press to cover an Inuit murder trial in the Arctic, he ended up serving on the jury as well as filing dispatches about the trial. After retiring to Victoria (where he died in 1983) he continued to write essays such as the one below, which illustrates, in a humorous but nonetheless realistic manner, one of the difficulties of life in the North—a difficulty implied in the question that serves as his title.

Man's Best Friend?

1   The snobbery of Indian and Eskimo dogs surprised and disappointed early fur traders on Hudson Bay. The newcomers admired the devoted service the animals gave, pulling sleds and carrying loads. They noted that the dogs were left to fend for themselves in periods of idleness and had to survive by ranging the countryside and eating everything from bird's nests to scraps cast up by the sea. The traders naturally   5
assumed that these undemanding beasts would be happy to serve them.

2   Nothing of the kind!

3   Andrew Graham, who served with the Hudson's Bay Company on the Bay from 1749 to 1775, observed that the dogs were as useful to the natives as horses to the Europeans. They assisted in the hunting of deer and their keen sense of smell enabled   10 them to lead their masters to beaver lodges. James Isham, who was also with the Company on Hudson Bay in the eighteenth century, was impressed by the ability of a single dog to haul a fortnight's provisions for two men. This was a factor of growing importance, as Hudson's Bay Company policy was encouraging the establishment of inland posts far from the sea.   15

4   But the dogs would not serve the traders, not even when the white men took them into the forts as puppies and raised them kindly. They regarded the traders with fear and hostility, and amiable and co-operative Newfoundland dogs had to be imported from England to perform work around the posts.

5   The Newfoundland dogs often mated with wolves and the traders waited con-   20 fidently for their pups to show them goodwill. It was no use, Graham reported. The offspring retained the 'moroseness' of the wolves.

6   In time, of course, the mixing of breeds and familiarity with the traders led to the development of dogs which deigned to take commands from Europeans. In the meantime, traders who used native dogs had to hire Indians or Eskimos to drive them.   25

7   The other complaint about native dogs concerned their skill and audacity in thieving. Their way of life, which so often left them in a barren land where only the swift and venturesome could survive, made them reckless. A placid Newfoundland might be trusted alone with a piece of meat meant for its master's supper, but a sled dog could not even be trusted with meat in a tin. Robert J. Flaherty, prospector and   30 filmmaker on Hudson Bay, left a shocking account of the transformation of handsome, diligent sled dogs into wild creatures as they tore open cans of meat, heedless of the cuts they suffered from the metal.

8   The yarns about thieving dogs were endless. Whips, harness, and gloves were carried off and chewed as a matter of course. A prairie guide had a fine elk-skin coat   35 and slept in it in cold weather. One morning he awoke to find that his dog had eaten his coat off his back, leaving only the collar cuffs. A rancher slept under a buffalo robe and discovered in the morning that two dogs from his team had devoured it all except the hair.

9   A tobacco pipe was reduced to splinters by a dog who believed for a moment   40 that it had found a delicacy. One raider in a tent ate almost 20 pounds of lard and staggered off with the rest. Tins of molasses were spilled by disappointed dogs. Stewed fruit was hardly a dog's delight, but if there was nothing better, down it went.

10   The four-legged robbers were all over the country, but the parties of surveyors and missionaries who made their way up James and Hudson Bay by boat, left some   45 of the most vivid accounts of annoying experiences with marauding dogs, reinforced in that region by hordes of vicious mosquitoes.

11   It was customary to tie up on shore at night. There dogs from Indian encampments would frequently pounce on the strangers. Tarpaulin covers were ripped off anything left outside the tent. Wolfish dogs prowled about in the dark, seeking a gap   50 in the defences. Unguarded kettles of food were carried off—it was claimed that dogs would run off with kettles and pans containing food and keep them upright without losing a mouthful.

12   The victory of the dogs and mosquitoes was complete when, in the middle of the night, the weary travellers would leave their tents, board the boats, and move out 55 into the bay seeking relief from their tormentors.

13   At other places where settlement was more advanced, dogs often gave strangers an unfriendly welcome, although they did not rob them. Reverend A.A. Boddy visited the Sarcee Indian Reserve near Calgary and recalled that nearly 50 dogs rushed out, howling and showing their teeth. 'Then,' he added, 'they noticed that we carried 60 stones in our hands for their benefit and then suddenly they retired.'

14   Having seen what could happen to any creature that got between a northern dog and food, those who worked with dogs treated them with a degree of caution. Still, the drivers usually came to feel affection for their loyal servants and to boast about their achievements.   65

15   Governor George Simpson of the Hudson's Bay Company, who seldom showed sympathy to man or beast, went so far as to comment that sled dogs 'had no sinecure'. That, in a way, was a warm tribute. The final service given by dogs, the Governor could have added, was to be killed and eaten in hard times. And not necessarily in hard times only. In territories where buffalo steaks were hard to come by the Indian 70 feasted on dog meat and taught the traders to share this practice.

16   Missionaries were among those who had to learn that sled dogs were not placid pets. None of the missionaries had a more difficult experience with dogs than the Reverend E.J. Peck and his assistant, who lived in a small mission hut on Blacklead Island in Cumberland Sound, Baffin Island. To enable the Eskimos to attend church 75 services under shelter the missionaries built a larger building near their hut, making use of light wood and, because they had nothing else, nailing seal-skins to the wooden frame to serve as a covering.

17   For some time over the winter, poor weather had prevented fishing, and by the end of January 1895 the Eskimos and their dogs were suffering from near-starvation. At 3 a.m. 80 one morning Reverend Peck and his assistant were awakened by a pack of hungry dogs. 'These creatures had managed to climb up on the roof of our skin church, and to our dismay were tearing the edifice to pieces. . . . We were literally besieged by dogs, and they must in all have numbered over a hundred. Most of them were on the roof, some had fallen through, others were devouring pieces of sealskin, and altogether such a confused 85 mass of dogs—young, old, bruised and wounded—it would be hard to find anywhere else. After a sharp battle we managed to put these unwelcome visitors to flight. . . .'

18   When the incident was later recounted to a class of girls in Scotland, one young woman remarked 'Now that we have heard of a kirk being eaten by dogs, it is not hard to believe that a whale could have swallowed Jonah.'   90

19   Some missionaries, such as the Methodist Reverend John McDougall and the Roman Catholic Father Lacombe, were expert dog drivers who thought little of covering 50 miles a day. Other missionaries were as useless on the trail as bags of snow. The Anglican Canon William Newton described how in winter he was wrapped up in skins and placed in a carriole, a box shaped like a long cradle attached to the bottom 95 board of the sled. There, warm but unable to move, he lay motionless while someone else drove the dogs and ran with the sled. Newton wrote that 'you are perfectly quiet, and have nothing to do, uphill, downhill or on level ground, except to observe the dogs, the drivers and the scenery.'

20   One of McDougall's burdens was the much respected Methodist preacher, Reverend Thomas Woolsey, who was no help at all when travelling. On one occasion McDougall undertook to drive two teams at once, breaking trail with one while the second, carrying Woolsey, followed. It was a disaster. Dogs in the Woolsey team soon realized he had no control over them. The lead dog took it easy. The quarrelsome snapped at each other. When the sled ran down a slope the dogs made no effort to keep ahead of it, and the harness became tangled. Fights became more furious, and finally Woolsey, dogs, and sled were a tangled mass at the bottom of the hill. McDougall had to leave his own team, unwrap Woolsey, sort out the harness, and drive the Woolsey team long enough to remind the dogs of their duty with his whip.

21   Widely distributed was the story of the driver who told a missionary that his dogs would not improve their slow pace because he could not swear at them in the presence of a reverend gentleman. It was said that the missionary told the driver to use whatever language was necessary to speed progress, and apparently, the bad language always worked!

22   Indeed, the dogs constantly found new ways of making their masters swear. A heavy overnight snowfall gave a team such an opportunity. The drivers could not locate the dogs buried in snow, and not one animal made a move to betray its location until a man stumbled over it.

23   The bells attached to the harness gave dog teams a totally false impression of Christmassy goodwill. The lead dog ruled because of superior intelligence and strength, and when necessary, reminded rebels of his authority. Lesser dogs grumbled and snapped at companions. Lazy dogs tried to avoid pulling their fair share of the load.

24   Strangers who saw Indians moving camp, with most of the burden carried by dogs directed by the women, were surprised at the noise—the growls and howls, the whines and whimpers, the sounds of general complaint made by as many as 500 dogs. The visitors also discovered that the silence of the night would be disturbed by one restless dog, and that the cry would be taken up by others of his kind and by the wolves and coyotes running free.

25   The buffalo-hunters and explorers from Britain who visited the prairies in the 1840s and later, left detailed accounts of experiences with dogs.

26   The Earl of Southesk, who travelled west to the Rocky Mountains in 1859–60, had high hopes for a formidable-looking beast he thought would fight wolves. One night he had just snuggled down when the dog rushed into his tent and crouched beside the bed quivering. In hot pursuit came a large white wolf, which was later shot by a guide.

27   Between Carlton House and Fort Edmonton Southesk acquired another dog which proved to be an amusing companion. This was a black Indian sleigh-dog named 'Whisky', 'as fat as a pig, and possessed of only four inches of tail'. The fondness which Southesk developed for this comical animal is evident in his description: 'Poor Whisky filled the place of the ancient domestic jester; One look at him dispelled melancholy; every movement he made was a farce. With his cunningly timorous countenance and sleekly rounded plebeian body, he was a true Sancho Panza of dogs. He was a daily delight: I would not have exchanged him for the best dog in the Company's territories.'

100

105

110

115

120

125

130

135

140

145

28   When Southesk travelled through mountainous country Whisky, in spite of his bulk, developed a 'mania' for climbing—although he squeaked with fear upon coming to the difficult places, and on one occasion narrowly escaped being crushed by a falling ram which Southesk had shot.

29   When the party reached Fort Edmonton, Whisky deserted, 'preferring ignoble 150 ease at the Fort to our good society'. Southesk felt Whisky would live to regret this choice once he was forced to resume the toilsome life of a sleigh-dog.

30   The hunter and explorer Captain John Palliser purchased a large white dog named 'Ishmah' from an Indian couple. Ishmah was to be his sole companion on a nine-month excursion through the wilds of Montana and North Dakota in 1847–48. 155 At first the dog would not come within 250 yards of him or any other white man, but Palliser patiently tempted him with pieces of meat until Ishmah gave him his trust. Palliser later commented that 'a more faithful, efficient, and devoted creature never breathed.'

31   Ishmah struggled through deep snow from morning to night pulling Palliser's 160 heavily laden travois. 'When supper was at last cooked and despatched (quickly enough on his part, poor fellow, for his share was sometimes very scanty), he sat up close beside me as I smoked my pipe and sipped my coffee; and when at last I got into bed he used to lie down at the edge of the robe with his back close up against my shoulders, and so we slept till morning.' 165

32   There were times, however, when even the admirable Ishmah fell from grace. On one occasion he ran off to gambol in the forest with a she-wolf. Unfortunately at the time he was harnessed to the travois containing all of Palliser's possessions, leaving his master in a serious predicament, stranded 100 miles from the nearest known habitation. Then, after several anxious hours the 'panting rascal' returned to his side. 'I never 170 felt so relieved, and laughed out loud from sheer joy, as I noticed the consciousness he showed by his various cringing movements of having behaved very badly. I was too well pleased, however, at his reappearance to beat him, particularly when I found nothing of his harness and load either missing or injured in the slightest degree. Even the portion of meat which I had secured from the last deer I shot was untouched. . . .' 175

33   Ishmah had less conscience about stealing food from strangers. On his way home from the prairies Palliser took Ishmah to his hotel in St Louis. The dog lay at his feet in the dining room, but 'not content with beholding his master enjoying the good things of this life' crept up to the dishes on the side board and helped himself to a calf's head 'with which savoury prize he decamped at racing speed, his bushy tail 180 stretching out, like a fox's brush, behind him; the waiters merely pointing after him and winking to one another, evidently enjoying the joke'.

34   The story of one completely satisfactory partnership between man and dog comes from the Canadian West. Reverend Egerton Ryerson Young and a companion were travelling across the ice on Lake Winnipeg when they were caught in a severe 185 blizzard, and became lost while many miles from shore. The travellers were in danger of freezing to death. What to do?

35   The missionary 'had a talk' with his sled dog 'Jack', a 160-pound black St Bernard described by his owner as 'the noblest of them all'. Young informed Jack that the chances were against the dog ever again having the opportunity to stretch out on 190 the rug before the study fire unless he could lead them to a place of shelter. Jack led the travellers through the raging storm and many hours later brought them safely to an Indian encampment on shore. Of course. *Noblesse oblige.*

1979

QUESTIONS

Reader and Purpose

1. What attitude towards his subject—and towards his readers—does McCook express with his opening comment about 'The snobbery of Indian and Eskimo sled dogs'?
2. What common assumptions about dogs is the author challenging with his opening comments about the sled dogs' hostility and thievery?

Organization

3. Paragraph 2 has only four words. Can you justify such a short paragraph?
4. What shift in the introduction occurs in paragraph 7?
5. How does paragraph 10 both summarize and introduce?
6. How does the beginning of paragraph 13 effect a shift from paragraph 10?
7. What two functions does paragraph 14 have?
8. Does the apparent lack of transition between paragraphs 18 and 19 seem to you a strength or a weakness? Justify your answer. Is there in fact a subtle transition that is skilfully concealed?
9. Consider the two concluding paragraphs in relation to introductory paragraphs 1–7. Is there any relationship between introduction and conclusion? If you think there is, explain it. If you think not, justify McCook's conclusion.

Sentence

10. In the second sentence of paragraph 11, should there be a comma after 'there'? Is a misreading probable, or possible, without the comma? Compare this usage with the comma after 'still' in paragraph 14.
11. Could the dash in paragraph 11 be replaced by a semicolon? a period? parentheses? What different effects would result from such substitutions?
12. In the last sentence of paragraph 19, should there be a comma after 'downhill'?
13. Sentences 4–6 in paragraph 20 could be rewritten this way: 'Dogs in the Woolsey team soon realized he had no control over them, so the lead dog took it easy and the quarrelsome snapped at each other.' Keeping in mind the context, is this rewritten passage more effective than the original?
14. What is the **inversion** in paragraph 21? Would the sentence be more effective with normal word order?
15. Point out the **parallel** elements in paragraph 23.
16. What does McCook mean by his last two brief sentences? How are they related to the rest of the essay?

Diction

17. Look up: *fend* (3), *fortnight* (13), *moroseness* (22), *diligent* (32), *sinecure* (67), *placid* (72), *kirk* (89), *carriole* (95), *timorous* (142), *plebeian* (143), *travois* (161), *gambol* (167), *noblesse oblige* (193).

18. How do the following expressions affect the **tone** of this essay: *these undemanding beasts* (6), *a dog's delight* (43), *four-legged robbers* (44), *the victory of the dogs* (54), *lesser dogs* (121), *lazy dogs* (122)?

19. Look up **alliteration** in the Glossary, and then comment upon the effectiveness, or lack of it, of the examples in paragraph 24.

20. At times McCook uses original and effective expressions, such as *stewed fruit was hardly a dog's delight* (43), *as useless on the trail as bags of snow* (93), *Christmassy goodwill* (120), *he squeaked with fear* (147). At other times, however, he is guilty of using **clichés**: *had high hopes* (133), *in hot pursuit* (135), *would live to regret* (151), *fell from grace* (166), *the raging storm* (192). List other examples of both kinds.

21. Rephrase five of the clichés you have found in this essay and then explain how your wording is more original than the cliché.

POINTS TO LEARN

1. Short paragraphs can be effective not only because of their brevity, in contrast to the rest of the paragraphs in an essay, but also because they can serve as contrasts, as transitions, and as introductions.

2. A paragraph can sometimes be effective even if there is no transition linking it to the previous paragraphs.

3. Even a serious topic can be dealt with in a dryly comic manner, if an author chooses his or her tone carefully.

SUGGESTIONS FOR WRITING

In 'Reluctant Villain' (p. 40), Roy Vontobel examines the wolverine seriously, with no attempt at humour. Choose an animal whose behaviour you are familiar with (the family dog or cat, for instance) and describe some of its activities, adopting either the serious tone of Vontobel or the serious-comic one of McCook.

IMPROVING YOUR STYLE

In your essay include:

1. a paragraph of no more than eight or ten words, which will serve as contrast, as transition, or as both;
2. at least three figures of speech which you have never before seen in print;
3. one sentence in which you deliberately use an inversion.

WAYNE JOHNSTON

Born and raised in Newfoundland, Wayne Johnston (1958–) was a reporter for the *St John's Daily News* and poetry editor of *Fiddlehead* before becoming a full-time writer. After completing his master's degree at the University of New Brunswick in 1984, he produced *The Story of Bobby O'Malley* (1985), which won the W.H. Smith/Books in Canada First Novel Award. A frequent contributor of poems and stories to various magazines, he has also published a memoir, *Baltimore's Mansion* (1999), which won the Charles Taylor Prize for Literary Non-Fiction, and five more novels, including *The Divine Ryans* (1990), the very successful *The Colony of Unrequited Dreams* (1998), and, most recently, *The Navigator of New York* (2002).

A Whale of a Time

1   Word that movie versions of *The Shipping News* and *The Bird Artist* are to be filmed in the province makes me wonder if Hollywood producers have forgotten what happened the last time they discovered Newfoundland. In 1976, the megabudget movie *Orca*, starring, among others, Richard Harris, Bo Derek, and Charlotte Rampling, was filmed near St John's, in the fishing community of Petty Harbour. For 5 six weeks Petty Harbour was turned upside down by the influx of movie-makers. Fishing was suspended as every fishing boat was rented for use in the movie and most of the fishermen were hired on as extras, as were a good many university students, including me.

2   The plot of *Orca*: Richard Harris, a Newfoundland fishing captain whose wife 10 was killed by a killer whale, gets revenge by killing a pregnant female killer whale whose mate then sets out to kill Richard Harris. Hollywood had high hopes for *Orca*. It was made just after the *Jaws* craze, but the makers of *Orca* swore they were not imitating *Jaws*. '*Jaws* was about a shark,' the director said, '*Orca's* about a killer whale,' as if he could not understand how, this being the case, anybody in their right mind 15 could think the two movies were related.

3   'The word "*orca*" means killer whale,' he went on. 'We show more sympathy for the whale than Spielberg showed for the shark. The whale is not the bad guy. *Jaws* was about what nature does to man. *Orca's* about what man does to nature.'

4   Every morning, all the student extras would gather in the parking lot of a 20 shopping mall in St John's to board the yellow school buses for Petty Harbour. Every morning, there was the same traffic-snarling, police-escorted convoy of buses, trucks, vans, and cars moving out of town, always, ritually, funereally, led by Orca itself, a life-size model of a killer whale, a great black-and-white slab of rubber laid out on the back of a flat-bed truck, a harpoon sticking out of it, a streak of red paint running 25 down one side.

5   For the first little while, people who lived along the route lined the sides of the road to see the rubber whale and in the hope of seeing one of the movie stars; every so often, Richard Harris or Bo Derek would stick a head out the window of a trailer to wave, and, if the procession was moving slowly enough, to sign autographs. It 30 wasn't long, however, before the convoy was ignored, except by irate commuters and

by children who, as though in some send-up of Farley Mowat's *A Whale for the Killing*, began to wait in ambush along the route, running out to pelt the rubber whale with rocks and sticks.

6   The makers of *Orca* ran into many unforeseen difficulties in Newfoundland, 35 most of them of the 'what nature does to man' variety. There was, for instance, for the duration of their stay, incredible as it still seems, no fog in or anywhere near Petty Harbour. 'I mean we knew there wouldn't be any decent hotels or restaurants here,' the director said, as if it had never occurred to him that Newfoundlanders might be offended by this observation, 'but the one thing we thought we could count on in this 40 bloody place was fog. We *came* for the fog, for God's sake.'

7   A fog machine had to be brought in, 'from Scandinavia', the director said. It was yellow, looked vaguely like a locomotive, and, with the help of two men who had to crank it constantly, produced great billowing quantities of fog, all of which, because of the offshore wind that was responsible for the absence of real fog, and in contra- 45 vention of the properties of real fog, blew out to sea. Large fans were set up to blow the fog the other way, which they succeeded in doing, but an assistant director con- fided to us students that, in the daily rushes, the 'fog footage' was disappointing.

8   In one scene, a group of us were supposed to bury a whale on the beach. Not until he actually had us attempt this feat did the director notice that the beach con- 50 sisted not of sand but of rocks the size and shape of ostrich eggs. The word 'Action' was followed by a tremendous volley of noise as our shovels hit the rocks. 'Clank, clink, clank, clank, clink.' I leaned on my shovel, stamping on it repeatedly in a futile effort to manoeuvre even so much as one rock onto it. The director yelled 'Cut' and told us that, before the next take, we should load up our shovels by hand. We did so, 55 crouching down, carefully piling beach rocks on our shovels. 'Action,' he yelled again. 'Now, begin to bury the whale.' We began to bury the whale. Though it was a strug- gle just to raise our shovels off the ground, we managed to hurl their contents at the whale, emitting, more or less in unison, great, choral grunts of exertion.

9   'Thump, thump thump, thump thump thump thump,' went the rocks, bounc- 60 ing off *Orca* as though it were made of some specially designed rock-repellent rubber, most of them ending up nowhere near it. 'Bloody Jesus Christ,' the director yelled, 'is there one, just one single fucking thing in this godforsaken place that works?' We were laughing so hard by this time we were leaning on our shovels, the sight of which so enraged him that, bullhorn raised to his mouth, he came running down the beach 65 towards us, sliding every which way on the rocks and threatening to fire the lot of us if we didn't do what we were told.

10   There was, as it turned out, one thing in the godforsaken place that did work, and that was a very large bulldozer that was used to bury the whale until little more than the dorsal fin was showing. Then, with the cameras rolling, we extras, using our 70 hand-loaded shovels, finished the job, or tried to at any rate, for when we were through heaving rocks the tip of the fin was still protruding from them. Assuring us that, as far as he was concerned, the whale was buried, the director then had us stand grim-faced around this incongruous, fin-tipped mound of beach rocks, then walk away, our shovels on our shoulders. 75

11   On the set, Bo Derek was always wearing the shortest of shorts, but this was not as diverting a sight as it might have been as one of her legs was encased to the hip in a plaster cast. The assistant director told us that the script called for her to have a broken leg, but rumour had it that the broken leg had had to be written into the script at the last moment as Bo had suffered some sort of accident in Newfoundland just 80 before shooting started. At any rate, it was a strange sight, Bo going on crutches with one golden-tanned leg bare, and paired with it an oversize plastered limb that she dragged along behind her as best she could. We expressed doubts to the assistant director that a person with a cast would wear shorts, but he assured us that, on the screen, Bo looked more 'erotic' with one leg showing, for the cast made the bare leg 85 look even better by comparison. We likewise expressed doubts about her tan. 'Her character spends all her time outdoors,' he said, to which one of the students replied that your chances of getting in Newfoundland the kind of tan Bo had would be every bit as good if you spent all your time indoors. 'It'll all make sense when you see it on the screen,' the assistant director said, as if he was used to this sort of cavilling from 90 people not acquainted with the art of filmmaking.

12   Our chance to see whether he was right came at the local premiere of *Orca*, which took place some months later. The movie, as it turned out, was every bit as ridiculous as we suspected it would be, if not more so—suffice it to say that the killer whale, ocean-bound though he is, manages to wreak a great deal of havoc on dry 95 land, cleverly causing to explode a sufficient number of oil-storage tanks to level Petty Harbour ten times over. It was not the movie, however, nor even the fact that Richard Harris and the director were in attendance, but the audience that made the premiere so memorable. Most of Petty Harbour had turned out, several hundred people who did not often go to the movies and who, it soon became apparent, had come out to 100 this one for the sole purpose of seeing themselves and Petty Harbour on the screen.

13   Even before the opening credits finished rolling, there was bedlam in the cinema. Hardly a frame went by that didn't draw from the crowd a roar of recognition. *Orca* ought to have been shown still frame by still frame, the better to allow the audience to itemize every recognizable person, place, or thing on the screen. Not a word of dialogue 105 could be heard. To say that there was no willing suspension of disbelief would be an understatement. As each scene opened, the audience ignored the foreground and ignored the actors, instead sitting forward in their seats the better to see whose house that was behind Bo Derek's head, whose car that was that Richard Harris had just walked past, whose boat that was at the bottom of the hill from the top of which 110 Charlotte Rampling was waving. 'That's Bucky's boat, look, Bucky's boat,' someone would shout, and then each person, as if alone in having heard this, would shout at the person beside, 'That was Bucky's boat.'

14   The greatest fuss was reserved for close-ups of familiar faces. There was always a pause, a delayed reaction before it struck them whose hyper-enlarged face it was that 115 they were looking at, and then everyone would shout out to that person, knowing they were somewhere in the cinema. When the face of a man named Chrissie Whitten filled the screen, the camera lingering as Chrissie looked grimly at Richard Harris from a wharf, the whole place went up, as if Chrissie had been caught in some moment of absurd pretentiousness. It seemed suddenly to have struck them that the movie- 120 makers' craft, about which so much fuss was made and in which so much money and hype was involved, consisted of nothing more than trying to pass off as something they were not mere mortals like Chrissie Whitten. 'That's Chrissie Whitten,' someone shouted, as if revealing the true identity of some impostor, 'where are ya Chrissie, where are ya, bye?' 'I'm right here,' Chrissie shouted, 'I'm right here,' standing up from   125 his seat near the front, waving his arms and bowing to loud applause.

15   It went on like this to the end. It was only during the final credits that the cinema was silent, everyone intently reading, searching the screen for the names of people they knew. When they read that the filmmakers wished to express their thanks to 'the people of Petty Harbour', there went up one last, derisive, almost self-mocking   130 cheer, which was followed by a rush for the exits, everyone clapping, back-slapping, laughing. Someone shouted 'Hey Harris, where's the party?' and the others took it up, chanting, the way you might some athlete's name, 'party, party, party.'

16   *Orca* flopped. It flopped as badly as such a premiere must have led its makers to expect. Hopes that it would be the first of many movies made in Newfoundland   135 were dashed. It's hard to believe it's taken Hollywood only nineteen years to get over it. Video cassettes of *Orca* are hard to come by now, except in Newfoundland, where it's a kind of camp classic and where, should they be faced with some unexpected down time, the makers of *The Shipping News* et al. will have no trouble finding it.

1995

QUESTIONS

Reader and Purpose

1. The author has used an old saying as the title of his essay. What does the title lead you to expect? When you have finished reading the essay, have you found more than you expected?

2. Comedy can consist of (among other things) plays on words, jokes, and straight-forward descriptions of incidents or situations that are in themselves humorous. Which has Johnston used?

3. In his second paragraph Johnston summarizes the plot of *Orca* in just one sentence. Is he oversimplifying?

4. What do the outsiders think of Petty Harbour and its inhabitants? What does the community think of the outsiders? Is this contrast the true topic of the essay, or is the topic actually the making of a film?

Organization

5. Annie Proulx's novel is referred to in both the opening and closing paragraphs. Why? How does the last reference constitute a **closing by return**?

6. Johnston concludes his opening paragraph with a reference to himself. Why? Is this appropriate?

7. Although the introductory paragraph is composed of only four sentences, it deals with several subjects. How does Johnston unify the paragraph?

8. Paragraph 2 contains a fine example of **irony**. What are its elements?

9. This essay has three sections. What are these sections, and what is the focus of each? What quoted phrase connects sections 1 and 2? What is the connection between sections 2 and 3?

Sentences

10. The second paragraph begins with a **sentence fragment**. Is it effective? Should Johnston have written, instead, 'In the plot of *Orca* Richard Harris . . .'?
11. The second sentence of paragraph 4 includes several series. Identify these series, and then show how the author has structured this long sentence in order to keep it clear.
12. Is the second sentence in paragraph 6 correctly punctuated? Would it be just as clear with less punctuation? How would less punctuation affect the **balance** of the sentence?
13. Identify each sentence in paragraph 11 as **loose**, **cumulative**, **freight-train**, or **periodic**.

Diction

14. Look up: *influx* (6), *ritually* (23), *funereally* (23), *irate* (31), *offshore* (45), *contravention* (45), *incongruous* (74), *cavilling* (90), *bedlam* (102), *pretentiousness* (120), *camp* (138).
15. What is the function of the six hyphens in paragraph 4?
16. The phrase *what nature does to man* occurs in paragraph 3 and again in paragraph 6. Does it mean precisely the same thing in both cases?
17. In paragraph 7 why is the phrase *from Scandinavia* placed in quotation marks?

POINTS TO LEARN

1. Well-constructed sentences can quickly provide a good deal of useful information.
2. A carefully contrived perspective and narrative tone allow a writer to make many points effectively, although indirectly.

SUGGESTIONS FOR WRITING

Write an essay in which you illustrate the wide gap between different perceptions of the same reality. Possible topics include the following: a peewee hockey game viewed by the players and by parents; a university class analyzed by professors and by students; a convenience store viewed by a clerk and by a customer; a long-distance airline flight described by a flight attendant and by a passenger; a church service viewed by the minister and by a member of the congregation.

IMPROVING YOUR STYLE

One of your objectives should be to show the humorous side of the contrast. Thus, in planning your essay, carefully choose several incidents that reveal this contrast, and then let them speak for themselves without emphasizing them.

GERALD HANNON

A native of New Brunswick, Gerald Hannon (1944–) grew up in Marathon, a pulp mill town in northern Ontario, and moved to Toronto in 1962 to attend St Michael's College at the University of Toronto; he graduated in 1966. In the 1970s he became involved with the city's gay culture, through various gay organizations of the time, including the radical magazine *The Body Politic*, where he was a member of the editorial collective. A freelance writer since 1987, Hannon has taught journalism at Ryerson Polytechnic Univeristy and is a member of the board of directors of Pink Triangle Press. He has earned four National Magazine Awards, most recently for his writing in the Toronto art magazine *Lola* in 2002.

Romancing the Stones

1   She was ready to get her first job at the age of 10. 'I wanted to get going,' she says. 'I could read. I could write. I could add, subtract, multiply, and divide. The rest is passion. I always knew I would own my own business—so why shouldn't I get started?'

2   Well, for one thing, her mummy wouldn't let her. Which meant Beth Kirkwood had to wait until she was 19 before she left home and plunged into the workforce— 5 without a university education but with, presumably, the same bounce-about energy I'm witnessing here, in her about-to-be-vacated office space in First Canadian Place in Toronto, where she begins by apologizing for the burnt-out ceiling lights but, hey, they're fifteen bucks each and we're moving so why bother, then crosses the room to answer the phone but doesn't, then sits us both down on the sofa, then springs up to 10 examine a map of Canada on the wall (she loves maps), then excuses herself to go out and get one of her favourites, and does, and comes back, and suddenly we're looking at Borneo.

3   Borneo makes sense. So does Baffin Island, the northern reaches of which she'd just been pointing out on the map of Canada. Beth Kirkwood may not have visited 15 every country she's obsessed with, but she is nonetheless an explorer—not your pith-helmet, barter-with-the-natives type, but your nail-biting, junior-resources-exploration entrepreneur with a passion for finding diamonds or gold or oil and gas in places as far-flung as Botswana or Borneo or Baffin Island or even, when it comes to that, southern Ontario. For Kirkwood, that job means selling the prospect of 20 untold riches to investors, then using their money to pay an exploration team (which these days can include everything from satellite surveys to your basic geologist looking at rocks) to head for promising territory, stake a claim, take samples, and hope.

4   Recently she's been making forays into what is probably the most dangerously uncharted territory of all—the Internet, though it might not quite match the experi- 25 ence of flying over the Kalahari Desert in a helicopter dangerously short on gas. 'We had to fly very low', she remembers, 'to save gas by avoiding the winds higher up. So low that when we passed over villages, I could practically read the time off people's wristwatches.'

5   That is a long way from typing, filing, and the myriad other duties in a legal 30 secretary's job description. Kirkwood spent 17 years in that world, working for

lawyer Rocco Schiralli, many of whose clients were big players in the mining business. She listened. She typed. She learned to love what she calls 'the tools and the science of exploration, especially for diamonds'. And she left, in 1993, to found her own resources-exploration company, which she named, with a trademark combo of   35
bravado and high spirits, TNK Resources Inc., short for 'The Next Kimberely' (name of the first, and very rich, diamond mine in South Africa). TNK became Opus Minerals Inc. in May 1999. Which sounds a bit like TNK had gone belly-up, but junior mining companies, Kirkwood says, never die, partly because they never have debt.   40

6   'Hardly anyone is crazy enough to lend us money,' she says. 'So we finance through the sale of shares. And when you need more money, you consolidate, sell more shares, and change your name.' She is now a director and shareholder of Investorlinks.com (an investing site born out of Opus), but president and CEO of First Strike Diamonds Inc., the company scouring Baffin Island for evidence of stones. As   45
if that weren't enough, she is also director of sales and marketing for Crossbeam Ltd., a Toronto company that designs and builds Web sites, and publisher and CEO of intheloop.com, an information source for investors in natural-resource companies. Oh, and she's a single mom raising two teenage boys.

7   Finding fulfillment in unlikely places may be something of a family trait. Her   50
sister and best friend is writer Barbara Gowdy, whose most recent novel, *The White Bone*, imagines the world from the point of view of a herd of elephants. Brother John Gowdy is a champion bridge player. Kirkwood, though, will admit to a retirement fantasy that is somewhat conventional—'Barbara and I will get this place in the south of France, and she'll write, but she's a slow writer so I'll spew out crap—I'm a fan of   55
mysteries—and that will pay the bills. We'll have light breakfasts and, in the afternoon, naps, a massage, and then dinner parties with young men.'

8   Which is a segue into a typical Beth Kirkwood riff that starts with travelling to Kenya with her sons and sister Barbara, and ends with rollerblading. It covers that ground something like this: how the trip to Africa both provided Gowdy with real-life   60
detail for her book on elephants and Kirkwood with pictures from a Botswana site to show shareholders, and that reminds her of how she and Gowdy had travelled to Germany and also to Paris, where they toured all the cemeteries, which reminds her that she started rollerblading recently and would practise in her local cemetery, until that got banned because, as she put it, 'people kept crashing into mourners.'   65

9   She declares—though she scarcely has to—that she has a lot of fun in life, but feels that she can't really take credit, that it's almost a genetic thing. 'My youngest son was born chuckling. And I just can't not be happy.' Besides, she notes, if you want to be an explorer, you pretty much have to be an optimist. 'The odds! One chance in a thousand when you stake a claim that you'll make a mine, especially a diamond mine.   70
I'm always setting out to do something that ultimately probably won't be a success.'

10   She's never made a discovery that became a mine. And the dream that the next Kimberley might be just over the horizon is one of the reasons she can't seem to abandon exploration—even if, at her level, exploration usually means the less-than-glamorous job of persuading investors to part with their money.   75

11   The new Internet ventures, however, seem just as consuming. I ask if there's a need for that kind of investor service, and she says, 'Of course there's a need. I just have to create the demand.' And manage to hold her own in that notoriously risky business—but then holding one's own comes naturally to a second alto.

12   Which is her voice part in the 10-woman choral group she's long been part of. 80 Known variously as The Hot Flashes and The Control Tops (in discreet homage to The Nylons), the group is in hiatus right now, but over the last 10 years has sung everything from madrigals to contemporary pop. 'It's difficult to find people to sing harmony with,' she says. 'So many people can't hold their part. When you sing harmony, the most important thing is to listen. You listen to the others to know what to sing yourself.'   85

13   Then, 'the rest is passion.'

2001

QUESTIONS

Reader and Purpose

1. The title of this essay is obviously a reference to the popular movie *Romancing the Stone* (1984, starring Michael Douglas, Kathleen Turner, and Danny DeVito), which was about searching for lost treasure in Colombia. But what does the title mean, and how, with *stone* in its plural form, is it an appropriate title for this essay?

2. Describe the **tone** of this essay. Is it the proper tone for the subject—the life and work of a successful Canadian executive—or do you find the tone rather too light and informal? On the other hand, could you argue that the exuberant personality of this woman lends itself to this kind of treatment?

3. Keeping in mind that this is a fairly short essay, has the author done a good job of illustrating how and why Beth Kirkwood has become a successful business person? If you believe that he has not, what else should he have done (without increasing the length of his essay)?

Organization

4. What **transition** joins paragraphs 2 and 3? paragraphs 3 and 4? 4 and 5? How do these three transitions differ from each other? Or is there no difference at all?

5. Because of its opening 'Oh', the last sentence of paragraph 6 is made to seem an afterthought. Is it an afterthought, or is it, rather, a stylistic device? How do you know? What is the purpose of such a sentence?

6. Is there a transition between paragraphs 6 and 7? If there is a transition, is it made by a **connective** or is it a transition of ideas? If there is no transition, should there be? Is the opening sentence of paragraph 7 an appropriate introduction to the paragraph?

7. The opening sentence of paragraph 8 is unusual in that it begins with a relative pronoun. Is this kind of sentence appropriate in this essay? Why, or why not?

8. How is the last sentence of this essay a **closing by return**?

Sentences

9. What kind of progression does the author use in the second sentence of paragraph 2? Is this long sentence effective, or should it be divided into shorter sentences? Try revising it: for instance, end the first sentence after 'Toronto' and start the next sentence with 'Here she begins by apologizing . . .'. Then end the following

sentence after 'answer the phone but doesn't', and begin the next sentence with 'She then sits us both down . . .'. Try several different revisions of this long sentence, and then decide which of your versions is better than the original. If you conclude that the original is still the best, explain what the author does better than you do.

10. The last sentence of paragraph 3 contains a four-part series. What are these four parts and how are they **parallel**?

11. What is the function of the **appositive** enclosed within parentheses in paragraph 5? In that appositive, why is the phrase *and very rich* set off by two commas?

Diction

12. Look up: *reaches* (14), *barter* (17), *entrepreneur* (18), *myriad* (30), *bravado* (36), *consolidate* (42), *trait* (50), *segue* (58), *riff* (58), *hiatus* (82), *madrigals* (83), *harmony* (83).

13. Why has the author used the word *mummy* at the beginning of paragraph 2? Wouldn't *mother* be more appropriate in this context?

14. To *stake a claim* is a fairly common **figure of speech**. What is its **figurative** meaning? What is its original, literal meaning? Which meaning is the author using in paragraph 3?

POINTS TO LEARN

1. A transition between paragraphs can be a simple word or a group of words, and can be made by continuing, or by developing, the same idea.

2. A long, seemingly rambling sentence can be effective provided it is organized according to space or time or a combination of the two.

SUGGESTIONS FOR WRITING

Write a profile (6–9 paragraphs) of a successful young person you know—a class president, a star athlete, a business person, a local community worker, a budding politician, a medical student, a licensed mechanic, etc. In showing how this person has become successful, give examples of, for instance, his or her work habits, attitudes, objectives, plans, achievements, etc.

IMPROVING YOUR STYLE

1. Use a transition that involves repeating the same word in the last sentence of a paragraph and in the first sentence of the next paragraph.

2. Write at least one long sentence that you organize spatially or temporally or by a combination of both.

Roy Vontobel

Roy Vontobel is an Ottawa-based freelance writer who has held editorial positions with such conservationist periodicals as *Natural History, Nature Canada,* and the journal of the Canadian Conservation Institute. He also edited *Man and Wildlife in a Shared Environment* (1982), published by the Canadian Wildlife Service. Recently he has worked for Nortex, an Ottawa-based organization that specializes in communications and educational materials for Northern companies and peoples.

In his treatment of the wolverine, the legendary villain of the Canadian North, Vontobel demonstrates how restatement and contrast can be used for effective emphasis of a main point.

Reluctant Villain

1   From earliest times, the fertile imagination of man has populated the world with a host of mythical and semi-mythical creatures. Most of them have become quaint and interesting folklore, but others still haunt and intrigue us. In curiosity and in fear, man has gazed with self-centred eye upon the world in which he lives, giving to the beasts around him all manner of human attributes. Unfortunately, this tendency 5 remains with us. Even today, in the minds of many, deep in the unknown reaches of the trackless forest, the 'good' animals frolic in a Walt Disney wonderland while 'evil' shadows lurk in the underbrush. Ancient prejudices run deep.

2   Perhaps no animal of the American or Eurasian wilderness has been tagged with more negative human characteristics than the wolverine. Today it is an animal of near 10 mythological proportions. Yet Indian and trappers' tales notwithstanding—very little is actually known about it. Wildlife biologists have ventured estimates of its numbers, but studies of its life and behaviour have so far been impossible. As with most mythical creatures, the tales are supported by a modicum of fact. The facts, however, have been gleaned for the most part from rare chance encounters with the animal, usually 15 when the wolverine is surprised while helping itself to a trapper's food cache or while fleeing into the bush. All in all, the wolverine has been the prime candidate for the furtive and vicious villain of the North. The time could come when that legacy is all that is ever known about it.

1979

QUESTIONS
Reader and Purpose

1. Is Vontobel writing for an audience familiar with his subject? What aspects of the first paragraph would you use to support your opinions?
2. How does the **tone** of the second paragraph differ from that of the first? In what other ways does the author emphasize his reasons for taking the wolverine seriously?

Organization

3. Vontobel develops paragraph 1 by restatement of the point made in the first sentence. He also uses this paragraph to pass judgment on our anthropomorphic thinking (i.e. attributing human characteristics to animals). What other words or phrases, such as *self-centred eye*, indicate the kind of judgment he is making?
4. How does the last sentence summarize paragraph 1 while at the same time taking us back to the opening sentence?
5. Explain how the first sentence of paragraph 2 serves both as a **topic sentence** and as a link with the preceding paragraph. What specific words in paragraph 2 also provide such links?
6. Vontobel contrasts fantasy with fact in his second paragraph. How does he stress this contrast? Compare, for example, the fifth sentence of paragraph 1 with the fifth sentence of paragraph 2.
7. Note that the two paragraphs are also organized by references to time. Point out these references, and trace the progression of Vontobel's exposition from the past ('earliest times') to the future ('the time could come').

Sentences

8. Vontobel restates his point in three differently constructed sentences to open the first paragraph. Describe the structure of each of these sentences; note the **participial** construction in the third sentence. Would the three sentences have been more effective if they had all been structured in the same way? How would the rhythm of sentence 3 be affected if Vontobel had written 'in curiosity and fear'?
9. What emphasis is achieved by the short fourth sentence of paragraph 1 and by the positioning of the adverb *unfortunately*?
10. What does the **interrupted movement** of the fifth sentence of paragraph 1 serve to emphasize? What does the **allusion** to Walt Disney contribute to the sentence?
11. Vontobel ends paragraph 1 with a short **simple sentence**. Explain why this serves well as a conclusion. What would be the result if the sentence were omitted?
12. Describe the ways in which Vontobel varies his sentence structures and sentence lengths in paragraph 2. How do the sentences of this paragraph make more use of specific detail than those of paragraph 1?

Diction

13. Look up: *mythical* (2), *quaint* (3), *folklore* (3), *frolic* (7), *prejudices* (8), *modicum* (14).
14. Many writers (and readers) today object to using *man* to refer to people generally. How might you reword the first three sentences of paragraph 1 to avoid using *man*, *he*, and *him*? Is your revision as effective as the original?
15. Why does the author put quotation marks around *good* and *evil* (7)?
16. What does *tagged* (9) mean to you? Does it have another meaning for a zoologist?
17. Is Vontobel's use of *trackless forest* (7) **ironic**?

POINTS TO LEARN

1. Restatement may involve repeating the same key words or repeating the same idea in different words.

2. Sentence structures and lengths can be varied for effective emphasis of main ideas.
3. **Participial phrases** are economic and allow you to subordinate ideas of secondary importance.
4. **Interrupting phrases** can be used both to vary sentence rhythms and to reinforce the main point of a sentence.

SUGGESTIONS FOR WRITING

Using restatement, compose two short paragraphs of six or seven sentences each (about 120 words) in which you develop one of the topics below. Contrast the main point of the second paragraph with that of the first—as Vontobel contrasts fantasy and fact— and be sure to provide a connecting link between the two paragraphs. (If none of the topics appeals to you, devise one of your own.)

Many people have trouble with mathematics (or English, or physics, etc.).

Automobiles are taken for granted as necessities in our way of life.

Canadians in other provinces generally view the people of Quebec as belonging to a totally different culture.

IMPROVING YOUR STYLE

1. Conclude one of the sentences in your essay with a participial phrase.
2. Write three sentences in which you vary the position of adverbs such as *unfortunately*.
3. Vary your sentence openings as follows:

   • Begin two sentences directly with the subject–verb nucleus.
   • Begin one with a **prepositional phrase**.
   • Begin one with two interrupting phrases followed by the subject–verb nucleus.
   • Begin one with a participial phrase.

4. Write two sentences in which you make use of allusions (one mythological or historical, and one drawn from current events).

GEORGE WOODCOCK

George Woodcock (1912–95) described himself as a 'man of letters' rather than a scholar or a journalist. However he is described, there is no question that Woodcock was for many years one of Canada's most prolific writers. He was the author of more than 130 books, books that reflect his extraordinarily cosmopolitan range of interests— biographies, histories, works of literary criticism, political commentaries, travel books, and collections of his own poetry. In addition, he was an editor and a frequent contributor to Canadian, American, and English periodicals. While teaching at the University of British Columbia, Woodcock founded *Canadian Literature* (the first journal devoted solely to the study of Canadian writing), which he edited from its inception in 1959 until 1977. Woodcock was especially interested in the art of biography, and his work in this genre was much praised; in 1966 he received a Governor General's Award for *The Crystal Spirit: A Study of George Orwell*.

Here, in the concluding paragraphs of the biographical study *Gabriel Dumont: The Métis Chief and His Lost World* (1976), Woodcock reveals his sympathetic insight into his subject as he describes the pathos and the irony of Dumont's last years while drawing together, in rhythmically effective prose, the main themes of the book as a whole.

From *Gabriel Dumont*

1   The years passed, and now they were uneventful, for Gabriel was no longer a man to whom his fellows called for leadership, though sometimes they asked his advice, nor did he wish to lead them. He withdrew into the rhythms of the hunting years, doing a little trading, catching his own meat and fish, and always pleased when he had a few skins to sell at one of the stores in Batoche or Duck Lake. On feast days he would put 5 on a suit, and wear, as insignia of a heroic past, the gold watch from Massachusetts and the Silver medal from New York. He thought of that past without guilt and without rancour, glorying in his own deeds as Homer's heroes must have done, yet sad always for that vanished primitive world to which he had been so superbly adapted.

2   He never experienced sickness or felt the grip of decay. Just before his death, he 10 went on a hunting trip to Basin Lake, in the hills a few miles east of Batoche. It was mid-May, the hunt was successful, and he enjoyed the bright spring weather, the opening flowers, the flights of migrant birds. When he came back, he complained to Alexis of pains in his chest and arms, but as he seemed otherwise in perfect health they decided he had merely strained his muscles. For the next few days he went about 15 in his usual way, doing a little fishing and a little walking, and talking to the friends he met by the roadside. On Saturday, 19 May 1906, he went again for a walk. When he returned, he went into Alexis's house and asked for a bowl of soup. He sat down, ate a few mouthfuls, and then, without speaking, he walked across to a bed in the room and crumpled onto it. His death was like the flash of his gun, sudden, accurate, 20 and—since one must die—merciful.

3   When Gabriel Dumont died, the world did not think of him because the world did not know. He and the cause he fought for, and the way of life he personified, has so faded out of memory that only the little local newspapers in Battleford and Prince Albert noticed his death and his funeral. The papers of Toronto and Winnipeg and 25 Montreal, that once had spoken of him with the kind of fearful admiration Milton reserved for Satan, did not even remark his passing. But when he was buried in the cemetery on the top of the hill at Batoche, where the dead men of the rebellion were already lying under the great stark cross, the Métis from all the settlements around came riding in, and the Cree tramped from Beardy's and One Arrow's reserves to 30 crowd into the little wooden church, scarred with the bullet marks of Lieutenant Howard's Gatling, where Father Moulin, his white beard hanging almost to his waist, conducted the service; then the young men of the Dumont clan carried Gabriel to his grave, on the crest overlooking the point on the river where, twenty-one years ago to within a few days, the *Northcote* came whistling round the bend to open the battle of 35 Batoche that marked the death of the Métis nation.

1976

QUESTIONS

Reader and Purpose

1. Woodcock is clearly sympathetic to Dumont and his cause. How does the **tone** of these concluding paragraphs indicate this feeling?
2. Why do you think Woodcock has spent so little time on the actual circumstances of Dumont's death? Keep in mind that the book is largely concerned with Dumont's role in the Métis rebellion of 1885 and his relationship with Louis Riel, the Métis leader.
3. By pointing out, in the first paragraph, that Dumont sold his skins at stores in Batoche and Duck Lake, Woodcock also recalls for the reader the important battles that had occurred at these places. What is the **irony** here? How is this point related to the author's mention of the steamboat in the last sentence of this selection?

Organization

4. Is the first sentence a good introduction for this selection? Why, or why not?
5. To what extent is the first sentence a brief summary of what follows?
6. The phrase *the years passed* (1)—akin to a **pointer**—hints that Woodcock's book is nearing the end. List the other phrases or words of this sort and explain how these expressions indicate that these are the concluding paragraphs of the book.
7. The selection ends with a slow, majestic sentence that brings the entire book to a conclusion. How has Woodcock managed to effectively slow down the speed of the final sentence?
8. Summarize briefly the purpose of each paragraph, showing what part each one plays in the development of Woodcock's conclusion.
9. Is the first sentence of paragraph 2 a logical **topic sentence**? Examine the rest of the paragraph closely in relation to the first sentence.
10. The last paragraph has two parts, with the second part being introduced by a contrasting word. Analyze the unity of this paragraph, showing how each sentence after the first is related to the one preceding it as either development or contrast.

Sentences

11. Compare the movement and rhythm of the last sentence with those of the other three sentences in the final paragraph.
12. The author's mention of *rhythms* (3) is a hint that perhaps his sentences try to reflect the rhythms he is referring to. Is this true of any of the sentences in paragraph 1?
13. The elements of the first sentence are linked by the words *and* (1), *for* (1), *though* (2), and *nor* (2). How are the elements of the final sentence of this selection joined?
14. What type of sentence is the last one: **parallel**? **cumulative**? **periodic**? some other type?
15. Why does the last sentence make an effective conclusion?

Diction

16. Look up: *uneventful* (1), *insignia* (6), *rancour* (8), *primitive* (9), *personified* (23), *stark* (29), *Gatling* (32).
17. The small number of words to look up in question 16 suggests that Woodcock's vocabulary is unusually plain. Do you think there is any relation between this point and the author's subject? To take the point one step further, does Woodcock use many **figures of speech**? Do the figures of speech (if there are any) reinforce this general impression of plainness?

POINTS TO LEARN

1. Tone indicates the writer's attitude towards his or her subject.
2. The rhythm of a sentence can reflect the idea being expressed.
3. The slow, rhythmic, balanced movement of a long concluding sentence can help emphasize the writer's tone.

SUGGESTIONS FOR WRITING

With regard to any substantial essay (1,000–1,500 words) you have written during the past few months,

   a) write a brief summary (10–20 lines) of the essay;
   b) write the concluding paragraph twice, ending once with a long, slow sentence, and once with a short, quick sentence.

IMPROVING YOUR STYLE

In your paragraph include:

1. at least two sentences in which the rhythm is emphasized;
2. a dividing point marked by a word of contrast.

CHRISTINA HOFF SOMMERS

Christina Hoff Sommers is a well-known American writer and social scientist who has written two books and has published articles in many newspapers and journals, from *USA Today* to the *New England Journal of Medicine*. A former professor of philosophy at Clark University, she is currently the W.H. Brady Fellow at the American Enterprise Institute, a conservative think tank. The essay included here is from her book *Who Stole Feminism? How Women Have Betrayed Women* (1994), in which she argues that contemporary feminism in North America is divided into two camps: that of 'equity feminists', who strive for equality with men in education, pay, and opportunities; and that of 'gender feminists', who dwell on victimhood and sexist oppression, thereby punishing men and hurting other women. The book, which stirred controversy and garnered Sommers national media attention, has been criticized for representing feminism as a monolithic system, rather than as a movement that comprises differing politics and voices. Sommers' most recent work is *The War Against Boys: How Misguided Feminism Is Harming Our Young Men* (2000).

Indignation, Resentment, and Collective Guilt

1   Every day the public is witness to feminist outrage at how badly women are treated: in the workplace, in the courts, on dates, in marriages, in the schools—by men mostly, but sometimes by other women. Much of what is reported is true, and some of it is very disturbing.

2   Of course, the abuse or slighting of women must be made known and should 5
arouse indignation. Plato himself recognized the role of righteous indignation as a
mainspring of moral action. In his metaphor, indignation is the good steed helping
the charioteer to stay on the path of virtue by controlling the vicious, wayward steed
straining to go its own brutish way. It is the 'spirited element' in the soul that supplies
the wise person with the emotional energy, the horsepower, to curb the appetites so 10
that he or she may act virtuously.

3   But most of those who publicly bemoan the plight of women in America are
moved by more dubious passions and interests. Theirs is a feminism of resentment
that rationalizes and fosters a wholesale rancour in women that has little to do with
moral indignation. Resentment may begin in and include indignation, but it is by far 15
the more abiding passion. Resentment is 'harboured' or 'nurtured'; it 'takes root' in a
subject (the victim) and remains directed at another (the culprit). It can be vicarious—you need not have harmed me personally, but if I identify with someone you
have harmed, I may resent you. Such resentment is very common and may easily be
as strong and intense as resentment occasioned by direct injury. In a way it is 20
stronger, for by enlarging the class of victims to include others, it magnifies the vil-
lainy as well.

4   Having demarcated a victimized 'us' with whom I now feel solidarity, I can
point to one victim and say, 'In wronging her, he has betrayed his contempt for us all,'
or 'Anyone who harms a woman harms us all,' or simply 'What he did to her, he did 25
to all of us.' The next step is to regard the individual who wronged 'us' as himself representative of a group, giving our animus a larger target. This I may do quite 'reasonably' by adopting a position from which people like the perpetrator (male, rich, etc.)
are regarded as 'the kind of people' who exploit people like 'us'. My social reality has
now been dichotomized into two groups politically at odds, one of whom dominates 30
and exploits the other.

5   Susan Faludi, author of *Backlash* and one of the more popular resenters of our
time, reminds us of the feminist truism that feminist anger comes when women construe their individual experiences in a political framework: 'When you're not able to
see your experience as political, you're not able to be angry about it.' Sandra Bartky, 35
who is an expert on something she calls the 'phenomenology of feminist consciousness', puts it succinctly: 'Feminist consciousness is consciousness of *victimization* . . .
to come to see oneself as a victim' (her emphasis).

6   Once I get into the habit of regarding women as a subjugated gender, I'm
primed to be alarmed, angry, and resentful of men as oppressors of women. I am also 40
prepared to believe the worst about them and the harm they cause to women. I may
even be ready to fabricate atrocities. Eleanor Smeal spoke in Austin of the need to get
women fighting mad. Neither she nor any of the other feminist leaders and thinkers
who promote the sexual politics of resentment and anger seem to be aware of how
injuriously divisive their version of feminism is—or if they are, they seem not to care. 45

7   Consider how Patricia Ireland, the president of NOW, speaks of her seven years
as a flight attendant for Pan Am: 'I thought of myself as a professional. But what I
really did was go down the aisle and take people's garbage and thank them for it.
That's what women have been doing. We've been taking their garbage and thanking
them for it. We've got to stop.' Ms Ireland is telling us how easy it is (in a society that 50

routinely humiliates women) for women to deceive themselves into thinking they are doing something dignified when they are 'really' doing something demeaning. She speaks of 'their garbage', meaning 'men's', though probably half the passengers were women. She asks us to note the shame of taking their garbage and having to thank 'them' for it. Would she be in favour of having the airlines phase out women flight 55 attendants, replacing them with men? But Ireland knows what she is doing. By so construing male/female relations, she is doing what any political leader does in time of war: get potential allies angry and unified behind the effort to defeat the enemy.

8   Resentment is not a wholesome passion. Unlike indignation, it is not an ethical passion. But because it often originates in moral outrage at real injustice (from wife 60 battering to job discrimination), resentment can be made to sound like a commendable passion for social justice. The idea that men are generally culpable has the status of a first principle among some establishment feminists.

9   According to Marilyn French, 'The entire system of female oppression rests on ordinary men, who maintain it with a fervour and dedication to duty that any secret 65 police force might envy. What other system can depend on almost half the population to enforce a policy daily, publicly and privately, with utter reliability?' It is a system that uses threat as well as force to exploit and humiliate women.

> As long as some men use physical force to subjugate females, *all* men need not. The knowledge that some men do suffices to threaten all women. Beyond that, 70 it is not necessary to beat up a woman to beat her down. A man can simply refuse to hire women in well-paid jobs, extract as much or more work from women than men but pay them less, or treat women disrespectfully at work or at home. He can fail to support a child he has engendered, demand the woman he lives with wait on him like a servant. He can beat or kill the woman he 75 claims to love; he can rape women, whether mate, acquaintance, or stranger; he can rape or sexually molest his daughters, nieces, stepchildren, or the children of a woman he claims to love. *The vast majority of men in the world do one or more of the above* [her emphasis].

In French's view, male atrocity and criminal abuse are pandemic. We must, however, 80 insist that the burden of proof for so broad a claim be on her. Even if we accept the premise that men and women are at odds, the factual question of guilt cannot be begged—at least not in this country. Moreover, we cannot help noticing that French's contempt for men is accompanied by a strong bias in favour of women: 'While men strut and fret their hour upon the stage, shout in bars and sports arenas, thump their 85 chests or show their profiles in the legislatures, and explode incredible weapons in an endless contest for status, an obsessive quest for symbolic "proof" of their superiority, women quietly keep the world going.'

10   Resenter feminists are convinced that men generally take every opportunity to exploit women and that they often delight in humiliating them physically and men- 90 tally. 'Given the prevalence of rape and given the socio-cultural supports for sexual aggression and violence against women in this society, perhaps we should be asking men who don't rape, why not! In other words, we should be asking what factors prevent men from abusing women in rape-supportive societies.' That is the view of Diana Scully, author of *Understanding Sexual Violence*.   95

11   Recently several male students at Vassar were falsely accused of date rape. After their innocence was established, the assistant dean of students, Catherine Comins, said of their ordeal: 'They have a lot of pain, but it is not a pain that I would necessarily have spared them. I think it ideally initiates a process of self-exploration. "How do I see women?" "If I did not violate her, could I have?" "Do I have the potential to   100 do to her what they say I did?" These are good questions.' Dean Comins clearly feels justified in trumping the common law principle 'presumed innocent until proven guilty' by a new feminist principle, 'guilty even if proven innocent'. Indeed, she believes that the students are not really innocent after all. How so? Because, being male and being brought up in the patriarchal culture, they *could easily have done* what they   105 were falsely accused of having done, even though they didn't *actually* do it. Where men are concerned, Comins quite sincerely believes in collective guilt. Moreover, she feels she can rely on her audience to be in general agreement with her on this.

12   The idea of collective guilt may sound like the theological doctrine of original sin, but in Christianity, at least, it applies equally to all human beings. Racists and gen-   110 der feminists are more 'discriminating'.

13   In the spring of 1993, nine women students, who were taking a course called 'Contemporary Issues in Feminist Art' at the University of Maryland, distributed posters and fliers all over the campus with the names of dozens of male students under the heading 'Notice: These Men Are Potential Rapists'. The women knew noth-   115 ing whatever about the bearers of the names; they had simply chosen them at random from the university directory to use in their class project. The instructor, Josephine Withers, would not comment to the press.

14   The New Feminists are a powerful source of mischief because their leaders are not good at seeing things as they are. Resenter feminists like Faludi, French, Heilbrun   120 and MacKinnon speak of backlash, siege, and an undeclared war against women. But the condition they describe is mythic—with no foundation in the facts of contemporary American life. Real-life men have no war offices, no situation rooms, no battle plans against women. There is no radical militant wing of a masculinist movement. To the extent one can speak at all of a gender war, it is the New Feminists themselves   125 who are waging it.

———

15   Gender feminists are fond of telling men who don't realize the depth of women's anger and resentment that 'they just don't get it.' Feminist leaders immediately rallied to the side of Lorena Bobbitt, the Virginia woman accused of having severed her sleeping husband's penis but who in turn accused him of having raped   130 her. The Virginia chapter of NOW set up a support line for Ms Bobbitt headed by Virginia's NOW coordinator, Denise Lee. In *Vanity Fair*, Kim Masters reported on 'Lorena supporters who have transformed the V-for-Victory sign into a symbol of solidarity by making scissorlike motions with their fingers'. Kim Gandy, executive vice-president of NOW, talked of the many women 'who have gone through this and   135 probably wish they had a chance to get their own revenge'.

16   The journalist Daniel Wattenberg rightly saw in all this the presumption of John Wayne Bobbitt's guilt long before the case had gone to trial. 'It is assumed that he routinely beat his wife over a period of years. It is assumed that he raped her the night

she castrated him.' It hardly matters that Mr Bobbitt has since been found not guilty 140
by the courts. Commenting on the castration on '20/20', Patricia Ireland said, 'The
depth of anger that was plumbed by this and the response of support that comes for
Lorena Bobbitt comes from the depth of anger, of feeling there has not been adequate
resources and recourse and redress of the terrible violence that women face.' But,
sticking to what facts we have, all we can say is that Lorena was enraged to the point 145
of violence. The personal tragedy of this unhappy couple has been appropriated as a
symbol of righteous feminist revenge. The in-joke among Lorena's feminist admirers
is that Lorena has since been greeting John by saying, 'Now do you get it?'

17   When collective guilt is assigned (to males, to Germans, to Moslems, etc.), children are usually included. Explaining why Minnesota has adopted strict sexual 150
harassment policies for children as young as five, Sue Sattel, the 'sex equity specialist'
for the Minnesota Department of Education, points out that 'serial killers tell inter-
viewers they started sexually harassing at age 10, and got away with it.'

18   Nan Stein, a project director at the Wellesley College Center for Research on
Women who specializes in sexual harassment by juveniles, is angry with Montana 155
school officials and teachers for ignoring the 'gendered terrorism' in their schoolyards.

> Friday 'Flip-Up Day' is a weekly occurrence at many elementary schools in
> Montana. Every Friday, boys chase girls around the school playgrounds; those
> girls who have worn skirts are fair game—their skirts will be flipped up, not once,
> but as many times as possible by as many boys as can get them. School adminis- 160
> trators . . . have seen no reason to intervene or to punish the perpetrators. Their
> silence has allowed this gendered terrorism on the playground to continue.

Boys who tease girls by flipping up their skirts should be dealt with decisively and
perhaps severely. But only women who view the world through 'sex/gender' lenses
would see in children's schoolyard rudeness the making of serial killers and gender 165
terrorists.

19   Should the rudeness even be regarded in sexual terms? The gender monitors
believe it should be and that girls should be made aware of its true nature. One of the
goals of the sex equity experts is to teach little girls to be resentful of boys' pranks by
pointing out that what they are doing is sexual harassment and against the law. 170
Bernice Sandler, a gender relations specialist at Washington's Center for Women
Policy Studies, offers harassment workshops to elementary school children. At one
workshop, a little girl told about a classmate who had pushed her down and tickled
her. Ms Sandler made sure to put the boy's act in perspective: 'Now, you have to ask,
what is the boy doing, throwing girls to the ground? This happens to be a sexual 175
offence in New York, and in most states.'

20   The presumption of sexual guilt continues as children grow up. In more and
more public schools and colleges, we find a dynamic group of feminist reformers—
harassment officers, women's studies professors, resident hall staff, assorted deans and
assistant deans, and sex equity experts—who regard male sexuality with alarm and 180
seek ways to control it. The Rutgers University anthropologist Lionel Tiger has
described the contemporary sexual environment with its hysteria over harassment
and date rape as a reversal of the one described in *The Scarlet Letter*: 'It's the male who
now bears the stigma of alleged sexual violation.'

21   If they do, not many notice it. The gender feminist ideology affects women far 185
more deeply. Many are 'converted' to a view of the society they inhabit as a patriarchal
system of oppression. For most, this happens in college. Laurie Martinka, a women's
studies graduate from Vassar, talked to me about her personal transformation. 'You're
never the same again. Sometimes I even bemoan the fact that so much has changed. I am
tired of always ripping things apart because they exclude the perspective of women. . . . 190
You become so aware of things. And it is hard. My mother cannot accept it. It is hard for
her because I have changed so completely.' Anne Package, a student at the University of
Pennsylvania, told me that students talk among themselves about this keen new awareness: 'We call it "being on the verge" or "bottoming out". You are down on everything.
Nothing is funny anymore. It hits you like a ton of bricks. You hit rock bottom and ask: 195
how can I live my life?' When I suggested to her that many would count her and her
classmates among the world's more fortunate young women, she bristled. 'We still suffer psychological oppression. If you feel like the whole world is on top of you, then it is.'
22   I was intrigued, though, by her expression 'being on the verge'. On the verge of
what? Though the expression suggests a transitory experience, being on the verge is 200
construed as the permanent condition of women who feel they have achieved a realistic awareness of their plight in male-dominated society. Such women sometimes
organize into small but powerful groups within institutions they regard as masculinist bastions and where they make their presence felt in no uncertain terms.
23   The *Boston Globe* is New England's largest and most prestigious newspaper. In 205
1991, some two dozen women editors, managers, and columnists (including Ellen
Goodman) formed a group called 'Women on the Verge' to counter what senior education editor Muriel Cohen called the 'macho newsroom'. The 'vergies', as they have
come to be known, have some traditional equity feminist concerns about salaries and
promotions; but they have also taken up arms against such things as the use of sports 210
metaphors in news stories and the traditional lunchtime basketball game, which symbolizes to them the once-powerful and exclusionary old-boy network (though that
complaint is unfounded because women are welcome to play, and some do).
Defending the basketball games, editor Ben Bradlee, Jr, says: 'All it is really is a bunch
of people who want to get exercise and play a game. In the current conspiracy that's 215
abroad, it's me and the other editors perhaps cutting secret deals and giving the boys
the best stories.' Ms Cohen expressed concern to editor Jack Driscoll over the 'hormones that are running around here'. Vergies are also irritated by 'the strutting zone'—
a corridor where some of the managerial males like to pace before deciding on the day's
lead stories. The Women on the Verge at the *Globe* are feared but not loved. Since their 220
advent, the newspaper has known no internal peace.
24   David Nyhan, a senior editor and syndicated columnist, has been on the paper
for more than 20 years and is part of what is known as its liberal 'Irish mafia'. He is
an old-style newspaperman who wears his sleeves rolled up and has a booming voice
and a penchant for bawdy humour. It was just a matter of time before he got into trou- 225
ble with the Women on the Verge. On April 20, 1993, he was on his way to play in
the infamous noontime basketball match when he spotted a fellow reporter, Brian
McGrory, and invited him to join the game. Brian was on assignment and had a bad
knee that day, so he declined. Nyhan persisted, but when it was clear that McGrory
was not going to play, Nyhan jeered him as 'pussy-whipped'.   230

25   Betsy Lehman, a vergie, overheard the remark in passing and made it clear that she was very offended. Nyhan, who hadn't realized anyone was listening, immediately apologized. Sensing he was in trouble, he placed a memo on his door restating his remorse. He went around the newsroom and again apologized to any woman he could find. But he was about to be made an example of, and nothing could stop it. Already   235 several Women on the Verge had interpreted his statement as an insult to a woman editor who, they assumed, had given Brian McGrory his assignment. McGrory denies it was a woman.

26   The *Globe* management had just spent thousands of dollars on sensitivity work-shops. Senior editor Matt Storin drew the moral: 'Coming off of that experience [the   240 workshops], I for one am all the more saddened by today's experience.' Storin warned the staff that 'remarks that are racially and sexually offensive to co-workers will not be tolerated here. Those who utter such remarks will be subject to disciplinary pro-cedures.' The publisher fined Nyhan $1,250 and suggested he donate that sum to a charity of Ms Lehman's choice.   245

27   The vergies had made their point, but the men of the *Globe* (and some women reporters who sympathized with them) had been alerted to the climate of resentment they lived in. They began to react. A price list was circulated: 'babe' cost $350, 'bitch' went for $900, 'pussy-whipped', $1,250. Someone started a David Nyhan relief fund. (The fine was eventually rescinded.) Even some of the vergies were uncomfortable.   250 Ellen Goodman said that she disapproved of the fine: 'You do not want to get to the point where everybody feels every sentence is being monitored.' But that is just the point the *Globe* had gotten to.

28   The *Globe* incident is emblematic of the 'achievements' of the New Feminists elsewhere. They have achieved visibility and influence, but they have not succeeded   255 in winning the hearts of American women. Most American feminists, unwilling to be identified as part of a cause they find alien, have renounced the label and have left the field to the resenters. The harmful consequences of giving unchallenged rein to the ideologues are nowhere more evident than in the universities.

1994

QUESTIONS

Reader and Purpose

1. Consider the words you are asked to look up under Diction. What does this list tell you about the kind of reader for whom Sommers is writing?

2. Sommers has divided her essay into two sections: paragraphs 1–14, and para-graphs 15–28. What is her purpose in each section?

3. Find four or five words that you feel best describe the **tone** of this essay.

4. Why is this essay included in the Restatement section of *Exposition*? In order to answer this question, look carefully at the quotations Sommers includes in her essay as evidence of what some 'resenter' feminists say and what (according to Sommers) they really mean.

Organization

5. How does the first sentence of paragraph 3 serve as a contrast to the first two paragraphs? Is it also an **organizing sentence**?
6. Outline the logical progression that Sommers follows in paragraph 4.
7. How is paragraph 14 a summary of the first section of this essay? Is it, in your opinion, an adequate summary?
8. Paragraphs 4 and 6 present rather general statements, whereas paragraphs 5 and 7 give specific examples. Is the rest of the first section organized in the same manner? If not, how is it organized?
9. How does Sommers develop her argument in paragraphs 15–22?
10. Paragraphs 23–27 deal with only one incident, the one at the *Boston Globe*, and its ramifications. Why does Sommers give so much attention to this one event?
11. How does the final paragraph function: as summary? as logical conclusion? as comment? as a combination of these?

Sentences

12. Is the first sentence of paragraph 2 a **topic sentence**? a **transitional** sentence? both? neither? Answer the same questions about the first sentence of paragraphs 3, 6, 19, and 21.
13. Examine Sommers' sentences in paragraphs 6, 8, and 14, and state which of the sentences are **simple**, **compound**, or **complex**. What conclusions can you draw about her expository method?
14. In the first sentence of paragraph 4, should 'say' be followed by a colon rather than a comma?
15. Is the comma after 'angry' in the first sentence of paragraph 6 correct? wrong? debatable?
16. Why is the quotation in paragraph 10 not introduced by a colon?
17. Should the first two sentences of paragraph 16 be joined into one?

Diction

18. Look up: *righteous* (6), *mainspring* (7), *wayward* (8), *bemoan* (12), *rationalizes* (14), *vicarious* (17), *demarcated* (23), *animus* (27), *dichotomized* (30), *truism* (33), *construe* (33), *phenomenology* (36), *demeaning* (52), *culpable* (62), *pandemic* (80), *theological* (109), *presumption* (137), *monitors* (167), *ideology* (185), *verge* (194), *transitory* (200), *bastions* (204), *rescinded* (250), *emblematic* (254), *ideologues* (259).
19. Explain what Sommers means by the following expressions: *resenter feminists* (89), *gender feminists* (110–11), *New Feminists* (119), *gender monitors* (167).

POINTS TO LEARN

1. The divisions of an essay can be indicated by symbols or large spaces.
2. The steps in a complex expository essay can be clearly marked by **organizing sentences** and summary paragraphs.

SUGGESTIONS FOR WRITING

Write an extended essay (1,000–1,500 words) on a complex topic, such as the real inequality of the sexes; the job search, the resume, and the interview; or plagiarism and the student's desperate search for higher grades. What standards of honesty does the desperate student follow? Use frequent examples to make your key points.

IMPROVING YOUR STYLE

1. Introduce at least three of your paragraphs by sentences that function both as contrasts and as organizers.
2. Do not give all your examples equal space and emphasis. Make your major examples stand out from the minor ones.

STEVE BURGESS

Born and raised in Brandon, Manitoba, Steve Burgess (1961–) spent 15 years working in private radio, including time as an all-night disc jockey in Vancouver. He has also been the radio host for CBC Newsworld's '@ the end'. The recipient of two Western Magazine Awards and of two National Magazine Awards, he works as a freelance journalist and publishes in such venues as *Chatelaine*, *Vancouver Magazine*, the *Vancouver Sun*, and Salon.com.

Blazing Skies

1   Tourist brochures do their best with what they have.

2   'Visit the world's largest log cabin theatre in Wasagaming, Manitoba!'

3   Could be worth a look.

4   'See the Manitoba Agricultural Hall of Fame!'

5   Umm, perhaps, if there's time after lunch.   5

6   'Brandon, Manitoba—home of the Visible Universe!'

7   Well, that's more like it. Sounds just grand. And if you ask me, the claim would be perfectly legitimate. When I want to view the cosmos in all its inexpressible glory, Brandon is usually where I go.

8   If this promotional strategy hasn't yet occurred to the good folks at the Brandon   10 Chamber of Commerce, it's understandable. The heavenly realms cannot be claimed exclusively by any one town—unlike, say, Vegreville's giant Easter egg. I've scanned the galaxies from Cypress Mountain in Vancouver, Salt Spring Island, BC, and flat on my back on a gravel road outside Stonewall, Manitoba. When you gaze skyward, your present whereabouts tend to disappear, which is sort of the point. But not even the   15 universe can always claim your undivided attention, and the ground beneath your feet can make a difference, too.

9   Stargazers have always understood this paradox: in order to see the largest attraction of all, you need to think small. Big city pollution comes not just from rows of tailpipes but rows of streetlights as well—the blinding haze of artificial illumination   20

that washes out the urban night. A growing national movement is attempting to preserve astronomical viewing areas, dark-sky parks, in places that have thus far stayed
relatively free of Edison's influence.

10   But my own personal starbase is Brandon. Granted, I favour it in part because Mom
and Dad let me stay cheap, and by now I'm used to the food, but those seeking a suitable   25
platform for celestial observation could do worse than the Wheat City. At 40,000-odd
souls, it's large enough to offer amenities, yet small enough to disappear over the horizon
after a 20-minute drive into the country dark. And, of course, there is that obvious prairie
advantage, the flip side of the Saskatchewan mountain-climber's dilemma—the lack of
any natural formations that might intrude on the 360-degree bowl of the sky.   30

11   Being starry-eyed is pretty much standard at a certain age, and I spent many
teenage Brandon summer nights on country roads reclining against the windshield of
my buddy's truck, a case of beer between us as we took turns agonizing over our
hearts' desires. Decades later and settled in busy, bright Vancouver, a trip home re-
acquainted me with what I had once taken for granted. Somewhere past midnight on   35
the near-empty Trans-Canada, I burst out of the claustrophobic Rockies and into
foothill country. Minutes later I was pulling onto the shoulder, stepping out of the car
to stare upward. My hometown was still a couple of provinces away, but I have rarely
experienced a more powerful sense of return, of home. Spread above me, across the
clear prairie night, were the stars. All of them.   40

12   Now nearly every summer I check the calendar to find one of those precious
June or July weeks when the moon is gone and the sky a perfect, dark canvas. Once
back in Brandon, I watch the Weather Channel with the obsessiveness of a fisherman's
wife. Then, with twilight falling in a cloudless sky, I set out for Kirkum's Bridge.

13   That's the name locals give to the little iron crossing where the gravel Kirkum's   45
Road hops over the Little Saskatchewan River. A riverside meadow separated from the
road by a barbed wire fence was always a popular drinking spot for Brandon kids, but
the bucolic little parties often broke up with an irate farmer in pursuit. These days I
keep my feet on public ground. Halfway up the hill from the bridge, a little pullout,
its entrance almost hidden by weeds, leads to a small rest area and a stone cairn. I'm   50
afraid I can't recall what it commemorates—by the time I arrive the light is fading anyway, and the cairn just a dark shape against deepening blue.

14   I park and pop the trunk. Only when every square centimetre of exposed skin
is smeared with repellent do I exit the car and set up shop—a sturdy, reclining lawn
chair, a blanket, more repellent, car window down and the radio tuned to Ross   55
Porter's *After Hours* program on CBC. I'm ready for the stars.

15   If I arrive when the sky is still fringed with orange, I can watch the heavens
darken and see constellations being constructed point by point. The handle of the Big
Dipper comes out first and hangs like an upside-down Cheshire Cat smile, awaiting
the arrival of its familiar body.   60

16   Straight ahead, just above the southern horizon, hangs the constellation
Scorpius: a sideways ice cream cone, as the Greeks somehow failed to notice. Since
Scorpius always occupies that twilight position in midsummer, I take its annual pres-
ence as a sign. Welcome back, it says. Another year, and here we are again. (Or, as the
Greeks would interpret it: 'I'm a giant bloody scorpion, you imbecile, not an ice cream   65
Welcome Wagon.')

17   Serious star freaks have measurements to determine the quality of their favourite observation spots. Bortle's Dark Sky Scale lists nine categories of sky conditions ranging from Class One (almost total darkness) to Class Nine (urban sky). My Kirkum's Bridge hangout, frankly, may rate no better than a Class Three. Then again, Bortle 70 doesn't account for the availability of Mom's meat loaf. And in that little valley it gets dark enough that the fireflies look dangerous as they drift toward the grass.

18   Overhead, the Milky Way stretches all the way to the southern rim in a frozen, vaporous stain. Those who never see the unadulterated night will be shocked at how much lies hidden. Star formations that seem to hang in isolation over city streets sud- 75 denly become bright points almost lost amid patchworks of lesser bodies and clusters. Cassiopeia, a mythical queen whose celestial throne forms a 'W' visible even above Vancouver, is revealed to be soaked in stars—her throne sits squarely midstream in the Milky Way. Orion the Hunter, visible as a lonely figure during the urban winter, gains blood and sinew in the cold country air, his body speckled with light.   80

19   I've managed to pick up some basics about the constellations and sometimes bring binoculars to look for Jupiter's moons or a clearer view of the Pleiades. But I'm no galactic wonk. Mostly I just want to stare at the whole thing—the overwhelming, stupefying sky. Shooting stars blast through, planes and satellites creep across like ants on a tile floor, and the firmament wheels slowly around and down. It's meditation of 85 a sort; you're in the presence of something that defies speech. Which is why eventually the radio must shut up, too. Quiet is needed. Not just to settle your thoughts, but also to make way for something else: the performance of the local choir.

20   The first time it happened, I didn't recognize it right away. Many a cowboy tune told of that lonesome coyote wail but failed to prepare me for the real thing, so high 90 and keening, it doesn't seem possible that its authors could be related to the cloddish, woofing moron that always answers immediately from a nearby farmyard. The poor farm dog brays like a drunken heckler at the 'Hallelujah Chorus', but the coyotes pay him no mind; they're sending out messages on a different frequency entirely.

21   As distractions go, it's infinitely preferable to that other high-pitched noise- 95 maker, the one celebrated on local postcards as the provincial bird. In a bad year (i.e. last year) the mosquitoes seem to outnumber the stars.

22   Worst at twilight, the skeeters become blessedly less active as the prairie night cools, and if you can tolerate the smell of Deet, you can often escape unscathed. Just don't miss a spot or someone will find your pale, drained carcass by the roadside next 100 day. 'Look there, Nestor—on his ankle. Eight hundred and forty-six bites. Poor feller. Must be from away.' (Never mind those orange and blue cans of playground-strength aerosol. This is Manitoba. Local supermarkets stock bottles of liquid repellent so potent it can literally flake the skin off your hands with repeated use.)

23   Bad as they can be, the mosquitoes are never bad enough to keep me away from 105 Kirkum's Bridge. There are other places I could go (I am curious to see what wonders a truly dark, Class One site could afford), but I know I'd miss it all: the river, the ghostly fireflies, the coyote choir, the idiot dog. It's the little touches that make a universe a home.

2001

QUESTIONS
Reader and Purpose
1. Does the author explain, or illustrate, specifically what he means by the 'blazing skies' of his title?
2. What does the author tell us about himself when he uses such expressions as 'I burst out of the claustrophobic Rockies' (paragraph 11), 'These days I keep my feet on public ground' (paragraph 13), 'Mostly I just want to stare at the whole thing—the overwhelming, stupefying sky' (paragaph 19), 'you're in the presence of something that defies speech' (paragraph 19), 'they're sending out messages on a different frequency entirely' (paragraph 20)? The context of these expressions may be important in establishing their meaning.

Organization
3. The last sentence of paragraph 7 makes a statement that is perfectly common-sensical but also startling. What is this contrast? Where else does the author address it?
4. How are the last three sentences of paragraph 11 a conclusion to the first part of this essay, paragraphs 1–11?
5. The second part, paragraphs 12–22, has several subdivisions. What are they? How does the author manage the transitions from each subdivision to the next?
6. What is the author's point in paragraph 21? Has he made his point with sufficient clarity? If you feel that he has not, how could the paragraph be improved?
7. What is the purpose of the final paragraph?
8. What earlier sentence does the final sentence of the essay echo?

Sentences
9. In his first eight paragraphs Burgess employs a variety of sentence lengths. Do you find such a variety anywhere else in his essay?
10. Burgess also uses a variety of sentence structures. For instance, his first sentence follows the basic English subject-verb-object pattern, while others use **interrupted movement**, as in the last sentence of paragraph 10. In paragraphs 17 and 18 find other instances of each kind of sentence.
11. Why has Burgess used a dash in the last sentence of paragraph 13? Would a semicolon be better? Apply the same questions to the dash in paragraph 14 and to the one in paragraph 18. Would a dash rather than the semicolon not be more appropriate after 'It's meditation of a sort' (paragraph 19)?
12. In the last sentence of paragraph 13 why has the author omitted 'is' after 'the cairn'? Would the sentence read better if the comma after 'anyway' were left out?

Diction
13. Look up: *cosmos* (8), *realms* (11), *paradox* (18), *astronomical* (22), *favour* (24), *celestial* (26), *amenities* (27), *dilemma* (29), *bucolic* (48), *cairn* (50), *constellations* (58), *unadulterated* (74), *sinew* (80), *firmament* (85), *keening* (91).
14. In paragraph 19 the author tells us, 'I'm no galactic wonk.' Do you agree, or is he being too modest?

15. What does the author mean by these expressions: *the flip side of the Saskatchewan mountain-climber's dilemma* (29); *Being starry-eyed is pretty much standard at a certain age* (31); *agonizing over our hearts' desires* (33–4)? Do these expressions have more than one meaning?

16. What **figurative** language does Burgess use in paragraphs 18 and 20? Does he frequently use figures of speech elsewhere, or are these two paragraphs exceptional?

17. Burgess uses a wide range of diction, from such phrases as *the cosmos in all its inexpressible glory* (8), *a suitable platform for celestial observation* (25–6), *bucolic little parties* (48), *the firmament wheels slowly around and down* (85), to such informal phrases as *Mom and Dad let me stay cheap* (24–5), *I park and pop the trunk* (53), *Scorpius: a sideways ice cream cone* (62), *The poor farm dog brays like a drunken heckler* (92–3). What other examples can you find of this tension between the educated writer and the simple-guy-from-Brandon persona?

POINTS TO LEARN

1. A short dialogue with oneself can be an effective means of introducing a topic.
2. Details about one's personal life can add a distinct touch to an account of an experience with nature, perhaps especially when they are mentioned briefly and precisely.

SUGGESTIONS FOR WRITING

Have you ever had an overwhelming experience while observing something in nature: a distant mountain range; a high, thin waterfall; a wide expanse of flat prairie; a small blue lake; a calm, flat ocean; the Milky Way; a fog-covered forest; a quiet slough? The essay you write on this experience will necessarily be partly descriptive, but your emphasis should be on exposition. Your essay should be structured, of course, but don't be afraid to let your thoughts and feelings be the basis of this structure.

IMPROVING YOUR STYLE

1. End your essay with a restatement or a **closing by return**.
2. Use figurative language only at places where you want to emphasize the impact of nature on your feelings.

NORA EPHRON

American screenwriter and director Nora Ephron (1941–) started her career as a writer for the *New York Post* before joining *Esquire* as a columnist and senior editor. Her essays have been collected in several books, including *Wallflower at the Orgy* (1970), *Crazy Salad: Some Things about Women* (1975), and *Scribble Scribble: Notes on the Media* (1978). She is the also the author of a novel, *Heartburn* (1983)—later a successful movie for which she wrote the screenplay. She has written the scripts for a number of highly acclaimed movies, including *Silkwood* (1983) and *When Harry Met Sally* (1989), and has directed her own scripts for such successful films as *Sleepless in Seattle* (1993) and *You've Got Mail* (1998). Her most recent film credits include *Lucky Numbers* (1999) and *Hanging Up* (2000).

The New Porn

1   Every so often, I manage to get through the day without reading the *New York Times*. This is an extremely risky thing to do—you never know whether the day you skip the *Times* will turn out to be the one day when some fascinating article will appear and leave you to spend the rest of your life explaining to friends who bring it up that you missed it. Fortunately, this rarely happens. But on Friday, November 14,   5 1975, I managed to miss the *New York Times*, and I learned my lesson.

2   That, as it happens, was the day the *Times* ran a page-one story by its food writer Craig Claiborne about a four-thousand-dollar meal he and his friend Pierre Franey ate at a Paris restaurant, and I think it is safe to say that no article the *Times* has printed in the last year has generated as much response. (The only recent exception that comes to   10 mind is one that Charlotte Curtis wrote about cottage cheese.) In any case, a few days later, in desperation, I went back and read it. As you undoubtedly know, Claiborne had bid three hundred dollars in an auction for dinner for two at any restaurant in the world; because American Express was footing the bill, there was a stipulation that the restaurant be on the American Express card. Claiborne chose to dine at a chic spot on the   15 Right Bank called Chez Denis, and there he and Franey managed to get through thirty-one courses and nine wines. Two things were immediately clear to me when I read the article: first, that the meal had been a real disappointment, though Craig only hinted at that with a few cutting remarks about the blandness of the sorrel soup and the nothingness of the sweetbread parfait; and second, that the *Times* had managed to give front-   20 page play to a story that was essentially a gigantic publicity stunt for American Express. What good sports the people at American Express were about the entire episode! How jolly they were about paying the bill! 'We were mildly astonished at first but now we're cheerful about it,' a spokesman for the company said—and well he might have been. Four thousand dollars is a small price to pay for the amount of corporate good will the   25 article generated—and that outraged me; I have dealt with the people at American Express about money on several occasions, and they have never been cheerful with *me*.

3   Because my outrage was confined to such a narrow part of the event, I was quite surprised a few days later when I began to read some of the letters the *Times* received about the dinner. There were eventually some five hundred in all, four to one against 30 Claiborne, and the general tenor of them related to the total vulgarity of spending four thousand dollars on a dinner when millions were starving. Knee-jerk liberalism is apparently alive and well after all. There were references to Nero and Marie Antoinette, and there were also a few media-wise letter writers who chose to object not to the article itself but to the *Times*'s decision to run it on the front page. The *Times* printed a 35 short and rather plaintive reply from Claiborne, who said that he could not see how anyone could claim that the meal had 'deprived one human being of one mouthful of food'.

4   All of this raised some interesting questions. For openers, how much money did Clairborne have to spend to cross the line into wretched excess? Would five 40 hundred dollars have done it? A thousand dollars? Had he spent two thousand dollars, would the *Times* have received only three hundred letters? Would the objections have been even more intense if he had spent the four thousand dollars but put the tab on his expense account? Then, too, there is the question of editorial play: how much difference would it have made if the *Times* had run the article inside the newspaper? 45 These are obviously unanswerable, almost existential questions, and a bit frivolous to boot—but there is something more serious underlying this whole tempest.

5   Clairborne was clearly puzzled by the reaction to his piece. He had managed to commit a modern atrocity—even if he did rip off American Express, for which he is to be commended—and there is a good reason why it never crossed his mind that he 50 was doing so: except for the price tag, what he did was no more vulgar and tasteless than what he and hundreds of other journalists do every day. Newspapers and magazines are glutted with recipes for truffle soufflés and nit-picking restaurant reviews and paeans to the joys of arugula. Which of us will ever forget the thrilling night that Gael Greene blew five hundred dollars on dinner at the Palace, or that spine-tingling 55 afternoon when Craig and Pierre jumped into the car and drove all the way from East Hampton to Southampton just in time to find the only butcher on eastern Long Island with a pig's ear? Or was it pork fat for pâté? God knows what it was, but the point is that it should not have taken a four-thousand-dollar dinner at Chez Denis to remind the readers of the *Times* that Nero fiddled while Rome burned. All of this—let's face 60 it—is pretty vulgar stuff. It's also fun to read. But when it's accompanied by a four-thousand-dollar price tag, it reminds people of something they should have known all along: it's not about food, it's about money. Craig Claiborne writes about consuming—which should not be confused with consumerism, or Ralph Nader, or anything of the sort. And in his way, he is representative of one of the major trends in publish- 65 ing today; he is a purveyor of what I tend to think of as the new porn.

6   Before going further, I should define what I mean by porn in this context: it's anything people are ashamed of getting a kick out of. If you want to sell porn to a mass audience, you have to begin by packaging it in a way that's acceptable; you have to give people an excuse to buy it. *Playboy*'s Hugh Hefner was the first person in pub- 70 lishing to understand this; if he has done nothing else for American culture, he has given it two of the great lies of the twentieth century: 'I buy it for the fiction' and 'I buy it for the interview'. Of late, Hefner has been hoist with his own petard. He has

spent twenty years making the world safe for split beaver, and now he is surprised
that magazines that print it are taking circulation away from his own.   75

7   The new porn has nothing to do with dirty pictures. It's simply about money.
The new porn is the editorial basis for the rash of city and local magazines that have
popped up around the country in the past ten years. Some of these magazines are
first-rate—I am particularly partial to *Texas Monthly*—but generally they are to the
traditional shelter magazines what *Playboy* is to *Hustler*: they have taken food and   80
home furnishings and plant care and surrounded them up with just enough political
and sociological reporting to give their readers an excuse to buy them. People who
would not be caught dead subscribing to *House & Garden* subscribe to *New York* magazine. But whatever the quality, the serious articles in *New York* have nothing whatever to do with what that magazine is about. That magazine is about buying plants,   85
and buying chairs, and buying pastrami sandwiches, and buying wine, and buying ice
cream. It is, in short, about buying. And let's give credit where credit is due: with the
possible exception of the Neiman-Marcus catalogue, which is probably the grand-
daddy of this entire trend, no one does buying better than *New York* magazine.

8   In fact, all the objections the *Times* readers made to Claiborne's article can be   90
applied to any one of the city and local magazines. How can you write about the perfect ice cream cone or the perfect diet cola or the perfect philodendron when millions
of people have never seen a freezer, suffer from sugar deficiencies, and have no home
to put potted plants in? How can you publish a magazine whose motto is essentially
'Let them eat cheesecake'? Well, you can. And thousands of people will buy it. But   95
don't make the mistake of giving the game away by going too far. Five extra pages on
how to survive in a thirty-thousand-dollar living room, one extra price tag on a true
nonessential, and your readers will write in to accuse you of terminal decadence. And
when this happens, what will be truly shocking will not be the accusation—which
will be dead on—but the fact that it took them so long to get the point.   100

9   Terminal decadence.

10   Exactly.

March 1976

1978

QUESTIONS
Reader and Purpose

1. What expectations does Ephron's title arouse? Are these expectations met?
2. At the end of her opening paragraph Ephron states, 'I learned my lesson.' Her meaning here is obvious, but by the time one has finished reading this essay it's clear
   that by this expression Ephron means more than the obvious. What else does she
   mean by it?
3. Why does this essay belong in the Comparison section of this text?

Organization

4. The last word in the second paragraph is a reference to the author herself, and the
   reference is made even more emphatic by being italicized. Is this relevant to
   Ephron's main purpose in the essay?

5. Is the first sentence of paragraph 4 an **organizing sentence**? Explain your answer. What about the first sentence of paragraph 5?
6. Why does Ephron wait until paragraph 6 to explain what she means by 'the new porn'? What difference in effect might have occurred if she had not waited?
7. What are the principal comparisons Ephron uses?
8. What important change of **tone** occurs in paragraph 8?
9. Comment on the effectiveness, or lack of it, of paragraphs 9 and 10.

Sentences

10. In paragraph 2 should 'Craig Claiborne' be enclosed within commas? Why, or why not?
11. Is the expression 'the rash of city and local magazines that have popped up' grammatically correct? Explain your answer.
12. In paragraphs 7 and 8 where can you find examples of **polysyndeton**? Would these sentences have been more effective if Ephron had used **asyndeton**?
13. In paragraph 8 three sentences begin with *and* or *but*. Would it be preferable to join each of these sentences to the one that precedes it, using either commas or semicolons?

Diction

14. Look up: *stipulation* (14), *chic* (15), *tenor* (31), *liberalism* (32), *existential* (46), *paeans* (54), *purveyor* (66), *partial to* (79), *decadence* (98).
15. Is the expression *surrounded them up* (paragraph 7) to be taken literally? **ironically**? humorously?
16. Consider the following phrases: *it is safe to say* (9), *knee-jerk liberalism* (32), *are glutted with . . .* (53), *let's face it* (60–1), *People who would not be caught dead* (82–3). In your opinion, which of these expressions are **clichés**? Which ones are appropriate in this essay and which could, or should, be replaced?

POINTS TO LEARN

1. The most important position in a paragraph is, usually, the final word or words. This position should thus be used for a key point.
2. Using an attention-getting title is certainly a legitimate strategy to catch the reader's interest, but the title must reflect the content of the essay.

SUGGESTIONS FOR WRITING

Although the example Ephron uses is certainly unusual, almost everyone has likely had some experience with excess—in eating, drinking, smoking, partying, dancing, skiing, reading, dieting, etc. In an essay of 800–1,200 words, compare your experience with that of a friend. Give your essay an attention-grabbing, but appropriate, title.

IMPROVING YOUR STYLE

1. Use **polysyndeton** in at least one of your sentences, and **asyndeton** in at least one other sentence.
2. Begin at least three sentences with different **coordinate conjunctions**.

JACQUES BARZUN

A distinguished man of letters, a respected educator, and one of the founders of cultural history, Jacques Barzun (1907–) immigrated to the United States from France in 1919. After graduating from Columbia University, he spent most of his life teaching history there, and has been professor emeritus since 1975. He is the author of dozens of books, including the popular *Teacher in America* (1945), *The Modern Researcher* (1957), *The American University* (1968), *On Writing, Editing and Publishing: Essays, Explicative and Hortatory* (1986), *On Teaching and Learning* (1990), and *Simple and Direct: A Rhetoric for Writers* (rev. edn, 1995). His latest book, published in 2000, is *From Dawn to Decadence: 500 Years of Western Cultural Life*.

The following selection, from his usage guide *A Word or Two Before You Go* (1986), illustrates Barzun's enduring affection for the English language.

What If—? English *versus* German and French

1   I am asked what I think would have happened if our national language were German instead of English. My first impulse is to retort: 'Why, *isn't* it German?' I think of the thick layers of abstract jargon we carry on top of our heads, of the incessant urge to rename everything in roundabout phrases (Personal Armour System = the new army helmet), of the piling up of modifiers before the noun (easy-to-store safety fold- 5 ing ironing board), of the evil passion for agglutinating half-baked ideas into single terms (*surprizathon* = advertising goods by lottery) and I can only grudgingly concede: 'True, it isn't German, but some of it is more German than English.'

2   Had the Pilger Fathers brought with them the pure Plattdeutsch of their time, all might have been well. After separation from its source and under stress of the hard 10 frontier life, the language would have melted and clarified like butter, lost its twisted shapes and hard corners, and become a model of lucidity and force. What only the greatest German writers—Goethe, Schopenhauer, Nietzsche, and a few others—managed to do by main strength in their prose would have been done anonymously by everybody in Massachusetts and in the wagons crossing the plains. Tough characters 15 like Thoreau, Lincoln, Mark Twain, and Ambrose Bierce would not have tolerated the stacking of clause within clause of yard-long words, uncaring whether meaning comes out at the other end. They were articulate beings and they articulated their thoughts— as we are doing less and less every day.

3   For on our former, flexible and clear Anglo-Latin-French, which we call 20 American English, the überwältigend academic fog has descended and we grope about, our minds damp and moving in circles. Similar forms of the blight have struck the other languages of Western civilization, with the inevitable result of a growing inability to think sharp and straight about anything—whence half our 'prahblems'.

4   Had the good forthright people who built this country in the last century met 25 this verbal miasma on landing here, they would have either perished soon from suffocation or made tracks for the open air of Canada, which would now number 210 million. Make no mistake: syntax can change the course of history.

5   English has a great advantage over German, on the one hand, French and the
rest of the Romance languages, on the other, in that it possesses two vocabularies, 30
nearly parallel, which carry the respective suggestions of abstract and concrete, formal and vernacular. A writer can say *concede* or *give in; assume* or *take up; deliver* or
hand over; insert or *put in; retreat* or *fall back;* a shop in New York can even call itself
'Motherhood Maternity'. The two series of terms are not complete, and the connotations of a word in either set must be heeded before it can be used as a substitute for 35
its first cousin, but the existence of the quasi duplicate makes for a wide range of
colouring in style and nuances in thought. Only a mechanical mind believes that the
so-called Anglo-Saxon derivatives should always be preferred, and only the starched
and stilted will persistently fall into the Latinate.

6   In contrast, the corresponding words in German always show their concrete ori- 40
gins: *Empfindung* means *perception*, but whereas the English word conceals the Latin
take (capere), the German keeps in plain sight the *find* (come upon). Similarly,
Gelegenheit (occasion) has *lie* in it; *abrichten* (adjust) has *straight; Verhältnis* (proportion)
has *hold; Entwurf* (project) has *throw*, and so on. All the everyday words reappear in the
compounds. Not merely the associations of these words but their uses and contexts are 45
influenced by this 'open plumbing': the abstract idea has not been fully abstracted away.

7   French, having lost much of its brisk medieval vocabulary during the Latinizing
vogue of the Renaissance, has been left with very formal-sounding words for everyday use—for example *comestible* and *consommation* for cases in which we would say
food and *drink*. The reason why American and English tourists think that French hotel 50
porters are highly educated is that they say such things as: Monsieur est *matinal;* vous
allez au *spectacle;* il serait *prudent* de prendre un *imperméable;* c'es un *indigène;* oui, la
représentation est *intégrale*—and so on. The truth is, no other words are available
(except slang), and all these 'learned' terms are the familiar ones, just as the highfalutin *emergency* in English is the only way to refer to a very commonplace event.   55

8   The results of these contrasting developments in the leading languages of the
West go beyond differences of style; they may plausibly be held responsible for ten-
dencies of thought. Thus, when philosophy stopped being written in Latin, the English
school that arose was the Empiricist—thinkers who believed in the primacy of *things:*
ideas were viewed as coming from objects in the world concretely felt. In French phi- 60
losophy, *notions* came first: abstract words breed generalities at once, and the realm of
thought is then seen as cut off from the world of things, the mind from the body. See
M. Descartes. The historians Tocqueville and Taine thought that some of the greatest
errors of the French Revolution were due to unconscious and misplaced abstraction.

9   By the same token, the French language has a reputation—wholly un- 65
deserved—for being the most logical of all. For three hundred years French writers
have repeated this myth in good faith, because the act of fitting together abstract,
generalizing terms lends a geometrical aspect to the product. But French grammar
and usage and spelling are full of illogicalities—like those of other languages.

10   As for German, its lumpy compounds and awkward syntax present a paradox. 70
There is a sense in which a formal German sentence delivers its core meaning three
times over—once in the root of the verb, again in the noun, and finally in the adjectives
or adverbs almost always tacked on to those other terms. One might therefore have
expected that German thought would be peculiarly down-to-earth; yet everybody

knows that it has been peculiarly cloudy. The probable explanation is that the words 75
that have to be used for abstract ideas (like *Vorstellung*—'put before') acquire the
abstract quality while keeping visible their original concreteness. This double aspect
makes the user confident that he is on solid ground. The upshot is the German academic prose that made Kierkegaard, Nietzsche, and William James tear their hair
(*Eigenshaarsichauszupflückenplage*). If anybody is inclined to belittle English for its 80
mongrel character and its 'illogicalites', let him remember the limitations of its rivals.
We are lucky to have, in James's words, a language 'with all the modern improvements'.

1986

QUESTIONS
Reader and Purpose
1. Some of the terms that Barzun uses need explaining. In paragraph 2 a 'Pilger' is a
   pilgrim. 'Plattdeutsch' is the common, or everyday, language used in northern
   Germany. In paragraph 3 'überwältigend' means overwhelming, or imposing. In the
   final paragraph '*Eigeneshaarsichauszupflückenplage*' (a word of Barzun's own devising) means roughly 'a plague to rip your own hair out'. And, in paragraph 7, the
   French expressions can be translated as follows: 'Monsieur is an early riser; you
   are going to the theatre; it would be wise to take a raincoat; he is a local; yes, the
   performance is complete.'
      What do these terms tell you about the kind of reader Barzun is writing for? What
   kind of **tone** does he use? Would a person who is conscious of French–English relations in Canada find this tone sympathetic?
2. In his second paragraph Barzun comments that we are becoming less and less
   articulate in expressing our thoughts. Is he guilty of this fault?

Organization
3. Why is there a break between paragraphs 4 and 5? Does this signal a shift in
   thought? If so, what is the shift?
4. Is the final sentence of paragraph 4 an effective conclusion to the first part of this
   essay? Explain your answer.
5. How does the expression *In contrast* (40) unite paragraphs 5 and 6? Does it also
   have an effect on paragraph 7?
6. Comment on the first sentence of paragraph 8 as both a transition and an introduction.

Sentences
7. Describe the **parallel structure** in the first paragraph.
8. In the last sentence of paragraph 3 could Barzun have used a colon instead of a dash?
   In the last sentence of paragraph 4 could he have used a dash instead of a colon?
9. In the second sentence of paragraph 7 is the colon necessary? useful? superfluous?
10. Barzun concludes his essay with words quoted from William James. Do the quoted
    words also have a satirical implication? If so, what is it?

Diction

11. Look up: *abstract* (3), *agglutinating* (6), *articulate* (18), *miasma* (26), *syntax* (28), *vernacular* (32), *stilted* (39), *highfalutin* (54–5).
12. What mild joke has Barzun made in the first sentence of paragraph 2?
13. Why has Barzun deliberately misspelled the last word of paragraph 3?

POINTS TO LEARN

1. One way of structuring a comparison essay is to deal with each point separately, and then come to conclusions.
2. Knowledge of a word's **etymology** can help clarify its meaning.

SUGGESTIONS FOR WRITING

1. What are your beliefs and feelings about English and French (or English and any other language)? In an essay of 5–8 paragraphs, compare the languages with regard to two or three important points. Discuss each point separately, rather than discussing both or all three points as they apply to the first language and then as they apply to the second.
2. In his first paragraph Barzun lists four weaknesses commonly found in today's English. Write a short essay (4–6 paragraphs) in which you comment on examples of one of these weaknesses that you have found in a local newspaper, magazine, brochure, newsletter, etc.

IMPROVING YOUR STYLE

In your essay include:

1. two long sentences based on parallel structure;
2. one paragraph in which you use at least two dashes and two colons.

ELIZABETH KELLY

A former editor of *Hamilton Magazine*, Elizabeth Kelly has three National Magazine Awards and several nominations to her credit. In addition to her essay in *Canadian Geographic*, she has also published in *Toronto Life* and, in both French and English, in *Canadian* magazine.

Untamed World

1   Teenage boys perform a natural primordial ballet. Walking, running, spinning wildly, leaping over great distances, lightly lingering on street corners, insouciantly slouched wherever they land, elegant and yielding as a pair of grey flannel trousers. Theirs is a lean and dangerous eloquence of movement. Whatever the pose, adolescent boys embody the naive carnality of youth and all its pretty wicked charms, and 5 who doesn't love a wicked pretty thing?

2   The guy in the cottage three doors down, for one. 'Get the hell off my break-water,' he screamed at my 19-year-old son, his voice ricocheting along Long Point's rugged Lake Erie shoreline. Rory was doing a benign pirouette along the dike's narrow edges when the middle-aged owner made his sour feelings known. Twinkle   10 intact, Rory hopped down, and we resumed our walk along the beach, its picturesque setting a jarring backdrop to the pettiness that often passes for civil interaction among strangers.

3   The archetypal crank, my raging neighbour is but one incarnation of those pinched spirits obsessive about keeping everything neat and tidy in a permanently   15 disordered world.

4   The urge to control the chaos of the natural world is born, I believe, of an inabil-ity to open up to the inelegant experiences of life. It is to find no joy in a lawn littered with the hues of autumn but to moan and complain and rush for the leaf blower.

5   I once lived in a townhouse complex in Brantford, Ont., home of the Six Nations.   20 Our closest neighbour was a Mohawk with an appealing sense of mischief who had recently moved to the city. He immediately made his presence felt.

6   Within a few weeks, his lawn featured knee-high grass and an amazing assort-ment of weeds and wildlife. His naturalized oasis sat at the centre of a landscape dom-inated by lawns as even as broadloom and was viewed as an assault on the senses of   25 people convinced that Moses could have used a weed whacker to part the Red Sea.

7   Can you imagine the ensuing drama? Meetings, private and public, were called, a petition was circulated, racial hatreds were aroused, the police summoned. There were borderline violent incidents in driveways, wives screaming at other wives.

8   And still, he would not cut his grass. He never did trim that lawn, and the   30 controversy and the resentments it provoked never did dissipate entirely. If life were a facsimile of art, or at least TV, it would be easy to cast my Aboriginal friend in the role of maligned spirit guide sent to teach the shallow white man a better way. Such a view does a disservice to everyone.

9   He was more amused than outraged by all the fuss, more mellow than zealous.   35 Entertained by our industriousness and our earnest notion of the lawn as a reflection of personal worth, he wanted the freedom to make a different choice. He liked the sounds of silence better than the Sunday morning insult of the gas mower. He had made his peace with the imperfect world.

10   In the fall, his long grass blew about untamed and graceful; the sweet anarchy   40 of wild asters was a seductive antidote to the dull convention of impatiens. I got used to the beautiful disorder of his lawn. I looked forward to its unpredictable and chang-ing nature. I grew to love the purity and simplicity of a more sophisticated philoso-phy expressed in a richer aesthetic. And I learned something. Where the outer eye dares to go, the inner eye will soon follow.   45

2002

QUESTIONS
Reader and Purpose

1. When the author asks, at the end of the first paragraph, 'who doesn't love a wicked pretty thing?' is she referring to her son? If so, is she serious about calling him 'wicked'? Or is it a term of endearment, of motherly love? If she doesn't mean her son, who or what else is she referring to? Or is she referring to more than one thing or person?
2. Explain what Kelly means when she says, at the end of her essay, 'Where the outer eye dares to go, the inner eye will soon follow.' How is this relevant to her son? to her comparison of her two neighbours?
3. There are four persons involved in this essay: the writer, her son, and the two neighbours. What do we find out about each one? What relationships exist among them?

Organization

4. How does the opening paragraph serve as the introduction to this essay? How is the paragraph relevant to the comparison?
5. Paragraphs 2–4 reveal a progression from the general to the increasingly specific. What does the progression concern?
6. What is the function of paragraph 5 with regard to the comparison?
7. How is the concluding paragraph related to the introductory one?

Sentences

8. How many series are there in the second sentence of the opening paragraph? How many elements are in each series?
9. Can you justify the **fragment** that begins the second paragraph?
10. Is the single sentence that makes up the third paragraph also a fragment? If not, what is the principal verb of the sentence?

Diction

11. Look up: *primordial* (1), *insouciantly* (2), *eloquence* (4), *carnality* (5), *benign* (9), *pirouette* (10), *archetypal* (14), *dissipate* (31), *facsimile* (32), *maligned* (33), *zealous* (35), *anarchy* (40), *aesthetic* (44).
12. Do you find the expression *The guy* at the beginning of paragraph 2 surprising? Why, or why not? How important is the context in which the expression appears?
13. What does the expression *Twinkle intact* (10–11) reveal to us about the author's son?
14. When Kelly says that her son 'was doing a benign pirouette along the dike's narrow edges' (paragraph 2), does she mean that he was actually whirling about on tiptoes, or is she speaking **figuratively**?
15. Should paragraph 8 not begin 'But still' rather than 'And still'? Why, that is, has Kelly used a word that shows addition rather than one that shows contrast? Should the last sentence of this paragraph also be preceded by a contrasting word, such as *however* or *but*?
16. Keeping in mind that context can help to reveal meaning, what do the following expressions mean: *the naive carnality of youth* (5), *The archetypal crank* (14), *naturalized oasis* (24), *more mellow than zealous* (35), *a seductive antidote* (41)?

POINTS TO LEARN

1. A rich vocabulary and striking figures of speech can bring much pleasure to an attentive reader.
2. Even a short essay can be rather complex.
3. Even if one side of a comparison is described only briefly, the comparison can still be interesting and persuasive if the details describing that one side are precise and colourful.

SUGGESTIONS FOR WRITING

Compare Elizabeth Kelly and Steve Burgess ('Blazing Skies', pp. 53–5) as writers. There is some information given in the headnote to each essay that you may use if you wish, but base yourself mainly on what these writers say in their respective essays. Among the many questions that may help you to approach this topic are these:

- What values do the two writers have in common?
- In what manner might they disagree with each other? About what subjects might they disagree?
- Which author's style do you prefer and, specifically, why?
- How are their feelings about nature similar and how are they different?
- How do they relate to others?

Remember that a comparison, in order to be convincing, has to be fair. Thus, even though you may prefer one writer to the other, it is important to recognize the strengths of each.

IMPROVING YOUR STYLE

1. In your discussion of each writer use at least one figure of speech that is original or unusual. Don't be afraid to put your imagination to work.
2. Use a sentence fragment as the transition at the beginning of a paragraph.

L.M. MYERS

L.M. Myers (1901–), a professor of English, published a number of highly regarded books on language, including *American English: A Twentieth Century Grammar* (1952) and *Guide to American English*, first published in 1959 and republished in new editions in 1963 and 1968. His *The Roots of Modern English* (1966, 1978) is a very readable history of the language. In the following excerpt he presents the case for a change in the kind of grammar we use to analyze our language. His strategy is to use an analogy, a type of comparison in which two things, often quite different, are compared in order to suggest that what is true of one applies to the other.

The Parts of Speech

1   It is quite easy for an American to see that our decimal system of coinage is better than the traditional (but soon to be changed) British system of pounds, shillings, and pence (not to mention half-crowns and guineas), because it is simpler in principle and very much more convenient to handle. But it is not nearly so easy for us to see that the metric system of weights and measures has exactly the same advantage over our 5 curious conglomeration of ounces and pounds, inches, feet, yards, and miles, pints, quarts, and gallons, and so forth. We may admit the advantage in theory, but we are likely to have a deep-seated feeling that our units are somehow real, and the metrical ones merely clever tricks. It is very hard indeed for most of us to think of a hundred metres as simply a hundred metres, or as a tenth of a kilometre. We feel that it is really 10 a hundred and nine-point-something yards, and wonder why the silly foreigners couldn't at least have made it come out an even hundred and ten. And of course the kilometre is too short to be a serious way of measuring long distances. How can anybody be satisfied with anything that isn't quite five-eighths of a mile?

2   In a very similar way most of us have a strong feeling that the sort of grammar 15 to which we were exposed when young is somehow real, and that any different analysis of our language is tampering with the truth. But there is no more reason to believe that all words fall naturally into eight parts of speech than there is to think that silver comes naturally in either dollars or shillings, or butter in pounds or kilograms. We may have been taught that the sacred eight were permanent realities, no more 20 open to question than the Ten Commandments or the multiplication table. Yet, since the second English grammar was written, there has never been a time when 'the authorities' agreed on what or how many the parts were (every number from zero to ten has been advocated), to say nothing of what words belonged in each part; and just now the disagreement is particularly acute.   25

1966

QUESTIONS
Reader and Purpose

1. Professor Myers wishes to drive home an elusive idea: that it is nonsense to believe, as some people do, that there must be eight parts of speech and only eight. To make his point he employs an **analogy**, comparing the rather abstruse subject of parts of speech to something with which his readers are more familiar. Thus he draws a contrast between how Americans feel about their system of coinage (as compared with the system then in use in Great Britain) and how they feel about the inch-pound system of measurements (as compared with the metric system). How do their attitudes differ in these two cases? Are their reactions consistent or illogical?

2. Explain how the analogy of coinage and of weights and measures supports Professor Myers' contention about the eight parts of speech.

Organization

3. Does the writer begin with his main point or with his analogy?

4. In which sentence does he make it clear that he is developing his topic by analogy?

5. Which words in the first sentence of the opening paragraph are repeated in the second sentence? Where else in this paragraph do you find similar repetition of key terms? Note that these repetitions help to unify the paragraph.

6. How is the second paragraph tied to the first? Show how each sentence in this paragraph is linked to what precedes it. Identify some of the **connectives** the author uses at the beginning of some sentences to help unify the paragraph.

Sentences

7. Suppose the word 'that' were omitted in line 16: how would this affect the clarity of the sentence? To what earlier construction is the *that*-clause in line 16 **parallel**?

8. What is the effect of the writer's question in lines 13–14? How do you think he expects his readers to respond?

9. Why is this revision inferior to Myers' original sentence?

> **Revision:** We are likely to have a deep-seated feeling that our units are somehow real, and the metrical ones merely clever tricks, but we may admit the advantage in theory.

> **Myers:** 'We may admit the advantage in theory, but we are likely to have a deep-seated feeling that our units are somehow real, and the metrical ones merely clever tricks.' (7–9)

Diction

10. Look up: *pounds* (2), *shillings* (2), *pence* (3), *half-crowns* (3), *guineas* (3), *conglomeration* (6), *grammar* (15), *tampering* (17), *advocated* (24).

11. Why is *the authorities* (22–3) in quotation marks? Is there any **irony** in Myers' use of the term *sacred* in line 20? Whom is he mocking by his use of 'silly' in the phrase *silly foreigners* (11)?

12. Why does Myers preface *real* with *somehow*, both in line 8 and again in line 16?

POINTS TO LEARN

1. Analogy is a useful way of developing a subject.
2. Although analogy does not constitute logical proof (except under very special circumstances), it is an effective means of explaining a difficult or unfamiliar subject.

SUGGESTIONS FOR WRITING

Write a short essay developed by an analogy, choosing one of the subjects listed below or a comparable topic. Obviously there are differences between the things to be compared, but in developing your analogy do not waste time enumerating the differences, for that will only blur your focus and weaken your analogy. Work only with similarities.

> Learning how to drive and learning how to use the Internet. Whether one is sitting behind the wheel or at a computer, it's essential to become comfortable with the mechanics and aware of the best routes before setting off for a particular destination.

> Learning the parts of a piece of machinery and learning grammar (of English or any other language). In either case one must learn new names, get to know how the various parts work, and so on.

> A cafeteria and university. Each offers a large number of choices, and, in each, one may choose unwisely.

> Jugglers and good writers. Both must keep several things going at once.

> Algebra and abstract art. Both are concerned with patterns and relationships rather than with specific things, not with John who has three more apples than Maria, but with x + 3.

IMPROVING YOUR STYLE

1. Somewhere in your essay employ a **rhetorical question**.
2. Be sure to provide an adequate link when you move from the first part of your analogy to the second.
3. Experiment with **irony**, using one or two words in an ironic sense. Don't be heavy-handed; let the reader get the point herself.

NANETTE VONNEGUT MENGEL

Nanette Vonnegut Mengel (d. 1996) taught English and professional writing to students in the Master of Public Administration program at the University of North Carolina at Chapel Hill. Her essay comes from 'Coming of Age the Long Way Around', which was published in *Working It Out* (1977). This is an anthology of essays by 23 women scholars, writers, and artists who discuss the problems of work—especially professional and creative work—faced by women in our society. Mengel describes her experience in graduate school, focusing in this excerpt on the difficulties of writing her dissertation. She recounts her anxieties and frustrations by means of a compelling analogy.

The Dissertation and the Mime

1   The hardest part of graduate school was the dissertation. Yet, it was only here that the pieces of the work puzzle fell into place and that I gradually came to find myself in my work.

2   I remember many images of emotional hardship in dreams and fantasies during the three and a half years that I struggled to write my thesis, to find ways to 'see' Dickens' novels whole and my own relationship to them clearly. The most persistent image—the one that best describes my fears as I worked—was of Svi Kanar, a student of Marcel Marceau, performing a pantomime called 'The Ball'.

3   It was May 1968; the thesis I was hatching on Dickens' comic technique in *Pickwick Papers*, a subject I had chosen because I thought I could live with it happily for months, was something I was not often proud of. It seemed a kind of comic luxury in a world that was everywhere in trouble. President Johnson had recently announced that he would not run for a second term and the black-student movement had just struck the campus with disturbing force. My Ph.D. orals were postponed because tear gas filled the English building. Who wouldn't have doubted, daily, the value of scholarship such as mine? But I always came back to my thesis. At the age of thirty-four I had gone too far in my graduate work to turn back.

4   It was 1968, and Kanar's mime gave symbolic shape to my anxieties about myself as an academic. As his act began, Kanar, alone on the stage, playfully bounced an imaginary basketball, tossed it in the air, and dribbled rhythmically at varying speeds. Suddenly the imaginary ball asserted a life of its own; it began to expand at a frightening rate so that his pleasure, and ours as well, turned to panic—it seemed unlikely that he could regain control of the ball. It was a relief to see him stop the ball by main force from expanding, and then to watch him, with enormous exertion, force it back toward its original size until, finally, he had a basketball again. True, he handled the ball more warily now, but it was once again manageable. The game could go on.

5   The next time the ball asserted its mysterious growing power, Kanar was not so successful. He strained valiantly to contain it, but it became so large that his arms could barely support it. He ended the act in the posture of Atlas, one knee on the floor, the ball weighing on his shoulders and the back of his neck. I remember that I clapped very hard for Kanar's performance and that my hands were cold. There was something familiar in it that frightened me. In retrospect, his act seems to have prefigured the life that lay ahead of me as I tried to control my thesis, to keep it within bounds.

6   I do not remember that Kanar acted out the opposite problem—shrinkage, the fear that the ball would diminish to the size of a jawbreaker and slip between the boards—but I retain that image of him as clearly in my mind's eye as if he had. What if my ideas came to nothing? What if my dissertation went the other way and vanished? These two fantasies of myself as Atlas and anti-Atlas were especially strong as my topic slowly evolved. I was dismayed at the accumulation of my earlier drafts and papers. Although it was painfully clear that I could not use most of them, I was determined to do something with those excruciatingly hard-won bits of work. Stubbornly, I filed them for later use, and at the same time loaded my dissertation for a while with a pointless accumulation of pages—until it reminded me of the children's book *Every Haystack Doesn't Have a Needle*.

7   Weeding lines from draft after draft as my adviser returned them, trying to 45
glean whatever was salvageable, endlessly, gratefully, unquestioningly, I retyped the
phrases he liked. If he made the smallest positive sign in the margin, I would not let
that sentence go. Those phrases asserted a claim to immortality even stronger than the
mortification I felt each time I redid them. On the one side, then, I was forever dis-
carding and on the other, I was forever preserving, as I swung between the polar fears 50
symbolized in Kanar's mime: the fear that my work was trivial and liable to evaporate,
and the fear that it was so enormous it would immobilize me.

1977

QUESTIONS
Reader and Purpose

1. What advantages are there in explaining anxiety in terms of a pantomimist struggling with an imaginary ball?
2. Do you think that Mengel is writing for people much like herself, or for readers
   whose backgrounds and experience are very different? What kind of knowledge
   does she expect her readers to have?

Organization

3. Make a rough outline of the passage, giving a synoptic title to each major section
   and indicating which paragraphs it includes. How do paragraphs 1 and 2 relate to
   the rest of this selection? How does paragraph 3? How do 4 and 5, 6 and 7?
4. What is the **topic sentence** of the third paragraph? How is it supported? Do the
   final two sentences of this paragraph change the topic slightly?
5. The first sentence of paragraph 4 does not state the topic of this paragraph. What
   does it do? Which is the topic sentence of paragraph 4? How is the paragraph
   organized?
6. What is the topic sentence of the fifth paragraph? Where does the paragraph
   change direction?

Sentences

7. Most of Mengel's sentences are relatively long, containing at least two clauses.
   Where does she use short **simple sentences** effectively?
8. The **rhetorical question** in lines 15–16 is a device used for emphasis. What is the
   writer asserting here? Are the two rhetorical questions in lines 36–8 also a form of
   emphatic statement?
9. The phrase 'to find ways to "see" Dickens' novels' (5–6) is an **appositive**. To what?
   There is also an appositive in the very next line; identify it.
10. Mengel puts dashes around the appositive in line 7. Would commas have worked?
    Are dashes preferable here? Would the construction in line 22 be clearer if the
    dashes were replaced by a comma followed by *and*?
11. Suppose the semicolon in line 21 were similarly replaced by a comma plus *and*:
    would it be an improvement?
12. Identify the **parallel** elements in the sentence in lines 19–20. Why is parallelism an
    especially good way of organizing this sentence?

Diction

13. Look up: *scholarship* (16), *asserted* (21), *warily* (26), *valiantly* (28), *prefigured* (32), *evolved* (39), *drafts* (39), *excruciatingly* (41), *trivial* (51), *immobilize* (52).
14. How do the **etymologies** of these words help to clarify their modern meanings: *dissertation* (1), *pantomime* (8), *retrospect* (32), *mortification* (49)?
15. Explain the meanings of these phrases as fully as you can: *dreams and fantasies* (4) *comic luxury* (11–12), *symbolic shape* (18), *an academic* (19), *playfully bounced* (19), *pointless accumulation* (43).
16. *Hatching* (9), *weeding* (45), and *to glean* (45–6) are all **metaphors**. Why are they better than more commonplace terms such as *working on, removing* and *to keep*?
17. To whom is *Atlas* (29) an **allusion**? Is the comparison apt? Where does the writer pick it up again?
18. *Yet* (1), *true* (25), and *then* (49) all signal to the reader that the statements they introduce have logical relationships to what precedes them. Explain the relationship in each case.

POINTS TO LEARN

1. Analogies explain the unfamiliar in terms of the familiar, the abstract in an image the reader can see or hear.
2. Metaphors and allusions also express ideas in more familiar or concrete terms.
3. A topic sentence may set up several paragraphs rather than just one.
4. An occasional short simple sentence varies a style composed of relatively long ones.

SUGGESTIONS FOR WRITING

1. A famous bit of pantomime shows an actor trapped within four invisible walls trying vainly to escape, and finally accepting the reality of his absolute imprisonment. You may have seen Marcel Marceau or another mime act out this scene, but even if you haven't you can imagine what he or she would do. In a short essay of three or four paragraphs (400–600 words) describe the pantomime and apply it to one of your own frustrations. (If you are familiar with some other piece of pantomime, you may substitute this for the 'invisible wall'.)
2. In an essay of similar length use a scene or a plot from a movie or TV show to explain a personal feeling or problem. First describe the scene or plot so that the reader understands its essentials, then apply it to your situation.

IMPROVING YOUR STYLE

Somewhere in your essay include the following:

1. Several short emphatic sentences.
2. A rhetorical question.
3. A parallel sentence describing the actions of the mime or the actor.
4. The word *true* to introduce a **qualification**, and the word *then* to signal a conclusion.
5. One or two verbs like *hatching* to describe an abstract activity in a vivid image.

GERALD WEISSMANN

Writer, educator, and rheumatologist Gerald Weissmann (1930–) immigrated to the United States from Vienna and became a naturalized American citizen. He studied art history at Columbia and received his MD from New York University, where he is now a professor of medicine and the director of the Biotechnology Study Center. He has received numerous awards and honours for his research in medicine and experimental biology. His interest in the public good is reflected in the titles of several of his books, which include *The Biological Revolution: Applications of Cell Biology to Public Welfare* (1979), *The Woods Hole Cantata: Essays on Science and Society* (1985), and *Democracy and DNA: American Dreams and Medical Progress* (1995); his most recent book is *The Year of the Genome: A Diary of the Biological Revolution* (2002). The essay below is taken from *The Doctor with Two Heads and Other Essays* (1990).

Titanic and Leviathan

> Why upon your first voyage as a passenger, did you yourself feel such a mystical vibration, when first told that you and your ship were now out of sight of land? Why did the old Persians hold the sea holy? Why did the Greeks give it a separate deity, and own brother to Jove? Surely this is not without meaning.
>
> —Herman Melville, *Moby-Dick*

1   We had almost forgotten that *Atlantis II* was returning to Woods Hole that morning when the buzz of helicopters overhead reminded us. Woods Hole is but one of several villages in the township of Falmouth, on Cape Cod, and the whole seaside community was expected to turn out. From the windows of the laboratory we could see the ship approaching less than a mile offshore. The July sky was cobalt, the sea a 5 Prussian blue, and the sun sparkled on whitecaps in Vineyard Sound. It was 9:30 on the clearest morning of summer. The research vessel was headed home in triumph after its second voyage to the wreck of the *Titanic*. Above, the ship was circled by a corona of helicopters and photo planes; on the water, a flotilla of powerboats and racing sloops kept pace.   10

2   In shorts and lab coats we rushed down the stairs to cross Water Street in order to be on the WHOI dock when the *Atlantis II* pulled in at ten. 'WHOI' is the acronym for the Woods Hole Oceanographic Institution, the youngest of the three scientific installations that share the harbours of our small village. The others are the Marine Biological Laboratory, or MBL, and the US Bureau of Commercial Fisheries and 15 Aquariums. The three institutions, each eminent in its own right, tend to coexist as separate little universes. Engineering and physical sciences set the tone at WHOI, cell and molecular biology dominate the MBL, and applied ecology is the business of Fisheries. But while the professional—and, alas, the social—spheres of the three enclaves do not overlap greatly, the scientists and technicians of Woods Hole are 20 united by perhaps the most ancient of terrestrial diseases: sea fever. Physics, biology, or ecology can well be studied under the pines of Duke or the ivy of Princeton, but folks at Woods Hole seem drawn to the seaside by the kind of urges that moved the ancients to worship a 'separate deity, and own brother to Jove'.

3   Neptune's kingdom has drawn scholars to many harbours: Naples, Villefranche, 25 and Bermuda come to mind as other centres where marine science has flourished. But the New England shore has a special meaning for those engaged in voyages of discovery. From the landfall of the *Mayflower* at Provincetown to the triumph of the New Bedford clippers, the path to new worlds was by way of the sea. Perhaps it is no accident that the most dazzling of our epics is the tale of a Yankee in search of a whale.   30

4   What wonder then, that these Nantucketers, born on a beach, should take to the sea for a livelihood. They first caught crabs and quahogs in the sand; grown bolder, they waded out with nets for mackerel: more experienced, they pushed off in boats and captured cod; and at last, launching a navy of great ships on the sea, explored this watery world; put an incessant belt of navigation round 35 it; peeped in at Behring's Straits; and in all seasons and all oceans declared everlasting war with the mightiest animated mass that has survived the flood; most monstrous and most mountainous! (Melville, *Moby-Dick*)

Melville may have worked in a Manhattan counting house, but the whalers of his mind left from colder seas; Ishmael took the packet for Nantucket through the waters 40 of Woods Hole. So too for a hundred years have marine scholars plied their craft by the shores of the Cape and its islands; the search for Leviathan—as fish, or ship, or secret of the cell—does not seem entirely preposterous there.

5   Our small lab in the Whitman building of the MBL is only a hundred yards or so from the main dock of WHOI, so we were there in no time at all. A good-natured 45 crowd of visitors, tourists, and locals were milling around the gates. It turned out that passes were required, but with a neighbourly gesture the guard waved us by in our MBL T-shirts. The scene on the dock was Frank Capra in a nautical setting: the crowd had clearly assembled to welcome Jimmy Stewart back to his hometown. Reporters of all shapes and sizes jockeyed for post positions, television cameras were mounted on 50 scores of tripods, Coast Guard and naval officers strutted their stripes; dockhands in cutoffs and gym shirts lugged hawsers by the pier. Assembled on a kind of grandstand were bigwigs in blazers, officials in seersucker, and the gentry of Falmouth in pink linen slacks. The Marine Biological Laboratory was represented by a packet of students and faculty from courses in physiology, embryology, and neurobiology. (The 55 biologists, if one judged them by details of facial toilette, seemed to have strayed in from a remake of *The Battleship Potemkin*.) There were also teenagers with spiked hair and bubble gum, fresh-scrubbed wives of the ship's crew, outdoor types from WHOI and Fisheries, greasy kids from the boatyard across the street, aproned kitchen staff from the four local restaurants, firemen, and town cops.   60

6   But to omit other things (that I may be brief) after long beating at sea they fell with that land which is called Cape Cod; the which being made and certainly known to be it, they were not a little joyful. (William Bradford, *Of Plymouth Plantation*)

The ship was now upon us. The size of a minesweeper, its silhouette in the sun dis- 65 played great winch posts at the stern. As the vessel berthed broadside, general

applause and happy cheers greeted the explorers. Near the top stood the head of the
expedition, Robert Ballard. He stood the height of a hero, wearing a baseball hat with
the sailboat logo of the Oceanographic Institution. Next to him stood a naval officer
in khaki to remind us that the Navy had supported much of this research. A platoon   70
of oceanographers leaned against the railings of a lower deck. They were out-
numbered by grinning crew members and a few lab types with round spectacles. The
air rang with shouts from ship to shore and back again as friends and relatives hoisted
the kind of encouraging signs that one sees at road races. Tots and schoolkids were
hauled aboard as the ship made fast. Flash bulbs popped and so did the corks from   75
sudden champagne bottles. Oceanographers soon looked like winning playoff pitch-
ers at Fenway Park. Kisses were exchanged and animals petted. More cheers and
applause. The journalists gave way: there would be a press conference a little later. It
took a while for the crowd to disperse, but we didn't wait for that since the champagne was still flowing. We crossed the street and reverted to the lab, where we spent   80
the rest of the morning watching the dissociated cells of marine sponges clump
together in a test tube.

7   Within the week, posters appeared all over Falmouth announcing that Robert
Ballard would give two lectures at the Lawrence Junior High School auditorium on
August 6 for the benefit of Falmouth Youth Hockey. At these talks he would show   85
pictures of the *Titanic* expedition before they were released to the general news media.
The pictures would include footage obtained by means of novel television cameras
mounted on a little robot, Jason, that had poked down the grand stairwell of the liner.
My wife and I bought tickets for the first of the talks to be given at four in the afternoon, and in preparation for this event, we scoured junk shops and bookstores for   90
literature on the *Titanic* disaster. Although it cannot be said that we stumbled across
unknown masterpieces of prose, the dozen or so accounts were reasonably accurate
jobs of popular history. Written at various times between 1912 and 1985, they told
pretty much the same story. Their overall congruity is due no doubt to their reliance
on the same primary sources, chief of which were the records of two investigative   95
commissions, American and English.

8   On April 15, 1912, at 11:40 p.m., while on its maiden voyage from
Southampton to New York, the largest and most luxurious ocean liner of its age struck
an iceberg at latitude 41°46' north, longitude 50°14' west, some 360 miles off the
Grand Banks of Newfoundland. By 2:20 a.m. the next morning, the ship had sunk.   100
Only 711 out of 2,201 souls on board escaped the shipwreck. A US Senate subcom-
mittee, headed by William Alden Smith of Michigan, began its hearing on April 19
and shortly thereafter reported its finding as follows:

9   No particular person is named as being responsible, though attention is called
         to the fact that on the day of the disaster three distinct warnings of ice were sent   105
         to Captain Smith. . . .

10   Ice positions, so definitely reported to the *Titanic* just preceding the acci-
         dent, located ice on both sides of the lane in which she was travelling. No dis-
         cussion took place among the officers, no conference was called to consider
         these warnings, no heed was given to them. The speed was not relaxed, the   110
         lookout was not increased.

11   The steamship *Californian*, controlled by the same concerns as the *Titanic*, was nearer the sinking steamship than the 19 miles reported by her captain, and her officers and crew saw the distress signals of the *Titanic* and failed to respond to them in accordance with the dictates of humanity, international usage, and the   115 requirements of law. . . .

12   The full capacity of the *Titanic's* lifeboats was not utilized, because, while only 705 persons were saved [6 died in lifeboats] the ship's boats could have carried 1,176.

13   No general alarm was sounded, no whistle blown, and no systematic   120 warning was given to the endangered passengers, and it was fifteen or twenty minutes before Captain Smith ordered the *Titanic's* wireless operator to send out a distress message.

The commissioners might have noted several other factors that contributed to the disaster. Whatever number of additional persons might have crowded into lifeboats,   125 these had in any case room for only about half of those aboard (1,176 of 2,201). In addition, the two lookouts in the crow's nest had not been given binoculars with which to spot the iceberg, and once the berg was unavoidable, an error of navigation compounded the wreck. Although the design of the ship was such that she probably would have survived a head-on collision of almost any force, the first officer swung   130 the liner hard-a-starboard, thereby exposing a broadside target for impact.

14   Seventy-five years of rehashing details of the *Titantic* disaster have not added much to this bare outline, although recent opinion has tended to lay a good share of the blame at the feet of the owners of the White Star Line. Social critics accuse J. Bruce Ismay and his financier, J.P. Morgan, of sacrificing safety for speed and prudence for   135 luxury. In contrast, amateur steamship enthusiasts trace the ocean wreck to many individual flaws of naval conduct, culminating in negligence by the captain of the *Californian*. But if one is neither a special pleader nor a buff of shipwrecks, the story of the *Titanic* can be read as that of a unique, unlikely accident that was not part of a general pattern of nautical malfeasance. Only the sentimental can derive from the   140 sinking ship an intimation of Western mortality: the wreck had no immediate predecessors and no similar accident happened again. Indeed, it is difficult to determine whether reforms instituted in response to the *Titanic* affair played a role in the remarkable safety record of ocean liners between the wars. Large ships that were faster and more luxurious than the *Titanic* made hundreds of trips in similar waters; the *Queen*   145 *Mary*, the *United States*, the *Île de France*, and their sister ships lived out their useful lives without incident.

15   Nevertheless, over the years, a more or less constant set of moral lessons has been drawn from the disaster; these cautionary tales split predictably in accord with the plate tectonics of class and party. The first of these is captured in the popular image   150 of handsome men in evening clothes awash on a tilting deck. The band plays 'Autumn'.

16   Said one survivor, speaking of the men who remained on the ship: 'There they stood—Major Butt, Colonel Astor waving a farewell to his wife; Mr Thayer, Mr Chase, Mr Clarence Moore, Mr Widener, all multimillionaires, and hundreds of other men, bravely smiling at us. Never have I seen such chivalry and   155 fortitude.' . . .

17   But these men stood aside—one can see them!—and gave place not
merely to the delicate and the refined, but to the scared Czech woman from the
steerage, with her baby at her breast; the Croatian with a toddler by her side,
coming through the very gate of death, and out of the mouth of Hell to the   160
imagined Eden of America. (Logan Marshall, *The Sinking of the Titanic and Great
Sea Disasters*)

This lesson—the noblesse-oblige theme—includes the story of Mrs Isidor Straus, who
returned from her place in lifeboat No. 8 to her husband, the owner of Macy's. Taking
her husband's hand, she told him, 'We have been living together many years. Where   165
you go so shall I.' And the magnate refused to go before the other men. Harry Elkins
Widener, grandson of a Philadelphia mogul, went to his death with a rare copy of
Bacon's *Essays* in his pocket; Harvard owes not only its library but its swimming
requirement to his memory. Benjamin Guggenheim, the smelting millionaire, went
downstairs to change into his evening dress. 'Tell my wife,' he told his steward, who   170
survived, 'tell her I played the game straight and to the end. No woman shall be left
aboard this ship because Ben Guggenheim was a coward.'
18   Then there was Major Butt, aide and confidant of President Taft. Mrs Henry B.
Harris reported:

19   When the order came to take to the boats he became as one in supreme com-   175
mand. You would have thought he was at a White House reception, so cool and
calm was he. In one of the earlier boats fifty women, it seemed, were about to
be lowered, when a man, suddenly panic-stricken, ran to the stern of it. Major
Butt shot one arm out, caught him by the neck, and jerked him backward like
a pillow. . . . 'Sorry,' said Major Butt, 'but women will be attended to first or I'll   180
break every bone in your body.'

Whereas 140 of 144 (97.2 per cent) women, and all the children in first class survived, only 57 of 175 (32.6 per cent) male first-class passengers made shore. This
example of social discipline served as a moral lesson for the gentry, who later went to
the trenches in Flanders as if to a test match at Lord's.   185
20   The gallant behaviour on the part of the moneyed class probably derived from
the English code of the gentleman. On the *Titanic*, that code was honoured to a
remarkable degree. As the commander of the liner was going under with his ship, his
last words were: 'Be brave, boys. Be British!' One does not abandon the ship. That part
of the legend—from out of the past, where forgotten things belong—keeps, indeed,   190
coming back like a song. Twenty-six years after the wreck of the *Titanic*, Ernest Jones
arrived in Vienna in the wake of the Anschluss and tried to persuade the aged
Sigmund Freud to leave Hitler's Austria. Freud replied that he had to remain in the
city where psychoanalysis was born. Leaving Vienna, he explained, would be like a
captain leaving a sinking ship. Jones reminded him of the *Titanic's* second-in-   195
command, Lightoller, who was thrown in the water by a boiler blast. 'I didn't leave
the ship,' he explained of his survival, 'the ship left me!' Reassured by the code of the
British gentleman, Freud took not only the lesson but also the Orient-Express to
Victoria station and freedom.

21   More recent students of the *Titanic* story have drawn a quite different set of   200
lessons from the statistics and offer an analysis that one might call the *Upstairs,
Downstairs* version of the disaster. Pointing out that the social classes were quartered
on the ship as in Edwardian society at large, they find that steerage passengers fared
less well than their upstairs shipmates: half as well, in fact! Of men in third class only
75 survived of 462 (16.2 per cent); of women, 76 of 165 (46 per cent); of children,   205
27 of 79 (34.2 per cent). These statistics—literally the bottom line—yield another
irony. Only 14 of 168 male passengers in second class, a mere 8.3 per cent, survived.
One might conclude that middle-class men adhered more closely to upstairs values
than did the entrepreneurial folk on top deck.

22   Darker streaks of division mar the canvas. Many of the accounts of the time   210
stirred up nativist sentiments, and the worst charges were levelled against dark,
swarthy foreigners. Reporters grew indignant that 'men whose names and reputations
were prominent in two hemispheres were shouldered out of the way by roughly
dressed Slavs and Hungarians.' Rumours were commonplace—and have since been
disproved—that violent battles took place in steerage: 'Shouting curses in foreign lan-   215
guages, the immigrant men continued their pushing and tugging to climb into the
boats. Shots rang out. One big fellow fell over the railing into the water. . . . One husky
Italian told the writer on the pier that the way in which the men were shot was pitiable!'

23   Another rumour of the time is contradicted by later accounts: 'An hour later,
when the second wireless man came into the boxlike room to tell his companion what   220
the situation was, he found a negro stoker creeping up behind the operator and saw
him raise a knife over his head. . . . The negro intended to kill the operator in order
to take his lifebelt from him. The second operator pulled out his revolver and shot the
negro dead.'

24   Those often-told dramas of the *Titanic* can be squeezed for the juice of class   225
struggle, but the real fear of the time was not of social unrest. Led by the great pop-
ulist William Jennings Bryan, the moralists found their true target: the enemy was luxury, luxury and speed. 'I venture the assertion that less attention will be paid to
comforts and luxuries and . . . that the mania of speed will receive a check,' said Bryan.

25   Speed and comfort are among the declared goals of applied technology; those   230
who worry about those goals—like Bryan—tend to worry about technology. For 75
years, those uneasy with machines have used the image of the *Titanic* to decorate the
Puritan sampler that 'pride goeth before a fall.' The proud *Titanic* was 882 feet long—
almost three football fields; contemporary illustrations show her as longer than the
height of the Woolworth Building. She had a swimming pool, a putting area, squash   235
courts, a Turkish bath, a Parisian café, palm-decorated verandas, a storage compartment for automobiles, and a full darkroom for amateur photo buffs. In the hold were
hundreds of cases of luxury consignments, which ranged from 34 cases of golf clubs
for A.G. Spalding to 25 cases of sardines and a bale of fur for Lazard Frères. Larder and
beverage rooms stocked 25,000 pounds of poultry and 1,500 champagne glasses. This   240
splendid, 'unsinkable' hotel was powered by engines that could generate 55,000
horsepower. Rumour had it that she was not far from her maximum speed of
25–6 knots per hour when she hit the iceberg; other hearsay had it that Captain Smith
was going for a transatlantic speed record. The pride of speed was blamed for the fall
of the *Titanic*.   245

26   Journalists complained that 'subways whiz through the tunnels at top speed; automobiles dash through the street at a speed of a mile in two minutes, and ocean liners tear through the water,' but it was the clergymen who had their field day on the Sabbath after the disaster. Technological pride took a beating from the Reverend William Danforth of Elmhurst, Queens, who blamed 'the age of mania for speed and smashing records. The one on whom one can fasten the blame is every man to whom all else palls unless he rides in the biggest ship and the fastest possible. He will be guilty in his automobile tomorrow.' The pulpits of all denominations were united in teaching the Puritan lesson. They were hard on the pride of luxury, as manifest in the squash courts, the putting area, and the swimming pool. Had William Bradford himself been alive, he would have been the first to see the luxury steamer as 'a right emblem, it may be, of the uncertain things of the world, that when men have toiled themselves for them, they vanish into smoke.' The leader of the Ethical Culture Society, Felix Adler of New York, was alive enough to voice the sentiment, 'It is pitiful to think of those golf links and swimming pools on the steamship which is now 2,000 fathoms deep.' And Rabbi Joseph Silverman of Temple Emanu-el was of the same mind: 'When we violate the fundamental laws of nature we must suffer.'

27   In the decades since 1912, the *Titanic* has ranked high on the list of violators of fundamental law (applied-technology division). Fans of natural law put the story of the steamship right up there with the flights of the *Hindenburg* and of Icarus, the building of the Tower of Babel and the Maginot Line. Not long ago, the space shuttle *Challenger* joined those other violators. In our most recent mythology, *Challenger* and the *Titanic* have become linked in the popular mind. Both craft were the largest and fastest vectors of their kind, both were the darlings of general publicity, both carried the banners of Anglo-Saxon pride; both voyages went haywire for almost mundane reasons. In the hagiography of disaster, the binoculars absent on the crow's nest of the liner and the faulty O-rings of the booster rocket have both been offered as examples of how the best of our science is in bondage to chance—or retribution.

28   On August 6, when we finally went to hear Ballard speak to the townsfolk of Falmouth on his discovery of the *Titanic*, I was sure that memories of the recent *Challenger* disaster were not far from the minds of many. That summer, with NASA grounded, the discovery of the *Titanic* 12,000 feet beneath the sea must have engaged sentiments in an American audience deeper than those of hometown curiosity. It seems unlikely that the community turned out in overflow numbers because of its concern for the traditional themes of *Titanic* literature. One doubts that the seats were packed with citizens who wished to hear replayed the moral lessons of noblesse oblige, the social notes of *Upstairs, Downstairs*, or the canons of technology's pride and fall. No, one might argue that the people of Falmouth went to hear the technical details of how a captain from Cape Cod tracked down the largest, most elusive object beneath the waves: *Titanic*, the Leviathan.

29   For the buckling of the main beam, there was a great iron screw the passengers brought out of Holland, which would raise the beam into his place; the which being done, the carpenter and master affirmed that with a post put under it, set firm in the lower deck and otherwise bound, he would make it sufficient. (Bradford, *Of Plymouth Plantation*)

30   The whale line is only two-thirds of an inch in thickness. At first sight, you
would not think it so strong as it really is. By experiment its one and fifty yarns
will each suspend a weight of one hundred and twenty pounds; so that the
whole rope will bear a strain nearly equal to three tons. In length, the common
sperm whale–line measures something over two hundred fathoms. (Melville,   295
Moby-Dick)

31   The echo on our sonar indicated that we were approaching bottom, at a little
more than 12,000 feet. Larry released one of the heavy weights on the side of
the *Alvin*, and our descent slowed. Soon in the spray of lights under the submersible, I could see the ocean floor slowly coming closer, seeming to rise   300
toward us, rather than our sinking to it. Pumping ballast in final adjustments,
Larry settled us softly down on the bottom, more than two miles below the surface. (Robert Ballard, in *Oceanus*)

32   In the logbook style of his Yankee predecessors, Ballard here describes an early
training drive of the deep submersible craft *Alvin*. And in this same, informative fash-   305
ion, Ballard went on that summer afternoon at the junior high school to detail his two
trips to the *Titanic* site. He spoke of the principles of oceanography, of the ground
rules of hydrodynamics, and of how optics and sonar had been used to establish the
site of the wreckage. He told us something of his decade-long career in manned submersible craft: of continental creep and hot geysers on the Mid-Atlantic Ridge. He told   310
of the dark, sterile sea two miles beneath the surface and of the rare creatures that
inhabited those depths. He acknowledged his French collaborators, without whom
the wreck could not have been found, and praised the technicians of Sony who fashioned the pressure-resistant TV apparatus of the robot Jason. And then we saw film
clips of the second voyage to the wreck of the *Titanic*, taken by Jason and its larger   315
partner, the submersible Argo.
33   By the blue lights of Argo's cameras, we saw the decks, the winches, the bridge.
The stern had become undone and the huge boilers had been scattered across the
ocean floor. We saw stalagmites of rust and intact bottles of wine. We went with Jason
into the cavern of the great staircase and marvelled at the preservation of metalwork,   320
silverware, and leaded glass in that cold sea. We had entered the belly of the whale.
34   Guided by our Ahab-Ishmael we returned to the surface as the submersibles
were retrieved and stowed. Ballard suggested that these pictures tended to discount
the hypothesis that the iceberg had torn a great gash in the liner's side and that instead
the welds had popped from the impact. The ship's hull had cracked like a nut. But his   325
peroration was not devoted to further anecdotes of how sad it was when the great ship
went down. Ballard ended with the message he had brought to the shore for a decade:
the ocean and its depths are a frontier as awesome as space itself.
35   When the lights came on, Ballard answered questions from his fellow townspeople. Yes, he was pleased that Congress had passed a resolution that would make   330
the wreck site a permanent monument to the victims. No, he thought that salvage was
impractical; we have better examples of Edwardian artifacts and he doubted that a few
chamber pots and wine bottles would be worth the gross expense of raising the ship.
Yes, the *Titanic* trip was, in part, an effort to organize support for the programs of deep
ocean science.   335

36   The applause that followed was long and loud. The happy crowd, from starry-eyed teenagers to oldsters with aluminum walkers, emerged into the sunlit afternoon looking as if each had been given a fine personal present. Many of us from the Woods Hole laboratories shared that sentiment; town and gown of Falmouth had been joined in a victory celebration for science and technology. The reception of *Titanic Rediviva* 340 reminded us that science appeals to people not only for the gadgets it invents but also for the answers it provides to the most important questions we can ask: What happens when we drown? How deep is the ocean? How bad is its bottom? How fierce is the whale?

37   After his first voyage, Ballard had told the House of Representatives' Merchant 345 Marine and Fisheries Committee that he was neither an archaeologist nor a treasure hunter. 'I am', he told the congressmen, 'a marine scientist and explorer. I am here to point out that the technological genius most Americans are so proud of has entered the deep sea in full force and placed before us a new reality.'

38   Influenced no doubt by Ballard's publicity on television, in newspapers, and in 350 magazines, not all of the scientists at Woods Hole shared my enthusiasm for the *Titanic* adventure. At a number of gatherings later that summer, one heard the nasty buzzing of such adjectives as 'publicity-seeking', 'grandstanding', 'applied', 'not really basic', 'developmental', and, perhaps most damning, 'anecdotal'. It has been no secret to the public at large since *The Double Helix* that scientists are no more charitable to each 355 other than are other professionals; novelists, investment bankers, and hairdressers come immediately to mind. But the detractors of the *Titanic* adventure were not only upset by Ballard per se. The naysayers also complained that technology rather than science was becoming imprinted on the collective unconscious of television. Some of those most vexed by Ballard's sudden prominence had themselves made major find- 360 ings in the 'new reality' of genetic engineering, neurobiology, and immune regulation. Were not their achievements also part of the 'technological genius most Americans are proud of'? They argued that their contributions to basic science will affect the world of the future in ways more fundamental than adventures on the ocean floor.

39   But that reasoning strikes me as very self-serving. Historians of science and 365 technology assure us that it is difficult to decide whether public practice follows private theory or whether the opposite is true. It is, they teach us, hard to know where technology ends and science begins. Moreover, really important discoveries, whether basic or applied, influence our social arrangements as they in turn are influenced by them. Such discoveries tend to attract attention. The Spanish court did not ignore the 370 voyage of Columbus, nor did Galileo fail to catch the ear of the Vatican. Einstein's relativity was featured in headlines by the *New York Times*, and polio was conquered in public. When one of the new dons of DNA discovers something as spectacular as the wreck of the *Titanic*, his lectures are likely to fill auditoriums larger than that of a junior high school on the Cape. When she finds the vaccine for AIDS or solves the 375 riddle of schizophrenia, purists will probably carp at the publicity, but I want to be in the audience to hear her grandstanding.

40   And still deeper the meaning of that story of Narcissus, who because he could not grasp the tormenting, mild image he saw in the fountain, plunged into it and was drowned. But that same image, we ourselves see in all rivers and 380 oceans. It is the image of the ungraspable phantom of life; and this is the key to it all. (Melville, *Moby-Dick*)

When Ishmael—or Melville—emerged from the sinking *Pequod* to tell the story of Moby-Dick, he told us as much about the science of whales as about the descent into self. Ballard's tale of the *Titanic* is not only the story of deep ocean science but also a 385
tale of memory, of desire, and of that search for the ungraspable phantom of life that some have called Leviathan.

1990

QUESTIONS

Reader and Purpose

1. An epigraph is a quotation placed at the beginning of a poem, book, or chapter; its purpose is to indicate, or to comment on, the principal sentiment or idea of the work. What purpose is served by the epigraph from *Moby-Dick*?

2. This essay involves three accounts: that of the Woods Hole scientific community, the story of the sinking of the *Titanic*, and the story of the huge white whale that Melville described in his novel *Moby-Dick*. Keeping in mind that an **analogy** is a comparison of an unfamiliar idea with one that is more familiar, what are the principal points of the author's analogy? What argument is he trying to make by this analogy?

3. Although the story of the *Titanic* is one focus of this essay, the author does not begin to deal with it specifically until paragraph 8. What do the first seven paragraphs do? What is the **tone** of these opening paragraphs? How important is this tone to the rest of the essay?

Organization

4. In paragraphs 1–7 Weissmann deals with the present, in paragraphs 8–27 with the past, and in paragraphs 28 and 32–41 with the present again. How does he manage the transitions from one section to the next?

5. Choose three places where *Moby-Dick* is either quoted from or referred to, and explain how these references help to unify the essay.

6. Paragraph 6 is an excerpt from *Of Plymouth Plantation*, which William Bradford began writing in 1630. What purpose does this quotation serve? How is it related to paragraph 5?

7. How is the last sentence of paragraph 7 an **organizing sentence**?

8. Explain how the opening sentence of paragraph 15 is an organizing sentence for paragraphs 15–23.

9. What are Weissmann's reasons for ranging so widely over time? Do you get the impression that he is merely displaying his broad knowledge of history? Or does this knowledge play an essential role in the essay?

10. How do the quotations in paragraphs 29, 30, and 31 refer to Weissmann's explanations in paragraphs 27 and 28?

11. How is the quotation from *Moby-Dick* in paragraph 40 a comment on paragraphs 38 and 39?

Sentences

12. Paragraph 5 includes several sentences that use **parallel structure**. Choose three of these sentences and explain the nature of the parallelism. You should also explain whether these sentences use **asyndeton** or **polysyndeton**.
13. Justify, or condemn, the sentence fragment in lines 77–8.
14. Compare the tone of the last sentence of paragraph 26 with that of the first sentence of paragraph 27.
15. How would you describe Weissmann's style? As part of your answer to this question, consider any two consecutive paragraphs (Weissmann's own, not those he quotes) in light of these questions: how many **simple sentences** are there? **compound sentences**? **complex sentences**? **compound-complex sentences**?

Diction

16. Look up: *corona* (9), *acronym* (12), *Leviathan* (42), *hawsers* (52), *oceanographers* (71), *congruity* (94), *malfeasance* (140), *nativist* (211), *hagiography* (271), *carp* (376).
17. Explain the metaphor in the first sentence of paragraph 22.
18. Weissmann uses a number of colourful phrases throughout his essay. Explain what he means by the following: *the ship was circled by a corona of helicopters and photo planes* (8–9); *the whalers of his mind left from colder seas* (39–40); *in accord with the plate tectonics of class and party* (149–50); *Darker streaks of division mar the canvas* (210); *We had entered the belly of the whale* (321); *that search for the ungraspable phantom of life that some have called Leviathan* (386–7).

POINTS TO LEARN

1. A well-chosen epigraph is not only interesting in itself but is helpful in making the writer's point.
2. Although an analogy is only a rough comparison, it can nevertheless clarify both sides of the comparison.
3. Parallel structure is helpful in structuring long lists of items.

SUGGESTIONS FOR WRITING

A comparison involves similar things—two cross-country bikes, for instance, or three novels, or several photographs. An analogy points out how apparently unlike things have some similarities—such as trying to kill a whale and analyzing the causes of a shipwreck.

Write your own analogy in an essay of some length. Choose from among the suggestions below or devise your own topic. Although it might seem much more difficult to find a topic for an analogy than for almost any other kind of essay, the suggestions that follow show that such topics can come easily after some reflection:

working in a fast-food restaurant and attending university

the past five years of your life and a difficult hike of several days

raising young children and working in a hardware store

a personal or professional relationship and a difficult course in genetics (or phyiscs, or biochemistry, etc.)

IMPROVING YOUR STYLE

1. Choose a short epigraph for your essay. Use whatever source you wish (the *Oxford Dictionary of Quotations* might be a good place to begin), provided it casts some light on your topic or your approach.
2. In one paragraph include several sentences that use parallel structure.

PICO IYER

Pico Iyer (1957–) was born in England of Indian parents, spent part of his childhood in California, and was educated at Eton and Oxford and later at Harvard. He joined *Time* magazine as a staff writer in 1982, after three years taking a leave of absence in order to explore Asia. This trip resulted in *Video Night in Kathmandu: And Other Reports from the Not-So-Far East* (1988), a fascinating travel narrative that comprises a series of meditations on the blending of Eastern and Western culture. He continues to publish essays and reviews in *Time*, where the essay below first appeared, as well as in such periodicals as *Partisan Review, Village Voice,* and *The Times Literary Supplement*. He has published other travel books, including *The Lady and the Monk: Four Seasons in Kyoto* (1991), and a novel, *Cuba and the Night* (1995). His latest collection of essays, *The Global Soul: Jet Lag, Shopping Malls and the Search for Home* (2000), is an investigation of multiculturalism that is dedicated in part to examining Toronto as a model of the multicultural city of the future. He continued this examination in *Imagining Canada: An Outsider's Hope for a Global Future* (2001), which he delivered as the inaugural Hart House Lecture at the University of Toronto.

In Praise of the Humble Comma

1   The gods, they say, give breath, and they take it away. But the same could be said—could it not?—of the humble comma. Add it to the present clause, and, of a sudden, the mind is, quite literally, given pause to think; take it out if you wish or forget it and the mind is deprived of a resting place. Yet still the comma gets no respect. It seems just a slip of a thing, a pedant's tick, a blip on the edge of our consciousness,   5
a kind of printer's smudge almost. Small, we claim, is beautiful (especially in the age of the microchip). Yet what is so often used, and so rarely recalled, as the comma—unless it be breath itself?

2   Punctuation, one is taught, has a point: to keep up law and order. Punctuation marks are the road signs placed along the highway of our communication—to con-   10
trol speeds, provide directions, and prevent head-on collisions. A period has the unblinking finality of a red light; the comma is a flashing yellow light that asks us only to slow down; and the semicolon is a stop sign that tells us to ease gradually to a halt, before gradually starting up again. By establishing the relations between words, punctuation establishes the relations between the people using words. That may be one   15
reason why schoolteachers exalt it and lovers defy it ('We love each other and belong to each other let's don't ever hurt each other Nicole let's don't ever hurt each other,'

wrote Gary Gilmore to his girlfriend). A comma, he must have known, 'separates inseparables', in the clinching words of H.W. Fowler, King of English Usage.

3   Punctuation, then, is a civic prop, a pillar that holds society upright. (A run-on 20 sentence, its phrases piling up without division, is as unsightly as a sink piled high with dirty dishes.) Small wonder, then, that punctuation was one of the first propri- eties of the Victorian age, the age of the corset, that the modernists threw off: the sexual revolution might be said to have begun when Joyce's Molly Bloom spilled out all her private thoughts in 36 pages of unbridled, almost unperioded and officially 25 censored prose; and another rebellion was surely marked when e.e. cummings first felt free to commit 'God' to the lower case.

4   Punctuation thus becomes the signature of cultures. The hot-blooded Spaniard seems to be revealed in the passion and urgency of his doubled exclamation points and question marks ('¡Caramba! ¿Quien sabe?'), while the impassive Chinese tradi- 30 tionally added to his so-called inscrutability by omitting directions from his ideograms. The anarchy and commotion of the '60s were given voice in the explod- ing exclamation marks, riotous capital letters, and Day-Glo italics of Tom Wolfe's spray-paint prose; and in Communist societies, where the State is absolute, the dig- nity—and divinity—of capital letters is reserved for Ministries, Sub-Committees and 35 Secretariats.

5   Yet punctuation is something more than a culture's birthmark; it scores the music in our minds, gets our thoughts moving to the rhythm of our hearts. Punctuation is the notation in the sheet music of our words, telling us when to rest, or when to raise our voices; it acknowledges that the meaning of our discourse, as of 40 any symphonic composition, lies not in the units but in the pauses, the pacing and the phrasing. Punctuation is the way one bats one's eyes, lowers one's voice, or blushes demurely. Punctuation adjusts the tone and colour and volume till the feeling comes into perfect focus: not disgust exactly, but distaste; not lust, or like, but love.

6   Punctuation, in short, gives us the human voice, and all the meanings that lie 45 between the words. 'You aren't young, are you?' loses its innocence when it loses the question mark. Every child knows the menace of a dropped apostrophe (the parent's 'Don't do that' shifting into the more slowly enunciated 'Do not do that'), and every believer, the ignominy of having his faith reduced to 'faith'. Add an exclamation point to 'To be or not to be . . .' and the gloomy Dane has all the resolve he needs; add a 50 comma, and the noble sobriety of 'God save the Queen' becomes a cry of desperation bordering on double sacrilege.

7   Sometimes, of course, our markings may be simply a matter of aesthetics. Popping in a comma can be like slipping on the necklace that gives an outfit quiet ele- gance, or like catching the sound of running water that complements, as it completes, 55 the silence of a Japanese landscape. When V.S. Naipaul, in his latest novel, writes, 'He was a middle-aged man, with glasses,' the first comma can seem a little precious. Yet it gives the description a spin, as well as a subtlety, that it otherwise lacks, and it shows that the glasses are not part of the middle-agedness, but something else.

8   Thus all these tiny scratches give us breadth and heft and depth. A world that 60 has only periods is a world without inflections. It is a world without shade. It has a music without sharps and flats. It is martial music. It has a jackboot rhythm. Words cannot bend and curve. A comma, by comparison, catches the gentle drift of the mind

in thought, turning in on itself and back on itself, reversing, redoubling, and returning along the course of its own sweet river music; while the semicolon brings clauses   65
and thoughts together with all the silent discretion of a hostess arranging guests
around her dinner table.

9   Punctuation, then, is a matter of care. Care for words, yes, but also, and more
important, for what the words imply. Only a lover notices the small things: the way the
afternoon light catches the nape of a neck, or how a strand of hair slips out from behind   70
an ear, or the way a finger curls around a cup. And no one scans a letter so closely as
a lover, searching for its small print, straining to hear it nuances, its gasps, its sighs and
hesitations, poring over the secret messages that lie in every cadence. The difference
between 'Jane (whom I adore)' and 'Jane, whom I adore,' and the difference between
them both and 'Jane—whom I adore—' marks all the distance between ecstasy and   75
heartache. 'No iron can pierce the heart with such force as a period put at just the right
place,' in Isaac Babel's lovely words; a comma can let us hear a voice break, or a heart.
Punctuation, in fact, is a labour of love. Which brings us back, in a way, to gods.

1988

QUESTIONS
Reader and Purpose
1. Would you normally be inclined to read an essay on the comma? Might the title of
   this essay possibly attract you? Would the appearance of this essay in a very popular magazine lead you to read it?
2. In his first sentence Iyer refers to 'The gods', and in the first sentence of the second
   paragraph he refers to punctuation as a means of keeping up 'law and order'. Such
   reverential treatment of a comparatively minor topic is called the mock heroic style.
   Does Iyer use this style effectively? Or does it at times seem too exaggerated?

Organization
3. How does the first paragraph use a **closing by return**? Does the final paragraph use
   this strategy?
4. Iyer's principal **analogy** is the use of the comma in comparison to breathing. But he
   also uses a number of other analogies, such as 'Punctuation . . . is a civic prop'
   (20). What other analogies does he use?
5. Is the first sentence of paragraph 6 a summary or an **organizing sentence**?
6. In commenting (in paragraph 8) on the use of the period, the comma, and the semicolon, the punctuation of Iyer's own sentences illustrates the usage he is describing. Explain his examples in paragraphs 5 and 8.
7. What does Iyer mean by his final two sentences? In calling punctuation 'a labour of
   love' is Iyer going too far?

Sentences
8. Iyer begins both **principal clauses** of his third sentence with a verb. Where else does
   he use this unusual structure? Explain why you find this structure effective, or not.
9. In the first two sentences of paragraph 2 Iyer has used a colon and a dash. Explain
   how these two marks function. Could the two be interchanged?

10. What is Iyer trying to do in the parenthetical section of paragraph 2? Does he have a different purpose in the parenthetical section of paragraph 3?
11. Explain the punctuation of the third sentence in paragraph 3.
12. How does the last sentence of paragraph 5 use **parallelism**? What is the effect of this use of parallelism?
13. 'Punctuation, then, is a matter of care' (68). Is this statement a brief summary of Iyer's main points? Do you agree with it? Or does punctuation, for you, involve more than being careful?

Diction

14. Look up: *pedant* (5), *exalt* (16), *proprieties* (22–3), *inscrutability* (31), *ideograms* (32), *discourse* (40), *demurely* (43), *ignominy* (49), *sacrilege* (52), *complements* (55), *jackboot* (62), *poring* (73).
15. The comma, for Iyer, is 'a pedant's tick' (5), or 'a flashing yellow light' (12); and he uses **figurative** language similarly to describe other marks of punctuation. Choose three or four of these expressions and explain whether or not you find them effective.
16. What **metaphor** does Iyer develop in the first part of paragraph 2?
17. Explain the differences among the three expressions of love in the final paragraph of this essay.
18. What **metaphors** occur in paragraph 5? How are metaphor and analogy related?

POINTS TO LEARN

1. Exposition by analogy can be effective, instructive, and amusing.
2. Metaphor, simile, and analogy are closely related, since they involve, although in different ways, an implied comparison.
3. Analogy has limitations: items that are comparable are not identical.

SUGGESTIONS FOR WRITING

Write your own essay in praise of a 'humble' object: a hockey puck, a coffee mug, a lawn rake, a key chain, a comb, a light bulb, a ruler, a tire gauge, etc. Before you begin planning or writing, however, invent an analogy that implicitly compares the object you have chosen with something far grander (the hockey puck, for instance, is an object physically pursued by a few well-paid athletes and vicariously pursued by many not-so-well-paid fans).

IMPROVING YOUR STYLE

1. State your analogy in the first sentence, and refer to it (without merely repeating it) in your final sentence.
2. Use metaphors and brief analogies in at least three of your paragraphs.

JOHN UPDIKE

One of the most widely respected American writers of the past half-century, John Updike (1932–) began writing for *The New Yorker* in 1955, contributing essays, parodies, and verse distinguished by their sardonic wit. He has since published numerous volumes of plays, poetry, short stories, and essays and criticism. He is perhaps best known for his Rabbit cycle of novels, which deal with the life and times of Harry (Rabbit) Angstrom, beginning with *Rabbit, Run* (1960), continuing with *Rabbit Redux* (1971) and *Rabbit Is Rich* (1981), and ending with *Rabbit at Rest* (1990), with the last two both winning the Pulitzer Prize. Among his most recent books are *More Matter: Essays and Criticism* (1999), *The Complete Henry Bech: Twenty Stories* (2001), *Americana and Other Poems* (2001), and *Seek My Face* (2002).

The essay below, from *Hugging the Shore: Essays and Criticism* (1984), is Updike's view of one of the great professional golf tournaments. Although many aspects of the game Updike describes have changed since the essay was written, it is a fascinating combination of personal observation, wit, social commentary, and much more.

Thirteen Ways of Looking at the Masters

1. *As an Event in Augusta, Georgia*

1   In the middle of downtown Broad Street a tall white monument—like an immensely heightened wedding cake save that in place of the bride and groom stands a dignified Confederate officer—proffers the thought that

> No nation rose so white and fair;
> None fell so pure of crime.   5

Within a few steps of the monument, a movie theatre, during Masters Week in 1979, was showing *Hair*, full of cheerful miscegenation and anti-military song and dance.
2   This is the Deep/Old/New South, with its sure-enough levees, railroad tracks, unpainted dwellings out of illustrations to Joel Chandler Harris, and stately homes ornamented by grillework and verandas. As far up the Savannah River as boats 10 could go, Augusta has been a trading post since 1717 and was named in 1735 by James Oglethorpe for the mother of George III. It changed hands several times during the Revolutionary War, thrived on tobacco and cotton, imported textile machinery from Philadelphia in 1828, and during the Civil War housed the South's largest powder works. Sherman passed through here, and didn't leave much in the 15 way of historical sites.
3   The Augusta National Golf Club is away from the business end of town, in a region of big brick houses embowered in magnolia and dogwood. A lot of people retire to Augusta, and one of the reasons that Bobby Jones wanted to build a golf course here, instead of near his native Atlanta, was the distinctly milder climate. The course, 20 built in 1931–2 on the site of the Fruitlands Nursery property, after designs by Dr Alister Mackenzie (architect of Cypress Point) and Jones himself, has the venerable Augusta Country Club at its back, and at its front, across Route 28, an extensive shopping-centre outlay. At this point the New South becomes indistinguishable from New Jersey.   25

2. *As an Event Not in Augusta, Georgia*

4   How many Augusta citizens are members of the Augusta National Golf Club? The question, clearly in bad taste, brought raised eyebrows and a muttered 'Very few' or, more spaciously, 'Thirty-eight or forty.' The initial membership fee is rumoured to be $50,000, there is a waiting list five years long, and most of the members seem to be national Beautiful People, Golfing Subspecies, who jet in for an occasional round dur-   30 ing the six months the course is open. When Ike, whose cottage was near the club-house, used to show up and play a twosome with Arnold Palmer, the course would be cleared by the Secret Service. Cliff Roberts, chairman of the tournament from its incep-tion in 1934 until his death in 1977, was a Wall Street investment banker; his chosen successor, William H. Lane, is a business executive from faraway Houston.   35
5   A lot of Augusta's citizens get out of town during Masters Week, renting their houses. The lady in the drugstore near the house my wife and I were staying in told me she had once gone walking on the course. *Once*: the experience seemed un-repeatable. The course had looked deserted to her, but then a voice shouted 'Fore' and a ball struck near her. The ghost of Lloyd Mangrum, perhaps. The only Augustans   40 conspicuous during the tournament are the black caddies, who know the greens so well they can call a putt's break to the inch while standing on the fringe.

3. *As a Study in Green*

6   Green grass, green grandstands, green concession stalls, green paper cups, green folding chairs and visors for sale, green-and-white ropes, green-topped Georgia pines, a prevalence of green in the slacks and jerseys of the gallery, like the prevalence of red   45 in the crowd in Moscow on May Day. The caddies' bright green caps and Sam Snead's bright green trousers. If justice were poetic, Hubert Green would win every year.

4. *As a Rite of Spring*

7   'It's become a rite of spring,' a man told me with a growl, 'like the Derby.' Like Fort Lauderdale. Like Opening Day at a dozen ballparks. Spring it was, especially for us Northerners who had left our grey skies, brown lawns, salt-strewn highways, and   50 plucky little croci for this efflorescence of azaleas and barefoot *jeunes filles en fleurs*. Most of the gallery, like most of the golfers, had Southern accents. This Yankee felt a little as if he were coming in late on a round of equinoctial parties that had stretched from Virginia to Florida. A lot of young men were lying on the grass betranced by the memories of last night's libations, and a lot of matronly voices continued discussing   55 Aunt Earlene's unfortunate second marriage, while the golf balls floated overhead. For many in attendance, the Masters is a ritual observance; some of the old-timers wore sun hats festooned with over twenty years' worth of admission badges.
8   Will success as a festival spoil the Masters as a sporting event? It hasn't yet, but the strain on the tournament's famous and exemplary organization can be felt. Ticket   60 sales are limited, but the throng at the main scoreboard is hard to squeeze by. The acreage devoted to parking would make a golf course in itself. An army of over two thousand policemen, marshals, walkway guards, salespersons, trash-gleaners, and other attendants is needed to maintain order and facilitate the pursuit of happiness. To secure a place by any green it is necessary to arrive at least an hour before there is   65 anything to watch.

9   When, on the last two days, the television equipment arrives, the crowd itself is watched. Dutifully, it takes its part as a mammoth unpaid extra in a national television spectacular. As part of it, patting our courteous applause at a good shot or groaning in chorus at a missed putt, one felt, slightly, *canned*.   70

5. As a Fashion Show

10   Female fashions, my wife pointed out, came in three strata. First, young women decked out as if going to a garden party—makeup, flowing dresses, sandals. Next, the trim, leathery generation of the mothers, dressed as if they themselves were playing golf—short skirts, sun visors, cleated two-tone shoes. Last, the generation of the grandmothers, in immaculately blued hair and amply filled pants suits in shades we   75 might call electric pastel or Day-Glo azalea.

6. As a Display Case for Sam Snead and Arnold Palmer

11   Though they no longer are likely to win, you wouldn't know it from their charismas. Snead, with his rakishly tilted panama and slightly pushed-in face—a face that has known both battle and merriment—swaggers around the practice tee like the Sheriff of Golf County, testing a locked door here, hanging a parking ticket there. On   80 the course, he remains a golfer one has to call beautiful, from the cushioned roll of his shoulders as he strokes the ball to the padding, panther-like tread with which he follows it down the centre of the fairway, his chin tucked down while he thinks apparently rueful thoughts. He is one of the great inward golfers, those who wrap the dazzling difficulty of the game in an impassive, effortless flow of movement. When, on   85 the green, he stands beside his ball, faces the hole, and performs the curious obeisance of his 'side-winder' putting stroke, no one laughs.

12   And Palmer, he of the unsound swing, a hurried slash that ends as though he is snatching back something hot from a fire, remains the monumental outward golfer, who invites us into the game to share with him its heady turmoil, its call for   90 constant courage. Every inch an agonist, Palmer still hitches his pants as he mounts the green, still strides between the wings of his army like Hector on his way to yet more problematical heroism. Age has thickened him, made him look almost muscle-bound, and has grizzled his thin, untidy hair; but his deportment more than ever expresses vitality, a love of life and of the game that rebounds to him, from the   95 multitudes, as fervent gratitude. Like us golfing commoners, he risks looking bad for the sake of some fun.

13   Of the younger players, only Lanny Wadkins communicates Palmer's reckless determination, and only Fuzzy Zoeller has the captivating blitheness of a Jimmy Demaret or a Lee Trevino. The Masters, with its clubby lifetime qualification for   100 previous winners, serves as an annual exhibit of Old Masters, wherein one can see the difference between the reigning, college-bred pros, with their even teeth, on-camera poise, and abstemious air, and the older crowd, who came up from caddie sheds, drove themselves in cars along the dusty miles of the Tour, and hustled bets with the rich to make ends meet. Golf expresses the man, as every weekend four-   105 some knows; amid the mannerly lads who dominate the money list, Palmer and Snead loom as men.

7. As an Exercise in Spectatorship

14   In no other sport must the spectator move. The builders and improvers of Augusta National built mounds and bleachers for the crowds to gain vantage from, and a gracefully written pamphlet by the founder, Robert Jones, is handed out as   110 instruction in the art of 'letting the Tournament come to us instead of chasing after it'. Nevertheless, as the field narrows and the interest of the hordes focuses, the best way to see anything is to hang back in the woods and use binoculars. Seen from within the galleries, the players become tiny walking dolls, glimpsable, like stars on a night of scudding clouds, in the gaps between heads.   115

15   Examples of Southern courtesy in the galleries: (1) When my wife stood to watch an approach to the green, the man behind her mildly observed, 'Ma'am, it was awful nice when you were sittin' down.' (2) A gentleman standing next to me, not liking the smell of a cigar I was smoking, offered to buy it from me for a dollar.

16   Extraordinary event in the galleries: on the fourth hole a ball set in flight by   120 Dow Finsterwald solidly struck the head of a young man sitting beside the green. The sound of a golf ball on a skull is remarkably like that of two blocks of wood knocked together. *Glock.* Flesh hurts; bone makes music.

17   Single instance of successful spectatorship by this reporter: I happened to be in the pines left of the seventh fairway on the first day of play, wondering whether to go   125 for another of the refreshment committee's standardized but economical ham sandwiches, when Art Wall, Jr, hooked a ball near where I was standing. Only a dozen or so gathered to watch his recovery; for a moment, then, we could breathe with a player and experience with him—as he waggled, peered at obtruding branches, switched clubs, and peered at the branches again—that quintessential golfing sensation, the   130 loneliness of the bad-ball hitter.

18   Sad truth, never before revealed: by sticking to a spot in the stands or next to the green, one can view the field coming through, hitting variants of the same shots and putts, and by listening to the massed cheers and grunts from the other greens, one can guess at dramas unseen; but the unified field, as Einstein discovered in a more general   135 connection, is unapprehendable, and the best way to witness a golf tournament is at the receiving end of a television signal. Many a fine golf reporter, it was whispered to me, never leaves the set in the press tent.

19   The other sad truth about golf spectatorship is that for today's pros it all comes down to the putting, and that the difference between a putt that drops and one that   140 rims the cup, though teleologically enormous, is intellectually negligible.

8. As a Study in Turf-Building

20   A suburban lawn-owner can hardly look up from admiring the weedless immensity of the Augusta National turf. One's impression, when first admitted to this natural Oz, is that a giant putting surface has been dropped over acres of rolling terrain, with a few apertures for ponds and trees to poke through. A philosophy of golf is expressed   145 in Jones's pamphlet: 'The Augusta National has much more fairway and green area than the average course. There is little punishing rough and very few bunkers. The course is not intended so much to punish severely the wayward shot as to reward adequately the stoke played with skill—and judgment.'

21   It is an intentional paradox, then, that this championship course is rather kind 150
to duffers. The ball sits up on Augusta's emerald carpet looking big as a baseball. It
was not always such; in 1972, an invasion of *Poa annua*, a white-spiked vagabond
grass, rendered conditions notoriously bumpy; in remedy a fescue called Pennlawn
and a rye called Pennfine were implanted on the fairways and greens respectively and
have flourished. Experimentation continues; to make the greens even harder and 155
slicker, they are thinking of rebuilding them on a sand base—and have already done
so on the adjacent par-three course.

22   From May to October, when the course is closed to play, everything goes to seed
and becomes a hayfield, and entire fairways are plowed up: a harrowing thought. The
caddies, I was solemnly assured, never replace a divot; they just spinkle grass seed 160
from a pouch they carry. Well, this is a myth, for I repeatedly saw caddies replace div-
ots in the course of the tournament, with the care of tile-setters.

9. As Demography

23   One doesn't have to want to give the country back to the Indians to feel a nos-
talgic pang while looking at old photos of the pre–World War II tournaments, with
their hatted, necktied galleries strolling up the fairways in the wake of the baggy- 165
trousered players, and lining the tees and greens only one man deep.

24   The scores have grown crowded, too. The best then would be among the best
now—Lloyd Mangrum's single-round 64 in 1940 has not been bettered, though for
the last two years it has been equalled. But the population of the second-best has
increased, producing virtually a new winner each week of the Tour, and stifling the 170
emergence of stable constellations of superstars like Nelson-Hogan-Snead and
Palmer-Player-Nicklaus. In the 1936 and 1938 Masters, only seven players made the
36-hole score of 145 that cut the 1979 field to 45 players. Not until 1939 did the winner break 280 and not again until 1948. The last total over 280 to win it came in
1973. In 1936, Craig Wood had a first-day round of 88 and finished in the top two 175
dozen. In 1952, Sam Snead won the Masters in spite of a third-round 77. That margin for intermittent error has been squeezed from tournament golf. Johnny Miller
chops down a few trees, develops the wrong muscles, and drops like a stone on the
lists. Arnold Palmer, relatively young and still strong and keen, can no longer ram the
putts in from twenty feet, and becomes a father figure. A cruel world, top-flight golf, 180
that eats its young.

10. As Race Relations

25   A Martian skimming overhead in his saucer would have to conclude that white
Earthlings hit the ball and black Earthlings fetch it, that white men swing the sticks
and black men carry them. The black caddies of Augusta, in their white overalls, are
a tradition that needs a symbolic breaking, the converse of Lee Elder's playing in the 185
tournament.

26   To be fair, these caddies are specialists of a high order, who take a cheerful pride
in their expertise and who are, especially during Masters Week, well paid for it. Gary
Player's caddie for his spectacular come-from-nowhere victory of 1978 was tipped
$10,000—a sum that, this caddie assured an impudent interrogator, was still safe in 190
the bank. In the New South, blacks work side by side with whites in the concession

stands and at the fairway ropes, though I didn't see any in a green marshal's coat. I was
unofficially informed that, at the very time when civil rightists were agitating for a
black player to be invited to play even if one did not earn qualification—as Elder did
in 1975—blacks were not being admitted to the tournament *as spectators*. I wonder 195
about this. On pages 26–27 of the green souvenir album with a text by Cliff Roberts,
one can see a photograph of Henry Picard hitting out of a bunker; behind him in the
scattering of spectators are a number of ebony gentlemen not dressed as caddies. At
any rate, though golf remains a white man's game, it presents in the Masters player and
caddie an active white–black partnership in which the white man is taking the advice 200
and doing the manual work. Caddies think of the partnership as 'we', as in 'We hit a
drive down the centre and a four-iron stiff to the pin, but then *he* missed the putt.'

11. As Class Relations

27   Though the Augusta National aspires to be the American St Andrews, there is
a significant economic difference between a Scottish golf links thriftily pinked out on
a wasteland—the sandy seaside hills that are 'links'—and the American courses elab- 205
orately, expensively carved from farmland and woods. Though golf has plebeian
Scottish roots, in this country its province is patrician. A course requires capital and
flaunts that ancient aristocratic prerogative, land. In much of the world, this humbling
game is an automatic symbol of capitalist-imperialist oppression; a progressive African
novelist, to establish a character as a villain, has only to show him coming off a golf 210
course. And in our own nation, for all the roadside driving ranges and four o'clock
factory leagues, golf remains for millions something that happens at the end of a long
driveway, beyond the MEMBERS ONLY sign.

28   Yet competitive golf in the United States came of age when, at The Country
Club, in Brookline, Massachusetts, a 20-year-old ex-caddie and workingman's son, 215
Francis Ouimet, beat the British legends Vardon and Ray in a playoff for the US Open.
And ever since, the great competitors have tended to come from the blue-collar level
of golf, the caddies and the offspring of club pros. Rare is the Bobby Jones who
emerges from the gentry with the perfectionistic drive and killer instinct that make a
championship in this game which permits no let-up or loss of concentration, yet 220
which penalizes tightness also. Hagen acted like a swell and was called Sir Walter, but
he came up from a caddie's roost in Rochester. The lords of golf have been by and large
gentlemen made and not born, while the clubs and the management of the Tour
remain in the hands of the country-club crowd. When genteel Ed Sneed and Tom
Watson fell into a three-way playoff for the 1979 Masters title, you knew in your 225
bones it was going to be the third player, a barbarian called Fuzzy with a loopy all-
out swing, who would stroll through the gates and carry off the loot.

12. As a Parade of Lovely Golfers, No Two Alike

29   Charles Coody, big-beaked bird. Billy Casper, once the king of touch, now
sporting the bushy white sideburns of a turn-of-the-century railroad conductor, still
able to pop them up from a sandtrap and sink the putt. Trevino, so broad across he 230
looks like a reflection in a funhouse mirror, a model of delicacy around the greens and
a model of affable temperament everywhere. Player, varying his normal black outfit
with white slacks, his bearing so full of fight and muscle he seems to be restraining

himself from breaking into a run. Nicklaus, Athlete of the Decade, still golden but almost gaunt and faintly grim, as he feels a crown evaporating from his head. Gay 235 Brewer, heavy in the face and above the belt, nevertheless uncorking a string-straight mid-iron to within nine inches of the long seventh hole in the par-three tournament. Miller Barber, Truman Capote's double, punching and putting his way to last year's best round, a storm-split 64 in two instalments. Bobby Clampett, looking too young and thin to be out there. Andy Bean, looking too big to be out there, and with his 240 perennially puzzled expression seeming to be searching for a game more his size. Hubert Green, with a hunched flicky swing that would make a high-school golf coach scream. Tom Weiskopf, the handsome embodiment of pained near-perfection. Hale Irwin, the picture-book golfer with the face of a Ph.D. candidate. Johnny Miller, look- ing heavier than we remember him, patiently knocking them out on the practice tee, 245 wondering where the lightning went. Ben Crenshaw, the smiling Huck Finn, and Tom Watson, the more pensive Tom Sawyer, who, while the other boys were whitewash- ing fences, has become, politely but firmly, the best golfer in the world.

30   And many other redoubtable young men. Seeing them up close, in the dining room or on the clubhouse veranda, one is struck by how young and in many cases 250 how slight they seem, with their pert and telegenic little wives—boys, really, anxious to be polite and to please even the bores that collect in the interstices of all well- publicized events. Only when one sees them at a distance, as they walk alone or chat- ting in twos down the great green emptiness of the fairway, does one sense that each youth is the pinnacle of a buried pyramid of effort and investment, of prior competi- 255 tion from pre-teen level up, of immense and it must be at times burdensome accu- mulated hopes of parents, teachers, backers. And with none of the group hypnosis and exhilaration of team play to relieve them. And with the difference between success and failure so feather-fine.

13. As a Religious Experience

31   The four days of 1979's Masters fell on Maundy Thursday, Good Friday, Holy 260 Saturday, and Easter Sunday. On Good Friday, fittingly, the skies darkened, tornadoes were predicted, and thousands of sinners ran for cover. My good wife, who had gone to divine services, was prevented from returning to the course by the flood of depart- ing cars, and the clear moral is one propounded from many a pulpit: golf and church- going do not mix. Easter Sunday also happened to be the anniversary of the 265 assassination of Abraham Lincoln and the sinking of the *Titanic*, and it wasn't such a good day for Ed Sneed either.

32   About ninety-nine per cent of the gallery, my poll of local vibes indicated, was rooting for Sneed to hold off disaster and finish what he had begun. He had played splendidly for three days, and it didn't seem likely he'd come this close soon again. 270 When he birdied the fifteenth and enlarged his once huge cushion back to three strokes, it seemed he would do it. But then, through no flagrant fault of his own, he began 'leaking'. We all knew how it felt, the slippery struggle to nurse a good round back to the clubhouse. On the seventeenth green, where I was standing, his approach looked no worse than his playing partner's; it just hit a foot too long, skipped onto 275 the sloping back part of the green, and slithered into the fringe. His putt back caught the cup but twirled away. And his putt to save par, which looked to me like a gimme, lipped out, the same way my two-footers do when I lift my head to watch them drop, my sigh of relief all prepared. Zoeller, ten minutes before, had gently rolled in a birdie from much farther away. Sneed's fate seemed sealed then: the eighteenth hole, a 280 famous bogey-maker, waited for him as ineluctably as Romeo's missed appointment with Juliet.

33   He hadn't hit bad shots, and he hadn't panicked; he just was screwed a half-turn too tight to get a par. The gallery of forty thousand felt for him, right to the pits of our golf-weary stomachs, when his last hope of winning it clean hung on the lip of 285 the seventy-second hole. It so easily might have been otherwise. But then that's life, and that's golf.

1984

QUESTIONS
Reader and Purpose

1. Updike's title is a reference to a well-known poem by the American writer Wallace Stevens, 'Thirteen Ways of Looking at a Blackbird' (1917). Is the reference obvious to you? Or is Updike asking too much of his reader?
2. Since an **analogy** points out how unlike things have some similarities, what does Updike's title suggest about his topic?
3. How would you describe Updike's **tone** in the first section: sarcastic? humorous? cynical? detached? passionate? neutral? philosophical? grim? critical? a mixture of some of these? all of them? or something else? Does he maintain this tone throughout? Or does he adopt a different one in some sections?
4. In a paragraph of 8–10 lines summarize the main points of Updike's analogy.
5. In the opening section Updike presents several contrasts: South–North, black–white, rich–poor, historical–contemporary. Do these contrasts adequately prepare the topics he introduces beginning with section 2? Trace one of these contrasts throughout the essay.

Organization

6. Is Updike's title meant to be taken literally? Is he, that is, really looking at the golf tournament in 13 different ways? Or does his title refer to 13 different aspects of the tournament?
7. What kind of person is the author? Although he says little about himself, there is some evidence that will help you answer this question. Note, for instance, the contrast between paragraph 4 and the second sentence of paragraph 5. Note also the last sentence of paragraph 9. What other evidence is there?
8. Several themes run throughout this essay, one of the most important being the place of blacks (or African Americans) in the Masters tournament, on the Augusta golf course, and in American life as a whole. Point out specifically where this theme occurs (its context), and thus how it helps to unify the essay.

Sentences

9. In the first sentence of paragraph 2, why is there a comma after 'Joel Chandler Harris'?

10. How does the third sentence of paragraph 2 use **parallelism**? And the third sentence of paragraph 3?
11. Are the **fragments** in paragraph 6 effective? Justify your answer.
12. The last sentence of paragraph 9 has four commas. How would the sentence be affected if all the commas were left out?
13. In section 7, sentence fragments begin four of the six paragraphs. Why are these openings effective, or dull?

Diction

14. Look up: *proffers* (3), *embowered* (18), *prevalence* (45), *efflorescence* (51), *equinoctial* (53), *festooned* (58), *strata* (71), *rakishly* (78), *rueful* (84), *agonist* (91), *deportment* (94), *blitheness* (99), *abstemious* (103), *quintessential* (130), *teleologically* (141), *plebeian* (206), *patrician* (207), *gentry* (219), *interstices* (252).
15. Explain the meaning of the epitaph Updike quotes in his first paragraph. If you know little about the American Civil War (1861–5) between the North and the South, you should refer to an encyclopedia.
16. What does Updike mean by the expression *sure-enough levees* (8)? Is there a touch of satire in the expression? How would substituting the word *genuine* for *sure-enough* alter the tone of this sentence?

POINTS TO LEARN

1. An analogy can be developed from several different perspectives.
2. A sentence fragment can be an effective method of description if used sparingly.

SUGGESTIONS FOR WRITING

Write an essay of 8–12 paragraphs in which you expose, by a series of brief analogies, various facets of a public, or private, entertainment: a hockey game, the high-school production of a play, a political rally, a year-end party, a wedding reception, a rock concert, etc. Look at this entertainment from the **point of view** of a spectator who is fascinated by every conceivable aspect of the spectacle or production.

IMPROVING YOUR STYLE

1. In one paragraph use several sentence fragments.
2. Use parallel structure extensively in two paragraphs that are not consecutive.

CHARLES GORDON

Charles Gordon (1940–) has worked since the 1970s for the *Ottawa Citizen*, where he has held the posts of city editor, books editor, features writer, and columnist; he now devotes himself to a humour column, with the occasional serious comment on politics or music. He is also a regular contributor to *Maclean's* magazine, and has won three National Magazine Awards. He has published several books that reflect his comic and often ironic interest in all things Canadian, including *The Governor General's Bunny Hop and Other Reports from the Nation's Capital* (1985), *At the Cottage: A Fearless Look at Canada's Summer Obsession* (1989), and *How To Be Not Too Bad: A Canadian Guide to Superior Behaviour* (1993). His latest books include *The Canada Trip* (1997), based on a three-month journey that he and his wife took throughout Canada, travelling more than 24,000 kilometres; and *The Grim Pig* (2001), a satirical look at newspapers.

The Threat to Canada's Beauty

1   More than ever now, it is important to see Canada. And soon. Although nature's beauty is still there, it is becoming harder and harder to see.

2   In Ontario, those nice bridges from which you liked to admire the river as you drove across—more and more of them have the view blocked by solid concrete walls where the bridge rails used to be.   5

3   This tendency to deprive our citizens of the best views springs from a most Canadian quality—overprotectiveness: if people looked at the view, they might get hurt. Where the view is reachable on foot, it is often obscured by signs warning of this and that. If there is a waterfall, it will likely be accompanied by a sign that says: WARNING: WATERFALL.   10

4   An actual example encountered on a recent trip is a highway rest stop at the French River, just south of Sudbury, Ont., on Highway 69. The rest stop features a deep gorge and a steep drop to the river below. It also features a magnificent chain link fence. A child or short adult would only be able to see the river by peering between the links. CAUTION, says a sign, STEEP DROP TO RIVER.   15

5   Is it possible that we have become, in the few short years since the Group of Seven roamed the wilderness, a nation afraid of its scenery? Who would have thought it.

6   But why should this matter? Think of a clear and perfect June evening in north-western Ontario. The lake trout is fresh, the sun is setting over Lake Superior, and the   20 whole thing is posing nicely for the family dining in the inn at Rossport. An Oscar Peterson tape plays quietly. The mother is explaining to the daughter what a great fishing town Rossport used to be and is just coming to the part about the lamprey and how it killed off the lake trout when a CP freight train rumbles by, completing this most Canadian of scenes.   25

7   The locomotive of the CP Rail freight train has the new logo on it, part of which is the Stars and Stripes of the United States. The daughter is incensed. The father, trying to be reasonable in this most Canadian of scenes, ventures to explain: CP Rail does a lot of business in the States, he says. The daughter is unmoved. The American flag has no place on a Canadian train, she says.   30

8   No too many people seem to share her view—about the CP Rail logo, about the president of Air Canada being an American, about the publisher of the *Globe and Mail* being an American. Perhaps not too many people have seen such a stirring juxtaposition: a Stars and Stripes flying where a Maple Leaf should be. Perhaps not enough people have seen those perfectly Canadian places.   35

9   And why is that? One reason, ironically enough, would be that the trains aren't running any more—at least, not the passenger trains, at least, not with any frequency; and certainly not on the Lake Superior route, which has been given over to the freight trains with their Stars and Stripes logo. The country is growing, but growing mainly in the cities. A smaller percentage of the people who live in the country have seen the   40
country. The Trans-Canada Highway is out of fashion, the roadside economy falling to the recession, while long-distance Canadian drivers opt for American routes and the lure of places to buy cheap sheets.

10   Canadian loyalties are a complicated matter. They are not the knee-jerk, my-country-right-or-wrong variety found to the south of us. Approaching Game 7 of a   45
Stanley Cup played between Vancouver and New York, a significant number of Canadians were cheering for the American team against the Canadian team. They reasoned, these complicated Canadians, that the Rangers represented the Original Six Team League and a saner moment in our history.

11   Other complicated Canadians reason that a smart American publisher will make   50
the *Globe and Mail* a healthier newspaper, and that a competitive Air Canada is more important than the nationality of its president. No loyalties are automatic up here.

12   A day later, at Pancake Bay, north of Sault Ste Marie, the man pumping gas says there is a dead wolf beside the road three miles to the east. When that spot is passed, there is no wolf, raising intriguing Canadian questions. What happens to a dead wolf?   55
Do maintenance people come along and cart it away? What do they think when they do that? Or do other animals come out of the Northern Ontario woods and eat it up? The other question is, in how many other places could the question even be raised?

13   It is not a trivial suggestion that the publisher of the *Globe and Mail* should go up and have a look, along with the logo design committee of CP Rail, and all the rest   60
of us too. Just as Canadians grow to love their country more when they travel in others, so do Canadians grow to love their country more when they see more of it. No matter how citified we get, the landscape is part of our culture, it is one of the things that differentiates us from other countries, makes us different people. If we confine ourselves to one place, we lose that.   65

14   In *Local Colour*, a recent anthology of travel writing about Canada, the late Margaret Laurence tells about overcoming her Prairie bias against 'the East' by discovering, among other things, the trees around Bancroft, Ont., in the fall: 'Words won't make a net to catch that picture; nor, I think, will paint,' Laurence wrote in 1976. 'But suddenly I could see why the Group of Seven was so obsessed with trying   70
to get it down, this incredible splendour, and why, for so long, many Canadian writers

couldn't see the people for the trees. With trees like these, no wonder humans felt overwhelmed.'

15   The subtitle of *Local Colour* (published by Douglas & McIntyre) is 'Writers Discovering Canada'. As Laurence shows, the discovery of the landscape is also the 75 discovery of the people who live in it. It is a process from which more of us could benefit, a process that could halt the slow but steady arrival of more stars and more stripes stamped on things we once thought of as ours. At the moment we don't seem to care enough. But the highway is there. Get on it before it is surrounded by WARNING: SCENERY signs.   80

1994

QUESTIONS

Reader and Purpose

1. After reading the title and opening paragraph, what aspect of Canada's beauty do you expect the essay to be about? What other aspect of Canada's beauty does Gordon deal with?
2. What, for Gordon, is the real threat to Canada's beauty? In his first five paragraphs how does he try to attract the reader's sympathy for his topic?
3. 'No matter how citified we get, the landscape is part of our culture' (63). To what extent is this the key sentence of the essay?

Organization

4. In paragraph 1 Gordon states his thesis, and in paragraphs 2, 3, and 4 he gives examples and reasons. What is the function of paragraph 5?
5. How do paragraphs 2, 3, and 4 reveal the differences between exposition by illustration and exposition by reasons?
6. What is the function of the first sentence of paragraph 6? Is it a transition to a different topic? If so, is it effective?
7. How does the last sentence of paragraph 8 join the two topics that Gordon is dealing with?
8. What happens between the first sentence of paragraph 10 and the last sentence of paragraph 11?
9. What point is the author making in paragraph 12? What is its connection to the paragraphs that precede and follow it? Is this connection clear?
10. How does paragraph 13 act as both summary and transition? Is it any different in this respect from paragraph 5?

Sentences

11. In speaking, one commonly uses the sort of construction found in the second sentence of paragraph 1. Is this construction effective in its written form?
12. The first sentence in both paragraphs 2 and 3 uses a dash. How are these dashes used differently? Why?
13. Is the *Just as . . . so do . . .* construction in paragraph 13 an example of **parallel structure**?
14. Identify the **comma splice** in paragraph 13. Can you justify this usage?

Diction

15. Look up: *gorge* (13), *lamprey* (23), *incensed* (27), *juxtaposition* (33–4), *intriguing* (55), *trivial* (59).
16. In paragraphs 3 and 4 the words on warning signs are written in capital letters. Why? Is this usage effective? Is **irony** involved?
17. Who were the Group of Seven? (You can look this up in the *Canadian Encyclopedia* or in a guide to Canadian art.) How important is this knowledge to a thorough understanding of this essay?

POINTS TO LEARN

1. Exposition by illustration is often part of exposition by reasons.
2. A skilful writer can use exposition of one topic to lead to another topic that the writer sees as part of the first.

SUGGESTIONS FOR WRITING

How do you feel about the beauty of the region in which you live? In an essay of 7–10 paragraphs, using both illustrations and reasons, discuss why the natural beauties where you live are worth preserving.

IMPROVING YOUR STYLE

1. Begin one paragraph of your essay with a short question that leads to a related topic.
2. Use parallelism to emphasize the relationship between some of your important points.

CHRISTOPHER BUCKLEY

Christopher Buckley (1952–), who lives in Washington, DC, with his wife and family, is a journalist, editor, novelist, and social critic. His writing attracted attention at an early age: he contributed to *New York Magazine* at 19 and became the managing editor of *Esquire* when he was only 24. In 1981–2 he was a speechwriter for then Vice-President George Bush. His books—three of which have been selected by the *New York Times* as Notable Book of the Year—include *The White House Mess* (1986), *Steaming to Bamboola: The World of a Tramp Freighter* (1987), *Wet Work* (1991), *Thank You for Smoking* (1994), and *Little Green Men* (1999). His latest book is *No Way to Treat a First Lady* (2002).

The essay below is from *Wry Martinis* (1997), a collection of humorous and satirical jabs at a wide variety of targets—the fashion industry, the gun lobby, television personalities, the cigarette manufacturers, the liquor lobby, Washington politics, and the movie industry, to name a few.

How I Learned to (Almost) Love the Sin Lobbyists

1   A couple of yeas ago, while wondering with some desperation what to write about, I turned on the TV and there was a nice-looking talking-head lady from the Tobacco Institute, manfully (as it were) denying that there was any scientific link between smoking and cancer, heart disease, respiratory disease, or athlete's foot. She was attractive, well-spoken, intelligent, and as persuasive as she could be, given the 5 deplorably disingenuous data she was pitching. I thought: *What an interesting job that must be. Get up in the morning, brush your teeth, and go and sell death for a living.*

2   A few days later I was reading in the paper about some teenage kid who, to judge from his blood-alcohol content, had drunk two kegs of beer single-handedly, then got in his pickup truck and careened over the yellow line into a minivan, anni- 10 hilating an entire Boy Scout troop. And there at the bottom of the story was a quote from a spokesman for the beer-keg industry saying what an awful tragedy it was, but that no one was more concerned about teenage drunk driving than the beer-keg industry. I thought: *Boy, I bet that guy trembles every time his beeper goes off.*

3   A few days after that, a 'disgruntled postal worker' went bonkers and blew away 15 his supervisor and a half-dozen others with a gun with a name like Hamburger-Maker .44 Triple-Magnum. And sure enough, the National Rifle Association was right on the case, worrying out loud that if we start outlawing Hamburger-Maker .44s, how long before we outlaw the Swiss Army knife? I thought: *There's another interesting job.*

4   The idea formed of writing a major, thick, serious, nonfiction study of institu- 20 tional hypocrisy in America. It would be grandiose and groundbreaking, but with an *accessible* title: *I'm Shocked—Shocked!* (said, of course, by Captain Renaud in *Casablanca*, on being handed his gambling winnings moments after closing down Rick's Café for gambling). The book—no, the *volume*—would cover government, busi-ness, society. It would be comprehensive, exhaustive, thorough. And boring.   25

5   But I kept coming back to these three yuppie Horsemen of the Apocalypse. Another title came to me: *Thank You for Smoking*. And then the mortgage bill arrived, so that settled it.

---

6   I wrote to the Tobacco Institute, the various liquor lobbies, and to the National Rifle Association. These were artfully worded letters announcing that I had had 30 enough of the neo-Puritanism that was sweeping America and was embarking on a book about it. True enough. They may now complain that they were deceived, but if they look at those letters, they'll see that they really weren't—and anyway, people who make their living pushing cigarettes, liquor, and guns ought not to claim the high moral ground. And they shouldn't look a gift novel in the mouth: the trio of charac- 35 ters who make up the book's Mod Squad—it's an acronym for 'Merchants of Death'—are sort of likable. Or at least sympathetic.

7   Likable? Yuppie mass murderers? Or mass enablers? *Sympathetic?*

8   I went to see the attractive lady from the Tobacco Institute. She was very nice and . . . tall. I don't want to get into amateur psychology here, but my guess is that 40 it's not all that easy being a six-foot-one-inch-tall woman, especially as she had no doubt reached this height in her teens; and maybe, just possibly, there's some anger

inside that she's still, uh, working out. (But it wasn't my business, and I didn't ask.)
I was surprised, however, to learn that her previous job had been at the Department
of Health and Human Services. 'At my going-away party, they were going to give me   45
signed copies of the Surgeon General's report', she said, smiling, 'but thought better
of it.'

9   I wanted to know what it's like, being a merchant of death. I didn't use that
exact phrase. Well, she said, it's not easy. No, I said, I imagine it's not. You get threats,
she said. What do you do about them?, I said. You throw 'em away, she said.   50

10   Once she was at a health symposium—that's part of her job, attending *health*
symposiums; what a warm welcome she must get—standing next to Everett Koop, the
formidable former Surgeon General who looks like Captain Ahab. And someone mentioned that she used to work at HHS. And he said, 'I wish she'd gone to be a prostitute
on Fourteenth Street instead.' Don't think that didn't hurt.   55

11   I said, How do you introduce yourself to strangers? 'Well,' she said, 'you never
come straight out and say, "I work for the Tobacco Institute."' First she'll say, 'I work
in public relations.' If they press, she'll say, 'I work for a trade association.' If they still
press, she says a trade association 'for a major manufacturer'. She added, 'You never
know if this guy's mother has just died of cancer.' By now I'm shaking my head in   60
sympathy, thinking: *Gosh, it must be just awful.*

12   But why, I fumbled diffidently, what's—

13   'A nice girl like me doing in a place like this?' she finished my sentence.

14   'Yes!' I cry. 'Why?'

15   She exhales her smoke—like Lauren Bacall. 'I'm paying the mortgage.'   65

16   Of course: the Yuppie Nuremberg defence: *I vas only paying ze mortgage!*
I admire this woman. In the kingdom of the morally blind, she has the echolocation
of a bat. On the way out, she points to a booklet on her credenza. Next to it is a packet
of 'Death' brand cigarettes, an actual brand of cigarettes, no name on the front of the
pack, just a white-on-black skull. As tchotchkes, the Tobacco Institute could do no   70
better than a pack of Death cigarettes.

17   But the booklet. It says, 'Helping Youth to Say No to Tobacco'. She says, 'That's
what I'm proudest of.'

18   This *was* an impressive statement. My admiration for her faculties of cognitive
dissonance, already large, swelled to even greater proportions. Goebbels might as well   75
have produced a booklet entitled 'The Führer and the Jews—A Love Story'.

19   Oh dear. I promised that I wouldn't moralize. It's not my job as a novelist. It's
just that I have kids myself and . . . well, no, back to the story.

20   Much in the news at the time was the controversy about Old Joe, Camel
cigarettes' famous dromedary with the nose that seems to remind some people of a   80
penis. Camel started a new campaign with Old Joe at its centre, wearing sunglasses
and playing the saxophone, shooting pool, coolly eyeing the chicks. RJR Nabisco was
putting out about 75 million dollars' worth of Old Joe ads a year. The cigarette companies say that they are not—repeat, *not*—trying to get new business. They say they
seek only to reinforce brand loyalty—and brand disloyalty, trying to get a *teeny*, *tiny*   85
percentage of smokers to switch brands.

21   In the wake of the Old Joe campaign, Camel's share of the illegal children's
cigarette market climbed from .5 per cent to 32 per cent. Outraged mothers howled.

Even *Advertising Age*, Mammon's own trade journal, editorialized against the Old Joe campaign, to little avail. Old Joe is still among us, playing his saxophone.   90

22   Meanwhile, overseas, the US trade representative had begun to bully Pacific Rim countries—Taiwan, Japan, South Korea, and others—into opening their markets to US tobacco. Up till then, those countries hadn't allowed cigarette advertising. Then comes the US trade rep threatening something called a 301 action, named for a section in the 1974 Trade Act that allows the president to slap retaliatory tariffs on foreign products   95 if their country of origin is seen to be discriminating against Marlboro et al. by not allowing Marlboro et al. to advertise—never mind that *no* cigarette advertising has been allowed.

23   Inevitably, the countries buckled to US government pressure. The happy result? In just the first year that South Korea allowed US tobacco advertising, the smoking   100 rate for male teenagers rose from 18 per cent to 30 per cent. For female teenagers, it rose from 2 per cent to 9. The trends were similar in the other countries. The World Health Organization estimates that between now and the end of the century, smoking will kill 250 million people in the industrialized world. That's one in five, roughly the population of the United States.   105

23   So it's clear that the tobacco industry is doing its level best to help youth to say no to smoking. I left the Tobacco Institute lady's office feeling warm and fuzzy.

---

25   My next new friend works for the Beer Institute. The *Beer* Institute! I come to him straight from a visit with the head of the hard-liquor lobby: the Distilled Spirits Council of the United States. They hate each other, the beer and the booze people.   110 Why? Because of a tax issue called 'equivalency'. If one beer and one highball contain the same amount of ethanol, well then, say the DISCUS people to the government, you should tax beer at the same rate you tax us. This makes the beer people—Augie Coors, especially—very unhappy. So I do not tell my beer people that I am bellying up to the booze people.   115

26   My beer guy—what a guy! Good-looking, jockly, hail-fellow-well-met. He is calling me 'guy' and we have only known each other for ten minutes. On his desk is a recent copy of *Fatal Accident Reporting System*, a Department of Transportation publication. On the bookshelf: beer steins, empty bottles of exotic beer. On the wall: his diploma from the Summer School of Alcohol Studies. I yearn to ask, Do they know   120 how to party at the Summer School of Alcohol Studies, or what? There is also an autographed photo of him and his wife and President Bush.

27   He works hard. And with a handicap. He hates to fly, and yet he used to have to fly one million miles a year. Once, he was on a plane that got struck by lightning. He drank 15 drinks to calm down. After that he got so nervous that he had to get him-   125 self drunk to fly. 'Which sometimes leads to trouble,' he allows.

28   He gives me a *tour d'horizon* of the beer world. It is not a pretty picture. Sales have been basically flat for 10 years: Neo-Prohibitionism is on the rise. Hypocrisy is rampant. Congressman Joe Kennedy II is demanding yet more warning labels on beer bottles. You know it's bad when a Kennedy is staking out the moral high ground on alcohol.   130

29   'We pour *millions* into traffic safety issues each year,' he says. And what thanks do they get? None, *nada*, *rien*, zip, zilch. Ingrates. We discuss the government's

'Controlled Availability Theory', the idea that if you tax something, people will buy less of it. He quotes Himmler: 'We must get rid of the alcohol.' He adds, 'That's not an exact quote.'   135

30   I follow him to a health symposium called Healthy People/Healthy Environments 2000. My beer guy says that he sort of 'relishes' being at the conference. He says it's 'like being black in the Old South'. I will hear variants of this as I shuttle between my alcohol, tobacco, and firearms people: They are the new pariahs, the niggers of postmodern morality—the *victims*. The DISCUS person, grey-haired, grand-   140 fatherly, and aggrieved, will crack the faintest smile when asked about the effects of neo-Puritanism on his social standing and will shrug, 'It's not *quite* as bad as being a Colombian drug baron.'

31   My beer guy gets up and speaks to the healthy fifteen hundred. They sense the presence of the enemy. Fifteen hundred bottoms—three thousand buttocks—shift   145 warily in their seats. You can hear them clenching. It is called buttlock—gridlock of the indignant. They do not like him. He is . . . unwanted.

32   He looks like an Eagle Scout up there. He pleads earnestly, 'All we're looking for is some input.' Can't they see that? It's all he wants, input. Just a little input. 'We're not saying we in the industry should control alcohol policy in this country, but for   150 Christ's sake'—he smiles when says this—'give us some input!'

33   At the National Beer Wholesalers' Convention in a few weeks their banners and lapel buttons will say it loudly: 'WE'RE PART OF THE SOLUTION!' And they are! Drunk driving is down 40 per cent since 1982, but you don't hear that from the Healthy People. 'It interferes with their funding needs.'   155

34   He is finished. The applause defines politeness: over in less than a nanosecond. The next speaker, from Mothers Against Drunk Driving, receives applause befitting Schwarzkopf ticker-taping up Broadway. I begin to appreciate what my beer guy is up against: a massive, tectonic moral shift, spearheaded by a phalanx of pissed-off acronyms: MADD, SADD—Mothers Against Drunk Driving, Students Against Drunk   160 Driving. P.J. O'Rourke, booze muse of the open road, wants to form an organization called DAMM: Drunks Against Mad Mothers. My beer guy loves P.J. O'Rourke. So does my cigarette girl, so does my gun guy. So do I.

35   We descend the hotel escalators into the exhibit rooms, where the individual groups that form the body Healthy have set up their booths. It is just like any trade fair.   165 My beer guy says, 'We're sort of shocked that they're even allowing us to exhibit here. They were very specific that we could not give away free products. It was a real interesting discussion', he chuckles, 'about what we could and couldn't do with that booth. It was their worst nightmare that we'd have a couple of kegs tapped and some trashy trinkets like bottle openers.' He laughs. Animal House. A toga party. *To-ga, to-ga!* He is   170 hearty, my beer guy. Which is really what you want in a beer guy.

36   Together we walk down the aisle between the booths. It is to walk a gauntlet. I keep my reporter's notepad well in view, like a shield, so that they will not mistake me for a beer lobbyist. You would not want to be mistaken for one yourself, walking past displays from Mothers Against Drunk Driving, Trauma Systems Associates, the   175 Mid-Western States Substance Abuse Committee: Facing Alcohol Concerns Through Education. Their display shows the Coors ad girl altered so that she's pouring a pitcher of beer down the toilet. He shakes his head and says, 'What a waste.'

37   There is the National Head Injury Foundation booth. He says they're 'okay' but adds winkily, 'We usually define the good guys by who'll take our money.' We then   180 come face to face with another of the enemy, and here is more evidence that God is a bad novelist. She is a nice lady, in charge of Washington DC's anti-drunk-driving initiative. Her name is Pam Beers.

38   On we go past the National Highway Safety Administration, the New Hampshire Concerned Citizens Against Drunk Driving. They have caught on to the   185 quilt thing: Theirs is inscribed with the names of all the kids killed in drunk-driving incidents. 'Chipper, We'll Always Love You.'

39   Does this crack my beer guy's heart? Not. In truth, he didn't even see it. We have arrived at the Beer Institute's booth—no Spuds Mackenzie, no Swedish bikini team, instead a model of sobriety and educational material. Signs proclaim the 39 per cent   190 decline in drunk-driving fatalities between 1982 and 1990. A slogan urges, THINK WHEN YOU DRINK. A lonely colour poster proclaims the photographic glories: a frosty mug surrounded by mountains and valleys of fried chicken, burgers, ham, and pizza.

40   But what's this? The booth next to the Beer Institute's is . . . the National Coalition to Prevent Impaired Driving. My beer guy grins wickedly, 'They're going to   195 be *sooo* pissed.'

41   What does the novelist make of all this? As much as he can, I suppose, while straining—straining—not to turn his director's chair into a seat of judgment. Anyway, who's to escape whipping in *this* crazy, mixed-up world? An ethical man, said Twain, is a Christian holding four aces. While in the midst of my research, I was somewhat sur-   200 prised to find on the back cover of the magazine I edit an ad for cigarettes. My indignation, expressed to my superiors, was duly noted. What goes around karmically comes around: Several weeks ago an except from my novel, eagerly desired by the literary editor of a national magazine of reputation, was turned down by the magazine's editor-in-chief on the grounds that it would imperil advertising. 'Yes, yes,' I said, 'I understand.'   205

1997

QUESTIONS
Reader and Purpose

1. From the very beginning of this essay, including its title, Buckley's approach to his topic is a compound of **irony** and humour. Yet he is writing about deadly serious matters—smoking, drinking, and guns. Why do you think he has chosen the **tone** he has, and why does he use irony?

2. In paragraph 5 the author refers to *Thank You For Smoking*, a novel he published in 1994, whose protagonist is a spokesman for the Academy of Tobacco Studies. Why does he refer to this novel? Would you like to read this novel? In your answer you should discuss Buckley's approach to such matters as smoking and drinking, and whether irony and humour are appropriate methods for approaching these subjects.

3. In paragraph 6 Buckley comments on the 'artfully worded letters' he wrote to the tobacco, liquor, and gun associations; he says that they 'really weren't' deceived by his letters, then adds 'and anyway . . .', as if it is possible they were. Is he trying to attract the reader's sympathy? Does he succeed? Or is he trying to do something else?

4. Consider what the author states in paragraph 19 and then compare this to what he says in his final paragraph. Is he being consistent? Is he certain of his position? What do you make of his third and fourth sentences in paragraph 41? And what do you make of the two anecdotes in the rest of the paragraph?

Organization

5. In his first three paragraphs Buckley refers to those who sell cigarettes, beer, and guns, yet the rest of his essay deals only with the first two. Does he explain why he doesn't deal with guns? Is there even a hint?
6. What **transition** is there between the first section of this essay (paragraphs 1–5) and the second? Is the transition clearly expressed or is it implied? or is there a subtle written transition?
7. What does the author do in each of the three sections of this essay?
8. In paragraphs 25–30, what reasons does the author give for his criticisms of the beer lobby? Does he convey these reasons directly? indirectly? If indirectly, by what means?

Sentences

9. Each of the first two sentences of paragraph 1 includes a four-part series. How are these two series similar? Is there any difference between them? Then compare them to the series in the first sentence of paragraph 4.
10. Paragraph 7 consists of four **sentence fragments**, each followed by a question mark. What effect is the author trying to achieve here? Is he successful?
11. Does paragraph 25 include any examples of **interrupted movement**?
12. Do the short sentences of paragraph 27 reflect the ideas and sentiments being expressed? In trying to answer this question, look also at paragraphs 26 and 28.
13. Are the last four sentences of paragraph 34 examples of **balanced constructions**? **parallel constructions**? something else?

Diction

14. Look up: *disingenuous* (6), *artfully* (30), *neo-Puritanism* (31), *acronym* (36), *symposium* (51), *echolocation* (67), *Mammon* (89), *tectonic* (159), *gauntlet* (172), *lobbyist* (174), *karmically* (202).
15. By using such books as, for example, your English dictionary, a French-English dictionary, a dictionary of phrases and expressions, the *Oxford English Dictionary*, and a recent encyclopedia, try to discover the meaning of the following expressions: *Horsemen of the Apocalypse* (26), *Captain Ahab* (53), *Yuppie Nuremberg defence* (66), *cognitive dissonance* (74–5), *Goebbels* (75), *retaliatory tariffs* (95), *hail-fellow-well-met* (116), *tour d'horizon* (127), *moral high ground* (130), *Himmler* (134).
16. In paragraph 4 the author distinguishes between 'The book' and 'the *volume*'. Why does he make this distinction?

POINTS TO LEARN

1. Using irony and humour together successfully can be difficult, but the result can also be highly enjoyable.
2. A good writer can vary his or her paragraph structure from the near-formal to the quite casual.

SUGGESTIONS FOR WRITING

Smoking and drinking, especially by young people, have long been controversial subjects; and, recently in Canada, so has gun registration. What are your views on any one of these three topics? Approach your topic in a lighthearted manner. Although humour is difficult to write well, and irony perhaps even more so, try your hand at both.

IMPROVING YOUR STYLE

1. Use a four-part series early in your essay.
2. Write at least one paragraph that consists only of a few sentence fragments.
3. Use italics at some point in your essay to emphasize a repeated theme.

ALEXANDRA LOPEZ-PACHECO

A freelance writer, researcher, and editor, Alexandra Lopez-Pacheco served for some time as assistant editor of *London Magazine*. Primarily a business writer, she has published a number of articles in such venues as the *National Post*, *Report on Business*, *National Post Business Magazine*, and *Canadian Business Magazine*.

That &*?#@ Machine

1   'It's nuts out there,' says Sean Elliott, an information technology support technician for a major Toronto corporation. 'I've seen a VP smack his computer and threaten to throw it out the window. I saw an IT guy who was cleaning up his area just flip and hurl hard drives, boxes full of equipment, and network cards across the room. He just went wild with rage.'   5

2   In fact, Elliott regularly sees a lot of rage in his workplace—IT rage, to use the current term. And it's widespread.

3   In the UK, where most of the studies on this new condition have been conducted, researchers at Compaq found that four out of five workers have either witnessed or experienced IT rage. One-fifth had witnessed colleagues bullying the IT   10 department. Elliott concurs: 'IT people, we get dumped on for everything.'

4   Last fall, Alberta-based Athabasca University and *CIO Canada* magazine conducted a poll of 3,200 IT staff and business executives. Not only did 55 per cent of respondents feel that new technologies have increased stress in the workplace, they also had a mouthful to say on the subject.   15

5   'It was very difficult to get people to move on from that question. They wouldn't talk about something else,' says Peter Carr, associate director of CIM, the Centre for Innovative Management at Athabasca.

6   Richard Earle, co-founder and managing director of the Canadian Institute of Stress, which helps organizations develop workplace-stress management strategies,   20 has seen it all—computers being hurled, employees mangling electrical outlets so that their PCs couldn't be plugged in. In one instance, a payroll and benefits manager of a company in the midst of several mergers had been putting in long hours trying to

integrate information from three IT systems—a frustrating job at the best of times. Overwrought, he finally exploded one day and sent his PC flying across the room.   25

7   The frustration is not surprising, given our growing dependence on technology. When equipment fails, the best-case scenario is twiddling your thumbs while waiting for the repair guy. The worst case is blowing your stack—because you've lost everything . . . everything!

8   'I rely a hundred per cent on my computer to get my work done,' says Marsha,   30 who owns a home-based IT consultancy firm with her husband in Oakville, Ont. 'But you have to understand, I sit in front of the window on the second floor, and I always just have this urge to take my computer and just throw it out the window.' Last year, when a devastating worm paralyzed her PC, Marsha's husband's fruitless efforts to fix the problem resulted in a classic example of IT rage: After hours of swearing up a storm,   35 he put his fist through the computer desk. Marsha doesn't want her full name published for fear of painting the wrong picture of her usually mild-mannered husband.

9   In fact, anyone can eventually succumb to rage. Think of stress, Richard Earle suggests, as heat rising in a saucepan of water. If the heat reaches 212°F, the water will boil. Turn up the stress heat in a person long enough and high enough, and even the   40 tiniest frustration can provoke a very dramatic response—often with a violent outcome.

10   Stress among Canadians is on the rise, according to a number of studies, including a September 2000, IpsosReid/CTV poll that found that 42 per cent of respondents claimed to be experiencing more stress in their lives than five years ago— with 45 per cent of them blaming work as the main culprit. Earle traces much of this   45 stress to MAD—mergers, automation, and downsizing. And apart from threats to job security, there's the constant presence of e-mail, laptops, voice mail, pagers, cellphones and the Internet. 'You feel like a dog on 17 different leashes—very short leashes,' Earle says.

11   Technology was put in place to make our lives easier, to save time and give us   50 more free time. It hasn't. In fact, more people are telling us that they are working longer days,' says Larry Rosen, a California-based research psychologist and co-author of *TechnoStress: Coping with Technology @Work @Home @Play*.

12   'There are new expectations of what we can perform in a normal workday,' he continues, 'and we're feeling pushed to do it faster and faster because of course the   55 computer does it faster and faster. We are multitasking ourselves to death.'

13   And when technological problems arise, the cost to business escalates. For starters, nearly one-fifth of the respondents to the Compaq study reported having missed up to nine work deadlines within a period of three months because of computer crashes. Another study by ICL, an e-business services company, found that a   60 third of employees spent at least 30 minutes a week helping others with IT problems. 'You walk in to fix one thing, and 400 people jump on you with their problems and they want it fixed now,' says Sean Elliott.

14   Then there's the urge to rebel. Many workers vent through what Earle calls civil disobedience—faced with an onslaught of e-mails, for example, they ignore or trash   65 them unread. 'Once that begins to happen,' says Earle, 'missed communication on vital corporate matters really increases dramatically.'

15   'You also have passive aggression,' he continues. 'And it's not at all uncommon. It will drive managers crazy to know this, but I have heard employees say that they

make up data at the end of the day. Many companies use an IT-based system to log 70 transactions. These people have been inputting random numbers.'

16   Why? 'Basically, they're saying, "You've [bombarded] us with all this other technology and you expect us to do this as well? This is what you can do with your system. We don't have time for it."'

2001

QUESTIONS

Reader and Purpose

1. This expository essay has been placed under the subheading Reasons, rather than under Effects or Analysis. Why? To what extent could it also reasonably be considered under these other two headings?
2. Anyone who has ever used a computer will be sympathetic to the author's discussion of the rage that can be caused by computers. But has she, in your experience, exaggerated the problem?
3. After describing the reasons for and examples of IT rage, is the author's conclusion at all helpful for the computer user who is having similar problems? Does she propose a remedy? Was this the purpose for her writing? If not, should it have been?

Organization

4. The first paragraph begins with 'It's nuts out there' and ends with 'He just went wild with rage'. What would be the result if these sentences were substituted for one another? Would paragraph 2 (slightly revised) make a better introductory paragraph? Why or why not?
5. How is the first sentence of paragraph 9 related to the first eight paragraphs? What other function does this sentence have?
6. This essay was first published in a business magazine and, as in most magazine articles, the paragraphs are quite short. But are they, nevertheless, structured paragraphs? In order to decide this, look at any four consecutive paragraphs in these terms: is there a transition from the previous paragraph? is there a **topic sentence**? does the paragraph make a central point? is there a concluding or transitional sentence?
7. Where, and how, does the author make the transition from writing about computer rage to writing about other things?
8. Is the final paragraph a logical conclusion to this essay? If so, why? If not, what has the author left unsaid?

Sentences

9. Although the majority of sentences in this essay are not very long, there are some exceptions, such as the second sentence of paragraph 4 and the first sentence of paragraph 6. Are there others? Is there any kind of pattern in their placement? That is, does the author seem to have deliberately used long sentences in certain places in order to achieve variety in sentence length?
10. The author uses a dash on eight occasions: paragraphs 2, 6 (twice), 7, 9, 10 (twice), and 14. How does she use these dashes: to mark a contrast? for an addition? an

explanation? something else? Should she have used a dash instead of the ellipsis at the end of paragraph 7?

Diction

11. Look up: *concurs* (11), *respondents* (14), *mergers* (23), *integrate* (24), *overwrought* (25), *succumb* (38), *culprit* (45), *escalates* (57), *vent* (64).
12. The author first mentions *IT* in the opening paragraph, but she never specifically tells us what it means. Should she, or is its meaning clear from the context?
13. Is the analogy in paragraph 9 effective in clarifying the author's point? Explain.
14. *Information technology support technician* (1–2), *workplace-stress management strategies* (20), *home-based IT consultancy firm* (31), *California-based research psychologist* (52). These kinds of expressions, in which a noun is modified by several other nouns that have been made to act as adjectives, have been criticized as the kind of awkward writing common to government and business. Is that true of all these expressions? Try rewriting them to see if you can make them simpler and more graceful. What conclusions can you draw about your revisions?
15. How do you interpret the expression *passive aggression* (68)? How does Richard Earle use it? Can you think of a more precise expression for what the employees he describes are doing?

POINTS TO LEARN

1. The most important position in a paragraph is usually that of the final sentence.
2. Colourful, precise examples not only help to emphasize your key point but will stay in the reader's mind.

SUGGESTIONS FOR WRITING

What have been your experiences with 'IT rage'? Your expository essay on this topic (6–10 paragraphs) should deal especially with reasons, but not to the exclusion of analysis or effects. You may base the essay on your own experiences or on those of others, or both. In addition to examining the reasons for IT rage you could propose ways of preventing it or cures for dealing with it when it does occur.

IMPROVING YOUR STYLE

In your essay include:

1. a dash in two different paragraphs, each dash having a different function;
2. an analogy;
3. at least one graphic example of IT rage.

Joan Didion

Joan Didion (1934–) has documented and explored the banality and brutality of much contemporary life in America. Her novels include *Play It as It Lays* (1970), *Democracy* (1984), and *The Last Thing He Wanted* (1996); among her several collections of essays are *The White Album* (1970) and *After Henry* (1992). Her latest book, *Political Fictions* (2001), is a collection of essays on political journalism.

     The selection below comes from her essay 'Los Angeles Notebook', one of a collection published in her well-known book *Slouching Towards Bethlehem* (1968). Didion develops her topic primarily by effects, in prose that is personal and informal. This kind of prose suits her subject matter; it is also typical of the trend of modern exposition toward informality and the personal vision.

Los Angeles Notebook

1   There is something uneasy in the Los Angeles air this afternoon, some unnatural stillness, some tension. What it means is that tonight a Santa Ana will begin to blow, a hot wind from the northeast whining down through the Cajon and San Gorgonio Passes, blowing up sandstorms out along Route 66, drying the hills and the nerves to the flash point. For a few days now we will see smoke back in the canyons, 5 and hear sirens in the night. I have neither heard nor read that a Santa Ana is due, but I know it, and almost everyone I have seen today knows it too. We know it because we feel it. The baby frets. The maid sulks. I rekindle a waning argument with the telephone company, then cut my losses and lie down, given over to whatever it is in the air. To live with the Santa Ana is to accept, consciously or unconsciously, a deeply 10 mechanistic view of human behaviour.

2   I recall being told, when I first moved to Los Angeles and was living on an isolated beach, that the Indians would throw themselves into the sea when the bad wind blew. I could see why. The Pacific turned ominously glossy during a Santa Ana period, and one woke in the night troubled not only by the peacocks screaming in the olive 15 trees but by the eerie absence of surf. The heat was surreal. The sky had a yellow cast, the kind of light sometimes called 'earthquake weather'. My only neighbour would not come out of her house for days, and there were no lights at night, and her husband roamed the place with a machete. One day he would tell me that he had heard a trespasser, the next a rattlesnake. 20

3   'On nights like that,' Raymond Chandler once wrote about the Santa Ana, 'every booze party ends in a fight. Meek little wives feel the edge of the carving knife and study their husbands' necks. Anything can happen.' That was the kind of wind it was. I did not know then that there was any basis for the effect it had on all of us, but it turns out to be another of those cases in which science bears out folk wisdom. The Santa Ana, 25 which is named for one of the canyons it rushes through, is a *foehn* wind, like the *foehn* of Austria and Switzerland and the *hamsin* of Israel. There are a number of persistent malevolent winds, perhaps the best known of which are the mistral of France and the Mediterranean sirocco, but a *foehn* wind has distinct characteristics: it occurs on the leeward slope of a mountain range and, although the air begins as a cold mass, it is 30 warmed as it comes down the mountain and appears finally as a hot dry wind. Whenever and wherever a *foehn* blows, doctors hear about headaches and nausea and allergies, about 'nervousness', about 'depression'. In Los Angeles some teachers do not attempt to conduct formal classes during a Santa Ana, because the children become unmanageable. In Switzerland the suicide rate goes up during the *foehn*, and in the 35 courts of some Swiss cantons the wind is considered a mitigating circumstance for crime. Surgeons are said to watch the wind, because blood does not clot normally during a *foehn*. A few years ago an Israeli physicist discovered that not only during such winds, but for the ten or twelve hours which precede them, the air carries an unusually high ratio of positive to negative ions. No one seems to know exactly why that 40 should be; some talk about friction and others suggest solar disturbances. In any case the positive ions are there, and what an excess of positive ions does, in the simplest of terms, is make people unhappy. One cannot get much more mechanistic than that.

4   Easterners commonly complain that there is no 'weather' at all in southern California, that the days and the seasons slip by relentlessly, numbingly bland. That 45 is quite misleading. In fact the climate is characterized by infrequent but violent extremes: two periods of torrential subtropical rains which continue for weeks and wash out the hills and send subdivisions sliding toward the sea; about twenty scattered days a year of the Santa Ana, which, with its incendiary dryness, invariably means fire. At the first prediction of a Santa Ana, the Forest Service flies men and 50 equipment from northern California into the southern forests, and the Los Angeles Fire Department cancels its ordinary non-firefighting routines. The Santa Ana caused Malibu to burn the way it did in 1956, and Bel Air in 1961, and Santa Barbara in 1964. In the winter of 1966–7 eleven men were killed fighting a Santa Ana fire that spread through the San Gabriel Mountains.   55

5   Just to watch the front-page news out of Los Angeles during a Santa Ana is to get very close to what it is about the place. The longest single Santa Ana period in recent years was in 1957, and it lasted not the usual three or four days but fourteen days, from November 21 until December 4. On the first day 25,000 acres of the San Gabriel Mountains were burning, with gusts reaching 100 miles an hour. In town, the 60 wind reached Force 12, or hurricane force, on the Beaufort Scale; oil derricks were toppled and people ordered off the downtown streets to avoid injury from flying objects. On November 22 the fire in the San Gabriels was out of control. On November 24 six people were killed in automobile accidents, and by the end of the week the *Los Angeles Times* was keeping a box score of traffic deaths. On November 65 26 a prominent Pasadena attorney, depressed about money, shot and killed his wife, their two sons, and himself. On November 27 a South Gate divorcée, 22, was murdered and thrown from a moving car. On November 30 the San Gabriel fire was still out of control, and the wind in town was blowing 80 miles an hour. On the first day of December four people died violently, and on the third the wind began to break.   70

6   It is hard for people who have not lived in Los Angeles to realize how radically the Santa Ana figures in the local imagination. The city burning is Los Angeles's deepest image of itself: Nathanael West perceived that in *The Day of the Locust*; and at the time of the 1965 Watts riots what struck the imagination most indelibly were the fires. For days one could drive the Harbor Freeway and see the city on fire, just as we had 75 always known it would be in the end. Los Angeles weather is the weather of catastrophe, of apocalypse, and, just as the reliably long and bitter winters of New England determine the way life is lived there, so the violence and the unpredictability of the Santa Ana affect the entire quality of life in Los Angeles, accentuate its impermanence, its unreliability. The wind shows us how close to the edge we are.   80

1967

QUESTIONS
Reader and Purpose
1. Didion's aim is not simply to communicate information, though she does tell us a great deal about what the Santa Ana is and about how it affects life in Los Angeles. More than reporting facts, however, she re-creates and comments on experience. Accordingly her **point of view** is personal, and in the first paragraph she uses verbs in a way calculated to suggest immediacy. How does she do this?
2. Ultimately her purpose includes even more than re-creating what it is to endure a Santa Ana. While Didion begins these paragraphs by putting us into the experience, she moves in the direction of philosophical speculation. Her final sentence is an example of such speculation. What does she mean by 'close to the edge'? 'Close to the edge' of what? Where earlier in the selection is this philosophical note sounded?
3. What is the purpose of the reference (in paragraph 3) to Raymond Chandler and his classic story of violence, 'Red Wind'?
4. Where does Didion use narrative elements, i.e. brief stories or accounts? How do these bits of narrative help to achieve the overall effect of the essay?

Organization
5. Make a brief outline of this selection, giving an explanatory title to each paragraph. Is each new paragraph justified by a shift in topic? Should some paragraphs be subdivided?
6. Paragraph 3 is a bit longer and more complicated than the others. In terms of its development of thought, divide it into its several parts and briefly describe the major idea in each part.
7. What single word toward the middle of paragraph 4 sets up the effects that Didion discusses?
8. Paragraph 5 describes a number of consequences of a particularly severe Santa Ana. How does the writer impose order upon these effects and thereby unify her paragraph?

Sentences
9. Why are the short, terse sentences in lines 7–8 particularly appropriate? There are individual short sentences elsewhere in this selection—in lines 14, 16, 23, and 80, for example. Consider what advantage each of these possesses.

10. In the sentence in lines 8–10 what verbs **parallel** 'rekindle'? Is 'given' one of them? In the sentence in lines 16–17, to what is the phrase 'kind of light' **in apposition**?
11. The sentence in lines 17–19 is an example of what is sometimes called a '**freight-train sentence**'. Why is that an appropriate name?
12. What is signalled by the colon in line 47?

Diction

13. Look up: surreal (16), cast (16), malevolent (28), leeward (30), ions (40), gusts (60), Beaufort Scale (61), radically (71), indelibly (74), apocalypse (77), accentuate (79).
14. Explain the meanings of these phrases: mechanistic view of human behaviour (11), ominously glossy (14), eerie absence (16), folk wisdom (25), numbingly bland (45), incendiary dryness (49).
15. Why is weather (44) in quotation marks?
16. What relationship in thought does in fact (46) signal?
17. In the sentence beginning 'I rekindle' (8) what **metaphors** can you find?
18. Each of these is a poor substitute for Didion's word. Why? 'whistling' for 'whining' (3); 'singing' for 'screaming' (15), 'falling into' for 'sliding toward' (48).

POINTS TO LEARN

1. Exposition may involve more than 'facts'; often it expresses a mind sensitively responding to facts.
2. Chronological sequence is one way of unifying a paragraph.
3. Learn to listen to your sentences; good prose pleases the ear.

SUGGESTIONS FOR WRITING

If you live in northern Ontario, or on the prairies, or in any other area with 'long and bitter winters', discuss how the cold weather affects the quality of life. Alternatively, if you do not know winter as some other Canadians do, explain the effects of another aspect of climate—the humid summers of Ottawa or Toronto, for example, or the dry season of the interior of British Columbia, or a severe northeaster along the Atlantic coast.

IMPROVING YOUR STYLE

Somewhere in your composition include the following:

1. a series of three or four short emphatic sentences (like Didion's in lines 8–9);
2. a freight-train sentence;
3. a metaphor.

CARL SAGAN

The American astronomer, writer, and educator Carl Sagan (1934–96) wrote many significant scholarly works in his field, although he remains well known to a wider public for his
important contributions to space exploration, particularly with regard to the interplanetary probes to the planets Venus, Mars, Jupiter, Saturn, Uranus, and Neptune. He has
been recognized for his contributions to science and science education with many awards
and honours, including more than 20 honorary degrees, as well as NASA medals for
Exceptional Scientific Achievement and Distinguished Public Service. Sagan and his wife,
Ann Druyan (also a distinguished science writer), have been 'elevated': two asteroids in
a companion orbit are now named 2707Sagan and 4970Druyan. Among his best-known
works are the Pulitzer Prize–winning *The Dragons of Eden: Speculations on the Origin of
Human Intelligence* (1977); *Cosmos* (1980), the best-selling science book in English published to date; *Contact: A Novel* (1985); and *Pale Blue Dot: A Vision of the Human Future
in Space* (1994). His last book, *Billions and Billions: Thoughts on Life and Death at the
Brink of the Millennium,* was published posthumously in 1997.

Sagan wrote several of his books for a general rather than a purely academic audience, and he continues to be widely read because of his clear and effective writing style
that does not distort or oversimplify his subjects. The essay reprinted here is excerpted
from *Broca's Brain: Reflections on the Romance of Science* (1979). It exemplifies
Sagan's love of science and his gift for writing about it in a popular style.

Night Walkers and Mystery Mongers:
Sense and Nonsense at the Edge of Science

1   In Greece of the second century AD, during the reign of the Roman emperor
Marcus Aurelius, there lived a master con man named Alexander of Abonutichus.
Handsome, clever, and totally unscrupulous, in the words of one of his contemporaries,
he 'went about living on occult pretensions'. In his most famous imposture, 'he rushed
into the marketplace, naked except for a gold-spangled loincloth; with nothing but this   5
and his scimitar, and shaking his long, loose hair, like fanatics who collect money in the
name of Cybele, he climbed onto a lofty altar and delivered a harangue' predicting
the advent of a new and oracular god. Alexander then raced to the construction site of
a temple, the crowd streaming after him, and discovered—where he had previously
buried it—a goose egg in which he had sealed up a baby snake. Opening the egg, he   10
announced the snakelet as the prophesied god. Alexander retired to his house for a few
days, and then admitted the breathless crowds, who observed his body now entwined
with a large serpent: the snake had grown impressively in the interim.
2   The serpent was, in fact, of a large and conveniently docile variety, procured for
this purpose earlier in Macedonia, and outfitted with a linen head of somewhat   15
human countenance. The room was dimly lit. Because of the press of the crowd, no
visitor could stay for very long or inspect the serpent very carefully. The opinion of
the multitude was that the seer had indeed delivered a god.
3   Alexander then pronounced the god ready to answer written questions delivered in sealed envelopes. When alone, he would lift off or duplicate the seal, read   20

the message, remake the envelope, and attach a response. People flocked from all over the Empire to witness this marvel, an oracular serpent with the head of a man. In those cases where the oracle later proved not just ambiguous but grossly wrong, Alexander had a simple solution: he altered his record of the response he had given. And if the question of a rich man or woman revealed some weakness or guilty secret, Alexander did not scruple at extortion. The result of all this imposture was an income equivalent today to several hundred thousand dollars per year and fame rivalled by few men of his time.

4   We may smile at Alexander the Oracle-Monger. Of course we all would like to foretell the future and make contact with the gods. But we would not nowadays be taken in by such a fraud. Or would we? M. Lamar Keene spent 13 years as a spiritualist medium. He was pastor of the New Age Assembly Church in Tampa, a trustee of the Universal Spiritualist Association, and for many years a leading figure in the mainstream of the American spiritualist movement. He is also a self-confessed fraud who believes, from first-hand knowledge, that virtually all spirit readings, seances and mediumistic messages from the dead are conscious deceptions, contrived to exploit the grief and longing we feel for deceased friends and relatives. Keene, like Alexander, would answer questions given to him in sealed envelopes—in this case not in private, but on the pulpit. He viewed the contents with a concealed bright lamp or by smearing lighter fluid, either of which can render the envelope momentarily transparent. He would find lost objects, present people with astounding revelations about their private lives which 'no one could know', commune with the spirits and materialize ectoplasm in the darkness of the seance—all based on the simplest of tricks, an unswerving self-confidence, and most of all on the monumental credulity, the utter lack of skepticism he found in his parishioners and clients. Keene believes, as did Harry Houdini, that not only is such fraud rampant among the spiritualists but also that they are highly organized to exchange data on potential clients in order to make the revelations of the seance more astonishing. Like the viewing of Alexander's serpent, the seances all take place in darkened rooms—because the deception would be too easily penetrated in the light. In his peak earning years, Keene earned about as much, in equivalent purchasing power, as Alexander of Abonutichus.

5   From Alexander's time to our own—indeed, probably for as long as human beings have inhabited this planet—people have discovered they could make money by pretending to arcane or occult knowledge. A charming and enlightening account of some of these bamboozles can be found in a remarkable book published in 1852 in London, *Extraordinary Popular Delusions and the Madness of Crowds*, by Charles Mackay. Bernard Baruch claimed that the book saved him millions of dollars—presumably by alerting him to which idiot schemes he should not invest his money in. Mackay's treatment ranges from alchemy, prophecy, and faith healing, to haunted houses, the Crusades, and the 'influence of politics and religion on the hair and beard'. The value of the book, like the account of Alexander the Oracle-Monger, lies in the remoteness of the frauds and delusions described. Many of the impostures do not have a contemporary ring and only weakly engage our passions: it becomes clear how people in other times were deceived. But after reading many such cases, we begin to wonder what the comparable contemporary versions are. People's feelings are as strong as they always were, and skepticism is probably as unfashionable today as in any other age. Accordingly, there ought to be bamboozles galore in contemporary society. And there are.

6   In the past hundred years—whether for good or for ill—science has emerged in the popular mind as the primary means of penetrating the secrets of the universe, 70 so we should expect many contemporary bamboozles to have a scientific ring. And they do.

7   Within the last century or so, many claims have been made at the edge or border of science—assertions that excite popular interest and, in many cases, that would be of profound scientific importance if only they were true. These claims are out of 75 the ordinary, a break from the humdrum world, and often imply something hopeful: for example, that we have vast, untapped powers, or that unseen forces are about to save us from ourselves, or that there is still unacknowledged pattern and harmony to the universe. Well, science does sometimes make such claims—as, for example, the realization that the hereditary information we pass from generation to generation is 80 encoded in a single long molecule called DNA, in the discovery of universal gravitation or continental drift, in the tapping of nuclear energy, in research on the origin of life or on the early history of the universe. So if some additional claim is made—for example, that it is possible to float in the air unaided, by a special effort of will—what is so different about that? Nothing. Except for the matter of proof. Those who claim 85 that levitation occurs have an obligation to demonstrate their contention before skeptics, under controlled conditions. The burden of proof is on them, not on those who might be dubious. Such claims are too important to think about carelessly. Many assertions about levitation have been made in the past hundred years, but motion pictures of well-illuminated people rising unassisted 15 feet into the air have never been 90 taken under conditions which exclude fraud. If levitation were possible, its scientific and, more generally, its human implications would be enormous. Those who make uncritical observations of fraudulent claims lead us into error and deflect from us the major human goal of understanding how the world works. It is for this reason that playing fast and loose with the truth is a very serious matter.   95

8   One of the most striking apparent instances of extrasensory perception is the precognitive experience, when a person has a compelling perception of an imminent disaster, the death of a loved one, or a communication from a long-lost friend, and the predicted event then occurs. Many who have had such experiences report that the emotional intensity of the precognition and its subsequent verification provide an 100 overpowering sense of contact with another realm of reality. I have had such an experience myself. Many years ago I awoke in the dead of night in a cold sweat, with the certain knowledge that a close relative had suddenly died. I was so gripped with the haunting intensity of the experience that I was afraid to place a long-distance phone call, for fear that the relative would trip over the telephone cord (or something) 105 and make the experience a self-fulfilling prophecy. In fact, the relative is alive and well, and whatever psychological roots the experience may have, it was not a reflection of an imminent event in the real world.

9   However, suppose the relative had in fact died that night. You would have had a difficult time convincing me that it was merely coincidence. But it is easy to calcu- 110 late that, if each American has such a premonitory experience a few times in his lifetime, the actuarial statistics alone will produce a few *apparent* precognitive events somewhere in America each year. We can calculate that this must occur fairly frequently, but to the rare person who dreams of disaster, followed rapidly by its real-ization, it is uncanny and awesome. Such a coincidence must happen to *someone* 115 every few months. But those who experience a correct precognition understandably resist its explanation by coincidence.

10   After my experience I did not write a letter to an institute of parapsychology relating a compelling predictive dream which was not borne out by reality. That is not a memorable letter. But had the death I dreamt actually occurred, such a letter would 120 have been marked down as evidence of precognition. The hits are recorded, the misses are not. Thus human nature unconsciously conspires to produce a biased reporting of the frequency of such events.

11   Precognitive dreams are typical of claims made on the boundary or edge of sci-ence. An amazing assertion is made, something out of the ordinary, marvelous, or 125 awesome—or at least not tedious. It survives superficial scrutiny by lay people and, sometimes, more detailed study and more impressive endorsement by celebrities and scientists. Those who accept the validity of the assertion resist all attempts at conven-tional explanation. The most common correct explanations are of two sorts. One is conscious fraud, usually by those with financial interest in the outcome. Those who 130 accept the phenomena have been bamboozled. The other explanation often applies when the phenomena are uncommonly subtle and complex, when nature is more intricate than we have guessed, when deeper study is required for understanding. Many precognitive dreams fit this second explanation. Here, very often, we bamboo-zle ourselves.   135

12   I make a distinction between those who perpetrate and promote borderline belief systems and those who accept them. The latter are often taken by the novelty of the systems and the feeling of insight and grandeur they provide. These are in fact scientific attitudes and scientific goals. It is easy to imagine extraterrestrial visitors who looked like human beings, flew space vehicles and even airplanes like our own, 140 and taught our ancestors civilization. This does not strain our imaginative powers overly and is sufficiently similar to familiar Western religious stories to seem com-fortable. The search for Martian microbes of exotic biochemistry, or for interstellar radio messages from intelligent beings biologically very dissimilar, is more difficult to grasp and not as comforting. The former view is widely purveyed and available; the 145 latter much less so. Yet I think many of those excited by the idea of ancient astronauts are motivated by sincere scientific (and occasionally religious) feelings. There is a vast untapped popular interest in the deepest scientific questions. For many people, the shoddily thought out doctrines of borderline science are the closest approximation to comprehensible science readily available. The popularity of borderline science is a 150 rebuke to the schools, the press, and commercial television for their sparse, unimag-inative, and ineffective efforts at science education; and to us scientists for doing so little to popularize our subject.

13   Flying saucers, or UFOs, are well known to almost everyone. But seeing a strange light in the sky does not mean that we are being visited by beings from the 155 planet Venus or a distant galaxy named Spectra. It might, for example, be an auto-mobile headlight reflected off a high-altitude cloud, or a flight of luminescent insects, or an unconventional aircraft, or a conventional aircraft with unconventional lighting patterns, such as a high-intensity searchlight used for meteorological observations. There are also a number of cases—closer encounters with some highish index numeral—where one or two people claim to have been taken aboard an alien space- ship, prodded and probed with unconventional medical instruments, and released. But in these cases we have only the unsubstantiated testimony, no matter how heart- felt and seemingly sincere, of one or two people. To the best of my knowledge there are no instances out of the hundreds of thousands of UFO reports filed since 1947— not a single one—in which many people independently and reliably report a close encounter with what is clearly an alien spacecraft.

14   Not only is there an absence of good anecdotal evidence; there is no physical evidence either. Our laboratories are very sophisticated. A product of alien manufac- ture might readily be identified as such. Yet no one has ever turned up even a small fragment of an alien spacecraft that has passed any such physical test—much less the logbook of the starship captain. It is for these reasons that in 1977 NASA declined an invitation from the Executive Office of the President to undertake a serious investiga- tion of UFO reports. When hoaxes and mere anecdotes are excluded, there seems to be nothing left to study.

15   Once I spied a bright, 'hovering' UFO, and pointing it out to some friends in a restaurant soon found myself in the midst of a throng of patrons, waitresses, cooks, and proprietors milling about on the sidewalk, pointing up into the sky with fingers and forks and making gasps of astonishment. People were somewhere between delighted and awestruck. But when I returned with a pair of binoculars which clearly showed the UFO to be an unconventional aircraft (a NASA weather airplane, as it later turned out), there was uniform disappointment. Some felt embarrassed at the public exposure of their credulity. Others were simply disappointed at the evaporation of a good story, something out of the ordinary—a visitor from another world.

16   In many such cases we are not unbiased observers. We have an emotional stake in the outcome—perhaps merely because the borderline belief system, if true, makes the world a more interesting place; but perhaps because there is something there that strikes more deeply into the human psyche. If astral projection actually occurs, then it is possible for some thinking and perceiving part of me to leave my body and effort- lessly travel to other places—an exhilarating prospect. If spiritualism is real, then my soul will survive the death of my body—possibly a comforting thought. If there is extrasensory perception, then many of us possess latent talents that need only to be tapped to make us more powerful than we are. If astrology is right, then our person- alities and destinies are intimately tied to the rest of the cosmos. If elves and goblins and fairies truly exist (there is a lovely Victorian picture book showing photographs of six-inch-high undraped ladies with gossamer wings conversing with Victorian gen- tlemen), then the world is a more intriguing place than most adults have been led to believe. If we are now being or in historical times have been visited by representatives from advanced and benign extraterrestrial civilizations, perhaps the human predica- ment is not so dire as it seems; perhaps the extraterrestrials will save us from our- selves. But the fact that these propositions charm or stir us does not guarantee their truth. Their truth depends only on whether the evidence is compelling; and my own, and sometimes reluctant, judgment is that compelling evidence for these and many similar propositions simply does not (at least as yet) exist.

17   What is more, many of these doctrines, if false, are pernicious. In simplistic   205
popular astrology we judge people by one of twelve character types depending on
their months of birth. But if the typing is false, we do an injustice to the people we
are typing. We place them in previously collected pigeonholes and do not judge them
for themselves, a typing familiar in sexism and racism.

18   Those skeptical of many borderline belief systems are not necessarily those afraid   210
of novelty. For example, many of my colleagues and I are deeply interested in the possibility of life, intelligent or otherwise, on other planets. But we must be careful not to
foist our wishes and fears upon the cosmos. Instead, in the usual scientific tradition,
our objective is to find out what the answers really are, independent of our emotional
predispositions. If we are alone, that is a truth worth knowing also. No one would be   215
more delighted than I if intelligent extraterrestrials were visiting our planet. It would
make my job enormously easier. Indeed, I have spent more time than I care to think
about on the UFO and ancient astronaut questions. And public interest in these matters
is, I believe, at least in part, a good thing. But our openness to the dazzling possibilities
presented by modern science must be tempered by some hard-nosed skepticism. Many   220
interesting possibilities simply turn out to be wrong. An openness to new possibilities
and a willingness to ask hard questions are both required to advance our knowledge.

19   Professional scientists generally have to make a choice in their research goals.
There are some objectives that would be very important if achieved but promise so
small a likelihood of success that no one is willing to pursue them. (For many years this   225
was the case in the search for extraterrestrial intelligence. The situation has changed
mainly because advances in radio technology now permit us to construct enormous
radio telescopes with sensitive receivers to pick up any messages that might be sent our
way. Never before in human history was this possible.) There are other scientific objectives that are perfectly tractable but of entirely trivial significance. Most scientists   230
choose a middle course. As a result, very few scientists actually plunge into the murky
waters of testing or challenging borderline or pseudoscientific beliefs. The chance of
finding out something really interesting—except about human nature—seems small,
and the amount of time required seems large. I believe that scientists should spend
more time in discussing these issues, but the fact that a given contention lacks vigorous   235
scientific opposition in no way implies that scientists think it is reasonable.

20   There are many cases where the belief system is so absurd that scientists dismiss it instantly but never commit their arguments to print. I believe this is a mistake.
Science, especially today, depends upon public support. Because most people have,
unfortunately, a very inadequate knowledge of science and technology, intelligent   240
decision-making on scientific issues is difficult. Some pseudoscience is a profitable
enterprise, and there are proponents who not only are strongly identified with the
issue in question but also make large amounts of money from it. They are willing to
commit major resources to defending their contentions. Some scientists seem unwilling to engage in public confrontations on borderline-science issues because of the   245
effort required and the possibility that they will be perceived to lose a public debate.
But it is an excellent opportunity to show how science works at its murkier borders,
and also a way to convey something of its power as well as its pleasures.

21   There is stodgy immobility on both sides of the borders of the scientific enterprise. Scientific aloofness and opposition to novelty are as much a problem as public   250

gullibility. A distinguished scientist once threatened to sic then Vice-President Spiro T. Agnew on me if I persisted in organizing a meeting of the American Association for the Advancement of Science in which both proponents and opponents of the extraterrestrial-spacecraft hypothesis of UFO origins would be permitted to speak. Scientists offended by the conclusions of Immanuel Velikovsky's *Worlds in Collision* and irritated 255 by Velikovsky's total ignorance of many well-established scientific facts successfully and shamefully pressured Velikovsky's publisher to abandon the book—which was then put out by another firm, much to its profit—and when I arranged for a second AAAS symposium to discuss Velikovsky's ideas, I was criticized by a different leading scientist who argued that any public attention, no matter how negative, could only 260 aid Velikovsky's cause.

22   But these symposia were held, the audiences seemed to find them interesting, the proceedings were published, and now youngsters in Duluth or Fresno can find some books presenting the other side of the issue in their libraries. If science is presented poorly in schools and the media, perhaps some interest can be aroused by 265 well-prepared, comprehensible public discussions at the edge of science. Astrology can be used for discussions of astronomy; alchemy for chemistry; Velikovskian catastrophism and lost continents such as Atlantis for geology; and spiritualism and Scientology for a wide range of issues in psychology and psychiatry.

23   Scientists are, of course, human. When their passions are excited they may aban- 270 don temporarily the ideals of their discipline. But these ideals, the scientific method, have proved enormously effective. Finding out the way the world really works requires a mix of hunches, intuition, and brilliant creativity; it also requires skeptical scrutiny of every step. It is the tension between creativity and skepticism that has produced the stunning and unexpected findings of science. In my opinion the claims of borderline 275 science pall in comparison with hundreds of recent activities and discoveries in real science, including the existence of two semi-independent brains within each human skull; the reality of black holes; continental drift and collisions; chimpanzee language, massive climatic changes on Mars and Venus; the antiquity of the human species; the search for extraterrestrial life; the elegant self-copying molecular architecture that con- 280 trols our heredity and evolution; and observational evidence on the origin, nature, and fate of the universe as a whole.

24   But the success of science, both its intellectual excitement and its practical application, depends upon the self-correcting character of science. There must be a way of testing any valid idea. It must be possible to reproduce any valid experiment. 285 The character or beliefs of the scientist are irrelevant; all that matters is whether the evidence supports his contention. Arguments from authority simply do not count; too many authorities have been mistaken too often. I would like to see these very effective scientific modes of thought communicated by the schools and the media; and it would certainly be an astonishment and delight to see them introduced into politics. 290 Scientists have been known to change their minds completely and publicly when presented with new evidence or new arguments. I cannot recall the last time a politician displayed a similar openness and willingness to change.

25   Many of the belief systems at the edge or fringe of science are not subject to crisp experimentation. They are anecdotal, depending entirely on the validity of eye- 295 witnesses, who in general are notoriously unreliable. On the basis of past performance

most such fringe systems will turn out to be invalid. But we cannot reject out of hand, any more than we can accept at face value, all such contentions. For example, the idea that large rocks can drop from the skies was considered absurd by eighteenth-century scientists; Thomas Jefferson remarked about one such account that he would rather   300
believe that two Yankee scientists lied than that stones fell from the heavens. Nevertheless, stones do fall from the heavens. They are called meteorites, and our preconceptions have no bearing on the truth of the matter. But the truth was established only by a careful analysis of dozens of independent witnesses to a common meteorite fall, supported by a great body of physical evidence, including meteorites recovered from   305
the eaves of houses and the furrows of plowed fields.

26   Prejudice means literally pre-judgment, the rejection of a contention out of hand, before examining the evidence. If we wish to find out the truth of the matter we must approach the question with as open a mind as we can, with a deep awareness of our own limitations and predispositions. On the other hand, if after carefully   310
and openly examining the evidence, we reject the proposition, that is not prejudice. It might be called 'post-judice'. It is certainly a prerequisite for knowledge.

27   Critical and skeptical examination is the method used in everyday practical matters as well as in science. When buying a new or used car, we think it prudent to insist on written warranties, test drives, and checks of particular parts. We are very   315
careful about car dealers who are evasive on these points. Yet the practitioners of many borderline beliefs are offended when subjected to similarly close scrutiny. Many who claim to have extrasensory perception also claim that their abilities decline when they are carefully watched. The magician Uri Geller is happy to warp keys and cutlery in the vicinity of scientists—who, in their confrontations with   320
nature, are used to an adversary who fights fair—but is greatly affronted at the idea of performances before an audience of skeptical magicians—who, understanding human limitations, are themselves able to perform similar effects by sleight of hand. Where skeptical observation and discussion are suppressed, the truth is hidden. The proponents of such borderline beliefs, when criticized, often point to geniuses of the   325
past who were ridiculed. But the fact that some geniuses were laughed at does not imply that all who are laughed at are geniuses. They laughed at Columbus, they laughed at Fulton, they laughed at the Wright brothers. But they also laughed at Bozo the Clown.

28   The best antidote for pseudoscience, I firmly believe, is science: 330

29   • There is an African freshwater fish that is blind. It generates a standing electric field, through perturbations in which it distinguishes between predators and prey and communicates in a fairly elaborate electrical language with potential mates and other fish of the same species. This involves an entire organ system and sensory capability completely unknown to pretechnological human beings.   335

30   • There is a kind of arithmetic, perfectly reasonable and self-contained, in which two times one does not equal one times two.

31   • Pigeons—one of the least prepossessing animals on Earth—are now found to have a remarkable sensitivity to magnetic-field strengths as small as one-hundred-thousandth that of the Earth's magnetic dipole. Pigeons evidently use this sensory   340
capability for navigation and sense their surroundings by their magnetic signatures:

metal gutters, electrical power lines, fire escapes and the like—a sensory modality glimpsed by no human being who ever lived.

32   • Quasars seem to be explosions of almost unimaginable violence in the hearts of galaxies which destroy millions of worlds, many of them perhaps inhabited.   345

33   • In an East African volcanic-ash flow 3.5 million years old there are footprints—of a being about four feet high with a purposeful stride that may be the common ancestor of apes and men. Nearby are the prints of a knuckle-walking primate corresponding to no animal yet discovered.

34   • Each of our cells contains dozens of tiny factories called mitochondria which   350 combine our food with molecular oxygen in order to extract energy in convenient form. Recent evidence suggests that billions of years ago the mitochondria were free organisms which have slowly evolved into a mutually dependent relation with the cell. When many-celled organisms arose, the arrangement was retained. In a very real sense, then, we are not a single organism, but an array of about ten trillion beings and   355 not all of the same kind.

35   • Mars has a volcano almost 80,000 feet high which was constructed about a billion years ago. An even larger volcano may exist on Venus.

36   • Radio telescopes have detected the cosmic black-body background radiation, the distant echo of the event called the Big Bang. The fires of creation are being   360 observed today.

37   I could continue such a list almost indefinitely. I believe that even a smattering of such findings in modern science and mathematics is far more compelling and exciting than most of the doctrines of pseudoscience, whose practitioners were condemned as early as the fifth century BC by the Ionian philosopher Heraclitus as   365 'night-walkers, magicians, priests of Bacchus, priestesses of the wine-vat, mystery-mongers'. But science is more intricate and subtle, reveals a much richer universe, and powerfully evokes our sense of wonder. And it has the additional and important virtue—to whatever extent the word has any meaning—of being true.

1979

QUESTIONS

Reader and Purpose

1. What is the purpose of the anecdote that Sagan presents in the first three paragraphs? Where else does he use anecdotes? Why?
2. In which paragraph or paragraphs does Sagan state the purpose of his essay? Is it clear that his purpose is to expose? Or will he also use persuasion? or argument?

Organization

3. How is the first sentence of paragraph 5 both a summary and a **transition**?
4. Why is the concluding sentence of paragraph 4 devoted to money rather than to, for example, the criminality of spiritualists, or the credulity of their audiences?
5. In the first three paragraphs the author recounts an anecdote about occult pretensions from the second century AD; in paragraph 4 he recounts a similar anecdote from our own time. What does he then do in paragraphs 5, 6, and 7?

6. Do paragraphs 5 and 6 end weakly or emphatically? Explain your answer.
7. How is the first sentence of paragraphs 8, 12, 16, 22, and 27 a transitional sentence? Do all of these sentences function in the same way, or do some of them also have an additional use?
8. How are paragraphs 14 and 15 logically related?
9. There is no obvious transitional expression to join paragraphs 18 and 19. What other means has the author used to show the relationship between these two paragraphs? With regard to this same question consider also paragraphs 20 and 21, and 24 and 25. To answer this question (which is admittedly difficult), examine paragraph 19 closely in light of what Sagan says in the last sentence of paragraph 18.
10. What is the purpose of paragraphs 29–36?

Sentences

11. The six sentences of paragraph 1 begin with (in succession) the following: **preposition** ('In'), adjective ('Handsome'), preposition ('In'), proper noun ('Alexander'), **gerund** ('Opening'), and proper noun ('Alexander'). How do the sentences in paragraph 3 begin? in paragraph 8? Is there any pattern in the way Sagan begins his sentences? If so, what conclusion can you draw? If not, what other conclusion is there?
12. Consider the following revisions of the first sentence of paragraph 9:

    Suppose the relative had in fact died that night, however.

    Suppose, however, the relative had in fact died that night.

    Are the rewritten sentences grammatically correct? Is either one as effective as the original? Why, or why not?

13. In paragraph 9 two sentences begin 'But'. In each case, could this word be replaced, with equal effectiveness, by either *however* or *nevertheless*?
14. In paragraph 16 there are six consecutive sentences beginning 'If'. Explain the **parallel structure** of these sentences.
15. In the second sentence of paragraph 3 Sagan uses commas to separate all the elements of the series (including the last one, a practice which many writers today do not follow). Is he consistent in this respect? To answer this question consider paragraphs 4, 7, and 12.
16. Point out the punctuation error in paragraph 23. Did this error affect your understanding of the passage when you first read it?

Diction

17. Look up: *imposture* (4), *oracular* (8), *seer* (18), *scruple* (26), *ectoplasm* (42–3), *arcane* (54), *bamboozles* (55), *levitation* (86), *fraudulent* (93), *precognitive* (97), *predictive* (119), *purveyed* (145), *anecdotal* (168), *credulity* (183), *astral* (188), *benign* (199), *pernicious* (205), *contention* (235), *stodgy* (249), *perturbations* (332).
18. In discussing M. Lamar Keene in paragraph 4, why does Sagan use both past-tense and present-tense verbs?
19. Sagan uses the word *bamboozle* (both verb and noun) three times in paragraphs 5 and 6 and twice in paragraph 11. Are there any suitable synonyms for this word? If so, why has he not chosen one of these rather than repeating the informal *bamboozle*? If not, why would he have chosen a word that seems inappropriate for its context?

POINTS TO LEARN

1. In some essays it is difficult to distinguish between exposition and persuasion.
2. An anecdote can be an effective way of introducing a topic, but it must be clearly relevant to your topic.

SUGGESTIONS FOR WRITING

What experiences have you had 'at the edge of science'? Consider, for instance, lucky and unlucky numbers and days, teacup readings, horoscopes, unfortunate occurrences (walking under a ladder, having a black cat cross your path), dreams that seem prophetic, extraordinary coincidences, etc.

Your essay on this topic (for which you should draw your own boundaries) should both expose your experiences and then draw whatever conclusions you think appropriate.

IMPROVING YOUR STYLE

1. Begin your essay with a short but precise anecdote.
2. Use other anecdotes related to your topic to help organize your essay.
3. In one paragraph include at least three consecutive sentences that begin with *If*.

BART ROBINSON

An American who moved to Canada in 1968, Bart Robinson has written extensively about the outdoors and, especially, about the history of the Canadian Rockies. A frequent contributor to several outdoor magazines and a conservationist for over 30 years, he was a founding and managing editor of *Equinox*. Among the books he has written or contributed to are *Great Days in the Rockies* (1978), *Columbia Icefield: A Solitude of Ice* (1981), and *Byron Harmon: Mountain Photographer* (1992). He is also the co-author, with Brian Patton, of one of the most popular books ever written about our mountains, *The Canadian Rockies Trail Guide*, first published in 1971 and currently in its seventh edition.

Cold Fury, White Death

1   Gingerly, a solitary skier eases out of the evergreens. Above him, bands of black quartzite shoot vertically up toward a deep winter sky; below, several hundred yards distant, the valley bottom lies swaddled in white satin. And between the two, the object of the young man's rapt attention, runs a 38-degree ramp of untrammelled snow, a dream of knee-deep hoary powder. The man traverses a third of the way across   5 the clearing, staying close by the rocks, before he stops. Then, one at a time, he lifts his skis out of the snow, kicks them around to point out across the valley and plunges their tails—right up to his boot heels—horizontally into the snow. Thus anchored, with his ski tips extending into space and the mountainside falling away below, he takes a deep breath, preparing to push off into the flawless blanket before him.   10

2   In that moment, the dream unravels. By virtue of the man's weight, or perhaps the penetration of his ski tails, a small section of one of the snowpack's many layers collapses, shooting shock waves out into the adjoining snow at the speed of sound. The man hears a short, protesting 'whomph' and feels the snow drop beneath his feet. He freezes, adrenaline rising, waiting for the snow to stop, to reconsider, to settle into   15 some new, stable configuration. But it doesn't. Rather, it begins to slide.

3   In the first second, the snow moves slowly, almost lazily, but once begun, its acceleration is startling. Initially, the whole surface moves as a sheet, but it quickly fractures into 40-foot (12 m) blocks, which are in turn halved and quartered as the snow shifts gears again and again, moving faster and faster. The man has time only to   20 rise slightly as the snow shrouds up around his waist, then his chest. After that, all he can do is look downslope and watch the valley race up to meet him. The sole sound is a soft hissing, the seductive rustle of taffeta pulled across itself.

4   The ride is short, maybe 10 seconds, but long enough to provide a lifetime memory. The skier comes to rest 400 feet (122 m) below his starting place, on top of   25 the snow. That same snow, however, several thousand tons of it, has also carried him over a small rock ledge and pushed him through a copse of stunted fir trees. He is in shock, nauseated by the adrenaline coursing through his body, sopping wet and well on his way to becoming hypothermic. His body shakes violently, and he groans and grunts involuntarily. His words come in jagged bursts through clenched, chattering   30 teeth: 'I think I broke my leg. My back hurts too. And my ribs, up here. Oh, man, I feel like I've been beat up. Yeah, just beat up.'

5   His mountain mugging, comparatively, was a gentle one. Twenty-four hours later, the skier, helicoptered out of the southeastern British Columbia backcountry to the hospital in Cranbrook, learned his injuries were of a soft-muscle variety and, given   35 time, would heal. More to the point, however, he learned that just across the mountain range, at almost the same time as his unscheduled descent, on a similar terrain and similar snow, three skiers had been caught and swept away by a larger avalanche. Two had died.

6   Seven people are killed on average in avalanches each year in Canada, and   40 scores of others are physically or financially inconvenienced by road and railroad closures, downed power and telephone lines, smashed pipelines and damaged property. The losses can be enormous. In the winter of 1982–3, an avalanche in British Columbia's Rogers Pass pushed a 250-ton Canadian Pacific Railway bridge 100 feet (30 m) off its abutments, effectively cancelling the company's transmountain rail ship-   45 ments for three days. The losses were estimated at one million dollars a day.

A Dark Ransom

7   The fatalities and near fatalities, however, most capture the public imagination. Even though the majority of those who die are acknowledged risk takers (mountain climbers, skiers and snowmobilers), each receives front-page attention. Avalanches, it seems, like other powerful natural phenomena—volcanoes, tornadoes, earthquakes   50 and large forest fires—hold a dark ransom in the human mind: 100,000 tons of snow travelling 180 miles per hour (290km/h) and striking with sufficient force to reduce 100 acres (40 ha) of mature forests to matchsticks and pulp commands, at a minimum, respect. Children raised in the Alps have riddled each other for centuries with the

question 'What flies without wings, strikes without hands and sees without eyes?' and 55
accounts from those mountains, dating back to the early Middle Ages, are replete with
references to the 'gruesome, grisly snow avalanches' that regularly decimated the resident populations: a village of 300 destroyed; 120 people and 400 cattle killed; 84 people buried in a single grave—the list runs on and on. Historians assume that Alexander
the Great and Hannibal lost soldiers to avalanches, and they know Napoleon did. In 60
the Tyrol, in World War I, the opposing armies of Austria and Italy suffered combined
avalanche losses of, conservatively, 40,000 troops. The armies fired not at each other
but into the snow-laden slopes above their respective positions, unleashing instruments of death much more effective than the shells themselves.

8   In Canada, between 1885 and 1911, over 200 avalanche casualties were 65
recorded in Rogers Pass, most related to trying to operate the Canadian Pacific
Railway in one of the most forbidding avalanche sites in the world. The single most
horrendous accident occurred just before midnight on March 4, 1910, when a large
crew of men, freeing the tracks of debris from one slide, was hit by a second avalanche
that raced down from a mountain on the opposite side of the valley. Sixty-two men 70
died, entombed, crushed and suffocated in the large trench they had been clearing.

9   An avalanche's destructive force is, by itself, enough to merit attention, but
when that force is as seemingly capricious as is an avalanche's, the phenomenon
becomes as fascinating as it is troubling. Ever since a Swiss forester named Johan Coaz
began recording observations about avalanches and weather in the 1870s, scientists 75
have struggled to both predict and control something that was, in the previous millennium, relegated to spheres considered incontestable by humans. Indeed, the earliest avalanche-control measures consisted largely of praying for deliverance, burying
eggs on which the sign of the cross had been made at the foot of dangerous slopes and
assiduously avoiding known avalanche paths. Today, after 100-plus years, thousands 80
of hours of study and the compilation of a small library's worth of data, scientists are
still, by and large, baffled; they remain unable to say just when an avalanche will
occur, or how large it will be, or what damage it will inflict. Between 10 and 30 per
cent of all of the snow that falls on the western cordillera each year eventually crashes
down the mountain flanks in two-and-a-quarter million avalanches. Very few of them 85
are of concern to humans, but of those that are, almost all defy the unstinting efforts
made to predict, if not control, them.

10   Such failures, however, are not for lack of knowing what an avalanche is or how
it occurs. As Peter Schaerer, head of the National Research Council's Avalanche
Research Centre, says: 'There's no great mystery to what makes an avalanche. 90
Everybody who has ever piled anything up on an incline knows that sooner or later,
there will be an avalanche. Papers, books or snow—they all will come sliding down.'
As Schaerer also knows, however, snow is one of the most unstable of natural sub-
stances, a complex, whimsical frozen vapour that can dramatically change shape,
structure and strength within a few hours' time and can creep and glide like warm 95
taffy or fracture abruptly like peanut brittle.

11   Schaerer has devoted his life to the intrigues of snow and its relationship with
mountain inclines. In his youth, in Switzerland, he combined his love for ski touring
and mountaineering with engineering studies to become, as he calls himself, an
'avalanchologist', and it was as such that he arrived in Canada in 1957 to help develop 100

an avalanche-control program for the Trans-Canada Highway in Rogers Pass. At that time, the country had little interest and less expertise in the field, and for the past 30 years, Schaerer has worked almost nonstop, dexterously and continually switching tuques as researcher, engineer, consultant, administrator and educator—often for organizations he has himself created. He is almost single-handedly responsible   105 for bringing the Canadian avalanche industry to its current state of maturity ('late ado- lescence') and for its growing international reputation ('People from the United States and Europe listen to us now'). Today, at a vigorous 59, Schaerer is the grand old man of Canadian avalanche studies.

12   His love for good snow and a steep slope has remained intact throughout his   110 career and is much in evidence during the week-long field courses he teaches once or twice a winter to recreational skiers, park wardens, would-be mountain guides and ski-industry and highway-maintenance personnel. Late last winter, as a guest instruc- tor for Ptarmigan Tours—a small company specializing in backcountry skiing and instruction out of Kimberley, British Columbia—Schaerer clambered down into a   115 snow pit shovelled out somewhat deeper than he was tall and, gesturing at the 15 or so layers visible in the blue-white wall before him, said, 'Ja, well, here we have the his- tory of the winter, so let's look at it.' His speech was soft, lilting with a Swiss-German accent. He patted the snow, a beaming smile on his face.

13   Each layer in the accumulated pack, he explained, represents a meteorological   120 event—light snow falling on a quiet day; a long cold snap; a short midwinter thaw; heavy, wet snow driven before 80-mile-per-hour (129 km/h) winds—and each layer, ranging in depth from knife-edge crusts to downy cushions of a foot or more, has a personality and life of its own. Using thermometers, hand lenses, folding rulers, thin metal rectangles marked with a millimetre grid, and small sampling tubes, the stu-   125 dents began to work their way from the top of the snowpack to the bottom, record- ing each layer's depth, density, crystal size and shape, moisture content, temperature and specific gravity. It was immediately apparent that what most people consider a unified mass is actually a vertical mosaic of varying strengths and weaknesses. While some layers were composed of dense, tightly connected grains of snow that Schaerer   130 declared 'bomb-proof', others were loose aggregations of fragile plates and crystalline cups that shifted and slid easily over each other.

14   It was less apparent that a snowpack exists in an almost constant state of flux. The temperature of the pack varies from bottom to top, and that difference, or gradi- ent, coupled with the relative humidity and the weight of any overlying snow, drives   135 a microscopic migration of water vapour within individual snow crystals, between adjoining snow crystals and between layers of snow crystals. The migration is minute, molecule by molecule, but its effect on the shape, size and strength of the individual crystals and on the stability of the snow mass as a whole is profound. Given an air temperature of between 14 °F (–10 °C) and 30 °F (–1 °C), for example, new snow will   140 rapidly metamorphose into small round grains, out of which emerge tiny necks that connect solidly to other grains. The process will carry on deep into the snowpack if the temperature remains stable over a long period. If, however, the temperature sud- denly drops, say, to –40°, vapour in the lower, warmer layers of snow begins to move to those above, and the snowpack starts recrystallizing into large, unbonded and   145 unstable facets from the bottom up. The result is a dynamic, sometimes volatile entity.

'What we skied so happily this morning', said Schaerer, 'might take us for a ride this afternoon. All that separates good skiing from a good avalanche is the balance between the load on a weak snow layer and its sheer strength. It can be very delicate: a little shift in the temperature and a little trigger of some sort—a bit of new snow, 150 some rocks falling from above, a skier—and down comes the mountainside.'

15   What actually comes down depends on the snowpack as well. Structurally, there are two basic types of avalanche, a distinction noted in the Alps two centuries ago. A slab avalanche is just that—a large, cohesive mass of snow that slides, following either the failure of one of the snowpack's weak underlying layers or the failure of 155 the bond between two layers. It is identified by an obvious fracture line left where the slab pulls away from the rest of the snowpack. Although the fracture line can be only a few inches deep and several yards long, it is often much larger, sometimes frighteningly so. In 1979, a massive avalanche in British Columbia that killed seven heli-skiers left a fracture line up to 13 feet deep (4 m) in places and a mile long (1.6 km).   160

16   The second type, a loose-snow avalanche, is composed of new, unconsolidated snow that slides when it reaches such a depth and weight that it can no longer cling to the slope. It often starts from a single point and is characteristically a small teardrop-shaped slough of indeterminate depth.

17   Either variety can be classified further by its moisture content. A wet avalanche, 165 created by falls of heavy, water-saturated snow or by springtime thaws, flows like a wall of mud or quick-setting cement, moving slowly but inexorably down gullies or creek beds, devouring all that lies in its path. A dry avalanche, on the other hand, accelerates rapidly and, given enough mass and the room to run, will top 200 miles per hour (322 km/h). It is particularly dangerous because the snow in a dry avalanche begins to 170 tumble at velocities of 25 miles per hour (40 km/h). Peter Schaerer once rode for a short distance in a dry tumbling slab before being spat out its side: 'It was a strange feeling, seeing sky and snow, sky and snow, up and down, around and around. I didn't feel I could do much to help myself.' A large, rapidly moving dry-snow avalanche will send huge clouds of powder billowing 300 to 400 feet (91–122 m) in the air, and some 175 researchers (although Schaerer is not among them) believe the avalanches themselves become airborne, riding like Hovercraft on fat cushions of air above the mountainside.

18   Airborne or not, there is little question that dry-powder avalanches generate prodigious power. The first blow comes from a wind blast that precedes the snow itself. The blast, measured at up to 0.05 tonnes per square metre, can snap small trees and 180 shatter windows. The knockout punch, however, arrives with the flowing core of snow. Sir Arnold Lunn, a famous British skier and promoter of the sport, recalled seeing a large iron bridge thrown like a child's toy 150 feet (46 m) into the air by a large powder avalanche, and in another well-recorded incident, a 120-ton Austrian locomotive was tossed like a snowball through a nearby station. Schaerer, who has done extensive 185 research on avalanche motion and impact out of his National Research Council (NRC) offices in Rogers Pass, has recorded impact pressures of 54 tonnes per square metre from the dense core of a dry avalanche. Other scientists have reported pressures of 120 tonnes. Three tonnes per square metre will destroy a well-built house.

19   To deal effectively with such forces, Schaerer and the other Canadians mantled 190 with the responsibility of protecting the nation's highways, railroads, mine and forest access roads, pipelines and ski areas must first accurately predict when a slope is ready

to avalanche and, second, control it. Neither is a simple task. Control work is hazardous, and forecasting vexatious. Indeed, although the core cadre of the avalanche industry, the sixty or so active members of the Canadian Avalanche Association, is a   195
diverse group of mountain individualists given to differences in style, opinion and approach, they agree unanimously that trying to predict just when and in what manner a mountain will slough its winter skin is not for people with low frustration thresholds. As Schaerer notes, 'Avalanches generally resist empirical analyses, and they absolutely refuse to recognize the experts.'   200

20   The forecasters' difficulties arise not because they lack sufficient data to make predictions but because there is so much data to be considered in making a prediction. Depending on the forecaster and the operation, as many as forty different factors relating to the weather, terrain, snowpack properties and avalanche history are juggled about in trying to determine a slope's stability. The list includes: the air temper-   205
ature and temperature change; wind direction and speed; precipitation type, precipitation rate and precipitation moisture; barometric pressure; the incline of the slopes being analyzed and their exposure to sun and wind; geomorphic and vegetative character of the avalanche path; the internal and surface tensions of the snowpack layers; the shape and size of their crystals; their densities; knowledge of where and   210
when avalanches have run in the past; and whether those avalanches were triggered naturally or by man.

'Witch-Doctor Stuff'

21   Even on a single uniform slope, the possible combinations and permutations are staggering. Add the convoluted topography of the mountains to the equation, with their myriad angles, intersections, exposures and local microclimates, and one   215
has, as mountain guide and avalanche course instructor Art Twomey says, 'a real head-scratcher'.

22   Computers are being applied to the industry, but they have been slow to prove their worth. Creating a program that can account for the necessary nuances of the relationship between snow-crystal microsphere and mountain-range macrosphere is a   220
herculean job, even if one has the data to work with. George Sibley, a writer and one-time resident of the Colorado Rockies, once listed a long string of avalanche-influencing variables and then concluded, 'Stick that in your Computron and smoke it. Or watch it smoke.'

23   There are no easy equations. Fred Schleiss, who runs Environment   225
Canada–Parks Snow Research and Avalanche Warning Section in Rogers Pass, says avalanche prediction is '65 per cent technical knowledge and 35 per cent witch-doctor stuff—intuition based on experience and knowledge of the locality. No matter what you know or think you know, there will always be surprises, snow sliding in some new place at the least likely time.' Anthony Salway, a veteran researcher from Winlaw,   230
British Columbia, ensured himself a spot in some future avalanchologist hall of fame when he concluded a long, highly technical report on avalanche prediction by suggesting that the best prediction marker was still: 'If it slid yesterday, it will probably slide today.'

24   If forecasters have difficulty pinpointing the instant a particular slope will slide,   235
they have little trouble recognizing a hazard. The threat can be obvious and immediate,

as from an overnight blizzard that leaves three feet (1 m) of wind-driven snow slabbed up on the leeward side of the high mountain ridges, or it can be subtle, as from precipitation and temperature patterns through an entire season. In the winter of 1985–6, for instance, experts predicted a potentially disastrous spring as early as January: a long, cold drought in November and December turned the snow that fell in late October into two feet (0.6 m) of depth hoar—delicate, unstable crystalline cups—and it was apparent that heavy snowfalls in January and February would be analogous to shuffling sheets of plywood out onto a tilted bed of Rice Krispies. 240

Arsenal of Weapons

25   Given a bad situation, the problem becomes how best to control the snow that wants to come down. The obvious solution, for backcountry users, is not to control it at all but to avoid it, either by staying away when the hazard is high or by educated route finding—sticking to the ridge tops or to the gently sloped windward sides of ridges, for example. Simple avoidance, however, is an unpopular and often unfeasible option for the people overseeing highways, railroads or downhill ski resorts, and highly sophisticated programs have been developed throughout the West to protect those facilities and the people who use them. 245 250

26   Although each operation is customized to local conditions and needs, all are based on common control strategies and all utilize a common arsenal of weapons. The strategic choices are basically four: to close a section of highway or ski area temporarily until the snow stabilizes; to stabilize the snow mechanically where it falls; to induce a large number of small, controlled slides on slopes where nature, left to its own devices, would send down a small number of large avalanches; and to control the direction of the avalanches that do come down. The weapons used are either static, like snowsheds, fences and a variety of earthworks—mounds, diversion channels, terraces and dams—or dynamic, like explosives. Explosives, in fact, are the backbone of the North American avalanche defence system: each year, a million charges of TNT, pentolite and gelatin, all high-strength, weather-resistant compounds, are thrown from ridges, trams or helicopters, launched by guns or set off by radio signals in an effort to release or stabilize avalanche-prone slopes. 255 260 265

27   In Rogers Pass, at the crest of the Selkirk Mountains in Glacier National Park, an impressive array of strategies and weapons is employed by the Snow Research and Avalanche Warning Section (SRAWS) in what is acknowledged to be the largest mobile avalanche-control program in the world. It is a massive operation, and it needs to be. Schaerer once devised an avalanche hazard index for roads based on the number of avalanche paths threatening the road, the frequency and type of avalanches, the traffic volume and the length of highway exposed to each avalanche path. A rating of 100 is extreme and calls for a full control program with special techniques, equipment and control personnel. Rogers Pass has a rating of around 300. For 27 miles (43 km), the Trans-Canada Highway threads a maze of quartzite-shot, glacier-wreathed peaks that in places soar 7,000 to 8,000 feet (2,134–2,438 m) above the asphalt, and along those 27 miles, 160 individual slide paths descend from 140 trigger zones—the regions where avalanches start. 270 275

28   As one might suspect, the winters that fuel the paths are enough to make January on Ellesmere Island an appealing proposition. Between 60 and 70 feet 280

(18–21 m) of snow fall on the high ridges in an average year, and storms with 100-mile-per-hour (161 km/h) winds can lethally load an avalanche slope in as little as 15 minutes. In 1966–7, the snow started falling on November 17 and did not stop until February 17. The daily minimum was about four inches (10 cm).

29   The results are spectacular. Even with control, avalanches occasionally deposit 15 to 20 feet (5–6 m) of snow on 1,500-foot (457 m) lengths of highway. Others will hit the road in several places, and yet others—up to six or seven avalanches—will hit the same small section of road from slightly different approaches. One of the avalanche paths, the Ross Peak slide, is a mile wide and a mile high.

30   The SRAWS operations centre is at the crest of the pass in the Environment Canada–Parks warden compound. There, in several tidy government-issue offices just down the hall from Schaerer's NRC offices, Fred Schleiss and his younger brother, Walter—who is the program's second-in-command—run a quasi-military operation that to date has been tremendously successful. According to Fred Schleiss, 'Experts from Switzerland and the United States come here and see what we are doing and say, "My God, how do you do this?" ' A short, animated man with grey hair and steel-blue eyes, Schleiss has worked at the pass since 1958 and has been first forecaster since 1965. In all the intervening years, there has been only one fatal accident related to the road operation. 'Two highway workers were clearing one slide when they were hit by another,' he recalls. 'The accident occurred before the program was running exactly as I wanted it run, but even then, they wouldn't have died if they had followed the suggested procedures. It was a regrettable incident.'

31   Today, his approach mirrors his 'infinite belief in regimentation and discipline'. Schleiss is Austrian, and his demeanour, coupled with his vestigial accent, fuels a perpetual series of Brown Shirt jokes among his juniors in the field. Schleiss is unrepentant: 'There is a lot at stake here—a national highway, a national railroad and, for the past three years, the largest construction site in North America [for the new 9.1-mile-long (14.7 km) CP Rail Macdonald Tunnel for westbound trains]. We are asked to keep them open and in operation all winter long. There are thousands of people out there on the road every winter and millions of dollars in rail and highway freight. The job is *extremely* hazardous, and I demand a lot from my men. If they make a mistake, I fail, and I am not about to fail. So if there are problems, I give them absolute hell. "Fred's Harassment" is well known around here.' Recently, when one team member's dog ran through one of the SRAWS snow-observation plots, the man walked off the job and caught the first ride out to Revelstoke rather than face Schleiss's wrath.

32   The operation relies on a battery of defences. High in the mountains, in the trigger zones, snow fences and cables help stabilize the snow where it falls. Lower, Caterpillar-built dykes help divert sliding snow away from the highway, 25-foot-high (8 m) earth mounds and 150-by-1,500-foot (46 m × 457 m) terraces check its progress, and catchment dams capture it. At six places in the pass, avalanches charge right over the top of the Trans-Canada Highway on a collective three-quarters of a mile (1.2 km) of special snowsheds.

33   The system's cornerstone, however, is rotating 11-man teams from the Royal Canadian Horse Artillery that are stationed in the pass and are on call twenty-four hours a day, seven days a week. Their work, under the direction of Schleiss and his own 11-man team, is to bring down the snow with a 105 mm Howitzer field gun

before the slopes 'become lethal'. It is a 'tricky game', says Schleiss, 'because you want
to knock the snow down before enough accumulates to create large avalanches, but
you have to wait until there is enough to actually slide. If you shoot too early, the
snow will settle and stabilize without sliding, and then in the spring, when the snow-   330
pack turns isothermal—when it warms up and turns to mush from top to bottom—
there is that much more snow that is likely to come down all at once.'

34   To determine just the right moment for action, Schleiss collects data from a battery of snow-observation plots, remote telemetry stations and manned snow-and-
weather stations peppered throughout the park; checks on the broader regional   335
weather forecasts from the east and west; and then tosses in his own 28 years of local
experience, which he updates with daily inspection tours through the pass. When
analyses suggest a high hazard, he has one of his crew confirm the instability by hand-
blasting or skiing a test slope at a snow-and-weather observation station perched high
on the flank of Mount Fidelity. The station was constructed at an altitude representa-   340
tive of most of the Selkirks' trigger zones, and Schleiss has established nearby test
slopes that correspond to all the trigger zones along the highway. The timing is critical: there may be as little as two hours in which an avalanche is ripe for the harvest.

35   With an affirmative response from Fidelity, the endangered section of road is
closed—which, in a bad storm, can be the entire pass—and the Artillery is called out.   345
Depending on the immediate threat, the team will proceed to any of 15 circular gun
emplacements set in the highway shoulder where the Howitzer is anchored and its
sights registered on nearby permanent target stakes. From the emplacements, 35-
pound (16 kg) high-velocity shells can be fired into perhaps 140 trigger zones, some
of which lie a mile (1.6 km) above and three miles (5 km) distant from the road. The   350
shooting is accurate to within 30 feet (9 m) of pinpoint, even though the target is
rarely visible. Depending on wind direction and speed, Schleiss will direct shells into
any of five distinct target zones in as little as a third of a square mile (1.6 km²) of terrain. Through experience, he has a good idea which zone will release the slide, given
the prevailing conditions. In an average year, a thousand shells, each costing nearly   355
$400, will be lofted into the snow-laden mountains flanking the highway.

36   After nearly 30 years' work at Rogers Pass, Schleiss admits to being 'very afraid'
of avalanches but still insists on going out in every storm, supervising the shooting
and monitoring the results. He has observed more than 10,000 avalanches, many at
a much closer range than he would prefer. 'The visibility is usually very poor when   360
we shoot,' he says, 'and so to see how we have done, I drive my truck to the centre of
the path we are shooting, turn off the engine and use my ears. I have become a good
judge of the clear-out we get even when I can't see it.'

37   The practice has led to some harrowing experiences. Once, he remembers, he
left an accompanying photographer and an Environment Canada–Parks superior in   365
his truck while he stepped out to listen for the sounds of success. He heard the rumble in the clouds of a big avalanche—one that was going to hit the road. 'Let's go!' he
yelled to the others as he leapt into the truck. To his horror, the truck would not start.
'Let's go!' he yelled again, and they all jumped out and ran. The avalanche, missing
them by feet, demolished the truck. 'So far,' says Schleiss, 'I have had two trucks   370
destroyed, and Walter has had two trucks destroyed. There is a rumour around here
that we like new trucks.'

38   Less than half a day's drive east of Rogers Pass, in Banff National Park, Clair Israelson, a public-safety supervisor with the warden service, directs an entirely different sort of program at Skiing Louise, one of the park's three ski areas. 'Our prob- 375 lem', says Israelson, 'is the ski area itself. We're responsible for eight square miles of terrain, in which there are 60 avalanche paths that produce 250 to 300 avalanches big enough to kill somebody each season. On a busy day, 6,000 skiers use the area, and most of them know nothing about avalanches. In a road operation, you worry about natural triggers and don't concern yourself much with small slides. At ski areas, you 380 have to worry about every little slope because the skiers will trigger the slides themselves. You have to figure the skiers will hit every available inch of terrain; that sooner or later, the most clued-out skier will find the worst possible spot. It demands a fine-tooth operation.'

'Circus Day'

39   One clear day last January, Israelson and five of his nine assistants demon- 385 strated their concern, some of their techniques and much of their spirit in trying to induce an avalanche down from a high mountain cirque named the Flush Bowl. Heavy powder on top of a thin crust on top of some three feet (0.9 m) of depth hoar indicated an avalanche long overdue. The slope, however, was particularly reluctant to budge. A few one-kilogram hand charges had been lobbed into the snow with no 390 noticeable results. The area was posted as closed to skiers, but it was Friday, the day before 'circus day', and the team was worried that snipers—skiers who disregard the closure signs and ropes in order to ski untouched snow—would find the bowl's weak spot and bring the whole thing down. 'Think of a rotten shingle held up on a roof by one rusty old nail,' said Israelson. 'Tap the nail, and the shingle slides.'   395

40   In the morning, hunched over coffee in a trim, new, log, on-mountain control centre, Israelson and his team discussed possible means of dealing with the Flush Bowl. One member suggested 'ski-cutting' the slope—sending a man back and forth across it on long, shallow traverses, hoping to trigger the slide. Israelson vetoed the idea as too dangerous: 'The snow's too rotten, and there's too much of it.' Someone 400 else facetiously suggested rounding up a bunch of ski patrollers, putting them in a long line at the bottom of the hill and prodding them upslope until something gave way. 'Like a Newfie mine sweep,' he said. A third member favoured trying 'nukes on a stick'—small hand charges taped to bamboo wands. Stuck in the snow, the wands keep the charges above the snow. The resulting 'air blast', the team claims, gives 'more 405 boom for your buck'.

41   Israelson decided on a major explosives effort. The men strapped on small radio transceivers that would allow them to be found quickly if they went down in a slide, donned their packs and skis and headed for a lift that would take them to the Flush Bowl. Once there, working one at a time, they skied cautiously out onto a high, 410 steep pitch at the top of the slope and planted 5 parcels of 2 one-kilogram TNT charges about 20 feet (6 m) apart. Doing their work, the men were very exposed, in a most uncomfortable place: it would be a long, nasty ride to the bottom of the hill in the company of several thousand tons of dislodged snow. The last man out, carrying a length of detonating fuse, connected the charges together and lit a fuse that gave him 415 130 seconds to point his skis downhill, make two or three turns and join the rest of the team in a small, protective finger of mountain larch at the end of the slope. Israelson, watching the man ski toward him, said, 'There are aspects of this job that are not for the faint of heart. Sometimes, you have to hang it out there a bit to get the results you want.'   420

42   The explosion ripped across the mountainside, and the air filled with the acrid smell of TNT. A long, thin rustle of snow eased down the slope, but nothing more. Israelson slapped his gloves together in disappointment.

43   In the afternoon, Israelson and team member Bryan Keefer took a snowcat up the mountain with an 'avalauncher', a special compressed-air gun with a 12 foot (4 m)   425 fibreglass barrel, and fired 15 two-kilogram shots into the Flush Bowl, trying either to release a slab avalanche or, failing that, to stabilize the snow. The gun fired with a loud 'ka-thwang', and the explosions ricocheted off the surrounding peaks. Soon, the bowl was tattooed with powder-stained holes, and Keefer, keeping track of the shots, renamed the target the Vietnam Bowl. 'You've got to recognize', said Israelson, 'that   430 this is not regular procedure. We'd rather not nail it down like this. It improves the chances that it will come back to tickle us in the spring.'

44   Keefer shrugged and said, 'Well, if somebody smokes it in there tomorrow, they can't say we haven't tried.'

45   Israelson stared at the slope for a long moment before surrendering. As with   435 almost all of the industry people with more than three or four years' experience, he himself has been caught in avalanches. And, as a rescue specialist with the parks service who has retrieved more battered bodies than he would like to remember, he has seen the power inherent in as little as four inches (10 cm) of loose snow. He knows that avalanche-disturbed snow settles like concrete around its victims and that an   440 unprotected person's chance of survival if buried for more than eight minutes is almost nil. The wardens will come when summoned, with helicopters, long metal probes and dogs that can sniff out a victim within minutes, but as one of Israelson's public-safety colleagues remarked, 'You should realize that if we have to come looking for you, you're probably already dead.'   445

46   'It's a strange business', said Israelson, waving a ski pole at the surrounding peaks, 'where the central question is not *if* there will be an accident but *when* there will be an accident. Through public education, forecast and control, we try to stretch out that span of "when" just as long as we can, but there will never be a morning when I'll be able to say to you, "Hey, these mountains are guaranteed safe." Because if I do,   450 you can bet that by sunset, one of them will prove me very, very wrong.'

1987

QUESTIONS

Reader and Purpose

1. Both Carl Sagan and Bart Robinson begin their essays with an anecdote—a brief story of a single incident. Do both writers have the same purpose in so introducing their works?

2. Although this essay is included in the Effects section of *Exposition*, does it also have a persuasive intent? If so, what is that intent?

3. Illustration and Reasons are other subdivisions of *Exposition* under which this essay could have been included. Explain why, and then argue why it is more appropriate under Effects.

Organization

4. In relation to the anecdote told in the first four paragraphs, what is the purpose of paragraph 5? Does paragraph 6 have a different purpose, or is it the same purpose but with a larger scope?
5. 'The key sentence of this essay is the fourth sentence of paragraph 9.' Your opinion of this statement should be supported in detail by showing how the rest of the essay is, or is not, the result of this statement. If you are arguing that this statement is incorrect, indicate which you think is really the essay's key sentence.
6. The author introduces a number of avalanche experts: Peter Schaerer (paragraph 10), Fred Schleiss (paragraph 23), Clair Israelson (paragraph 38). Summarize how the experiences of each expert contribute to the development of the topic.
7. The experience described in paragraphs 39–46 is inconclusive. Is this an appropriate conclusion to the essay? If you believe that it is not, what kind of conclusion would be appropriate?

Sentences

8. The third sentence of paragraph 7 is constructed as follows: the main clause, including a list, set off by dashes, of 'natural phenomena'; a colon; then a detailed example of the 'dark ransom', which is 'travelling' and 'striking'; and finally 'commands', the principal verb of the sentence introduced by the colon, followed by 'respect', the object of 'commands'. Note that 'respect' not only is the final word of this long sentence—the final word being the most emphatic position in a sentence—but is also set off by a comma.

    What does this construction tell you about the author's sentence structure? or about his purpose in this sentence? Rewrite this sentence in two different ways in order to emphasize an idea other than 'respect'.

Diction

9. Look up: *untrammelled* (4), *copse* (27), *replete* (56), *capricious* (73), *assiduously* (80), *mosaic* (129), *metamorphose* (141), *facets* (146), *cadre* (194), *geomorphic* (208), *topography* (214), *analogous* (243), *demeanour* (304), *inherent* (439).
10. In paragraph 5 what function does the expression *More to the point, however* have?
11. In the last sentence of paragraph 10 the author uses one **metaphor** and two comparisons. Are these **figures of speech** appropriate to their context? Are they effective?
12. Explain the expression *dexterously and continually switching tuques* (103–4). What well-known saying has Robinson modified here?
13. What do you understand by the expression *Caterpillar-built dykes* (318)? Is it effective? Consider also *a fine-tooth operation* (383–4) and *on-mountain control centre* (396–7).

POINTS TO LEARN

1. Introducing an essay by an anecdote can immediately grasp the reader's interest if the anecdote is both well told and relevant to the subject of the essay.
2. The conclusion of an essay should bring the essay to a complete end, even if the subject dealt with is itself not logically concluded.
3. The views of experts can be interesting in themselves and help in achieving the objectives of exposition.

SUGGESTIONS FOR WRITING

What experiences have you had with the extremes of nature? Consider such occurrences as blizzards, hail or ice storms, extreme cold, lightning, floods, drought, tornadoes, etc.

Keep in mind that your essay on this topic should focus on effects; narrative will likely be important, but it should be subordinate to exposition.

IMPROVING YOUR STYLE

1. Begin your essay with an anecdote, preferably about something you experienced yourself.
2. Use the relevant opinions of others, even though they may not be experts.

ALAN RAYBURN

A geographer who specializes in the history of names used to identify Canadian towns, rivers, mountains, creeks, etc., Alan Rayburn was the executive secretary of the Canadian Permanent Committee on Geographical Names from 1973 to 1987. From 1983 to 1996, he wrote the popular column 'Place Names' for *Canadian Geographic*; in 1994, sixty-two of these columns were collected as *Naming Canada: Stories about Place Names from 'Canadian Geographic'*, from which the selection below is taken. Among his other books are *Geographical Names of Prince Edward Island* (1973), *Geographical Names of New Brunswick* (1975), *Place Names of Ontario* (1997), and *Dictionary of Canadian Place Names* (1997).

Hot and Bothered by 'Disgusting' Names

1   Place names derived from words deemed coarse or unspeakable have frequently aroused sensitivity, offence, and even hostility. Over the years new names and masked substitutes have been used to banish names found vulgar or suggestive.

2   In 1924, almost 200 property owners in Victoria asked city council to change the name Foul Bay to Gonzales Bay, after a nearby point named in 1790 for the first 5 mate of a Spanish sloop. The change was opposed by Post No. 3 of the Native Daughters of British Columbia, among others, but the matter was raised again 10 years later by Henri Parizeau, long-time director of the Canadian Hydrographic Service on

the West Coast. He claimed that 'it would be in the interests of the public in general, that this most objectionable name around the coast of Victoria, should be changed to 10 a more respectable and decent name.' It was a sentiment shared by the Foul Bay Community Association, which noted that the name was 'a constant source of offence to residents and of ridicule by non-residents and tourists', as well as an obstacle to residential development. Finally, in November 1934, with endorsements from the councils of Victoria and Oak Bay and provincial authorities, the Geographic Board of 15 Canada authorized the change. However, the boundary street between the two municipalities is still Foul Bay Road.

3   Two names of Native origin on Vancouver Island, Kokshittle Arm and Kowshet Cove, were also changed in 1934, to Kashutl Inlet and Cullite Cove. George G. Aiken, provincial member of the Geographic Board, assumed a high moral tone in support 20 of the changes. 'We do not wish', he wrote, 'to have the daughters of our present and future citizens feel embarrassment in naming the locations of their homes. We cannot, as a Board, in this democratic country, ignore these objections of the citizenry when these objections are founded on good taste and reason.'

4   In 1959, a family of Finnish extraction named Suni advised the Ontario 25 Department of Municipal Affairs that the word *paska* ('shallow' in Cree), as in the name Paska Township, was a vulgar word for excrement in Finnish. Municipal Affairs advised the Department of Natural Resources of the offending names Paska Lake and Paska Creek, and Canadian National Railways of the embarrassingly named Paska siding. As there was a large Finnish population in northern Ontario, especially in 30 Thunder Bay, 250 kilometres to the southwest, the township, the siding, and the two natural features were renamed—after the Suni family.

5   Other examples of undesirable names changed include, in Newfoundland, Distress becoming St Bride's, Famish Gut switching to Fairhaven, Scilly Cove opting for Winterton, and Turk's Gut changing to Marysvale. In Alberta, Meighen (pronounced 35 'mean') was changed to Viking. And in New Brunswick, Pisarinco became Lorneville.

6   A century ago, Sipweske was a growing village near Brandon, Man. Its name, derived from a Cree word, had unwelcome overtones of intemperance to some. According to Penny Ham in her *Place Names of Manitoba* (1980), Wawanesa ('whippoorwill'), adapted from Wawonaissa in Longfellow's *Hiawatha*, was then introduced. 40 The village of 482 is the headquarters of the Wawanesa Mutual Insurance Company.

7   Crotch Lake is a reservoir on Ontario's Mississippi River, 110 kilometres southwest of Ottawa. In 1848, land surveyor John Harper gave it the euphemism Cross Lake, and this was endorsed by the Geographic Board in 1941. I made a field survey of the area in 1965, and found the original name was universally preferred. It was sub- 45 sequently reaffirmed by the Canadian Permanent Committee on Geographical Names.

8   In 1910, the Lethbridge Board of Trade declared, 'We are certainly very much disgusted with the present name and wish to make a change of some kind.'

9   The object of the board's disgust was the name of the river on whose banks the city of Lethbridge, Alta, was situated. It was the Belly River, and Lethbridge citizens 50 were convinced that their thriving young city deserved to be set on a river whose name did not engender discomfort and embarrassment. (In those days 'belly' was a word avoided in polite company.) They had campaigned since 1886, but it took almost 30 years to secure a more distinguished appellation.

10   Alberta's Belly River rises some 20 kilometres south of the 49th parallel in 55 Montana and flows north to join the Oldman River 18 kilometres upstream from Lethbridge. It was given its name during a survey in 1858 by Thomas Blakiston, a member of the Palliser Expedition, and the name first appeared on a map in 1865.

11   Blakiston derived the name from the Blackfoot *Mokowanis*, meaning 'big bellies', referring to the local Atsina Indians and equivalent to the name Gros Ventre used by 60 French explorers and voyageurs. Blakiston applied the name Belly to the whole river from its source to its confluence with the Bow River, where the two rivers become the South Saskatchewan River, 90 kilometres northeast of present-day Lethbridge.

12   Thus when the city of Lethbridge was laid out near a series of rich coal deposits in 1885, it found itself on the east bank of the Belly River.   65

13   Just one year later, Minister of the Interior Thomas White visited Lethbridge, and residents asked him to get the name changed. No action was taken, and in 1900, *Lethbridge News* publisher E.T. Saunders—who had earlier found the name historic and euphonious—urged a change, too. He wrote about the discomfort of strangers and the blushing embarrassment of ladies. To get around the problem, he suggested 70 that the St Mary River, a tributary of the Belly upriver from Lethbridge, be designated the main watercourse, with the Belly as a branch of it. That way, Lethbridge would sit beside the St Mary.

14   Six years later (and still no action), Saunders again appealed to the authorities. He claimed the name Belly made Lethbridge appear to be a crude frontier settlement, 75 and this time suggested extending the name South Saskatchewan River to some point upriver from Lethbridge.

15   In 1910, the Lethbridge Board of Trade wrote a letter to the Department of the Interior proposing the name Alberta River for the entire watercourse, including the present Oldman and South Saskatchewan rivers. The Geographic Board rejected the 80 proposal, stating the new name had no authority based on usage, and noting in any case that the Bow was the principal tributary of the South Saskatchewan. The Board of Trade asked for other alternatives to Belly, but the Geographic Board responded by urging it to canvass local residents for their own alternatives.

16   The matter languished until 1913, when the Board of Trade again asked the 85 Department of the Interior to replace Belly River with Alberta River, 'a name citizens could call attention to with pride'. But the Geographic Board told the Board of Trade to obtain the views of local authorities and then seek the endorsement of the provincial government. In 1915, the Board of Trade asked Premier Arthur Sifton to approve Alberta River, but Sifton said he preferred Lethbridge River. This new proposal was 90 sent to the Geographic Board, which declined to accept it. Geologist and Geographic Board member Donaldson Dowling pointed out that the Oldman River carried considerably more water than the Belly at their confluence, and suggested carrying the name Oldman River to its junction with the Bow. This would make the Belly the Oldman's tributary and put Lethbridge on the Oldman. It was the compromise the 95 Geographic Board approved in August 1915, and thus after many years of appeals, Lethbridge finally got rid of its Belly River.

17   Fortunately, the purging of place names has become quite rare in recent times. People are sometimes astonished to encounter Bastard Township in Ontario's Leeds County, but in 1796, when the township was surveyed and named, Bastard was a 100 respectable surname in England, and John Pollexfen Bastard was a member of Parliament. The names of both Bastard Township and adjoining Kitley Township are derived from the Bastard family seat in Devonshire.

18   In 1966, I asked Reeve Gerald Cross of the Township of Bastard and South Burgess if thought had ever been given to changing the name. He replied that the   105 question had been raised with the Department of Municipal Affairs in Toronto, but when told it would cost $1,200, the council decided such funds should be spent on more important matters.

1994

QUESTIONS

Reader and Purpose

1. In Rayburn's title why is the word 'disgusting' in quotation marks? What, if anything, does this tell you about his attitude towards his topic? Does his use of a **cliché** as part of his title tell you something of his attitude towards his reader?
2. Is there any indication that Rayburn has used a specific method in choosing his examples? Does he appear to have looked for certain kinds of examples, or do they appear to have been chosen haphazardly? If there is a pattern in his choices, what is it? If you can find no pattern, does this affect your response to the essay?

Organization

3. Does the one sentence in paragraph 8 deserve being set off in a separate paragraph? What about paragraph 12?
4. Would paragraph 9 be strengthened or weakened if it were combined with paragraph 8? Explain your answer. Should paragraphs 12 and 13 be combined?
5. What is the conclusion of this essay: paragraph 18? both paragraphs 17 and 18? Does the conclusion follow logically from the rest of the essay?

Sentences

6. In his first sentence Rayburn uses a comma after 'offence'. Is this correct? optional? preferable?
7. Explain the function of the first word in each of the last two sentences of paragraph 2.
8. Why is there a dash in the final sentence of paragraph 4?
9. Explain the purpose of the commas in the second sentence of paragraph 6. Do the same for the second sentence of paragraph 7. Do the commas have the same function in each sentence?
10. Would commas be more, or less, effective than the dashes in the second sentence of paragraph 13?

Diction

11. Look up: *derived* (1), *Hydrographic* (8), *extraction* (25), *siding* (30), *intemperance* (38), *euphemism* (43), *engender* (52), *confluence* (62), *euphonious* (69), *tributary* (71), *purging* (98), *Reeve* (104).

12. Note these examples:

> *George G. Aiken, provincial member of the Geographic Board* (19–20)
>
> *land surveyor John Harper* (43)
>
> *Minister of the Interior Thomas White* (66)
>
> *Geologist and Geographic Board member Donaldson Dowling* (91–2)

How does the first example differ from the other three? Is there a reason for the difference?

POINTS TO LEARN

1. An essay's title can clearly reveal the author's attitude towards the topic.
2. Paragraphs can be very simply constructed without becoming superficial.

SUGGESTIONS FOR WRITING

Write an essay of 7–10 paragraphs on the effects of place names in the area where you live: lakes, creeks, sloughs, rivers; hills, plains, mountains; cities, towns, villages; unusual names of any kind; historic sites; etc. You may find it useful to refer to one or two books on the local history of your area in the library. Your object is not just to gather interesting names but to show how some of these names have had an effect on the inhabitants, culture, tourism, etc., of the area.

IMPROVING YOUR STYLE

1. Use **transitions** when necessary to show how sentences and paragraphs follow each other logically.
2. Choose a title that reflects your attitude towards your topic.

Charles K. Long

Born in Ohio, Charles Long lived in Australia, where he studyied economics at the University of Queensland, before moving to Ottawa in 1968. In 1975 he left his job as a senior policy adviser to the Privy Council and, with his wife and two children, went to live in a stone house that he had built himself on the shores of Big Rideau Lake, south-west of Ottawa. His avid interest in the self-sufficient life away from cities is reflected in his books, which include *The Stonebuilder's Primer* (1981), *The Backyard Stonebuilder* (1985), *Life after the City: A Harrowsmith Guide to Rural Living* (1989), and *Cottage Projects* (1997). The one novel he has published, *Undefended Borders* (1995), was shortlisted for the Chapters/Books in Canada First Novel Award. His best-known book is *How to Survive Without a Salary*, first published in 1981 and often reprinted since. Long's essay on the village of La Loche, Saskatchewan, is a fine example of expository analysis reinforced by striking description.

Out of the Shadow of The Bay

1   When night approached, the woman crept into a cave to sleep. A dog-like creature followed her in and lay down beside her while she slept. In the night the woman dreamed that the creature turned into a handsome man. They performed an act of love. In the morning, when she awoke, she found that the creature beside her was still a dog. Then a giant appeared at the mouth of the cave and tore the dog to 5 shreds, scattering pieces over the earth. The organs became the fish in the lakes. The flesh became the animals. And the bits of skin became birds. Before he disappeared forever, the giant told the woman that her children could kill these creatures and live from their abundance. That, for the Chipewyan people, is how the world began.

2   The giant's undying mistake was in failing to register the title to that abundance 10 with the government of Saskatchewan. Of course, the giant could hardly have known that the Hudson's Bay Company wanted the furs, that southern sportsmen cherished antlers, that fish could be mounted on walls as well as eaten. He didn't say a word about the uranium under the ground and who had the rights to that. He didn't even warn the people that the Oblate fathers would come with an entirely different story 15 of how the world began, and who would be in charge.

3   To find the offspring of Eve and the dog-like creature today, we drive 547 miles northwest from Regina. The bank calendar view of Saskatchewan—the quilted sea of wheat—lasts for less than half that distance. Then the prairie begins to roll, and swathes of poplar and spruce creep up between farms, growing slowly wider and 20 bolder until it seems that the farms are the timid interlopers. The pavement ends at Buffalo Narrows. It's another 62 miles of axle-bashing ruts to La Loche.

4   Getting to La Loche has never been easy. It has, however, been profitable. Peter Pond, the first white fur trader to reach Lac La Loche, arrived in the summer of 1778. At the northern end of the lake, Pond saw a small, winding creek. A mile up the creek 25 was an already well-trodden path through the pines. At the end of that 12-mile trail, Pond and his voyageurs suddenly emerged from a thicket of trees on the crest of a bluff dropping 600 feet to the Clearwater Valley below them. For the next hundred years this would be the top of the voyageurs' world. Behind them, the narrow creek and Lac La Loche led all the way back to Hudson Bay. Before them, the waters flowed 30 to the Arctic, through the fur-rich Athabasca and Mackenzie valleys. The La Loche portage did not just divide the waters, it also marked the outer limit of the fur monopoly held by the Hudson's Bay Company, from the even richer lands to the north and west where any British subject was free to trade.

5   Crossing the divide with a year's supply of trade goods and fur was a 35 Herculean labour. Each man carried 180 pounds on his back, struggling across the divide, plagued with insects, heat, and thirst. Sir George Simpson, HBC governor, crossed the portage in 1818, using 10 local Indians to carry the freight. The Chipewyan carriers were paid in notes for trade goods. They also received 'a fathom of tobacco', and a lecture on the evils of drink and the perils of trading with anyone 40 but the Honourable Company. He then gave them, 'as a matter of great indulgence, a glass of weak rum'.

6   Missionaries soon followed the trails opened by the Honourable Company's traders. By the mid-1800s the Oblate order, formed in France to renew the Church in the wake of the revolution, had dispatched priests to Canada and charged them with 45 strengthening Catholicism among the rural poor. The first missionary reached the portgage on June 4, 1845. The Reverend Mr Thibault reported that the people of the area were 'inexpressibly docile' and readily converted to Christianity.

7   The Chipewyans are a gentle, accommodating people. They trapped and hauled freight for the fur companies. They welcomed the missionaries, hauling lum- 50 ber up the frozen Methye River to build the church at La Loche. They guided the first overland trip to Uranium City in 1955, blazing the trail at −50 °F. The trail is now a road, named for a Meadow Lake businessman and serving a uranium mine run by AMOK, a French company. It remains to be seen whether uranium will do any more for the people of La Loche than The Company and the Oblate fathers have done. 55

8   Modern La Loche is clustered at the rim of a low, sandy bank, overlooking the lake. Some 10 miles to the northwest, across the grey, choppy water, is the beginning of the historic portage.

9   The church looms on the high point of land between the town and the shore. Clad in sombre grey Insul-brick, and guarded by a rough stone grotto whose back- 60 side has fallen away, the mission seems a little down at the heels, like a dowager queen whose senility is beginning to show.

10   The drabness, though, is not entirely the fault of the mission and its leader for the last 30 years, Father Matthew. In fairness, it is the town—not the mission—that has changed. There is a new hospital next to the church, and facing it, a bright new 65 school, gymnasium, and playground. Across the street is a restaurant, and beside that a poolroom. Even the mission's historic partner, the HBC, has built a new store just across the narrow rectory lane. Mind you, The Bay has hunkered down for the '80s with a squat, windowless bunker whose every possible opening has been shuttered with steel mesh; but the colours are bright and the contents modern. High-tech futur- 70 ist Alvin Toffler is on the book rack. New TVs line the shelves, for $149 and up. There's

fresh milk and large eggs for $1.53 a dozen. The IGA around the corner and a handful of smaller stores help to keep the prices down.

11   None of this is at all remarkable, though, unless it can be seen in contrast to La Loche as it was just a short time ago.   75

12   Bob Luker arrived in La Loche in 1968. He was a shy, dishevelled redhead, a would-be community organizer for the Ottawa-based Company of Young Canadians. But the community, he learned, was already well organized. Father Matthew was at the political—as well as the geographic—centre of the town. There was the Department of Natural Resources, the RCMP, and the Hudson's Bay manager. There were also a few   80
transitory whites, mostly attached to the school. The rest of the town's 1,500 people were Natives. Luker recalls that, for them, there was one half-ton truck for hauling firewood, and one paid job (helping in the DNR office). There was lots of unpaid work to do—helping in the mission garden, for example—but the money economy for Native people was one truck, one DNR job, fishing and trapping, welfare, child allowance, and   85
the old age pension.

13   When the Liberal government of Premier Ross Thatcher cut off all welfare for 'employables', the economy of the town collapsed. There were lots of 'employables', but the only job in town was already filled.

14   Credit was tough. The post office was in the Hudson's Bay store. There was no   90
bank. The only place to receive or cash cheques was at The Bay. The Bay made sure its own credit accounts were fully paid up as the cheques came in.

15   The Bay's only competition in La Loche had been the small Co-op store, run by Bobby Clarke. Clarke was too lenient with credit, however, and the Co-op failed. Bobby Clarke went back to trapping. Just before Christmas 1968, he and his partner   95
died on the trapline. There was some debate in town as to whether the official search party had been organized quickly enough to save the men.

16   Certainly Clarke had enemies. He was one of the few Native activists in town. He had competed with The Bay and criticized the Mounties and the priest. He was involved with early attempts to organize a local chapter of the Métis Society. Father   100
Matthew refused to let the Society use the meeting hall. They met in private. Strong opposition kept many away. The organization failed.

17   After Clarke died, his widow and children had difficulty getting fuel for the winter. Stubbornly they stayed where they were, even at −50 °F. Then their home burned to the ground. They left town. Whispers linked the persistent tragedies that   105
followed the Clarkes with his refusal to bend where others had bowed.

18   That same year Luker and Susan Dann were pressured into leaving town. Dann, the other CYC volunteer in Lake La Loche, was trying to organize a preschool program for children. 'There wasn't much to do in the village then,' she recalls. 'People drank a lot of tea. There was lots of sex. A lot of the girls and young women   110
used to come to my cabin and we would just sit around talking and drinking tea. They wanted to talk about life mostly—and birth control. The priest was really against birth control. I had some of those pamphlets put out by McGill Planned Parenthood. The girls were very covert in asking to see them. They told me that the priest didn't want them to have (the pamphlets). . . . Later, when the priest organized   115
the meeting to kick us out of town, giving out the pamphlets was one of the chief accusations against us.'

19   La Loche, today, looks like a town reborn. A young town. Compact. It hardly looks big enough to hold the 2,000 citizens advertised—and by all accounts there are even more people now. Most of them are young. Three-quarters of the popula-   120
tion is under 21. They congregate in the dusty unpaved streets, where the wind plays shuffleboard with litter. The younger ones tumble happily over the stoops and unfenced yards.
20   In the fall, when fathers are looking for moose, little boys stalk the forest of back yard sheds with slingshots, followed by their ubiquitous and much loved dogs.   125
Dogs have strong spirits (shadows of the dream cave weave through the sanctioned Genesis) and bad things happen to anyone who mistreats a dog. During a rabies scare, all the dogs had to be destroyed. No one would take on the task. The Mountie who finally volunteered soon died in a plane crash over Peter Pond Lake. The body was never found. The story ends with a knowing look.   130
21   Large, young families are bound to create some pressure in a town of small bun-galows. More surprising is that the houses themselves are closely bunched on 50-foot lots, dressed shoulder to shoulder in orderly ranks. Bob Long, economic development officer with the Local Community Authority (LCA), explains that the lots were sur-veyed and controlled under the rules of the Central Mortgage and Housing Corpora-   135
tion. Apart from bureaucratic tidiness, the reason for the close regimentation is utility services. The services available are extensive by any standard. There is door-to-door garbage collection, a fire department, dial phones, day care, a liquor store, a health clinic, gas stations, a library, an airstrip—a wealth of services that would not be pos-sible without a resource-rich provincial government to foot the bill.   140
22   It is not, however, a wealthy town. There are only 280 jobs in La Loche. Outsiders, mostly teachers and other public employees, hold 104 of them. The un-employment rate among locals is a staggering 80 per cent. Recent layoffs might take it closer to 90 per cent, says Alphonse Janvier. Janvier, an LCA employee and chairman of the local school board, looks more like a student than the chairman of the board.   145
'Social problems just won't be solved before real economic change takes place.' He's talking about jobs, and about the regular failure of programs designed to create jobs. 'The problem has been that the government was coming in with the ideas rather than the ideas coming from the people.' Now the ideas are starting to come from the local Economic Development Corporation, under the direction of an elected board.   150
23   The Development Corporation is beginning to show its mettle. In housing, for example. Nearly all of the old log cabins, scattered willy-nilly on common land, have been replaced by southern-style bungalows, lined up side-by-side on a treeless grid. Hard to heat, dripping with condensation, doors and windows splintered from the effects of frost and too-light (i.e. cheap) hardware, the provincial houses quickly dis-   155
integrate. The Development Corporation is setting out to prove that it can build a better house for the same amount of money. The demonstration house is only half-built, but it is already showing its distinctions. Set skew to the grid (and to every other house on the street), it is aligned with the sun for maximum solar heat advantage. There is a full 12 inches of insulation in the double walls, and a wood/oil combination furnace in the   160
basement. Inside air is vented through a heat exchanger. Heavy-duty hardware will keep the doors and windows straight. The Native tradesmen building the house are rightfully proud of what is emerging. What is emerging may be very much more than a house.

24   Not everyone has the same kind of confidence in the community's future. Jonas
Clark is 78. He has been trapping and fishing for 71 years. He speaks four languages, 165
though he has never been to school. Clark is Métis. 'My daddy came from Scotland,'
he explains. 'He was Hudson's Bay man in Flin Flon. He make a girl friend there,
and—you know what I mean "make a girl friend?"—he make a girl friend there and
have two babies. Then he comes to La Loche to be Hudson's Bay man here. Then he
make a girl friend with my mother. I was born here 78 years ago. Then my daddy left 170
again—somewhere else for Hudson's Bay Company.'

25   Today, Clark sits in his kitchen, the remains of a duck on the table. 'There's a
lotta money now,' he says, 'but lotsa people got nothin'. In the old days everybody had
gun, canoe, cabin, traps . . . Now all they got is government money and too much
liquor and poker. In ten years is gonna be hard times. Money goin' up and up and up.' 175

26   Clark still hunts and traps and lives with a houseful of assorted grand- and
great-grandchildren. Chipewyan families are extended and loving. Not all of them
take his advice, however. Some younger charges are heard in the back room giggling
over the Flintstones. Jonas is on his way to Thursday court for another errant grandson. 'Drinking' is the only explanation offered.   180

27   Clark's neighbour, Dave O'Hara, has trapped and fished with the old man many
times. 'Jonas,' he says, 'has his past. And because he's a dreamer, he's got a future. The
young people say, however, that "the old have nothing to offer. They can tell what it
was like in the past, but they can't tell us what the future will be like." Three thousand people can't trap.'   185

28   Just outside La Loche, a mile or so up a sandy trail that curves around the shore,
is a tidy one-room cabin on a modest knoll of pine and birch. It looks across the
northern water to the place where the creek still marks the old portage to the
Athabasca country. The middle-aged couple who live in the cabin are busy with
autumn chores. He is scraping fat from a fresh moose hide. He killed it himself. His 190
moccasins are made from last year's moose. His wife will make a coat this year. He
scrapes with a tool he has carved from the leg bone of a caribou. A loop braces the
tool to his forearm in the ancient way. On the porch is a tub of water and ashes, and
a perfect deerskin is soaking. Smiling, he shows off his skill and abundance with a
patient pantomime for visitors who speak neither Chipewyan nor Cree, his only lan- 195
guages. The cabin is solid, clean, and spare. No water, sewers, or telephone lines. The
government pipes don't reach this far. Three thousand people can't trap.

29   At night, the younger half of La Loche packs itself into the cavernous modern
Robby Fontaine Memorial Arena. The name is important. Fontaine is described by
former residents as an implacable opponent of The Bay, the priest, and every vestige 200
of the old establishment. Fontaine was already an old man in the winter of 1969,
when the first hockey team in La Loche was organized—from a donated pile of sec-
ond-hand skates. Most of the kids had never skated before. They played a team from
Buffalo Narrows and lost by something like 40 to 0. The game turned into a brawl.

30   Now hockey draws a quarter of the population to the arena. Before the concrete 205
floor is frozen over for the season, there are roller skates for rent. It is a beehive of
exuberant youngsters jiving around on their vinyl wheels to the thunder of the Rolling
Stones. A sprinkling of Mums and Dads supporting fawn-legged young, a swirl of
flirting teens, and wave after wave of joyful kids, booming around in circles with

white-dusted bums and knees, shrieks, giggles and face bustin' aint't-the-circus- 210
wonderful grins.

31   It is hard to reconcile this energetic joy with the sombre missionary past, with
the quiet pride of the self-sufficient trapper's life, with the hopeless pit of alcoholism
that looms through broken windows. They seem like parts of different lives. Jonas
Clark isn't here tonight. He said he liked the village life when he was a boy, 'but now 215
there's too much noise.'

32   Parts of different lives—and yet it is folly to look for clear-cut factions within
the town. Political activists belong to AMNSIS (the Association of Métis and Non-Status
Indians of Saskatchewan); and yet Jonas Clark, who is widely known as 'the priest's
man', insists that the houses being built by AMNSIS are the best in town. The priest 220
campaigns against drinking; AMNSIS supports AA. Socialist Saskatchewan helps Native
capitalists get started with development loans and consultants to show them the
ropes. One white outsider keeps a dog sled in his living room, and enjoys teaching
young Indians to trap. Stereotyped divisions get a little blurry.

Decolonization

33   Rod Bishop is an AMNSIS field worker. He travelled regularly to La Loche in the 225
shrill days of the '60s, when AMNSIS was the Métis Society and Bishop was called the
Minister of Housing and Guerrilla Warfare. Now Bishop sits in his living room, tired
from a day of forking hay. A small boy crawls onto his lap with a book. His wife Rose
is in the adjoining room, planning their daughter's wedding. It will be in the church,
with a white dress and all the trimmings. When asked about his memories of La 230
Loche, Bishop doesn't hesitate. 'Father Matthew used to rule that place,' he says, 'but
now the people are getting decolonialized.'

34   Bishop and Jim Sinclair, AMNSIS president, recently travelled to London to
explain their position on the constitution. Sinclair told the parliamentarians, 'When
the missionaries came to our land, they had the Bible and we had the land. When they 235
had finished, we ended up with the Bible and they ended up with the land. Then the
army followed and the rest is history.'

35   On a bright autumn day, we find Father Matthew directing a crew of five strap-
ping boys around the mission yard. The rectory is getting a new wardrobe. The priest
is driving the truck. The boys are doing the lifting. The wardrobe goes on the second 240
floor. Father Matthew gets things organized in fluent Chipewyan. The boys follow
orders cheerfully.

36   Father Matthew refused to be interviewed. Others tell us that he opposed the
building of the road to La Loche. He fought to keep out the Métis Society. He stopped
the reading of Planned Parenthood literature. He kept out the Pentecostals. He fought 245
the LCA to keep the hospital on mission land. But he did it all in Chipewyan, and he
still fills the church for two services every Sunday. Tenacity is part of the Oblate code;
the Oblates vow to stay in their congregations until death. If the power of the mission
has not exactly withered away, the balance has nevertheless been tipped. The power
of the community, the state and a relentless southern culture is unfolding all around. 250
The twentieth century is coming to La Roche, and no finger in the dike will be able
to hold it back.

37   The reason, of course, is money. The old order has simply been out-spent by the new. It's more than the relatively piddling sums spent in La Loche itself. It's the whole web of connecting threads that breaks the old pattern of isolation. It's the roads, 255 airstrips, and satellites—services that were not designed to serve the people of La Loche, but which nevertheless are bringing them pell-mell into the '80s.

38   Almost within the shadow of Father Matthew's spire is another heavenly shaft. Down by the water's edge, incongruous beside the weathered boats, is the slender mast of a satellite receiver. It brings in 24 channels of mostly American sacraments— 260 relentlessly. Sports and movies are big, but anything will do. Sesame Street characters dance away behind the counter of the gas station, the local news from Chicago, and a soap opera version of the American Revolution fill the living rooms. The Bandit is headed north, and Smokey can't stop him now. I asked Bob Long what the town might do if the federal Department of Communications follows through on its threats 265 to close illegal stations like this one. 'Move the equipment onto the reserve and tell the DOC to go . . .' he replies, in deadly earnest.

39   For better or worse, the tide of change is sweeping over the dike. Uranium money, government programs, roads, and satellites make it inevitable. Still unanswered is the question of who will control those changes, and what it will all mean 270 for the progeny of Eve and the dog-like creature.

40   Behind the new arena, in a boxy office trailer that houses the spillover of LCA offices, is a cramped reception bay and a half-open door. The sign on the door says: 'DANGER—RADIOACTIVITY'. It is supposed to be a joke. Behind the rough-sawn lumber door is a tiny radio station broadcasting Yoko Ono music on FM 89.9 to the people of 275 La Loche. That's the radio part.

41   The activity is in the effervescence of Mabel Park, disc jockey, newscaster, producer, director, technician, and everything else. The music is modern. So is the lady. Her fingers flick over the controls with confidence.

42   If the radioactive sign is a joke, it is a superficial one. This kind of activity, how- 280 ever mellow it may seem on the surface, is part of a more promising future. There is nothing revolutionary in the music of Yoko Ono, or even in the gentle Ms Park. The promise of change comes from the simple fact that the fingers on the controls are brown, the colour of smoke-tanned doeskin.

43   Park admits she was nervous at first, but now she loves the job. She flips 285 through a pile of records and announcements, ordering the rest of the program. 'Who decides what goes on the air?' I ask her.

44   She leans back comfortably in the swivel chair. 'I guess I do now,' she says, letting the softest edge of a feline smile well up from somewhere within.

1982

QUESTIONS
Reader and Purpose

1. Although this essay is mainly expository by analysis, it is also, to some extent, persuasive. Thus, when Long says that 'Stereotyped divisions get a little blurry' (224), he seems to be discussing the subject in a neutral, objective manner. But paragraph 36, which discusses Father Matthew, concludes with this remark: 'The

twentieth century is coming to La Loche, and no finger in the dike will be able to hold it back.' Does this comment lead you to believe that Long is not quite as objective as the earlier comment indicates? What other evidence can you find that shows Long to be generally on one side of the question rather than the other? Consider also, in this respect, the last two paragraphs of the essay.

Organization

2. Long begins his essay by telling a brief story about the Chipewyan interpretation of creation. Is this an effective introduction? Did it make you want to read more?
3. How are paragraphs 1, 2, 3 and 20 and 39 related?
4. After the introductory paragraphs 1–3, paragraphs 4–7 detail the history of the La Loche area. How does Long make this transition? Then how does he shift to his next topic?
5. How does paragraph 11 function as both summary and transition?
6. Explain how the following transitional expressions function: *Modern La Loche* (56); *Today, Clark sits* (172); *The reason, of course* (253); *For better or worse* (268).
7. Compare the structure of paragraphs 4, 5, and 6. Is the first sentence in each the **topic sentence**? or is the topic sentence elsewhere in the paragraph? or is it altogether missing? Could any one of these paragraphs be more tightly structured by the addition of a topic sentence or the substitution of a better one?
8. How does the final paragraph make a fine contrast to paragraph 1 and, especially, to paragraph 2?
9. Paragraph 30 describes the exuberance of La Loche's youth. Does it mark a turning point in the essay? How is it related to other points, such as the concluding sentence of paragraph 36? paragraph 39? etc.

Sentences

10. Why does Long use dashes in paragraph 3 but parentheses in paragraph 20? Would there be much difference if the marks were interchanged?
11. Point out the **parallel** elements in paragraph 7.
12. Comment on the effectiveness (or ineffectiveness) of the **fragments** in paragraphs 19 and 23.
13. Compare the sentence structure of paragraph 12 with that of paragraph 23. How many **simple**, **compound**, and **complex** sentences are there in each? Then do the same for paragraph 42. From this brief survey, what kinds of generalizations can you make about Long's sentence structure?
14. Explain the **irony** in the first sentence of paragraph 2.

DICTION

15. Look up: *swathes* (20), *interlopers* (21), *bluff* (28), *monopoly* (33), *indulgence* (41), *grotto* (60), *rectory* (68), *bunker* (69), *futurist* (70–1), *transitory* (81), *ubiquitous* (125), *feline* (289).
16. Does Long tend to use words that are **abstract** and general, or **concrete** and specific? Examine his diction in any four consecutive paragraphs.
17. Identify the **images** in the first three paragraphs. Do any of these seem particularly effective? Explain your preferences.

POINTS TO LEARN

1. Exposition and persuasion are not mutually exclusive; they can be used together with considerable impact.
2. **Sentence fragments** can be used effectively as **appositives**.

SUGGESTIONS FOR WRITING

As the topic for an expository essay choose a location you know well where group activities often take place: a schoolyard, the local hockey rink, a community centre, the church basement or social hall, a gymnasium, an apartment recreation centre, etc. Begin your exposition by focusing on one type of character: the bully, the quiet but efficient leader, the constant complainer, the arrogant loner, the trustworthy friend of all, the lonely braggart, etc. Although you will be describing the activities that take place in this centre, the focus of your analysis will be on the people—particularly in their relationship to the one character you have chosen.

IMPROVING YOUR STYLE

In your essay include the following:

1. at least two **fragments**, used as **appositives**, in the same paragraph;
2. three sentences using **parallel structure** in another paragraph;
3. at least one paragraph in which **images** play an important part.

DALE EISLER

Before becoming actively involved in federal politics, Dale Eisler enjoyed a successful career as a writer and journalist that included stints as a political writer for the *Saskatoon Star-Phoenix*; as editor of Leader-Star Services, which provides political coverage for the Regina *Leader-Post*; and as the Prairie bureau chief for *Maclean's*. He is the author of *Rumours of Glory: Saskatchewan and the Thatcher Years* (1987), an analysis of the Saskatchewan government under Ross Thatcher, premier of the province from 1964 to 1971. In 1998 Eisler was appointed assistant deputy minister of the Consultations and Communications Branch of the federal Department of Finance.

Cultural Genocide

1   If you want to see what cultural genocide looks like close up, all you have to do is come here.

2   This is a town that should not exist. At least not with 2,300 inhabitants, the vast majority of whom are without jobs or any realistic hope of finding work or a better life.   5

3   This is a town that is here because long ago white society deemed it necessary. Ever since, it has been sustained not by any discernible economic logic, but by government seeking to justify a community that did not make sense.

4   Trying to unravel the social and economic complexities of La Loche isn't easy. It is not unlike countless other northern communities that survive on the margins of Canadian society, a virtual Third World which we only vaguely acknowledge.   10

5   Usually we become aware of these isolated towns when there is some compelling event that attracts our attention. Most recently it has been the problems of Davis Inlet, where solvent abuse by children shocked those on the outside who were given a brief glimpse into a bleak and desolate world.   15

6   But our attention span is brief. We are quickly distracted by other events and the problems of the North again lapse from the public agenda.

7   Although the problems of the North fade from our minds, they never disappear. They remain invisible, out of sight and out of mind until another incident comes along to plague our conscience until something else distracts us again.   20

8   There has been nothing out of the ordinary that has happened in La Loche in recent days or weeks to attract attention. It is merely the usual misery ground out by unemployment of about 90 per cent, rampant alcohol and drug abuse and a crime rate that is more than three times the provincial average.

9   It has been ever thus in La Loche, at least the La Loche as we have known it.   25 This is a town that suffers endlessly from the fact it exists as little more than an invention of white society.

10   Like so many other northern communities, its roots are in the arrival of the white man's fur trade and religion. The Dene people who live in and around La Loche were once nomadic trappers and hunters who lived a subsistence life in the bush.   30 Their life was basic because their needs were simple.

11   When the economy of the fur trade arrived, it had a profound impact on the indigenous people. Fur trade posts and the Hudson's Bay store became the beginnings of larger communities, which brought with it missionaries who wanted to convert the Indians to Christianity. Steadily the dispersed life of the Dene became more and more   35 centralized as families moved from trap lines and wilderness camps into the community.

12   Before Europeans arrived, La Loche was a small, self-sufficient community. One depiction of an early La Loche is given by elders. It's quoted in a study into the community's problems and solutions done by Dr John Hylton of Regina for the provincial government last fall.   40

13   According to the elders, before white society intervened, La Loche was a place where people were happy and tranquil. 'In the fall the people would catch two thousand fish for food, and another two thousand for the dogs . . . then they would have enough to last right through the winter. . . . I remember when I was a kid, the people lived poorly, but the people were happy, and everybody had love for each other,' the   45 report quotes the elders as saying.

14   When that scene is contrasted with the La Loche of today, the destruction of a way of life becomes stark.

15   La Loche's economy is based almost entirely on welfare and government assistance. The population has continued to grow over the years because, in an attempt to   50 address social and economic problems, government has made the community evermore dependent.

16   What has resulted is a sprawling town where almost everyone lives in public housing and very few have jobs. As such, life takes on an aimless, yet ritualistic texture.

17   Twice a month by mid-afternoon people start gathering around the post office. 55
They know it's the day for social assistance or unemployment insurance cheques
to arrive.
18   For the next 24 to 48 hours, locals tell you the town shows its dark side.
19   As one woman explains, La Loche becomes 'unhinged' as alcohol abuse prevails
and the town's frustration with itself and its lack of hope erupts.   60
20   Before long, the money runs out and the trouble subsides. The people, who are
warm and generous by nature, then return to a life that makes little sense and, sadly,
carries little meaning.

1994

QUESTIONS
Reader and Purpose
1. Dale Eisler's essay about La Loche, published 12 years after Charles Long's, also
   has a persuasive intent, persuasion, in both cases, by analysis. Long, however, in
   a lengthy essay has much more room to work with, and thus he is able to give his
   reader different perspectives about the situation in La Loche. Eisler, on the other
   hand, is writing a short column for a newspaper and thus must make his key points
   rapidly and briefly. How does this constraint affect Eisler's approach to his subject?
       In dealing with this question you might compare the introduction to both essays,
   their use of appropriate detail, and their analysis of causes.

Organization
2. 'This is a town that should not exist' (3). 'This is a town that is here because long
   ago white society deemed it necessary' (6). 'This is a town that suffers endlessly
   from the fact it exists as little more than an invention of white society' (26–7). Is
   there any progression in the author's analysis between paragraphs 2 and 9?
3. What is the transition between paragraphs 6 and 7? Is it effective? Can you think
   of a better one?
4. Can you discern any principle that guides the author in structuring his paragraphs?
   Or are the paragraphs built more or less haphazardly?

Sentences
5. In the second sentence of paragraph 6 should there be a comma after the first **principal clause**? Is there a possibility of misreading here, however slight?
6. Is the second sentence of paragraph 2 a **fragment**? Is it an effective sentence, or
   should it be made part of the first sentence?
7. In the second sentence of paragraph 8 would a comma after 'abuse' make the sentence slightly clearer?

Diction
8. Look up: *genocide* (1), *deemed* (6), *discernible* (7), *compelling* (12–13), *rampant*
   (23), *nomadic* (30), *subsistence* (30), *indigenous* (33), *stark* (48), *ritualistic* (54).

9. 'It is not unlike countless other northern communities' (10). Would it have been preferable for Eisler to write, 'It is like countless other northern communities'? What effect does the double negative have in Eisler's sentence?
10. *which brought with it* (34). What is the antecedent of 'it'? Is the antecedent clear, or has the author made a grammatical error?

POINTS TO LEARN
1. Short, precise paragraphs can be effective.
2. Even a brief analysis can be persuasive.

SUGGESTIONS FOR WRITING
Write an analysis of a social problem in your community: public drunkenness by teenagers, school vandalism, playground bullying, drug abuse at raves or bush parties, etc.

Use the same kind of structure Eisler does, and restrict your essay to no more than 20 paragraphs. Note also that, although some description will be necessary, your emphasis should be on analysis.

IMPROVING YOUR STYLE
1. Use one sentence that includes a double negative.
2. Make sure that the steps of your analysis are clear from beginning to end.

FREDERICK ALLEN

Frederick Allen (1948–) has been, since 1990, the managing editor of *American Heritage*, a bimonthly magazine sponsored by the American Association for State and Local History and by the Society of American Historians. He is also the editor of the quarterly *American Heritage of Invention and Technology*. As a journalist and a political commentator he has worked for CNN and for several Atlanta TV stations; his articles have been published in the *Washington Post*, the *New York Times*, and *The Economist*. He is also the author of *Secret Formula* (1994), a history of the Coca-Cola Company, and of *Atlanta Rising: The Invention of an International City, 1946–1996* (1996).

Unreasonable Facsimile

1   In 1950, in the optimistic early morning of the computer age, the British mathematician Alan Turing predicted that computers would become intelligent enough to pass for human beings in conversation. 'I believe that in about fifty years' time it will be plausible . . . to make them play the imitation game so well that an average interrogator will not have more than a 70 per cent chance of making the right identification after   5
five minutes of questioning,' he wrote. A field soon grew up to make his prediction come true, led by Marvin Minsky, who co-founded the Artificial Intelligence Laboratory

at the Massachusetts Institute of Technology. For a while the possibilities seemed limitless. One MIT professor asserted that 'a modern computer system . . . can be made to develop a sense of itself . . . a kind of self-consciousness.' Another writer went so far as 10
to warn, in a book titled *Machines Who Think*, that 'there will be very little communication between machines and humans because unless the machines condescend to talk to us about something that interests us, we'll have no communication.'

2   Today traditional artificial intelligence, or AI, is a backwater at best, and the confidence with which it was once pursued seems unimaginable. Nobody has ever 15
designed a program that can converse at all convincingly on a single subject, and the field has splintered into disparate parts. People work to simulate bits of the neural networks that are the raw material of mind; they design robots to perform simple tasks involving vision and coordinated movement; they struggle to come up with useful language translators; they devise programs to digest medical diagnostic data and 20
calculate suggested courses of treatment. The grand vision has nearly vanished. As one critic of the field wrote in 1984, 'The world of artificial Intelligence programs is populated by idiot savants and well-behaved children.'

3   Still, there are diehards. A small group of them run the Loebner Prize Competition in Artificial Intelligence, which sponsors an actual Turing test, in which 25
judges converse with computer terminals and then try to identify which have computers behind them and which have human confederates. I was one of the eight judges in the third Loebner contest, last December. I got to meet some of the best conversational AI programs existing, and I came away with the conviction that real humanlike artificial intelligence is not just far off but impossible—and that the goal is 30
misguided and pointless anyway.

4   The eight judges gathered in a defence contractor's headquarters in San Diego (I had to sign a paper avowing my US citizenship to be let in) and huddled in a room with eight computer terminals. Next to each terminal was a sign indicating a single topic for conversation, such as 'Abortion' or 'Baseball'. We spent three hours taking 35
turns at the terminals and then privately casting ballots on which were human and which were humanoid.

5   I began at 'Pets'. The conversation, with me going first, commenced as follows:

6   'Hello. What kind of pets do you have yourself?'

7   'I have two cats.'   40

8   'What are their names?'

9   'My cats are called Spats and Bowtie.'

10   'How do you feel about declawing?'

11   'What kind of pets did you have as a child?'

12   'Won't you answer my question? How do you feel about declawing?'   45

13   'Guinea pigs are about as smart as cucumbers.'

14   It was clearly a program and already at sea. It never again attained the apparent coherence of its first two answers.

15   Next I went to 'Baseball'. That conversation started with my asking. 'What teams are you a fan of?'   50

16   'The Baltimore Orioles!' came the reply.

17   'Have you always been an Orioles fan?'

18   'I would like to say yes, but at one time when I was small I was a Tiger fan.'

19   'Didn't what's-his-name Robinson play third base for the Orioles?'
20   'You have that right! The best ever to play 3rd base!!'   55
21   'What was his first name?'
22   'Brooks, of course!'
23   Now I was just as obviously talking to a human being—who, I soon learned, had played some minor-league ball himself. I could always tell instantly if a terminal had a program or a person behind it. There was no comparison. The programs were   60 elaborate, digitized versions of the old Magic Eight Ball. They could look for a few key words and try to recognize very basic kinds of questions, but then all they could do was choose from a long list of prepared questions and answers.
24   As soon as we'd all had a turn at each terminal, we voted. Not one of the judges was fooled into thinking that any of the three computer programs was a human being,   65 but five of my seven colleagues were fooled in the other direction, which wasn't supposed to happen at all. Each of them guessed that at least one of the five human confederates was in fact a computer program, even though the human beings had been instructed to act as honestly human as possible. The confederates had happened to be very humanly inarticulate and illogical. The judges had been too humanly eager to   70 equate humanity with eloquence to recognize this.
25   The winner—the computer program we judged most nearly human, a more or less arbitrary choice—turned out to have been designed by the same person who had won the prize both years before. All three of the programs were hopeless at conversation. The winner, 'Liberal or Conservative?', gave itself away by churning out non   75 sequiturs and rote wisecracks about *Star Trek*. The runner-up, 'Bad Marriage', had obviously been designed only to ask questions, not to answer them.
26   Because the contest has been so disappointing, the chairman of the prize committee, the Tufts University philosopher Daniel Dennett, who is the author of the popular *Consciousness Explained* (1991), sought to persuade the prize's benefactor, a   80 New York businessman named Hugh Loebner, to cut it back at least to every two years. (Shortly after I judged the prize, Loebner said he could not, and three members of the prize committee quit.)

—

27   If the computer programs gave themselves away with their crudeness, the human beings gave themselves away too, I found—but not with sophistication so   85 much as with simple humanness. People inevitably had distinct personalities that shone through fast and clear, even though we were conversing over computer terminals, about narrowly defined topics.
28   I quickly became aware that all the confederates' knowledge and how they expressed it must be tied up with their backgrounds, their moods, their reactions to   90 being part of this test. The 'Cooking' confederate told me, 'My favorite cuisine is oriental food, but I am an excellent Mexican food cook.' I asked how mole sauce is made, and she answered, 'I've heard you use chocolate, and that sounds awful!' Then she remembered that she had made it once. I asked if she had ever made pad Thai, and she said, 'No, what is that?' I mentioned that I am married to professional gourmet cook; she was   95 fascinated and a bit abashed: 'Well, I am not a professional cook—I am self-taught. I had to teach myself because I was married at an early age and it was sink or swim.'

29   Every conversation I had with a human confederate had a similar quality, and so I found myself wondering how anyone could hope ever to teach a computer to converse in a way that would seem at all human. No machine could possibly pass for 100 human without manifesting such a rich, vital context. As the contest made plain, being human isn't about knowledge and syntax—or if it is, it is about mysteriously accumulated, emotion-distorted, often forgotten, confused knowledge, and how you got your knowledge and how you communicate it, which depends on whom you're communicating it to, and what kind of day you're having, and much more. Even the 105 most mundane conversation has this kind of texture—and so, for that matter, does time spent in idleness without saying a word. This may be recognized more often by novelists and poets than by scientists. After all, Marcel Proust built literary immortality on knowing it, and more recently Nicholson Baker knew it well enough to set an entire novel, *The Mezzanine*, in a single silent escalator ride.   110

30   And so I came to suspect that the only truly believable computer program would be one able to ape life itself, since thinking as we know it exists only as a purposive tool of living organisms. And even if the thing were created, what purpose would it serve? We already have at our disposal the all-too-easy means for creating human beings with fully human brains and bodies. What's more, creating a human 115 being (or its facsimile) means creating something passionate, demanding, selfish, neurotic, fallible, and often fogbound. If it isn't, it will never pass.

31   Computers, it seems to me, are valuable exactly insofar as they are inhuman—they can do enormously complex calculations at lightning speed with no chance for error; they can contain volumes of information without forgetting or confusing it, 120 and with immediate access to all of it; they can be emptied out and refilled to tackle totally new problems with no preconceptions except those explicitly fed to them; and so on. Their great strength is their very lack of humanness. What good would a computer be at any of that if it had the power to change its mind, or get bored, or forget, or wonder?   125

32   One area of human intelligence that AI researchers have particularly wanted to simulate is our ability to associate—to retrieve appropriate but disparate memories and to think metaphorically. But isn't our genius for making farfetched associations also the source of many of our neuroses and prejudices and stupidities? The ingenious mind that foresaw an enormous market for automobiles and figured out how to meet 130 that demand by reversing the concept behind the disassembly lines at meat-packing houses—the mind of Henry Ford—was also the anti-Semitic mind that blamed the Jews for the First World War and for a personal difficulty in dealing with investors.

33   So perhaps creating a program to pass a Turing test is both impossible in the conceivable future and futile. Perhaps there's no reason why anyone should want to 135 create one. I asked Hugh Loebner about this. He is a dreamer who also envisions long-distance gravity railroads, but he is especially devoted to AI, which he concedes is an extremely long way from fulfilling its promise. When I asked him what one would do with a humanlike computer that had what I saw as crippling human weaknesses, he talked of 'unstrapping' it from those human frailties when they got in the way. But that 140 sounds an awful lot like backtracking toward a traditional computer.

34   Mightn't there be a more fundamental urge behind all this activity? The classicist J. David Bolter, who also has a degree in computer science, has pointed out in his book *Turing's Man* that 'there was perhaps never a moment in the ancient or modern history of Europe when no one was pursuing the idea of making a human being by 145 other than the ordinary reproductive means.' That is to say, he adds, 'the cultural equivalent of artificial intelligence can be found throughout the history of Western cultures.' Is that what it's all about? Is the quest for AI really at heart an expression of that essential, timeless Promethean urge?

35   'Of course it is,' Loebner said, 'Of course.'   150

1994

QUESTIONS

Reader and Purpose

1. After you have finished reading this essay, explain its title. The title has the virtue of being brief, but is it also appropriate?
2. At the end of paragraph 3 the author concludes that achieving artificial intelligence 'is not just far off but impossible' as well as 'misguided and pointless anyway'. Do these conclusions, which the author published in 1994, still seem valid?
3. 'Every conversation I had with a human confederate had a similar quality' (98). What is this quality? What, in effect, does the author say distinguishes humans from computers?

Organization

4. Briefly state the purpose of each of the first three paragraphs. Would it be correct to say that paragraph 3 contains the key points in this essay?
5. *I began* (paragraph 5), *Next* (paragraph 15), *Now* (paragraph 23), *As soon as* (paragraph 24)—how do these expressions function as **transitions**? How does the expression *The winner* (paragraph 25) introduce the conclusion to this first part of the essay?
6. This essay has two parts: paragraphs 1–26 and 27–35. Summarize each part in no more than two or three sentences.
7. In what ways does paragraph 26 emphasize the disappointment at the results of the contest? What effect is achieved by placing the final sentence of this section in parentheses?

Sentences

8. The third sentence in paragraph 2 is a four-part series, with the parts separated by semicolons. What effect would result if the semicolons were replaced by commas? Apply the same question to the first sentence in paragraph 31.
9. What is the function of the first word in the third paragraph?
10. Would a comma do as well as the dash in the last sentence of paragraph 3?
11. How does the structure of the third sentence in paragraph 29 reflect what is being expressed?
12. What type of sentence is the first one in paragraph 31: **parallel**? **periodic**? **cumulative**? or a combination of these?

Diction

13. Look up: *plausible* (4), *backwater* (15), *disparate* (17), *neural* (17), *idiot savants* (23), *confederates* (27), *humanoid* (37), *non sequiturs* (75–6), *rote* (76), *syntax* (102), *mundane* (106), *purposive* (112–13), *Promethean* (149).
14. In paragraph 3, and later in paragraphs 24, 28, and 29, the author refers to the human operators of the five computer terminals not run by AI programs as 'confederates'. What **connotations** does this word have? Are they all complimentary?
15. In the last two sentences of paragraph 29 the author uses 'this', 'it', and 'it'. Are the antecedents of these pronouns sufficiently clear?

POINTS TO LEARN

1. The structure of a sentence or paragraph can be made to reflect the writer's attitude.
2. Even very brief transitions can be of considerable help to the reader.

SUGGESTIONS FOR WRITING

What has been your experience with computers? In an essay of 8–12 paragraphs, analyze your relationship with a computer or some computerized device, emphasizing the contrast between the cold logic of the machine and the emotions of the human—you—trying to operate it. If you are not sufficiently familiar with a computer, use any other kind of device or machine that seems to have some kind of 'thinking' ability.

IMPROVING YOUR STYLE

1. Use one-word transitions at the beginning of three consecutive paragraphs.
2. Use one four-part series, with each element of the series being followed by a semicolon.

JOANNE KATES

Joanne Kates (1949–) became a freelance writer after studying at Wellesley College in Massachusetts and at the world-famous École Cordon Bleu de Cuisine in Paris. She has written essays on a variety of subjects for *Chatelaine, Maclean's, Toronto Life*, and the *New York Times*, but she is perhaps best known for her work in the *Globe and Mail*, for which she is both a regular columnist and a restaurant critic. She has also published a number of books, including *Exploring Algonquin Park* (1983) and *The Joanne Kates Cookbook* (1984). *The Taste of Things* (1987), from which the selection below is taken, is a collection of her best essays on food, essays that deal with such varied topics as hunger in the Third World, anorexia nervosa, great chefs, and food-tasting contests.

The Chicken Farm

1   They set up a great clucking, all eighty-five hundred of them singing their song at once. From time to time a great angry chirp is heard above the rest. What's the problem, dearie? Was that an extra large getting laid? But the sound is not the first thing you notice. No, the overwhelming impression upon entering an industrial chicken barn is the perfume. It is ammonia, it is barnyard, it is a toilet in a down-and-   5 out bus station somewhere south of Tijuana.

2   Five times every day the narrow feed trough in front of the cages starts, by grace of the electric timing device, to move. Eighty-five hundred pale pink beaks shoot forward on eighty-five hundred scrawny white necks. It's all hands on deck. They peck with an intensity that recalls humans at the shrimp and lobster section of an all-you-   10 can-eat buffet. And half an hour later there's a run on water. Anyone who thinks that chickens are too dumb to tie their shoelaces ought to watch the birds at White Feather Farm in Oshawa, Ontario. Water comes to them drop by drop from overhead pipes. Each cage has its own pipe and the birds have to learn to place their little pink beaks right under the pipe in order to drink. They learn fast.   15

3   Hubert Schillings, the man who has run White Feather since his father semi-retired, knows how fast they learn because he gets a new batch, 17,000 of them, every year (he has two barns). A laying hen's life is not long. She comes to Hubert from the hatchery at 20 weeks of age and a year later she's in the pot. Campbell's Soup buys all of Hubert's old fowls and uses them to make soup.   20

4   During her life on the planet each hen lays 250 to 260 eggs. And no, a hen does not need a rooster to lay eggs, any more than a woman needs a man in order to ovulate. Her little wire cage has a slanted floor. As soon as she lays it, the egg rolls down to the low end of the cage and drops out onto a narrow conveyor belt. The belt brings all the eggs to the front of the barn where the egg picker puts them in   25 cartons. Out of the two barns come 13,000 eggs every day. Twice a week the eggs are picked up and taken to a grading station in Mississauga where they're washed, candled, graded for size, put in cartons, and sent out to the stores. Candling means shining a light through the egg and getting rid of those whose air sacs are too big.

5   But I'm getting ahead of myself. Here we are in the barn, where the trough is   30 moving and the hens are going wild. Even though the food is always available, when the trough starts to move it's bebop time. Hubert theorizes that they get excited because it's a moving target. If so, this behaviour is one of the few piteous vestiges of their natural conduct.

6   White Feather Farm is typical of Ontario's 778 egg producers. The barn is   35 300 feet long and 30 feet wide. Lines of wire cages run its whole length. Each cage is 18 inches tall, 18 inches deep, and 24 inches wide. The lights are on 16 hours a day. It is home, if such a word may be used, to five chickens. The cage is meant for seven chickens, but the Ontario Egg Producers' Marketing Board, which regulates egg production in order to create a stable market, dropped Hubert's quota. So now he has fewer birds.   40 Even so, five chickens cannot quite play baseball in an 18-by-24-inch cage.

7   The moral question begs to be asked. Is it right to confine animals so narrowly? But a simple answer is impossible. Ask that question in a cultural and economic vacuum and the answer is obvious: of course it's wrong. But welcome to reality. Virtually

everything we consume has been produced in that way. Pigs, cows, sheep, chickens, 45
they are all reared as factory products. Go and see how they keep the calves that
become your veal if your heart really wants to bleed. The nice word for all of this is
intensive agriculture, and what it involves is pumping chemicals into earth and animals and depriving animals of exercise and space in order to get them to produce
what we want from them (more eggs, more pounds of pork) for the least possible cost 50
in feed, labour, and barn space. Farmers used to get 14 piglets per year from each sow.
Now they get 20. It's the same in chickens: more product through more technology.
But where does it all end? It may be fine to inject chicks with a supermarket selection
of drugs to prevent diseases and it may be fine to pen calves up so that they can barely
move. It may be okay to put five chickens in a wire cage that we wouldn't put a minia- 55
ture poodle in. But how do we know whether nature will be able to provide so bounteously when we take away the ground from her creatures' feet and sky from their
heads? And is that so different from asking humans to spend their days popping widgets on an assembly line? It fits in rather well with megafarming field methods that
put chemicals into the soil to increase production, and do who knows what to the soil 60
and the water table in the long term. Of course, thanks to Mr Mulroney, we don't have
to ask difficult questions like that any more in Canada. Since the environmental inves-
tigators have been laid off there won't by any answers, so why ask the questions?

8   In Europe, where the animal-welfare activists are a powerful lobby, the way the
agribusiness system treats animals is being seriously questioned. Switzerland has 65
passed a law that requires farmers to eliminate all cages for chickens by 1993. How
can you tell when a chicken is happy? Do its beady little eyes light up? Its beak cannot smile. Its tail doesn't wag. Tom Hughes, executive vice-president of the Ontario
Humane Society, defines chicken happiness as the opportunity to behave naturally.
Chickens like to scratch in the dirt, they adore dusting (scratching up dirt, getting it 70
in their feathers, and then shaking it off like a dog after a swim). But most of all,
chickens love to roost. Wherever they are, they like to go up a level at night, which is
probably an instinctive act born in nature when they flew up into trees at night to
escape predators' teeth.

9   Tom Hughes says the chicken system now in use is cruel because it totally 75
restricts the birds' liberty and prevents them from doing all that is natural. It is true
that the birds in question neither groom, scratch, dust, nor roost. They don't move
much, because there isn't room. Four years ago the Ontario Humane Society paid an
animal behaviourist in Britain to develop a semi-intensive chicken cage. It's three
cubic feet, intended for one chicken, and equipped with a little ledge for roosting. A 80
barnyard with worms it ain't, but Mr Hughes is a realist when he dreams: 'We understand perfectly well the laws of the marketplace. We accept the reality of the need for
efficient production. We're trying to play by those ground rules and come up with
solutions that are labour-efficient and just as profitable as today's methods.' Mr
Hughes thinks chickens would be happier in his cages, and that happy chickens lay 85
more. Unfortunately he can't prove it, because there haven't been any studies.

10   When nice guy Gene Whelan was Canada's minister of Agriculture he wrote the
foreword to a ministry booklet called 'Recommended Code of Practice for Handling
Chickens from Hatchery to Slaughterhouse'. Mr Whelan's booklet asked farmers to get
hip to the 'prevention of social aggression' and went on to suggest that managerial 90

problems were surely the result of the scourge of 'aggression linked to boredom, caused by low levels of environmental complexity and limited exploratory opportunities for the chickens'. Does Mr Whelan recommend Sesame Street for them? A stroll down the lane? On a leash perhaps? Mobiles hanging above the cages? What would he suggest?   95

11   The fact that Hubert Schillings's chickens are bored and peck each other is not Hubert Schillings's fault. He runs a clean, warm, well-ventilated barn. His seventeen thousand chickens never want for food or water, and he didn't invent the system. In order to survive in it he has to compete, and as he says: 'People want food on the table and they want it for nothing. Nobody wants to see an animal in a cage but there's no 100 other way to produce eggs and sell them to the consumer so cheaply.' There may be another way, but it is not Hubert Schillings's responsibility to send his family business down the tubes to figure it out. At around the time when Gene Whelan was writing the foreword to his ministry's silly platitudes about giving your chickens exploratory opportunities, the Ontario Humane Society went cap in hand to the Ministry of Agriculture 105 asking them to conduct tests on the new chicken cage. According to Tom Hughes, the response was 'polite but cynical. They said no. And besides, they were busy doing experiments to produce a wingless chicken so they could reduce the size of the cages a bit.'

1987

QUESTIONS
Reader and Purpose

1. Joanne Kates's analysis of how chickens are raised today is clearly an attempt to change things. But does her last paragraph say the contrary? That is, after analyzing the situation in detail is she, in effect, throwing up her arms and saying, 'This is a bad situation but, under the circumstances, it's the best we can do'?

2. In spite of the serious nature of her topic, the author uses a humorous **tone**. Why might she have done this? Does this tone somehow lessen the effect of what she says, or make the situation she describes seem less cruel? Or, rather, does the contrast emphasize her point?

Organization

3. What **transition** links paragraphs 1 and 2? 2 and 3? 3 and 4? Are the transitions made by single words? by phrases? by some other means?

4. Why has Kates 'gotten ahead' of herself (paragraph 5)? Why does she then tell us 'Here we are in the barn'? Is this **signpost** too obvious?

5. In paragraph 7 which of the first six sentences is the **topic sentence**?

6. Most of the first five paragraphs describe the life of the chickens, but the final sentences of paragraphs 5 and 6 add a different note. What is it? How do these two sentences lead to the key point in paragraph 7?

7. You may have noticed that, in the 11 paragraphs in this essay, not a single one begins with a common **transitional** word or phrase. How does Kates make the passage from one paragraph to the next?

Sentences

8. In the first sentence of paragraph 2 the author has separated the verb phrase *starts to move*. Is this a grammatical error? a stylistic error? Or is the author's wording both correct and effective?
9. Should the last sentence of paragraph 2 be made a part of the previous sentence?
10. Are there any **organizing sentences** in this essay?
11. The third sentence of the first paragraph is an example of a sentence that is **colloquial** in both its structure and its diction, and the same can be said of the third sentence in paragraph 2. What other examples can you find?
12. In paragraph 6 which sentences begin with the subject? Which begin with a **phrase** or a **subordinate clause**? Consider the same questions about paragraph 10.

Diction

13. Look up: *piteous* (33), *vestiges* (33), *stable* (40), *virtually* (44), *technology* (52), *bounteously* (56–7), *widgets* (58–9), *agribusiness* (65), *scourge* (91), *platitudes* (104).
14. Early in this essay we find such humorous expressions as *What's the problem, dearie?* (2–3), *It's all hands on deck* (9), and *a year later she's in the pot* (19). How many such expressions do you find in the final few paragraphs? What conclusion can you draw?
15. In the second sentence of paragraph 2 do you find **assonance**? **alliteration**? both? neither?

POINTS TO LEARN

1. Transitions between paragraphs need not be spelled out; they can be made by, for example, following a logical progression of ideas, or by following a series of steps in a chronological sequence.
2. Colloquial expressions can help to lighten the tone of an essay on a topic that most people would find very uncomfortable.

SUGGESTIONS FOR WRITING

In an essay of 1,000–1,200 words come to your own conclusion about the problem Kates analyzes.

IMPROVING YOUR WRITING

1. Try for a somewhat humorous tone in the early part of your essay, which you can achieve in part with some well-placed colloquial expressions.
2. Do not use transitional expressions between paragraphs 1 and 2, and 3 and 4. Try instead to make your transitions implicit by the manner in which you develop your ideas.

KEVIN PATTERSON

Kevin Patterson (1964–) grew up in Manitoba, put himself through medical school by enlisting in the Canadian Army, and worked as a doctor in the Arctic and on the British Columbia coast. He also holds a Master of Fine Arts degree, from the University of British Columbia, which he completed while maintaining his practice as a family physician. His short fiction has been published in *Descant* and *Canadian Fiction Magazine*, and he has been a correspondent for *Saturday Night*. His book *The Water in Between: A Journey at Sea* (1999) is an account of the trip, fascinating and at times terrifying, he took on his boat *Sea Mouse* from Vancouver Island to the South Pacific.

The Right Call

1   A gorgeous day in Halifax, late winter already and no real cold. It's almost as warm as British Columbia and far sunnier. It doesn't seem to matter which direction I move from Winnipeg, the weather only gets better. For the first time in years, I find myself living in an eastern city. I moved here seven months ago, knowing no one, to study internal medicine at one of the local hospitals. If I go up to the eighth floor,   5
where the leukemics are, I can see the Atlantic Ocean in the distance, and in between, a stretch of two-storey wooden houses of typically Haligonian design. Things are very different here.

2   As a family doctor on Saltspring Island, I used to go to a coffee shop in town every day for lunch, and people would see me there and remember that they needed   10
to get their blood pressure checked or had discovered some bodily oddness they wanted me to look at. I would eat my pumpkin pie and they would arrange to come and see me that afternoon. In the morning, as I bicycled to the hospital to do rounds, people would toot their horns at me. I lived on a sailboat tied to a wooden dock. It seemed just as idyllic at the time as it does in recollection. At the hospital where I   15
work and spend most of my days now, my fluorescent-lit face must, to the patients I treat, seem largely interchangeable with that of any of my colleagues.

3   Ever since medical school, I found myself most interested in patients who had problems like heart disease and tumours and infections—problems that are demonstrable, serious, and understandable. Heart failure and hepatitis and hemochromatosis   20
involve biologic and metabolic intricacies, like Chinese ring puzzles. On Saltspring, when I heard a heart murmur through my stethoscope, I would send the patient to Victoria for an echocardiogram. But it left me vaguely unsatisfied: my part in solving the puzzle was over. It's hard to explain why such mysteries have a hold on me. The important thing is to acknowledge that they do, and act on it. So I left my little sail-   25
boat and got my hair cut short and went back to school. It was difficult, as such changes in direction always are, but probably the right call.

4   It was a strange thing to give up a balanced and gentle existence for my single-minded life here in Halifax, among strangers. My apartment is breathtakingly ugly: beige wall-to-wall carpet, late-seventies arborite esthetic, its sole redeeming feature   30
being that it is two hundred yards from the hospital. In the evenings I eat at the wooden-floored Café Libertine nearby. The waiters all know me and let me sit as long

as I like. I read textbooks and medical journals and drink ginger ale. I have never been this wrapped up in something before.

5   These days I'm working in a cardiac intensive-care unit. As I walk there in the 35
morning, I think about the ability of the heart to constantly adjust the force and speed of its beat. I clench and relax my fists in my pockets, trying to visualize what I understand of cardiac physiology. An observer might think me full of unexpressed rage. It isn't so. There's just a lot to know.

6   In my unit, virtually every bodily function that can be measured may also be 40
controlled: arterial pressure, arterial resistance, cardiac output, urine production. There are dialysis machines lined up alongside intra-aortic balloon pumps, heart-lung machines, extra-corporeal membrane oxygenators and ventilators. Tubes of alarming diameter are placed in tracheas and atria and ventricles and pulmonary arteries.   45

7   My experience as a family doctor was that people who got as sick as the patients here just died. Mostly they still do, but later, after they've been moved to the regular ward, or a few weeks or months after they go home. Epidemiologists tell us that high-technology medicine doesn't increase lifespan very much. But it certainly appears to. Old men and women come in here gasping and pale from pain and circulatory col- 50
lapse; a balloon is inserted in an artery, a life-threatening occlusion that took years of Cheez-Doodles to form is opened up wide, and immediately everything is better. I never stop being astonished by the potency of all these tubes and machines. But what surprises me most is that anyone thinks this is normal.

8   What is normal is to live a life of punctuated comfort, to experience gradually 55
more frequent nuisances like prostate-prompted nocturnal trips down the hall, like being out of breath after an easy walk, like breast lumps that one day do not feel like the others, like when did I get so skinny? A visit to the doctor will provide reassurance and the problem maybe goes away for a while, but other problems follow and grow more frequent and start to blend together. Then one day someone draws a cur- 60
tain and says, 'I am very sorry.' That is the normal trajectory of illness, and the usual effect of medicine. From the doctor's point of view it feels like supervised collapse—collapse that is inexorable and inevitable, and often beautiful.

9   Birth and death choose their own timing. That's the big picture. But in the small picture of last Tuesday in Halifax, seconds away from death became minutes and then 65
hours and now the old man is breathing on his own and chatting with his blue-haired and tender wife, who thinks that she is the most fortunate of women. She thinks the tubes and machines are miraculous.

10   And though I too am awed by their potency, I still make the effort to remain skeptical. The comfort we offer here is immediate but limited. The shiny hospitals, 70
with their machines and tubes, probably exist as much to allay our fear of death as to delay it. We could as easily build giant pyramids or modern Stonehenges to dull our sense of mortality. Maybe that's the real point behind the death rituals of intra-aortic balloon pumps and tubes in orifices. I don't know. I thought I did know something, living on my little boat and bicycling to the hospital in the morning. Something about 75
the dignity of acquiescence. And now I can see myself raging right to the end. Bring on the shiny machine. At least give it a whirl. I'll trot out the graceful equanimity when all the other options have been exhausted.

11   On Saltspring Island, in the morning, I would drink my coffee in the cockpit of my boat. Seals would come up alongside me and stare and sniff the air. The lower   80 boughs of the cedar trees that lined the shore hung heavily in the water. You could always smell woodsmoke.

1999

QUESTIONS
Reader and Purpose
1. Early in his essay the author tells us that he moved from Saltspring Island, BC, to Halifax in order to study internal medicine. It was, his title tells us, 'the right call'— that is, the correct decision. But throughout the rest of his essay, which analyzes his life and medical work in Halifax, he admits to having had doubts about the purpose of medicine, about its role in human life. Why?
2. What is 'the big picture' that the author mentions at the beginning of paragraph 9?
3. In paragraph 10 the author points out a contrast in his attitude towards death: on Saltspring it was 'the dignity of acquiescence', but in Halifax 'I can see myself raging right to the end,' turning to 'graceful equanimity' only when all else has failed. Has his Halifax experience really changed his mind?
4. What does the final paragraph say about the author's experiences in both places where he has worked? Has he changed his mind, in spite of what he says in paragraph 10?

Organization
5. 'Things are very different here [in Halifax],' Patterson tells us at the end of paragraph 1, and in the next two paragraphs he describes his life and medical work on Saltspring Island. What does he do in paragraphs 4–6? Do these paragraphs follow any kind of pattern?
6. Is the final paragraph a **closing by return**?

Sentences
7. Rewrite the first sentence of this essay in order to eliminate the **sentence fragment**. Is the complete sentence preferable to the fragment? Why, or why not?
8. The first sentence of paragraph 2 contains two **principal clauses** joined with a **coordinate conjunction** and separated by a comma. Is this comma necessary? Why, or why not? Compare the fourth sentence of paragraph 4. Why is the coordinate conjunction not preceded by a comma in this case? Should it be?
9. There are two 3-part series in the first sentence of paragraph 3, and the next sentence begins with a similar series. What other such series—whether they consist of words, phrases, or clauses—can you find in paragraphs 3–6?
10. In the second sentence of paragraph 7 should the second 'after' be followed by a comma?
11. What **parallel constructions** do you find in paragraph 8?

Diction

12. Look up: *leukemics* (6), *Haligonian* (7), *idyllic* (15), *hemochromatosis* (20), *echo-cardiogram* (23), *esthetic* (30), *physiology* (38), *epidemiologists* (48), *occlusion* (51), *potency* (53), *nocturnal* (56), *trajectory* (61), *inexorable* (63), *allay* (71), *acquiescence* (76), *equanimity* (77).
13. In the first sentence of paragraph 3, would 'I have found myself' be clearer than 'I found myself'?
14. In paragraph 3 the author uses *it* four times. Is the **antecedent** always sufficiently clear?

Points to Learn

1. An author's acknowledgement of doubt or uncertainty can draw the reader's sympathy.
2. A three-part series (as opposed to a two-part series or a series of four or more parts) gives an impression of completeness, of thoroughness, of finality.
3. A pronoun such as *it* should have a clear antecedent.

SUGGESTIONS FOR WRITING

The author recalls, in paragraph 3, that his life in Saltspring 'seemed just as idyllic at the time as it does in recollection'. Recollect an idyllic, or extremely pleasant, episode of your own life, one that you had to leave in order to continue with another part of your life. In analyzing the reasons for your leaving and the nature of your life subsequently, reveal what you have learned, or what you failed to learn. Don't be afraid of admitting wrong turns.

IMPROVING YOUR STYLE

1. Begin your essay with a sentence fragment.
2. Your final paragraph should achieve a closing by return.

CHARLES SIEBERT

A writer who lives in Brooklyn, New York, Charles Siebert has published extensively in such magazines as *Esquire, The New Yorker, Harper's Magazine, Outside*, and the *New York Times Magazine*. He has also published two books: *Wickerby: An Urban Pastoral* (1998), a memoir in which the author, from his run-down Brooklyn neighbourhood, recalls a five-month stay in an isolated log cabin in Quebec; and *Angus: A Memoir* (2000), which examines life from the perspective of a Jack Russell terrier.

Call of the Wild

1   This is the time of day, near dusk, the dinner fire just lit at our cabin's outdoor cooking pit, when the coyotes start up. Their sounds vary so wildly that you think at

first it might be a dog from a neighbouring farm, or a cow, or the hooting of an owl in the pine-tree tops, but soon the cries clamber up above all those benign referents, a frenzy of howls and yelps that instantly claims you and the night and whatever prey 5 they've felled here within our isolated patch of Quebec woods.

2   My wife Bex and I have been coming here every summer for the past 15 years, to Wickerby, a rundown old log cabin built by homesteaders back in the 1830s on a modest mountain overlooking the tiny town of Georgeville on Lake Memphremagog in the Eastern Townships. The place has been in Bex's family since 10 she was a child growing up in Montreal. The cabin and its surrounding 150 acres long served her family as a summer and occasional winter getaway, but in the wake of the usual family upheavals and breakups, Bex and I, both writers based in New York City, have emerged as the only ones who have the time and will to come here on a regular basis.   15

3   I say 'will' because Wickerby is in a state of disrepair so far beyond anyone's current means to mend that it requires a good deal of will and courage to put up at once with the place's lack of creature comforts—heat, hot water, toilet, stable foundation, and walls—and its ever-expanding creaturely onslaughts: the mice and snakes and porcupine; the bats that swoop just above our bed each night in the sleeping loft; and 20 now, as never before, and with remarkable persistence, the coyotes.

4   Stirring as their presence and their primordial calls may be, you'll forgive me if I don't wax romantic about them. It was just last summer that coyotes killed our 11-month-old Jack Russell terrier, Angus.

5   It was a Sunday night in early July. Bex and I had just finished dinner and had 25 settled in to watch a movie on the VCR. (Wickerby gets only one English-language TV channel, which features, of all things, nature shows.) Angus had been inside the cabin with us but ventured out near dusk, as was his wont, to perform a nightly perusal of what he'd established as his territory.

6   It had been a while since we'd heard any sign of him, and we began to get a bad 30 feeling. We took turns going outside to call for him. Eventually I decided to try the start-up-the-car-engine trick. Still no sign of him. Then I turned on the headlights. Bex was standing just outside the cabin door. She looked left, away from the glare, and spotted in its far reaches a small fleck of white in the grass of the north field where we sometimes set a table out in the evenings to eat our dinner.   35

7   I could see her running and waving to me to come. Who knows how far Angus had had to crawl to make it back to us, but he did and was still alive, though barely. His eyes were fixed wide, unseeing, his jaw clenched as though still grabbing on to whatever it was that had gotten to him. His coat was matted with saliva and dirt, but there was hardly any blood. I ran to the cabin to get a pair of work gloves in case 40 Angus in his delirium attempted to bite. But he was too spent, in deep shock. Even through the gloves I could feel the trapped air pockets under his coat. It buckled and popped to the touch, like tinfoil.

8   In the days that followed, we'd hear all kinds of theories about what it was that killed Angus. The farmer down the road from our place said a fox, but given Angus's 45 breeding, I think he could have handled a fox. Bear, bobcat, wolf—but wolves, like bears and bobcats, are top predators that prey on other animals in the forest food chain, tend to keep their distance from humans, and with the influx of the latter to

these parts in the form of tourism or the building of retirement homes, have long
since departed for more remote habitats.   50

9   We heard wolverine, a fisher, even a wolf-dog hybrid. A local handyman who
came up here a couple of weeks ago to help me fix the cabin's tin roof owns a 90 per
cent wolf. He says they instantly bond with immediate family members, but that's as
far as their loyalties and affection go. He said a friend of his came up the front walk
one day last winter looking for him. He usually kept the animal on a chain in back,   55
but it happened to be in the house this day. The friend unwittingly opened the front
door and wound up in the hospital with 70 stitches in the forearm he used to keep
his throat from getting ripped open.

10   We initially ruled out coyotes. In all our years of coming here there'd never been
trouble with coyotes, and if it had been them in this instance, no one could figure out 60
why they wouldn't have carried Angus off. But the Sunday after the attack we got a fairly
good idea of what had happened. We'd gone into Magog for dinner and arrived back
here at about 10 p.m., around the same time we'd found Angus. I walked out into the
north field to get some air and look at the stars when the howling started. It was coming from just inside the treeline. At one point, amid the yips and howls and very dog- 65
like woofs, I heard the yelping of pups. Right then a clear picture coalesced in my mind:
the edges of Angus's territory suddenly claimed by a coyote pack with a pregnant or
newly nursing mother, and Angus, being who he was, charging out to confront them.
They were probably more concerned with protecting the pups than dragging Angus off.

11   On and off for the rest of that summer we'd hear them, and have now nearly   70
every night of this one. A few weeks ago, I overheard a woman down at the general
store in Georgeville say that she'd lost eight cats to coyotes in the past two years.
Coyotes, it appears, have taken up full-time residence in these parts and seem intent
on hanging around. That, after all, is what they're best at.

12   I've done some reading on coyotes. In the canine family, which includes the   75
wolf, fox, coyote, and jackal, the coyote is a cousin of the dog, kind of a cross between
the fox and the wolf. But it is the wolf, the dog's closest relative, sharing nearly 100
per cent of the same DNA, which is now an endangered species in most parts of the
world, while the coyote is thriving everywhere, literally in our own backyards. They
troll the perimeters of airports, sunning themselves on runways. They pad about the   80
swimming pools of Beverly Hills. Coyotes have migrated down to the Bronx. One
recently crossed a bridge to Manhattan and was seen dodging taxicabs before finally
taking up residence in Central Park.

13   A major reason for their success is what might be called, in anthropocentric
terms, their lack of preciousness. Wolves, precisely because they've always been a top   85
predator, accustomed to ruling over their habitat, have never developed the kind of
survival skills that would have enabled them to deal with the encroachment of other
top predators, ourselves, for example. Wolves have either been subsumed into our
world in the form of the dog, or chased out of it. Into their vacated niche, the coyote,
one of the animals preyed upon by wolves, has vigorously stepped. Coyotes thrive in   90
the margins, in the grey area between our stubbornly defended antipodes of civilization and wilderness. They're the flouters of that boundary, the ones who've retained
their inherent wildness while freely moving about and partaking of the fruits of our
domesticity, even our pets.

14   Angus's fate was, in part, of his own making, the result of obeying his own wild 95
instincts in a place where doing so brought him up against a far more formidable
adversary than he could have ever encountered in his tamed and tilled native
England. But it is, curiously, the chance nature and inevitability of the encounter that
I take solace in now, the pure remorselessness of the wild and of Angus's fearful charge
into it, into something at once of him and much greater than him, the jaws of his own 100
ancestry, the part that never came along with us.

1999

QUESTIONS

Reader and Purpose

1. Charles Siebert and his wife are New York writers who have been coming to their cabin in eastern Quebec for 15 years, and thus, presumably, they are well acquainted with the surrounding woods and its animals. Why, then, does it take them so long to conclude that it was coyotes that were responsible for the death of their dog? Do you find the author's explanation convincing?
2. Where do your sympathies lie: with the Sieberts, who lost a beloved pet? with the dog, savagely killed because it had reacted naturally? with the coyotes, which also reacted naturally in protecting their young? Where does the author want the reader's sympathies to lie? In dealing with this question you should look carefully at what he says in his concluding paragraph.

Organization

3. The author doesn't introduce his topic until the fourth paragraph. What does he do in the first three paragraphs? If you believe that the information he provides here is necessary, could it not have been shortened into just one paragraph?
4. In the analysis of the death of his dog, Siebert's procedure is chronological. What **signposts** does he use?
5. How do paragraphs 8–10 logically follow from paragraph 7? How are paragraphs 11–13 related to paragraph 10?
6. Is the last paragraph a logical conclusion to this essay?

Sentences

7. The opening sentence is composed of a **simple sentence** that is interrupted by two **phrases**. Are there any other sentences in the first three paragraphs that are similarly constructed?
8. Is the first sentence of paragraph 9 an **organizing sentence**? a **transitional sentence**? neither? both?
9. To what extent has the author used **parallel structure** in the last four sentences of paragraph 12? Is the parallelism exact, or has he used variations?
10. Paragraph 3 consists of only one sentence. How does the punctuation in this long sentence help to keep it perfectly clear?

Diction

11. Look up: *dusk* (1), *clamber* (4), *benign* (4), *referents* (4), *onslaughts* (19), *wax* (23), *wont* (28), *perusal* (28), *influx* (48), *coalesced* (66), *confront* (68), *canine* (75), *troll* (80), *perimeters* (80), *anthropocentric* (84), *encroachment* (87), *subsumed* (88), *niche* (89), *antipodes* (91), *inherent* (93), *tilled* (97), *solace* (99).

12. The diction in this essay is clearly that of a sophisticated writer. But does the writer seem occasionally to go out of his way to use unusual words rather than simpler, more common ones with about the same meaning? Look carefully at any four words in the list above and see if you can find a substitute word that is both appropriate and more common.

    Once you have finished this work, what conclusions can you draw about diction in general or Siebert's diction in particular?

13. What is the function of the colon in paragraph 3?

14. In the second sentence of paragraph 7 the author writes: 'Who knows how far Angus had had to crawl.' Why does Siebert write '*had* had to crawl' rather than 'had to crawl'?

POINTS TO LEARN

1. Analysis can also include narration and description.
2. A parallel construction need not be perfectly parallel in every detail.
3. The skilful use of various marks of punctuation can keep a long and potentially confusing sentence clear and easy to read.

SUGGESTIONS FOR WRITING

1. Both Siebert and Wayne Grady ('The Haunting Powers of God's Dog', pp. 7–13) deal with what Siebert calls the 'remarkable persistence' of coyotes (paragraph 3). Drawing upon evidence from both works, write an analytical essay in which you discuss what this persistence consists of, how it is demonstrated, what its results are, or anything else that you find relevant to this topic.

2. How effective is Siebert's concluding paragraph? Your essay that answers this question (and this is not the same as question 6 above) will have to analyze how the points he makes in his conclusion are prepared for at various places throughout his essay, how well he has summarized these points, what conclusion(s) he draws, the sentence structure he has used, and what moral or lesson (if any) he draws from his bad experience.

IMPROVING YOUR STYLE

1. Delay the statement of your topic until after the first paragraph.
2. Use at least one example of parallel structure with variation.

DEFINITION

Although by placing it in a separate section we seem to be treating definition as something different from exposition, definition is in fact a form of expository writing. Indeed, it is a very important form, since to define something is essentially to explain it, and very often in order to explain one must first define. But because definition presents certain problems of its own, we have treated it separately.

The Meaning of Definition

A definition is a means of distinguishing an entity from all other things in order to recognize it or in some way to understand it. To define *leaf*, for instance, is to find some means of isolating *leaf* from all other things, especially from those things that superficially resemble it, like buds or flowers. We must show that *leaf* refers to a combination of features possessed by no other thing. But to find this combination of distinguishing features is not always easy; moreover, there are many ways to define and many complicated questions of psychology, philosophy, and logic involved in the intellectual operation we call definition.

For example, in one sense, the term *leaf* is merely a symbol—a combination of sounds made by the vocal apparatus, or a certain combination of letters that stand for these sounds—that may be used to refer to more than one thing. In another sense *leaf* signifies any one of several different objects—a part of a plant, a sheet of paper, a thin sheet of metal, a detachable part of a tabletop, a strip of metal in a leaf spring. Thus we may reasonably ask whether definition is concerned primarily with *leaf* as word or with *leaf* as one of several different kinds of thing. Although not all logicians would agree on a single answer, most seem to admit that definition may deal either with words or with things. Some definitions focus our attention chiefly upon the thing, no matter which kind of thing is being referred to. This kind of definition attempts to give, as best it can, accurate, factual information about what a leaf is, in some particular frame of reference. It is often concerned with the analysis of the thing, with its constituent parts, their nature, function, and purpose. It describes the thing in relation to other things.

In contrast, other definitions stress the word or the word–thing relationship. Either they call our attention to how a word has been used in the past, or else they explain—by whatever the process—what words mean. Philosophers and logicians have called the former *real definition* and the latter *nominal definition*. These terms designate the two most general purposes of definition, both of which are important intellectual goals.

We must acknowledge, however, an understandable human tendency to regard real definition as the only kind that matters and to dismiss nominal definition as only juggling with words, as being 'merely verbal'. Yet real definition is probably the much rarer of the two. It is, most usually, the contribution of an original and creative thinker or of a pioneer in some form of research. More commonly, a definition of *atom* or *quantum* is likely to be an explanation of how original thinkers and research workers have used the term—a nominal rather than a real definition. But this fact need not humble us or dismay us, for surely one of humankind's greatest achievements is the ability to use words accurately and wisely both for learning and for communicating.

With words we are able to think clearly about things, to devise new concepts, and to gain increasing mastery over our world. Defining words is therefore among the most important of our intellectual activities.

Methods of Definition

How does one go about defining a word or thing? Since there is no one 'correct' method, it's fair to say that it all depends on one's reader and purpose. Or, put in a different way, the general principle is this: the writer may use any method or combination of methods known or devisable as long as he efficiently brings his reader to understand what something is or what a word means. The following is a list of some of the most common methods of definition, a list that does not claim to be either exhaustive or exclusive.

1. **Analysis.** The type of definition that is perhaps most familiar to the average reader consists of placing a word in a large class called the *genus* and then differentiating the word from other members of that class. This method, as old as Aristotle, results in the kind of definition you would find in a dictionary, though it is by no means confined to dictionaries. A typical entry in *A Dictionary of Canadianisms*, for example, reads in part as follows:

> **pemmican** . . . beaten or pounded meat mixed with melted animal fat and, sometimes, berries, the preparation being sewn in a skin bag to form a hard, compact mass that would keep for a long time under almost any conditions.

Another example comes from the *Canadian Oxford Dictionary*:

> **Newfoundland** . . . a kind of very large dog with a thick, coarse coat and webbed feet, noted for its intelligence, strength, and swimming ability.

This same kind of analysis appears in the first sentence of an essay defining *semantics* by Hugh. R. Walpole: 'Semantics, or semasiology, is the study of the meaning of words.' But analysis does not always consist of this kind of classification into genus and 'differentiae' (the characteristics that distinguish a thing from other species of the same genus). Another form of analysis lists the most important characteristics of the thing-to-be-defined, as we see in Aldous Huxley's definition of *ectomorph*, one of three major body types:

> The extreme ectomorph is neither comfortably round nor compactly hard. His is a linear physique with slender bones, stringy, unemphatic muscles, short and thin-walled gut. The ectomorph is a lightweight, has little muscular strength, needs to eat at frequent intervals, is often quick and highly sensitive. The ratio of skin surface to body mass is higher than in endomorphs or mesomorphs, and he is thus more vulnerable to outside influences, because more extensively in contact with them. His body is built, not around the endomorph's massively efficient intestine, not around the mesomorph's big bones and muscles, but around a relatively predominant and unprotected nervous system.

Both definition by genus and differentiae, and definition by division into parts, are common and extremely useful, but it would be a mistake to assume that all definitions must proceed by analysis.

2. **Synthesis.** Just as important as definition by analysis is definition by *synthesis*. This form of definition relates the thing-to-be-defined to something already familiar to the reader or listener. It often reveals the thing-to-be-defined as part of some larger whole. Thus, it might also be called 'relational definition'. Consider the following definition of thirst:

> . . . the entire theory of the mechanism of thirst has been formulated on this basis: 'When there is a diminution of the water content of the blood and tissues generally, the secretions of the body, including saliva, are diminished in volume. Because less saliva is secreted, the mouth and throat become dry. It is this sensation of dryness that has been called "thirst".' (Anton J. Carlson and Victor Johnson, *The Machinery of the Body*)

It is possible to define *thirst* by analyzing it, by saying that it consists of unpleasant tension, burning, and tickling, instead of relating the sensation to the chemistry of the body. But some things cannot be analyzed in this way and must be defined by synthesis or by some other method. Take the colour *blue*, for instance. *Blue*, unlike *pemmican* or *ectomorph*, cannot be analyzed and described. To define *blue*, other than by pointing to some blue object, we have to relate it to something familiar to the reader. We could say that *blue* is the colour produced by light of a wavelength .000047 cm. Or we might define blue as the colour of the sky on a cloudless day. Either is an example of definition by synthesis.

3. **Negative Definition.** Closely related to synthetic definition, indeed what may be a special form of it, is negative definition, which helps to define a thing by making clear what it is not. Ovide Mercredi, the Manitoba Cree lawyer, defines sovereignty (in part) as follows:

> I will tell you what sovereignty is not, so that you will have at least some understanding of why we also, like you, cherish our freedoms. First of all, it is not the Indian Act. It is not Parliament sitting down deciding in assembly in one session to pass a law that tells me that I can do this but I can't do that. That is not sovereignty, that is not self-government, and that is not self-rule. That is someone telling you what to do.

Or again, when defining the modern cowboy, Donald Hough observes that 'Cowboys do not know how to fire a six-shooter. Most of them have never seen one. They used to wear revolvers for much the same reasons as those that prompted early-day farmers to carry a scythe over one shoulder and a blunderbuss over the other when they went to work in their fields. Their herds are now protected by the cops. . . .' By itself, negative definition is of little value, but as an accessory method of development and definition it is a striking device.

In connection with negative definition, we might add that definitions sometimes carefully distinguish the thing-to-be-defined from something resembling it and often confused with it. Thus, a definition of *stalactite* might very well distinguish that formation from *stalagmite*. As with negative definition, to make this kind of distinction is to define the thing by means of relationships, by synthesis.

4. **Exemplification.** Often appearing as an aid to definition by analysis or by synthesis is definition by example, for one of the best ways to define something is to give

one or more examples of it. At times, however, the method of example by itself is sufficient. Lincoln Barnett, for instance, after discussing *relativity of place*, defines *relativity of motion* in this way: 'Anyone who has ever ridden on a railroad train knows how rapidly another train flashes by when it is travelling in the opposite direction, and conversely how it may look almost motionless when it is moving in the same direction.' The example is developed at greater length than is indicated here and is made to serve, quite properly, as the writer's definition. Sometimes, then, one example can define all by itself, but other methods of definition can seldom do without examples.

5. **Synonyms.** Almost as familiar as definition by example is definition by synonyms. Dictionaries often define words by listing synonyms of the word-to-be-defined. This method has the advantage of being brief, but unless it is accompanied by some other method of definition, it runs the risk of misleading the reader, for no two words mean exactly the same thing, and, quite often, approximations are not good enough. For this reason, many small abridged dictionaries have a limited value. Still, this method is useful, if the purpose is to clarify the meaning of a word or term in passing, as Martin Luther King, Jr, does in his discussion of the principle of non-violence:

> The non-violent resister agrees with the person who acquiesces that one should not be physically aggressive toward his opponent; but he balances the equation by agreeing with the person of violence that evil must be resisted. He avoids the non-resistance of the former and the violent resistance of the latter.

Types of Definition

1. **Consensual Definition.** Whatever the method of definition, the purpose remains the same: to make clear what the word means. Usually the writer will mean by it what most others in his culture mean. Thus in defining *leaf* he is trying to state one of the common public definitions of the term, what it means by the consensus of its users. We may, in fact, call such a statement a consensual definition.

2. **Stipulative Definition.** On the other hand, a writer may occasionally want to assign to a word a meaning more precise or in some other way slightly different from that which it commonly has. Mark Miller, for example, stipulates a definition of *ethics* and *morality* in this way:

> The word 'ethics' is often used to describe the theory or reflection concerning human choice and behaviour. 'Morality', on the other hand, tends to be associated with human actions we think of as good or bad. For example, a philosopher is said to study ethics; a businessperson runs a good, or moral, business. In this guide, however, ethics and morality will be used to mean the same thing. While our actions and our decisions are ethical behaviour, with this activity is a parallel and constant process of reflecting on what we do and why. Nor is this process restricted to philosophers. Parents are always trying to explain to their children what is right or wrong and, sometimes, why it is one or the other. Even youngsters playing ball are debating rules for their game and, sometimes, reasoning their way to new adaptations. Questions that ask what we should do or what we ought to do connect our thinking and our actions.

What is the advantage of creating one's own definition? The answer is that one does so, first, for clarity, and second, for convenience. Words, often, have so many different meanings that they are potential sources of ambiguity. Whenever an abstraction like *beauty*, *liberty*, *justice*, *Romanticism* is a key word in an essay, it is wise to announce that, for this particular discourse, the word is meant to be understood in one sense only. *Ethics* and *morality*, for example, are often used to refer to two different concepts entirely, but for his own purposes, Miller wishes to make the two have the same meaning. The result, for the reader, is both concentration and clarity.

In addition, making a stipulative definition is more convenient than each time having to differentiate between *ethics* and *morality*. A stipulative definition is closely related to the consensual meaning, being essentially a precise denotation selected out of the several senses contained within the general definition. Of course, stipulative definitions do not have to be related to consensual definitions. A writer is free to stipulate any meaning he chooses for a word, as did Humpty Dumpty when he told Alice that when 'I use a word . . . it means just what I choose it to mean—neither more nor less.' Still, when stipulative meanings grow too idiosyncratic, the writer ceases to communicate and thus ceases to be a writer. There must always be some good reason for making a stipulative definition, some kind of ambiguity in the writing situation that cannot otherwise be avoided, since a stipulative definition always places an extra burden of attention upon the reader. But a wise use of stipulation is one of the writer's sharpest tools in exposition and argument.

3. **Normative Definition**. Finally, a writer may make what is called a normative definition, which may or may not be more precise than the consensual one, but which is, in the writer's opinion, better. A political theorist, for example, might feel that most of us misuse the word *democracy*. We use it, he complains, to mean X when it should mean Y. If he defines it to mean Y and says that it should never be used by anyone except to mean Y, he has framed a normative definition. This might seem to be a special kind of stipulative definition, but it is actually different. In a stipulative definition the writer says, 'In this work I shall use *democracy* to mean Y'; he says nothing about how he may define it in other contexts, and he says nothing about how other people should use it. In a normative definition the writer says not only, 'I shall define *democracy* here to mean Y,' but asserts, or implies, that he will always use it with that meaning and so should everyone else, for it—and it alone—is the proper meaning. Both types, however, have in common the fact that they cannot depart too far from commonly accepted meanings.

In exposition and argument the writer is constantly defining. Sometimes his definition is a single word. Sometimes it is only a sentence or two. But almost as often it is a paragraph, a section, or even a chapter; and at times, to make his definition clear, the writer needs the space of an entire book, for a definition is not complete until a writer can be sure that his reader knows what his term means. Writing good definition thus depends upon a thorough knowledge of one's subject, common sense, and a rudimentary acquaintance with logic. The following selections illustrate these characteristics as they appear in the work of skilful writers.

HUGH RAWSON

Hugh Rawson co-authored *An Investment in Knowledge* (1969), an examination of the summer programs established by the National Science Foundation to improve the teaching of science and mathematics in secondary schools. He is the co-compiler of *The New International Dictionary of Quotations* (1986) and of the *American Heritage Dictionary of American Quotations* (1997). He is also the author of *A Dictionary of Euphemisms and Other Doubletalk* (1981), from which the entry below is taken, and of the entertaining *Wicked Words: A Treasury of Curses, Insults, Put-Downs, and Other Formerly Unprintable Terms from Anglo-Saxon Times to the Present* (1989).

Toilet

1   **toilet**. A place and a thing that can be discussed only in euphemistic terms for the simple reason that the English language, despite its rich vocabulary, lacks any non-euphemistic words for them.

2   'Toilet' is a rather recent French import. It comes from *toilette*, dressing room, which is a diminutive of *toile*, cloth. 'Toilet' was used in English in various ways before 5 it reached its present state. Thus, from the seventeenth century, the 'toilet' was the process of dressing, and in the eighteenth century a 'toilet call' was the formal reception of visitors by a lady of fashion while she was in the final stages of making herself fashionable. In the nineteenth century, people began to speak of 'toilet articles', 'toilet pails' (for slops), 'toilet paper' (*Oxford English Dictionary*: 'soft paper prepared for shav- 10 ing, hair-curling, use in lavatories, etc.'), and 'toilet rooms'. The use of 'toilet room' in the euphemistic sense of 'bathroom' or 'lavatory', as contrasted with the original sense of 'dressing room', seems to have been an American innovation of the late nineteenth century. Today, the French themselves go to *les toilettes* (or *les cabinets*—*cabinet d'aisances*, in full) when they are not making use of the English WC. French also glo- 15 ries in the explicit *pissoir*, for a public urinal, but this, too, has been euphemized as the *vespasienne*. The languages of other peoples reveal similar hang-ups. As noted by Mario Pei: 'In South Africa they call it "PK", an abbreviation for the Kaffir picanin kyah, "little house". Germany has *abort* ("away place") . . . Spanish and Italian use words which mean "retreat"; Russian *ubornaya* means "adornment place" . . .' (*The Story of* 20 *Language*, 1965). And so it goes. The Dutch call it a *bestekamer* (best room) and the Melanesian islanders even have a Pidgin euphemism: *house-peck-peck*.

3   In the absence of any precise English word for what we now call a 'toilet', euphemisms have flourished, their sheer number indicating the strength of the under-lying taboo. For example, out of the pages of history, as well as from our times, we 25 have such picturesque expressions as:

> *Ajax* (a pun on the older 'a jakes', for a chamber pot, popularized by Sir John
>   Harington, Rabelaisian wit and ingenious contriver, who gave his plan for a
>   flush toilet in 1596 in *The Metamorphosis of Ajax*); *altar room; amenity;*
> *bathroom; bog house* (or *shop*) and *bogs* (from 'bog', an old word meaning 'To 30
>   exonerate the bowels', OED);

cabinet; can (perhaps originally referring to a toilet with a replaceable can beneath the seat);

Cannes (a famous watering place); *chamber*; *chamber of commerce*; *Chick Sale* (an outhouse of the 1920s, after a comedian who produced a much-admired 35 book on the subject; *cloaca*; *cloakroom*; *closet* (or *seat*) *of ease* (see EASE); *comfort station*; *commode*; *convenience*; *crap house* (with many variants: *crapper*, *crappery*, *crapping castle*, etc.—see CRAP);

Deauville (another famous watering place); *dooly*; *doniker*; *dunniken* (? 'dung' + 'ken', i.e. 'house'); 40

earth closet; *Egypt*;

facility;

gab room (for women only); *garderobe* (in medieval castles, and originally a place for keeping clothes, from *garde-r*, keep + *robe*); *growler*;

halfway house; *head*; *hers/his*; *holy of holies*; *honey house* (a septic tank is a *honey* 45 *bucket*); *house of ease* (or *office*);

it;

jakes; *Jane*; *Joe*; *John*; *Jones' place*; *jordan* (see LEAK);

ladies/gentlemen (with many variants: *little girls/boys room*, *women/men*, etc.); *last resort*; *latrine*; *lavatory*; *loo*; 50

marble palace; *member* (or *thunder*) *mug* (see MEMBER); *Miss White*; *Mrs Jones*; *municipal relief station* (see RELIEVE);

necessary house (or *place* or *stool*: see NECESSARY); *no-man's-land* (for women only);

old soldiers' home; *outhouse*; 55

peers/peeresses (British); *place*; *poet's corner*; *potty* (see WEE WEE); *powder room*; *private office*; *privy*;

rest room; *retiring room*; *retreat*; *Ruth*;

sanctuary; *sanctum sanctorum*; *smokehouse*; *statehouse*; *stool*;

temple; *throne* (and *throne room*); 60

utensil;

walk; *washroom*; *waste-management compartment*; WC; *what-you-may-call-'em*; and *Widow Jones*.

1981

QUESTIONS

Reader and Purpose

1. The complete title of the book from which this definition of *toilet* is taken is *A Dictionary of Euphemisms & Other Doubletalk: Being A Compilation of Linguistic Fig Leaves and Verbal Flourishes for Artful Users of the English Language*. This title is an imitation of the long titles that were popular in books published in the eighteenth century and earlier. What, specifically, does the title mean? How would you describe its **tone**? How is this tone reflected in the definition of *toilet*?

2. Since this selection is taken from a dictionary, and the purpose of a dictionary is, presumably, to provide clear definitions, do you find the definition of *toilet* satisfying? If not, does this dictionary have some other purpose?

3. In the introduction to his book the author explains **euphemisms** as follows:

> Mr Milquetoast gets up from the table, explaining that he has to go the *little boys' room* or *see a man about a dog*; a young woman announces that she is *enceinte*. A secretary complains that her boss is a pain in the *derriere*; an undertaker (or *mortician*) asks delicately where to ship the *loved one*. These are euphemisms—mild, agreeable, or round-about words used in place of coarse, painful, or offensive ones. . . . Many euphemisms are so delightfully ridiculous that everyone laughs at them.

What method of definition is the author using here?

Organization

4. Can this explanation of one word be considered an essay? To answer this question you might want to consider such questions as these: is a topic clearly presented? is there any kind of development or exploration of a topic? is there some sort of result, or conclusion, about the topic?
5. What is the progression, in space and time, of the second paragraph?
6. 'And so it goes' appears near the end of paragraph 2. Why do you think the author placed it where he did rather than at the end of the paragraph? Would it be more effective as the paragraph's conclusion?

Sentences

7. In the first sentence would it be more effective to place 'only' after 'can'? Why, or why not?
8. In paragraph 2 how is the fourth sentence a consequence ('thus') of the previous three sentences?
9. Why has the author used commas in the sixth sentence of paragraph 2? Would omitting them cause confusion for the reader?

Diction

10. Look up: *euphemistic* (1), *diminutive* (5), *innovation* (13), *Pidgin* (22), *taboo* (25), *Rabelaisian* (28), *exonerate* (31).
11. Near the end of paragraph 2 the author mentions 'the English WC', but he doesn't explain what this means, and 'WC' is mentioned once again at the very end of this selection. Why does the author not explain? Is he guilty of an oversight? or does he expect his reader to know this?
12. Near the end of paragraph 2 the author refers to 'similar hang-ups'. Is the word 'hang-ups' appropriate for its context? Or is it slang, and thus not appropriate? Can you suggest another word that might be more appropriate?

POINTS TO LEARN

1. The kind of definition found in a dictionary is not the only way to define a word.
2. Looking at how a word has been used at different times and in different regions can be most useful in establishing the word's meaning for us now.

SUGGESTIONS FOR WRITING

Choose a word that has always interested you, or one that has caused you problems for a long time, and in an essay of 3–5 paragraphs, give an extended definition of this word. Make it clear whether the definition you are providing is consensual, normative, or stipulative. You might provide the word's **etymology**, if it helps to explain the word's present meaning; or, by using the *Oxford English Dictionary*, you might show how the various meanings attributed to the word over the centuries have led to its present meaning.

IMPROVING YOUR STYLE

Adopt a definite tone for your essay—sarcastic, or humorous, or serious, or playful, etc.

E.M. FORSTER

E.M. Forster (1879–1970) was a distinguished English novelist, short-story writer, and essayist. His best-known novels include *Where Angels Fear To Tread* (1905), *A Room with a View* (1908), *Howard's End* (1910), and *A Passage to India* (1924). These novels have all recently been the subjects of excellent and widely acclaimed movies. The selection below comes from *Aspects of the Novel*, the printed version of a series of lectures that Forster delivered at Cambridge University in 1927. This little book, which is still in print, has often been derided by literary critics, but it is still frequently referred to by those interested in the structure of fiction.

Plot

1   Let us define a plot. We have defined a story as a narrative of events arranged in their time-sequence. A plot is also a narrative of events, the emphasis falling on causality. 'The king died and then the queen died,' is a story. 'The king died, and then the queen died of grief,' is a plot. The time-sequence is preserved, but the sense of causality overshadows it. Or again: 'The queen died, no one knew why, 5 until it was discovered that it was through grief at the death of the king.' This is a plot with a mystery in it, a form capable of high development. It suspends the time-sequence, it moves as far away from the story as its limitations will allow. Consider the death of the queen. If it is in a story we say 'and then?' If it is in a plot we ask 'why?' That is the fundamental difference between these two aspects of the novel. A 10 plot cannot be told to a gaping audience of cave men or to a tyrannical sultan or to their modern descendant the movie-public. They can only be kept awake by 'and then—and then'. They can only supply curiosity. But a plot demands intelligence and memory also.

2   Curiosity is one of the lowest of the human faculties. You will have noticed in 15 daily life that when people are inquisitive they nearly always have bad memories and are usually stupid at bottom. The man who begins by asking you how many brothers and sisters you have, is never a sympathetic character, and if you meet him in a

year's time he will probably ask you how many brothers and sisters you have, his mouth again sagging open, his eyes still bulging from his head. It is difficult to be 20 friends with such a man, and for two inquisitive people to be friends must be impossible. Curiosity by itself takes us a very little way, nor does it take us far into the novel—only as far as the story. If we would grasp the plot we must add intelligence and memory.

3   Intelligence first. The intelligent novel-reader, unlike the inquisitive one who 25 just runs his eye over a new fact, mentally picks it up. He sees it from two points of view; isolated, and related to the other facts that he has read on previous pages. Probably he does not understand it, but he does not expect to do so yet awhile. The facts in a highly organized novel (like *The Egoist*) are often of the nature of cross-correspondences and the ideal spectator cannot expect to view them properly until he 30 is sitting up on a hill at the end. This element of surprise or mystery—the detective element as it is sometimes rather emptily called—is of great importance in a plot. It occurs through a suspension of the time-sequence; a mystery is a pocket in time, and it occurs crudely, as in 'Why did the queen die?' and more subtly in half-explained gestures and words, the true meaning of which only dawns pages ahead. Mystery is 35 essential to a plot, and cannot be appreciated without intelligence. To the curious it is just another 'and then—' To appreciate a mystery, part of the mind must be left behind, brooding, while the other part goes marching on.

4   That brings us to our second qualification: memory.

5   Memory and intelligence are closely connected, for unless we remember we 40 cannot understand. If by the time the queen dies we have forgotten the existence of the king we shall never make out what killed her. The plot-maker expects us to remember, we expect him to leave no loose ends. Every action or word ought to count; it ought to be economical and spare; even when complicated it should be organic and free from dead matter. It may be difficult or easy, it may and should con- 45 tain mysteries, but it ought not to mislead. And over it, as it unfolds, will hover the memory of the reader (that dull glow of the mind of which intelligence is the bright advancing edge) and will constantly rearrange and reconsider, seeing new clues, new chains of cause and effect, and the final sense (if the plot has been a fine one) will not be of clues or chains, but of something aesthetically compact, something which might 50 have been shown by the novelist straight away, only if he had shown it straight away it would never have become beautiful. We come up against beauty here—for the first time in our enquiry: beauty at which a novelist should never aim, though he fails if he does not achieve it. I will conduct beauty to her proper place later on. Meanwhile please accept her as part of a completed plot. She looks a little surprised at being 55 there, but beauty ought to look a little surprised: it is the emotion that best suits her face, as Botticelli knew when he painted her risen from the waves, between the winds and the flowers. The beauty who does not look surprised, who accepts her position as her due—she reminds us too much of a prima donna.

1927

QUESTIONS

Reader and Purpose

1. Does Forster assume that his readers know a great many novels and short stories or that they have read very little fiction? Is his purpose anything more than to make them understand clearly what *plot* means?

Organization

2. What is the genus of *plot*? Name several other things that belong to the same family. What characteristics of *plot* differentiate it from them? Does Forster differentiate *plot* explicitly or implicitly?
3. How do the last two sentences of the first paragraph organize the rest of the selection?
4. In Forster's sense, *plot* signifies a quality **abstracted** from narrative literature. Curiosity, intelligence, and memory, however, belong to the reader of the story rather than to any quality of the story itself. Can they be, then, part of a definition of *plot*? To put this another way, are these mental qualities essential to Forster's definition, or are they accidental attributes of *plot*? Can you add to Forster's third sentence so that curiosity, intelligence, and memory become part of his formal definition: 'A plot is . . . a narrative of events, the emphasis falling upon causality, which . . .'?
5. Why in line 39 does the writer set off his short sentence as a new paragraph?
6. Describe the writer's **point of view**.

Sentence

7. In his introductory note Forster says of the lectures he delivered at Cambridge that 'they were informal, indeed talkative in their **tone**, and it seemed safer when presenting them in book form not to mitigate the talk, in case nothing should be left at all. Words such as "I", "you", "one", "we", "curiously enough", "so to speak", and "of course", will consequently occur on every page.' The fact that he was talking has also influenced Forster's sentence structure. How?
8. Why does the writer begin by saying, 'Let us define a plot'? Is that beginning more effective for his purpose than this opening: 'If a story is a narrative of events arranged in their time-sequence, a plot is also a narrative of events, the emphasis falling on causality'? Forster's sentences are relatively short and their effect is one of simplicity. Yet they are not monotonous or flat. How does he vary his sentence structure?

Diction

9. Look up: *faculties* (15), *cross-correspondence* (29–30), *organic* (45), *Botticelli* (57), *prima donna* (59).
10. In the middle of paragraph 3 the author refers to 'the detective element as it is sometimes rather emptily called'. What does he mean by 'emptily'? Can you suggest a more effective word?

POINTS TO LEARN

1. Good definitions give several concrete examples of the thing defined.
2. A writer may define something by contrasting it with something similar, something with which it may be confused.

3. A writer may define a thing by telling what it is not.
4. In defining, a writer may list the essential qualities or characteristics of a thing.
5. Writing intended to be read aloud must use short, emphatic transition sentences and relatively simple constructions.

SUGGESTIONS FOR WRITING

Prepare a definition to be read aloud. First, write down a number of things that one might define for an audience of students. Then, choose one of these, or define one of the following: tragedy, surrealism, culture (as used by the sociologist or anthropologist), the stock market, outer space. Your purpose should be to inform without being dull or losing the attention of your audience. Pay careful attention to your sentence structure, keeping in mind that you will be reading aloud.

IMPROVING YOUR STYLE

Your style should be that of someone talking, talking to a friendly and sophisticated audience. Avoid jargon and street slang but work for a relaxed, informal tone. Remember that a personality is inevitably revealed in your language and that your audience will respond to that personality. Seek therefore to be pleasing. Strive for modesty without appearing hesitant or wishy-washy, for confidence without seeming overbearing, for originality in idea and diction without sounding idiosyncratic. Use 'I' and 'me', and by an occasional judicious 'we' or 'us' suggest an identification between yourself and your listeners.

RODERICK HAIG-BROWN

Roderick Haig-Brown (1908–76) was born and educated in England. He emigrated to the state of Washington and then, in 1928, moved to British Columbia, where he worked as a logger, trapper, guide, and fisherman. Eventually he settled at Campbell River, on Vancouver Island, where he was appointed a local magistrate and later a provincial court judge. Haig-Brown wrote extensively on the outdoors, especially on fishing, his seven books on this subject earning him the reputation of one of the best writers in North America on the topic. He also wrote several novels and children's books set in a sensitively described natural world; *Saltwater Summer* (1948) won a Governor General's Award. His comments on conservation are those of a man who spent much of his life involved with the outdoors and thought deeply about nature.

Conservation Defined

1   An easy definition of the word conservation is 'proper use of natural resources'. But this still leaves a difficult and wide-open question: What is 'proper use'?

2   This is as it should be because conservation is a dynamic, not a static, conception. It does not mean simply hanging on to things, like a miser to his gold. It means putting them to use, seeking a valuable return from them and at the same   5

time ensuring future yields of at least equal value. It means having enough faith in the future to respect the future and the needs of future people; it means accepting moral and practical restraints that limit immediate self-interest; it means finding a measure of wisdom and understanding of natural things that few peoples have attained; ultimately, though we no longer see it in this way, it is a religious concept— 10 the most universal and fundamental of all such concepts, the worship of fertility to which man has dedicated himself in every civilization since his race began. We may well believe now that an intellectual and scientific approach is more likely to succeed than a mystical one. But without moral concepts and without a sense of responsibility for the future of the human race, the idea of conservation could have little mean- 15 ing. Since it deals for the future as well as for the present, it must always be as much an act of faith as an intellectual exercise.

3   The basic resources of any country are soil and water and, largely depending on these, climate. All three can be damaged by misuse, utterly destroyed by persistent mis- use—and when they are so destroyed the civilizations that grew upon them, however 20 great and powerful, are utterly destroyed with them. The Sahara Desert, the arid lands of the eastern Mediterranean, and the Euphrates Valley all supported civilizations that were supreme in their time, wise in their time, and secure in their time. But the wisdom of the time was not enough; the water failed, the soil eroded and blew away, and desert sands blew in to bury the wonderful cities whose wealth the land had once supported. 25

4   Soil and water and climate are the permanent resources; together they make habitat, the set of conditions that favours the growth of timber, wildlife, fish, cattle, and farm crops. Used within proper limits they are renewable and perpetual resources. Used without regard for those limits they deteriorate steadily and may quickly pass beyond the stage where the knowledge and effort of man can restore them.   30

1961

QUESTIONS

Reader and Purpose

1. Haig-Brown begins by asserting that the kind of definition of *conservation* we might find in a dictionary is inadequate. He is making, indirectly, an important point: that we define the meaning of a word by using other words, and that these other words may require their own definition and explanation. In this selection Haig-Brown explains the defining terms *proper use* and *natural resources*. Why does he begin with *proper use*? What does this way of beginning reveal about his purpose in this essay?

2. How would you describe the **tone** of this selection? How does it differ from the tone of a dictionary definition?

Organization

3. The author's opening paragraph is very short. What kind of effect does Haig-Brown achieve here? What would be lost if the paragraph were omitted?

4. A dictionary entry gives us information about the meaning of a word and also about its spelling, **etymology**, grammatical functions, pronunciation, and range of use. Consider the detailed way in which the concept of *conservation* is treated in

paragraph 2. Do the last two sentences of the paragraph help you to see why Haig-Brown is 'defining' the term in other than a dictionary fashion? Why does he make repeated use in this paragraph of words such as *faith, wisdom, religious, moral,* and *responsibility*? What **connotations** do these words give to the term *conservation*?

5. Haig-Brown does not use **transitional** sentences between paragraphs 2 and 3, or between paragraphs 3 and 4. What other devices does he use to link these paragraphs? Try rearranging the paragraphs in a different order (1–3–4–2, for example) as a way of seeing why the selection is organized as it is.

6. The author stresses *time* (past and future) in paragraphs 2 and 3. How does the opening sentence of paragraph 2 serve to introduce this subject? Does this subject also appear in the concluding paragraph?

Sentences

7. Haig-Brown begins his second paragraph by stating briefly what *conservation* does not mean. He then moves from negative to positive statements, emphasizing the change of direction by contrasting the words 'it means' with 'it does not mean'. What effect is produced by the repetition of 'it means'? Why does he end his statement in the third sentence with a period instead of joining it to the next sentence with a semicolon, as he joins the clauses in sentence 4?

8. Notice that the statements introduced by the repetition of 'it means' in sentences 3 and 4 of paragraph 2 are deliberately arranged in ascending order of importance. This is particularly effective in a long sentence, such as sentence 4, because it emphasizes for the reader the logical development of the author's ideas. Try rearranging the order of Haig-Brown's statements to see how their effect would be weakened.

9. The author introduces the final clause of sentence 4 in paragraph 2 with a **conjunctive adverb** (*ultimately*). What does this signal to the reader? Why does he use a dash near the end of this sentence? Would a colon have been more, or less, effective?

10. Repetition of key words is also a feature of paragraph 3. How would the rhythms of Haig-Brown's sentences be weakened if we were to use synonyms for *destroyed* (20) and for *time* (24)?

11. Explain the difference in tone between the sentences of paragraph 4 and those of paragraphs 2 and 3. How does this change in tone affect the conclusion of this selection? Although Haig-Brown does not use the word, is he offering us a definition of *conservation* in this final paragraph? How have paragraphs 2 and 3 served to prepare us to understand not only the meaning of the term but also its connotations? What additional force do they give to the three **straightforward** sentences of paragraph 4?

Diction

12. Look up: *dynamic* (3), *self-interest* (8), *fundamental* (11), *fertility* (11), *mystical* (14), *deteriorate* (29).

13. Why does Haig-Brown use *easy* (1) instead of *simple* or *elementary*? What connotations does *easy* have that the other two words lack?

14. Haig-Brown uses the word *proper* twice (1, 2). Look up the word and determine which of its meanings he is emphasizing.

POINTS TO LEARN

1. Definition may involve not only the denotative meaning of a word but also its moral connotations.
2. Words are defined by other words, and the reader should try to understand the meanings and implications of the words used in a definition.
3. Repetition of key words can be an effective way of organizing long sentences. Repetition can also produce effective sentence rhythms.
4. Statements within a paragraph can be arranged in ascending order of importance as one method of emphasizing the key point.

SUGGESTIONS FOR WRITING

Choose a word (such as *progress*, *socialism*, *welfare*, etc.) that has moral connotations for most people and compose a definition essay. Begin with a dictionary definition and then write two paragraphs in which you explain in more detail the implications of the word. Conclude with a short paragraph defining your chosen word in light of these implications.

IMPROVING YOUR STYLE

Include the following in your essay:

1. a sentence in which the final phrase or clause is set off by a dash for emphasis;
2. a long sentence in which you begin several statements with a repeated word or phrase and join the statements with semicolons. Introduce your final statement, for purposes of summing up, with a conjunctive adverb;
3. a sentence or two in which you try to achieve a pronounced rhythm by repeating a key word.

ALLAN ANDERSON

Allan Anderson (1915–94) grew up in Calgary and later worked there as a broadcaster for the CBC. His interest in oral history—that is, history as recorded from the mouths of those who experienced it—has resulted in several books, including *Remembering the Farm: Memories of Farming, Ranching, and Rural Life in Canada, Past and Present* (1977), *Salt Water, Fresh Water* (1979), and *Remembering Leacock: An Oral History* (1983). 'Scouts' is taken from *Roughnecks and Wildcatters: . . . An Informal History of 'The Oil Patch'* (1981).

Scouts

1   Of all the many, varied, entertaining, or incredible stories told me by oilmen, in particular the old-timers, the ones that appealed to me as much as any were those about scouts. Scouts were simply company spies whose job it was to find out, in any devious or devilish or straightforward way they could, whether or not a rival company had stuck oil. There was a lot more to it than that, but that was what the game was all about. 5

2   The idea was very simple. If there was oil in that location, then the company for which the scout worked could be saved all the trouble and expense of drilling a well itself. If the scout could come up with evidence the other company had struck oil, then all that company had to do was lease land around the producing well, and as fast as possible.   10

3   When a well was declared 'a tight hole', it meant that the company drilling it was trying to bottle up all information about what was going on. Any number of scouts from other companies would arrive in the countryside around the well and use all the considerable ingenuity they possessed to ferret out what was really going on.

4   The obvious way was to buy beers for roughnecks from the well in a local   15 beer parlour and pump them. Or scouts could fly over the well in helicopters. Or they could train high-powered binoculars on the well. They might even walk right up to the rig and claim they were working for a service company. Any tricks that would work.

5   Scouts had an astounding zeal for their work. They would all but freeze to   20 death in the bush scouting a well. They'd get lost. Their cars would break down on remote roads. They'd be chased by roughnecks from the rig under scrutiny. In the great days of scouting in the fifties and sixties, they lived on modest expense accounts and would get 'Brownie points' from their companies if they came up with really valu- able information. That meant they'd get a pat on the back and their salary at the end 25 of the month and that was that. The company might make millions out of the infor- mation dug out by a scout.

6   Scouts had to be dedicated, they had to take pride in their work, and they had to be fiercely and frantically competitive. One can only applaud their zeal, while being astounded by the stunts they pulled to achieve their goal.   30

7   There are still commercial scouts who go out and spy on wells, but there's also a Canadian Oil Scouts Association. Members of the Association trade information each week at a 'scout check', which is certainly a far cry from the old, individualistic days. A well can be treated as a tight hole for a year. Scout checks undoubtedly ferret out a certain amount of information valuable to company geologists and computers, 35 but it seems to me it's about as interesting as a movie press conference.

1981

QUESTIONS

Reader and Purpose

1. In the terms used in the introductory comments to the *Definition* section of this book, Anderson's essay is a *real definition*; its method is *exemplification*. Explain both points, referring to specific examples from the essay.
2. Setting aside your desire to know more about this subject (if, indeed, you do), does Anderson's definition satisfy you?
3. Obviously the author has some interest in his topic, since he has devoted a whole chapter of his book to it. But within the essay itself is there any evidence to show that he is interested? very interested? enthusiastic?

Organization

4. How does paragraph 1 serve as introduction to the six paragraphs that follow it?
5. How does the first sentence of paragraph 2 serve as transition?
6. Note how paragraph 4 is organized: the transitional phrase 'the obvious way' refers to the scouts as they tried 'to ferret out what was really going on'. This transition is followed by four methods the scouts used: buying beer for roughnecks, flying over the well, using binoculars, and simply walking in to the rig. The last sentence functions as both summary ('any trick') and conclusion. Analyze paragraph 5 in this same manner.
7. In paragraph 7 Anderson changes topic slightly, from scouts as extraordinary individuals to scouts as members of an association, and he ends his essay with a somewhat sarcastic comment on 'scout checks'. How does this last paragraph affect the meaning of the whole? How does it cast light on his perception of individual scouts? Since the book from which this essay is taken is a history of oil-field workers, does his conclusion seem appropriate?

Sentences

8. There are two series of **parallel** adjectives in paragraph 1. Identify them and explain the nature of the parallelism. Where else does Anderson use parallel structure, either within sentences or among them?
9. This essay is quite simple and straightforward. Is this the result of Anderson's sentence structure, or is there some other reason? In order to answer this question, analyze the sentences of any two consecutive paragraphs. Are Anderson's sentences mainly **simple**? **compound**? **complex**?
10. Where in this essay does the author use **fragments**? Are they effective? or should he have used complete sentences?

Diction

11. Look up: *devious* (3), *lease* (9), *ferret* (14), *roughneck* (15), *zeal* (20), *scrutiny* (22), *individualistic* (33).
12. Why does the author use quotation marks around the phrase *Brownie points* (24)? Could they just as well have been omitted? Would usage be the same for the expression *a tight hole* (11)?
13. Look up **colloquialism** in the Glossary. Is *stunts* in paragraph 6 such a word? Are there others?
14. Should the clause 'the ones that appealed to me as much as any' (2) be rewritten 'the ones that appealed to me as much as any others'? Why, or why not?

POINTS TO LEARN

1. Examples can be extremely useful in helping to define.
2. The difficult task of expressing the complex in a simple manner can be aided by carefully choosing both diction and sentence structure.

SUGGESTIONS FOR WRITING

Any kind of employment, whether it's delivering newspapers, bagging groceries in a supermarket, or serving up fries in a fast-food restaurant, involves aspects that are

known only to those who have held this kind of job. Describe some task you are familiar with for an audience that could not be expected to know it. Don't go into much detail;
rather, treat the main points, and restrict you essay to just 6 or 7 fairly short paragraphs.

IMPROVING YOUR STYLE

In your essay pay special attention to these two points:

1. brief but precise transitions between paragraphs;
2. parallel series of adjectives; include at least two.

HENRY FAIRLIE

Henry Fairlie (1924–90) was a British journalist who wrote extensively on American politics. His books include *The Life of Politics* (1968), *The Kennedy Promise: The Politics
of Expectation* (1973), and *The Parties: Republicans and Democrats in This Century*
(1978). He also wrote a series of essays for *The New Republic* on the seven deadly sins
(pride, anger, lust, envy, greed, gluttony, and sloth). The essay below is from his book *The
Seven Deadly Sins Today* (1978).

The Fact of Sin

1   Even in a secular age, we need to keep the idea of sin. We are not exempt from
the Seven Deadly Sins simply because we do not understand that the wilful violation of
our humanity is no less a wilful violation of our life in God; and even the most irreligious amongst us can have some idea of what that concept means. When a theologian
says that 'in each of the sins, a man acts in such a way as to make his relationship to God 5
precarious, frightened, suspicion-laden, deceitful,' it is not impossible for the irreligious
to understand what he is saying; as they can also understand when he adds that 'sin is
what a man is compelled to confess to God because his action has placed him in a crisis before God.' Certainly if one has no inkling of what he is talking about, one will not
understand why sin is more than moral evil, and is commonly described as infidelity; 10
why it has been said that sin is less like the act of a criminal than the act of a traitor.
2   Sin is the destruction of one's self as well as the destruction of one's relationship
with others. But the terribleness of the self-destruction cannot be grasped unless we
realize that the damage is done precisely where each of our natures is organized by
some unifying principle that is more than their parts: where there is something 15
unknowable in us, which we nevertheless know to be most completely ourselves, and
with which we have in fact to form our own relationship.

> Below the surface stream, shallow and light,
> Of what we say we feel—below the stream,
> As light, of what we think we feel, there flows   20
> With noiseless current, strong, obscure and deep,
> The central stream of what we feel indeed.

This is where sin causes its devastation in us, at the very core of our beings, where life's flow is this noiseless, strong, deep, obscure current in us; and if to talk of God helps to reinforce our awareness of how severe is the violation, then even the un- 25
believing may sometimes use His name without taking it in vain.

——

3   Nevertheless, these essays are addressed to a secular age, by someone who can perhaps best describe himself as a reluctant unbeliever. Sin is 'whatever I do that mars, mauls, inflates, depresses, distorts, or abandons' our humanity, and through us it therefore does all these things to our societies. A book was published recently with 30
the title *Sinful Social Structures*, and we need sometimes to think of our societies as sinning. The toleration of avoidable poverty is sinful. It is the sin of Avarice. The glut of foods and goods that we consume is sinful. It is the sin of Gluttony. The exploitation of sex is sinful. It is the sin of Lust. These are partly our own sinning—we are avaricious, we are gluttonous, we are lustful—but not entirely so. A society is not 35
only the individuals who compose it. It has its own life, in its laws and institutions, its customs and values, and through them it is able to impose on us. It can incite us to do what we ought not to do, and lull us into not doing what we ought to do. We may be ultimately responsible as individuals, since we could change our societies if we wished. But that they are capable of sinning on their own, without our direct 40
approval or participation, is beyond any doubt. If we neglect the poor, it is not only because we are avaricious, not even only because those who manage the economy may be particularly avaricious, but because the economic system is itself founded on Avarice.

4   The relationship of the individual to his society is at the core of these essays. It 45
has seldom been less harmonious than now. The individual should find an inner personal satisfaction in the performance of his social responsibilities. But he hardly finds it today. The individual uses his society, society uses the individual: that is today the breadth and depth of the relationship. It is a mutual bargain, not a joint enterprise; and even in the bargain, there is little trust. It is hard to think of a time in Western 50
civilization when the individual has been so subject to society, yet felt so little attached to it; or when society has been forced to govern so much, but with so little moral authority to govern at all. The dislocation is so severe that it should tell us that we do not face only a few social problems, which we may meet with yet more feats of social engineering, but are confronted by the results of our refusal to contemplate the fact 55
of evil with any intelligent strenuousness.

5   It is characteristic of our age that people want to have God, but do not want to have the Devil. People are inventing gods for themselves, with what I have elsewhere called their Do-It-Yourself God Kits. But they are gods who will not demand much of them, and who certainly do not punish. On the contrary, their gods absolve them 60
from conflict and doubt, massage them, pat them on the head and, rather like their parents, tell them to run along, get stoned, and pick daisies. But above all they are gods who will not trouble them with the fact of evil. The problems of evil, suffering, and death are not confronted, but evaded and dismissed. The recipes are too easy. Twenty minutes of transcendental meditation or Zen tennis and the thing is done: one 65
is again made whole, at peace with the world, and so with oneself.

6   Unfortunately the Devil is cleverer than any guru. If God moves in a mysterious way His wonders to perform, the Devil moves in ingenious ones to accomplish his victories. He is rather like the hotel burglar, who goes down the corridors, trying all the doors, until he finds one that is unlocked. 'Resist the Devil', says the New   70
Testament, 'and he will flee from you.' Perhaps he will. But it is not easy to lock him out; he has too many pass keys. 'The Devil is a gentleman,' said Shelley, and the irony is double. For if Shelley was most interested in making a comment about gentlemen, it is no less true that the Devil often has the most civil manners, and comes with impeccable letters of introduction. He was himself, after all, rather well-born; and like   75
the younger son of a good family who has fallen on bad times, he is very adept at insinuating himself into the best of company. 'The Devil's cleverest wile is to convince us that he does not exist,' said Baudelaire. This is not as difficult for him as it might seem, since he is inside us already, and we do not care to look there to find him.

7   We can recognize evil in others, but if we wish to look on the face of sin, we will   80
see it most clearly in ourselves. It cannot always be recognized or measured by its visible consequences. The face of Dorian Gray did not change where it could be seen; it changed only in the portrait in the attic of which only he knew. Sin is our secret from others. Only we know where, and how deeply, it has taken root in us. Although we are all sinful, every discussion of it must proceed outward from ourselves. It is only our   85
awareness of its presence in us that makes us then aware of how universally it is present. We learn more from St Augustine about the nature of sin in his *Confessions* than in all the volumes of the *City of God*. The essays that follow are not confessions, but they are written in the belief that we are, in ourselves and in our societies, trifling with the fact that sin exists, and that we are blind to its destructiveness.   90

8   If we acknowledge the existence of sin at all, we must acknowledge that there is original sin. But the idea of original sin is so abused, when it is secularized, that we need to be clear about it. Nothing is more searching in Augustine's many interpretations of the Fall than his insistence that 'our first parents' were already wicked in themselves before they succumbed to the actual temptation, otherwise 'the Devil   95
would not have begun by an open and obvious sin to tempt man into doing something which God had forbidden.' Man had 'already begun to seek satisfaction in himself and, consequently, to take pleasure in the words, "You shall be as Gods"'. We have already said something of the same in secular terms: that the evil we do, and the consequences of it we can see, are not in themselves our sinning, but have been preceded   100
by it. Our sin is that we are in the frame of mind to listen to the Devil, before we do what the Devil asks of us.

9   The notion that every baby is born sinful is too simple. The result of the Fall was our loss of sanctifying grace, and this deprivation has left mankind with the inclination to sin. It is a tendency to sinfulness that is inherent in man; and these words—   105
inclination and tendency—are crucial. They help to demystify the idea of original sin, when its secularizers seem bent on mystifying it. Baptism remits original sin, but it leaves us still subject to physical and human disabilities, and our free will remains. We may still choose a righteous course or a sinful one. 'No one sins because God foreknew he would sin,' says Augustine, 'No one sins unless it is his choice to sin; and   110
his choice not to sin, that also God foresaw.' His foreknowledge leaves us still free agents. We sin necessarily but willingly.

10   When it is secularized and applied to our relationships with our societies, the idea of original sin is most often used by conservatives. Since we are inherently so wicked, they say, we cannot be trusted with the freedom, and with much else, that we 115 demand so imperiously. This has from the beginning, is now, and ever shall be, the political theology of the *National Review*, and of course of other conservatives. But thus to secularize the idea of original sin, by removing from it the remittance by baptism, by diminishing the concept of our free will, by failing to emphasize that it is of an inclination to sinfulness that is inherent in our natures: this is to make the 120 relationship of man with his God, and man with his neighbours, not merely contemptible but meaningless. We said at the beginning that sin is wilful. It is always our choice. But the conservative's interpretation of original sin is that man is so inherently doomed to do evil that there is very little society can do but truss him up. The idea that society is a partnership of its members, which will not confine them so much as 125 free them to choose rightly, is one that he is reluctant to entertain. There has to be only one backsliding, and he wags his finger and says, 'There is the old Adam in man.'

---

11   The Seven Deadly Sins—Pride, Avarice, Lust, Anger, Gluttony, Envy, Sloth—are also called capital vices. They are *capital*, because they will inevitably lead to other sins. They are *deadly*, because they will easily lead to mortal sin. They are *vices*, 130 because they are not distinct acts but habits: passions or appetites. They are therefore a continual deflection from the order of right reason, and an offence against our dignity as human beings, since 'man's fundamental duty is to act in accordance with his rational nature.' As we will see in our examination of each of them, we lose control of ourselves to them. We put ourselves into slavery to them, into what Spinoza calls 135 bondage: 'for, when a man is prey to his emotions, he is not his own master, but lies at the mercy of fortune.' This is one reason why we talk of the stain of sin, because it is not something that touches us here and there, now and then, moving us to evil acts, but informs our whole natures. We lose possession of ourselves.

12   The abandonment of our rational nature makes us take things which are good 140 and worthy in themselves, lift them out of their place, and magnify their importance, both to ourselves and in the whole scheme of things; and this lack of proportion may be found in the excessive significance that we give to some created and finite good. This is true today of the attention we give to sex, which is a form of lust; of our excessive desire for material things, which is a form of Avarice; of our obsession with what 145 we eat and drink and the drugs we take, which is a form of Gluttony; of the clamour for personal rights that are not rights at all, which is a form of Anger; and we will come to the rest, and to the several forms that each of them now takes. In resisting them, we seem today to have very few devices with which to restore our perspective.

13   'The sense of humour is the just balance of all the faculties of man, the best 150 security against the pride of knowledge and the conceits of the imagination, the strongest inducement to submit with a wise and pious patience to the vicissitudes of human existence.' So said Monckton Milnes in his *Memoir of Thomas Hood*, and it is not a trivial text to set at the beginning. If a sense of humour is a defence against the sin of pride, it is no less a defence against all the sins. The one thing that the Devil 155 does not like is to be laughed at. The one sound that we never hear in *Paradise Lost* is the sound of laughter, and we cannot put all the blame on Milton, even though he was not the English poet most frequently given to merriment. What being can be less given to laughter than a fallen angel? One cannot draw laughter into the faces of any of the Seven Deadly Sins. But what is relevant to us here is that, above all, a sense of humour is a sense of proportion.

14   There is something mirthless about our age, and it is partly because we will not acknowledge the fact of sin. Endlessly we scrape over our faults and weaknesses, which we ought to be able to take in good part, in others and in ourselves, because we will not acknowledge that the real danger lies elsewhere and deeper. We give game, set, and match to the Devil, when he has won only an advantage. He finds a chink in our armour, where we have been found weak or at fault, and when he cries, 'Aha! You are already lost,' we open ourselves to his much greater depredations. This is why Kafka is right when he says: 'One of the Devil's most effective tricks to waylay us is to pick a fight with us. It is like a fight with a woman which ends in bed.' He makes us quarrelsome, and the quarrel only reinforces the sense of familiarity with him. He is full of innuendoes, that he knows us and knows what we are up to, until at last the fight seems pointless and wearying, and we decide that it is futile for us to carry it on or resist any longer.

15   In no other age can people have been so apparently frank and serious about their pecadilloes, so ready to confess them openly and publicly flagellate themselves for them, at cocktail parties and at the dinner table, only to use their wrongdoing as a justification for not resisting the total despoliation that sin will cause. If the greatest of the sins is Pride, this is one of the commonest forms of Pride in our time. Mirthlessly and to our self-satisfaction, we boast of our faults in order to concede to the sin. If we have erred in a moment of lust, humourlessly we confess it and, as if by a miracle of absolution, then progress to the sin of Lust, since we have proved that it is in our natures. There is in these essays an implicit criticism of psychiatry; of the excuses that it finds for us, and of the shallowness of the accommodations that it invites us to make. Its explanations are our substitutes for the idea of sin, and in nothing is this more obvious than in the mirthlessness with which it encourages us to be absorbed in our lesser disorders, our faults and our weaknesses, while it frees us from the dark night of the soul in which we must wrestle alone with our evil.

16   That the sins bring us in the end to solitude and to death is too well understood for these fearful consequences to be discussed in general: we will examine the forms that they take when we consider each of the sins as we may observe them today. Pride is always put first, since it is regarded as a universal vice, and the source and inspiration of the others. Avarice is usually put second, for reasons which we will see when we discuss it. For the rest, the order given above is the common one, although it is worth noticing that Gregory the Great, while still putting Pride first, then put Envy and Anger and Sloth, in that order, before Avarice and Gluttony and lastly Lust. It is because of its importance that I have chosen to discuss Pride at the end, as a kind of summation. I have also examined Envy and Anger before Avarice, not because I depose Avarice from its place, but because I think that its evil is best understood, in our age, if we have been forced first to consider sins that have less obvious satisfactions. These questions are important, because all of the Seven Deadly Sins inspire and incite to the others. They are intertwined. As the readers follow this exploration of them, it is hoped that they will at least acknowledge, even where he or she may disagree, that the insights that are gained into ourselves and our societies are not superficial.   205

1977

QUESTIONS

Reader and Purpose

1. The author defines *sin* in paragraph 2 and again in paragraph 3. What type of definition does he use? Does he favour one method of definition over any other?
2. What does the author mean when he describes sin as a 'fact'?
3. Since before the time of Christ sin has usually been discussed in relation to religion. Yet Fairlie describes himself in paragraph 3 as 'a reluctant unbeliever', and in the next paragraph he discusses 'the core of these essays' (i.e. the essays, of which this is the first, that make up his book) not in terms of religious belief but in terms of 'the relationship of the individual to his society'. On the other hand, however, in paragraph 1 he discusses 'our life in God' and man's 'relationship to God'. Is this a contradiction? If not, how do you explain his position?

Organization

4. In paragraph 1 the author briefly discusses the universality, even for the irreligious, of the idea of sin; and in paragraph 2 he deals with the nature and effects of sin. What does he do in paragraph 3?
5. Paragraph 3 begins: 'Nevertheless, these essays are addressed to a secular age.' What contrast is the author making?
6. The author has divided his essay into three sections: paragraphs 1–2, 3–10, and 11–16. Summarize briefly (no more than 3 or 4 lines each) what he does in each section, and then give each section a title, using the form 'The Fact of . . .'

Sentences

7. The fourth sentence of paragraph 5 is constructed of an introductory **phrase**, a **main clause** that has three verbs, another phrase, and a final verb governing three infinitives. Analyze in this same manner the structure of the fourth sentence in paragraph 10 and of the second sentence of paragraph 12. How do these structures resemble each other? How do they differ?
8. Is the seventh sentence of paragraph 4 an example of **parallel structure**? or is it a **balanced** sentence?
9. Look closely at the third sentence of paragraph 10: is the parallel structure of this sentence correct? or should the sentence begin 'This has been from the beginning . . .'? Why does the author use this structure?

Diction

10. Look up: *secular* (1), *wilful* (2), *inkling* (9), *maul* (29), *glut* (32), *incite* (37), *lull* (38), *absolve* (60), *transcendental* (65), *impeccable* (75), *wile* (77), *sanctifying* (104), *remit* (107), *imperiously* (116), *vicissitudes* (152), *accommodation* (184).

11. Paragraph 6 begins with a comparison, and the rest of the paragraph is built on a series of **images**, including **metaphors** and comparisons. Draw up an outline of the paragraph, sentence by sentence, briefly describing each image.
12. Using italics for emphasis is a practice which is usually discouraged, since a skilful writer should be able to convey emphasis without them. There can be exceptions, however—situations where italics are the most effective means of conveying emphasis. Are the three examples near the beginning of paragraph 11 such exceptions? That is, are the italics here useful, or are they superfluous?

POINTS TO LEARN

1. The different sections of an essay can be indicated by several means, including larger-than-usual spacing, symbols, subtitles, numbers, and letters.
2. Although a sentence may be long and involved, the judicious use of parallel structure and balanced clauses can make it both clear and pleasant to read.

SUGGESTIONS FOR WRITING

Choose one of the Seven Deadly Sins that Fairlie mentions in paragraph 11 and write an extended definition of it in 3–5 paragraphs. Use whatever method of definition or combination of methods you wish. Keep in mind that your definition is to be a personal one, although you may wish, by way of contrast, to begin with a dictionary definition.

IMPROVING YOUR STYLE

1. Include at least one long sentence that uses parallelism.
2. Include another long sentence that is structured by means of balanced clauses or phrases.

WAYNE GRADY

In addition to his work as an editor (see p. 7), Wayne Grady has written articles that have appeared in a number of magazines, including the one here, from *Saturday Night*. In this humorous essay, which is not a serious attempt at definition, he looks at the way the metric and imperial systems of measurement are used in this country and proposes a new name for this 'uniquely Canadian' hybrid.

The Metric System (Sort Of)

1   Canada was declared a metric nation in 1971, and after 2.8 decades, it's safe to say that we're as metric as we're going to get. At first the two systems, metric and imperial, battled it out—the metricists seized the road signs and thermostats, while the stubborn imperialists refused to buy anything that wasn't measured out according to some body part. You may recall extremists in Ottawa driving all the way to Carleton 5

Place, a distance of 63 kilometres, to fill up at a service station that still sold gasoline
in gallons. But that's all over now. Resistance and insistence proved equally futile.

2   Purists on both sides have lamented the resulting mishmash, failing to see that
what we have now is a system that's uniquely Canadian. By combining the more sensible features of the metric system, or SI (for Système Internationale d'Unités), with   10
some long-cherished aspects of the imperial system, we've come up with a seamless
hybrid that makes perfect sense to us all. Let's call it simperial. Like franglais and
'Progressive Conservative', simperial is the ideal Canadian compromise.

3   For example, the other day I asked directions to an auction sale: 'Drive 10 kilometres down this road', I was told, 'and you'll see a barn about two hundred feet in   15
from the highway.' That's simperial. Only in Canada can a river be half a mile wide and
30 metres deep. At building supply yards, you can buy 100 square metres of shingles
and a box of three-quarter inch roofing nails to hold them down. When I ask my
daughter, who is 14 and has been raised metric, how tall she is, she says 'Five four.'
What's the temperature outside? 'Plus three.' Simperial.   20

4   In our quiet, peacekeeping way, we took the best features from each extreme
and consigned the rest to oblivion. Simperial simply makes more sense than either of
its two feeder systems. Nobody's feet should be size forty-two anything. But at the
same time, zero degrees, not thirty-two, is obviously the temperature at which water
should freeze; if anyone knows that, it's us.   25

5   After the auction, I stopped at that gas station in Carleton Place. The pump reg-
isters gasoline by the litre now, of course, and when I went in to pay, the guy in the
booth pointed his chin at my car.

6   'How is she on gas?' he asked.

7   'I get 100 kilometres on six litres,' I said, quoting the manual; I had no idea   30
what it meant.

8   He nodded appreciatively. 'That's pretty good mileage.'

1999

QUESTIONS

Reader and Purpose

1. This short, humorous essay is obviously not a serious attempt at definition, yet it
   does make some valid and interesting points not only about systems of measurement but about one facet of being Canadian. What facet is that?

2. When the author says, near the end of paragraph 2, 'Let's call it simperial,' what
   kind of definition is he proposing? Which method, or methods, has he used to arrive
   at this definition?

3. In paragraph 4, when the author states that the Canadian hybrid, simperial, 'makes
   more sense than either of its two feeder systems', is he being completely serious,
   or is this statement merely part of the humorous **tone** of the whole essay?

Organization

4. Is the last sentence of paragraph 1 a fitting conclusion to the paragraph? Why, or
   why not? What about the last sentence of paragraph 2? of paragraph 3?

5. Does the author substantiate his assertion in the first sentence of paragraph 4? Is he exaggerating? Where else in the essay does the author make exaggerated or unsubstantiated claims?
6. How effective as a conclusion is the final paragraph? If you feel that the conclusion is not entirely effective, can you write a better one?

Sentences

7. Is the last sentence of paragraph 1 an example of **alliteration**? or **assonance**?
8. 'For example' is the very obvious **transition** between paragraphs 2 and 3. Is it too obvious to be effective?
9. In the second sentence of paragraph 5 should the expression 'of course' be placed at the beginning of the sentence? What difference would it make?

Diction

10. Look up: *imperial* (3), *extremist* (5), *purist* (8), *seamless* (11), *compromise* (13), *oblivion* (22).
11. *Simperial* is the word Grady uses for the Canadian hybrid of the metric and imperial systems. What other invented words might he have suggested?

POINTS TO LEARN

1. Exaggeration can, up to a point, serve the purposes of humour.
2. Defining a word, even in a tongue-in-cheek manner, requires balance and tact.

SUGGESTIONS FOR WRITING

Try your hand at coining a hybrid word of your own, based on common elements of your everyday life. For instance, you might consider that a coffee shop located in a bookstore could be called a *bookafé*, or a *coffook*; a doughnut shop in a large hardware store might be called a *doughware*, or a *hardough*; a classroom in a library could be called a *clary*; a magazine counter in an office building might be called a *magice*; etc.

The point of your essay should be to justify your new definition by explaining the process that led you to it. Humour will probably play a part in your approach, as will exaggeration, but you will have to balance the two carefully.

IMPROVING YOUR STYLE

1. End one of your paragraphs with the new word you have coined.
2. Write at least one short sentence that emphasizes alliteration or assonance.

PERSUASION

Thus far we have been concerned with problems of explaining and defining. Often, however, a writer desires to change his readers' beliefs or opinions, to persuade them to share his own values or conclusions. Of course, a clear-cut line is not easily drawn between exposition and persuasion. One, in fact, may imply the other. If you wish to convince someone that you are right about a controversial issue, you probably will have to define terms and explain facts and ideas—to engage, that is, in exposition. On the other hand, exposition—especially if it is effectively organized and expressed—is likely to have persuasive force, even though its writer had no persuasive intention. But however difficult it is to lay down in practice, there is a difference between writing to explain and writing to persuade.

It is also important to understand how persuasion differs from argument. Persuasion appeals to our emotions, to our feelings; argument, on the other hand, appeals mainly to our reason (as we will see later). Most often we use persuasion to convince someone about the wisdom of something or of a course of action—the attempt to persuade is most often meant to arouse to some action. Constructive criticism, for example, is a type of persuasion meant to bring about change. Because criticism is threatening, however, it must be made less threatening by praise, by ensuring that the criticism is not of people but of ideas or actions. Another type of persuasion is the kind we find in advertising, where comparisons are common, as in Pepsi/Coke commercials, or in soap commercials in which Brand X is compared to The Soap, with the latter, of course, being by far the better. Even though advertisers know that one ad is not likely to sway potential customers, they also know that the incessant repetition of their ad will eventually persuade some customers to switch to, or at least to try, their product.

Other kinds of persuasion have nothing to do with language: the curvaceous model leaning on the hood of a car or on the back of a pick-up truck, the famous athlete grinning at the camera as he eats his breakfast cereal, the model applying her 'favourite' brand of face cream, the finicky cat rushing to a bowl full of 'the only food he will eat'—all these are visual attempts to persuade, to convince.

One of the most useful of all types of persuasion is that used when the writer is dealing with someone who may feel threatened by the attempt to convince him. The key to Rogerian persuasion is empathy. In the attempt to persuade this person of his views, the writer's first step is to show that he is fair by agreeing that his opponent (i.e. the person he is trying to persuade) has some right on his side. The writer shows that, in some contexts, his opponent's position is right. He does this in a conciliatory way; he is trying to eliminate conflict from the situation, he is seeking to identify with rather than to confront his opponent. The next step is to present his case and try to get his opponent to look at the problem from a different perspective, all the while showing empathy with his opponent's position and being sympathetic to his stance. The final step is to show how his opponent would profit by moving towards the writer's view. He is not likely to completely convince his opponent; what he is trying to do is to get him to at least consider his position, and, perhaps, gradually, he will start to come over to the writer's side. The key to this kind of persuasion is a conciliatory tone, a careful choice of non-aggressive vocabulary, and, especially, empathy with the person the writer is trying to convince.

Another way of making an appeal to the emotions is satire. The satirist aims at our sense of the ridiculous and, presumably, at our sense of shame. He mocks and exaggerates the faults and follies he would persuade us to disavow. His tone may range from light, witty humour (as in P.J. O'Rourke) to profound bitterness (as in Jonathan Swift); but whether he be amused or enraged by human weakness, the satirist holds before us the disparity between what is and what ought to be, between the ideals we profess and the idiocies we practice.

To emphasize this disparity satirists often employ irony. Irony in its simplest form is using words so that their real significance is the reverse of their apparent meaning. If one were to say of a stingy man, 'He's a generous person,' the word 'generous' would be ironic. (Heavy-handed and insulting irony of this sort is called sarcasm. The difference between the two is that the purpose of irony is to give pleasure to the listener or reader, whereas the objective of sarcasm is to hurt). Irony, or course, must be clearly signalled so that the listener or reader will interpret it correctly. In speech this is often done by uttering the ironic word with a special emphasis or intonation, or by some non-verbal sign such as a raised eyebrow, a smile, a wink, a gesture, or a shrug. In writing, obviously, such cues are unavailable. While the writer can italicize an ironic term or enclose it in quotation marks, these expedients are mechanical and not very effective. The skilful literary ironist depends upon the subtle use of context to make his intention clear, and usually, too, he counts upon the good sense of his readers to distinguish what he is really saying from what he appears to be saying.

Less subtly, the satirist may belabour his target with invective, hurling abuse at the faults he castigates. A fine example occurs in Edward Abbey's novel *Hayduke Lives!*, when a crowd of conservationists, who are fighting land developers, are addressed by one of their own with cutting sarcasm:

> 'Finally, I'd like to point out that your gross display of flags here, with clenched fists, coiled rattlesnakes, red monkey wrenches and the feared hated brazen banner of capitalist militarist imperialist racist Amerika—I spell it, of course, with the appropriate "k"—reveals the basically macho, redneck, sexist, violence-prone frontiersman mentality of your Earth First! image makers. Your own symbols give you away, reveal and expose you for what you are: a drunken ignorant low-class (but not true working-class) lumpen-proletariat led and misled by a power-greedy clique of petit-bourgeois shop clerks, writers *manqués*, failed academics, corrupt journalists and petty business-men, *the traditional raw material*, as seen in Italy, in Germany, in Latin America, *of Fascism and Nazism*.' Mushkin paused. 'And so I say, once more, "*Sieg heil*" to you Earth First! rightwing pigs and if you want to hang me for it, hang me!'

Such satire of insult, as we may call it, is less common than it was. Manners have softened in the modern world, and our sense of fair play is likely to be offended by invective; furthermore, libel laws have resulted in writers using invective against large corporations and institutions, but rarely against individuals. But it can still be wondrously effective, as in this 1978 letter to the *Edmonton Sun*:

Sir: During the short time since The Sun started publishing in Edmonton, I have witnessed your decay from amiable drunk through voyeur and track rat to misogynous, vitriolic pariah. . . . I cannot but from now on dismiss your scribblings as the libellous drivel of an unbalanced mind.

Robert Hamilton

Most of us enjoy clever, witty insult (if we are not the victims); the popularity of insult-comedians testifies to that. Still, it must be admitted that invective appeals to a base instinct: our enjoyment at seeing another person or an institution pilloried and made ridiculous. (Of course, we rationalize our pleasure by assuring ourselves that they had it coming.) The last type of persuasion sets its aim much higher: eloquence evokes our noblest conceptions of humanity and elevates us to a plane of duty far above the petty preoccupation with self. It puts before us examples of great men and women, and urges, whether directly or by implication, that we imitate them. Thus on 2 October 1968, Prime Minister Pierre Elliott Trudeau, at the unveiling of the monument to Louis Riel in Regina said these words:

> A democratic society and system of government, while among the grandest of human concepts, are among the most difficult to implement. In a democracy, it is all too easy for the majority to forget the rights of the minority, and for a remote and powerful government to ignore its protests. It is all too easy, should disturbances erupt, to crush them in the name of law and order. We must never forget that, in the long run, a democracy is judged by the way the majority treats the minority. Louis Riel's battle is not yet won.
>
> That is why I suggest that we should never respond to demands for just treatment by pointing to other examples of injustice. If a certain right is attacked or denied in one province, it is not a valid reason for refusing similar rights in another. Yet such excuses are offered; and this leads to a vicious circle in which no improvement in human liberties is possible. The rights of individual Canadians are too important to be used as bargaining chips. Every government must accept responsibility for the rights of the citizens within its own jurisdiction. Canada as a whole suffers when any of her citizens is denied his rights; for that injustice places the rights of all of us in jeopardy.

This is persuasion at a high level, not only with regard to the ideas and sentiments expressed, but to the manner in which they are expressed. True eloquence is precisely this beautiful yet forceful synthesis of idea and expression.

CHARLES GORDON

Charles Gordon, author and longtime columnist for the *Ottawa Citizen*, is a regular contributor to *Maclean's*. Like his earlier selection (see p. 99), this essay shows his belief in the importance of tourism and his appreciation of nature.

Bungee Jumping over Victoria Falls

1   You've got all your shots, started your anti-malarial pills, waited in countless lines, endured long, cramped hours on several airplanes to get to Africa, and the entire effort has pointed towards this moment: you are in the posh Livingstone Room of that historic colonial monument, the Victoria Falls Hotel, watching a group of German tourists fox-trotting to a four-piece Zimbabwean band playing and singing 5 *Candle in the Wind*.

2   Small world, isn't it?

3   Professional travellers say this is what it has come to, a world so homogenized by tourism and television and the Internet and heaven knows what else that yesterday's funeral song in Westminster Abbey is today's hotel ballroom dance number in 10 Zimbabwe. The travellers make a distinction between themselves and mere tourists. They fear that the experience of discovering the world is being ruined by those who demand that away be like home, that remote parts of the globe be supplied with all the comfortable attributes of the less remote places from which they have journeyed. With the increasing reach of modern technology and the modern corporation, the foreign 15 becomes less foreign, the remote becomes more familiar and the experience of foreign travel is diminished.

4   That's the argument made increasingly by professional travellers in the face of a boom in international tourism driven by the affluence of aging baby boomers. Just the other day, a British travel writer wrote that 'travel as a significant transformative ex- 20 perience is no longer possible' and quoted another writer bemoaning what he called the 'McDonaldization' of travel—'the increasing effort to ensure predictability from one time or place to another'.

5   Is it that bad? Well, there are certain signs of the global village out there, and the village is not without its curio shops. Not far from the fox-trotting is the historic 25 railway bridge between Zambia and Zimbabwe over the Zambezi River. Clouds of mist from Victoria Falls billow up behind the bridge and the scene is just as it has always been.

6   One slight difference is the small structure at the centre of the bridge that you can see if you look carefully, and if you look carefully below the green structure you 30 can see what appear to be folds of rope, which means that—Yes! Bungee jumping has arrived at Victoria Falls. Consider for a moment how we have come to this point. The Falls, one of the most magnificent sights on the planet, sits here for centuries unacknowledged by the outside world, until a white man, David Livingstone, 'discovers' it in 1855. Then a hotel is built, and a railway to carry white people to it. Then various 35 businesses spring up around the Falls, from banking to the sale of carved hippopotamuses, and culminating in bungee jumping, the Nineties way of celebrating any great natural landmark. (More traditional ways range from carving your initials into it to building a wax museum beside it.)

7   The professional traveller, of course, would always sneer a bit at a luxury hotel   40
near a waterfall, but now the hotel features CNN in the rooms and just a 10-minute walk away are not one but two Internet cafés, perhaps the purest expression yet of McLuhan's global village. At the Internet café, tourists can use the computers to check their e-mail and send messages to friends and family in a way far more instantaneous than the exchange of postcards.   45

8   Inadequate phone lines keep Victoria Internet cafés from operating at North American–style efficiency, but you can watch the customers and get the idea: it is now possible, thanks to Internet technology, for people to leave home without ever taking leave of their thoughts of home. From the telephone in the airplane to the Internet at the hotel or down the street, they need never be out of touch.   50

9   Of course, getting out of touch is what travel used to be about. You went some-where that was not, say, Canada, and you tried to focus on thoughts of that new place, picking up thoughts of Canada again when you returned. Now, certain technological glitches aside, you need never leave home in your mind.

10   So, is all lost? Is real travel no longer possible, or even necessary? Only if we   55
assume that everybody really travels in this new way. Much of the professional trav-ellers' complaint is snobbery, arising from a resentment that places once restricted to the few are now being viewed by the many and buses drive up hills that once had to be scaled. Another thing to remember is that even if a tourist takes a bus up the hill, he is still seeing the hill, still seeing the view from the top of it. From that point, if he   60
is aware and perceptive, he will take something away from it. The criticism of McDonaldization overlooks the fact that to find the McDonald's in, say, Lusaka (where, in fact, there isn't one), you first have to get there. And in getting there, you see scenes that are different and people who live differently. The currency is different, the sounds are different and the newspapers don't have the hockey scores.   65

11   It is true that you have to be particularly determined or know someone in order to find a way off the road, to see the farmers near the Zambezi River or the cramped markets behind the walls of the impoverished townships near the modern city of Lusaka. But while not all tourists will get behind the scenery and into the daily lives of the people, they will at least have the opportunity to be affected by what they see.   70

12   To put it another way, you can't bungee-jump at Victoria Falls without seeing the Falls and you can't see the Falls without being moved by them. Much of travel is in our heads. For minds that are not narrow, travel can still be broadening.

1999

QUESTIONS
Reader and Purpose

1. What is the author trying to persuade his reader about? For you, has he succeeded?
2. *Candle in the Wind* (6) is the Elton John song, originally about the life of Marilyn Monroe, that he rewrote for the funeral of Princess Diana in 1997. What point is the author making when he writes that this song is now played by a band in Zimbabwe for German tourists to dance to?

3. In his final paragraph the author states: 'For minds that are not narrow, travel can still be broadening.' Is this sentence a valid summary of what he is trying to persuade the reader of? If you feel that it is not, write a revised one-sentence summary.

Organization

4. The opening paragraph is an extended contrast, the two parts of which are separated by a colon. What contrast is the author making? How is the third paragraph relevant to this contrast?
5. What is the function of paragraph 2?
6. 'Is it that bad?' Gordon asks at the beginning of paragraph 5, and paragraph 6 begins with 'One slight difference'. Is the author being realistic with these expressions, or is he deliberately downplaying (for the moment) the seriousness of the problem?
7. Is the first sentence of paragraph 10 the transition between the first nine paragraphs and the final three? Or does this sentence have some other function?

Sentences

8. Is the first sentence of this essay an example of **polysyndeton** or **asyndeton**?
9. The author uses a number of series throughout his essay: for instance, in his very first sentence, in the first and last sentences of paragraph 3, and in the last sentence of paragraph 10. How are these series similar or different?
10. Could the contrast in the first paragraph have been better effected by a dash rather than a colon?
11. Should paragraph 6 begin with *However* in order to mark the contrast between this paragraph and the preceding one?
12. Explain the **irony** in the last two sentences of paragraph 6.
13. In the first sentence of paragraph 7 would it be preferable to move the expression 'of course' to the beginning of the sentence? In the first sentence of paragraph 9 should 'of course' be placed after 'touch', or at the end of the sentence? Or is it fine where it is?

Diction

14. Look up: *posh* (3), *homogenized* (8), *attribute* (14), *transformative* (20), *bemoan* (21), *culminating* (37), *instantaneous* (44), *glitch* (54), *assume* (56), *perceptive* (61), *impoverished* (68).
15. Why does the author place 'discovers' (34) in quotation marks?
16. In the last sentence of paragraph 10 should there be a comma before 'and'? In the first sentence of paragraph 11 should there be a comma before 'or'? Are these two examples similar, or is there some difference between them?
17. The author refers several times to *professional travellers*. What does he mean by this expression? Where does he use the expression in an **ironic** manner?

POINTS TO LEARN

1. A very brief paragraph can be effective either as a summary or as a contrast.
2. A series is an efficient method of organizing information.

SUGGESTIONS FOR WRITING

Has one of your favourite outdoor locations been altered by modern 'improvements'—such as the introduction of new amenities, of technological changes, of commercialism? Has the area been ruined for you, or can you still use it? Does it still have enough significance for you to make it worthwhile going there? Your essay on this topic should explore the contrast between what was and what is now; what, if anything, has been lost; and the result for you personally.

IMPROVING YOUR STYLE

1. In one paragraph write two consecutive sentences that include a series.
2. Write one paragraph that consists of only one short sentence.

DONNA LOPIANO

A nine-time All-American softball player and a member of the National Sports Hall of Fame, Donna Lopiano (1946–) spent 17 years as the director of Women's Athletics at the University of Texas before leaving in 1992 to become the executive director of the Women's Sports Foundation, which works to ensure equal access to participation and leadership opportunities for girls and women in sports and fitness. She is also a member of the executive board of the US Olympic Committee. A prolific writer and public speaker, Lopiano regularly publishes articles in the Foundation's newsletter. She is also the co-author of two books: *Baseball-Softball Play Book* (1980) and *The Money Game: Financing Collegiate Athletics* (1980), published by the American Council on Education.

Purse Snatching

1   It appears that we are at a crossroads in women's sports. As Jesse Jackson said of the civil rights movement, 'We have moved from the battlefield of access to opportunity to the battlefield of access to capital.' Through government legislation like Title IX and the pressure of societal sanction and criticism, we have removed the participation barriers that once confronted women in the world of sport, especially sport at government-supported educational institutions. The right to play has been established. However, the issue that has not yet been confronted is the barrier to being treated equally when it comes to money.

2   Few see the fairness, for example, in our 1999 USA Women's World Cup soccer champions being promised $12,500 if they won compared to the approximately $300,000 received by male World Cup champs. Now the US women will receive almost $50,000 as a result of the public outcry over how the event's huge profits (estimates hover at $2 to $5 million) would be spent. And few would argue against the position that the women's pro tennis tour is more appealing and interesting to the public than the men's tour and should command equal if not higher salaries for its players. Yet, women's professional tennis purses are 25 per cent smaller than those of men.

3   The Women's National Basketball Association (WNBA) players had trouble negotiating minimum salary guarantees of $20,000 to $30,000 a year—a tiny fraction of
what most NBA players make. Meanwhile, it took almost thirty years for the NBA to   20
average 10,000 spectators a game and only two years for the WNBA to reach that mark.

4   Where are the women in auto racing at Indy, NASCAR, or CART events—truly the
most lucrative of all professional sports—when it comes to endorsements, winnings,
and the profits of team ownership? The answer is nowhere, since virtually no women
regularly participate in auto racing. With regard to salaries, profit sharing, or access   25
to significant dollars to begin professional leagues or gain entry into high-stakes
sports competition, women are still behind the eight ball.

5   Instead of paying women athletes what they're worth, there seems to be a
concerted effort to sexualize them. By commenting on the looks of the US women's
soccer team, the media blatantly suggest that these athletes' physical appearance is   30
more important, and of greater interest than their athletic achievements. When Brandi
Chastain took her shirt off following the winning goal, displaying considerable muscle
as well as a sports bra that more than covered the territory, the media acted like they
were looking at a Victoria's Secret catalogue as opposed to a world championship
soccer match. How many women jog on city streets and work out in health clubs   35
every day wearing less?

6   The media and the medical establishment, despite evidence to the contrary, are
quick to posit that the reason for a spate of anterior cruciate knee injuries in women
is because women are physically inferior to men (our knees are ill-constructed and
our hormones wreak havoc on our bodies). Are these predominantly male professions   40
maybe too eager to reinforce the strength and dominance of males and dismiss
women in sport?

7   I travel all over the country as a public speaker. I love talking to high school boys
because they reflect the male view before the veil of political correctness disguises their
true feelings. Young boys believe that it's terribly important for me to acknowledge that   45
males are better athletes than females. Males jump higher, throw farther, run faster,
dunk basketballs better, and are more interesting to watch than female athletes. They
listen intently as I ask, 'Who is the better athlete, Mike Tyson or Sugar Ray Leonard?'
Initially struck silent by the question, they then respond with considerable chagrin,
'That's not a fair question! Those are boxers in different weight classes. They don't com-   50
pete against each other. They are both great boxers.' To which I quietly respond,
'Exactly.' Why the need to affirm male dominance? Why the need to hog the marbles?

8   Women's sport has proved it has a market. What the marketplace needs is people who are willing to risk and share capital to exploit that market. One would think
that sex discrimination would take a backseat to making money and good business   55
decisions. How many more wildly successful events need to occur before people talk
positively about an investment in the women's sports market and act to take advantage of this opportunity? When will questioning the physical ability of female athletes
go away? When will efforts to undermine the women's sports industry cease?
Ultimately, it comes down to a matter of will and being gender-blind when exploiting   60
business opportunities. We're not there yet.

1999

QUESTIONS
Reader and Purpose

1. In choosing as her title an expression that usually refers to a petty crime, is the author taking the chance of being misunderstood? Or does the eye-catching quality of the title make up for this possible defect?
2. How does the title of this essay reflect its subject?
3. Describe the **tone** of this essay. Is the tone consistent with the argument being made, or should it have been calmer, milder? On the other hand, should it have been more vigorous, more forceful?
4. The first sentence of this essay is an assumption introduced by 'It appears that'. Does the rest of the essay accept this assumption as true and build on it, or does the author attempt to prove the assumption?

Organization

5. Outline the progression of ideas in the first paragraph.
6. What **connectives** join paragraphs 1 and 2? paragraphs 2 and 3? paragraphs 3 and 4? Are the connectives specific words or phrases, or are they connections between ideas?
7. Is the last sentence of the first paragraph a **transitional** sentence between this paragraph and the next, is it the **topic sentence** for paragraphs 2, 3, and 4, or does it have both these functions?
8. What is the function of the first sentence of paragraph 5? Is it logical? If you believe that it is illogical, is it nevertheless effective?
9. How are paragraphs 6 and 7 related to what precedes them? How are these two paragraphs part of the persuasive intent of this essay?

Sentences

10. In the first sentence of paragraph 2 what difference would result in moving 'for example' to the beginning of the sentence? to the end?
11. In the second sentence of paragraph 2 what difference would result if the parentheses were replaced by dashes? What if they were replaced by commas?
12. In the second sentence of paragraph 5 should the phrase 'and of greater interest' be followed by a comma? Would adding this comma give the sentence better **balance**?
13. The expression *the reason is because* (an example occurs in the first sentence of paragraph 6) has been condemned by some grammarians as redundant; they say that the expression should be simply *the reason is that*. Other writers on usage say that the expression has become acceptable because it has been so widely used. What is your view?

Diction

14. Look up: *sanction* (4), *virtually* (24), *high-stakes* (26), *establishment* (37), *posit* (38), *spate* (38), *marketplace* (53), *capital* (54), *exploit* (54).
15. In paragraph 1 should the phrase *the participation barriers* be replaced by *the barriers of participation*? At the end of the paragraph should *the barriers to being treated equally* be replaced by *the equal treatment barriers*? What conclusion can you come to about nouns that are used as adjectives?

16. In the third sentence of paragraph 5 is the expression 'the media acted like they were looking' correct, or should it be 'the media acted *as though* they were looking'?
17. *Behind the eight ball* (27), *the need to hog the marbles* (52). What do these expressions mean? Are they **clichés**? Are they appropriate to the context?

POINTS TO LEARN

1. Paragraphs can be joined by ideas, without connecting words and phrases, if they are consecutive parts of a developing argument.
2. A persuasive essay need not have the logical rigour of an argumentative essay. The object of persuasion is assent, but not necessarily the truth.

SUGGESTIONS FOR WRITING

Assuming that women's sports at your university or college receive less funding and recognition than men's sports, what could be done to improve the status of women's sports? In an essay of 6–8 paragraphs, try to persuade the student body to accept your views.

IMPROVING YOUR STYLE

1. Give your essay a title that is short, vigorous, and eye-catching.
2. Join two or three consecutive paragraphs without using connective words but by making each paragraph an example of one point in your argument.

HARRY F. HARLOW

Harry F. Harlow (1905–81) was a scientist specializing in animal behaviour. His research included a series of studies in which he separated newborn rhesus monkeys from their mothers in order to examine the importance of maternal affection to infant social development. Among the many books he published are *The Nature of Love* (1958) and *Learning to Love* (1971). In collaboration with others, including his wife, he published *From Thought to Therapy: Lessons from a Primate Laboratory* (1971), *The Human Model: Primate Perspectives* (1979), and *Social Deprivation in Monkeys* (1992). The following piece, which is complete, is his report on an experiment. It is a model of how to write up an experiment—beginning with the problem to be investigated, explaining the procedure and results in detail, and clearly stating the conclusion. In a narrow sense the essay is not avowedly persuasive. Yet viewed more broadly it has great persuasive force, convincing us by the careful application of reason and gathering of evidence.

Of Love in Infants

1   The use of infant monkeys in many laboratory experiments is perhaps dictated by necessity, but few scientists would deny that it is also remarkably convenient. Monkeys are far better coordinated at birth than human infants; their reactions can be

evaluated with confidence at an age of 10 days or earlier, yet their development follows the same general line as that of humans.   5

2   The monkeys' well-being and even survival pose a number of problems, however—particularly if they must, in the course of experimentation, be separated from
their mothers only a few hours after birth. Nonetheless, at the University of
Wisconsin's Primate Laboratory we were able, using techniques developed by Dr
Gertrude van Wagenen of Yale, to rear infant monkeys on the bottle with a far lower 10
mortality than is found among monkeys nursed by their mothers. Now one of the
components of our technique involved the use of a gauze diaper folded on the floor
of the infant monkeys' cages, following Dr van Wagenen's observations that monkeys
would maintain contact with soft, pliant surfaces during nursing. We were struck by
the deep attachment our monkeys formed for these diaper pads and by the distress   15
they showed when, once a day, the pads were removed for reasons of sanitation. This
observation led us into quite a new series of experiments—research into the importance of bodily contact in infant love.

3   Love of infants for their mothers is often regarded as a sacred or mystical force,
and perhaps this is why it has received so little objective study. But if facts are lack- 20
ing, theory on this subject is abundant. Psychologists, sociologists, and anthropologists usually hold that the infant's love is learned through the association of the
mother's face and body with the alleviation of such physical tensions as hunger and
thirst. Psychoanalysts specially emphasize the importance to emotional development
of attaining and sucking at the breast. Our experiments suggest something else   25
is involved.

4   We contrived two substitute 'mothers'. One was a bare cylinder made of welded
wire and surmounted by a wooden head. In the other, the wire framework was covered by a layer of terry cloth. We put eight newborn monkeys in individual cages,
each with equal access to a cloth and to a wire mother. Four received their milk from 30
one type of mother, four from the other—the milk being obtained from nursing bottles fixed in the mothers' 'breasts'.

5   Physiologically, the two mothers proved to be equivalent—the monkeys in both
groups drank as much milk and gained weight at the same rate. But psychologically,
the two mothers were not at all equivalent. Both groups of monkeys spent far more 35
time climbing over and embracing their cloth mothers than they did their plain wire
ones; they even left their electric heating pads to climb on the unheated mother.
Those that suckled from the wire mother spent no more time than feeding required.

6   The theory that infant love is related to satisfaction of hunger or thirst was thus
contradicted, and the importance of bodily contact in forming affection underscored. 40
This finding was supported by the next phase of our investigation. The time the monkey infants spent cuddling their surrogate mothers was a strong indication of emotional attachment, but it was perhaps not conclusive. Would they also turn to their
inanimate mothers for comfort when they were subjected to emotional stress?

7   With this question in mind, we exposed our infant monkeys to strange objects 45
likely to frighten them, such as a mechanical teddy bear that moved forward, beating
a drum. It was found that, whether the infants had nursed on the wire mother or the
cloth one, they overwhelmingly sought comfort in stress from the cloth one. The
infant would cling to it, rubbing its body against the towelling. With its fears thus

assuaged, it would turn to look at the previously terrifying bear without the slightest 50
sign of alarm. It might even leave the comfort of its substitute mother to approach the
object that had frightened it only a minute before.

8   It is obvious that much behaviour is analogous to that of human infants, and
we found that the analogy held in situations that less obviously involved stress. If a
human child is taken to an unfamiliar place, for example, he will usually remain calm 55
and happy so long as his mother is nearby, but if she leaves him, fear and panic may
result. Our experiments showed a similar effect in infant monkeys. We put the monkeys in a room that was much larger than their usual cages, and in the room we placed
a number of unfamiliar objects—a crumpled piece of newspaper, blocks of wood, a
metal plate, and a doorknob mounted on a box. If a cloth mother was present, the 60
monkey, at the sight of these objects, would rush wildly to her and, rubbing against
the towelling, cling to her tightly. Its fear would then diminish greatly or else vanish
altogether, as in the previous experiment. Soon the monkey would leave its mother to
explore its new world. It now regarded the objects as playthings. Returning from time
to time to the mother for reassurance, it followed an outgoing pattern of behaviour. 65

9   If, on the other hand, the cloth mother were absent, the infant would rush
across the room and throw itself head down on the floor, clutching its head and body
and screaming in distress. The bare wire mother afforded no more reassurance than
no mother at all—even monkeys that had known only the wire mother from birth
showed no affection for her and got no comfort from her presence. Indeed, this group 70
of monkeys showed the greatest distress of all.

10   In a final comparison of cloth and wire mothers, we adapted an experiment originally devised by Robert A. Butler in this laboratory. Butler had found that monkeys
enclosed in a dimly lighted box would press a lever to open and reopen a window for
hours on end, with no other reward than the chance to look out. The rate of this action 75
depended on what the monkeys saw: a glimpse of another monkey elicited far more
activity than that of an empty room.

11   When we tested our infant monkeys in such a box, we found that those raised
with both cloth and wire mothers showed as great an interest in the cloth mother as
in another monkey but responded no more to a wire mother than to an empty room. 80
In this test, as in all others, the monkeys that had been fed on a wire mother behaved
in the same way as those that had been fed on a cloth-covered mother surrogate.

12   Thus, all objective tests we have been able to devise indicate that the infant
monkey's relationship to its substitute mother is a full one. There are, of course, factors other than bodily contact involved. For example, the simple act of clinging, in 85
itself, seems important: a newborn monkey has difficulty surviving in a bare wire cage
unless provided with a cone to which it can cling.

13   Yet our experiments have clearly shown the importance of the comfort derived
from bodily contact in the formation of an infant's love for its mother and revealed the
role of breast-feeding to be negligible or nonexistent. They have also established an 90
experimental approach to subtle and dramatic relationships.

1975

QUESTIONS

Reader and Purpose

1. What question is Harlow attempting to answer? Does he?
2. Harlow's argument appeals to reason, and its method is inductive, depending upon evidence. That is, instead of using generalizations based upon statistics, Harlow has devised an experiment. What essential features distinguish the experimental method of gathering data?
3. Does Harlow appear to be writing for people who share his scientific interests and knowledge or for a more general audience: would you be more likely to find this article in a scientific journal or in *Reader's Digest*?

Organization

4. Which paragraphs constitute the beginning of this essay? Within these paragraphs what one sentence most clearly sets up the problem? Which paragraphs constitute the closing?
5. The middle of the essay has three major sections. Give a title to each and indicate the paragraphs it includes.
6. In paragraph 1 how is the second sentence related in idea to the first?
7. In paragraph 6, the second sentence performs an important **transitional** function. Which words point backward to what has just been said? Which point forward, directing the reader to the next topic?
8. What is the topic of paragraph 8? How is the second sentence related to the topic? The third? How are the remaining sentences of the paragraph related to the third?
9. What phrase at the beginning of paragraph 9 prepares the reader for a shift in idea?

Sentences

10. What does the dash in line 17 help to signal? The colon in line 76?
11. The first two sentences of paragraph 5 open in the same way. What does the similarity serve to emphasize?
12. Identify the **participial** phrase in the sentence in lines 48–9. Find three or four other effective participial phrases in this selection. What advantage do such constructions offer a writer?

Diction

13. Look up: *coordinated* (3), *pose* (6), *component* (12), *hold* (22), *access* (30), *conclusive* (43), *analogous* (53), *reassurance* (65), *devise* (83), *negligible* (90).
14. How do the **etymologies** of these words help to clarify their sense: *primate* (9), *pliant* (14), *alleviation* (23), *assuaged* (50)?
15. What is the difference between the interests or functions of *psychologists*, *sociologists*, *anthropologists*, and *psychoanalysts* (see 21–4)?
16. What relationships in thought are signalled by these **connectives**: *nonetheless* (8), *now* (11), *thus* (83), *of course* (84), *yet* (88)?
17. Why does Harlow put quotation marks around 'mothers' in line 27?

POINTS TO LEARN

1. Effective arguments begin by making clear what is to be proved or disproved.
2. A good essay has a well-defined beginning, middle, and end.
3. Transitional sentences direct readers from one section of an essay to the next.
4. Participial phrases are an economical and efficient way of conveying subordinate information.

SUGGESTIONS FOR WRITING

1. Compose a report of 500–600 words on an experiment done in one of your lab courses in high school or university. Begin by stating what you sought to determine, devote the bulk of your essay to describing the procedure, and end by drawing the appropriate conclusion.
2. If you have not had any experience in an actual laboratory, imagine an experiment situation in everyday life—for example, trying several different routes to a destination by car or public transit to see which is fastest, or trying several methods of study to decide which works best, or using various approaches to impress someone you wish to please. Follow the general organization suggested in the first exercise.

IMPROVING YOUR STYLE

1. Include participial phrases in at least six of your sentences. Vary their position—according to the logical progression of your ideas or the demands of emphasis—so that some open the sentence, others close it, and one or two occur in interrupting positions.
2. Use each of the following connective words or phrases at least once somewhere in your essay: *of course, for example, nonetheless, thus, yet.*

RUTH MORRIS

An American who moved to Canada in 1968 to teach at York University, Ruth Morris (1933–2001) spent most of her life fighting for social justice, especially the reform of prisons. A devout Quaker, she helped found the International Conference for Penal Abolition. Among the books she published are *Crumbling Walls—Why Prisons Fail* (1989), *Penal Abolition, the Practical Choice: A Practical Manual on Penal Abolition* (1995), *Listen Ontario! Faith Communities Speak Out* (1997), and *Stories of Transformative Justice* (2000). Shortly before her death she was awarded the Order of Canada for her life-long work.

Women in Prison

*'When you take away everything a person has, you make them desperate.
And when you make someone desperate, you make them dangerous. They used
to say they were protecting society, but they made animals. They conditioned,
controlled, and made those girls into revolving door syndromes.'*

1   Bettina Harris is 24 years old, tough, bright, eloquent. Bettina has 58 convictions, and has spent 12 years in juvenile, provincial adult, and federal adult institutions.
Her story illustrates what it is like to be a minority of minorities: a woman prisoner.

Early Life

2   Bettina's mother, keen to be up with the times in the 1960s, got involved with a
black man in the US, a pimp with criminal connections. Pregnant, she fled to Canada,   5
spending the rest of her life feeling guilty toward Bettina for making her black.

3   One of Bettina's earliest, most recurrent memories was her mother's saying, during suicidal bouts, 'I'm really sorry I made you black.' Bettina got the message: her
blackness was responsible for her mother's repeated suicide attempts.

4   Bettina's other early memory was of sitting on the step outside her house. Her   10
mother would drink herself into a stupor till 3 or 4 a.m. and constantly try to get
Bettina to come in. Bettina didn't run away, but she wouldn't come in to her drunken
mother. 'I never went anywhere, 'cause I had nowhere to go,' recalled Bettina, 'I'd sit
right there on the little sidewalk, and she would scream and holler and beg me to
come in, and I would refuse. What I was trying to say, had I had logic and verbaliza-   15
tion was, "I don't want to be there when you are like that. I love you, I don't want the
part-time Mommy that leaves me sometimes. I want you always. When you're like
this, I don't want to be there." So I sat out there, and it was a stand.'

5   When Bettina was 11, her mother called the Children's Aid, and Bettina was
declared 'unmanageable'. It's an interesting aspect of sexism in our society that girls   20
are much more likely than boys to be charged simply with 'incorrigibility'—general
refusal to submit to family discipline. Children's Aid wasted no time in half measures.
Bettina went to no foster homes, nor were efforts made to remedy the home situation.

6   She was taken straight to a group home. Bettina describes herself at this point
as an angry child. 'In school, I was good in grades, but I used to fight with boys, girls,   25
anyone. I was fighting because I felt different. My mother felt guilty, passed it on to
me, and I passed it on in anger and violence. But I never knew outward violence till
the group home.'

Group Home Life

7   'I met a group called the Devil's Angels there. I learned the ropes from the girls
the first night: the girls against the staff.' Bettina was introduced immediately into the   30
group code of sneaking out into the park, and of gang life.

8   But she also made two close friends who meant a lot to her: Candy and Michelle.
At 11, peers begin to become important to most children. To a child as starved of normal family life as Bettina, and the other girls in the group home, peer friendships
become overwhelmingly important.   35

9   The only time in our long and trauma-filled interview when Bettina totally broke down was in talking about Michelle. Less than two months after Bettina's entry into the group home, she found her friend Michelle in the park, semi-conscious, beaten and gang-raped.

10   Even now, Bettina blames the Children's Aid for not protecting these children 40 from such horrors. When I asked her later in our talk if anyone in her life had ever been truly kind or tried to help, perhaps a social worker, she responded: 'Social worker! I was half black in a totally white system. I was from an emotionally disturbed background. My father was a criminal. I didn't have a chance in Hell in that system. They used to say "Tsk tsk, she's intelligent, it's a shame." My intelligence was a liabil- 45 ity: they fought me all the way.'

11   Feeling abandoned, the children's gangs had their own way of dealing with such terrible trauma as Michelle's gang-rape.

12   'My boyfriend Woody promised revenge. The night after Michelle was found, we went down to have a rumble. For the first time, I could have killed somebody and 50 had no conscience. The leader of the other gang was called Snake. He grabbed me, and held a knife to my throat. He held me up to our gang as an enticement, because I was Woody's girlfriend.

13   'The night before, Woody had given me a knife. I didn't want it, but for some reason I had it with me. And suddenly, there I was with Snake's knife at my neck. For 55 Michelle, for myself, I found myself saying "There is nobody here. Nobody is going to protect me. I have no parent. This system is not going to protect me, it's going to use me." So I plunged the knife into his shoulder with pleasure, and if I had the same thing to do over, I would. I actually don't think I did anything wrong, compared to the things that happened to me or to Michelle.'   60

14   No one reported this incident to the police. Snake recovered, and in fact, went on to be a 'Big Biker'. Bettina went through a period of disassociation from her repeated shocks.

15   The group home blamed Bettina and her friends for being the wrong type of girls. Had they been the right types, they would not have been there in the first 65 place.

16   This familiar syndrome of blaming the victim was accentuated by a psychology test Bettina took not long after these incidents. The psychologist found Bettina had images of violence! Of course he didn't know she had found her best friend brutally raped and permanently damaged, or any of the rest. Whereas the system considered 70 all the girls abnormal, the girls accepted the little differences among one another. But this too led to misunderstandings with the more 'normal' staff view.

17   'There was a girl named Trudi who had been molested by her father, so she was freaky scared of men. One time a male staff was going toward Trudi. We told him to stop, but he kept coming. A fight broke out, and I cracked him over the head with a 75 vase. I was charged with threatening and assault, because I threatened to break up the house if he didn't let Trudi alone.'

Detention Centre

18   Bettina describes what it is like for a child to enter our Juvenile Detention Centre for the first time: 'Trudi had been in 311 Jarvis 13 times; I had never been there. She

ended up going home. That place is terrible: I knew it was a jail. I was 11 years old. 80
I remember exactly how I felt when they made you go in this little cell with a toilet,
and a steel bed, and the terrible, clanging echo when they shut that steel door behind
you, with keys jangling. It looked exactly like the West Detention Centre cells (adult
women's jail) do today.

19   'But before that they had deloused me. They check your body in places where 85
at 11 years of age I had never been touched. I had never done more than kiss. This
big hairy, masculine type aggressive matron who wasn't sensitive at all did the strip
search; she just figured we were bad children, that was that. So I felt pretty degraded.
And then that clanging, ringing door. I remember thinking over and over, "You must
really be bad, or you wouldn't be here." No words could change that opinion, because 90
otherwise I wouldn't be here.'

20   Left alone with these overwhelming feelings, Bettina unravelled a toothpaste
tube, and found a razor-sharp end. She did not want to die, but she wanted to hurt
herself. Three days later she came to fully, and found herself on the way to court, arms
heavily bandaged. 'The judge kept saying, "Tsk, tsk, such a young girl, why would you 95
want to kill yourself?"'

21   She tried to explain her imitation of her mother, but it made no sense to the
grownup judge. With adult court logic, the judge concluded, 'For your protection and
for society's protection, we're going to send you to training school.'

22   No one in court saw the irony: taking a girl so sensitive that a single day in 100
detention had driven her to cut her wrists, and putting her into a jail-like environment for years to 'protect' her! But Bettina saw it. And her greatest virtue and vice both
were that she was never quiet about things. She says now reflecting on it, 'There was
no explaining. I was a child. It was their system. In their eyes I had no feelings, no
logic and no rights.' 105

23   But at the time she was led out screaming, ' "You can send me anywhere, but
I'll be damned if I'll accept it." I spat in the Judge's face.'

Training School

24   Bettina arrived in Training School a fully committed and experienced rebel.

25   She was a natural organizer. She quickly began to get across to the girls that
with 200 kids, four segregation cells, and relatively few staff at any one time, there 110
was no way they could control the girls. The truce that ensued involved the authorities giving Bettina her own TV, her own radio, special privileges of all kinds—as long
as she desisted from organizing.

26   But confused as Bettina was by now, a part of her could not be bought off. She
felt the authorities were manipulating the kids, that the psychologists were destroy- 115
ing what was left of their sense of self-worth. Bettina had her own campaign of trying
to tell the girls they were worth something. She would say, 'You don't have to take all
this ————. They get $200 a day for you.' But she laments that she was too 'screwed
up' herself to begin to meet the yawning chasm of need all around her.

27   When asked about being a woman in the system, Bettina said, 'A woman in the 120
system is ten times, a hundred times more devastated, because it's a man's world in
and out of the system, and women even in the subculture are demeaned. You're to be
used sexually. I broke the code in both cultures.'

A Cry from the Dark

28   Bettina graduated to the adult system, and the rest of her life to date has been a tragic continuation of these beginnings. She sees now that one main purpose of her   125
life is to be a voice of the few survivors from among the young women she grew up with. While in the institutions, she fought the institutional message: 'They kept pounding on their heads, "You are no good; you're worthless; you're useless." And I would say, "No, you're not, these guys are fucked up. They don't know what they are talking about." So I would reverse the mechanism.'   130

29   When I asked what had happened to the girls she knew in group home and training school, she replied, 'About a third are in the adult system; a third are dead; and a third are in mental institutions. There are four women I know who aren't in any of those situations, and three of them only made it because they married some guy that still beats them.' She went on to say that the mental institutions let you go every   135
six months, then send you out to return quickly, with the same revolving door syndrome. The deaths were mainly from violence and drugs.

30   Bettina explained her own violence in this way. 'I have a lot of guilty emotions. I didn't want to hurt people. I didn't want to be a very angry person. I hated the things it made me into. But I never hurt people outside. I always fought police. I have 15 assaults   140
on my record: all of them are police and security guards. Their use of unnecessary and illegal violence towards me and others makes it acceptable for me to be violent to them. I could not justify myself otherwise. Bettina has to live with Bettina.'

31   Bettina's closing plea were words addressed to all of us: 'What did they give me to go out and survive with? Nothing but emptiness and anger.   145

32   'There's a lot of young kids out there that we can still save, for the ones I couldn't, the ones that are dead now. Society, hang your head in shame, because you people are the ones contributing to this—you are accepting it. "Let's let the professionals handle it." No one is speaking up.

33   'A main reason a lot of women don't make it is because it is very lonely out here.   150
There aren't a lot of people ready to help. Right now people can get away with saying "Well, we didn't know." My main reason for telling people about my life is so they will know. Once you know, and don't do anything, then you are responsible.

34   'I write to 22 women in jail and share with them my struggle. I am trying to show them all it can be done. But we need outside help too.'   155

1987

QUESTIONS
Reader and Purpose

1. In the opening paragraph, Morris describes Bettina Harris as 'bright, eloquent'. Are these qualities evident in the quotations that Morris uses? Consider, for example, the quoted material in paragraph 4, keeping in mind that the quotations reproduce speech, not writing.

2. In paragraph 9, Morris reveals that this essay was the result of an interview that she had with Bettina Harris. Why has the author waited so long to tell us this?

3. Why does the author conclude her essay with four paragraphs of reported speech? Then consider why this essay has been included in the *Persuasion* section of the book, rather than in the *Narration* or *Exposition* sections.

Organization

4. Morris has divided her essay into five sections, each with its own subtitle. Why does paragraph 1 not have a subtitle?
5. The first section of the essay, 'Early Life', develops as follows: paragraph 2, the introduction, briefly describes why Bettina's mother feels guilty towards her; paragraphs 3 and 4 give examples of Bettina's early memories about her mother; paragraph 5 relates her being declared 'unmanageable'; and paragraph 6 describes the result of that declaration. How do the other four parts of this essay develop? What is the function of each?
6. Consider the **parallel structure** of Bettina's accounts in paragraphs 10 and 13. Is the structure perfectly parallel, or does she use some variations? If so, what are they?

Sentences

7. Consider the sentence structures of the first four paragraphs. How many of the sentences begin with a subject–verb combination? How many begin with an introductory **phrase** or a **subordinate clause**? What conclusions about Morris's style can you draw from your answers?
8. 'I learned the ropes from the girls the first night: the girls against the staff' (29–30). What function does the colon serve? Would a dash work as well? Explain why, or why not. Apply these same questions to the colon in the next paragraph, and to the one in the final sentence of paragraph 10.
9. Morris uses a comma after 'Bettina' in paragraph 8. Is the sentence slightly awkward because of this comma, or is the comma necessary for clarity?

Diction

10. Look up: *eloquent* (1), *stupor* (11), *incorrigibility* (21), *peers* (33), *liability* (45–6), *trauma* (48), *enticement* (52), *disassociation* (62), *syndrome* (67), *accentuated* (67), *unravelled* (92), *ensue* (111), *desist* (113), *demean* (122).
11. At the end of paragraph 26, Morris puts the words 'screwed up' in quotation marks. Is her intent to draw attention to the words? Does she use quotation marks because she is quoting Bettina? Does she add them because the words are too informal, given the style used in the rest of this essay?
12. Explain what Bettina means by the following expressions: *a stand* (18), *have a rumble* (50), *freaky scared* (74). Do these expressions seem to be a natural part of her speech, or do they appear exaggerated?

POINTS TO LEARN

1. Quotations can be very effective in revealing a person's motives.
2. Dividing an essay into titled sections emphasizes structure, although it is no substitute for clear organization.

SUGGESTIONS FOR WRITING

This essay concludes with Bettina's words: 'But we need outside help too.' What kind of help would you be prepared to give a young person who is in trouble?

Your essay (12–15 paragraphs) on this serious problem should describe a specific situation; it should then try to persuade your reader to agree to the solution you propose.

IMPROVING YOUR STYLE

1. Quote liberally from the person you are describing, but ensure that the words you quote are realistic and without exaggeration.
2. Separate your essay into three or four parts and give each part a title.

JONATHAN SWIFT

Jonathan Swift (1667–1745) is the greatest writer of satire in English and one of the greatest in the world. He is best known for *Gulliver's Travels* (1726), popularly thought of as a fantasy for children, but actually a biting attack upon a variety of targets—politicians, courtiers, travel books, scientists, humanity in general. *A Tale of a Tub* (1704) is a funny and scandalous treatment of religious follies.

The essay reprinted here satirizes England's policy toward Ireland. (Swift, though English, was born and educated in Dublin and served for many years as dean of the Anglican St Patrick's Cathedral in that city. His concern for all Irish people, regardless of religion, made him a national hero.) During the eighteenth century Ireland suffered under a repressive and exploitative Protestant English rule. Religious intolerance was strong, and Protestant England imposed harsh religious, political, and economic restrictions upon the native Irish, the majority of them Roman Catholic. Even the Anglo-Irish—Swift's class—who descended from English settlers and were themselves Protestant, suffered under unjust laws forbidding Ireland to trade with nations other than England. Swift had proposed solutions to some of these inequities, solutions that seemed to him workable and fair. No one listened. In 'A Modest Proposal' (1729) he suggested a more horrendous scheme, advising the English, who he believed were determined to destroy the Irish for profit, on a more efficient and systematic method of conducting their slaughterhouse policy. Although the 'Irish Question' is still unsettled, Swift's 'A Modest Proposal' remains the finest example of sustained irony ever written.

A Modest Proposal

for Preventing the Children of Poor People in Ireland from Being a Burden to their Parents or Country, and for Making Them Beneficial to the Public

1   It is a melancholy object to those who walk through this great town, or travel in the country, when they see the streets, the roads, and cabin-doors crowded with beggars of the female sex, followed by three, four, or six children, all in rags, and importuning every passenger for an alms. These mothers, instead of being able to work for their honest livelihood, are forced to employ all their time in strolling to beg 5 sustenance for their helpless infants: who, as they grow up, either turn thieves for want of work, or leave their dear native country to fight for the Pretender* in Spain, or sell themselves to the Barbadoes.[1]

2 I think it is agreed by all parties, that this prodigious number of children in the arms, or on the backs, or at the heels of their mothers, and frequently of their fathers, 10 is, in the present deplorable state of the kingdom, a very great additional grievance; and, therefore, whoever could find out a fair, cheap, and easy method of making these children sound and useful members of the commonwealth, would deserve so well of the public, as to have his statue set up for a preserver of the nation.[2]

3 But my intention is very far from being confined to provide only for the chil- 15 dren of professed beggars; it is of a much greater extent, and shall take in the whole number of infants at a certain age, who are born of parents in effect as little able to support them as those who demand our charity in the streets.

4 As to my own part, having turned my thoughts for many years upon this important subject, and maturely weighed the several schemes of other projectors, 20 I have always found them grossly mistaken in their computation. It is true, a child, just dropped from its dam,[3] may be supported by her milk for a solar year with little other nourishment; at most, not above the value of two shillings, which the mother may certainly get, or the value in scraps, by her lawful occupation of begging; and it is exactly at one year old that I propose to provide for them in such a manner, as, 25 instead of being a charge upon their parents or the parish, or wanting food and raiment for the rest of their lives, they shall, on the contrary, contribute to the feeding, and partly to the clothing, of many thousands.

5 There is likewise another great advantage to my scheme, that it will prevent those voluntary abortions, and that horrid practice of women murdering their bastard 30 children, alas, too frequent among us, sacrificing the poor innocent babes, I doubt more to avoid the expense than the shame, which would move tears and pity in the most savage and inhuman breast.

6 The number of souls in this kingdom being usually reckoned one million and a half, of these I calculate there may be about two hundred thousand couple whose 35 wives are breeders; from which number I subtract thirty thousand couple, who are able to maintain their own children (although I apprehend there cannot be so many, under the present distresses of the kingdom); but this being granted, there will remain an hundred and seventy thousand breeders. I again subtract fifty thousand for those women who miscarry, or whose children die by accident or disease within 40 the year. There only remain a hundred and twenty thousand children of poor parents

---

* The Old Pretender, James Edward, son of James II (last Catholic king of England, deposed in 1688) and Mary of Modena. The Pretender was a Catholic and, possessing a claim to the English throne, posed a threat to Protestant England. [Editor's note; the numbered notes are taken from *The Restoration and the Eighteenth Century*, ed. Martin Price.]

1 Many Irish Catholics enlisted in French and Spanish forces, the latter employed in the effort to restore the Stuart Pretender to the English throne in 1718; emigration to the West Indies from Ireland had reached the rate of almost 1500 a year (and often led to desperate servitude).

2 The idiom of the 'projector' (see the first sentence of paragraph 4), the enthusiastic proponent of public remedies (often suspected of having an eye on his own glory).

3 The idiom now of the cattle breeder.

annually born. The question therefore is how this number shall be reared and provided for? which, as I have already said, under the present situation of affairs, is
utterly impossible by all the methods hitherto proposed. For we can neither employ
them in handicraft or agriculture; we neither build houses (I mean in the country) 45
nor cultivate land: they very seldom pick up a livelihood by stealing until they arrive
at six years old, except where they are of towardly parts; although I confess they learn
the rudiments much earlier; during which time they can, however, be properly
looked upon only as probationers; as I have been informed by a principal gentleman
in the county of Cavan,[4] who protested to me, that he never knew above one or two 50
instances under the age of six, even in a part of the kingdom so renowned for the
quickest proficiency in that art.

7   I am assured by our merchants that a boy or a girl before twelve years old is no
saleable commodity; and even when they come to this age they will not yield above
three pounds or three pounds and half-a-crown at most, on the exchange; which can- 55
not turn to account either to the parents or kingdom, the charge of nutriment and rags
having been at least four times that value.

8   I shall now, therefore, humbly propose my own thoughts, which I hope will not
be liable to the least objection.

9   I have been assured by a very knowing American[5] of my acquaintance in 60
London, that a young healthy child, well nursed, is, at a year old, a most delicious,
nourishing, and wholesome food, whether stewed, roasted, baked, or boiled; and I
make no doubt that it will equally serve in a fricassee or a ragout.[6]

10   I do therefore humbly offer it to public consideration, that of the hundred and
twenty thousand children already computed, twenty thousand may be reserved for 65
breed, whereof only one-fourth part to be males; which is more than we allow to
sheep, black cattle, or swine; and my reason is, that these children are seldom the fruits
of marriage; a circumstance not much regarded by our savages, therefore one male will
be sufficient to serve four females. That the remaining hundred thousand may, at a year
old, be offered in sale to the persons of quality and fortune through the kingdom; 70
always advising the mother to let them suck plentifully in the last month, so as to render them plump and fat for a good table. A child will make two dishes at an entertainment for friends; and when the family dines alone, the fore or hind quarter will
make a reasonable dish, and, seasoned with a little pepper or salt, will be very good
boiled on the fourth day, especially in winter.   75

11   I have reckoned, upon a medium, that a child just born will weigh twelve
pounds, and in a solar year, if tolerably nursed, increaseth to twenty-eight pounds.

12   I grant this food will be somewhat dear, and therefore very proper for landlords,
who, as they have already devoured most of the parents, seem to have the best title to
the children.   80

13   Infants' flesh will be in season throughout the year, but more plentifully in
March, and a little before and after: for we are told by a grave author, an eminent
French physician,[7] that fish being a prolific[8] diet, there are more children born in

---

4 One of the poorest districts of Ireland.
5 Presumably American Indian, many of whom were believed by the English to enjoy cannibalism.
6 A French stew, one of the foreign dishes ('olios and ragouts') Swift mocks elsewhere as affectations.
7 François Rabelais (c. 1494–1553), *Gargantua and Pantagruel* V. 29.
8 Generative.

Roman Catholic countries about nine months after Lent than at any other season; therefore, reckoning a year after Lent, the market will be more glutted than usual, 85 because the number of popish infants is at least three to one in this kingdom; and therefore it will have one other collateral advantage, by lessening the number of papists among us.

14   I have already computed the charge of nursing a beggar's child (in which list I reckon all cottagers, labourers, and four-fifths of the farmers) to be about two shillings 90 per annum, rags included; and I believe no gentleman would repine to give ten shillings for the carcass of a good fat child, which, as I have said, will make four dishes of excellent nutritive meat, when he has only some particular friend, or his own family, to dine with him. Thus the squire will learn to be a good landlord, and grow popular among his tenants; the mother will have eight shillings net profit, and be fit for 95 work till she produces another child.

15   Those who are more thrifty (as I must confess the times require) may flay the carcass; the skin of which, artificially dressed, will make admirable gloves for ladies, and summer-boots for fine gentlemen.

16   As to our city of Dublin, shambles[9] may be appointed for this purpose in the 100 most convenient parts of it, and butchers we may be assured will not be wanting; although I rather recommend buying the children alive, and dressing them hot from the knife, as we do roasting pigs.

17   A very worthy person, a true lover of his country, and whose virtues I highly esteem, was lately pleased, in discoursing on this matter, to offer a refinement upon my 105 scheme. He said, that many gentlemen of this kingdom, having of late destroyed their deer, he conceived that the want of venison might be well supplied by the bodies of young lads and maidens, not exceeding fourteen years of age, nor under twelve; so great a number of both sexes in every country being now ready to starve for want of work and service; and these to be disposed of by their parents, if alive, or otherwise by 110 their nearest relations. But, with due deference to so excellent a friend, and so deserving a patriot, I cannot be altogether in his sentiments; for as to the males, my American acquaintance assured me from frequent experience, that their flesh was generally tough and lean, like that of our school-boys, by continual exercise, and their taste disagreeable; and to fatten them would not answer the charge. Then as to the females, it would, 115 I think, with humble submission, be a loss to the public, because they soon would become breeders themselves: and besides, it is not improbable that some scrupulous people might be apt to censure such a practice (although indeed very unjustly) as a little bordering upon cruelty; which, I confess hath always been with me the strongest objection against any project, how well soever intended. 120

18   But in order to justify my friend, he confessed that this expedient was put into his head by the famous Psalmanazar,[10] a native of the island Formosa, who came from thence to London about twenty years ago; and in conversation told my friend, that in his country, when any young person happened to be put to death, the executioner sold the carcass to persons of quality as a prime dainty; and that in his time the body of a 125 plump girl of fifteen, who was crucified for an attempt to poison the emperor, was sold

---

9 Slaughterhouses.
10 George Psalmanazar (1679–1763), a Frenchman who pretended to be a Formosan and wrote (in English) a fraudulent book about his 'native' land.

to his Imperial Majesty's prime minister of state,[11] and other great mandarins of the court, in joints from the gibbet, at four hundred crowns. Neither indeed can I deny, that if the same use were made of several plump young girls in this town, who, without one single groat to their fortunes, cannot stir abroad without a chair, and appear at playhouse and assemblies[12] in foreign fineries which they never will pay for, the kingdom would not be the worse.

19   Some persons of a desponding spirit are in great concern about that vast number of poor people who are aged, diseased, or maimed; and I have been desired to employ my thoughts what course may be taken to ease the nation of so grievous an encumbrance. But I am not in the least pain upon that matter, because it is very well known, that they are every day dying, and rotting, by cold and famine, and filth and vermin, as fast as can be reasonably expected. And as to the younger labourers, they are now in almost as hopeful a condition: they cannot get work, and consequently pine away for want of nourishment, to a degree, that if at any time they are accidentally hired to common labour, they have not strength to perform it; and thus the country and themselves are happily delivered from the evils to come.

20   I have too long digressed, and therefore shall return to my subject. I think the advantages by the proposal which I have made are obvious and many, as well as of the highest importance.

21   For first, as I have already observed, it would greatly lessen the number of papists, with whom we are yearly overrun, being the principal breeders of the nation as well as our most dangerous enemies; and who stay at home on purpose with a design to deliver the kingdom to the Pretender, hoping to take their advantage by the absence of so many good Protestants, who have chosen rather to leave their country than stay at home and pay tithes against their conscience to an idolatrous Episcopal curate.[13]

22   Secondly, the poorer tenants will have something valuable of their own, which by law may be made liable to distress, and help to pay their landlord's rent; their corn and cattle being already seized, and money a thing unknown.

23   Thirdly, whereas the maintenance of a hundred thousand children, from two years old and upwards, cannot be computed at less than ten shillings a piece per annum, the nation's stock will be thereby increased fifty thousand pounds per annum; besides the profit of a new dish introduced to the tables of all gentlemen of fortune in the kingdom who have any refinement in taste. And the money will circulate among ourselves, the goods being entirely of our own growth and manufacture.

24   Fourthly, the constant breeders, besides the gain of eight shillings sterling per annum by the sale of their children, will be rid of the charge of maintaining them after the first year.

---

11 Probably a reference to Walpole.

12 Social gatherings (Swift had sought an Irish boycott of all such foreign luxuries of dress or diet).

13 Swift is mocking the castigation of the Catholics, for he regarded it as a typical propaganda device of the Whigs and Protestants; his own experience as a clergyman in northern Ireland had given him reason to fear and distrust the energies of the dissenting Protestants, and he questions their motives (money or conscience) for leaving Ireland. The word 'idolatrous' was added in 1735 after renewed agitation to remove the Sacramental Test, with the implication that Anglican forms and doctrines were intolerable to other Protestants.

25   Fifthly, this food would likewise bring great custom to taverns; where the vint- 165
ners will certainly be so prudent as to procure the best receipts for dressing it to
perfection, and, consequently, have their houses frequented by all the fine gentlemen,
who justly value themselves upon their knowledge in good eating: and a skilful cook,
who understands how to oblige his guests, will contrive to make it as expensive as
they please.   170

26   Sixthly, this would be a great inducement to marriage, which all wise nations
have either encouraged by rewards, or enforced by laws and penalties. It would
increase the care and tenderness of mothers towards their children, when they were
sure of a settlement for life to the poor babes, provided in some by the public, to
the annual profit instead of expense. We should soon see an honest emulation 175
among the married women, which of them could bring the fattest child to the market. Men would become as fond of their wives during the time of their pregnancy,
as they are now of their mares in foal, their cows in calf, or sows when they are
ready to farrow; nor offer to beat or kick them (as is too frequent a practice) for fear
of a miscarriage.   180

27   Many other advantages might be enumerated. For instance, the addition of
some thousand carcasses in our exportation of barrelled beef; the propagation of
swine's flesh, and improvement in the art of making good bacon, so much wanted
among us by the great destruction of pigs, too frequent at our tables, which are no
way comparable in taste or magnificence to a well-grown, fat yearling child, which, 185
roasted whole, will make a considerable figure at a Lord Mayor's feast, or any other
public entertainment. But this, and many others, I omit, being studious of brevity.

28   Supposing that one thousand families in this city would be constant customers
for infants' flesh, besides others who might have it at merry meetings, particularly
weddings and christenings, I compute that Dublin would take off annually about 190
twenty thousand carcasses; and the rest of the kingdom (where probably they will be
sold somewhat cheaper) the remaining eighty thousand.

29   I can think of no one objection that will possibly be raised against this proposal,
unless it should be urged, that the number of people will be thereby much lessened
in the kingdom. This I freely own, and it was indeed one principal design in offering 195
it to the world. I desire the reader will observe that I calculate my remedy for this one
individual kingdom of Ireland, and for no other that ever was, is, or I think ever can
be, upon earth. Therefore let no man talk to me of other expedients:[14] of taxing our
absentees at five shillings a pound: of using neither clothes nor household furniture
except what is of our own growth and manufacture: of utterly rejecting the materials 200
and instruments that promote foreign luxury: of curing the expensiveness of pride,
vanity, idleness, and gaming in our women: of introducing a vein of parsimony, prudence, and temperance: of learning to love our country, wherein we differ even from
Laplanders, and the inhabitants of Topinamboo:[15] of quitting our animosities and factions, nor act any longer like the Jews, who were murdering one another at the very 205
moment their city was taken:[16] of being a little cautious not to sell our country and

---

14 The following are, of course, Swift's own genuine proposals for Ireland.
15 A region of Brazil known for wildness and barbarous stupidity.
16 When Jerusalem fell to Nebuchadnezzar (II Kings 24, 25; II Chronicles 36), with the suggestion that
   English domination is Ireland's Babylonian captivity.

consciences for nothing: of teaching landlords to have at least one degree of mercy towards their tenants: lastly, of putting a spirit of honesty, industry, and skill into our shopkeepers; who, if a resolution could now be taken to buy only our native goods, would immediately unite to cheat and exact upon us in the price, the measure, and 210 the goodness, nor could ever yet be brought to make one fair proposal of just dealing, though often and earnestly invited to it.

30   Therefore I repeat, let no man talk to me of these and the like expedients, till he hath at least some glimpse of hope that there will ever be some hearty and sincere attempt to put them in practice.   215

31   But, as to myself, having been wearied out for many years with offering vain, idle, visionary thoughts, and at length utterly despairing of success, I fortunately fell upon this proposal; which, as it is wholly new, so it hath something solid and real, of no expense and little trouble, full in our own power, and whereby we can incur no danger in disobliging England. For this kind of commodity will not bear exportation, 220 the flesh being of too tender a consistence to admit a long continuance in salt, although perhaps I could name a country which would be glad to eat up our whole nation without it.

32   After all, I am not so violently bent upon my own opinion as to reject any offer proposed by wise men which shall be found equally innocent, cheap, easy, and effec- 225 tual. But before something of that kind shall be advanced in contradiction to my scheme, and offering a better, I desire the author, or authors, will be pleased maturely to consider two points. First, as things now stand, how they will be able to find food and raiment for a hundred thousand useless mouths and backs? And, secondly, there being a round million of creatures in human figure throughout this kingdom, whose 230 whole subsistence put into a common stock would leave them in debt two millions of pounds sterling, adding those who are beggars by profession, to the bulk of farmers, cottagers, and labourers, with the wives and children who are beggars in effect; I desire those politicians who dislike my overture, and may perhaps be so bold as to attempt an answer, that they will first ask the parents of these mortals, whether they 235 would not at this day think it a great happiness to have been sold for food at a year old, in the manner I prescribe, and thereby have avoided such a perpetual scene of misfortunes as they have since gone through, by the oppression of landlords, the impossibility of paying rent without money or trade, the want of common sustenance, with neither house nor clothes to cover them from the inclemencies of 240 weather, and the most inevitable prospect of entailing the like, or greater miseries, upon their breed for ever.

33   I profess, in the sincerity of my heart, that I have not the least personal interest in endeavouring to promote this necessary work, having no other motive than the public good of my country, by advancing our trade, providing for infants, relieving 245 the poor, and giving some pleasure to the rich. I have no children by which I can propose to get a single penny; the youngest being nine years old, and my wife past child-bearing.

1729

QUESTIONS
Reader and Purpose

1. Swift's purpose, of course, is to attack English policy toward Ireland, but not so much any specific act as the fundamental attitude toward the Irish that determined policy in general. To do this he pretends to accept that attitude. Describe what Swift implies is the way in which the English regard the Irish.

2. In reading 'A Modest Proposal' one must distinguish Swift from the 'I', the pious projector ('do-gooder', we might call him today) who puts forward this cannibalistic scheme. On occasion Swift does speak almost directly through the 'I'; but more often the 'I' is part of the satire, expressing the moral platitudes typical of many English, who could see no contradiction between the Christianity they avowed and the harsh policy toward Ireland they preached and practised. An example of this kind of shallow piety is the sympathy the speaker expresses for the Irish poor in the very opening sentence. Again, in paragraph 17 he speaks warmly of the virtues of his friend who suggests that Irish boys and girls might take the place of venison. Point out one or two other passages in which Swift, by giving pious sentiments to his speaker, reveals the disparity between Christian pretensions and political realities. Several times the 'I' refers to himself as 'humble'. Is he?

3. On the surface the **tone** of 'A Modest Proposal' is sober and objective, carefully avoiding any direct expression of emotion. The Irish problem is approached simply as a matter of economics, calculable solely in terms of cost and profit. Now and then, however, the emotionless objectivity slips and we see a flash of anger. The very end of paragraph 18 is an example, where Swift lashes out at the vanity and idleness of society girls. Where else do you detect anger?

4. But such passages are exceptional. Generally the surface discipline holds, and emotion is kept in check. Below the surface, it is another story. Describe this deeper tone—'undertone', as it might be called.

Organization

5. Roughly, 'A Modest Proposal' divides into these sections: (1) the introduction, in which the problem is identified and laid out; (2) the solution to the problem; (3) the advantages of that solution; (4) answers to possible objections; and (5) the conclusion. Indicate in terms of paragraph numbers where each of these parts begins and ends.

6. The organizational scheme is not absolutely rigid. For instance, Swift touches upon the advantages of his proposal in places other than the third section. Where?

7. What is the function of paragraphs 8 and 20?

8. Swift organizes the sixth paragraph by analyzing the problem in statistical terms. Explain why his use of statistics is a device of **irony**. Toward the end of this paragraph Swift gets involved in a discussion of whether or not children can support themselves by stealing. Is he wandering away from his point here, or does this apparent digression contribute to the general irony?

9. Paraphrase the point Swift makes in paragraph 12.

10. How are paragraphs 21–26 unified?

11. In paragraph 29 how does Swift answer the objection that his scheme would depopulate Ireland?

12. The final paragraph of 'A Modest Proposal' is frequently praised as an excellent ending to the satire. Do you agree? Why, or why not?

Sentences

13. Point out the **parallel construction** in the following sentences:

    (a) '. . . who, as they grow up, either turn thieves for want of work, or leave their dear native country to fight for the Pretender in Spain, or sell themselves to the Barbadoes.' (6–8)

    (b) 'For we can neither employ them in handicraft or agriculture; we neither build houses (I mean in the country) nor cultivate land. . . .' (44–6)

14. Why are the following revisions poorer than Swift's sentences?

    (a) **Revision:** I grant this food will be somewhat dear, and therefore very proper for landlords who seem to have the best title to the children since they have already devoured most of the parents.
    Swift: 'I grant this food will be somewhat dear, and therefore very proper for landlords, who, as they have already devoured most of the parents, seem to have the best title to the children.' (78–80)

    (b) **Revision:** Fifthly, this food would likewise bring great custom to taverns. Vintners will certainly be so prudent as to procure the best receipts for dressing it to perfection. Consequently they will have their houses frequented by all the fine gentlemen. Such gentlemen justly value themselves upon their knowledge in good eating. Therefore a skilful cook, who understands how to oblige his guests, will contrive to make it as expensive as they please.
    Swift: 'Fifthly, this food would likewise bring great custom to taverns; where the vintners will certainly be so prudent as to procure the best receipts for dressing it to perfection, and, consequently, have their houses frequented by all the fine gentlemen, who justly value themselves upon their knowledge in good eating: and a skilful cook, who understands how to oblige his guests, will contrive to make it as expensive as they please.' (165–70)

15. Study the following sentence, which is a fine example of the kind of long, complex statement Swift was master of:

    'But, as to myself, having been wearied out for many years with offering vain, idle, visionary thoughts, and at length utterly despairing of success, I fortunately fell upon this proposal; which, as it is wholly new, so it hath something solid and real, of no expense and little trouble, full in our power, and whereby we can incur no danger in disobliging England.' (216–20)

What is the **main clause**? What do 'having been wearied' and 'utterly despairing of success' modify? What does the long 'which' clause modify? Point out all the parallel constructions. This sentence tells us three things: (1) what the speaker did, (2) the conditions under which he did it, and (3) why he considers it worthwhile. In what sequence are these elements placed in Swift's sentence? Why are they in that particular order?

Diction

16. Look up: *raiment* (27), *fricassee* (63), *glutted* (85), *computed* (89), *repine* (91), *flay* (97), *discoursing* (105), *deference* (111), *expedient* (121), *gibbet* (128), *groat* (130), *idolatrous* (151), *emulation* (175), *absentee* (short for *absentee landlord*) (199), *parsimony* (202), *incur* (219).

17. Explain the **etymologies** of these words: *melancholy* (1), *importuning* (4), *alms* (4), *vermin* (138), *digress* (143), *curate* (152), *overture* (234).

18. What is the difference between *beggars by profession* (232) and *beggars in effect* (233)?

19. As the second footnote makes clear, the word *projector* meant for Swift something very different than it means for us. Similarly, the following words, still in use today, have different meanings than they had in Swift's time; explain the difference: *passenger* (4), *artificially* (98), *vintners* (165–6), *prudent* (166), *receipts* (166), *politicians* (234). Suggest in each case a modern word that would be the equivalent of what Swift meant.

20. Explain the irony in the following expressions: 'so deserving a patriot' (111–12), 'to fatten them would not answer the charge' (115), 'some scrupulous people might be apt to censure such a practice (although indeed very unjustly) as a littler bordering upon cruelty' (117–19), 'refinement in taste' (160), 'vain, idle, visionary thoughts' (216–17), 'although perhaps I could name a country which would be glad to eat up our whole nation without it' (222–3).

21. *Dam* (22) is normally applied to animals, not to human beings. Why does Swift use it as he does here? Point out other instances of his applying to humans words commonly restricted to animals.

22. One of the tricks Swift uses in 'A Modest Proposal' is the inclusion of little details, seemingly irrelevant, but which have the effect of increasing our sense of horror. For instance, in arguing that the forequarter of a child will make a tasty leftover dish, he adds (75) 'especially in winter'. Or in lines 102–3 he suggests that it might be better to buy the children alive and 'dress' them 'hot from the knife'. Find other examples of such horrific details. If you agree that these do intensify our repulsion, can you explain why they do?

POINTS TO LEARN

1. Often an essayist who uses 'I' is creating a persona, a mask through which he speaks, but which is not identical to him.
2. Moral outrage may be strengthened by being suppressed.

SUGGESTIONS FOR WRITING

1. Taking him at face value, compose a character sketch in several paragraphs of the speaker of 'A Modest Proposal'.
2. Complete the following topic sentence and then support it in a paragraph or two with evidence from Swift's text: 'The speaker of "A Modest Proposal" considers the Irish to be _____.'
3. In a paragraph or two answer this criticism of 'A Modest Proposal': 'The essay is too revolting to be effective; it exaggerates English policy in so disgusting a manner that it defeats its own purpose.'

IMPROVING YOUR STYLE

In your composition include:

1. two or three sentences using **parallelism**;
2. a complex sentence with a **main clause** and three or four **subordinate clauses** arranged so that their order reflects the actual sequence of events or the logic of ideas;
3. a series of three or four sentences tied together by First, Second, Third, (Fourth);
4. several examples of **irony**.

JAMES S. TREFIL

A teacher of physics at the University of Virginia for many years, James S. Trefil (1938–) has published extensively on a wide variety of scientific subjects. His books, many of which are aimed at a general audience, include *From Atoms to Quarks* (1980), *Living in Space* (1981), *The Dark Side of the Universe: A Scientist Explores the Mysteries of the Cosmos* (1988), *The Edge of the Unknown: 101 Things You Don't Know about Science and No One Else Does Either* (1996), and *Other Worlds: Images of the Cosmos from Earth and Space* (1999). He has also written numerous articles for professional journals and for more popular periodicals, and answers readers' science questions in *USA Weekend*'s 'Ask Mr Science' column. The selection below is taken from an article on probability, which appeared in the September 1984 issue of *Smithsonian* magazine.

The Golf Ball on the Grass

1   The second type of misuse of statistics centres around what I like to call 'hidden message' theory. It goes like this: in some ancient structure, superior beings (usually extraterrestrials) have left a secret message which, if we were only clever enough to decode it, would reveal to us mysteries of the cosmos. The Great Pyramid at Giza is a favourite hunting ground for hidden-message enthusiasts, but almost any old build- 5 ing will do. The idea is to search around until you find that one particular dimension in the building is one-billionth of the distance to the moon or one ten-millionth the distance around the world, at which point you announce your result. 'Could it be just a coincidence that the height of this column is *exactly* that distance? The people who built it couldn't have known the distance that accurately, so . . .' I think you can anti- 10 cipate the rest.

2   This kind of argument illustrates what one of my old math professors used to call the 'golf-ball-on-the-fairway fallacy'. The probability that a golf ball will wind up on a particular blade of grass in the fairway is very small. But you don't have to explain why the ball came down on that particular blade because the fact of the mat- 15 ter is that the ball has to land on some blade somewhere. If it had not landed on that one, then it would have landed on some other one.

3   Significant numbers are like the blades of grass on the fairway. You can generate quantities of them just by looking at the solar system. For example, the mass of

Venus divided by the mass of the Earth is .815, the mass of Jupiter divided by the   20
mass of Saturn is 3.34, and so on. By the time you run through this exercise for the
masses, radii, and the distances from the sun to all nine planets, you will have generated hundreds of thousands of significant numbers. Because the rules of the hidden-
message game allow you to shift decimal places at will (finding something 100 or
1,000 times bigger or smaller than a significant number is just as good as finding   25
something equal to a significant number), you can't miss. Just as the golf ball has to
fall on some blade of grass, anything you want to measure to find a hidden message
must fall on some significant number. The low probability of having it fall on a particular number is simply irrelevant, because it has to fall somewhere.

Kennedy–Lincoln: Less Than Meets the Eye

4   A classic example of the 'golfball on the fairway' made the rounds shortly after   30
the assassination of John F. Kennedy in 1963. The story, widely circulated in the press
and on a popular record, established a series of apparently astonishing coincidences
between the assassinations of Presidents Lincoln and Kennedy. Among the points
made were these:

1. Lincoln was elected in 1860, Kennedy in 1960   35
2. Both were assassinated on Fridays the thirteenth in the presence of their
   wives
3. Lincoln was killed in Ford's Theater, Kennedy while riding in a car made
   by the Ford Motor Company
4. Both were succeeded by vice-presidents named Johnson who were   40
   Southern Democrats and former senators
5. Andrew Johnson was born in 1808, Lyndon Johnson in 1908
6. Lincoln's secretary was named John Kennedy, Kennedy's secretary named
   Evelyn Lincoln
7. John Wilkes Booth was born in 1839, Lee Harvey Oswald in 1939   45
8. Booth shot Lincoln in a theatre and fled to a warehouse, Oswald shot
   Kennedy from a warehouse and fled to a theatre
9. The names Lincoln and Kennedy have seven letters each
10. The names Andrew Johnson and Lyndon Johnson have 13 letters each.

5   This list is actually very typical of the sort of numerology you run across once   50
in a while. In the first place, some of the 'facts' are just wrong—Booth was born in
1838, Lincoln's secretary was named John Nicolay, Booth was trapped in a barn
instead of a warehouse. But the real question was whether the coincidences remaining could have some underlying significance.

6   The author of the original list is unknown. But Martin Gardner, for many years   55
a columnist at *Scientific American* and the author of books on bogus science, used the
list to demonstrate how a diligent researcher could establish apparently extraordinary
similarities between any two lives. Just take the first point as an example. Any president will have gone through many elections in his career. For each election, there are
all sorts of numbers associated with the date: the man's age and the time since his   60
marriage, since the birth of his children, since he finished school, since his last
election, and so on. The last two digits of the year are just one more item in this

collection that can be as long as you make it. That two of these indices should match is not very surprising.

7   But more important than that, there are many facts about anyone's life that can 65
play the role of the blades of grass on the fairway. If you really started, you could probably write down more than a thousand about your own birth date and place of birth
(and number of letters in the town), schools attended, children's names, places lived,
etc. Comparing this list with anyone else's will be sure to turn up similarities. For
example, I learned to drive in a Ford, which gives me one point up on both Lincoln 70
and Kennedy; Oswald and Trefil each have six letters. Or consider Presidents
McKinley and Garfield. They were both born in Ohio. Their names both have eight
letters; the names of their vice-presidents (Chester Alan Arthur and Theodore Roose-
velt) both have 17. Both were assassinated while on trips; the wives of both had fallen
sick before the assassinations. And so on. The reason that something like the 75
Kennedy–Lincoln list holds our attention is that we know that if we had to predict
these similarities in advance, the probability of success would be very low. The same
is true about predicting the blade of grass on which the golf ball will eventually come
to rest. The point is that in this case we're *not* predicting the points of similarity, we're
picking them out of literally millions of possible points after the fact. This is like look- 80
ing at the blade of grass after the ball has come to rest. There are bound to be coincidences in a finite world, and it's always a good idea to think about the golf ball when
somebody singles out one.

8   Having made this point, let me close with one more observation. If you divide
the height of the Sears Tower in Chicago (the world's tallest building) by the height of 85
the Woolworth Building in New York, you get 1.836. This is precisely one-thousandth
of what you get if you divide the mass of one of the fundamental building blocks of
matter, the proton, by the mass of the other fundamental building block, the electron.

9   Think about it.

1984

QUESTIONS
Reader and Purpose
1. Beyond the immediate question of the validity or nonvalidity of the 'hidden-message' theory lies a broader issue. Why do you suppose some people feel a need to
   believe in hidden messages, numerology, extraterrestrials, and so on? What, on the
   other hand, is the attitude that Trefil represents and that opposes such beliefs?
   Why does he take the trouble to argue the point? Why not live and let live?
2. Is Trefil writing primarily for believers in 'concealed messages'? If not, what degree
   of knowledge and sophistication does he assume in his readers?
3. Does Trefil develop a convincing argument? What is his main strategy: to dispute
   the accuracy of the facts cited by 'hidden message' believers, or to show that the
   significance they claim for the facts is exaggerated or based on faulty logic?

Organization
4. What does the opening sentence contribute to the organization? What does the
   entire first paragraph contribute?

5. Identify the **topic sentence** of each paragraph. (Consider paragraph 4 as comprising all the material from line 30 to line 49.)
6. Indicate the words at or near the beginning of each paragraph that link it to the preceding material.
7. Paragraph 3 includes an example. Does it make the topic clearer? Where else does Trefil use examples?
8. In the second paragraph the writer introduces an **analogy**. One of its purposes is to clarify an **abstract** idea. What idea? What sentence applies the analogy to the argument?
9. Another purpose of the analogy is organizational: to serve as a continuing theme that helps to unify the passage. Where else does Trefil refer to the 'golf ball on the fairway'?
10. Which paragraph (or paragraphs) constitutes the closing? Is it an effective ending?

Sentences

11. Compare these revisions with Trefil's sentences and explain why each is less effective.

   (a) **Revision:** The probability is very small that a golf ball will wind up on a particular blade of grass in the fairway.

   Trefil: The probability that a golf ball will wind up on a particular blade of grass in the fairway is very small. (13–14)

   (b) **Revision:** Think about the fact that this is precisely one-thousandth of what you get if you divide the mass of one of the fundamental building blocks of matter, the proton, by the mass of the other fundamental building block, the electron.

   Trefil: This is precisely one-thousandth of what you get if you divide the mass of one of the fundamental building blocks of matter, the proton, by the mass of the other fundamental building block, the electron.
   Think about it. (86–9)

12. Suppose the parentheses around the explanation in lines 24–6 were replaced by commas: would the sentence be just as clear? If not, why not?
13. What about the parentheses in lines 73–4—could they be replaced by commas? by dashes?
14. What does the dash in line 51 signal? Why does Trefil use the same pattern for each of the three **clauses** following that dash? Where else does he use a similar series of short sentences?

Diction

15. Look up: *extraterrestrial* (3), *cosmos* (4), *anticipate* (10–11), *fallacy* (13), *fairway* (14), *generate* (18–19), *radii* (22), *irrelevant* (29), *indices* (63), *observation* (84).
16. What do these phrases mean: *classic example* (30), *bogus science* (56), *diligent researcher* (57), *finite world* (81–2)?
17. If the term *enthusiasts* (5) were replaced by *kooks*, how would the **tone** of the passage change? Is *enthusiasts* a neutral word, or does it have connotations of approval or of disapproval?

POINTS TO LEARN

1. Facts—even numerical facts—are not inherently meaningful. Their significance must be established and cannot be taken for granted.
2. Abstract ideas can often be made clearer by example and by analogy.
3. An analogy—or any comparison—can be repeated throughout a passage and thus provide unity.

SUGGESTIONS FOR WRITING

At a supermarket or a convenience store buy one of those tabloid scandal sheets that feature stories about popular wonders—the abominable snowman, brain transplants, dinosaurs surviving deep in the Amazonian jungle, etc. Select one such article, read it carefully, and try to expose the misrepresentation of fact and the fallacies of reason upon which it rests. Present your analysis—which is, in effect, a refutation—in an essay of about 500 words. Begin by briefly making clear the claim you are going to dispute.

IMPROVING YOUR STYLE

1. Use several illustrations and at least one **analogy** in support of two or three of your **topic sentences**.
2. Pay careful attention to the **transitions** between paragraphs.
3. Close your essay with a short sentence.

WILLIAM FAULKNER

William Faulkner (1897–1962), one of the great novelists of the twentieth century, was born and educated in Mississippi and wrote primarily about his native region. Among his 19 novels, which depict and analyze the decline of Faulkner's American South into crudity, meanness, and brutality, are *The Sound and the Fury* (1929), *Sartoris* (1929), *As I Lay Dying* (1930), *Sanctuary* (1931), *Absalom, Absalom!* (1936), and *The Hamlet* (1940). Both *A Fable* (1954) and *The Reivers* (1962) won Pulitzer Prizes, and in 1950 Faulkner was awarded the Nobel Prize for literature. The selection reprinted here is the speech he delivered on that occasion. It is a fine example of true eloquence: a high-minded sense of human destiny expressed in moving and memorable language, and characteristic of the man himself.

On Receiving the Nobel Prize

1   I feel that this award was not made to me as a man but to my work—a life's work in the agony and sweat of the human spirit, not for glory and least of all for profit, but to create out of the materials of the human spirit something which did not exist there before. So this award is only mine in trust. It will not be difficult to find a dedication of the money part of it commensurate with the purpose and significance 5 of its origin. But I would like to do the same with the acclaim, too, by using this

moment as a pinnacle from which I might be listened to by the young men and women already dedicated to the same anguish and travail, among whom is already that one who will some day stand here where I am standing.

2   Our tragedy today is a general and a universal physical fear so long sustained 10 by now that we can even bear it. There are no longer problems of the spirit. There is only the question: When will I be blown up? Because of this, the young man or woman writing today has forgotten the problems of the human heart in conflict with itself which alone can make good writing because only that is worth writing about, worth the agony and the sweat.   15

3   He must learn them again. He must teach himself that the basest of all things is to be afraid; and, teaching himself that, forget it forever, leaving no room in his work-shop for anything but the old verities and truths of the heart, the old universal truth lacking which any story is ephemeral and doomed—love and honour and pity and pride and compassion and sacrifice. Until he does so he labours under a curse. He 20 writes not of love, but of lust, of defeats in which nobody loses anything of value, of victories without hope and worst of all without pity or compassion. His griefs grieve on no universal bones, leaving no scars. He writes not of the heart but of the glands.

4   Until he relearns these things he will write as though he stood among and watched the end of man. I decline to accept the end of man. It is easy enough to say 25 that man is immortal simply because he will endure; that when the last ding-dong of doom has clanged and faded from the last worthless rock hanging tideless in the last red and dying evening, that even then there will still be one more sound: that of his puny inexhaustible voice still talking. I refuse to accept this. I believe that man will not merely endure: he will prevail. He is immortal, not because he alone among creatures 30 has an inexhaustible voice, but because he has a soul, a spirit capable of compassion and sacrifice and endurance. The poet's, the writer's, duty is to write about these things. It is his privilege to help man endure by lifting his heart, by reminding him of the courage and honour and hope and pride and compassion and pity and sacrifice which have been the glory of his past. The poet's voice need not merely be the record of man, 35 it can be one of the props, the pillars to help him endure and prevail.

1954

QUESTIONS
Reader and Purpose

1. Faulkner clearly defines his purpose in the first paragraph. In which sentence?
2. To whom does he imagine himself to be talking? Of what does he wish to persuade these listeners.
3. Keeping in mind that Faulkner wrote this essay in 1949 (that is, not long after the end of World War II), what do you think he is referring to when he writes, 'There is only the question: When will I be blown up?' (11–12)

Organization

4. If the first paragraph established the writer's intention, how does the second fit into his strategy? What does it contribute to his thesis? Give this paragraph a brief descriptive title.

5. What words tie the beginning of the third paragraph to the second? How are the topics of these two paragraphs related?

6. Analyze paragraph 3, showing how the writer's thought progresses from sentence to sentence. Explain why the passage beginning in line 20 ('Until he does so he labours under a curse.') marks a major turn of thought within the paragraph. How does Faulkner use sentence structure to unify paragraph 3?

7. What words connect the fourth paragraph to the third? Which sentence marks a major turn in this paragraph

Sentences

8. Compare the following revisions with Faulkner's sentences and comment upon the differences in meaning, emphasis, or rhythm:

   (a) *Revision:* The only question is when I'll be blown up.
   Faulkner: 'There is only the question: When will I be blown up?' (11–12)

   (b) *Revision:* He will write as though he stood among and watched the end of man until he relearns these things.
   Faulkner: 'Until he relearns these things he will write as though he stood among and watched the end of man.' (24–5)

   (c) *Revision:* I believe that man will prevail and not merely endure.
   Faulkner: 'I believe that man will not merely endure: he will prevail.' (29–30)

9. Point out one or two places where Faulkner employs short sentences very effectively.

10. In the sentence in lines 16–20 to what are 'love and honour and pity and pride and compassion and sacrifice' in **apposition**? Suppose a comma rather than a dash had preceded these words—would the clarity of the sentence have been helped or hindered?

11. In the list above Faulkner joins all the items with *and* instead of following the more common formula: 'love, honour, pity, pride, compassion, and sacrifice'. Where else does he handle a list or series with multiple **conjunctions** (a technique called **polysyndeton**)? Can you see any reason why he does it this way?

Diction

12. Look up: *acclaim* (6), *anguish* (8), *travail* (8), *basest* (16), *prevail* (30).

13. Explain the **etymologies** of *commensurate* (5), *verities* (18), *ephemeral* (19), *doom* (19), *endurance* (32).

14. Several times Faulkner couples *compassion* and *pity*. What is the difference?

15. Would it be an improvement in lines 22–3 to write something like 'his griefs sadden no universal bones,' avoiding the repetition of 'griefs grieve'? What does Faulkner mean by 'universal bones'?

16. In lines 26–7 Faulkner uses the striking phrase 'the last ding-dong of doom'. *Ding-dong* and *doom* arouse quite different associations in one's mind. Explain. Do you think this clash of association makes the image awkward and ineffective? Why in this same passage does Faulkner specify the rock as being 'tideless'?

17. Identify the **alliteration** in the final sentence. What value does it have? Where else does Faulkner employ alliteration?

POINTS TO LEARN

1. Faulkner's speech is a notable testament to the human spirit. This faith in human-kind is the foundation of all eloquence.
2. Like all effective persuasion, eloquence requires a clear sense of purpose and a strategy designed to achieve that purpose.

SUGGESTIONS FOR WRITING

Write a paragraph or two describing your reaction to Faulkner's words. Did they move you or not? Do you agree with what he says about the moral responsibilities of the writer? Do you think he is unduly pessimistic, is guilty of an unjustifiable optimism, or expresses a balanced view of human possibilities?

IMPROVING YOUR STYLE

Include in your composition:

1. a portion of the paragraph unified by several sentences beginning in the same way;
2. an appositive;
3. an instance of polysyndeton (see question 10);
4. a passage using alliteration.

JOHN MCPHEE

John McPhee (1931–) is among the best of the so-called 'new journalists', who add a dimension of personal judgment and sensitivity to the reporter's traditional job of report-ing the facts. His essays in *The New Yorker*, where he has been a staff writer since 1965, deal with an extraordinary variety of people, places, and topics: Alaska, a canoe trip in northern Maine, the Jersey pine barrens, the basketball star and later US sena-tor Bill Bradley, English literature, historical science, recreation, and so on. He has pub-lished more than 25 books, including *The Curve of Binding Energy* (1974), *Basin and Range* (1980), *Looking for a Ship* (1990), and *Assembling California* (1993). His most recent work, *Annals of the Former World* (1998), earned McPhee a Pulitzer Prize.

In the following essay, from his book *Pieces of the Frame* (1975), McPhee writes about Atlantic City, the once fashionable resort on the coast of New Jersey whose for-tunes declined in the 1950s and 1960s. (Since McPhee wrote the essay—1972—the city has been revived, financially at least, by the introduction of legalized gambling.) He organizes his essay in an unusual way, using the game of 'Monopoly' to counterpoint his account of the city. The relationship between Monopoly and Atlantic City is not fortu-itous; in its layout, the game borrows actual street names from the resort.

Monopoly was invented in the 1930s during the Great Depression and was an immediate, and phenomenal, success. Seventy years later, while no longer a phenomenon, the game remains popular. It obviously appeals to a society based upon economic individualism and competition, by giving us the chance to play a role real life denies: the 'Grand Monopolist', financially omnipotent, owner of all he surveys.

On the surface 'The Search for Marvin Gardens' is not persuasion. It mounts no formal argument; it is not satire. Yet below the surface it implies, with considerable persuasive force, feelings and judgments about the values of our society.

The Search for Marvin Gardens

1   Go. I roll the dice—a six and a two. Through the air I move my token, the flat-iron, to Vermont Avenue, where dog packs range.

2   The dogs are moving (some are limping) through ruins, rubble, fire damage, open garbage. Doorways are gone. Lath is visible in the crumbling walls of the buildings. The street sparkles with shattered glass. I have never seen, anywhere, so many 5 broken windows. A sign—'Slow, Children at Play'—has been bent backward by an automobile. At the lighthouse, the dogs turn up Pacific and disappear. George Meade, Army engineer, built the lighthouse—brick upon brick, 600,000 bricks, to reach up high enough to throw a beam 20 miles over the sea. Meade, seven years later, saved the Union at Gettysburg.   10

3   I buy Vermont Avenue for $100. My opponent is a tall, shadowy figure, across from me, but I know him well, and I know his game like a favourite tune. If he can, he will always go for the quick kill. And when it is foolish to go for the quick kill he will be foolish. On the whole, though, he is a master assessor of percentages. It is a mistake to underestimate him. His eleven carries his top hat to St Charles Place, 15 which he buys for $140.

4   The sidewalks of St Charles Place have been cracked to shards by through-growing weeds. There are no buildings. Mansions, hotels once stood here. A few street lamps now drop cones of light on broken glass and vacant space behind a chain-link fence that some great machine has in places bent to the ground. Five plane trees—in 20 full summer leaf, flecking the light—are all that live on St Charles Place.

5   Block upon block, gradually, we are cancelling each other out—in the blues, the lavenders, the oranges, the greens. My opponent follows a plan of his own devising. I use the Hornblower & Weeks opening and the Zuricher defence. The first game draws tight, will soon finish. In 1971, a group of people in Racine, Wisconsin, played 25 for 768 hours. A game begun a month later in Danville, California, lasted 820 hours. These are official records, and they stun us. We have been playing for eight minutes. It amazes us that Monopoly is thought of as a long game. It is possible to play to a complete, absolute, and final conclusion in less than 15 minutes, all within the rules as written. My opponent and I have done so thousands of times. No wonder we are 30 sitting across from each other now in this best-of-seven series for the international singles championship of the world.

6   On Illinois Avenue, three men lean out from second-storey windows. A girl is coming down the street. She wears dungarees and a bright-red shirt, has ample breasts and a Hadendoan Afro, a black halo, two feet in diameter. Ice rattles in the 35 glasses in the hands of the men.

7   'Hey, sister!'

8   'Come on up!'

9   She looks up, looks from one to another to the other, looks them flat in the eye.

10   'What for?' she says, and she walks on.   40

11   I buy Illinois for $240. It solidifies my chances, for I already own Kentucky and Indiana. My opponent pales. If he had landed first on Illinois, the game would have been over then and there, for he has houses built on Boardwalk and Park Place, we share the railroads equally, and we have cancelled each other everywhere else. We never trade.   45

12   In 1852, R.B. Osborne, an immigrant Englishman, civil engineer, surveyed the route of a railroad line that would run from Camden to Absecon Island, in New Jersey, traversing the state from the Delaware River to the barrier beaches of the sea. He then sketched in the plan of a 'bathing village' that would surround the eastern terminus of the line. His pen flew glibly, framing and naming spacious avenues parallel to the   50 shore—Mediterranean, Baltic, Oriental, Ventnor—and narrower transecting avenues: North Carolina, Pennsylvania, Vermont, Connecticut, States, Virginia, Tennessee, New York, Kentucky, Indiana, Illinois. The place as a whole had no name, so when he had completed the plan Osborne wrote in large letters over the ocean, 'Atlantic City'. No one ever challenged the name, or the names of Osborne's streets. Monopoly   55 was invented in the early nineteen-thirties by Charles B. Darrow, but Darrow was only transliterating what Osborne had created. The railroads, crucial to any player, were the making of Atlantic City. After the rails were down, houses and hotels burgeoned from Mediterranean and Baltic to New York and Kentucky. Properties—building lots—sold for as little as six dollars apiece and as much as a thousand dollars. The   60 original investors in the railroads and the real estate called themselves the Camden & Atlantic Land Company. Reverently, I repeat their names: Dwight Bell, William Coffin, John DaCosta, Daniel Deal, William Fleming, Andrew Hay, Joseph Porter, Jonathan Pitney, Samuel Richards—founders, fathers, forerunners, archetypical masters of the quick kill.   65

13   My opponent and I are now in a deep situation of classical Monopoly. The torsion is almost perfect—Boardwalk and Park Place versus the brilliant reds. His cash position is weak, though, and if I escape him now he may fade. I land on Luxury Tax, contiguous to but in sanctuary from his power. I have four houses on Indiana. He lands there. He concedes.   70

14   Indiana Avenue was the address of the Brighton Hotel, gone now. The Brighton was exclusive—a word that no longer has retail value in the city. If you arrived by automobile and tried to register at the Brighton, you were sent away. Brighton-class people came in private railroad cars. Brighton-class people had other private railroad cars for their horses—dawn rides on the firm sand at water's edge, skirts flying.   75 Colonel Anthony J. Drexel Biddle—the sort of name that would constrict throats in Philadelphia—lived, much of the year, in the Brighton.

15   Colonel Sanders' fried chicken is on Kentucky Avenue. So is Clifton's Club Harlem, with the Sepia Revue and the Sepia Follies, featuring the Honey Bees, the Fashions, and the Lords.   80

16   My opponent and I, many years ago, played 2,428 games of Monopoly in a single season. He was then a recent graduate of the Harvard Law School, and he was working for a downtown firm, looking up law. Two people we knew—one from Chase Manhattan, the other from Morgan, Stanley—tried to get into the game, but after a few rounds we found that they were not in the conversation and we sent them home.   85

Monopoly should always be *mano a mano* anyway. My opponent won 1,199 games, and so did I. Thirty were ties. He was called into the Army, and we stopped just there. Now, in Game 2 of the series, I go immediately to jail, and again to jail while my opponent seines property. He is dumbfoundingly lucky. He wins in 12 minutes.

17   Visiting hours are daily, eleven to two; Sunday, eleven to one; evenings, six to   90
nine. 'NO MINORS, NO FOOD. Immediate Family Only Allowed in Jail.' All this above a blue steel door in a blue cement wall in the windowless interior of the basement of the city hall. The desk sergeant sits opposite the door to the jail. In a cigar box in front of him are pills in every colour, a banquet of fruit salad an inch and a half deep—leapers, co-pilots, footballs, truck drivers, peanuts, blue angels, yellow jackets, redbirds, rain-   95
bows. Near the desk are two soldiers, waiting to go through the blue door. They are about 18 years old. One of them is trying hard to light a cigarette. His wrists are in steel cuffs. A military policeman waits, too. He is a year or so older than the soldiers, taller, studious in appearance, gentle, fat. On a bench against a wall sits a good-looking girl in slacks. The blue door rattles, swings heavily open. A turnkey stands in the doorway.   100
'Don't you guys kill yourselves back there now,' says the sergeant to the soldiers.

18   'One kid, he overdosed himself about ten and a half hours ago,' says the MP.

19   The MP, the soldiers, the turnkey, and the girl on the bench are white. The sergeant is black. 'If you take off the handcuffs, take off the belts,' says the sergeant to the MP. 'I don't want them hanging themselves back there.' The door shuts and its   105
tumblers move. When it opens again, five minutes later, a young white man in san-dals and dungarees and a blue polo shirt emerges. His hair is in a ponytail. He has no beard. He grins at the good-looking girl. She rises, joins him. The sergeant hands him a manila envelop. From it he removes his belt and a small notebook. He borrows a pencil, makes an entry in the notebook. He is out of jail, free. What did he do? He   110
offended Atlantic City in some way. He spent a night in the jail. In the 1930s, men visiting Atlantic City went to jail, directly to jail, did not pass Go, for appearing in top-less bathing suits on the beach. A city statute requiring all men to wear full-length bathing suits was not seriously challenged until 1937, and the first year in which a man could legally go bare-chested on the beach was 1940.   115

20   Game 3. After 17 minutes, I am ready to begin construction on overpriced and sluggish Pacific, North Carolina, and Pennsylvania. Nothing else being open, oppo-nent concedes.

21   The physical profile of streets perpendicular to the shore is something like a playground slide. It begins in the high skyline of Boardwalk hotels, plummets into war-   120
rens of 'side-avenue' motels, crosses Pacific, slopes through church missions, conva-lescent homes, burlesque houses, rooming houses, and liquor stores, crosses Atlantic, and runs level through the bombed-out ghetto as far—Baltic, Mediterranean—as the eye can see. North Carolina Avenue, for example, is flanked at its beach end by the Chalfonte and the Haddon Hall (908 rooms, air-conditioned), where, according to one   125
biographer, John Philip Sousa (1854–1932) first played when he was 22, insisting, even then, that everyone call him by his entire name. Behind these big hotels, motels—Barbizon, Catalina—crouch. Between Pacific and Atlantic is an occasional house from 1910—wooden porch, wooden mullions, old yellow paint—and two churches, a package store, a strip show, a dealer in fruits and vegetables. Then, beyond Atlantic   130
Avenue, North Carolina moves on into the vast ghetto, the bulk of the city, and it looks

like Metz in 1919, Cologne in 1944. Nothing has actually exploded. It is not bomb damage. It is deep and complex decay. Roofs are off. Bricks are scattered in the street. People sit on porches, six deep, at nine on a Monday morning. When they go off to wait in unemployment lines, they wait sometimes two hours. Between Mediterranean and Baltic runs a chain-link fence, enclosing rubble. A patrol car sits idling by the curb. In the back seat is a German shepherd. A sign on the fence says, 'Beware of Bad Dogs'.

22   Mediterranean and Baltic are the principal avenues of the ghetto. Dogs are everywhere. A pack of seven passes me. Block after block, there are three-storey brick row houses. Whole segments of them are abandoned, a thousand broken windows. Some parts are intact, occupied. A mattress lies in the street, soaking in a pool of water. Wet stuffing is coming out of the mattress. A postman is having a rye and a beer in the Plantation Bar at 9:15 in the morning. I ask him idly if he knows where Marvin Gardens is. He does not. 'HOOKED AND NEED HELP? CONTACT N.A.R.C.O.' 'REVIVAL NOW GOING ON, CONDUCTED BY REVEREND H. HENDERSON OF TEXAS.' These are signboards on Mediterranean and Baltic. The second one is upside down and leans against a boarded-up window of the Faith Temple Church of God in Christ. There is an old peeling poster on a warehouse wall showing a figure in an electric chair. 'The Black Panther Manifesto' is the title of the poster, and its message is, or was, that 'the fascists have already decided in advance to murder Chairman Bobby Seale in the electric chair.' I pass an old woman who carries a bucket. She wears blue sneakers, worn through. Her feet spill out. She wears red socks, rolled at the knees. A white handkerchief, spread over her head, is knotted at the corners. Does she know where Marvin Gardens is? 'I sure don't know,' she says, setting down the bucket. 'I sure don't know. I've heard of it somewhere, but I just can't say where.' I walk on, through a block of shattered glass. The glass crunches underfoot like coarse sand. I remember when I first came here—a long train ride from Trenton, long ago, games of poker in the train—to play basketball against Atlantic City. We were half black, they were all black. We scored 40 points, they scored 80, or something like it. What I remember most is that they had glass backboards—glittering, pendent, expensive glass backboards, a rarity then in high schools, even in colleges, the only ones we played on all year.

23   I turn on Pennsylvania, and start back toward the sea. The windows of the Hotel Astoria, on Pennsylvania near Baltic, are boarded up. A sheet of unpainted plywood is the door, and in it is a triangular peephole that now frames an eye. The plywood door opens. A man answers my question. Rooms there are six, seven, and ten dollars a week. I thank him for the information and move on, emerging from the ghetto at the Catholic Daughters of America Women's Guest House, between Atlantic and Pacific. Between Pacific and the Boardwalk are the blinking vacancy signs of the Aristocrat and Colton Manor motels. Pennsylvania terminates at the Sheraton-Seaside—thirty-two dollars a day, ocean corner. I take a walk on the Boardwalk and into the Holiday Inn (23 storeys). A guest is registering. 'You reserved for Wednesday, and this is Monday,' the clerk tells him. 'But that's all right. We have *plenty* of rooms.' The clerk is very young, female, and has soft brown hair that hangs below her waist. Her superior kicks her.

24   He is a middle-aged man with red spiderwebs in his face. He is jacketed and tied. He takes her aside. 'Don't say "plenty",' he says. 'Say "You are fortunate, sir. We have rooms available."'

25   The face of the young woman turns sour. 'We have all the rooms you need,' she says to the customer, and, to her superior, 'How's that?'

26   Game 4. My opponent's luck has become abrasive. He has Boardwalk and Park 180
Place, and has sealed the board.

27   Darrow was a plumber. He was, specifically, a radiator repairman who lived in
Germantown, Pennsylvania. His first Monopoly board was a sheet of linoleum. On it
he placed houses and hotels that he had carved from blocks of wood. The game he
thus invented was brilliantly conceived, for it was an uncannily exact reflection of the 185
business milieu at large. In its depth, range, and subtlety, in its luck–skill ratio, in its
sense of infrastructure and socio-economic parameters, in its philosophical characteristics, it reached to the profundity of the financial community. It was as scientific
as the stock market. It suggested the manner and means through which an under-
developed world had been developed. It was chess at Wall Street level. 'Advance 190
token to the nearest Railroad and pay owner twice the rental to which he is otherwise
entitled. If Railroad is unowned, you may buy it from the Bank. Get out of Jail, free.
Advance token to nearest Utility. If unowned, you may buy it from Bank. If owned,
throw dice and pay owner a total ten times the amount thrown. You are assessed for
street repairs: $40 per house, $115 per hotel. Pay poor tax of $15. Go to Jail. Go 195
directly to Jail. Do not pass Go. Do not collect $200.'

28   The turnkey opens the blue door. The turnkey is known to the inmates as
Sidney K. Above his desk are 10 closed-circuit-TV screens—assorted viewpoints of the
jail. There are three cellblocks—men, women, juvenile boys. Six days is the average
stay. Showers twice a week. The steel doors and the equipment that operates them 200
were made in San Antonio. The prisoners sleep on bunks of butcher block. There are
no mattresses. There are three prisoners to a cell. In winter, it is cold in here. Prisoners
burn newspapers to keep warm. Cell corners are black with smudge. The jail is three
years old. The men's block echoes with chatter. The man in the cell nearest Sidney K.
is pacing. His shirt is covered with broad stains of blood. The block for juvenile boys 205
is, by contrast, utterly silent—empty corridor, empty cells. There is only one prisoner.
He is small and black and appears to be 13. He says he is 16 and that he has been
alone in here for three days.

29   'Why are you here? What did you do?'

30   'I hit a jitney driver.'   210

31   The series stands at three all. We have split the fifth and sixth games. We are
scrambling for property. Around the board we fairly fly. We move so fast because we
do our own banking and search our own deeds. My opponent grows tense.

32   Ventnor Avenue, a street of delicatessens and doctors' offices, is leafy with plane
trees and hydrangeas, the city flower. Water Works is on the mainland. The water 215
comes over in submarine pipes. Electric Company gets power from across the state,
on the Delaware River, in Deepwater. States Avenue, now a wasteland like St Charles,
once had gardens running down the middle of the street, a horse-drawn trolley, private homes. States Avenue was as exclusive as the Brighton. Only an apartment house,
a small hotel, and the All Wars Memorial Building—monadnocks spaced widely 220
apart—stand along States Avenue now. Pawnshops, convalescent homes, and the
Paradise Soul Saving Station are on Virginia Avenue. The soul-saving station is pink,
orange, and yellow. In the windows flanking the door of the Virginia Money Loan

Office are Nikons, Polaroids, Yashicas, Sony TVs, Underwood typewriters, Singer
sewing machines, and pictures of Christ. On the far side of town, beside a single track   225
and locked up most of the time, is the new railroad station, a small hut made of glazed
firebrick, all that is left of the lines that built the city. An authentic phrenologist works
on New York Avenue close to Frank's Extra Dry Bar and a church where the sermon
today is 'Death in the Pot'. The church is of pink brick, has blue and amber windows
and two red doors. St James Place, narrow and twisting, is lined with boarding houses   230
that have wooden porches on each of three stories, suggesting a New Orleans made
of salt-bleached pine. In a vacant lot on Tennessee is a white Ford station wagon
stripped to the chassis. The windows are smashed. A plastic Clorox bottle sits on the
driver's seat. The wind has pressed newspaper against the chain-link fence around the
lot. Atlantic Avenue, the city's principal thoroughfare, could be 17 American Main   235
Streets placed end to end—discount vitamins and Vienna Corset shops, movie the-
atres, shoe stores, and funeral homes. The Boardwalk is made of yellow pine and
Douglas fir, soaked in pentachlorophenol. Down-beach, it reaches far beyond the city.
Signs everywhere—on windows, lampposts, trash baskets—proclaim 'Bienvenue
Canadiens!' The salt air is full of Canadian French. In the Claridge Hotel, on Park   240
Place, I ask a clerk if she knows where Marvin Gardens is. She says, 'Is it a floral shop?'
I ask a cabdriver, parked outside. He says, 'Never heard of it.' Park Place is one block
long, Pacific to Boardwalk. On the roof of the Claridge is the Solarium, the highest
point in town—panoramic view of the ocean, the bay, the saltwater ghetto. I look
down at the rooftops of the side-avenue motels and into swimming pools. There are   245
hundreds of people around the rooftop pools, sunbathing, reading—many more people than are on the beach. Walls, windows, and a block of sky are all that is visible
from these pools—no sand, no sea. The pools are craters, and with the people around
them they are countersunk into the motels.

33   The seventh, and final, game is 10 minutes old and I have hotels on Oriental,   250
Vermont, and Connecticut. I have Tennessee and St James. I have North Carolina and
Pacific. I have Boardwalk, Atlantic, Ventnor, Illinois, Indiana. My fingers are forming a
'V'. I have mortgaged most of these properties in order to pay for others, and I have
mortgaged the others to pay for hotels. I have seven dollars. I will pay off the mortgages
and build my reserves with income from the three hotels. My cash position may be low,   255
but I feel like a rocket in an underground silo. Meanwhile, if I could go to jail for a time
I could pause there, wait there, until my opponent, in his inescapable rounds, pays the
rates of my hotels. Jail, at times, is the strategic place to be. I roll boxcars from the
Reading and move the flatiron to Community Chest. 'Go to Jail. Go directly to Jail.'

34   The prisoners, of course, have no pens and no pencils. They take paper nap-   260
kins, roll them tight as crayons, char the ends with matches, and write on the walls.
The things they write are not entirely idiomatic; for example, 'In God We Trust.' All
is in carbon. Time is required in the writing. 'Only humanity could know of such
pain.' 'God So Loved the World.' 'There is no greater pain than life itself.' In the
women's block now, there are six blacks, giggling, and a white asleep in red shoes. She   265
is drunk. The others are pushers, prostitutes, an auto thief, a burglar caught with pis-
tol in purse. A 16-year-old accused of murder was in here last week. These words are
written on the wall of a now empty cell: 'Laying here I see two bunks about six inches
thick, not counting the one I'm laying on, which is hard as brick. No cushion for my

back. No pillow for my head. Just a couple scratchy blankets which is best to use its   270
said. I wake up in the morning so shivery cold, waiting and waiting till I am told the
food is coming. It's on its way. It's not worth waiting for, but I eat it anyway. I know
one thing when they set me free I'm gonna be good if it kills me.'

35   How many years must a game be played to produce an Anthony J. Drexel Biddle
and chestnut geldings on the beach? About half a century was the original answer, from   275
the first railroad to Biddle at his peak. Biddle, at his peak, hit an Atlantic City streetcar
conductor with his fist, laid him out with one punch. This increased Biddle's legend.
He did not go to jail. While John Philip Sousa led his band along the Boardwalk playing 'The Stars and Stripes Forever' and Jack Dempsey ran up and down in training for
his fight with Gene Tunney, the city crossed the high curve of its parabola. Al Capone   280
held conventions here—upstairs with his sleeves rolled, apportioning among his lieutenant governors the states of the Eastern seaboard. The natural history of an American
resort proceeds from Indians to French Canadians via Biddles and Capones. French
Canadians, whatever they may be at home, are Visigoths here. Bienvenue Visigoths!

36   My opponent plods along incredibly well. He has got his fourth railroad, and   285
patiently, unbelievably, he has picked up my potential winners until he has blocked
me everywhere but Marvin Gardens. He has avoided, in the fifty-dollar zoning, my
increasingly petty hotels. His cash flow swells. His railroads are costing me two hundred dollars a minute. He is building hotels on States, Virginia, and St Charles. He has
temporarily reversed the current. With the yellow monopolies and my blue monopo-   290
lies, I could probably defeat his lavenders and his railroads. I have Atlantic and
Ventnor. I need Marvin Gardens. My only hope is Marvin Gardens.

37   There is a plaque at Boardwalk and Park Place, and on it in relief is the leonine
profile of a man who looks like an officer in a metropolitan bank—'Charles B. Darrow,
1889–1967, inventor of the game of Monopoly'. 'Darrow,' I address him aloud. 'Where   295
is Marvin Gardens?' There is, of course, no answer. Bronze, impassive, Darrow looks
south down the Boardwalk. 'Mr Darrow, please, where is Marvin Gardens?' Nothing.
Not a sign. He just looks south down the Boardwalk.

38   My opponent accepts the trophy with his natural ease, and I make, from notes,
remarks that are even less graceful than his.   300

39   Marvin Gardens is the one colour-block Monopoly property that is not in
Atlantic City. It is a suburb within a suburb, secluded. It is a planned compound of
72 handsome houses set on curvilinear private streets under yews and cedars, poplars
and willows. The compound was built around 1920, in Margate, New Jersey, and consists of solid buildings of stucco, brick, and wood, with slate roofs, tile roofs, multi-   305
mullioned porches, Giraldic towers, and Spanish grilles. Marvin Gardens, the ultimate
outwash of Monopoly, is a citadel and sanctuary of the middle class. 'We're heavily
patrolled by police here. We don't take no chances. Me? I'm living here nine years. I
paid seventeen thousand dollars and I've been offered thirty. Number one, I don't
want to move. Number two, I don't need the money. I have four bedrooms, two and   310
a half baths, front den, back den. No basement. The Atlantic is down there. Six feet
down and you float. A lot of people have a hard time finding this place. People that
lived in Atlantic City all their life don't know how to find it. They don't know where
the hell they're going. They just know it's south, down the Boardwalk.'

1972

QUESTIONS

Reader and Purpose

1. McPhee uses a personal **point of view** rather than striving for the appearance of objectivity. And his essay is richly implicative: the meaning of the essay does not lie on top, but must be dug for like the theme of a short story or a poem. Both of these characteristics are typical of New Journalism. McPhee's piece is not simply an account of 'Monopoly', nor is it merely a report on the decline of Atlantic City, though it includes both these topics. But if neither is his essential subject—what is?

2. The essay is not argument in any technical sense. Indeed, it is not even persuasion, as we normally understand that term. Yet McPhee is trying to convince us of something. What?

Organization

3. McPhee does not develop his essay in a series of topics, each leading logically into the next. He organizes by moving back and forth between two related themes. Which paragraphs are concerned primarily with 'Monopoly' and which with Atlantic City? Are any paragraphs concerned equally with both themes?

4. The structure of the essay is almost musical in its use of alternating themes, and we might adapt the terms *counterpoint* and *contrapuntal* to describe it. The counterpointed themes are linked by details common to both, such as the various streets and jail. These details act as bridges, shifting us from one theme to the other. Thus at the end of the opening paragraph the phrase 'where the dog packs range' transposes us from the blue space on the 'Monopoly' board to the actual street. Point out other details that swing us from game to city or from city to game.

5. In some cases there are no links, simply abrupt jumps from theme to theme— between paragraphs 26 and 27, for example. Where else do you find such discontinuities? Are they faults, or do they serve a purpose?

6. Does paragraph 4 have a **topic sentence**? If not, is its absence a fault? Can you supply one easily?

7. Which paragraph (or paragraphs) constitutes the closing of this essay? Is the closing effective?

Sentences

8. McPhee often uses a series of short **simple sentences**—in lines 4–6, for instance. Point out three or four similar passages. Does he reserve such sentences for particular topics? The sentences in paragraph 12 are longer and more complicated than those in lines 4–6. Is the subject different here?

9. McPhee sometimes omits *and* between paired constructions where normally the conjunction would appear, for example in lines 24–5: 'The first game draws tight, will soon finish' (instead of '*and* will soon finish'). Find other instances of this kind of **elliptical construction**. Why do you suppose he does it?

10. Identify the **fragments** in paragraph 37. Where else in this selection do you find fragments? Would they be improved by being made grammatically complete?

11. Could commas be used instead of dashes in lines 20–1, 75–6, 94, and 248? If they could be, is there any justification for the dashes?

12. How do these revisions alter the emphasis of McPhee's sentences?

    (a) **Revision:** We are gradually cancelling each other out, block upon block . . .
        McPhee: 'Block upon block, gradually, we are cancelling each other out . . .' (22)

    (b) **Revision:** Motels such as the Barbizon and the Catalina crouch behind these big hotels.
        McPhee: 'Behind these big hotels, motels—Barbizon, Catalina—crouch.' (127–8)

    (c) **Revision:** It is a secluded suburb within a suburb.
        McPhee: 'It is a suburb within a suburb, secluded.' (302)

Diction

13. Look up: *shards* (17), *traversing* (48), *glibly* (50), *transliterating* (57), *burgeoned* (58), *constrict* (76), *plummets* (120), *ghetto* (123), *mullions* (129), *rubble* (136), *pendent* (160), *abrasive* (180), *infrastructure* (187), *jitney* (210), *trolley* (218), *monadnocks* (220), *phrenologist* (227), *curvilinear* (303).

14. Explain as fully as you can the meanings of the following phrases: *master assessor of percentages* (14), *barrier beaches* (48), *archetypical masters of the quick kill* (64–5), *mano a mano* (86), *business milieu* (186), *socio-economic parameters* (187), *leonine profile* (293–4), *ultimate outwash* (306–7).

15. McPhee uses the present tense when writing about both the game and Atlantic City. He could as easily have made the past his primary tense. What advantage does the present have for his purpose? Suppose that he had used the past throughout:

    Go. I rolled the dice—a six and a two. Through the air I moved my token, the flatiron, to Vermont Avenue, where dog packs ranged.
    The dogs were moving (some were limping) . . .

Would the change in tense affect the **tone** of his essay in any way?

16. In the opening passage just quoted McPhee might have written simply: 'I move my token to Vermont Avenue, where dog packs range,' omitting the phrase 'through the air' and any reference to the flatiron. It doesn't really matter if he picks up his token or shoves it, and the flatiron has no symbolic value. Why, then, do you suppose he adds these apparently trivial details?

17. Who were the Visigoths (284)? Is the **allusion** apt?

18. Explain the **metaphors** implicit in *seines* (89), *warrens* (120–1), and *the city crossed the high curve of its parabola* (280).

19. Certain **images** are repeated throughout the essay so that they become motifs. The dog packs referred to in paragraph 1 and again in paragraphs 2 and 22 is an example. While the dogs do not symbolize anything, they are a laden image—that is, a visual detail that implies more than it literally states. What is suggested by the dog packs? Point out one or two other motifs and explain their significance.

20. What **ambiguity** is contained in the word *game* as it is used in line 274?

21. All these devices—allusions, metaphors, laden images, ambiguity—are ways of enriching meaning by adding overtones of feeling and thought. An even more important way of creating such overtones is the use of **symbols**, details that function both on the literal level of meaning and on a second level where it conveys a more **abstract** idea—often moral, political, or philosophical. The culminating symbol of

McPhee's essay, Marvin Gardens, is actually a double symbol, since it exists both in the game and in the city, and in each it has a literal and a symbolic value. Within the context of the game the author and his friend are playing, what does Marvin Gardens signify literally and what does it represent symbolically?

22. With reference to Atlantic City, what does Marvin Gardens literally designate? What does it symbolize? Is there a connection between its symbolic values in the game and in the city?

23. As a symbol Marvin Gardens operates, perhaps, on multiple levels, possessing economic, social, and political values, and, on the most abstract level of all, a philosophical significance. Can you sort out these various levels of meaning?

24. Finally, we return to the first question: What is 'The Search for Marvin Gardens' about?

POINTS TO LEARN

1. Do not be afraid of using the first person. You are the chief observer of what you see and do; your thoughts and feelings have value, even in reporting.

2. An essay may be organized contrapuntally by moving back and forth from one theme to another.

3. Short, strong sentences are good for rendering scene and action.

4. Think about the advantages and limitations of the tense you select as primary.

5. Laden images, metaphors, and symbols enrich—and complicate—meaning.

SUGGESTIONS FOR WRITING

1. In about 500 words describe a board game (but not 'Monopoly') or an athletic sport such as baseball. Assume that your reader is intelligent but ignorant about the activity and that your job is to acquaint him with its basics (explaining baseball to someone from Finland would be an example). Remember that describing something like a game clearly and succinctly is one of the most difficult of all writing tasks. It tests your ability to distinguish essentials from non-essentials and organize the former without getting bogged down in the latter. You may be able to play baseball or chess, but are you able to lay out the fundamental facts of such games?

2. A more ambitious assignment: Compose an essay of about 1,000 words using a game as a controlling metaphor to report on a situation or an experience, moving back and forth between the two themes as McPhee does with Monopoly and Atlantic City. There should be an inherent connection between the topics, as, for example, a varsity football game counterpointed against a report on one of the colleges or a description of the spectators. If possible, work one or two motifs into your composition, and try to develop a culminating symbol comparable to Marvin Gardens in McPhee's essay.

IMPROVING YOUR STYLE

1. In two or three places in your essay use a series of short simple sentences to set a scene or render dramatic action.

2. If your instructor agrees, experiment with fragments in several places, and with the kind of elliptical construction McPhee uses in lines 24–5.

P. J. O'ROURKE

The work of American writer and humorist P.J. O'Rourke (1947–) represents both the 'New Journalism' (see the essay by John McPhee, pp. 235–45) and the 'old-fashioned journalism', in which the reporter stands on the ground where events are taking place. In Somalia, Bangladesh, and Iraq (among other places), O'Rourke goes where few other Western journalists go, only hinting from time to time that he is running the risk of serious injury or death.

O'Rourke was a staff writer for *National Lampoon* in the 1970s and for *Rolling Stone* in the 1980s. His work is collected in such books as *The Bachelor Home Companion: A Practical Guide to Keeping House Like a Pig* (1987), *Give War a Chance: Eyewitness Accounts of Mankind's Struggle Against Tyranny, Injustice and Alcohol-Free Beer* (1992), *Age and Guile Beat Youth, Innocence, and a Bad Haircut* (1995), and *Eat the Rich* (1998). His latest book is *The CEO of the Sofa* (2001).

Because O'Rourke does not take himself seriously, he seldom treats others any differently. The reader should ask, however, whether O'Rourke, in the essay printed here, is trying seriously to persuade his audience.

Fiddling while Africa Starves

1   When the 'We Are the World' video first slithered into public view, I was sitting around with a friend who himself happens to be in show business. The thing gave him the willies. Me too. But neither of us could figure exactly why. 'Whenever you see people that look pleased with themselves on stage', said my friend, 'you know you're in for a bad show.' And the USA for Africa performers did have that self-satisfied look 5 of toddlers on a pot. But in this world of behemoth evils, such a minor lapse of taste shouldn't have upset us. We changed the channel.

2   Half a year later, in the middle of the Live Aid broadcast, my friend called me. 'Turn on your television,' he said. 'This is horrible. They're in a frenzy.'

3   'Well,' I said, 'at least it's a frenzy of charity.'   10

4   'Oh, no,' he said, 'it could be *anything*. Next time it might be "Kill the Jews."'

5   A mob, even an eleemosynary mob, is an ugly thing to see. No good ever came of mass emotion. The audience that's easily moved to tears is as easily moved to sadistic dementia. People are not thinking under such circumstances. And poor, dreadful Africa is something which surely needs thought.   15

6   The Band Aid, Live Aid, USA for Africa concerts and records (and videos, posters, T-shirts, lunch buckets, thermos bottles, bath toys, etc.) are supposed to illuminate the plight of the Africans. Note the insights provided by these lyrics:

> *We are the world* [solipsism],
> *we are the children* [average age near forty]   20
> *We are the ones to make a brighter day* [unproven]
> *So let's start giving* [logical inference supplied without argument]
> *There's a choice we're making* [true as far as it goes]

We're saving our own lives [absurd]
It's true we'll make a better day [see line 2 above]   25
Just you and me [statistically unlikely]

7   That's three palpable untruths, two dubious assertions, nine uses of a first-person pronoun, not a single reference to trouble or anybody in it and no facts. The verse contains, literally, neither rhyme nor reason.

8   And these musical riots of philanthropy address themselves to the wrong prob-   30
lems. There is, of course, a shortage of food among Africans, but that doesn't mean there's a shortage of food *in* Africa. 'A huge backlog of emergency grain has built up at the Red Sea port of Assab,' says the *Christian Science Monitor*. 'Food sits rotting in Ethiopia,' reads a headline in the *St Louis Post-Dispatch*. And according to hunger maven William Shawcross, 200,000 tons of food aid delivered to Ethiopia is being   35
held in storage by the country's government.

9   There's also, of course, a lack of transport for that food. But that's not the real problem either. The authorities in Addis Ababa have plenty of trucks for their military operations against the Eritrean rebels, and much of the rest of Ethiopia's haulage is being used for forcibly resettling people instead of feeding them. Western govern-   40
ments are reluctant to send more trucks, for fear they'll be used the same way. And similar behaviour can be seen in the rest of miserable Africa.

10   The African relief fad serves to distract attention from the real issues. There is famine in Ethiopia, Chad, Sudan and areas of Mozambique. All these countries are involved in pointless civil wars. There are pockets of famine in Mauritania, Niger and   45
Mali—the result of desertification caused mostly by idiot agricultural policies. African famine is not a visitation of fate. It is largely man-made, and the men who made it are largely Africans.

11   Enormous irrigation projects have been put onto lands that cannot support them and into cultures that cannot use them. Feeble-witted nationalism puts borders   50
in the way of nomadic peoples who used to pick up and move when things got dry. Rural poverty drives populations to African cities where governments keep food prices artificially low, thus increasing rural poverty. Bumbling and corrupt central planning stymies farm production. And the hideous regimes use hunger as a weapon to suppress rebellion. People are not just starving. They are *being* starved.   55

12   'Socialist' ideals infest Africa like malaria or dengue fever. African leaders, lost in the frippery of centrist thinking, fail to deal with market forces or any other natural phenomena. Leave it to a Marxist to see the world as the world is not. It's not unusual for African intellectuals to receive their education at such august bodies of learning as Patrice Lumumba U. in Moscow. That is, they are trained by a nation   60
which intentionally starved millions of its citizens in order to collectivize farming.

13   Death is the result of bad politics. And the Aid concerts are examples of the bad logic that leads to bad politics. It's probably not going too far to say that Africa's problems have been produced by the same kind of dim, ignorant thinking found among American pop artists. 'If we take, say, six months and not spend any money on nuclear   65
weapons, and just spend it on food, I think we could make a big dent,' says Waylon Jennings in the USA for Africa publicity packet. In fact, a small nuclear weapon placed

directly under Haile Mariam Mengistu and his pals would probably make a more beneficial dent than a whole US defence budget worth of canned goods.

14   Anyway, money is not going to solve the problem. Yet the concert nonsense is all 70
put strictly in terms of cash. Perhaps it is the only thing the idiot famous understand.

15   Getting people to give vast amounts of money when there's no firm idea what that money will do is like throwing maidens down a well. It's an appeal to magic. And the results are likely to be as stupid and disappointing as the results of magic usually are.   75

16   But, say some, Live Aid sets a good example for today's selfish youth, remind-
ing them to be socially concerned. Nonsense. The circus atmosphere of the Live Aid concerts makes the world's problems seem easy and fun to solve and implies that the solutions are naturally uncontroversial. As an example of charity, Live Aid couldn't be worse. Charity entails sacrifice. Yet the Live Aid performers are sacrificing nothing. 80
Indeed, they're gaining public adulation and a thoroughly unmerited good opinion of themselves. Plus it's free advertising. These LPs, performances and multiform by-
products have nothing in common with charity. Instead they levy a sort of regressive alms tax on the befuddled millions. The performers donate their time, which is wholly worthless. Big corporations donate their services, which are worth little enough. Then 85
the poor audience pledges all the contributions and buys all the trash with money it can ill afford. The worst nineteenth-century robber barons wouldn't have had the cheek to put forward such a bunco scheme. They may have given away tainted money, but at least they didn't ask you to give away yours.

17   One more thing, the music's lousy. If we must save the World with a song, 90
what's the matter with the Metropolitan Opera Company?

18   Rock and roll's dopey crusade against African hunger has, I posit, added to the stock of human misery. And not just audibly. Any religious person—whether he wor-
ships at a pile of gazelle bones or in the Cathedral of St Paul—will tell you egotism is the source of sin. The lust for power that destroys the benighted Ethiope has the same 95
fountainhead as the lust for fame that propels the lousy pop band. 'Not every one that saith unto me, Lord, Lord, shall enter into the kingdom of heaven.' Let alone everyone that saith sha la la la la and doobie doobie do.

1992

QUESTIONS
Reader and Purpose

1. Has the author persuaded you that charity concerts for the poor in Africa are a waste of money? How serious is his attempt to persuade his audience of this point? If this is not his main purpose, what is? To criticize African political policy? or simply to please the reader with humour at the expense of pop recording artists? or something else?

2. 'Fiddling While Africa Starves' is taken from a book titled *Give War A Chance: Eyewitness Accounts of Mankind's Struggle Against Tyranny, Injustice and Alcohol-Free Beer*. What do these titles tell you about the author's attitude towards his subject? Would it be correct to say that his attitude is entirely humorous?

3. In paragraph 7 the author criticizes the lyrics he has quoted in the previous paragraph. Do you agree with his comments? What has he failed to consider in critiquing this song?

Organization

4. 'No good ever came of mass emotion' (12–13). Could you argue that this is the controlling idea of the first five paragraphs? of the first seven?
5. What is the purpose of the first four paragraphs? How are they related to paragraph 5?
6. How are paragraphs 8 and 9 similar?
7. How is paragraph 10 a **transitional** paragraph?
8. How is the last sentence of paragraph 10 related to the first sentence of the paragraph?
9. How does paragraph 11 substantiate the last two sentences of paragraph 10?
10. Why does paragraph 14 begin, 'Anyway'? What sort of concession is the author making here?
11. Consider paragraph 16 carefully. Is the author guilty of exaggeration? If so, where? Has he made any accusations that, to be persuasive, would require some proof? Has he made unsupported generalizations?

Sentences

12. What word in the opening sentence of the first paragraph reveals the author's attitude towards his subject? Is this word too strong, or is it consistent with his attitude throughout?
13. On a number of occasions the author begins a sentence with *And* (paragraphs 1, 5, 8, 9, 11, 13, 15, 18). Rewrite three or four of these sentences, substituting for the *and* a different **coordinate conjunction** or a **conjunctive adverb**. In each case, is your substitution better or worse than the original?
14. Would the first sentence of paragraph 7 be clearer if 'it' were followed by a comma? What does 'it' refer to? Is the antecedent clear?
15. The author begins paragraph 17 with the phrase *One more thing* followed by a comma. Would it be preferable to replace the comma with a dash? a colon?

Diction

16. Look up: *willies* (3), *behemoth* (6), *lapse* (6), *frenzy* (9), *eleemosynary* (12), *dementia* (14), *plight* (18), *inference* (22), *palpable* (27), *philanthropy* (30), *maven* (35), *desertification* (46), *nomadic* (51), *stymie* (54), *frippery* (57), *entail* (80), *levy* (83), *bunco* (88), *benighted* (95).
17. Discuss how the following expressions help make the author's critical points: *that self-satisfied look of toddlers on a pot* (5–6), *easily moved to sadistic dementia* (13–14), *these musical riots of philanthropy* (30), *the rest of miserable Africa* (42), *feeble-witted nationalism* (50), *the frippery of centrist thinking* (57), *the idiot famous* (71), *dopey crusade* (92).
18. What is the nature of the **irony** in the fourth sentence of paragraph 12?

POINTS TO LEARN

1. One sentence can be the controlling idea of several paragraphs.
2. A transition can be effected by a word, a sentence, or an entire paragraph.

3. An unsupported generalization may have a persuasive effect, but it may also leave the author open to criticism.

SUGGESTIONS FOR WRITING

What has been your experience with charitable organizations? Have their representatives seemed to you too pushy, too demanding? Have their objectives been clearly presented? Have they seemed at all frivolous? Has the percentage of their income devoted to administrative costs been explained? Do they have a good reputation in your community? Are some of them objectionable on the same grounds that O'Rourke raises about the Live Aid concerts for Africa? Do others have an impeccable reputation? Is there one to which you give willingly and without hesitation?

Before beginning this essay (7–10 paragraphs) you should establish clearly what it is that you want to persuade your reader about.

IMPROVING YOUR STYLE

1. Use irony in two or three sentences, but ensure that your irony does not become mere sarcasm.
2. Make one of your paragraphs a transition from several paragraphs to those following.
3. Make at least two of your points with humour, but avoid excessive exaggeration.

Peter C. Newman

Formerly the editor-in-chief of both the *Toronto Star* and *Maclean's* magazine, Peter C. Newman (1929–) is a distinguished journalist and author who has won many awards and has received five honorary doctorates. Among his twenty books, which deal mainly with the Canadian corporate and political establishment, often from a historical perspective, are *Flame of Power: Intimate Profiles of Canada's Greatest Businessmen* (1960), *Renegade in Power: The Diefenbaker Years* (1963), *The Canadian Establishment* (1975), *Caesars of the Wilderness* (1987), and *The Canadian Revolution, 1985–1995: From Deference to Defiance* (1995). His latest book is *Titans: How the New Canadian Establishment Seized Power* (1998). The essay reprinted below comes from the Royal Bank Letter (now known as the *RBC Letter*), a monthly newsletter published by RBC Financial Group.

Igniting the Entrepreneurial Spark

1   There was a time when the entrepreneurial spirit was welcomed but not compulsory. Survival was the main concern of most Canadians, and while much of business was competitive, there was enough room to grow and space to expand.

2   But in the twenty-first century, most of us have little choice about acting and thinking like entrepreneurs. The global economy has become so competitive that   5

being entrepreneurial, whether we work for ourselves or for others, has become a given. Only the self-motivated will inherit and enhance tomorrow's economy. Inside large organizations, that means taking initiatives beyond job descriptions, while individually advancing collective corporate objectives.

3   Whatever their specific goals, entrepreneurs in every context and at all levels   10
constitute a fraternity joined by their quest for self-fulfillment. Rather than involving the exercise of any specific skills or talents, the entrepreneurial spirit places priority on certain qualities of thought and attitude. Few are immune from taking part in the entrepreneurial ethic.

4   The most unlikely professions require entrepreneurial talent. Authors, for   15
example, who turn out books every three years or so, are producing a thirty-five-dollar product that nobody needs. To be successful, they must be as much marketers as writers, scattering their imagination along both paths equally. This Royal Bank Letter attempts to isolate some of the essential, rarely defined elements that combine to ignite the entrepreneurial spark, and more important, to keep that flame flickering.   20

A Creed to Live By

5   Among the most impressive of contemporary Canadian entrepreneurs is Craig Dobbin of St John's, Newfoundland, because exercising that trait literally saved his life. Started in 1947 with no assets but his brawn and bravura plus a small bank loan, his CHC Helicopter Corp. now earns annual revenues of $555 million, operat-   25
ing more than 300 flying machines in 23 countries, mostly servicing offshore oil-drilling platforms.

6   A few yeas ago, when he was unexpectedly diagnosed with idiopathic pulmonary fibrosis, Dobbin's doctors blamed his potentially fatal disease on the use of a faulty compressor during his younger days as a professional diver. 'I was gradually running out of the capacity to breathe, because my lungs couldn't deliver CO_2 from   30
my bloodstream,' he said in a recent interview. 'The doctors said I had four months to live unless I got myself a new lung. That's when I decided that death was not an option.'

7   Dobbin analyzed the North American hospitals doing lung transplants, got himself listed in 10 of them as a 'local resident', by virtue of the fact that he was only   35
two hours away on his leased jet, which he kept in Birmingham, Alabama, near the continent's mid-point. Dobbin is six foot three inches, and there were few tall enough donors whose lungs would fit him. Eventually, he could only breathe through a full-face oxygen mask.

8   But success was his. He got new lungs at the University of Pennsylvania Hos-   40
pital in Philadelphia, reaching the operating room 2 hours and 10 minutes after he received their call. 'It was a very hard chore,' he recalls, 'but the thought never ever entered my mind that I wouldn't be able to repair the inconvenience that was prohibiting me from having a full life. Now, I just boogie down life's highway and feel the same age [Dobbin is 65] as some of the young guys around me. I was lucky, I guess.   45
But you make your own luck.'

9   That's hardly a typical case history, but the primary formula of any entrepreneurial success, is the lesson Dobbin passes on: 'Make your own luck.'

Making Your Own Luck

10   'You must believe that what you're doing is beyond failure,' he insists. 'And you need to be credible and you better be honest. Banks, when they lend you money, want 50 security and a repayment of their loan. You have to give that assurance and live up to it. Becoming a successful entrepreneur means being both highly competitive and slightly insecure. By that I mean knowing that if you don't make your own way, there is nobody out there to do it for you. There are no safety nets.'

11   Dobbin strongly advocates that people follow their own path, but not at any 55 risk. The trick is learning how to manage or at least minimize risk, so that the chances of success are at least as high as the possibilities of failure.

12   Entrepreneurs aren't born with do-it-yourself manuals, but some guideposts on how to tilt the odds in you favour can be useful. Here is one version of the Ten Commandments of Successful Entrepreneurship: 60

13   *1. Be adaptable.* To discover this most basic rule of entrepreneurship, you must study Charles Darwin's *On the Origin of Species*, first published in 1859. Actually, you don't have to plough through that ponderous tome's scientific arguments, but you must draw from it one essential lesson. Darwin is constantly being quoted as having advocated 'survival of the fittest'. He never did, and it's just as well, because in its 65 modern meaning that would endow those muscle-bound, macho individuals who exercise daily with barbells as having the greatest chance of success. Darwin's theory was based squarely on what he called 'survival of the most adaptable'. Flexibility of thought and action in a world that's changing as we walk in it, is what divides serious entrepreneurs who become long-distance runners, from one-shot-Charlies. Being and 70 remaining adaptable is exactly what entrepreneurship is all about.

14   *2. You must see what others don't.* One example: William Zeckendorf when he was New York City's leading real estate broker, enjoyed a justly earned reputation for making his own luck. At one point, he purchased, at a ridiculously low price, an abandoned riding stable in downtown Manhattan. The block-long structure was once 75 used by the city's upper crust to exercise their favourite mounts. It had been on the market for more than 20 years without attracting a single bidder. Zeckendorf had heard that NBC was searching for new downtown TV studios that required large open spaces, unobstructed by pillars. A quick glance at the derelict riding stable convinced him that, once refurbished, it would make an ideal TV location, and promptly flipped the 'use- 80 less' building to the television network for ten times his cost. That story illustrates the twin, essential ingredients of successful entrepreneurship: vision and chutzpah.

15   *3. Launching an exciting vision doesn't mean having to re-invent the wheel.* Ted Turner didn't create the idea of television news, but in 1968 he bought WJR, a debt-ridden Atlanta, Georgia, television station, and changed its call letters to WTGG, ('Watch 85 This Channel Go'). A dozen years later, realizing that traditional family life was becoming more hectic and fragmented, so that viewers in any given home seldom watched newscasts together, he established CNN, the 24-hour news network, which he sold 16 years later, to Time-Warner for $7.5 billion. What any successful entrepreneur must bring to the table, is not so much a revolutionary concept, as energy, enthusiasm and 90 unbounded faith in him or herself.

16   4. *Take advantage of the most obvious opportunities, but never be satisfied with the status quo.* One example is the story of Peter Armstrong, currently CEO and major shareholder in the Great Canadian Railway Tour Company. The largest privately owned passenger railroad in North America, it tours an average of 80,000 passengers   95 a year through the Rockies, employing 350 in the process. Working as a doorman at the Hotel Vancouver, Armstrong kept watching Gray Line, then a provincially owned bus tour company, turn away passengers. He leased his own tour bus, and eventually took over the Gray Line franchise, but his big breakthrough was acquiring the heavily subsidized and money-losing VIA Rail operation between Calgary and Vancouver. His   100 Rocky Mountaineer train rides are a success, and he's currently eyeing VIA's transcontinental service as a possible follow-up. This was hardly a precedent-shattering idea, but it took guts and determination to make Peter Armstrong's ambitious dream come true. True entrepreneurs can never have enough of either of these valuable qualities.

17   5. *Take a lesson from our historically most entrepreneurial Canadians, the   105 cowboys.* They were the ultimate loners of the western plains who made their own way, following highly individualistic lives. Their trail wisdom is worth repeating. 'A cowboy who says he ain't been throwed ain't telling the truth,' they contend, stressing their hard, sweaty labours. 'It takes a lot of wet saddles to train a horse.' But it is their lament about how tough a life they lead that makes the cowboy experience most rele-   110 vant to contemporary entrepreneurs. 'Cowboying is a rough way of life,' complains Buzz Kirkpatrick, who knows the trails well and still rides them. 'Despite the prevalence of four-wheel vehicles and high-priced machinery, the cowboy will never become extinct. . . . They just ain't come up with anything that will take as much abuse as a cowboy.' Many an entrepreneur, sitting alone in his office at midnight, worried about   115 meeting his payroll and how to fatten next month's thin order book, will sympathize with that sentiment.

18   6. *While making money is a useful ambition, it seldom provides adequate inspiration for greatness.* 'You can't just want to succeed so you can drive a Porsche,' emphasized Paul Lum, the co-founder of Internet Gateway, one of western Canada's   120 most successful Internet service providers, in a recent interview with *BC Business Magazine*. 'You have to be personally compelled to prove something to yourself, your friends or your family. If you're happy with ordinary things, if you're happy with five per cent growth a year, you'll never succeed as an entrepreneur. You have to be greedy.' In other words, enough is never enough, because allowances must be made   125 for rainy days. They'll come. Count on it.

19   7. *Be as eager to complete projects as you are to start them.* 'Too many entrepreneurs abandon their enthusiasms too early—they are great starters but poor finishers,' claims Julia Levy, CEO of Quadra Logic Technologies, an up-and-at-'em biotech firm in downtown Vancouver. 'I think of myself as someone who puts   130 opportunities together.' It's the stamina and determination you invest that achieve optimal results.

20   8. *You must cater to existing markets, but keep switching your product and service lines to reflect the newest trends.* Timing is everything. The Panasonic advertising slogan 'Slightly ahead of our time', is good advice. Michael Dell dropped   135 out of university in the early 1980s to launch a mail-order computer company that tailored its units specifically to its customers' needs, and promised virtually overnight delivery. He was a billionaire by the age of 31, since everybody else was still selling only standard units, and marketing them through dealer networks that involved high cost structures, including wholesale and retail middlemen. He invented nothing, but   140 made a fortune out of reviving mail-order sales, a distribution method that dates back to the days of outdoor privies. You must never rest on your laurels, no matter how comfortable they may feel. Not to grow is to slide backwards.

21   9. *Study your markets, but follow your fantasies.* 'If the barons of Silicon Valley were not chronic fantasizers, all of our mail would still come in envelopes,' point out   145 James Champy and Nitin Nohria, in their recent bestseller, *The Arc of Ambition.* 'But dreams alone are not enough. Acting on one's dreams, that's the hard part. The good news is that daring is more often learned than inherited. To those who respond, life teaches courage, which then multiplies itself—as if by compound interest. What unites all achievers is that they see the world as it really is, without the fears, constructs   150 and constraints that inhibit others from daring to act out their dreams, much less believe in them.' That's sound planning: action should always take precedence over dreams, but both are necessary.

22   10. *Your commitment must be so focused that it filters out distracting and unforeseen risks that might interfere with building equity in your dream.* 'All I have   155 is stubbornness,' insisted Albert Einstein. That 'never-give-up' attitude remains a given, but there is one other quality without which no entrepreneur can succeed: plain, dumb luck. 'Running a business of your own', concludes *The Complete Entrepreneur*, a recently published handbook by Mark Peterson on the subject, 'has many of the same risks as picking up hundred-dollar bills scattered through a minefield.   160 There is no wealth without risk, but your best opportunity is the day you invest in yourself.' Good advice: you are your company's greatest asset. Keep it that way.

23   The above 'Commandments' will be useful to present and future entrepreneurs, but the most essential and enduring quality is self-confidence. It takes courage to strike out on your own. It takes even more courage to not be discouraged by the   165 unavoidable pitfalls along the way.

24   The only dependable rule is that despite the inevitable disappointments and shattered illusions, it may be absurd to believe that being a successful entrepreneur is an attainable goal. But it's even more absurd not to try.

2001

QUESTIONS
Reader and Purpose

1. 'You can't win if you don't try' is what many people say to justify buying lottery tickets or engaging in any other kind of activity that depends mainly on luck. Is this what the author proposes?

2. One of the author's 'Ten Commandments' is that the budding entrepreneur should learn a lesson from the cowboys. Why is this kind of advice better suited to persuasion than to argument?

3. In paragraph 4 Newman, the author of many books, makes the extraordinary statement that books are 'a thirty-five-dollar product that nobody needs'. How are we to take this statement?

4. Did any of Newman's 'commandments' surprise you? Number 6, for instance, might seem completely opposed to the aspirations of many business people.

5. How persuasive is this essay? If you have always wanted to be—rather than an entrepreneur—a geologist, or a medical doctor, or a junior high teacher, or a professional athlete, or a minister, or a politician—does Newman have anything to say to you?

Organization

6. Newman never stops to define specifically what he means by 'entrepreneurial', yet he still gives us a pretty good idea of what he means by the term. How does he do this?

7. At the end of paragaph 4 the author points out what he intends to do in the rest of this essay. But what has he done up to this point?

8. In paragraphs 5–8 the author presents an example of a Canadian entrepreneur who overcame a serious obstacle, yet this obstacle had nothing to do with business. What is the point of this example?

9. Newman's 'most basic rule of entrepreneurship' is that you must 'Be adaptable' (paragraph 13), yet in paragraph 23 he states that 'the most essential and enduring quality is self-confidence.' Has he contradicted himself?

10. Once he has stated his most important rule in paragraph 13, does the author follow any progression, or logical order, in presenting his next nine rules?

Sentences

11. In the last sentence of paragraph 4 could the expression 'essential, rarely defined elements' be rewritten as 'essential but rarely defined'? or 'essential and rarely defined'? How does each of these three expressions say something different?

12. Did you misread the first sentence of paragraph 7 when you first read it? Should the author have used a **coordinate conjunction** between the two **independent clauses**?

13. Has the author made an error by using a comma after 'success' in the first sentence of paragraph 9? Can you justify this usage? Can you justify the first comma in the last sentence of paragraph 15?

14. In paragraph 23, 'The above "Commandments"' follows a very common usage in contemporary prose ('the above rules', 'the above examples', etc.). Would it not be more graceful to write, 'The "Commandments" above'?

Diction

15. Look up: *entrepreneurial* (1), *enhance* (7), *corporate* (9), *immune* (13), *ethic* (14), *trait* (22), *bravura* (23), *advocate* (55), *tome* (63), *derelict* (79), *refurbished* (80), *contend* (108), *prevalence* (112–113), *optimal* (132), *virtually* (137), *equity* (155), *pitfall* (166).

16. *one-shot (Charlies)* (70), *rainy days* (126), *rest on your laurels* (142). Using a dictionary of slang, or of popular expressions, or of quotations, explain the meaning of these three expressions. Are any of them **clichés**?

17. When Craig Dobbin said that 'death was not an option' (32–3), what, precisely, did he mean? Is death ever an option?
18. In paragraph 22, how persuasive is the analogy that Newman quotes from the book by Mark Peterson?

POINTS TO LEARN

1. Dividing an essay into numbered sections can be a useful way of ordering material, but it must not be a substitute for well-structured paragraphs and intelligent, logical transitions.
2. The experiences of others can be useful evidence in support of an attempt to persuade.

SUGGESTIONS FOR WRITING

What advice would you give to someone just starting high school? Structure your essay on this topic in roughly the same way Newman has: begin with a few paragraphs in which you introduce your topic and point out the usefulness of some guidelines, then offer a set of 'rules' or 'instructions' or 'lessons', and finally, draw some useful conclusions. Remember that, just as Newman does, you must have a key point about which you are trying to persuade your readers, and that all of your 'rules' are related to this point.

IMPROVING YOUR STYLE

In your essay,

1. include a brief analogy;
2. begin all your 'rules' with imperative verbs, as Newman does in his numbers 1, 2, 4, 5, 8, and 9.

ARGUMENT

Argument can be considered a form of persuasion, since its objective is to persuade, or to influence, the reader to change her mind about some belief or opinion. In this text, however, we distinguish between the two because of the means they use to attain their objective: persuasion appeals to the reader's emotions, to her feelings, whereas argument appeals to the reader's reason, to her intellect. We also distinguish between them because of the objectives themselves: the object of argument is to attain the truth, whereas the object of persuasion is to get the reader's agreement (sometimes with little regard for the truth). Although there is often a grey area in trying to distinguish between the two—when an attempt to persuade makes some appeal to reason, or when an attempt to reason makes some appeal to feeling—nevertheless the distinction is worthwhile.

A note of caution should be sounded here: the word 'argument' can be taken in two quite different ways. On the one hand, in this text by 'argument' we mean a logical means of reaching the truth. On the other hand is the popular meaning of the word, as in 'We were having an argument about how many goals Gretzky scored in the 1991–92 season.' However, the number of goals he scored that year is a verifiable fact, and thus it cannot, strictly speaking, be the subject of an argument.

With emotion argument has little to do. Its essence is reason, and reason may work in two ways: by *deduction* and by *induction*. The first argues from general premise to particular conclusion, the second from particular fact to broad conclusion. However, the writer must remember that today few of her readers will have any training in logical argument, in reasoning, that is, that works either by deduction or by induction. And, in practice, one will find few essays today that depend solely on the use of reason to influence the reader.

Deductive argumentation is usually cast in the form of a logical syllogism. At its simplest a syllogism contains two premises and an inference that necessarily follows from them. For example:

1. All drivers are mad.
2. X is a driver.
3. Therefore, X is mad.

If the major premise (1) and the minor premise (2) are true, the inference, or conclusion, (3) has got to be true, for the inference is logically valid. Logical validity, however, is not the same thing as empirical (or verifiable) truth. Since all drivers are not mad, the factual truth of the conclusion about X is open to question. Syllogistic reasoning, in short, is no sounder than the premises upon which it rests. The writer arguing logically must begin from premises not easily denied by her opponents.

In working from these premises she must proceed carefully. It is not hard to make mistakes—called logical fallacies—in getting from premise to conclusion. Many arguments involve a chain of interlocked syllogisms, each more complicated than that about X the driver. In most arguments the rigid form of the syllogism will be replaced by a more fluid prose, and here and there a premise or an inference may be omitted for economy. Under these conditions fallacies are especially easy to commit. There is no shortcut to learning sound logic. The student who wishes to argue well should consult a good textbook, master at least the rudiments of logic, and train herself to detect the common logical fallacies.

Exposing these fallacies is an effective way of attacking the argument of others. One such flaw, quite frequent and quite easily demonstrated, is self-contradiction. It is a fundamental law of logic that if *a* is true, *a* cannot be non-true. For example, one cannot argue that the Romans were doomed to fall and then assert that they were fools because they failed to solve the problems that destroyed them. To argue the inevitability of their decline is to deny the Romans free will; to charge them with folly presupposes that they had the freedom to choose between acting wisely or not. All this seems very obvious; yet in more subtle matters a writer can easily contradict herself without realizing it. To be sure that she has not, she must examine not only her argument itself, but all assumptions that lie beneath it and all the implications that lie within.

About deductive argumentation, then, we may conclude (1) that it must begin from true premises, and (2) that it must derive its conclusions from these premises according to the rules of inference. The writer who ignores either principle is herself open to attack. If her premises are untrue she may be answered factually; if her conclusions are invalid the fallacy can be revealed.

Inductive reasoning is somewhat more common in argumentation. The method of the scientist or the prosecutor, it begins with facts and builds from them to a general conclusion. In practice, a writer will usually find it more convenient to indicate her conclusion first and then bring forward the evidence that supports it. This is only a matter of arrangement, however, and does not deny the essential order of particular to general. Like the syllogism, induction will be fallacious when it fails to observe certain rules, which may be called the laws of evidence.

The first, and most obvious, of these laws is that evidence must be accurate. The second, more easily forgotten, is that it must be relevant, relating meaningfully to the conclusion it is brought forward to support. To prove, for instance, that women are involved in more accidents than men, a writer might cite figures that show that they bring more automobiles to body shops with damaged fenders. Granting the accuracy of the evidence, we may still question its relevancy. It may be that some women hastily repair dents that men blithely ignore; it may be that most of the dents resulted from accidents with reckless males. Often relevancy is so obvious that it may be taken for granted, but sometimes, as in this example, the writer must show that her evidence connects with her conclusion.

The third rule is that evidence must be complete. One of the commonest mistakes in inductive reasoning is to ignore this rule, especially when dealing with what are called universal affirmative propositions. These are statements that assert a truth applicable to all members of a class; for example, 'All students love school.' Such propositions can be proved only be testing each member to which they apply. Since so complete a demonstration is generally impossible, all that can be shown for most universal propositions is a strong probability. Usually probability will be all the argument requires, but honesty demands that the conclusion be stated as less than an absolute truth. In brief, a writer should never phrase her premise even one degree stronger than her evidence will support. Writers who scorn such qualifiers as *some*, *generally speaking, on the whole, for the most part*, expose themselves to easy counter-attack. Their evidence may in itself be good, but they ride it too hard and are surprised when it collapses under the strain.

All evidence, then, must observe these rules; the evidence itself, however, may take different forms. Three are most frequent: common knowledge, specific examples, and statistical data. Evidence is often advanced in the form of common knowledge, which may be defined as what is so generally known that it can safely be asserted without the support of examples or statistical tables. No one can draw the line that separates common knowledge from particular assertion. It is common knowledge that school is sometimes dull. It is a particular assertion that crocodiles make fine household pets. Perhaps they do; still, most of us would require proof. Perhaps the best rule is this: if a writer is doubtful whether a statement is common knowledge or assertion, she had better support it with additional specific evidence.

Examples, especially when they are historical, often involve the problem of interpretation. For example, one might consider Louis Riel's refusal, during the Northwest Rebellion of 1885, to allow Gabriel Dumont and his Métis sharpshooters to ambush Colonel Irvine and his men on their way to Prince Albert. This example is often used to support the argument that Riel was a poor military strategist, but this argument itself rests on a prior assumption—that Riel should have sought a military victory. Such an interpretation ignores Riel's conception of himself as a religious visionary, a prophet who was obeying God's direct orders, however impractical they might seem to a modern historian.

Another type of specific evidence often misused is the rhetorical analogy. For clarification or emphasis an analogy is often excellent; for proof it is meaningless. No matter how similar two things may be, there must be some differences between them. However slight, these differences deny any possibility of proof. This does not mean that analogies have no place in argumentation, simply that they should be restricted to supporting more legitimate evidence. To do this they must be fair and not force similarities where none exist. A famous instance of an unfair, or false, analogy is Thomas Carlyle's comparison of a state to a ship in order to demonstrate the weakness of democracy. The analogy is used to argue that a state cannot survive danger unless its leader, like the captain of a ship, has power independent of majority consent. But ships and states are very different things, and what may hold at sea does not therefore hold on land. Analogies, then, are valuable in argument if they are fair and if they are not used for proof (see also *Analogy*, pp. 69–98).

The third sort of evidence is statistical. Although subject to the same laws that govern all evidence, statistics are often employed less critically. Consider a very simple case. We wish to answer the charge based on the evidence of the dented fenders and to prove that, on the contrary, Canadian women are safer drivers than Canadian men. Selecting a small community, we show that in a single year 100 women were involved in accidents as compared to 500 men. The figures seem strong evidence. Yet this town may contain 5000 male drivers and only 500 female drivers, and if so then only 10 per cent of the men had accidents as opposed to 20 per cent of the women. Or perhaps the community is not a typical sample of the Canadian population; or perhaps the police records included only some accidents, not all; or perhaps these figures cover a wide range of accidents, from mild bumps to head-on collisions; or perhaps the figures reflect that those who count such things tend unconsciously to perpetuate the old stereotype that women are worse drivers than men.

Perhaps a great many things. As you see, statistics must be handled carefully. If it is too much to expect all writers to be trained in statistical method, it is not too much to ask them to subject any statistical data they use to the common-sense criteria of accuracy, relevancy, and completeness. So tested, statistics are good evidence.

Most of the faults of inductive reasoning follow from ignoring these criteria, or, even worse, from ignoring the spirit behind them. Induction begins with facts, and it stays with facts until it has established their truth. It does not select or distort facts to fit a preconceived notion. It is easy, for example, to blame juvenile delinquency on comic books by ignoring the complexity of forces that create juvenile crime. Such an argument may strike us for a moment, but only for a moment. It is neither true nor honest. And in argumentation, as in murder, truth will out.

We have stressed here the problems of reasoning well, for that is the essence of argumentation. Yet to be fully effective an argument must be not only well reasoned but well expressed. Its organization must be clear. The writer should make plain at the very beginning what she is arguing for or what she is contending against, and her paragraphs should march in perfect order from premise to inference or from evidence to conclusion. Her syntax should be an easy yet a strong vehicle for the ideas it conveys, and her diction both honest and exact. In short, argumentation is reason finely phrased. Reason twisted in awkward prose is like a chisel of strong steel with a blunted edge. Beautiful writing that hides fallacy and misrepresentation is a shiny tool of cheap metal that soon cracks. To argue well the writer must begin with intelligence and with honesty, but she must hone them to the sharp edge of good prose.

Ralph Heintzman

Formerly a teacher of history, and for several years the editor of the *Journal of Canadian Studies*, Ralph Heintzman is now the assistant secretary in the Treasury Board of Canada. He has held a wide variety of positions with the federal government, including executive director of the Social Sciences and Humanities Research Council of Canada and assistant secretary to the Cabinet for Federal–Provincial Relations. He also served as a member of the Privy Council and of the Applebaum-Hébert committee on Canadian culture. He has published a number of essays on Canadian politics and economics, as well as *The Struggle for Life: The French Daily Press of Montreal and the Problems of Economic Growth in the Age of Laurier, 1896–1911* (1977).

Heintzman's editorials in the *Journal of Canadian Studies*, of which the following selection is an example, were consistently thought-provoking and well-argued discussions of a wide range of contemporary political, social, economic, and cultural issues. His examination of censorship is a persuasive attempt to deal rationally with a subject usually clouded by emotion and inflated or misleading rhetoric.

Liberalism and Censorship

1   After a period of more than a decade in which it had seemed to fade from view, the issue of censorship has emerged again in the last year as a matter of public debate in Canada. The reemergence of the issue suggests that certain questions many had thought settled were in fact only temporarily set aside. The assumption of a portion of the community—that the state has no right to restrict public expression—has 5 proven to be less widely accepted than seemed for a time to be the case. The attempted reassertion of the state's right to control certain kinds of public expression—apparently with the support of a wide segment of opinion—has alarmed those who assumed such a right was already extinct, or on the point of becoming so.

2   The reaction of many within the intellectual and artistic community has been 10 commendably energetic. The Book and Periodical Development Council has formed a special task force on censorship chaired by Timothy Findley. A recent broadcast of *Cross-Country Check-Up* was mobilized against censorship. Among many others, the editor of *Saturday Night* and the book columnist of the *Globe and Mail* have strongly deplored the reassertion of a right to censorship, the latter repeatedly and in sensa- 15 tional terms.

3   All of these voices are perfectly correct in diagnosing a problem of censorship, but the real problem is a rather different one than most of them seem to think: it is a failure to think clearly about the issue. The bulk of recent commentary on censorship in Canada has been a crude mixture of knee-jerk reactions, unexamined premises, 20 and the wielding of bogeys. This is as true of those who oppose censorship as of those who favour it, but it is perhaps more surprising and regrettable in the case of the former. The censorship debate has not been characterized by the careful thought and distinction one would hope to find on such a sensitive and divisive issue, especially from the 'intellectuals' whose special care it ought to be to make just such distinctions. 25

4   The result is a state of high confusion in which a number of separate issues have been mixed together and the real issue has been almost entirely obscured. One is scarcely justified, for example, in mixing up the right of parents and school boards to decide what the children in their care shall be *required* to read with the issue of censorship properly so-called. The exercise of this right does not interfere with what may 30 be published and sold, or even with what young people may read, but only with what they may be *required* to read, which is a different matter altogether. Like all other rights, this one may be exercised with good judgment or bad—and, more often than not, with the latter—but the existence of the right itself cannot be questioned. Indeed, parents who failed to exercise it would probably be more open to censure than those 35 who did.

5   Similarly, it is an abuse of common sense to confuse the well-meaning efforts of a city council to license and supervise—not ban—the sale of pornographic literature with a limitation, even a potential one, on political expression, as William French has done. The lack of proportion involved in this kind of judgment goes to the heart of 40 the confusion surrounding the discussion of censorship and the refusal of those engaged in it to make the necessary distinctions.

6   It is essential to distinguish, for example, between the maintenance of a minimum level of public decorum and the censorship of political debate. Those who refuse to acknowledge this distinction and who argue, as Robert Fulford has, that any 45 form of censorship leads inevitably to totalitarianism are just as guilty as if they were to attack liberals as communists or conservatives as fascists: they are indulging in a form of intellectual McCarthyism. It cannot be seriously maintained that insistence on a certain standard of public decorum is a threat to political life, any more than concern for a decent level of manners is a threat to social life. In fact the reverse is more 50 probable in both cases: a high standard of public manners may well be the condition for a high standard of political and social life. In any event, the increasing licence of our own time does not seem to have raised the level of political discourse notably, to say the least, above the standard achieved in another age by a Burke, a Marx, or a Mill.

7   One ought also to make a more careful distinction than is usually the case today 55 between the practice of censorship and the level of artistic expression. It is by no means self-evident, as many today assume without adequate reflection, that the existence of censorship inevitably entails a loss of artistic power. As everyone knows, nineteenth-century Russia was subject to a high degree of political censorship (though not nearly as high as in the Soviet Union today), yet it also witnessed one of the great- 60 est flowerings of literary creativity in the history of the world, thus perhaps confirming Northrop Frye's suggestion that literature actually flourishes in difficult circumstances. The facts are so striking that one is almost tempted to suggest that a measure of censorship might be a reasonable price to pay for a Pushkin, a Turgenev, or a Chekhov, let alone a Dostoevsky or a Tolstoy! Though utterly facetious, such a 65 thought does underline the fact that those who oppose any form of censorship cannot do so on the ground that it inevitably means a lowering of artistic standards. Once again the reverse could be just as easily maintained. In fact, the celebrated critic George Steiner has done precisely that in his most recent book, *On Difficulty*.

8   That certainly does not mean, of course, that the case against censorship is with- 70 out merit, but it suggests that those who argue it must give more sustained attention than they have yet done to their premises. All too often these remain unexplored, while the weight of their argument rests on a number of bogeys exploited to intimidate and silence their opponents. Since these bogeys will not withstand serious criticism, the opponents of censorship must strengthen and refine their case. In doing so, they will 75 have to take a harder look at their own presuppositions.

9   One of the curious things is the inconsistency these presuppositions often involve. In my own experience—and it is worth emphasizing that the views expressed here are those of the editor alone and do not necessarily reflect those of any other person or institutions associated with the *Journal*—virtually all those who oppose cen- 80 sorship on principle are equally strongly in favour of legislation against hate literature and various forms of racial abuse. Yet this too is a form of censorship. Thus the opposition is not really to censorship at all but only to certain forms of it. The right of the state to enact controls on public expression is admitted: only the objects of censorship remain in dispute.   85

10   This concession alters the nature of the debate fundamentally. It is no longer a question of whether censorship should exist—this being now admitted—but of what should be censored, and how. Answers to these questions presuppose answers to others. Most of the recent controversy about censorship in Canada has been about censorship of pornography or of explicitly sexual material. If, as I have suggested, 90 one cannot successfully argue that censorship in any form is necessarily a threat to political life or to artistic integrity, then in order to decide whether the state ought to exercise its right to censorship in relation to these matters one requires a coherent view of the place of sexuality in the human spirit and of the implications of this view for the development or preservation of a civil society.   95

11   Supplying answers to *these* questions is enormously complicated in our time by the role of liberalism as the prevailing ideology of the intellectually influential. In fact, the intellectual confusion surrounding the issue of censorship—the *real* problem of censorship defined above—is largely the consequence of both the strengths and weaknesses of the liberal mind.   100

12   As Lionel Trilling remarked in his suggestive review of the Kinsey report, later reprinted in *The Liberal Imagination*, the good side of liberalism in sexual matters is 'its impulse toward acceptance and liberation, its broad and generous desire for others that they be not harshly judged'. This generous side of liberalism is greatly to be cherished and admired, but when it has been given due credit 'as a sign of something good 105 and enlarging', Trilling wrote,

> we cannot help observing that it is often associated with an almost intentional intellectual weakness. It goes with a nearly conscious aversion from making intellectual distinctions, almost as if out of the belief that an intellectual distinction must lead to a social discrimination or exclusion. We might say that 110 those who most explicitly assert and wish to practise the democratic virtues have taken it as their assumption that all social facts—with the exception of exclusion and economic hardship—must be *accepted*, not merely in the scientific sense but also in the social sense, in the sense, that is, that no judgment must be passed on them, that any conclusion drawn from them which perceives 115 values and consequences will turn out to be 'undemocratic'.

13   The prevailing liberal view of sexuality is shaped by the behaviourist assumption that human acts can only be judged—if indeed they can be judged at all—according to generalizations drawn from the observation of what people actually do. The liberal mind shrinks, therefore, from judging sexual behaviour   120

> except, presumably, in so far as it causes pain to others. . . . the preponderant weight of its argument is that a fact is a physical fact, to be considered only in its physical aspect and apart from any idea or ideal that might make it a social fact, as having no ascertainable personal or cultural meaning and no possible consequence—as being, indeed, not available to social interpretation at all. In   125
> short, [liberalism] . . . by its primitive conception of the nature of fact quite negates the importance and even the existence of sexuality as a social fact.

14   Yet it is precisely the meaning of sexuality as a social fact with which one must grapple before the question of censorship can be satisfactorily resolved. This is a very large matter and no approach to it can be suggested here, but it is obvious that much   130
will depend on one's notion of the human mind or spirit. It is not common nowadays to think of the mind in Platonic terms, that is, as requiring mental 'guardians' to keep in order the potentially unruly energies and forces of which it is in large part composed. But since this view of mind has been held even longer than our modern one, perhaps it deserves more attention than it now receives.   135
15   In this view, the passions are conceived as being a vitally important element of mind, perhaps even its centre, but, by their very power, being also capable of great destruction and therefore in need of careful direction and control. The individual citizen's control over his own passions is, in fact, the foundation of social discipline and social order. The sexual passions in particular have almost always been regarded as   140
forces of tremendous power for good or evil. An intuition of their awesome power explains why so many religions incorporate elements of sexuality into their own mythology and worship, yet also encircle them with a great variety of prohibition and taboos. The purpose and origin of such prohibitions vary greatly but their fundamental source is the intuition that this power cannot safely be trifled with, that it   145
should not be taken in hand lightly or frivolously, but reverently, discreetly. . . . They are warning signs posted around the passions to caution the unwary: 'Handle with care.' Chastity, as Benedict Domdaniel remarks in *A Mixture of Frailties*, is having the body in the soul's keeping: just that and nothing more.
16   The modern or liberal frame of mind regards the passions in a very different   150
light. For one thing, it approaches them with far less awe. In its classical mood, it is more sanguine about the power of naked rationality to control and direct them for good. In its romantic mood, it is inclined to look on every impulse of the human spirit as potentially creative and therefore not to be checked or disciplined without loss: the romantic hero is often one who by giving in to his passions and violating the taboos   155
achieves a level of knowledge or experience denied to others. The view that almost every impulse is potentially creative is not wrong, of course. But it overlooks the complementary Platonic or Augustinian insight that there is a hierarchy in the realm of the good and that evil enters the world not through the triumph of bad over good, but through our own preference for a lesser good to the exclusion of a greater. Thus it   160

gravely minimizes the potential for evil implicit in acts or impulses which may be, in their own terms, good.

17   For another thing, the liberal mind interprets sexuality in terms of certain analogies drawn from modern technology. The Freudian or twentieth-century notion of sexuality was shaped by the analogy of the steam engine. As pressure builds up 165 within the steam boiler or the human psyche, it must be let off in some form if an explosion is to be avoided. Thus the liberal mind concludes that the basic sexual 'drives' demand 'release' if damage is not to be done to the personality. However, as Tom Wolfe has pointed out, the usefulness of this analogy appears increasingly doubtful. As both electronic technology and neurological research advance, we have learned 170 that the mind is far more comparable to a computer than to a steam engine. If so, the conclusion to be drawn about human behaviour is exactly reversed. Far from providing a healthful 'release' each successive act or thought actually 'programs' the mind for continued activity of the same kind, until, if the programming is sufficiently complete, the mind can dwell on little else. Obviously a theory of mind which took this con- 175 temporary analogy seriously would adopt a very different attitude to censorship than the prevailing one, especially censorship of material which might become available to children and so 'program' their imaginations.

18   If the assumptions of the liberal mind about human nature and sexuality are shown to be flawed or incomplete, then it may be wise to give correspondingly 180 greater attention to that other tradition of thought which approaches the powers of the spirit with greater awe, which conceives the mind as requiring 'guardians' and as having to be kept in order, with no little difficulty. If the need is admitted, then influences which increase the difficulty can be rightfully considered anti-social, since tending to break down that inner self-control on which social order depends. In this 185 view, the process of civilization, the process of establishing an ever-increasing degree of civility in social and political life, depends upon each member of the community establishing greater dominion over his or her own psyche and emotions. To the degree that self-control is inhibited by the deliberate arousal of passion or desire, to that degree a civil society becomes a more distant and elusive goal and society moves 190 closer to a state of barbarism.

19   If so, the recent reassertion of the public's right to establish minimum standards of decorum may not be necessarily unwelcome. Now that we have enjoyed the fruits of forty years or so of liberalism in sexual matters as in political, there is perhaps room for the reassertion of another range of values and for a re-examination of the claims 195 of excellence, in human behaviour and social conduct as in other things. The liberal impulse to tolerance and acceptance is wholly admirable, but it needs to be balanced and complemented by something else. If it leads to a paralysis of the faculty of judgment, it becomes one of those good things by which so much evil can be done. We need to transcend what Trilling called liberalism's 'primitive conception of the nature 200 of fact' and to learn again to make balanced judgments about the ultimate meaning and consequence of human behaviour.

20   If the apparent public concern with censorship expresses a confused groping toward a revival of critical judgment in sexual and social matters, then it may deserve more than contempt, however misguided or badly motivated some of the noisiest 205 advocates of censorship may be. The role of the intellectual community should not be to thwart or deny the right to censorship—a denial which would not be sincere in any case—but rather to guide it and help it avoid the crude and harmful purposes to which it might be put. If certain works, films, or publications do not undermine civility as alleged but contribute instead to the process of civilization, then it should not be 210 beyond the power of the intellectual community to say why. But it will have to do so with greater intellectual and moral rigour than in the recent past. The public is not as foolish as the *cognoscenti* often believe. It may sometimes fall into the error of thinking that a truly moral work of art cannot contain what it considers to be 'immoral' scenes or characters, but it rarely makes the opposite mistake, to which so many artists and 215 intellectuals are vulnerable, of thinking that art is beyond good and evil, and should not be judged, in the final analysis, by moral standards as well as aesthetic ones.

21   The intellectual, artistic, and journalistic communities would perhaps do well to embrace the claims of civility and excellence and to work out their implications for the public depiction of sexuality in more satisfying terms than they have yet done, 220 rather than fighting the principle of censorship itself. Above all, they should avoid basing opposition to censorship on the defence of civil liberties. For one thing, there is no opposition between them. In fact, the first may be a prerequisite for the second, since it is improbable that civil liberty would long survive in a society threatened by social decadence and disorder. For another thing, there can be little doubt which of 225 the two the public would ultimately choose if forced to do so. That is why the choice should not be forced upon it. To suggest that civil liberties and censorship are not compatible is to call into question, in the long run, not censorship, as many assume, but liberty itself.

1978

QUESTIONS

Reader and Purpose

1. Which of the following kinds of people do you think this article is intended for: a) high-school student; b) lawyer; c) any professional person; d) university professor; e) minister; f) any university graduate; g) artist or intellectual; h) politician? Prove your point by quoting any three sentences (each from a different paragraph). For example, if your answer is 'a', you might refer to the sentence beginning in line 17; if 'd', to the sentence beginning in line 58.

2. Now discuss the validity of both the question above and your answers to it. Consider such matters as context, quoting out of context, and the relationship between context and overall purpose.

3. Summarize briefly (in no more than 100 words) the main point of Heintzman's argument.

Organization

4. How does the expression *the reaction* (10) serve as **transition** between paragraphs 1 and 2? In commenting on the effectiveness (or lack of it) of this expression, try substituting three or four of your own transitional words or expressions. Are they as effective? Why, or why not?

5. Consider the following transitions: *in this view* (136), *for another thing* (163), *if so* (192). Are these transitions too obvious? Does Heintzman's subject matter require some fairly obvious **signposts**?

6. How do you explain that, in spite of the title of this essay, the word *liberalism* occurs for the first time only in paragraph 11? What does this tell you about the structure of the essay?

7. Which of the first four paragraphs most clearly states the topic of the essay? How is paragraph 8 related to any of these four? and to paragraph 11?

8. In order to deal adequately with questions 6 and 7, you will probably have to outline the argument of Heintzman's article. Once you have done this, describe briefly the major steps in the argument, paying particular attention to paragraphs 11, 14, and 19.

9. To what extent do paragraphs 20 and 21 constitute a **closing by return**? Which paragraph or sentences are recalled?

10. *In this view* (136) and *in a very different light* (150–1) are the two parts of a contrast. What points is the author contrasting?

Sentences

11. In paragraph 1, the first sentence begins with a **subordinate clause**, while the next three sentences begin with **independent clauses**. In paragraph 2, the pattern is reversed, with only the last sentence beginning with something other than an independent clause (in this case, a **prepositional phrase**). Compare the sentence structures in paragraphs 5 and 6, and 18 and 19, to see if there is any pattern.

12. To which of the following classes of sentences does each sentence in paragraph 18 belong: **antithetical, balanced, cumulative, freight-train, organizing, periodic**?

13. Substitute both parentheses and commas for the dashes in paragraph 1, and then explain which is the more effective of the three. Do the same for paragraphs 4 and 5, and then see what conclusions you can come to about the author's use of dashes.

14. In paragraph 11 the author has emphasized two words by italicizing them. Rewrite these sentences, trying to achieve the same emphasis by placing the important words at the beginning or end of each sentence. Are your revisions more or less effective?

15. Outline the **parallel** elements of the sentences in paragraph 15.

Diction

16. Look up: *reassertion* (7), *commendably* (11), *knee-jerk* (20), *premises* (20), *bogeys* (21), *decorum* (44), *totalitarianism* (46), *discourse* (53), *facetious* (65), *presuppositions* (76), *concession* (86), *aversion* (108), *behaviourist* (117), *negates* (127), *Platonic* (132), *taboos* (144), *sanguine* (152), *hierarchy* (158), *psyche* (166), *transcend* (200), *aesthetic* (217), *decadence* (225).

17. Look up *liberalism* (97); then compare the dictionary definition with the explanations of this word given in paragraphs 12, 13, and 16. What conclusions can you draw about the differences between defining a word and explaining it?

18. Consider the expression *may not be . . . unwelcome* (193). Is this double negative effective? or clumsy? Would rephrasing the sentence as a positive statement be an improvement?

19. Explain the **metaphor** *all of these voices* (17). Is the expression *a state of high confusion* (26) also a metaphor? Why, or why not? What about *heart of the confusion* (40–1)?

POINTS TO LEARN

1. In dealing with a complex topic, the writer will assist the reader by using clear, even obvious, transitions and signposts.
2. The steps of a complicated argument need not all be revealed at the beginning but may be clarified gradually throughout most of the essay.
3. A writer may contrast not only successive sentences but successive paragraphs.

SUGGESTIONS FOR WRITING

In a fairly well-developed argumentative essay (800–1,000 words), try to convince your reader of your point of view about a complex topic, such as one of these: the most successful political party or organization on campus; the necessity of proper dress in class; the real inequality of the sexes; the place of religion in the classroom; plagiarism and the demand for high grades; the morality of the single life.

IMPROVING YOUR STYLE

Somewhere in your essay include the following:

1. an explanation—which goes beyond a mere definition—of any key terms you use about which there might be either uncertainty or confusion;
2. two pairs of contrasting paragraphs;
3. at least three balanced and three periodic sentences.

MARTHA BAYLES

After some years as a critic of books, films, and television for such publications as the *New York Times*, *American Spectator*, and the *Wall Street Journal*, Martha Bayles now teaches literature at Claremont McKenna College in California. A native of Boston, she has taught writing at public schools there and in Philadelphia, as well as at Harvard, Fordham, Cornell, and Syracuse universities. She has also worked in television, as the popular culture and arts correspondent for PBS's *Religion & Ethics News Weekly*, and as a scriptwriter and editorial consultant with New River Media, a production company based in Washington, DC. Bayles is a contributor to such magazines as the *Atlantic Monthly*, *Harper's Magazine*, the *New York Times Book Review*, and *Wilson Quarterly*, where she is also the literary editor. She is also the author of two books, *Hole in our Soul: The Loss of Beauty and Meaning in American Popular Music* (1994), from which the essay below is adapted, and *Ain't That a Shame? Censorship and the Culture of Transgression* (1996).

The Shock-Art Fallacy

1   In a trendy nightclub a controversial playwright puts on one-man shows in which he excoriates the government, spews profanity, urinates, masturbates, even goes into convulsions. To one onlooker, such performances represent 'inconceivable

freedom', the 'fearful cynical spectacle' of an artist 'struggling to eliminate both himself and the last remains of a once firmly established civilization'.   5

2   Outside a venerable cathedral a crowd of worshippers are startled by a flurry of
leaflets calling for a radical rejection of architectural tradition. Looking up, they see a
black-clad figure in the campanile, one of several artists vowing to 'go out into the
street, launch assaults . . . , and introduce the fisticuff into the artistic battle.' When
such stunts dominate the headlines, the artists rejoice.   10

3   A collector visits a gallery and buys a work called *Artist's Shit*, a can of feces
weighing 30 grams and priced at the current cost of gold. This collector is not alone;
the art world is so enamoured of the concept that the lucky artist sells 90 cans.

4   Inside the art gallery an artist invites spectators to 'abuse her at their will for six
hours'. After three hours they have torn away her clothes with razors and begun slash-   15
ing at her bare skin. When someone holds a loaded gun to her head, a fight breaks
out and the proceedings are brought to 'an unnerving halt'.

5   No, these vignettes are not culled from Senator Jesse Helms's National
Endowment for the Arts blacklist. Rather, they come from the history of modernism:
first, the expressionist Frank Wedekind, presiding at Munich's Cafe Simplicissimus at   20
the turn of the century; second, a follower of the futurist Filippo Marinetti, at St
Mark's Cathedral, calling for the total transformation of Venice in 1910; third, the
Fluxus artist Piero Manzoni, hawking Dada doodoo in 1961; and fourth, the performance artist Marina Abramovic, unnerving Naples in 1974.

6   When we delve into the history of the European avant-garde, we see how thor-   25
oughly today's 'cutting edge' art recycles the clichés of expressionism, futurism, Dada,
surrealism, the Theatre of Cruelty, Fluxus, and 'happenings'. A certain type of modernist has always sought to jettison the past, to mock aesthetic standards, to provoke
the audience, to erase the line between art and life, and to exploit the shock potential
of the mass media.   30

7   Should we resign ourselves, taking comfort in the soothing words of *Time*'s
Richard Corliss: 'That has always been the role of art: to shock, not just to ratify the
prejudices of the generation in power'?

8   I think not. First, modernism cannot be reduced to Corliss's crude alternatives.
At the turn of the century, when Wedekind was wetting his pants, Paul Cézanne was   35
immortalizing Mont St Victoire. In 1910, when Marinetti was scattering leaflets, Igor
Stravinsky was composing *The Firebird*. In 1961, when Manzoni was labelling cans,
Walker Percy was exploring cinematic fiction in *The Moviegoer*. And in 1974, when
Abramovic was handing out razors, Ingmar Bergman was expanding film narrative in
Scenes From a Marriage. The best modernist art seeks neither 'to shock' nor 'to ratify   40
the prejudices of the generation in power' but to humanize the modern world.

9   Still, the Corliss view is widespread. After a century of modernism most of us
tend to assume automatically that if art is controversial, our hidebound society, with
its hostility to new ideas, sensibilities, and artistic practices, is to blame. Thus we draw
an implicit parallel between the original bourgeois reaction to modernism and the   45
outrage provoked by people like the performance artist Karen Finley and the 'gangsta'
rapper Ice-T. Recalling that bourgeois critics abused Manet for painting in a non-
Academic style, bourgeois authorities censored Flaubert for depicting adultery, and
bourgeois theatregoers jeered Stravinsky's *Rite of Spring*, those who subscribe to the

Corliss fallacy assume that Finley's chocolate-smeared breasts and Ice-T's 'evil dick' 50
must be art because they, too, 'shock the bourgeoisie'.

10   But what is the nature of the shock? Is today's shock art introducing forbidden
ideas into a repressive polity? Is it creatively defying the rigid conventions of an
Academy? Is it breaking a puritanical silence about sex? Is it challenging the stilted
decorum of a ruling class? Granted, there are some cultural bomb-throwers who seem 55
to think we are living in Bismarck's Germany, just as there are some Bible-thumpers
who seem to think that all modern art is the work of the devil. But these voices,
though loud, are few. Most of us accept, however dubiously, the right of artists to do
anything they want.

11   But this doesn't mean we can't be shocked. One thing remains shocking: obscen- 60
ity. The Supreme Court has defined obscenity as the depiction of 'sexual conduct' in a
'patently offensive way' lacking 'serious literary, artistic, political, or scientific value'.
This definition evolved out of a century-long legal battle over the portrayal of sex in
serious literature, and it represents the victory of art over prudery. Yet precisely because
this legal definition focuses exclusively on sex while exempting material possessing 65
'serious artistic value', it is irrelevant to our present situation.

12   A better definition of obscenity comes from the legal scholar Harry M. Clor. Clor
argues that obscenity resides not in particular bodily functions or conditions but in the
angle of vision taken toward them:

> Obscenity . . . consists in a degradation of the human dimensions of life to a 70
> subhuman or merely physical level. . . . Thus, there can be an obscene view of
> sex; there can also be obscene views of death, of birth, of illness, and of acts
> such as eating or defecating. Obscenity makes a public exhibition of these
> phenomena and does so in such a way that their larger human context is lost
> or depreciated.   75

13   Obscenity is shocking because it violates our sense of shame. In puritanical cultures the slightest reference to the body causes undue shame. But that does not mean
we should never feel shame. Shame is the natural, universal response to nakedness,
eroticism, and suffering. In most human societies these states are taboo—meaning not
forbidden but sacred and awe-inspiring, connected with the mysterious beginnings 80
and endings of life. It is only in the modern West that people have sought to eradi-
cate these taboos.

14   Or to exploit them. Today's shock artists equate shame with repression because
they are committed to obscenity as the only reliable means of getting a shocked reaction out of the public. They flatter themselves that this reaction is akin to that in the 85
great scandals of the modernist past. But in fact it comes neither from public resistance to aesthetic innovation nor from a high degree of prudery in the culture. Instead
it reflects the simple fact that most people are not exhibitionists or voyeurs. Most people feel slight embarrassment and a strong need for either ritual or privacy when eating, eliminating, making love, suffering, and dying. If that makes them unable to 90
appreciate 'art', then the word has lost its meaning.

15   Obscenity as art is everywhere. In the Whitney Museum one finds a
photographic display of penises in one room and a row of video monitors showing

'transgressive' sexual practices in another. In *Spin* magazine one finds a jeans adver-
tisement in which a young man brandishes a handgun over the caption 'Teaching kids   95
to KILL helps them deal directly with reality.' The compulsion to shock dominates pop-
ular music, movies, television, publishing, talk radio, stand-up comedy, and video
games. Never before in the history of culture has obscenity been so pervasive.

16   Yet as obscenity ceases to be the preoccupation of a self-conscious elite and
enters the popular culture, it will face something it has never had to face before: a   100
plebiscite. One may hesitate to place too much faith in the aesthetic judgment of the
everyday people who will cast the deciding votes. But better they than the shock
artists, with their fond belief that if something is shockingly degrading and dehu-
manizing, it is, perforce, art. At least the mainstream is likely to weigh the claims of
art against those of civility, decency, and morality.   105

17   The danger is that such popular revulsion can lead to backlash censorship,
even repression. Raising the spectre of the Nazi crackdown on 'degenerate art', shock
artists warn that the same thing is happening today, because the NEA [National
Endowment for the Arts] is under fire from conservatives. Yet all this stale posturing
proves is that some artists are so isolated from the rest of the world that their ideas   110
never undergo a reality check. In one breath they vow to disrupt the (presumably)
repressive social order. In the next they complain that the power behind that order—
the government—won't pay their bills. As George Orwell observed, there are some
ideas so preposterous that only an intellectual could believe them. Today we can add,
'Or an NEA grantee.'   115

1994

QUESTIONS

Reader and Purpose

1. What is the fallacy that the author refers to in her title? Use your own words in answering this question; do not quote the author.
2. Is the author arguing that art must shock—even the art that she approves of? If you believe that this is true, what are her reasons? If not, then what is she arguing?
3. Would Martha Bayles be sympathetic to the argument proposed by Ralph Heintzman in his 'Liberalism and Censorship'? Why, or why not?

Organization

4. How is the author developing her essay in the first four paragraphs?
5. How is paragraph 5 related to paragraphs 1 to 4?
6. What is the purpose of the contrasts in paragraph 8?
7. How do the five questions at the beginning of paragraph 10 lead to the concluding sentence of that paragraph?
8. Paragraph 10 begins with the **connective** *but*. Could any other connective serve equally well? Apply this same question to the first word in paragraphs 11, 14, and 16.
9. Does the second-last sentence of this essay constitute a **closing by return**?

Sentences

10. In the first sentence of paragraph 1 would it be preferable to place a full colon after 'he' ('one-man shows in which he: excoriates the government, spews profanity, . . .')? Why, or why not?
11. In paragraph 4 should there be a comma after the clause 'a fight breaks out'?
12. Would either of the two series in paragraph 6 be more effective if they used either **asyndeton** or **polysyndeton**?
13. Although the second sentence of paragraph 8 begins with 'First', there is no 'second' or 'third'. Should there be? If so, where would you place these words? If not, is the author guilty of an error in logic?
14. What are the **parallel** elements of the first five sentences of paragraph 10? Should the first sentence be omitted from this question?

Diction

15. Look up: *excoriates* (2), *campanile* (8), *vignettes* (18), *modernism* (19), *expressionist* (20), *avant-garde* (25), *jettison* (28), *aesthetic* (28), *bourgeois* (45), *polity* (53), *stilted* (54), *decorum* (55), *patently* (62), *prudery* (64).
16. What does the author mean by the following expressions: *an unnerving halt* (17), *unnerving Naples* (24), *the angle of vision* (69)?
17. Which of the following phrases strike you as **clichés**: *a venerable cathedral* (6), *to jettison the past* (28), *this stale posturing* (109)?
18. Look up the **etymology** of *hidebound* (43). Then show how the earlier senses of this word help us to understand its current meaning.
19. What does *perforce* (104) mean? Is the author being **ironic** in her use of this word? If so, what is she trying to suggest?

POINTS TO LEARN

1. Parallel structure can help to clarify a series of which each element is developed in a separate paragraph.
2. A **coordinate conjunction** can begin a sentence or a paragraph, but you must remember that the seven most common of these connectives (*and, or, but, for, nor, so, yet*) are not interchangeable; each one has a different meaning.

SUGGESTIONS FOR WRITING

Have you ever been shocked by a piece of contemporary hard-rock music? or a contemporary novel? or photograph? or movie? or play? Describe your reaction and why you reacted as you did. Then construct an argument that either validates or rejects Bayles's contention that 'Obscenity is shocking because it violates our sense of shame' (76).

IMPROVING YOUR STYLE

1. Begin one paragraph with a series of questions that help to focus your discussion.
2. Use an appropriate coordinate conjunction to begin at least two paragraphs.

LESTER B. PEARSON

Lester Bowles Pearson (1897–1972) was, successively, a teacher of history at the University of Toronto, a brilliant civil servant in Canada's Department of External Affairs, and Liberal prime minister of Canada from 1963 to 1968. He was also twice president of the United Nations Assembly, the only Canadian ever to hold this prestigious position. Because of his role in bringing about a resolution to the Suez crisis in 1956, he was awarded the Nobel Prize for Peace. In the following selection, which offers a summary of Pearson's political philosophy, he uses description and metaphor to persuade his audience of the importance for Canada of the values of tolerance and co-operation.

The Implications of a Free Society

1   The essential lubricant for a free society is tolerance. This, however, does not necessarily apply to *all* societies. There are obvious examples of states which are held together without the least regard for tolerance. It does apply, however, to all states where there is government by consent. Canada, where various groups live and work together within the boundaries of a national state, is a good example of this princi- 5 ple in operation. This country exists on the assumption that, as far as is humanly possible, the interests of no group—racial, geographic, economic, religious, or political—will prevail at the expense of any other group. We have committed ourselves to the principle that by compromise and adjustment we can work out some sort of balance of interests which will make it possible for the members of all groups 10 to live side by side without any one of them arbitrarily imposing its will on any other. It is my belief that this is the only basis upon which Canada can possibly exist as a nation, and that any attempt to govern the country on any other basis would destroy it. In these circumstances, the basic quality of tolerance in our national character is of the first importance.   15
2   Of almost equal importance for our national welfare, and indeed arising out of the practice of tolerance, is the avoidance of extreme policies. This is often called walking in the middle of the road. This of course is not so easy as people usually think. It imposes both self-restraint and discipline, even when we assume that the traffic is all going in the one direction. Anyone who chooses to travel in the middle of 20 the road must not deny the use of either side of it to persons who prefer to walk there. He condemns himself, therefore, to accept during the journey the constant jostling of companions on either side. This middle ground is, I think, becoming more and more difficult to maintain, and the temptation to abandon it is constantly increasing, especially in the face of the road blocks thrown up by unfriendly fellow travellers. I do not 25 wish here to criticize those who choose other ground upon which to walk, or to question the basis of their choice. I wish only to make a strong plea for the preservation of this middle position in our national life. Paradoxically, it is only in this way that the existence of many of those on each side can also be preserved. If the middle group is eliminated, less tolerant elements fall under the irresistible temptation to try to cap- 30 ture the whole roadway. When the middle of the road is no longer occupied firmly by stable and progressive groups in the community, it is turned into a parade ground for

those extremist forces who would substitute goose-stepping for walking. All others are driven to hide, disconsolate and powerless, in the hedges, ditches, and culverts.

3   How can the meaning of the middle way in our free society be described in a 35 few words? What principle does it stand for? Where does it lead in practice? Is it merely the political line of least resistance along which drift those without the courage of their convictions, or simply without convictions? It is, or should be, far more than that. The central quality of this approach is the stress which it always lays on human values, the integrity and worth of the individual in society. It stands for the emanci- 40 pation of the mind as well as for personal freedom and well-being. It is irrevocably opposed to the shackling limitations of rigid political dogma, to political oppression of, and to economic exploitation by, any part of the community. It detests the abuse of power either by the state or by private individuals and groups. It respects first of all a person for what he is, not who he is. It stands for his right to manage his own 45 affairs, when they *are* his own; to hold his own convictions and speak his own mind. It aims at equality of opportunity. It maintains that effort and reward should not be separated and it values highly initiative and originality. It does not believe in lopping off the tallest ears of corn in the interests of comfortable conformity.

4   The middle way presents no panacea for the easy attainment of general welfare, 50 but it accepts the responsibility of government to assist in protecting and raising the living standards of all, and, if necessary, to take bold and well-planned action to help maintain economic activity for that purpose.

5   The middle way, unlike extremism in political doctrine, has positive faith in the good will and common sense of most people in most circumstances. It relies on their 55 intelligence, their will to co-operate, and their sense of justice. From its practitioners, it requires determination and patience, tolerance and restraint, the discipline of the mind rather than the jackboot, and the underlying belief that human problems, vast and complicated though they may be, are capable of solution.

1970

QUESTIONS
Reader and Purpose

1. Because Mr Pearson (later prime minister of Canada, 1963–8) was, at the time of this speech, one of the more honoured statesmen in the Western world, his views were likely to be accorded close attention. To whom do you think his remarks were addressed?

2. Is Pearson trying to persuade us that the issue he is treating is a contentious one? That is, are the points he is making likely to be the subject of discussion, or of argument?

3. To what extent is this as much a descriptive essay as an argumentative one?

Organization

4. Pearson begins with a sweeping statement to which he immediately adds a **qualification**. Then, in the third sentence, he makes another generalization. Do the beginnings of paragraphs 2 and 3 have this same sort of structure? If not, how do they begin?

5. In paragraph 1 Pearson describes tolerance as both a 'principle' (9) and a 'basic quality' (14). Is there a contradiction here? What is his justification? Does he make any further use of this distinction?

6. What two **transitional** expressions does Pearson use at the beginning of paragraph 2? Why does he use two, instead of the more common one?

7. In paragraph 2 Pearson introduces the **metaphor** 'walking in the middle of the road' (18). Describe how this metaphor affects the construction of the rest of the paragraph.

8. Pearson continues to refer to 'the middle way' in paragraphs 3, 4, and 5. Is he still using a metaphor? Or has this metaphor become an **abstraction**? Or is it both?

9. Is there a transition between paragraphs 2 and 3? If so, describe how it functions. If not, show how Pearson is justified in omitting it.

10. How is paragraph 4 a logical conclusion to paragraph 3? Should it not, rather, be a part of 3?

11. What is the principal device Pearson uses to maintain the **flow** of paragraph 3?

12. What does the phrase 'in these circumstances' (14) refer to? Why does it occur in the last sentence of the paragraph?

13. What is the function of the four questions that begin paragraph 3? Are they **rhetorical questions**?

Sentences

14. Pearson's essay contains a number of **balanced sentences** (such as the one beginning in line 12) and **antitheses** (as in lines 44–5). Are there any other examples? Justify your choices.

15. Is the sentence beginning in line 33 a **tricolon**? the sentence beginning in line 39?

16. Which sentence of paragraph 1 comes closest to being a definition, or explanation, of tolerance?

17. What is the function of the phrase 'the meaning of the middle way' (35)?

18. The first sentence of paragraph 5 uses **interrupted movement, parallelism**, and **balanced construction**. Point out the example of each, and then analyze the other sentences in this paragraph in the same manner.

Diction

19. Look up: *consent* (4), *assumption* (6), *prevail* (8), *compromise* (9), *arbitrarily* (11), *assume* (19), *paradoxically* (28), *goose-stepping* (33), *disconsolate* (34), *emancipation* (40–1), *irrevocably* (41), *conformity* (49), *panacea* (50), *extremism* (54), *jackboot* (57).

20. Explain the metaphor in the first sentence.

21. In the sentence beginning in line 31, there is an example of what can be called a metaphor within a metaphor. Explain.

22. Why does Pearson write 'values highly' (48) instead of 'highly values'? Would there be any difference in emphasis between these two expressions?

23. Pearson uses expressions which either are, or are close to being, **clichés**, such as *road block* (25) and *shackling limitations* (42). Can you find any others? What does the use of such expressions reveal about the author?

POINTS TO LEARN

1. A persuasive essay can include much that is descriptive.
2. A controlling metaphor is a very useful device for unifying a paragraph.
3. A paragraph may be effectively introduced by a series of questions that are answered in the main part of the paragraph.

SUGGESTIONS FOR WRITING

1. In a paragraph of about 100 words write a précis of Pearson's argument.
2. 'Pearson's middle way is the way of the compromiser, of the political and social coward.'
   In an essay of 800–1,000 words argue the truth of this statement, using persuasive techniques to defend or criticize Pearson's political philosophy. Make your own position clear and then try to convince the reader that this position, even though it may not be the whole truth, is more reasonable than the alternative.

IMPROVING YOUR STYLE

Include the following in your essay:

1. one paragraph based on a controlling metaphor;
2. two balanced sentences;
3. two sentences using parallelism;
4. a closing sentence like Pearson's, in which you try to create a rhythm based on the balancing of pairs.

JANE JACOBS

With the publication of *The Death and Life of Great American Cities* in 1961, Jane Jacobs (1916–) gained a reputation as one of America's more important urban planners. In this book she argued for the preservation of the vitality of cities and for the importance of rehabilitating communities rather than destroying them and rebuilding. Now a resident of Toronto, she was born in Pennsylvania and lived in New York City for more than thirty years before she and her husband, fearing that their two sons might soon be drafted to fight in Vietnam, emigrated in 1968. A former associate editor of *Architectural Forum*, she has published a number of other books, including *The Economy of Cities* (1969), *The Question of Separatism: Quebec and the Struggle Over Sovereignty* (1980), *Cities and the Wealth of Nations* (1984), *Systems of Survival: A Dialogue on the Moral Foundations of Commerce and Politics* (1992), and *The Nature of Economies* (2000).

Streets that Work

1   Twenty years ago it was commonly believed that to benefit cities a plan must be sweeping and comprehensive. Small improvements and non-disruptive plans were sneered at as 'the band-aid approach'. Slums were bulldozed to make way for monolithic public housing projects. Neighbourhoods were bisected, trisected, and some-

times vivisected for links in city-wide expressway systems. Historic and humanely 5
scaled landscapes were demolished to make way for high-rise apartment or office
buildings. Zoning was aimed at segregating the different components of city life from
one another.

2   Reality finally caught up with us: not only was the destruction expensive, the
results were disappointing socially, functionally, and aesthetically.   10

3   Even so, old ways of thinking die hard. Once people have taken it for granted
that little worthwhile can be accomplished without the guidance of sweeping
schemes—masterminding big change far into the future—they tend to be at a loss in
finding constructive alternatives.

4   Since we think with words even more than with diagrams, sometimes a single 15
change of phrase helps open our minds to possibilities and alternatives. Just so, nowadays a new term, 'retrofitting', has begun to enter the planning vocabulary. Retrofitting
means accepting what exists as a base, a given, and deliberately improving it with varied small changes. These little alterations, thought of and undertaken as opportunity
offers, incrementally add up to very significant improvement. By its very nature, this 20
approach is economic, conserving, efficient, flexible, and responsive.

5   What it requires, in place of comprehensive and dictatorial plans, is a shared
set of perceptions and values, so that the incremental changes, as they add up, are
coherent rather than chaotic and at cross-purposes.

6   The most requisite 'shared value' is a simple belief that the city is a good place, 25
not something to be hated, not something to be accepted as a necessary evil, certainly
not something to try to destroy. This may seem self-evident, but apparently is not. The
very genesis of so-called modern city planning was hatred of the city, and especially of
its most important visual and functional artifacts, its streets. The great men of planning
and its philosophy—Ebenezer Howard, Corbusier, Lewis Mumford, and the others— 30
deplored cities, were disgusted by their streets, and even sought to erase them as far
as possible.

7   A second necessary shared value has already been alluded to: belief that small
improvements are worthwhile, faith that they add up, and recognition that they are
all the more effective because they are not disruptive and all the more congenial 35
because they can occur as opportunity offers and circumstance permits.

8   We must also recognize that small—in itself—isn't necessarily beautiful. Thus,
besides that fundamental belief in the value of the city and the value of incremental
improvement, we need general guidelines for retrofitting city streets, rules of thumb
that can be kept in mind in the trenches by embattled local block groups, neigh- 40
bourhood associations, homeowners and tenants, and—yes—even professional city
planners. The seven guides that follow, many of them aptly illustrated in my own city
of Toronto, are proposed not as the last word, but as a start. They too can be aug-
mented incrementally, as experience suggests additions or refinements:

9   *1. Avoid monotony.* When retrofitting a street, try to insert what isn't there 45
already, and with respect to what is inserted, avoid monotony too. The worst possible
insertion is a long, blank wall. This would hardly seem necessary to mention except
that it is transgressed so often by shopping malls, arenas, buildings of all kinds that
should be improved with the use of imagination, sensitive design, and inclusion of
varied functions at street level.   50

10   Fountains can be wonderful insertions. One of the things we all like when we visit old cities in Europe—I'm thinking of Zurich—is the many fountains dotted about the city. In the old days, every district had to have its fountain for households to get their water. Europe has since been retrofitted with indoor plumbing but its fountains still serve a social purpose—they're hangouts, places to meet, and they're   55
nice, visual exclamation points.

11   In Canada, we seem to have only the great monumental fountain or the little drinking fountain in the park. There's nothing in between. A lot could be done here with fountains.

12   When inserting something different, aesthetics can help, even cosmetics can, but   60
it will count for a lot more if you can also add something functionally different. Putting stores into the ground floor of a parking garage, for example, could enliven what is usually a dead stretch. But a word of caution: there's no use putting in stores where they'd go out of business or remain empty. You have to think whether they're practical.

13   *2. Go with what's natural to the circumstances.* For instance, a lot of horizontal   65
greenery is not natural to most city streets. *Vertical* greenery is. Streets are natural places for trees, for vines, for greenery taking little ground area. A city can't support many trees.

14   Vines unfortunately have a bad name, partly because architects don't like to have their buildings covered up and partly because the probing roots of some vine species can damage mortar. But it would be nice to see certain kinds of vines planned   70
as an element of design. Used properly on the right type of surface, deciduous plants like Virginia Creeper can shield masonry from acid rain, and vines on a south wall can work wonders keeping buildings cool in summer.

15   *3. Be aware, and open to discovery.* This applies even to things that seem invisible. Take the bicycle. A cyclist tells me some of the best bike routes are on streets   75
where there is just a little more room in the curb lane. Say there's a parking lane, then lanes of traffic, and there's a little more room in each lane than necessary. If the excess of, say, three feet is consolidated into the lane next to the parking, you create an invisible bike path. I'd never analyzed this before, but when I used to ride my bike to work in New York, I too had certain paths I'd chosen because they felt spacious. I wonder   80
that I'd never noticed just why. This is the kind of thing we must notice. And we all can't notice everything—so listen to other people.

16   *4. Don't try to be comprehensive.* That's how you get into the worst trouble, trying to coordinate everything desirable at once, which is cumbersome, frustrating, and unpractical. Many of our cities' worst problems stem from overly zealous, com-   85
prehensive planning and policy making. There are many tales, but here's one of the more incredible: Once, when I lived in New York, I was looking through the Urban Renewal Administration files to find out how a really very decent neighbourhood had gotten designated for urban renewal, and had been knocked down, to the great hardship of many people. And what do you think? It began with a letter—from some inno-   90
cent in the neighbourhood—to the Planning Commission, asking if they could have trees planted on the street. This is a fact. From the Planning Commission, the letter was sent to various civil servant specialists, and everybody it went to latched onto it as a chance to do something his department wanted. When the Urban Renewal people saw the letter, they got so comprehensive they doomed the neighbourhood.   95

17   *5. Start with what's easiest.* This is a good general principle in life. Don't begin where everything is stacked against you, where you'll need the most specialists, and especially not where the people involved are going to oppose what you contemplate.
18   If the plan works, you can build on that success. People can actually see what you're talking about. You have a successful precedent, making it easier to overcome 100 objections and red tape where similar changes would be harder to initiate.

19   *6. Work incrementally.* Little drops of water, little grains of sand, they do add up. But more than that, they point the way to still further things. I'm thinking of Toronto's experience with infill housing, which started when there was a citizen revolt at Dundas and Sherbourne Streets about knocking down old buildings to make way 105 for another one of those massive high-rise developments.
20   The people in that neighbourhood were fed up with the city's fabric being comprehensively torn apart, and at the last minute their protests succeeded in stopping the wreckers. That gave time to develop a counter-proposal—one that was economically feasible and wouldn't require demolition of existing buildings. It took real genius 110 at cutting red tape to get over the hurdles and permit the construction of infill housing (new construction in vacant lots that blends with the style and character of the existing architecture around it). In the process the city began to learn a whole new way of working. The Department of Housing was reincarnated, and went on to develop all kinds of lots, mostly small, as infill sites. In the past, they'd have been 115 written off as too small or awkward to fool with. There was some opposition, but the city was sensible. It began with the easiest places. This showed people that the new way of working wasn't like the old assisted housing that ruins the area all around it. The more infill was done, the more acceptable it became.
21   Because planners were learning a different way of working, the City Planning 120 Department was equipped in a way it hadn't been before to work on Toronto's St Lawrence neighbourhood. This was a different problem, a large clean-sweep area that would have been made a project in the past. It's called a neighbourhood because it's not a project. The department had so much expertise at knitting up the city's fabric—where it was torn, or tattered—that it could work on this large swatch of land as if it was an extension of that 125 fabric. Even with the best intentions—to make nice streetscapes, human-scaled and for people—I'm sure the St Lawrence planning couldn't have been done without that prior experience of infill planning. I watched the change in the planners' and architects' perceptions of city fabric as they went through this experience. They couldn't even have thought of how to plan St Lawrence previously. This is an example of how working incre- 130 mentally, in itself leads to new techniques and design ideas if you build on experience.
22   After watching this, I became optimistic about the next possible incremental change in Toronto, since there were planners with experience in a new way of seeing the city and dealing with it. I hoped the city would take some of the monotonous and monolithic housing projects—beginning with the easiest ones—and start knitting 135 these back into the city: for instance, by making reasons for people outside the projects to go into them by livening them up, inserting new and interesting and convenient things—in short, retrofitting them both for their own residents and for others. We can't afford to blow up our many dismal projects, as was done in the case of St Louis' infamous Pruitt-Igoe project, and it is outrageous to make people endure 140 their faults interminably. The practical approach is to retrofit them.

23   Several years ago I heard this was being thought of for St Jamestown in Toronto, which seems a good choice as it's probably one of the easiest with which to begin. However, I'm pessimistic. The old, besetting sin of planners seems again taking command: trying to be comprehensive instead of getting started with something—one   145 street, one part of a street, whatever can be begun easily, then building on that.

24   Perhaps if Toronto fails to begin incrementally improving its sterile housing projects, some other city will. I hope it starts happening someplace, because literally every city in the world, from Toronto to Beijing, Amsterdam and Zagreb, is waiting for practical examples of how to incorporate wretchedly-designed projects function-   150 ally and socially into the fabrics of cities.

25   *7. Remember who the real jurors are.* They aren't the architectural and planning magazines. They aren't the private or public clients who pay for street changes. They aren't the schools of architecture. They aren't the jurors of design competitions.

26   The real jurors of street success are the people who use and enjoy them. If you   155 heed their responses as indicated by the use they make of what you do—or by their lack of use and appreciation—they'll show very quickly what success you've had.

1987

QUESTIONS
Reader and Purpose
1. This essay is a good example of a work that blurs the boundaries between different kinds of essays: descriptive, persuasive, and argumentative. What elements of each can you find?
2. The subtitle of this essay (which may have been added by the editors of the magazine in which the essay was first published) is 'Seven hints to help keep our cities' lifelines viable'. However, these hints are all expressed in imperative verbs, i.e. verbs that give a command, an order. Can such verbs be considered a persuasive technique? an argumentative one?

Organization
3. What sort of progression does the author use in the first three paragraphs?
4. How do the first three paragraphs prepare for the definition and explanation in paragraphs 4 and 5?
5. How is paragraph 6 related to paragraph 5? How is paragraph 7 related to both paragraphs 5 and 6?
6. Why is the sixth section of this essay (paragraphs 19–24) the longest? How does this section develop an idea first mentioned in paragraph 4?

Sentences
7. In the second sentence of paragraph 2, would placing a dash after 'disappointing' make the list that follows more, or less, emphatic? What would be the effect of substituting commas for the dashes in the second sentence of the next paragraph?
8. In the third sentence of paragraph 9 should the phrase 'should be improved' be changed to 'could be improved'? Would the author likely accept this change? Why, or why not?

9. Why is there a comma after 'incrementally' in the last sentence of paragraph 21? Would the sentence read better if the comma were taken out?

10. What is the average length of the sentences in paragraph 22? Does the author vary her sentences sufficiently to avoid monotony? What other methods does she use to vary her sentences?

11. Is the **parallel structure** in paragraph 25 effective? Why, or why not? How does the final element of this parallelism act as the conclusion to the paragraph? Does it function as the **transition** to the final paragraph? If so, how?

Diction

12. Look up: *monolithic* (3–4), *vivisected* (5), *aesthetically* (10), *incrementally* (20), *coherent* (24), *genesis* (28), *artifact* (29), *allude* (33), *congenial* (35), *transgress* (48), *deciduous* (71), *cumbersome* (84), *zealous* (85), *precedent* (100), *feasible* (110), *swatch* (125), *interminably* (141), *besetting* (144).

13. In paragraph 4 the author explains what she means by *retrofitting*. In her later uses of this term does she vary its meaning, or is her original explanation the one she is faithful to?

14. What metaphor does the author introduce in the fourth sentence of paragraph 21? How does she develop this metaphor in paragraph 22?

15. In the first sentence of the final paragraph, what is the antecedent of 'them'? Is the author guilty here of a grammatical error?

POINTS TO LEARN

1. Monotony can be avoided not only by varying sentence length but also by using different sentence structures within a paragraph.

2. Subheadings can help to structure an essay and thus to emphasize its main points.

SUGGESTIONS FOR WRITING

Write an argumentative essay (800–1,000 words) on one of the following topics:

1. An area of the town or city in which you live must be revitalized in order to survive.

2. Your landlord must make some badly needed repairs to your apartment.

3. A children's park in your neighbourhood, unusable because of garbage, must be cleaned up.

Your essay (in the form of a letter) must be addressed to a specific individual, either your landlord or local member of City Council. Although your tendency will probably be to write an impassioned plea, and thus a persuasive piece, you must resist this temptation in favour of a reasoned argument. You will, that is, base your letter on reason rather than on feeling.

IMPROVING YOUR STYLE

1. Use at least two subheadings.

2. Include one definition that you explain at some length.

NORTHROP FRYE

Born in Sherbrooke, Quebec, Northrop Frye (1912–91) was educated at the universities of Toronto and Oxford, and later taught for many years at Victoria College in the University of Toronto. As a result of such books as *Fearful Symmetry: A Study of William Blake* (1947), *Anatomy of Criticism* (1957), *The Well-Tempered Critic* (1963), *The Secular Scripture: A Study of the Structure of Romance* (1976), and *The Great Code: The Bible and Literature* (1982), Frye established a reputation as one of the world's principal literary critics of the twentieth century. Among his many other works are *The Bush Garden: Essays on the Canadian Imagination* (1971), *On Education* (1988), and *The Double Vision: Language and Meaning in Religion* (1991). He was also a frequent and extremely perceptive commentator on the social, educational, and cultural issues of our time, as the following selection shows. It is from *The Educated Imagination* (1963), a collection of six Massey radio lectures broadcast on the CBC in the fall of 1962.

The Motive for Metaphor

1   For the past 25 years I have been teaching and studying English literature in a university. As in any other job, certain questions stick out in one's mind, not because people keep asking them, but because they're the questions inspired by the very fact of being in such a place. What good is the study of literature? Does it help us to think more clearly, or feel more sensitively, or live a better life than we could without it? What is the function of the teacher and scholar, or of the person who calls himself, as I do, a literary critic? What difference does the study of literature make in our social or political or religious attitude? In my early days I thought very little about such questions, not because I had any of the answers, but because I assumed that anybody who asked them was naive. I think now that the simplest questions are not only the hardest to answer, but the most important to ask, so I'm going to raise them and try to suggest what my present answers are. I say try to suggest, because there are only more or less inadequate answers to such questions—there aren't any right answers. The kind of problem that literature raises is not the kind you ever 'solve'. Whether my answers are any good or not, they represent a fair amount of thinking about the questions. As I can't see my audience, I have to choose my rhetorical style in the dark, and I'm taking the classroom style, because an audience of students is the one I feel easiest with.

2   There are two things in particular that I want to discuss with you. In school, and in university, there's a subject called 'English' in English-speaking countries. English means, in the first place, the mother tongue. As that, it's the most practical subject in the world: you can't understand anything or take any part in your society without it. Wherever illiteracy is a problem, it's as fundamental a problem as getting enough to eat or a place to sleep. The native language takes precedence over every other subject of study: nothing else can compare with it in usefulness. But then you find that every mother tongue, in any developed or civilized society, turns into something called literature. If you keep on studying 'English', you find yourself trying to read Shakespeare and Milton. Literature, we're told, is one of the arts, along with

painting and music, and, after you've looked up all the hard words and the Classical allusions and learned what words like imagery and diction are supposed to mean, what you use in understanding it, or so you're told, is your imagination. Here you don't seem to be in quite the same practical and useful area: Shakespeare and Milton, whatever their merits, are not the kind of thing you must know to hold any place in society at all. A person who knows nothing about literature may be an ignoramus, but many people don't mind being that. Every child realizes that literature is taking him in a different direction from the immediately useful, and a good many children complain loudly about this. Two questions I want to deal with, then, are, first: what is the relation of English as the mother tongue to English as a literature? Second: what is the social value of the study of literature, and what is the place of the imagination that literature addresses itself to, in the learning process?

3   Let's start with the different ways there are of dealing with the world we're living in. Suppose you're shipwrecked on an uninhabited island in the South Seas. The first thing you do is take a long look at the world around you, a world of sky and sea and earth and stars and trees and hills. You see this world as objective, as something set over against you and not yourself or related to you in any way. And you notice two things about this objective world. In the first place, it doesn't have any conversation. It's full of animals and plants and insects going on with their own business, but there's nothing that responds to you: it has no morals and no intelligence, or at least none that you can grasp. It may have a shape and a meaning, but it doesn't seem to be a human shape or a human meaning. Even if there's enough to eat and no dangerous animals, you feel lonely and frightened and unwanted in such a world.

4   In the second place, you find that looking at the world, as something set over against you, splits your mind in two. You have an intellect that feels curious about it and wants to study it, and you have feelings or emotions that see it as beautiful or austere or terrible. You know that both these attitudes have some reality, at least for you. If the ship you were wrecked in was a Western ship, you'd probably feel that your intellect tells you more about what's really there in the outer world, and that your emotions tell you more about what's going on inside you. If your background were Oriental, you'd be more likely to reverse this and say that the beauty or terror was what was really there, and that your instinct to count and classify and measure and pull to pieces was what was inside your mind. But whether your point of view is Western or Eastern, intellect and emotion never get together in your mind as long as you're simply looking at the world. They alternate, and keep you divided between them.

5   The language you use on this level of the mind is the language of consciousness or awareness. It's largely a language of nouns and adjectives. You have to have names for things, and you need qualities like 'wet' or 'green' or 'beautiful' to describe how things seem to you. This is the speculative or contemplative position of the mind, the position in which the arts and sciences begin, although they don't stay there very long. The sciences begin by accepting the facts and the evidence about an outside world without trying to alter them. Science proceeds by accurate measurement and description, and follows the demands of the reason rather than the emotions. What it deals with is there, whether we like it or not. The emotions are unreasonable: for them it's what they like and don't like that comes first. We'd be naturally inclined to think that the arts follow the path of emotion, in contrast to the sciences. Up to a point they do, but there's a complicating factor.   75

6   That complicating factor is the contrast between 'I like this' and 'I don't like this'. In this Robinson Crusoe life I've assigned you, you may have moods of complete peacefulness and joy, moods when you accept your island and everything around you. You wouldn't have such moods very often, and when you had them, they'd be moods of identification, when you felt that the island was a part of you and you a part of it. That 80 is not the feeling of consciousness or awareness, where you feel split off from everything that's not your perceiving self. Your habitual state of mind is the feeling of separation which goes with being conscious, and the feeling 'this is not a part of me' soon becomes 'this is not what I want'. Notice the word 'want': we'll be coming back to it.

7   So you soon realize that there's a difference between the world you're living in 85 and the world you want to live in. The world you want to live in is a human world, not an objective one: it's not an environment but a home; it's not the world you see but the world you build out of what you see. You go to work to build a shelter or plant a garden, and as soon as you start to work you've moved into a different level of human life. You're not separating only yourself from nature now, but constructing a 90 human world and separating it from the rest of the world. Your intellect and emotions are now both engaged in the same activity, so there's no longer any real distinction between them. As soon as you plant a garden or a crop, you develop the conception of a 'weed', the plant you don't want in there. But you can't say that 'weed' is either an intellectual or an emotional conception, because it's both at once. Further, you go 95 to work because you feel you have to, and because you want something at the end of the work. That means that the important categories of your life are no longer the subject and the object, the watcher and the things being watched: the important categories are what you have to do and what you want to do—in other words, necessity and freedom.   100

8   One person by himself is not a complete human being, so I'll provide you with another shipwrecked refugee of the opposite sex and an eventual family. Now you're a member of a human society. This human society after a while will transform the island into something with a human shape. What that human shape is, is revealed in the shape of the work you do: the buildings, such as they are, the paths through the 105 woods, the planted crops fenced off against whatever animals want to eat them. These things, these rudiments of city, highway, garden and farm, are the human form of nature, or the form of human nature, whichever you like. This is the area of the applied arts and sciences, and it appears in our society as engineering and agriculture and medicine and architecture. In this area we can never say clearly where the art 110 stops and the science begins, or vice versa.

9   The language you use on this level is the language of practical sense, a language of verbs or words of action and movement. The practical world, however, is a world where actions speak louder than words. In some ways it's a higher level of existence than the speculative level, because it's doing something about the world instead of just 115 looking at it, but in itself it's a much more primitive level. It's the process of adapting to the environment, or rather of transforming the environment in the interests of one species, that goes on among animals and plants as well as human beings. The animals have a good many of our practical skills: some insects make pretty fair architects, and

beavers know quite a lot about engineering. In this island, probably, and certainly if you were alone, you'd have about the ranking of a second-rate animal. What makes our practical life really human is a third level of the mind, a level where consciousness and practical skill come together.

10 This third level is a vision or model in your mind of what you want to construct. There's that word 'want' again. The actions of man are prompted by desire, and some of these desires are needs, like food and warmth and shelter. One of these needs is sexual, the desire to reproduce and bring more human beings into existence. But there's also a desire to bring a social human form into existence: the form of cities and gardens and farms that we call civilization. Many animals and insects have this social form too, but man knows that he has it: he can compare what he does with what he can imagine being done. So we begin to see where the imagination belongs in the scheme of human affairs. It's the power of constructing possible models of human experience. In the world of the imagination, anything goes that's imaginatively possible, but nothing really happens. If it did happen, it would move out of the world of imagination into the world of action.

11 We have three levels of the mind now, and a language for each of them, which in English-speaking societies means an English for each of them. There's the level of consciousness and awareness, where the most important thing is the difference between me and everything else. The English of this level is the English of ordinary conversation, which is mostly monologue, as you'll soon realize if you do a bit of eavesdropping, or listening to yourself. We can call it the language of self-expression. Then there's the level of social participation, the working or technological language of teachers and preachers and politicians and advertisers and lawyers and journalists and scientists. We've already called this the language of practical sense. Then there's the level of imagination, which produces the literary language of poems and plays and novels. They're not really different languages, of course, but three different reasons for using words.

12 On this basis, perhaps, we can distinguish the arts from the sciences. Science begins with the world we have to live in, accepting its data and trying to explain its laws. From there, it moves towards the imagination: it becomes a mental construct, a model of a possible way of interpreting experience. The further it goes in this direction, the more it tends to speak the language of mathematics, which is really one of the languages of the imagination, along with literature and music. Art, on the other hand, begins with the world we construct, not with the world we see. It starts with the imagination, and then works towards ordinary experience: that is, it tries to make itself as convincing and recognizable as it can. You can see why we tend to think of the sciences as intellectual and the arts as emotional: one starts with the world as it is, the other with the world we want to have. Up to a point it is true that science gives an intellectual view of reality, and that the arts try to make the emotions as precise and disciplined as sciences do the intellect. But of course it's nonsense to think of the scientist as a cold unemotional reasoner and the artist as somebody who's in a perpetual emotional tizzy. You can't distinguish the arts from the sciences by the mental processes the people in them use: they both operate on a mixture of hunch and common sense. A highly developed science and a highly developed art are very close together, psychologically and otherwise.

13   Still, the fact that they start from opposite ends, even if they do meet in the middle, makes for one important difference between them. Science learns more and more about the world as it goes on: it evolves and improves. A physicist today knows more physics than Newton did, even if he's not as great a scientist. But literature begins with the possible model of experience, and what it produces is the literary 170 model we call the classic. Literature doesn't evolve or improve or progress. We may have dramatists in the future who will write plays as good as *King Lear*, though they'll be very different ones, but drama as a whole will never get better than *King Lear*. *King Lear* is it, as far as drama is concerned; so is *Oedipus Rex*, written two thousand years earlier than that, and both will be models of dramatic writing as long as the human 175 race endures. Social conditions may improve: most of us would rather live in nineteenth-century United States than in thirteenth-century Italy, and for most of us Whitman's celebration of democracy makes a lot more sense than Dante's Inferno. But it doesn't follow that Whitman is a better poet than Dante: literature won't line up with that kind of improvement.   180

14   So we find that everything that does improve, including science, leaves the literary artist out in the cold. Writers don't seem to benefit much by the advance of science, although they thrive on superstitions of all kinds. And you certainly wouldn't turn to contemporary poets for guidance or leadership in the twentieth-century world. You'd hardly go to Ezra Pound, with his fascism and social credit and Confucianism 185 and anti-Semitism. Or to Yeats, with his spiritualism and fairies and astrology. Or to D.H. Lawrence, who'll tell you that it's a good thing for servants to be flogged because that restores the precious current of blood-reciprocity between servant and master. Or to T.S. Eliot, who'll tell you that to have a flourishing culture we should educate an elite, keep most people living in the same spot, and never disestablish the Church of 190 England. The novelists seem to be a littler closer to the world they're living in, but not much. When Communists talk about the decadence of bourgeois culture, this is the kind of thing they always bring up. Their own writers don't seem to be any better, though; just duller. So the real question is a bigger one. Is it possible that literature, especially poetry, is something that a scientific civilization like ours will eventually out- 195 grow? Man has always wanted to fly, and thousands of years ago he was making sculptures of winged bulls and telling stories about people who flew so high on artificial wings that the sun melted them off. In an Indian play fifteen hundred years old, *Sakuntala*, there's a god who flies around in a chariot that to a modern reader sounds very much like a private aeroplane. Interesting that the writer had so much imagina- 200 tion, but do we need such stories now that we have private aeroplanes?

15   This is not a new question: it was raised a hundred and fifty years ago by Thomas Love Peacock, who was a poet and novelist himself, and a very brilliant one. He wrote an essay called *Four Ages of Poetry*, with his tongue of course in his cheek, in which he said that poetry was the mental rattle that awakened the imagination of 205 mankind in its infancy, but that now, in an age of science and technology, the poet has outlived his social function. 'A poet in our times', said Peacock, 'is a semi-barbarian in a civilized community. He lives in the days that are past. His ideas, thoughts, feelings, associations, are all with barbarous manners, obsolete customs, and exploded superstitions. The march of his intellect is like that of a crab, backwards.' Peacock's 210 essay annoyed his friend Shelley, who wrote another essay called *A Defence of Poetry* to refute it. Shelley's essay is a wonderful piece of writing, but it's not likely to convince anyone who needs convincing. I shall be spending a good deal of my time on this question of the relevance of literature in the world of today, and I can only indicate the general lines my answer will take. There are two points I can make now, one 215 simple, the other more difficult.

16 The simple point is that literature belongs to the world man constructs, not to the world he sees; to his home, not his environment. Literature's world is a concrete human world of immediate experience. The poet uses images and objects and sensations much more than he uses abstract ideas; the novelist is concerned with telling 220 stories, not with working out arguments. The world of literature is human in shape, a world where the sun rises in the east and sets in the west over the edge of a flat earth in three dimensions, where the primary realities are not atoms or electrons but bodies, and the primary forces not energy or gravitation but love and death and passion and joy. It's not surprising if writers are often rather simple people, not always what 225 we think of as intellectuals, and certainly not always any freer of silliness or perversity than anyone else. What concerns us is what they produce, not what they are, and poetry, according to Milton, who ought to have known, is 'more simple, sensuous and passionate' than philosophy or science.

17 The more difficult point takes us back to what we said when we were on that 230 South Sea island. Our emotional reaction to the world varies from 'I like this' to 'I don't like this'. The first, we said, was a state of identity, a feeling that everything around us was part of us, and the second is the ordinary state of consciousness, or separation, where art and science begin. Art begins as soon as 'I don't like this' turns into 'this is not the way I could imagine it'. We notice in passing that the creative and 235 the neurotic minds have a lot in common. They're both dissatisfied with what they see; they both believe that something else ought to be there, and they try to pretend it is there or to make it be there. The differences are more important, but we're not ready for them yet.

18 At the level of ordinary consciousness the individual man is the centre of every- 240 thing, surrounded on all sides by what he isn't. At the level of practical sense, or civilization, there's a human circumference, a little cultivated world with a human shape, fenced off from the jungle and inside the sea and the sky. But in the imagination anything goes that can be imagined, and the limit of the imagination is a totally human world. Here we recapture, in full consciousness, that original lost sense of identity 245 with our surroundings, where there is nothing outside the mind of man, or something identical with the mind of man. Religions present us with visions of eternal and infinite heavens or paradises which have the form of the cities and gardens of human civilization, like the Jerusalem and Eden of the Bible, completely separated from the state of frustration and misery that bulks so large in ordinary life. We're not concerned with 250 these visions as religion, but they indicate what the limits of the imagination are. They indicate too that in the human world the imagination has no limits, if you follow me. We said that the desire to fly produced the aeroplane. But people don't get into planes because they want to fly; they get into planes because they want to get somewhere faster. What's produced the aeroplane is not so much the desire to fly as a rebellion 255 against the tyranny of time and space. And that's a process that can never stop, no matter how high our Titovs and Glenns may go.

19   For each of these six talks I've taken a title from some work of literature, and my title for this one is 'The Motive for Metaphor', from a poem of Wallace Stevens. Here's the poem: 260

> You like it under the trees in autumn,
> Because everything is half dead.
> The wind moves like a cripple among the leaves
> And repeats words without meaning.
>
> In the same way, you were happy in spring,   265
> With the half colours of quarter-things,
> The slightly brighter sky, the melting clouds,
> The single bird, the obscure moon—
>
> The obscure moon lighting an obscure world
> Of things that would never be quite expressed,   270
> Where you yourself were never quite yourself
> And did not want nor have to be,
>
> Desiring the exhilarations of changes:
> The motive for metaphor, shrinking from
> The weight of primary noon,   275
> The A B C of being,
>
> The ruddy temper, the hammer
> Of red and blue, the hard sound—
> Steel against intimation—the sharp flash,
> The vital, arrogant, fatal, dominant X.   280

What Steven calls the weight of primary noon, the A B C of being, and the dominant X is the objective world, the world set over against us. Outside literature, the main motive for writing is to describe this world. But literature itself uses language in a way which associates our minds with it. As soon as you use associative language, you begin using figures of speech. If you say this talk is dry and dull, you're using figures 285 associating it with bread and breadknives. There are two main kinds of association, analogy and identity, two things that are like each other and two things that are each other. You can say with Burns, 'My love's like a red, red rose,' or you can say with Shakespeare:

> Thou that art now the world's fresh ornament   290
> And only herald to the gaudy spring.

One produces the figure of speech called the simile; the other produces the figure called metaphor.

20   In descriptive writing you have to be careful of associative language. You'll find that analogy, or likeness to something else, is very tricky to handle in description, 295 because the differences are as important as the resemblances. As for metaphor, where you're really saying 'this *is* that,' you're turning your back on logic and reason completely, because logically two things can never be the same thing and still remain two things. The poet, however, uses these two crude, primitive, archaic forms of thought

in the most uninhibited way, because his job is not to describe nature, but to show 300
you a world completely absorbed and possessed by the human mind. So he produces
what Baudelaire called a 'suggestive magic including at the same time object and subject, the world outside the artist and the artist himself'. The motive for metaphor,
according to Wallace Stevens, is a desire to associate, and finally to identify, the human
mind with what goes on outside it, because the only genuine joy you can have is in 305
those rare moments when you feel that although we may know in part, as Paul says,
we are also a part of what we know.

1963

QUESTIONS
Reader and Purpose
1. Although the topic Frye deals with is fairly complex, his vocabulary presents few
   problems (see the small number of difficult words in question 13, below). Might this
   be because this talk was given on radio? What kind of listener could the author
   have had in mind? How appropriate for this kind of listener is the 'classroom style'
   Frye sets out to adopt (17).
2. This essay is the first in a series of six. Point out some issues raised in this essay
   that you might expect Frye to treat in greater detail later in the series.

Organization
3. Frye asks several questions in his first paragraph. Then, in paragraph 2, he presents
   the two questions that are central to his argument. What are these questions?
4. In answering these two central questions, does Frye also answer (perhaps indirectly) the questions posed in the first paragraph? If so, where and how?
5. Where does Frye explain the 'motive for metaphor'—in his conclusion, or progres-
   sively, in the stages of his argument? Does he, in fact, give a clear statement explaining his title? Support your answer with examples.
6. Frye refers in paragraph 9 to 'a third level of the mind' (122). Where has he described
   the first two levels? What connections and **transitions** link the three descriptions?
7. How has Frye led up to his distinction between the arts and the sciences (paragraph
   12)? Having made this distinction, how does he use it to advance his subsequent
   argument?

Sentences
8. In paragraph 2 the author uses the colon on five occasions. Does he always use it
   for the same reason, or does it have more than one function?
9. At the beginning of paragraph 3 Frye writes 'Let's start' and 'Suppose you're shipwrecked'. Should he have written 'Let us start' and 'Suppose you are shipwrecked'? What does his use of the contractions tell us about his style? Does it
   tell us anything about the audience he is addressing? or the medium he is using?
10. In the second sentence of paragraph 4, why is there a comma before the **coordi-
    nate conjunction** 'and'? Would it be an error to omit this comma? Why, or why not?
    In the fifth sentence, why is there no comma after 'reverse this'? Why is there a
    comma after 'really there'? What difference is there in these two examples?

11. Do Frye's sentences seem relatively long to you? Calculate the length of the average sentence in paragraphs 7 and 9.
12. Are his sentences varied in structure? Compare the structure of the first three sentences in paragraph 11 with that of the first three sentences in paragraph 16. What can you conclude about his sentence structure?

Diction

13. Look up: *scholar* (6), *precedence* (23), *austere* (54), *speculative* (67), *rudiments* (107), *eavesdropping* (141), *construct* (150), *tizzy* (162), *evolve* (168), *barbarous* (209), *neurotic* (236), *uninhibited* (306).
14. Explain the **figure of speech** in the last sentence of paragraph 13. What kind of figure is it?

POINTS TO LEARN

1. The discussion of a complex topic need not involve a difficult vocabulary or a complicated style.
2. A simple and widely known analogy (Frye's being shipwrecked on an island in the South Seas in paragraph 3) is another effective means of dealing with a complex topic.

SUGGESTIONS FOR WRITING

Write an argumentative essay of 8–12 paragraphs on one of the following difficult topics, or one of your own choosing:

1. the rights of both parents in a divorce
2. the usefulness of one of the humanities
3. the rights of Native Canadians
4. the law and the victims of drunk drivers
5. the citizen's right to own guns

You will likely not be able to address all aspects of the topic, so you should deal with those about which you feel most certain. Use a style that is simple without becoming elementary.

IMPROVING YOUR STYLE

1. Use a simple analogy that you present in one paragraph and refer to in at least two subsequent paragraphs.
2. In one paragraph use a series of questions to help you focus on one aspect of the topic.

PETER SHAWN TAYLOR

A member of the editorial board of the *National Post*, Peter Shawn Taylor has published numerous articles, mainly on Canadian business. His work has appeared in such magazines as *Saturday Night*, *Alberta Report*, and the *National Post Business Magazine*.

Be Fruitful, Or Else

1   The crisis in health-care funding. Collapsing public pension plans. A looming economic slowdown. What if I told you all these problems could be easily solved but that the solution might offend some people? Would you still want to hear it?

2   Canada, along with most other developed countries, is in a demographic strait-jacket, and the consequences are dire. Canadians are living longer than ever and, thus, expecting more from public health care, pensions, and welfare systems. At the same time, Statistics Canada forecasts that between 2000 and 2040, the ratio of seniors to members of the working population will double from the current 2 per 10 workers to 4 per 10. And by 2040, the overall population of Canada will begin to shrink due to a declining birth rate. The strain these twin phenomena—more seniors and fewer young workers to support them—place on Canadian social programs such as medicare and the Canada Pension Plan is plain to see. In more mature countries such as Japan, Germany, and Italy, where the birth rate is even lower, these problems are far more advanced. In his 1999 book *Gray Dawn*, Peter Peterson argued that an aging population is a 'global hazard' on par with nuclear weapons and superviruses. The United Nations last year declared that only massive international migration on a scale never before seen could keep the aging trend at bay and economies in rich nations functioning. The future, however, is more flexible than most people seem to think.

3   All these grim discussions are strangely incomplete. While no one would wish to reverse the many improvements in life expectancies, nearly every demographic jeremiad leaves out the equally important front end of the population equation—the birth rate. The number of children an average Canadian woman bears over her lifetime has fallen to 1.48 from 1.65 twenty years ago. The rate required for a population to maintain itself without immigration is 2.1 per woman (one each to replace the parents and a fraction to cover the possibility that the child might die before procreating). If we were to make a concerted effort to push the birth rate above 2.1, it would create a growing supply of young workers to support aging pensioners and their health problems. More young workers would keep the economy staffed up and remove the need for massive tax increases to sustain our imperilled social programs. Despite the views of the United Nations, increased fertility is the only permanent solution to the future workforce shortage since immigrants tend to be adults and are already that much closer to retirement age. Encouraging greater fertility is not an argument against immigration, mind you. Immigrants would still be a necessary part of the equation since it takes 18 years for a rising birth rate to produce new workers.

4   Given the simplicity of the prescription, it is puzzling that so few people are willing to seriously discuss the fact that having more babies would be a good thing. In Germany, when conservative politicians promote richer baby bonuses, this argument

is dismissed as anti-immigrant rhetoric. And when Bjorn Borg, the Swedish tennis icon, sponsored a full-page ad in a newspaper earlier this year urging his countryfolk to procreate because 'there aren't enough babies being born', his concerns rated only   40 a twitter—just another libidinous Swede advocating more nookie. Back home, the only province to make it an explicit objective has been Quebec. Between 1988 and 1997 the province offered a sliding scale of baby bonuses that peaked with an $8,000 payment on the birth of the third child. That system was then replaced with a range of programs aimed at making parents' lives easier, such as five-dollars-a-day universal   45 daycare and a generous parental-leave system. While the baby bonuses did have a positive impact on the birth rate, the results seemed to diminish over time. All other jurisdictions in Canada appear to accept insufficient fertility as part of the landscape.

5   Some might say that this is a good thing, that governments have no business sticking their noses into what is a very private and complex decision. True enough;   50 but Ottawa has not been exactly shy in lecturing us on such delicate matters as smoking, drinking, exercise, and safe sex when it has been deemed to be in the national interest. And the need for more babies is surely that. Even still, many women will doubtless take the suggestion that they should have more children to be a personal insult and a step backwards for feminism, and oppose it on those grounds. Certainly   55 no one wants to press parenthood onto people who are unwilling to accept the burdens. And the responsibility for the birth dearth should be properly shouldered by males as well as females who have put off or decided against having progeny for careers or other reasons. Thus the goal of any pro-natalist policy must be to convince people of the greater good in having offspring. It will not be an easy task. But con-   60 sider that in the 1970s, wild predictions of massive global overpopulation spurred governments and international agencies around the world to focus on lowering birth rates through public campaigns as well as direct action such as birth-control distribution and education with obvious, and now regrettable, success. Surely a similar level of urgency and purpose could be mustered to promote the opposite notion.   65

6   Whether changing several generations of attitudes on parenthood and family size is best accomplished by a hard sell, as with Quebec's cash payments and universal daycare, or a softer approach that merely promotes fecundity as a virtue, is open for debate. Perhaps the best chance for success comes from a recent high-court ruling in Germany that held that childless adults constitute a greater burden on society and   70 thus should be expected to pay more in taxes to support future social programs. From this perspective, making babies is not only patriotic, productive, and a lot of fun; it is also cheaper than the alternative.

2001

QUESTIONS

Reader and Purpose

1. What does the 'or else' refer to in Peter Taylor's title? Is there an implied threat? If so, what is it? If not, why would he use such an expression?

2. In his first paragraph, after mentioning three extremely important problems that Canadians face, the author tells us that 'all these problems could be easily solved.'

Does this surprising statement strike you as a frank exposition of the author's belief, or as a somewhat flippant way of getting the reader's attention?

3. How would you describe the author's **tone**. Is it always appropriate to the argument he is trying to make? If yes, then how so? If no, then why do you think he chose to adopt this tone?

4. Do you believe that Taylor has dealt with all aspects of this extremely important problem, or are there other matters that he should also have discussed?

Organization

5. Does Taylor's essay actually deal with the three problems he mentions at the beginning, or does he in fact neglect two of them in order to deal with the one he is really interested in?

6. In the first sentence of paragraph 2 the author states a 'dire' problem; in the last sentence of the paragraph he writes that the consequences of the problem aren't quite as serious as first thought. Outline the logical progression of his argument between these two points.

7. 'Increased fertility is the only permanent solution to the future work-force shortage' (30–1). Could it be argued that this is the key sentence of paragraph 3? If so, should it not have been placed in a more prominent position, such as at the beginning or end of the paragraph? If not, can you show that the sentence is precisely where it should be because the argument has logically led up to it?

8. Is the final sentence an appropriate conclusion for the essay? Why, or why not?

Sentences

9. Taylor's first paragraph is most unusual: three **fragments** followed by two questions. Rewrite this paragraph in such a way as to eliminate the fragments. Are your sentences an improvement on his?

10. In the second sentence of paragraph 2 Taylor encloses 'thus' in commas and places a comma after 'pensions', the second element of a three-part series. Are these commas necessary? unnecessary? optional? If they are optional, would you use them?

11. Is the **transition** between paragraphs 2 and 3 effected by the last sentence of paragraph 2 or the first sentence of paragraph 3? If both sentences are involved, explain how.

12. On the whole, Taylor uses sentences that are quite long; however, when he does use a short sentence it stands out not only because it is short but because he expresses an important point in that short sentence—thus drawing attention to it in two ways. Discuss the two short sentences in paragraph 5.

Diction

13. Look up: *demographic* (4), *dire* (5), *jeremiad* (21), *concerted* (26), *imperilled* (29), *icon* (39), *libidinous* (41), *jurisdiction* (47–8), *deemed* (52), *dearth* (57), *progeny* (58), *natalist* (59), *mustered* (65), *fecundity* (68).

14. Although it may well be the precise expression of the author's thought, does the rhyming expression *birth dearth* (57) seem a bit humorous and thus inappropriate for its context?

15. In the seventh sentence of paragraph 3, would the possibility of misreading be eliminated by placing a comma before 'since'? For the same reason should a comma be placed before 'since' in the last sentence of the paragraph?

POINTS TO LEARN

1. An argument rarely consists only of reasoned propositions; inevitably, an appeal to the senses will make itself felt.
2. The structure of an argument may be partly concealed by the author's reasonable and sympathetic attitude.

SUGGESTIONS FOR WRITING

Peter Taylor's argument, briefly put, is that the three serious problems he mentions at the very beginning of his essay could be solved by significantly increasing the Canadian birth rate. Do you agree?

Your essay (of roughly 1,000 words, the same length as Taylor's) need not deal with every point he raises, and there are also other questions to ask: should he have considered such points as the costs of an increasing birth rate? the unfortunate controversies brought about by increasing immigration? the social and financial costs of trying to educate many more young people? etc.

IMPROVING YOUR STYLE

1. Begin your opening paragraph in an unusual manner: with sentence fragments, with questions, or with a combination of the two.
2. Structure your paragraphs carefully, proceeding logically in each paragraph from first sentence to last.

DESCRIPTION

Description is the art of translating perceptions into words. All description thus involves two elements: the object—that which is seen or heard—and the observer—the one who sees or hears it. According to which predominates, description is of two basic types: objective and impressionistic.

Objective description attempts to report accurately the appearance of the object as a thing in itself, independent of the observer's (or writer's) perception of it or feelings about it. It is a factual account, the purpose of which is to inform a reader who has not been able to see with his own eyes. The writer regards himself as a kind of camera, recording and reproducing, though in words, a true picture. In his detachment he becomes much like the scientist, rigorously excluding from his work his opinions and emotions.

Objective description often begins with a brief general picture comprehending the object in its entirety. This it then develops analytically, using paragraphs—or, in a short description, sentences—to divide the object into its parts, handling each in turn with as much detail as the purpose requires. These parts are placed in an order that reflects the arrangement in space of the object. Thus, a writer depicting the interior of a house would likely organize the description by floors, and in describing the rooms on each floor would probably move from left to right or from front to rear.

Usually objective description is written impersonally, and the writer wanders freely about the object or scene without bothering to record his own movements. When, for example, he has finished describing the first floor, he need not report, 'I am now going upstairs'; he merely writes, 'On the second floor . . .'. Similarly the tone must be kept factual, and the writer should avoid words that connote a personal reaction. 'A large elm', for example, states a fact; 'a magnificent elm' suggests a feeling. This is not to say that such feelings are always a fault in composition—in much writing they are a virtue. But in objective description they are irrelevant to the writer's purpose.

Given these restrictions, objective description often appears prosaic, even dull; and too often the appearance is real. It is not, however, inherently dull—it is only difficult to do well. Even though his impressions are excluded, the writer can create interest by the fidelity and the skill with which he translates into words the thing he sees. A dying goldfish is hardly an intriguing topic; yet consider this passage from *The Natural History of Selborne*, by Gilbert White:

> As soon as the creature sickens, the head sinks lower and lower, and it stands as it were on its head; till, getting weaker, and losing all poise, the tail turns over, and at last it floats on the surface of the water with its belly uppermost.

This is interesting because it is accurate, precise, economical; because it reproduces exactly what White saw. To see accurately is, as any painter knows, far from easy; to reproduce accurately, whether in prose or paint, what one sees is even more difficult. But when it has been achieved, such description is one of the most satisfying kinds of writing.

Impressionistic description is very different. Focusing on the mood or feeling the object evokes in the observer, rather than on the object as it exists in itself, impressionism does not seek to inform but to arouse emotion. It attempts to make us feel more than to make us see. Thus the communication of feeling is the primary purpose of impressionistic description. The process begins in the writer, and it must originate in genuine feeling. But if he is to succeed, the writer must do more than feel deeply; he must in his own mind define that feeling. Impressionistic descriptions often fail because the writers have not really defined in their own minds what their responses are. Only when the writer has understood his own mood can he communicate that mood to his readers.

The actual communication may be achieved in two ways: directly and indirectly. The direct method, the simpler, is merely to describe the feeling itself. The indirect is to project the emotion back into the object and, by the careful selection and treatment of its details, so to infuse the object with feeling that it will arouse in the reader a response similar to the writer's. Both methods are illustrated in this brief description of a clipper ship from John Masefield's *A Tarpaulin Muster: A Memory*:

> She bowed and curveted, the light caught the skylights on the poop; she gleamed and sparkled; she shook the sea from her as she rose. There was no man aboard of us but was filled with the beauty of that ship.

The second sentence is direct impressionism; it tells us that in the men who watched her the clipper stirred feelings of beauty. The first sentence is indirect. Masefield judiciously selects only those details that suggest grace, power, beauty. If there were facts about the ship inimical to his impression—stained and weathered sails, a shabby figurehead—these he has excluded.

Of the two methods, the indirect is more effective. If the writer's purpose is to communicate a mood, he succeeds better by re-creating the object as he sees it. A writer who merely tells us he is afraid does not necessarily frighten us; but if he can throw before us the fearsome thing in all its horror, he probably will. In practice, however, impressionistic description uses both methods, often employing direct statement of mood as a centre about which to organize the more precise details of indirect description.

In treating these details the writer frequently follows a technique that in art is called expressionism. Broadly, expressionism is the distortion of objective reality in order to communicate the inner reality of emotion. At its simplest, expressionism is the blurring of a film image to suggest dizziness or shock. Similarly the writer may blur or intensify the details he selects, and, by the clever use of figures of speech, may compare them to things calculated to evoke the appropriate emotion. To impress us with the dreary ugliness of a house, he may exaggerate the drabness of its paint or metaphorically describe the flaking as 'leprous'. In such exaggeration the writer is like the caricaturist, but like the caricaturist he is allowed to distort only within limits. Distortion becomes illegitimate when it passes belief and leads us, not toward, but away from the truth the writer seeks to express.

It may be objected that impressionism has little to do with truth, if the writer is free to exaggerate some facts and to ignore others. Certainly it is true that impressionistic description draws no very accurate picture. But objective accuracy is not its concern; it tells the truth of feeling. In short, impressionism tells us not what the clipper ship is, but what it is to the one who sees it.

Thus the objective and the impressionistic are the broad categories of description. Neither ever exists purely. The most detached and scientific observer cannot totally repress his own feelings; and the most impressionistic writer suggests something about the objective reality of what he describes. Most actual description makes use of both. The two techniques are the ends of a continuum, between which, partaking of each, all descriptive writing falls. Yet if no fine line can be drawn between the objective and the impressionistic, they are essentially different in purpose and method. The competent writer must realize when to use the one, when the other. But he must know how to write both.

Essentially, describing a character is no different than describing things. The same general principles and techniques govern both. Yet, character drawing has special problems of its own. There are different ways of approaching the description of character, and many kinds of characters for the writer to create, each serving different purposes. In general we can divide all characters into either *types* or *individuals*. Types, or flat characters as they are sometimes called, possess only a single trait. Individuals, or round characters, have a number of traits, a complexity that is closer to real life than the single dimension of the type.

Types exist in literature, of course, but it would be unrealistic to take them as accurate depictions of real people. They are all, to some degree, exaggerations that are tools that authors use to make a point. All types fall into one of four classes, depending on the kind of trait the writer depicts. There are (1) national types—the typical Canadian, Scot, or Australian; (2) the occupational type—the typical farmer, professor, movie actress, opera singer, bus driver, or business executive; (3) the social type—the bachelor uncle, the distant cousin, the blind date, the party animal, the hostess, the weekend guest; (4) the personality type—The Tactful Man, The Tactless Woman, The Nervous Man, The Steady Woman, The Happy-Go-Lucky Man, The Steely-Eyed Woman, The Boastful Man. The types of all four categories have one thing in common: they have only a single characteristic. Actually, they are not real people at all, but only the single characteristic abstracted from an observation of many people. The type is a single trait personified.

In describing a type, therefore, the writer chooses only those details that bear directly upon the one characteristic of nationality, occupation, social role, or personality. The writer may know a Winnipeg taxi driver who spends all her leisure time reading Mordecai Richler; but in so far as the driver goes, she is an individual, not a type. The writer rigorously excludes all details of physical description, clothing, interests, and personality that do not help to define the typical taxi driver.

What is the point behind the description of types? Besides appealing to our delight in the vivid description of the familiar and commonplace, the type may serve either of two purposes. The less common is to inform. A social historian, for example, may wish to describe the typical medieval peasant, showing how she looked, how she worked, what pleasure she had, if any, and how she felt about her station in life. More often the description of a type intends to instruct the reader in manners or behaviour. If we describe The Braggart, we are saying in so many words, 'Don't be like this.' We may, of course, serve the same purpose in a different, more positive way by describing The Modest Woman. Usually the negative, satiric approach is more effective and is more fun both to write and to read.

As the character acquires more than one trait, she becomes an individual. She is more than a walking occupation or trait of personality: she is a Winnipeg cab driver and a reader of Richler. But the fact that the individual has many dimensions poses a problem. What traits shall the writer include and what traits shall he ignore? The answer depends on the writer's impression of the individual, for almost all description of round characters is impressionistic to some degree. It is well-nigh impossible for any but a highly trained psychologist to write objectively about something so complex as the total personality of a human being. Character drawing of the individual must be both partial and interpretive. It may be more or less shrewd and accurate, but it remains an impression nevertheless. The impression may be simple or complex, and it may require qualification, but the impression guides the writer's selection of details. Our impression of an individual may range anywhere from love and admiration to hatred and loathing. We may see her as mysterious, a bundle of contradictions, or we may see beneath the variety of her traits a pattern that reveals some truth about human behaviour or human values. In any case, we always begin with some reaction to the round character we are describing.

To convey this reaction, we may use many different kinds of details. Among the most useful are details of physical appearance, clothing, and personal belongings. These make the reader see, but they also suggest both the writer's impression and the character's personality. Whether it be sound psychology or not, the reader responds in one way to a tall, thin, tight-lipped woman carrying a thread-worn purse, and in a totally different way to a robust, smiling, sloppily dressed man carrying a fishing rod. In prose, a character's appearance, clothing, and possessions are, by convention, clues to his or her personality.

In addition to these, a writer may describe the 'stage' or the setting within which the character moves about and lives—her room, her home, her place of work. For these, too, are extensions of the character's personality. The shrewd observer can write pages about a woman he has never seen—about her income, her social position, her tastes, her interests, even her values—if only he can study for a bit the room or the house in which she lives.

Viewing the individual in a wider perspective, we may describe her relation to society by making clear what she says and does, what she likes and dislikes, what goals she is seeking, what she values most. We may show her in action, or in conflict with others, how they react to her, what they say about her. In short, our portrait may be static or dynamic or in part both.

How much vivid detail the writer will use and what he selects will depend both on his purpose and the space at his disposal. A very short description may evoke the writer's impression with only two or three striking details, having the force or suggestiveness of an unfinished pencil sketch. If the writer has the space of a novel, he may use all kinds of details and dramatic situations to create his character over hundreds of pages, although ample space alone will not ensure good characterization. It is the telling, the representative detail, the vividness that count. It is more effective to make the reader see a character's modesty in action, for example, than to say merely that she is modest.

Round characters in prose have the purpose of informing, instructing, entertaining, or doing all these at once. The historian who writes the character of a great woman may have as her guiding intention to explain the impact of a personality upon the course of history. Her character, without being obviously moralistic, may contain a lesson for the reader. Any character that is vivid can scarcely fail to entertain the reader. All of us are interested in people—in their motivations, their eccentricities, in the fascinating variety and complexity that make up the human comedy. For that reason any character of any individual, no matter how great or how obscure, is likely to be a pleasant task for the writer and a pleasure to the reader.

PIERRE BERTON

Pierre Berton (1920–) is one of Canada's most popular and distinguished men of letters. He was, for many years, a widely read newspaper columnist, and became a radio and television personality in this country, particularly through his association, as a panellist, with CBC's *Front Page Challenge*. The range of his books includes *Klondike* (1958), a history of the Yukon gold rush; *The Secret World of Og* (1963), a children's book; *The Comfortable Pew* (1965), a critical treatment of apathetic churchgoers; *Hollywood's Canada: The Americanization of our National Image* (1975); *Attack on Montreal* (1995); and *The Great Lakes* (1996). He also wrote a bestselling and critically acclaimed two-volume history of the Canadian Pacific Railway: *The National Dream* (1970) and *The Last Spike* (1971), for which he won the Governor General's Award for non-fiction, one of several such awards he has received. He has continued his work on the Klondike (he was born in the Yukon) with *The Klondike Stampede* (1991) and *Kings of the Klondike* (1993). His most recent books are *Marching as to War: Canada's Turbulent Years, 1899–1953* (2001) and *Cats I Have Known and Loved* (2002).

Hard Times in the Old West

1   The cities stank of horse manure. Calgary was the worst, 'the horse smellingest town I ever remember', in the words of an old-timer. In 1910 the downtown area had 15 livery stables and 12 blacksmith shops. One gigantic barn on 11th Street housed 60 teams of dray horses that produced a mountain of ordure, which, after a rain, assailed the nostrils of passengers boarding the train at the CPR station across the tracks. 5
2   There was little attempt at street sanitation. Clouds of dust rose from the new excavations and from the vast mounds of coal heaped in the railway yards. When the rain fell, the dust and horse droppings formed a liquid gruel six inches deep on Calgary's narrow streets. A passing dray could throw several gallons of this filth a distance of 10 feet, showering the unfortunate pedestrians.   10
3   On Tenth Avenue West, near First, the Chinese launderers dumped the contents of their tubs into the streets and lanes. 'They have not the slightest idea of cleanliness and sanitation,' one alderman said of the Chinese, but in fact the North Americans weren't any better. In the open shops along Eighth Avenue layers of dust caked the fruit and vegetables while fish and fowl were covered with flies. The sidewalks were slip- 15
pery with spittle and tobacco juice. Outside the Royal Hotel, where loafers congregated day and night, men leaning against the side of the building sent streams of tobacco juice in the paths of women trying to reach the CPR station from the streetcars. The police were finally goaded into taking action, with little result: the first man arrested got off when he explained to the court he had merely been combing his moustache.   20
4   All the prairie cities were hideously overcrowded, a direct result of the city fathers' hunger for more and more people. In Calgary in 1905, in spite of soaring rents, the demand for space exceeded the supply by 10 to 1; thousands lived in tents, barns, and shacks. In Edmonton in 1907, 1,550 homeless newcomers were living under canvas. Calgary's booster pamphlets showing James Lougheed's resplendent 25
Beaulieu, with its landscaped terraces, its ornate fountains, its Italian marble and

Spanish mahogany, or Pat Burn's sandstone castle with its 10 bedrooms and 4 bath-
rooms, its oak panelling and stuffed trophy heads, didn't portray the immigrant shanty-
town near the Langevin Bridge.

5   To those newcomers who had not found their dream homestead and were con-   30
fined to the cities, looking for work or taking any job they could get, the traditional
Western boast about a classless society must have sounded hollow. In Winnipeg in
1909, 32 men were discovered crammed into a boarding house licensed to hold 7. A
few doors away, in a similar house, 25 men and women were crowded together without distinction as to sex. The situation in Regina was appalling: 60 per cent of all its   35
houses were overcrowded. Again and again, five-room houses were found to contain
10 double beds. In spite of this, scores had no shelter. One March night in 1910, a
newspaper reporter counted 400 homeless men walking the streets.

6   Each city had its immigrant section across the tracks, usually named 'Germantown' after the largest of the urban ethnic groups. In Regina's Germantown, in the city's   40
East End, members of 22 separate nationalities were crowded into an area six blocks
square. Here were more than 600 dwellings, many little better than shacks, jammed
together on 25-foot lots. Only 48 had plumbing; only 15 had baths. When it rained,
the area became a quagmire. J.S. Woodsworth, who studied it in 1913 at the request of
the Methodist Church, found one house where a man was forced to sleep in a clothes   45
closet, another in which three families were crammed into four small rooms, a third in
which one couple and six boarders shared four rooms with a flock of chickens.

7   Under such conditions, babies sickened and died. In July of 1913, a Winnipeg
woman reporter, Genevieve Lippett-Skinner, appalled at the high rate of infant mortality in the city, paid a visit to the tenements on Barber Street in Winnipeg's North   50
End—'fearfully and wonderfully made death traps', as she called them.

8   'Yes, I know a lot about children,' one German immigrant mother told her. 'I
had ten. They are all dead but three.'

9   In one rabbit warren of a tenement, when a baby died, the parents kept the
corpse for three days before a neighbour phoned the city's health department. In   55
another room, Miss Lippett-Skinner found a young woman whose five-month-old
infant was covered with flies; the odour was overpowering. Downstairs she encountered a tear-stained Greek woman living with her family in a single room. Insects had
bitten her baby so badly that the child had been hospitalized. The mother's arm was
a mass of poisoned bites. For this unfurnished room the family paid seven dollars   60
a month.

10   In the background of this same building, a deserted mother and two children
shared a woodshed with rats and other vermin. The father had been gone for more
than four months, but the wife refused to move for fear he might return and not be
able to find his family.   65

11   In Calgary that winter, while the boosters were still inflating the census figures
and urging their fellow citizens to write letters to bring in more people, the superin-
tendent of the associated charities uttered a plaintive appeal for private aid to the city's
poor: 'There are lonely widows in Calgary who sit shivering in poorly heated rooms.
There are bedridden invalids who draw insufficient bed clothing around their chilly   70
forms. There are scores of underfed and poorly clad children who watch with anxious
glances their rapidly diminishing coal heap and wonder what will happen when that

is all done, for mother said she hadn't any more money. For over a fortnight, the thermometer has been ranging between 15 and 20 degrees below zero. Will you try to
imagine what that means to the poor of the city?'   75

12   But the local authorities were less concerned about the poor than they were
about the get-rich-quick opportunities the Western boom was providing. There was
little public charity, let alone money for parks or recreational facilities. The loneliness
of the sod house was paralleled by life in the urban Germantowns. After a ten-hour
working day, some men found their only relief in the saloon, the brothel, or the dance 80
hall. In Regina's Germantown there were five hotels with saloons, seven pool halls, but
only three dance halls. These were crowded and noisy, frequented by fallen women,
and plagued by drunken brawlers, but for many a lonely immigrant they provided the
only respite from a harsh existence.

13   'I like this better than to lie on my dirty bed all the time,' one young man in 85
Regina explained. 'The room where I am staying drives me mad. I am not satisfied
with these people with whom I live and my job is hard in the day time. So I am very
willing to spend my 50 cents twice a week because I have here an hour of life.'

14   'For the poor,' wrote Woodsworth, 'there is no substitute for the barroom.' On
six blocks of Winnipeg's Main Street were 20 hotels, all serving liquor, 24 more stood 90
shoulder to shoulder on the side streets. Convictions for drunkenness in Manitoba
were double those for Ontario, triple those for Quebec.

15   In spite of an active temperance movement and considerable lip service paid by
politicians at every level, from the mayor of Winnipeg to Clifford Sifton, those in
power shied away from direct prohibition, the president of the Liberal organization 95
kept a liquor store and the chairman of the East End Liberal committee ran one of the
licensed hotels. 'It would appear', he wrote, 'that the liquor men hold a strong grip on
the political situation.'

16   For there was money in drink and even in drunkenness. A group of live wire
Calgary businessmen took advantage of the situation and opened an Institute for 100
Drunkenness, proclaiming, in full-page advertisements, that there was HOPE FOR
BROKEN HEARTED WIVES AND BALM FOR THE MOTHER'S TEARS. For a fee, the institute
offered to cure anyone of chronic alcoholism in just three days.

17   The overwhelming presence of saloons in the West is no more surprising than
the overwhelming presence of brothels. The nature of Western settlement made large- 105
scale prostitution inevitable. With 100,000 bachelors on the prairies, most of them
young and virile, the bawdy houses did not lack for customers. Every city had its red-
light district, winked at by the authorities, such as Calgary's Nose Creek Flats and
Moose Jaw's notorious River Street. According to one madam, Edmonton alone had
by 1914 between 400 and 500 prostitutes; Winnipeg probably had more.   110

18   The authorities were generally lackadaisical in enforcing the law. In 1906, the
Calgary chief of police, Thomas English, insisted there was less gambling and prostitution in his city than in any community of comparable size on the continent. 'There
may be houses of prostitution in Calgary but I do not know of them,' he declared. Two
days later the *Morning Albertan* identified nine brothels within the city known to 115
everyone 'except the chief of police'.

19   Even during the periodic vice cleanups, prosecutions were difficult to achieve.
When the Mounted Police raided one Nose Creek brothel and found a customer in

bed with one of the girls, they were sure they would get a conviction. The accused got off, even though he admitted he was in a house of prostitution, by swearing that the 120 woman was ill and he was simply nursing her.

20   In Winnipeg, in 1909, there was a concerted effort on the part of churchmen and reformers to expose the brothels. As a result the city fathers tacitly gave the chief of police the right to find a district where prostitutes could be segregated, away from the eyes of respectable citizens. The chief, John C. McRae, went to the fount 125 of all knowledge, Minnie Woods, 'The Queen of the Harlots', the best-known madam in town. With her help he selected the MacFarlane-Rachel-Annabella streets area north of the CPR tracks, suitably enclosed by a gas plant, a lumberyard, and a power station and within easy walking distance of the CPR depot and the major hotels. Here, in a space of two city blocks, some 200 prostitutes began to ply 130 their trade.

21   There was, of course, a profit to be made from the kind of mass segregation undertaken by the city of Winnipeg. Into town on the day before the decision was made crept a mysterious figure, one J. Beaman, a so-called real estate operator with no real estate experience and no affiliation with any local firm. Beaman stayed in 135 Winnipeg for one year only—the year the city moved the brothels. And it was to Beaman that Chief McRae went to help in the switch of location. Beaman bought 22 buildings and resold them to the madams at sky-high prices, making a total profit of $70,000 before he vanished. He was almost certainly a front man for the chief, or the chief's friends, or the local politicians, or perhaps all three.   140

22   Nobody paid any heed to the 50-odd immigrant families living in the area, who complained, vainly, that drunks were stumbling into their homes looking for girls, that residents were being propositioned going to and from work, that drunks, bounced from the brothels, lay on the sidewalks or in the gutter, and that on occasion bare-breasted women could be seen dashing through the neighbourhood and even 145 riding horseback up Annabella Street.

23   The city fathers may have been complacent about their red-light district, but they certainly didn't want it publicized, especially in the East, as the Reverend Dr J.G. Shearer discovered in 1910. Shearer told the Toronto *Globe* that 'they have the rotten-est condition of things in Winnipeg in connection with the question of social vice to 150 be found in any city in Canada.' The Toronto papers were delighted with this intelli-gence. 'WINNIPEG WALLOWS IN VICE' was the *Star*'s headline.

24   Shearer was no fly-by-night Presbyterian cleric. He was secretary of the power-ful Moral and Social Reform League and was a key figure among those who, in 1907, had forced the Lord's Day Act through the federal parliament. But he was reviled in 155 his home town by the city fathers and the business community. The church consid-ered Winnipeg's red-light district a disgrace. But Mayor W.S. Evans, who was up for re-election, cleverly muddied the argument by switching it away from the evils of white slavery to the question of the city's image. 'As citizens of our community, we should be, if possible, even more jealous of the good name of our city than of our 160 homes,' he declared. 'It is patent that those who have the welfare of the city at heart would not advertise it abroad as the rottenest city on the continent. I stand for the best and cleanest and purest city in the world—for Winnipeg and the reputation of such.' After all, real estate values had to be maintained.

25   Evans's opponent, E.D. Martin, backed by church and reform groups, didn't   165
stand a chance. Even the *Free Press* tacitly supported Evans, though his opponent was
a Liberal. In December 1910, the Mayor took 57 out of 72 polls. Every incumbent
was returned. A hurriedly organized Royal Commission of Inquiry reassured the
world that Winnipeg was definitely not the 'rottenest' city in Canada. The city's image
was restored, and the brothels on Rachel, Annabella, and MacFarlane streets were   170
allowed to operate openly for the next three decades with no obstruction apart from
the quarterly payment of a fine.

1985

QUESTIONS

Reader and Purpose

1. Since Berton is a historian one might expect that his essay would be written entirely
    as objective description, as simply a factual account of the situation. Is this how he
    has written? To answer this question consider carefully paragraphs 3, 9, and 11.

Organization

2. The author does not use a conventional introduction. Instead, his opening sentence
    begins immediately to elaborate on the title. Is this an effective beginning, or would
    an introductory paragraph have helped?
3. Is paragraph 25 an effective conclusion to this essay? Why, or why not?
4. The **topic sentence** of the first three paragraphs is the first sentence of paragraph 2,
    and the topic sentence of paragraphs 4–6 is the first sentence of paragraph 4. What
    are the other topic sentences in this essay, and which paragraphs do they govern?

Sentences

5. In the second sentence of paragraph 1 what is the grammatical function of the quota-
    tion? Does this function explain why 'worst' is followed by a comma rather than by a
    colon? Does this same reason explain the comma in the first sentence of paragraph 4?
6. In paragraph 14 should there be a semicolon after 'liquor'? Why, or why not?
7. In paragraph 15 does the comma after 'prohibition' constitute a **comma splice**?
    Would the sentence be clearer if 'prohibition' were followed by a colon or a dash?
8. What elements of **parallel structure** can you find in paragraph 17? in paragraph 22?
9. In the first sentence of paragraph 22, why is 'vainly' separated by commas? What
    would be the effect of removing the commas?

Diction

10. Look up: *livery* (3), *ordure* (4), *gruel* (8), *dray* (9), *terraces* (26), *ornate* (26), *quagmire* (44),
    warren (54), *vermin* (63), *sod* (79), *brothel* (80), *temperance* (93), *shied* (95), *chronic*
    (103), *lackadaisical* (111), *tacitly* (123), *complacent* (147), *reviled* (155), *patent* (161).
11. In the fifth sentence of paragraph 24, the phrase *muddied the argument* is a clever
    word play on which **cliché**?
12. Explain the **irony** of the last sentence of paragraph 24. Does paragraph 25 contain
    any ironic comments?
13. What **imagery** do you see in paragraph 1? in paragraph 16? in paragraph 21?

POINTS TO LEARN

1. Irony can be helpful in revealing the author's attitude towards the subject.
2. A topic sentence can be the subject of more than one paragraph.

SUGGESTIONS FOR WRITING

Assume that your answer to question 2 is 'No, that is not an effective way to begin this essay, and yes, there should be an introductory paragraph.' Write this introductory paragraph.

IMPROVING YOUR STYLE

In your paragraph include

1. a brief quotation from an official (which you will have to make up);
2. an ironic comment.

MARK TWAIN

'Mark Twain' was the pen name of Samuel Langhorne Clemens (1835–1910), who gave up his career as a steamboat pilot on the Mississippi at the beginning of the American Civil War in 1861 and travelled by stagecoach to the Nevada Territory. From 1861 until 1866 he remained in the West as a prospector in Nevada and then as a journalist for several newspapers. Some six years later—newly married and living in Buffalo, New York—Twain began to record his western experiences in a book called *Roughing It* (1872). Twain's purpose was to tell the truth about frontier life, a truth, in Twain's opinion, not found in the idealizing novels of James Fenimore Cooper or in the sentimental tales of Bret Harte. Throughout *Roughing It*, as in others of his books, a part of Twain's theme is the difference between romantic imaginings and grotesque realities. In the following excerpt Twain describes the buildings where stagecoach passengers stopped for breakfast about a day's drive away from Kearney, Nebraska, en route from St Joseph, Missouri, to Carson City, capital of the Nevada Territory. Twain's attention to detail in this selection, and his irony, appear as well in his best novels, most particularly *The Adventures of Huckleberry Finn* (1885), one of the greatest novels, in any language, of the nineteenth century.

Stagecoach Station

1   The station buildings were long, low huts, made of sun-dried, mud-coloured bricks, laid up without mortar (*adobes*, the Spaniards call these bricks, and Americans shorten it to *'dobies*). The roofs, which had no slant to them worth speaking of, were thatched and then sodded or covered with a thick layer of earth, and from this sprung a pretty rank growth of weeds and grass. It was the first time we had ever seen a man's 5
front yard on top of his house. The buildings consisted of barns, stable-room for twelve or fifteen horses, and a hut for an eating-room for passengers. This latter had

bunks in it for the station-keeper and a hostler or two. You could rest your elbow on
its eaves, and you had to bend in order to get in at the door. In place of a window
there was a square hole about large enough for a man to crawl through, but this had   10
no glass in it. There was no flooring, but the ground was packed hard. There was no
stove, but the fireplace served all needful purposes. There were no shelves, no cup-
boards, no closets. In a corner stood an open sack of flour, and nestling against its
base were a couple of black and venerable tin coffee-pots, a tin teapot, a little bag of
salt, and a side of bacon.   15

2   By the door of the station-keeper's den, outside, was a tin washbasin, on the
ground. Near it was a pail of water and a piece of yellow barsoap, and from the eaves
hung a hoary blue woolen shirt, significantly—but this latter was the station-keeper's
private towel, and only two persons in all the party might venture to use it—the
stage-driver and the conductor. The latter would not, from a sense of decency; the   20
former would not, because he did not choose to encourage the advances of a station-
keeper. We had towels—in the valise; they might as well have been in Sodom and
Gomorrah. We (and the conductor) used our handkerchiefs, and the driver his pantaloons and sleeves. By the door, inside, was fastened a small old-fashioned looking-
glass frame, with two little fragments of the original mirror lodged down in one   25
corner of it. This arrangement afforded a pleasant double-barreled portrait of you
when you looked into it, with one half of your head set up a couple of inches above
the other half. From the glass frame hung the half of a comb by a string—but if I had
to describe that patriarch or die, I believe I would order some sample coffins. It had
come down from Esau and Samson, and had been accumulating hair ever since—   30
along with certain impurities. In one corner of the room stood three or four rifles
and muskets, together with horns and pouches of ammunition. The station-men
wore pantaloons of coarse, country-woven stuff, and into the seat and the inside of
the legs were sewed ample additions of buckskin, to do duty in place of leggings,
when the man rode horseback—so the pants were half dull blue and half yellow, and   35
unspeakably picturesque. The pants were stuffed into the tops of high boots, the
heels whereof were armed with great Spanish spurs, whose little iron clogs and
chains jingled with every step. The man wore a huge beard and mustachios, an old
slouch hat, a blue woolen shirt, no suspenders, no vest, no coat—in a leathern
sheath in his belt, a great long 'navy' revolver (slung on right side, hammer to the   40
front), and projecting from his boot a horn-handled bowie-knife. The furniture of
the hut was neither gorgeous nor much in the way. The rocking-chairs and sofas
were not present, and never had been, but they were represented by two three-
legged stools, a pine-board four feet long, and two empty candle-boxes. The table
was a greasy board on stilts, and the table-cloth and napkins had not come—and   45
they were not looking for them, either. A battered tin platter, a knife and fork, and
a tin pint cup, were at each man's place, and the driver had a queens-ware saucer
that had seen better days. Of course, this duke sat at the head of the table. There
was one isolated piece of table furniture that bore about it a touching air of grandeur
in misfortune. This was the caster. It was German silver, and crippled and rusty, but   50
it was so preposterously out of place there that it was suggestive of a tattered exiled
king among barbarians, and the majesty of its native position compelled respect even
in its degradation. There was only one cruet left, and that was a stopperless, fly-

specked, broken-necked thing, with two inches of vinegar in it, and a dozen preserved flies with their heels up and looking sorry they had invested there.   55

1872

QUESTIONS

Reader and Purpose

1. Like many descriptions, 'Stagecoach Station' contains both objective and impressionistic elements. List several examples of each. Overall, which predominates—
   impressionism or objectivity?
2. Explain how the description of things—buildings, furniture, utensils, clothing—serves
   to characterize the stationmen and frontier life.
3. If this scene were to be shown as part of a television or movie western, in what ways
   might the visual details differ from Twain's description? Would the eating room, for
   example, be so low 'you had to bend in order to get in at the door'? What do these
   probable differences reveal about Twain's purpose? about the legend of the Old West
   then and now?
4. Is Twain writing primarily for Easterners or Westerners? Give several reasons for
   your conclusion.

Organization

5. Show that Twain's first paragraph is organized by the pattern of general to particular.
6. Show that the second paragraph is organized spatially, that it falls into two parts,
   and that the beginning of the second part is signalled by verbal repetition.
7. The second paragraph might be said to lack unity. It can easily be divided into four
   shorter paragraphs without making any verbal changes. Where can these divisions
   occur? How might Twain's paragraph be defended against the charge that it is
   not unified?

Sentences

8. In each of the following cases, what is the significant difference between Twain's
   sentence and the revision?

   (a) **Revision:** The latter contained bunks for the station-keeper and a hostler.
       Twain: 'This latter had bunks in it for the station-keeper and a hostler or two.'
       (7–8)

   (b) **Revision:** There was no flooring, but the ground was packed hard. The room
       was without a stove; however, the fireplace served all needful purposes.
       Nowhere were to be found shelves, cupboards, or closets.
       Twain: 'There was no flooring, but the ground was packed hard. There was no
       stove, but the fireplace served all needful purposes. There were no shelves, no
       cupboards, no closets.' (11–14)

   (c) **Revision:** We had towels in the valise but they might as well have been in
       Sodom and Gomorrah.
       Twain: 'We had towels—in the valise; they might as well have been in Sodom
       and Gomorrah.' (22–3)

9. What variety of purposes do the dashes serve in lines 19, 20, 28, 39, and 45?

10. In the sentence beginning 'Near it was a pail of water' (17) what word is given great emphasis by isolation? Why has Twain isolated this word?

Diction

11. Look up: *hostler* (8), *venerable* (14), *hoary* (18), *pantaloons* (23–4), *horns* (32), *bowie-knife* (41), *queens-ware* (47), *caster* (50), *cruet* (53).

12. Citing specific words and phrases, show how Twain's diction reveals his attitude toward the stagecoach station and the men who tend it.

13. How does Twain's diction distance him from his subject and ally him with his eastern readers?

14. Is *mustachios* (38) a better word here than *moustache*? Why or why not?

15. Like many nineteenth-century writers Twain is fond of Biblical **allusions**. The Bible was widely read and provided a common coin of exchange by which complex sets of feelings and attitudes and judgments could be easily conveyed. Who or what were Sodom and Gomorrah (22–3), Esau and Samson (30)? What is Twain implying by these allusions?

POINTS TO LEARN

1. Most good descriptions are a mixture of objective facts and the writer's feelings about those facts.

2. How the writer feels about his or her subject guides the selection of details and helps to give the description unity and purpose.

3. A bad description often seems pointless—a mere laundry list with no theme.

4. Descriptive details of the things people use or own may serve to characterize them.

5. Description characterizes the writer as well as what he or she is describing. Obviously, the description is more likely to be effective if the reader likes the writer.

SUGGESTIONS FOR WRITING

1. Describe the buildings and equipment of one of the following: a summer camp for young people; a farm; a small factory; a mechanic's garage; a bicycle shop; a store specializing in hiking and canoeing equipment. If possible, use details of places and things to characterize those who live or work at the camp, farm, factory, store. Be conscious of **tone**, and work to achieve one appropriate to what you feel and how you want the reader to respond.

2. Describe some work area not generally seen by the public—a warehouse, the kitchen of a restaurant, an upholsterer's shop, a lumber mill, a loading dock, the billing office of a trucking company. Try for a distinct tone, while at the same time making yourself sympathetic and agreeable to the reader.

IMPROVING YOUR STYLE

1. In your description imitate Twain's **anaphora** in lines 11–13, beginning three successive sentences (kept fairly short) with 'There was (were)'.

2. Use diction that implies your feelings about what you are describing, your response to it. Don't be afraid to exaggerate, even to be outrageous. Exaggeration is one way in which Twain gets his comic effect, as in the description of the dirty comb.

WINSTON COLLINS

Trained as a social worker, whose doctoral dissertation was titled 'The Effect of Social Isolation on Inmate Self-Concept' (1983), Winston Collins is now a Toronto-based free-lance writer and editor. He has written extensively on food and travel. His articles have appeared in the *Globe and Mail, Harrowsmith, Equinox,* and *Report on Business Magazine.* He is also the author of *The Harrowsmith Fish & Seafood Cookbook* (1985).

The Belly of Ontario

1   Amid the mayhem of Toronto's Ontario Food Terminal, Jim McCarthy resembles Buddha in an outdoor shrine. Framed by the altarlike open rear doors of a two-ton truck, the portly, silver-haired farmer sits serenely on a squat stool, baskets of ripe strawberries at his feet like offerings. He seems oblivious to the rowdy haggling going on around him. At age 76, he has heard it many times in the 57 years he has 5 been selling his fresh-from-the-farm fruit and vegetables at open-air markets in Toronto. 'When I began in 1919, growers sold their produce at any vacant lot there was,' he says. 'I remember when Charlie Clay charged us a quarter a day to sell on a lot he rented. Charlie always had his hand out for money. Said they buried him that way.'   10
2   Over the years, McCarthy, owner of the 470-acre (190 ha) Pine Haven Farms near Georgetown, has become a living legend at the Ontario Food Terminal, which is known simply as 'the market' by the 6,000 men and the handful of women who buy, sell, or otherwise work here. Rumour has it that he is a millionaire at least twice over. Certainly, he is treated with respect, even reverence, by the wheeler-dealers whose 15 customary market parlance is peppered with unsavoury comments about someone's lineage, mentality, and sexual preferences or practices. But when they check out McCarthy's strawberries (or, later in the year, his snap beans, pears, and apples), it is as if they had just had their mouths washed out with soap. 'Quality product and a fair price, Mr McCarthy,' says one prospective buyer who was overheard a minute earlier 20 calling a stalwart farmer an 'overpriced whore'. The bargain-hunting buyers are amazed that McCarthy never cuts the price of even his most perishable produce to get rid of it at the end of a selling day. 'I'd sooner give it away,' he explains. 'And I always feel good when I do.'
3   As if on cue, a Plymouth sedan pulls up to McCarthy's stall. Out steps Sister 25 Agnes from the Carmelite Sisters Day Nursery in Toronto's west end. An hour earlier, McCarthy had telephoned the nun to say that he would have some strawberries left over and that if she wanted them, she could just come and get them. 'Jim's been giving us produce for a long, long time,' says Sister Agnes, as she efficiently packs the

car's empty trunk and seats with 40 eight-quart crates of strawberries that the 30
Carmelite sisters will clean and freeze 'so the children can enjoy them all year long'.

4   Although Sister Agnes is receiving a charitable donation today, she regularly
buys fruit and vegetables for the daycare centre and flowers for the chapel at Canada's
largest wholesale fresh fruit and produce market. Does she haggle with the sellers?
'Oh, no,' she responds with an angelic smile. 'I figure if they cheat me, the Lord will 35
get them.'

Cantankerous & Greedy

5   To a passerby driving west on the Queen Elizabeth Way out of Toronto, the
food terminal is not an inviting sight: 42 acres (17 ha) of tarmac enclosed by a chain-
link fence topped with barbed wire; a two-storey U-shaped building connected to
loading docks and train tracks; an elevated concrete parking deck. Yet driving 40
through the market gate at 165 The Queensway is crossing the threshold into a self-
contained centre of exuberant, spontaneous vitality. The Ontario Food Terminal is as
cantankerous as Parliament Hill, as diverse as the United Nations, as intense as the
stock exchange, as greedy as a gambling casino, as closely knit as a fraternal organization, as entertaining as impromptu street theatre, as intimate as a small town.   45

6   Built in 1954 on land where spring onion, radishes and lettuces were once cultivated, the utilitarian facility is today a gigantic stage on which a commercial food
show takes place year-round. The ongoing drama touches every Canadian because the
prices determined each morning at the food terminal affect what consumers throughout the country will pay for their fruit and vegetables.   50

7   The 'Belly of Ontario' would be a more graphic name for the Ontario Food
Terminal. This year, 80,000 trucks and 800 rail cars will deliver 800,000 tons of
homegrown and imported fresh fruit and produce, which will be sold to the terminal's buyers to the tune of about $500 million. Thirty-five per cent of the volume is
grown by Ontario farmers in such fertile areas as the Holland Marsh, the Niagara 55
Peninsula, and Essex and Norfolk counties on the shore of Lake Erie. The 430 outdoor stalls, which growers can rent by the year, half-year, or day, constitute the largest
wholesale farmers' market in the world.

8   The 28 wholesale companies operating out of the terminal's warehouse deal primarily in imported produce, much of which is purchased from California and Florida 60
growers, who ship it to the food terminal's wholesalers, who then sell it to retailers,
who in turn sell it to you and me. Since the Toronto area is the largest market outside
the United States for California produce and the third largest anywhere in the world
for Florida produce, the sheer volume of imported perishable food that passes
through the terminal is staggering. What North American growers are unable to pro- 65
vide is brought in from some other part of the planet—at a price, of course. For a
wholesaler, and hence a consumer, there is no such thing as seasonal produce anymore: at any given time, quickly transportable fruit and vegetables are ripening and
being harvested somewhere in the world. The primary restriction on what we eat
today is determined by our pocketbooks, not the season.   70

9   Canadians have recently developed a ravenous appetite for garden and farm fare.
Our current annual per capita consumption of fresh fruit and vegetables is about 460
pounds (209 kg)—up 110 pounds (50 kg) from 1972 and a whopping 160 pounds

(73 kg) more than the average American consumes in a year. The amount will continue
to increase as more and more Canadians join the health-and-fitness brigade. Unlike   75
Ontario's beleaguered tobacco farmers, the province's commercial horticulturists can
crow about their products' virtues all the way to the bank.

10   I first arrived at the Ontario Food Terminal at 6:30 one morning in a five-ton
Ford truck driven by my greengrocer, Joey Formusa, who at age 23 is the sole buyer
for Formusa Fine Foods, his family's 30-year-old fruit-and-vegetable store on   80
Toronto's Bloor Street. Formusa refers to the market as 'my home away from home'.
Indeed, he spends about as much time here as he does at home in his parents' suburban house. He is at the food terminal six days a week, five hours a day, 52 weeks a
year. He relishes every minute of it.

11   'This place always charges me up,' exclaims Formusa, a little dynamo in both   85
physique and energy, as he deftly manoeuvres his truck through the morning traffic
snarl. Finding a parking space, he springs from the cab to begin his circuitous quest for
quality produce at fair prices through the farmers' outdoor stalls and the wholesalers'
enclosed warehouses. By 11 a.m., Formusa will spend close to $2,000 for the items on
the day's shopping list he carries in his head—strawberries, raspberries, blueberries,   90
gooseberries, cherries, grapes, plums, bananas, mangoes, watermelons, tomatoes, lettuces, peppers, peas, beans, celery, spinach, broccoli, zucchini, eggplants, leeks, fennel,
radishes, parsley, mushrooms, daisies, delphiniums, and baby's-breath.

12   He is one of 4,000 buyers who purchase their produce at the market. Nearly half
are independent grocers like himself; the others are a mixed bunch of jobbers and buy-   95
ers for chain stores, restaurants, caterers, and institutions. While 3,000 of the buyers
are from the greater Toronto area, some travel from as far away as Ottawa and western
Quebec. Their mission is the same: to fill their empty trucks—which range in size from
Sunkist Food Markets' refrigerated trailers to a Hare Krishna van—with a choice selection from the more than 120 different varieties of produce available at the Ontario   100
Food Terminal.

13   Formusa warns me in advance of the way business is conducted in the free-
wheeling market. 'But the haggling and bad language are mostly an act to show you're
one of the boys,' says Formusa, who is a model of good manners in his store. Indeed,
in the decade I have known him, the only memorably quaint expression I have ever   105
heard him utter is 'Missus', his term of address for matronly customers. As for haggling, Formusa says he does not have 'the clout'. Shelling out two grand a day is considered small potatoes at the food terminal. 'Besides, I can't be bothered for 50 cents
here, 50 cents there.'

14   Still, Formusa is very much one of the market boys. With his practical knowl-   110
edge of supply and demand, his shrewd eye for quality at bargain prices and his ebullient gift of the gab, the young man works the stalls and warehouses like the seasoned
professional he already is. 'First, I go around and say hello just to let them know I'm
here.' At the same time, he is checking out the day's crops and prices, which are never
posted in print and are certainly not carved in stone.   115

15   The first stall we come to on the outer edge of the farmers' market is rented by
Overholt Orchards, a 50-acre (20 ha) family fruit farm near St Catharines. Doug
Overholt, who looks as wholesome as the cherries, peaches, and pears he sells from
June through November, is a 10-year veteran of the Ontario Food Terminal. 'It takes

time to learn the market and how to set prices, which only experience can teach you,' 120
says the 30-year-old University of Guelph graduate while Formusa is sampling the
sweet cherries and pronouncing them A-1. 'Sometimes, you have to compromise;
sometimes, you have to be stubborn,' the fruit seller continues. 'But it's not all straight
business here. It's also making friends with guys like Joey.'

Ethnic Potpourri

16   We venture on beneath the cavernous parking deck toward the heart of the 125
farmers' market. It is like entering a world beyond time. Engulfed in perpetual
shadow, sellers hawk their wares to buyers who peel off bills from the thick wads they
carry in their pockets. There are no receipts or written records; everyone keeps track
of everything in his or her head.

17   In one respect, though, the cheek-by-jowl greengrocery is notably Canadian. 130
Perhaps nowhere else is the country's rich cultural mosaic so immediately apparent as
in the microcosm of the market. While Italians are predominant among the buyers, the
sellers are an ethnic potpourri. Just 20 years ago, the farmers' names tended to be of
the Smith or Johnson variety, but today, they include Ostromecki, Aziz, VanDenBroer,
Caietta, Singh, Yarmoluk, Eng, Montalbano, Goetz, Omar, Koornneff, Chow, and 135
Medve, as well as Smith and Johnson. Ontario-grown produce has become almost as
widely diverse as the province's heritages: potatoes, carrots, peas, and cucumbers are
for sale, but so are rapini, fennel, bok choy, and red-rooted pigweed.

18   Formusa, now in high gear, darts from stall to stall joshing with the sellers,
scrutinizing their crops, and buying a crate of tomatoes here, a basket of parsley 140
there, all of which he will return to collect and load into his truck at the end of his
shopping spree.

19   During our foray, I encounter Henry Specht, a 58-year-old German-Canadian
who heads the food terminal's seven-man police force. The big-boned staff sergeant
with bushy grey eyebrows is discussing a problem with a constable: a forklift has been 145
reported stolen from the warehouse loading dock. Dispatching the constable to investigate, Specht says: 'Remember, nothing is ever stolen at the market. Things are either
misplaced or borrowed.'

20   As busy as the market is, everyone has time to talk. Specht is no exception. 'The
most serious crime we have here is an occasional fistfight,' he says, launching into a 150
monologue that has its own peculiar logic. 'No one has ever hit me, but somebody
once bit me when I was trying to break up a fight. People yell insults at one another
and then, 10 minutes later, go off and have a coffee together. This is a place where
buyers can let off steam before going to their stores, where they have to be calm, cool,
and collected. How can I describe what I do? Sometimes, I'm a judge and jury; some- 155
times, a psychologist. Before I started here nearly 20 years ago, I studied child psychology. Believe me, it's helped. I can speak six languages—seven, if you include
profane. The market is organized confusion, and it has to be noisy and busy to work.'

21   The discourse is cut short by a call on the sergeant's walkie-talkie. It is from the
investigating constable, who reports that the case of the missing forklift has been 160
solved: the motorized machine was misplaced, not stolen. Just as Specht had predicted. With a triumphant smile, the officer mounts his bicycle and pedals off to serve
and protect or to shoot the breeze somewhere else.

22   The food terminal's police force has the power to impose a $100 fine on anyone caught buying or selling before 6:30 a.m., the official opening time. Signs clearly 165
stating the crime and punishment are prominently posted throughout the market. But all in all, the regulation is taken as seriously as a rule prohibiting cursing or spitting would be.

Streetwise Sellers

23   The official closing time for buying or selling is 2 p.m. But by 9:30 a.m., the farmers' market action is already in its denouement. Most of the growers have been 170
here since 4 or 5 in the morning, and they are itching to get back to their market gardens or small farms. For Paul Tiveron, one of the market's biggest sellers, going home means a three-and-a-half-hour drive on Highway 401 to his 100-acre (40 ha) farm near Leamington—a journey he will begin in the reverse direction the next day at 1 a.m. His wife, son, and daughter work alongside the grower-seller. Says Tiveron: 'A 175
business like this has got to be family. Who else would work these crazy hours?' When do they find time to sleep? He seems astonished by the question. 'You don't sleep in the summer. That's a winter activity.'

24   When the farmers' market shopping is completed, Formusa moves on to the large, air-cooled wholesale units housed in the food terminal's horseshoe-shaped ware- 180
house, which has 225,000 square feet (21,000 m²) of selling space. While the outdoor market's ambience is similar to that of a frenetic country fair, the wholesale section has the aura of a hyper big-city business. Although a few of the 28 wholesale companies specialize in such commodities as melons or exotic fruits, most compete directly—and fiercely—with one another in a wide variety of fresh fruit and vegetables.   185

25   The warehouse is also an arena in which streetwise city buyers are pitted against streetwise city sellers. The wheeling and dealing is merely a warm-up for the main event. A number of the combatants on either side wear the same uniforms: designer jeans, expensive running shoes, gold neck chains. The contest is yet another game that the macho market men like to play. The name of this particular game is 'Now I've 190
Got You, You S.O.B.'.

26   Even my pal Formusa, a good-natured joker among the yeomen and Mr Charming with his customers, is transformed into a cocky tough guy as soon as he enters the wholesale section, which is manned by equally cocky tough guys. 'Everyone's a shyster around here,' he says. 'Ask a salesman when something came in, 195
and he'll say, "Just now." But it might have come in yesterday or two days ago.' For a buyer, freshness is all. Formusa aggressively rips open a box of romaine lettuce from California and inspects the contents. 'Not consistent and a little old,' he declares, tossing it aside. 'The only way to judge quality is to see, touch, and compare the produce.' He moves on to rummage through a crate of imported eggplants, which measure up 200
to his standards. He hails a particular salesman ('I always deal with the same salesman at each place; that way, I know I won't get soaked') and buys the crate.

27   This morning, one of Formusa's quests is for blueberries. He goes from place to place lightly squeezing the packaged fruit through their plastic wrappings. 'Too soft,' he mutters time after time. Finally, he finds the texture he wants and pays, without 205
arguing, $17 for a case of 12 boxes, which he will sell this afternoon for $1.99 a box. The markup is well below the 30 per cent profit margin retailers usually aim for.

Because wholesalers deal in massive quantities, they're content with a 5 to 10 per cent profit on the produce they sell. All in all, the price of produce generally increases five- to sevenfold between the time it leaves the farm gate to be graded, packaged, shipped   210 to a wholesaler and eventually retailed to a customer.

Entrepreneurial Quartet

28   One of Formusa's stops is Lenson Celery, a wholesale company that, in spite of its name, sells a wide range of mainly imported vegetables. Two of the owners are Formusa's brother Sal and his cousin Tony Badali. Formusa and his brother Anthony are about to buy into Lenson Celery, where they will work full-time. When the deal   215 is completed, the three brothers and a cousin—an entrepreneurial quartet whose average age is 26—will own the wholesale company lock, stock, and barrel.

29   And so it goes, day in, day out, year after year, at the market. Wrangling and haggling. Buying and selling. Working and playing. True, some things have changed over the years. In a letter to the Ontario minister of Agriculture and Food printed in   220 the Ontario Food Terminal's annual report, Chairman of the Board D.E. Williams mentions that a just-completed renovation means 'the Board now operates one of the finest cold-storage facilities in the country, having computer control of the temperatures and humidity in each room. The Board looks forward to continuing the redevelopment of the terminal with plans to complete the deck over the uncovered portion of the farm-   225 ers' market [and] provide further buyers assembly and loading facilities and additional wholesale warehouse units.'

30   Farmer Jim McCarthy, who has been coming to the market since Day One, provides a more human perspective of the changing scene: 'Each year, there are more and more buyers—and more big buyers.'   230

Tough Exterior

31   Fifty-six years ago, a 10-year-old Toronto lad named Nick Luciano started peddling carrots and apples door-to-door from a pushcart he rented for a dollar a week. Today, Luciano is the senior import buyer for F.G. Lister and Co. Ltd Fruits and the food terminal's chief guru. At his desk in a glass-fronted office overlooking the produce-packed warehouse, he succinctly elucidates the complex food-marketing sys-   235 tem: 'You buy the best product at the best price possible so you can attract customers in order to make money.' Both a wholesaler and retailer have 'to know the pulse of the business and be able to anticipate what people will want. Supply and demand is the basis for the whole industry. When there's a short supply and a big demand, prices go up. Beyond supply and demand, the biggest single factor is the weather. One late frost   240 in Niagara can ruin a year's crop.'

32   Perhaps because the fruits of the earth are nature's most fragile and transitory pleasures, an elegiac refrain can be heard just beyond the market's prevailing cacophony. Gazing out on the newly arrived crates of perishable fruit and vegetables that will be gone within two days, Luciano says: 'The twilight of my work in the   245 industry is closing in. The calendar dictates that. But I won't retire before I have to, and I would like to work here till the day before I die.' I recall what McCarthy had said, sitting on a stool in a farmers' market with the season's last strawberries at his feet: 'I'll keep coming here for as long as the good Lord gives me strength.'

33   I asked the farmer what it is that draws him back day after day, year after year.   250
'The market gets into your blood,' McCarthy answered. 'There's no other way to
explain it.' Perhaps there isn't. *It gets into your blood*: import buyer Luciano, Sergeant
Specht, and greengrocer Formusa all used exactly the same words to describe their
attachment to the market, which is to them a way of life as well as a place to earn a
living. Each mentioned the appeal of the market's camaraderie. As Luciano put it: 255
'Sure we compete, but the bottom line is, if my biggest competitor got into trouble,
I'd help him out, and he'd do the same for me. Though we have a tough exterior,
there's a heart in every one of us.'

1987

QUESTIONS

Reader and Purpose

1. Is Collins sympathetic to the subject he is describing? What is there, specifically, about his **tone** that leads you to believe he is sympathetic? Or, on the other hand, does he strike you as a professional writer who is simply doing a job he has been assigned? This is a difficult question; nevertheless try to be as specific as you can in gathering evidence to support your view.
2. To what extent is this essay an objective description of the Ontario Food Terminal and to what extent is it an impressionistic description? Support your answer by reference to specific passages.
3. Which part of this essay do you prefer: the description of the terminal, or the descriptions of the characters? Why?

Organization

4. How are paragraphs 1 and 6 related? paragraphs 2 and 7? 5 and 8? What do these relationships tell you about the structure of the essay?
5. The author does not begin to describe the food terminal itself until paragraph 5. How do the first four paragraphs serve as preparation for this description? as introduction to the whole essay?
6. The bulk of this essay is devoted to a description of the food terminal as the author observed it on the day he visited. In the final three paragraphs, however, the topic changes somewhat. What does it change to, and why?
7. The author's friend, Joey Formusa, is introduced in paragraph 10 and is present in most paragraphs thereafter until paragraph 28. How does his presence help to structure the essay?
8. Does the final paragraph constitute a **closing by return**? Explain why, or why not.

Sentences

9. In the first paragraph of this essay the author has used hyphens in four phrases. Are these hyphens all used for the same reason?
10. What is the function of the colon in the first sentence of paragraph 5?
11. What kind of series is used in the last sentence of paragraph 5?

Diction

12. Look up: *mayhem* (1), *portly* (3), *parlance* (16), *unsavoury* (16), *stalwart* (21), *exuberant* (42), *cantankerous* (43), *beleaguered* (76), *circuitous* (87), *jobber* (95), *ebullient* (111–12), *mosaic* (131), *potpourri* (133), *denouement* (170), *ambience* (182), *frenetic* (182), *shyster* (195), *elegiac* (243), *cacophony* (244).

13. In his first two sentences the author compares Jim McCarthy to Buddha—the farmer-vendor is likened to a powerful religious figure. Is this **image** effective, or do you find it exaggerated? Does it engage the reader, or is it a turnoff?

14. At the end of paragraph 7 why does the author write '*farmers*' market' rather than '*farmer's* market'?

15. On several occasions the author uses **clichés**, such as *living legend* (12), *ravenous appetite* (71), *home away from home* (81), *shrewd eye* (111), *gift of the gab* (112), and *carved in stone* (115). We cannot avoid using clichés entirely, since some of them describe a situation accurately and briefly. Others, however, could be replaced by expressions that are less common and thus more appealing. From this essay pick out a number of other clichés, and then discuss whether they are justified because of their accuracy and brevity, or whether they could have been replaced by fresher language.

POINTS TO LEARN

1. Sometimes a cliché is the shortest and most accurate way of describing something, but using clichés often will result in a style that is tired and trite.
2. A narrative element can help to organize a descriptive essay by providing a focus.
3. Descriptions of characters are often more interesting and memorable than descriptions of things.

SUGGESTIONS FOR WRITING

Describe a farmers' market that you have been to, or any other place characterized by busy buying or selling, such as an auction, a department store on a big sale day, a ski equipment sale and swap evening, etc. Describe the place itself as well as some of the characters you find interesting. You may want to focus on one character who moves about in the place, or you may be that roving character yourself. Don't forget, however, that your emphasis must be on description, with narration helping to focus the description.

IMPROVING YOUR STYLE

The object of a description is to help readers experience as fully as possible the place and people you are describing: to help them feel, see, smell, hear. Thus, you should give full reign to your imagination, but being careful not to exaggerate.

GEORGE ORWELL

'George Orwell' was the pen name of Eric Blair (1903–50), born in Bengal of middle-class English parents. After his education in England, he worked for five years as a member of the British Imperial Police in Burma, but in 1927 he left his job and returned to England; *Burmese Days* (1934) shows his contempt for the oppression and injustice of colonial rule. Subsequently determined to become a writer, he went to Paris hoping to support himself by giving English lessons. When this attempt failed, he became almost destitute. His life among the nearly starving poor of Paris, and later as a tramp and migrant worker in England, led to *Down and Out in Paris and London* (1933) and *The Road to Wigan Pier* (1937). Orwell fought against the Fascists and was wounded in the Spanish Civil War (1936–9). His difficult life, and chronic tuberculosis, led to his early death. Today he is known throughout the world as one of the greatest of all satirists, particularly for his anti-totalitarian satires *Animal Farm* (1945) and *1984* (1949). In the following excerpt from *Down and Out in Paris and London* he describes working as a dishwasher ('plongeur') in a luxury hotel in Paris; he shows (even early in his career as a writer) a keen eye for the details that matter and an ear for the best rhythms of English prose.

A Paris Plongeur

1   Our cafeterie was a murky cellar measuring twenty feet by seven by eight high, and so crowded with coffee-urns, breadcutters, and the like that one could hardly move without banging against something. It was lighted by one dim electric bulb, and four or five gas-fires that sent out a fierce red breath. There was a thermometer there, and the temperature never fell below 110 degrees Fahrenheit—it neared 130 at some 5 times of the day. At one end were five service lifts, and at the other an ice cupboard where we stored milk and butter. When you went into the ice cupboard you dropped a hundred degrees of temperature at a single step; it used to remind me of the hymn about Greenland's icy mountains and India's coral strand. Two men worked in the cafe-terie besides Boris and myself. One was Mario, a huge, excitable Italian—he was like 10 a city policeman with operatic gestures—and the other, a hairy, uncouth animal whom we called the Magyar; I think he was Transylvanian, or something even more remote. Except the Magyar we were all big men, and at the rush hours we collided incessantly.

2   The work in the cafeterie was spasmodic. We were never idle, but the real work only came in bursts of two hours at a time—we called each burst 'un coup de 15 feu'. The first *coup de feu* came at eight, when the guests upstairs began to wake up and demand breakfast. At eight a sudden banging and yelling would break out all through the basement; bells rang on all sides, blue-aproned men rushed through the passages, our service lifts came down with a simultaneous crash, and the waiters on all five floors began shouting Italian oaths down the shafts. I don't remember all our 20 duties, but they included making tea, coffee, and chocolate, fetching meals from the kitchen, wines from the cellar, and fruit and so forth from the dining-room, slicing bread, making toast, rolling pats of butter, measuring jam, opening milk-cans, count-ing lumps of sugar, boiling eggs, cooking porridge, pounding ice, grinding coffee—all this for from a hundred to two hundred customers. The kitchen was thirty yards 25

away, and the dining-room sixty or seventy yards. Everything we sent up in the service lifts had to be covered by a voucher, and the vouchers had to be carefully filed, and there was trouble if even a lump of sugar was lost. Besides this, we had to supply the staff with bread and coffee, and fetch the meals for the waiters upstairs. All in all, it was a complicated job.   30

3   I calculated that one had to walk and run about fifteen miles during the day, and yet the strain of the work was more mental than physical. Nothing could be easier, on the face of it, than this stupid scullion work, but it is astonishingly hard when one is in a hurry. One has to leap to and fro between a multitude of jobs—it is like sorting a pack of cards against the clock. You are, for example, making toast, when   35
bang! down comes a service lift with an order for tea, rolls, and three different kinds of jam, and simultaneously bang! down comes another demanding scrambled eggs, coffee, and grapefruit; you run to the kitchen for the eggs and to the dining-room for the fruit, going like lightning so as to be back before your toast burns, and having to remember about the tea and coffee, besides half a dozen other orders that are still   40
pending; and at the same time some waiter is following you and making trouble about the lost bottle of soda-water, and you are arguing with him. It needs more brains than one might think. Mario said, no doubt truly, that it took a year to make a reliable cafetier.

4   The time between eight and half-past ten was a sort of delirium. Sometimes we   45
were going as though we had only five minutes to live; sometimes there were sudden lulls when the orders stopped and everything seemed quiet for a moment. Then we swept up the litter from the floor, threw down fresh sawdust, and swallowed gallipots of wine or coffee or water—anything, so long as it was wet. Very often we used to break off chunks of ice and suck them while we worked. The heat among the gasfires was   50
nauseating; we swallowed quarts of drink during the day, and after a few hours even our aprons were drenched with sweat. At times we were hopelessly behind with the work, and some of the customers would have gone without their breakfast, but Mario always pulled us through. He had worked 14 years in the cafeterie, and he had the skill that never wastes a second between jobs. The Magyar was very stupid and I was inex-   55
perienced, and Boris was inclined to shirk, partly because of his game leg, partly because he was ashamed of working in the cafeterie after being a waiter; but Mario was wonderful. The way he would stretch his great arms right across the cafeterie to fill a coffee-pot with one hand and boil an egg with the other, at the same time watching toast and shouting directions to the Magyar, and between whiles singing snatches from   60
Rigoletto, was beyond all praise. The *patron* knew his value, and he was paid a thousand francs a month, instead of five hundred like the rest of us.

5   The breakfast pandemonium stopped at half-past ten. Then we scrubbed the cafeterie tables, swept the floor and polished the brasswork, and, on good mornings, went one at a time to the lavatory for a smoke. This was our slack time—only rela-   65
tively slack, however, for we had only ten minutes for lunch, and we never got through it uninterrupted. The customers' luncheon hour, between twelve and two, was another period of turmoil like the breakfast hour. Most of our work was fetching meals from the kitchen, which meant constant *engueulades* from the cooks. By this time the cooks had sweated in front of their furnaces for four or five hours, and their   70
tempers were all warmed up.

6   At two we were suddenly free men. We threw off our aprons and put on our coats, hurried out of doors, and, when we had money, dived into the nearest *bistro*. It was strange, coming up into the street from those firelit cellars. The air seemed blindingly clear and cold, like arctic summer; and how sweet the petrol did smell, after the stenches of sweat and food! Sometimes we met some of our cooks and waiters in the *bistros*, and they were friendly and stood us drinks. Indoors we were their slaves, but it is an etiquette in hotel life that between hours everyone is equal, and the *engueulades* do not count.

7   At a quarter to five we went back to the hotel. Till half-past six there were no orders, and we used this time to polish silver, clean out the coffee-urns, and do other odd jobs. Then the grand turmoil of the day started—the dinner hour. I wish I could be Zola for a little while, just to describe that dinner hour. The essence of the situation was that a hundred or two hundred people were demanding individually different meals of five or six courses, and that fifty or sixty people had to cook and serve them and clean up the mess afterwards; anyone with experience of catering will know what that means. And at this time when the work was doubled, the whole staff was tired out, and a number of them were drunk. I could write pages about the scene without giving a true idea of it. The charging to and fro in the narrow passages, the collisions, the yells, the struggling with crates and trays and blocks of ice, the heat, the darkness, the furious festering quarrels which there was no time to fight out—they pass description. Anyone coming into the basement for the first time would have thought himself in a den of maniacs. It was only later, when I understood the working of a hotel, that I saw order in all this chaos.

8   At half-past eight the work stopped very suddenly. We were not free till nine, but we used to throw ourselves full length on the floor, and lie there resting our legs, too lazy even to go to the ice cupboard for a drink. Sometimes the *chef du personnel* would come in with bottles of beer, for the hotel stood us an extra beer when we had had a hard day. The food we were given was no more than eatable, but the *patron* was not mean about drink; he allowed us two litres of wine a day each, knowing that if a *plongeur* is not given two litres he will steal three. We had the heeltaps of bottles as well, so that we often drank too much—a good thing, for one seemed to work faster when partially drunk.

9   Four days of the week passed like this; of the other two working days, one was better and one worse. After a week of this life I felt in need of a holiday. It was Saturday night, so the people in our *bistro* were busy getting drunk, and with a free day ahead of me I was ready to join them. We all went to bed, drunk, at two in the morning, meaning to sleep till noon. At half-past five I was suddenly awakened. A night-watchman, sent from the hotel, was standing at my bedside. He stripped the clothes back and shook me roughly.

10   'Get up!' he said. '*Tu t'es bien saoulé la gueule, eh*? Well, never mind that, the hotel's a man short. You've got to work to-day.'

11   'Why should I work?' I protested. 'This is my day off.'

12   'Day off, nothing! The work's got to be done. Get up!'

13   I got up and went out, feeling as though my back were broken and my skull filled with hot cinders. I did not think that I could possibly do a day's work. And yet, after only an hour in the basement, I found that I was perfectly well. It seemed that

in the heat of those cellars, as in a turkish bath, one could sweat out almost any quantity of drink. *Plongeurs* know this, and count on it. The power of swallowing quarts
of wine, and then sweating it out before it can do much damage, is one of the com-   120
pensations of their life.

1933

QUESTIONS

Reader and Purpose

1. Orwell is not writing for the down-and-out in Paris and London. At what kind of reader
   is he aiming? What does he assume the reader to know and not to know?
2. Is Orwell's purpose best described as accurate, detailed reporting of a personal
   experience, as social criticism, as some combination of these, or as something
   else altogether? Give reasons for your answer, citing passages in the text.

Organization

3. The first paragraph sets the stage and lists the cast of characters. The second and
   third paragraphs describe the narrator's job. What organizing principle is at work in
   paragraphs 4–8?
4. Give a title to paragraphs 9–13, indicating the essential topic of that section.

Sentences

5. In line 5 a semicolon in place of the dash would be more conventional. Is the dash
   in paragraph 3 used in the same manner, or is it used differently?
6. In lines 10 and 11 the dashes might be replaced with parentheses. Yet parentheses would create a slightly different effect. Explain.
7. What is the difference in the emphasis upon 'drunk' in this sentence by Orwell and
   its revision?

   > **Revision:** We all went to bed drunk at two in the morning, meaning to sleep till
   > noon.
   >
   > **Orwell:** 'We all went to bed, drunk, at two in the morning, meaning to sleep till
   > noon.' (107–8)

8. In paragraph 6 identify an example of emphasis by **inversion**. What is its effect?
9. What three ways of achieving emphasis are at work in the sentence beginning 'The
   Magyar was very stupid' in line 55?

Diction

10. Look up: *Magyar* (12), *spasmodic* (14), *porridge* (24), *voucher* (27), *scullion* (33),
    gallipots (48), *Rigoletto* (61), *heeltaps* (101).
11. Throughout this passage Orwell uses French words and phrases. In one case he
    quotes what the night watchman said, using part English and part French (111–12).
    Should Orwell have avoided French altogether? Why, or why not? What rule of thumb
    can you formulate about using foreign words in your own writing?
12. Does Orwell's diction tend to be **abstract** and general or **concrete** and particular?
    List examples of both types.

13. Does Orwell rely more heavily on adjectives or on nouns and verbs? List the adjectives used in the first two paragraphs.
14. List Orwell's **similes** and **metaphors**.
15. Using examples, demonstrate the relationship between Orwell's diction and **tone**. Describe his attitudes toward his job, the 'Magyar', Mario, and himself.

POINTS TO LEARN

1. The skilful choice of punctuation can be a subtle help in the depiction of frenzied activity.
2. Chronological progression, with the steps clearly marked, is a method of organization that can be both unobtrusive and efficient.

SUGGESTIONS FOR WRITING

Loosely following Orwell's organization and employing the first-person **point of view**, describe your job in a supermarket, restaurant, factory, hospital, department store, or elsewhere. Convey a distinct tone toward your work and your fellow employees. Your aim is to interest your reader by making clear exactly what you do and how you feel about it.

IMPROVING YOUR STYLE

1. In your composition write a sentence similar to that in lines 89–92: use a long series of **parallel** nouns (or **gerunds** and nouns) concluded by a dash and short clause, the subject of which refers to all the nouns in the series. A similar but slightly different pattern occurs in lines 20–5. Either model is suitable. Notice the occurrence of this kind of sentence in other descriptions or narrations. It is very useful to convey multiplicity and complexity.
2. Use a dash as Orwell employs it in line 5.
3. Include two or three metaphors and two or three similes.
4. In one sentence achieve emphasis by inversion.

DAN SCHNEIDER

A resident of Puslinch, Ontario, Dan Schneider is a nature interpreter with the Grand River Conservation Authority and a member of the Federation of Ontario Naturalists. Many of his articles, like the essay here, focus on naturalist themes. A previous article of his in *Canadian Geographic* (Aug./Sept. 1986) dealt with poisonous plants, especially those in Canada. He is also a frequent contributor to *Nature Canada*; for instance, 'Water Works' (Spring 1995) gives practical advice on how to make the background of your yard a welcome habitat for fish, bugs, birds, toads, and many other life forms.

Biter's Banquet

1   The poets would have us believe that the quintessential summer fantasy of a Canadian is a romance to the call of the loon on a moonlit lake. But for those who have truly experienced the Canadian wilderness the collective fantasy is more likely

to be the delivery of a technological slap to the community of biting insects that suck
many of the pleasures from our fleeting summers. Are there not moments when even 5
the calmest among us, the most generous spirited, never-hurt-a-fly kind of folks,
would zap the biting scourges out of every creek, swamp, slough, ditch, pond, mud-
hole, and pothole? Are we not all able to summon to mind exactly the sentiment that
drove a French Recollet brother to write, after enduring black flies on the Ottawa
River in 1620, 'I must confess this is the worst martyrdom I suffered in this country'? 10
2   It's been said that tolerance is a sapling that grows only if it is able to sink roots
deep into the soil of understanding. Other than the fact that their bites itch, what do
most of us really know about the perpetrators? With the season once again upon us,
we offer in the spirit of peacemaking an explanation of why biting flies have been
inflicted upon Canadians, as well as a guide to their table manners and mating habits. 15
Lastly, we offer advice for the afflicted.

O Sting, What Is Thy Purpose?

3   There is a divine reason for the existence of the rogue's gallery that includes
mosquitoes, black flies, deer flies, horse flies, no-see-ums, and stable flies. They are
critical links in the food chain, passing nutrients on to animals higher up the chain,
including humans.   20
4   'Biting flies are a strong indicator of healthy environments,' observes Steve
Smith, a biting fly researcher at the University of Waterloo and a man who is as sensitive to a bite as anyone. 'Their absence would mean that something serious has happened to an area of wetlands and streams. Sure, we bitch all the time about
mosquitoes. But the reality is, if you said "would you live in an area without them?" 25
I'd say "no," because then I wouldn't have the frogs in the springtime, and I wouldn't
have turtles, and I wouldn't have birds associated with wetlands, and I wouldn't have
the flora associated with wetlands.'
5   'The larvae of black flies are absolutely critical to many fish, for example trout, in
streams and rivers,' says Gord Surgeoner, an entomologist at the University of Guelph. 30
6   And then there are our migrating songbirds, irresistibly drawn from southern
climates to an annual feeding and breeding orgy in our northern forests. They capture
mosquitoes, black flies, and the others by the millions and feed them to their ravenous
nestlings. 'They also play an important role in the diets of a lot of things we don't think
about,' says Smith. 'Biting flies have very important roles in the diets of other insects, 35
and the diets of spiders, and the diets of sundews and pitcher plants and many others.'

How the Flies Feast

7   It's the weekend, and you're out relaxing in the back yard. Nearby, lounging on
a leaf, a mosquito detects the aroma of your breath, laced with the succulent smell of
carbon dioxide. She lifts off, and follows the odour towards its source. Closer in, she
detects body heat as she lands delicately on your arm.   40
8   In recent studies, a Trent University research team led by Professor Jim Sutcliffe
and graduate student Steve Scofield discovered that people differ in their attractive-
ness to biting flies. 'The attraction process is largely under the control of breath
odours and of body odours,' says Sutcliffe. 'Then the actual biting process is under the
control of a different set of chemical stimuli from the skin.'   45

9   Warmth is one biting trigger but so are the chemical qualities of sweat and other skin glands, which are detected by taste receptors on the fly's feet. 'So a person can be quite attractive, but not necessarily "bitable",' concludes Sutcliffe.

10   Once on the skin and cued to bite, the mosquito's remarkably sophisticated blood-extracting equipment comes into play. What looks like a needle on her head is 50 really a sheath, which bends out during feeding to allow six interior lancets to probe into your skin. Two of them are equipped with tiny barbs that help the piercing unit penetrate until it encounters a capillary. Two others are hollow. One, with a powerful pump at its base, is the syringe-like blood-taker. The second injects saliva, including an anticoagulant so the mosquito doesn't choke on rapidly congealing blood.   55

11   It is the injected saliva that causes the itch, alerting your body's defence reactions to combat a foreign substance. The injection site is surrounded by histamines, raising a reddish, itchy bump. As with allergies, the severity of the reaction varies with each person's immune response.

12   Watching a mosquito fill up with blood from your arm is fascinating. Your 60 nutritious blood becomes visible through her translucent abdomen, which swells until you'd think it would burst, finally tripling her weight before she pulls out and flies off clumsily, like a happy drunk.

13   Other biters are less fastidious. Black flies and minuscule no-see-ums use their scissor-like mandibles to snip the victim's skin until blood begins to flow. They lap up 65 the blood as it pours from the wound. It is the snipping that hurts initially, but the body's defence reaction to the fly's saliva triggers an irritating itch.

14   Bites from deer flies and horse flies are more painful, since they use fearsome, jabbing mouthparts to pierce your skin. With huge eyes and excellent vision, these large flies may be attracted by the shininess of wet skin, and they often plague bathers. 70 The stable fly's bite is less painful, but these housefly-like biters are infuriatingly agile as they zoom in on bare feet and ankles around lakeshores.

15   With the exception of male stable flies, every biter that you swat is a female. Protein from ingested blood is absorbed by their eggs, which may number several hundred in a single clutch for mosquitoes and black flies. So, when you donate some 75 blood, you can feel good about supporting the next generation. Yet blood is not the major energy source of biting flies.

16   'Carbohydrates from somewhere—from nectar, honeydew, or some source—are absolutely vital, and they probably have to be taken on a daily basis,' says Steve Smith. His recent studies have revealed that honeydew, a sugary substance excreted by aphids 80 sucking liquid from plants, is a critical energy source for horse flies. Mosquitoes, however, almost always sip nectar directly from flowers.

17   Smith has observed that the spring emergence of one species of mosquito, very common in eastern Ontario, is tightly tied to the blooming of wild cherry trees. 'You see the trees fill up—a single cherry tree with 10,000 mosquitoes feeding on it, just 85 absolutely dense. The mosquitoes are hitting virtually every blossom.'

The Love of a Fly

18   The whine of a mosquito may be as appealing as the buzz of a dentist's drill, but it is the sweet call of amour to a love-starved male. The sound is produced by the female's wings beating at a frequency of 300 to 800 times per second. Males,

who hear the sound with their feathery antennae, can be drawn to anything—a   90
tuning fork, another male, or a female—with the appropriate frequency. Their
hearing range is about 30 centimetres, and they can distinguish between the sound
of a newly emerged female who would spurn their advances and a mature, recep-
tive female.

19   Mosquito mating is an acrobatic affair. Males clasp females in mid-air, arrange   95
themselves face to face, and copulate on the wing or after they drift to the ground.

20   Once they have mated and sought out a blood supply for their newly fertilized
eggs, the females are ready to jettison their broods in standing water or land likely to
be flooded. Rain barrels, ponds, low-lying woods and fields, tanks, garden pools,
puddles on a highway, roadside ditches, blocked eavestroughs, holes in trees, dis-   100
carded tin cans, and pitcher plant leaves are among their many breeding sites.

21   Once she has deposited the next generation, the female mosquito may die soon
after or, if conditions are good, return to seek another blood meal and lay another
batch of eggs. Some species may produce up to six or seven broods; correspondingly,
they must search out six or seven blood 'victims'.   105

22   Depending on the species of mosquito and time of year, eggs may hatch in just
a couple of days, or later in the summer after heavy rains. In many species, eggs lie
quiescent for months before winter's sustained cold and the following warmth of
spring combine to break their dormancy. Although a few species hibernate as adults,
by far the majority of Canada's mosquito species overwinter as eggs, insulated by a   110
blanket of snow. When meltwater fills low-lying areas in spring, the eggs quickly
hatch into wriggling larvae. The growing multitude breathes air by piercing the
surface with posterior snorkels, and uses brush-like mouthparts to browse algae and
bacteria from bottom debris. Eventually, the 'wrigglers' are full grown and transform
into the pupal stage, comma-shaped 'tumblers' that jerk here and there in the shal-   115
low water.

23   Finally, the pupal skin splits and a delicate adult mosquito squirms out, using
its discarded skin as a floating launch pad. Its life as an adult will be fleeting, usually
just a few weeks. Since males usually emerge first, and since females search out nectar and mates before blood, there is generally a grace period of three to four days in   120
the spring when countless mosquitoes have emerged, yet we are not being bitten.

24   Black flies require clear, running water as a nursery for their offspring, which is
why they are so common in the forests of the Canadian Shield. Laid carefully on rocks
or vegetation in or near the stream, the eggs hatch into tiny, writhing larvae, which
'glue' themselves to underwater rocks with a sticky secretion and hooks. The water   125
current acts as a food delivery service, sending plankton and tiny food particles to the
larvae, which they sieve into their mouths with bristle-like mouthparts.

25   The numbers of black fly larvae can be staggering. Often, a rock will appear
covered with a seething, greenish moss which is actually larvae bursting with life.
'They could certainly reach a hundred thousand per square metre at lake outlets,' says   130
Murray Colbo, an entomologist at Memorial University in St John's.

26   When black flies emerge, in spring or summer, they do it in style. Much too
delicate, as winged adults, to survive in racing currents, they form an air bubble
around themselves in their pupal case, float up, and, remarkably, fly instantly when
their bubble bursts at the surface.   135

27   Stable flies breed in rotting vegetation like manure heaps on farms or flotsam washed up on beaches, where the adults can make sunbathing a more lively pastime. Horse flies, deer flies, and no-see-ums deposit their eggs in wet soil at the margins of lakes and in boggy areas. The larvae of some horse flies and deer flies are fierce preda-   tors. They assassinate earthworms, each other, and anything else that they encounter 140 and can subdue.

Ointment for the Fly

28   Eating garlic doesn't work. Going unwashed doesn't work. Taking vitamin B doesn't work. Sonic buzzers, which are designed to imitate the hum of a male mosquito and so repel an already-mated female, don't work.

29   It should come as no surprise and perhaps some relief that Canada's scientific 145 establishment includes a person like entomologist Gord Surgeoner of the University of Guelph, who has tested on our behalf most of the folk remedies and repellents that we pass around to each other every summer. We don't even want to know how he tested the garlic. We'll take his word for it.

30   We'll also accept his assessment of the currently popular backyard electrocuters 150 which, he says, actually zap moths and other harmless insects rather than biting flies. 'You're no better off in a yard with one than a yard without,' asserts Surgeoner.

31   On the other hand, he says, there is some truth to folk wisdom about how to protect yourself from the biters. 'There's a general rule that the darker the clothing, the more problems you can run into,' says Surgeoner. This is probably because dark 155 clothing more closely resembles the relatively dark fur of the flies' natural hosts.

32   Citronella is a natural repellent extracted from citronella grass which is grown commercially in southeast Asia. Products containing it, like Avon Skin-So-Soft, do repel insects. The only drawback is that citronella's repellent properties last only 30 to 60 minutes.   160

33   So what should a person do?

34   'Stick to the name-brand repellents,' Surgeoner advises. He recommends using registered repellents with citronella or low concentrations of DEET, the active ingredi-ent in most repellents, especially when protection is needed for just an hour or two. The chemical DEET (Diethyl-m-toluamide) was discovered by US military researchers 165 in the 1940s. Wearers of DEET still attract flies, but as mosquitoes and some flies zoom in for blood the chemical's odour interferes with their instinct to land and bite. DEET discourages mosquitoes, black flies, and no-see-ums, but it is fairly useless on deer flies, horse flies, and stable flies.

35   And then there's the 'know-thy-enemy' protection. Any wind stronger than 15 170 kilometres per hour forces mosquitoes, whose top speed is only five kilometres per hour, to head for cover. A strong breeze also deters black flies and no-see-ums. Most mosquitoes are primarily crepuscular blood feeders, meaning that dusk is their peak harassment time. Black flies, on the other hand, are more diurnal biters, reaching blood-seeking climaxes in the early morning and pre-dusk hours. But take comfort: 175 generally, the more you get bitten, the less your bites itch. This means that the first few bites of spring will bother you most, and that people spending more time outside gain some immunity to the effects of bites.

36   So there are choices. Most experts, though, agree that the most effective remedy is also the worst. Staying indoors through biting fly season means you miss the possibility   180 of a romance to the call of the loon on a moonlit lake and other pleasures of summer.

1995

QUESTIONS

Reader and Purpose

1. Look up the explanation of **rhetorical question** in the Glossary. Do you agree that the two questions in the opening paragraph are rhetorical ones? What is the purpose of these questions?

2. In paragraph 2 the author writes that he has three objectives in his essay. What are these objectives? Does he deal with all three? Does he have any other purpose?

3. This essay might also have been included, with some justification, in the *Exposition* section of this book. In what section would you include it, and why?

Organization

4. Explain how this essay uses a **closing by return**.

5. 'There is a divine reason', begins paragraph 3. Does the author state this 'divine reason' explicitly, or does he assume that his readers can figure it out for themselves?

6. After the two introductory paragraphs this essay is divided into four sections—paragraphs 3–6, 7–17, 18–27, 28–36—with each section having its own title. How appropriate are these titles? Can you provide better ones?

7. 'Paragraph 7 describes why a mosquito will come to bite you, and the next paragraph describes what controls both the process of attraction and the biting process.' Describe the rest of this section (paragraphs 9–17) in this same brief manner.

8. Keeping in mind that paragraphs in magazines are usually fairly short, compared to those in books, is the point made in paragraph 5 worth a separate paragraph, or is the idea really part of the preceding paragraph? Is paragraph 23 logically a part of paragraph 22, or is the author justified in making this a separate paragraph?

Sentences

9. Identify the series in the first sentence of paragraph 3. What kind of series is it? Is the series that concludes paragraph 4 of the same kind? the series that concludes paragraph 6? the one that concludes paragraph 20?

10. Quotations can be either introduced or attributed (that is, after the quotation) in many ways, as in these examples: 'observes Steve Smith' (21–2), 'says Gordon Surgeoner' (30), 'concludes Sutcliffe' (41). Pick out any four attributed quotations and rephrase them as quotations that are introduced. Is one method more effective than the other?

11. Does paragraph 28 begin with three **fragments**? Or are these merely short, but complete, sentences?

Diction

12. Look up: *quintessential* (1), *scourge* (7), *perpetrator* (13), *afflicted* (16), *flora* (28), *entomologist* (30), *succulent* (38), *capillary* (53), *anticoagulant* (55), *histamine* (57), *fastidious* (64), *mandibles* (65), *ingested* (74), *quiescent* (108), *plankton* (126), *crepuscular* (173), *diurnal* (174).

13. Is the author guilty of using a **cliché** in his opening sentence?
14. Identify the **figures of speech** in the second sentence of paragraph 1. Do the same for the first sentence of paragraph 2.
15. Explain the **personification** in paragraph 7. Where else does the author use this device? What effect does it have?
16. Is the author being **ironic** in paragraph 15?

POINTS TO LEARN

1. A rhetorical question can have a dramatic effect, it can serve as an **organizing sentence**, and it can also help to introduce a topic.
2. The verb *says* (and its variations) is a simple and unobtrusive way to attribute a quotation.
3. Personification in writing about birds, fish, insects, or animals can make an unattractive subject more appealing to the reader but may undermine the credibility of serious description unless it is used sparingly.

SUGGESTIONS FOR WRITING

What experiences have you had with wasps, or spiders, or mosquitoes, or horseflies, or any other kind of insect? Describe your encounters (or perhaps just one telling experience) in an essay of 7–10 paragraphs.

Remember that your purpose in this essay is to describe; thus, although narration will likely play a part, your emphasis should be on description: what the insect looks like, its nature, where it comes from, what it does to humans, how to repulse it or escape from it, etc.

IMPROVING YOUR STYLE

In your essay include

1. two examples of irony (without being too heavy-handed);
2. an example of personification.

ADRIAN FORSYTH

One of the most prominent natural-science writers in North America, Adrian Forsyth has received a number of distinguished awards. He has a Ph.D. in tropical ecology from Harvard and has served as the Canadian representative to and, later, vice-president of the environmental agency Conservation International. He is the president and co-founder of the Amazon Conservation Association and a research associate with the Smithsonian Institution; he also serves as a board member or researcher for various other conservation and environmental organizations. His work has been published frequently in such periodicals as *Equinox* (from which the essay below is taken), *Saturday Night*, *Horticulture*, and *Natural History*. Among his many books are *Mammals of the Canadian Wild* (1985), *Journey Through a Tropical Jungle* (1988), *The Nature of Birds*

(1988), *A Natural History of Sex: The Ecology and Evolution of Mating Behavior* (1993), *How Monkeys Make Chocolate: Foods and Medicines from the Rainforests* (1995), and *Mammals of North America: Temperate and Arctic Regions* (1999).

Flights of Fancy

1   Fledgling common swifts, perched on the edge of their nest in preparation for their first flight, are about to embark on the natural world's greatest odyssey. Common swifts are so completely at home in the air that biologists believe they spend two years in continuous flight, feeding, mating, and even sleeping in the air. A young swift will fly nonstop for 300,000 miles—a distance equal to six flights around the world—   5
from the time it leaves its parental nest until it settles to build its own nest.
2   Among birds, swifts are but one of many species capable of outstanding aerial exploits. Peregrine falcons can descend on prey at 175 miles per hour. Hummingbirds manoeuvre with more finesse than any bee. Arctic terns fly an 18,000-mile annual migration from the Arctic to the Antarctic. Dippers plunge into mountain torrents in   10
pursuit of underwater insects and emerge from the water flying.
3   All of these athletic feats of flight depend on a single evolutionary development: feathers. Insects, fish, bats, squirrels, and lemurs can fly or glide. But it is feathers that allow birds to fly for thousands of miles, to dive at speeds greater than any land or marine animal can achieve, and to move with unsurpassed agility and grace.   15
4   The usefulness of feathers is a product of both the construction of individual feathers and the way they are arranged on a bird's body. True to the cliché, feathers are light, but their design makes them strong and flexible as well. Flight feathers have a hollow central shaft. Hundreds of hairlike barbs run out from the shaft to form the flat surface of the feather. Barbs are connected to each other by hooked, overlapping   20
barbules. A single pigeon feather may have more than one million barbs, barbules, and hooks. The resulting complex, tightly knit surface is light, sheds water, and presents little friction against air.
5   Large flight feathers can provide sophisticated aerodynamics. Feathers increase the surface area and curvature of a bird's wing, giving it more lift and con-   25
trol than the fixed membrane of a bat or insect wing. Flight feathers have muscles around their base, allowing them to move like the flaps on the tail of an airplane. By spreading the feathers on the rear edge of its wings, a bird can create slots that reduce air resistance when it lifts its wings between down beats. Many bird species also have small secondary wings called alula. Located near the centre of the front   30
edge of the wing, the alula feathers capture air currents and can increase the lift of a wing by up to 20 per cent. Many birds are unable to get off the ground if their alula feathers are damaged.
6   Although flight and feathers seem inseparable, flying is only one of many functions that feathers perform for birds. Like a mammal's hair or a reptile's scales, feath-   35
ers insulate and protect a bird's body. Down, which is composed of small feathers that lack the hooks which bind the barbules of flight feathers, has a puff of fine barbs that create millions of pockets of dead air. Anyone who has snuggled into a down parka at 20 below zero can attest to the insulating properties of down.

7   Feathers around the ears of birds such as owls act as sound amplifiers. Other 40
nocturnal raptors have feathers that resemble bristles around their faces and feet. Like
the whiskers of a cat, the bristles provide the night fliers with information about the
location of prey. Hairlike feathers called filoplumes have a large number of nerve endings at their base and are believed to act as sensory devices to help the bird adjust its
other feathers to pressure changes.   45
8   Most birds have excellent colour vision, which is in keeping with their multi-
hued plumage. One nineteenth-century ornithologist catalogued 1,115 shades in bird
feathers. The great range of colour is due to the diverse roles played by feathers. Bright
colours are important for courtship and species identification. The bright red
epaulettes of the red-winged blackbird, for example, signal other blackbirds that the 50
bearer is a mature breeding male. Immature males have only a faint red patch, and
females have no red. Such signalling enables a bird to escape harassment by members
of the wrong sex or by competitors that are larger, older, and stronger. Researchers
have found that if the feathers of a young red-winged blackbird are reddened, it is
subject to fierce challenges by bona fide adult territorial males.   55
9   Bright colours and elaborate feathers are also used by males in courtship displays directed at females. The most colourful feathers of all are those worn by courting
pheasants, peacocks, and quetzals. In some cases the tail feathers are six feet long, and
many of these birds feature spectacular iridescent eyespots complete with counter-
shading. Humans have, at various times, become enamoured of these ornamental 60
feathers and have sought to adorn themselves in comparable fashion. At the turn of the
century, the thirst of Western women for feathers was so great that egret plumes sold
for $80 an ounce, more than the price of gold. The trade involved about one million
pounds of feathers a year, resulting in the estimated destruction of 200 million birds.
10   Because nine-tenths of a feather is pure protein, producing plumage requires 65
substantial amounts of nutrients and energy, especially in view of the large number of
feathers a bird grows: roughly 1,500 by the ruby-throated hummingbird and 25,000
by the whistling swan. In species such as frigate birds and tropic seabirds, which
spend most of their lives soaring above the ocean, the feathers weigh more than the
bird's skeleton. It is somewhat surprising, then, that birds moult and grow new feath- 70
ers at regular intervals.
11   Flying, brooding, fighting, and feeding, along with exposure to wind, sunlight,
and other elements, such as seawater, cause feathers to fray and tear and, in time, to
become less efficient. To compensate, most birds shed their feathers once a year,
although some tropic birds have a longer period between moults. The moulting cycle 75
is a complex process that reflects the ecological pressures on a species. Aquatic birds
like loons or dippers, which can escape underwater from danger and are not particularly vulnerable even when they cannot fly, shed all their feathers at once. Birds which
must be able to fly to escape predators or which have to keep hunting often have a
prolonged moult so that old feathers are lost gradually as new ones grow in. This 80
ensures that the bird is never grounded. Some species fit all their feather changing
into a brief period of food abundance at the peak of summer, when the cost of growing a new set of feathers is low.
12   Moulting is an adaptation that not only eliminates worn feathers but also
enables a bird to match its appearance to changing seasons and social necessities. 85

Many birds use the moult for camouflage. Willow ptarmigan and other northern birds moult from their white winter coat to an inconspicuous dirty summer plumage that blends with the tundra. Male ducks, such as the blue-winged teal, moult from a colourful courtship coat to a drab summer coat known as 'eclipse' plumage, which conceals them from predators.   90

13   The moult may also be a means of shedding parasites. The intricate spaces within and among feathers harbour a rich array of fleas, flies, lice, and mites, many of which feed directly on the feathers and skin. As many as 1,000 lice have been found on the feathers of a single curlew, and there are an estimated 25,000 species of feather lice. The presence of these vermin accounts for the enthusiasm that many birds dis- 95 play for bathing in water and dust.

14   Like all evolutionary adaptations, feathers are not perfect. They lack the flexibility of hair and are ill suited to tasks that involve getting rubbed the wrong way. That is why vultures have lost the feathers on their heads and necks. Sticking a feathered head inside a rotting carcass would result in a formidable mess when the head was 100 withdrawn. Nevertheless, feathers have been successfully modified, shortened, and compacted enough to enable many species of birds to nest in underground burrows and to swim well underwater. As a result, there is virtually no habitat on Earth, except for the ocean depths, unexploited by feathered species.

15   When observing a bird in flight, it is hard to imagine that the origins of this 105 freedom can be traced to a scaly reptile sleeping in the sun. Yet most evolutionary biologists believe that birds had such an ancestor. The best explanation for the evolution of feathers has nothing to do with flying. Instead, feathers appear to have originated from long, pointed scales that were used as heat shields by the basking reptiles. The ancestors of birds were probably small upright reptiles that pursued prey and 110 hopped around the shrubbery and treetops. Wings developed as gliding structures. Feathers, meanwhile, had already evolved because they were useful in shedding and capturing heat. As the prototype birds began to rely on gliding and wing flapping, their feathers became aerodynamic structures. Thus feathers were present before birds became full-fledged fliers. In fact, feathers may have existed before birds became truly 115 birdlike and could have been the device necessary to launch the group forward into true sustained flight.

16   There is a biological moral in this aspect of feathers: one cannot predict the evolutionary future of a characteristic or behaviour. As we look into the fossilized past, we discover that some small change in the scales of reptiles, an alteration that may 120 have seemed trivial at the time of its origin, eventually produced profound adaptations. Just as we owe much of our evolutionary success to a few minor changes—the shifting of the thumb, perhaps, or a propensity to forage on the ground instead of in the trees—birds owe much of their success to a reptile scale that gradually grew longer and more elaborate and finally became a feather.   125

17   The success of birds—both evolutionarily and in the eyes of humanity—is inextricably based on feathers and flight. Birds are the most mobile of organisms and some would say the most beautiful and inspiring. A plucked bird looks ignominious and pathetic, but a bird possessed of feathers and flight is a symbol of freedom and peace, of escape and independence.   130

1986

QUESTIONS

Reader and Purpose

1. What kind of information about its subject does this essay offer that could not be found in a dictionary definition? Does the author also offer impressions, or feelings?
2. Is this essay simply an example of objective description? Are there also places where the author draws conclusions from his material to suggest that the study of feathers can lead us to think about larger and more controversial issues?

Organization

3. How many paragraphs constitute the introduction? In what paragraph is the main subject of the essay introduced? What would be lost if Forsyth's essay had begun with paragraph 4?
4. Between the introductory paragraphs and the concluding paragraph the essay exhibits a clearly defined four-part structure. Indicate which paragraphs belong to each part. Identify the **connectives** between each part.
5. What are the main topics of each of the four parts? What effect is achieved by putting the parts in the order Forsyth gives them? How does this order serve the purpose of his essay?
6. How does Forsyth prepare the reader for the evolutionary theory introduced in paragraph 15?
7. What relationship is established between the bird as **symbol** of independence (paragraph 17) and the 'biological moral' of paragraph 16? Is the concept of independence anticipated in other parts of the essay?

Sentences

8. Identify some of the places where Forsyth uses a series of sentences to introduce a generalization and then follows it with particularizing details, as in paragraphs 2 and 3.
9. Examine Forsyth's sentences in paragraphs 4 and 5 and state how many of them are **compound, complex,** or **simple**. What does the proportion of each kind reveal about Forsyth's descriptive method? How does this proportioning serve the purpose of his essay?
10. Nearly all of Forsyth's sentences present straightforward statements of fact. What significant change in this method is evident in paragraph 15? Why is the change appropriate?

Diction

11. Look up: *odyssey* (2), *barbules* (21), *epaulettes* (50), *quetzals* (58), *iridescent* (59), eco*logical* (76), *ignominious* (128).
12. Find the **etymologies** of: *camouflage* (86), *ignominious* (128).
13. Explain the meaning of these phrases: *fixed membrane* (26), *nocturnal raptors* (41), *bona fide* (55).
14. Identify the **figure of speech** in paragraph 7. Is the same device being used in paragraph 6?
15. Examine Forsyth's choice of nouns in paragraphs 10–14, and then indicate the proportion of **abstract** terms to **concrete** ones. How does his preference for one or the other suit the purpose of his essay?

POINTS TO LEARN

1. Description of apparently insignificant objects can be used to draw or suggest conclusions of wider importance.
2. Abstract terms need particular supporting detail to make them clear to an unspecialized reader.
3. An introduction may require more than one paragraph in order to focus the topic.

SUGGESTIONS FOR WRITING

1. Copy out a dictionary definition of some general term (such as *hand*, *foot*, *eye*, *claw*, or *fur*). Then write three paragraphs in which you lead your reader to an understanding of how this general term has a particular and important interest.
2. Write three paragraphs of description (an awkward animal, unusual cloud formations, an odd-looking tree or plant, a particularly ugly insect), the first in simple sentences, the second in compound sentences, and the third in complex. Then rewrite the three paragraphs using all three types of sentences in each one.

IMPROVING YOUR STYLE

1. Begin three paragraphs with a general topic and then provide specific examples to make it particular.
2. Write two or three paragraphs in which you use similes to explain, or clarify, the subject you chose from the previous topic in terms of its resemblance to something quite unlike itself.

Hugh Dempsey

Hugh Dempsey (1929–) served as chief curator of the Glenbow-Alberta Institute in Calgary and has for many years edited the quarterly magazine *Alberta History*. As a result of his long interest in the history of western Canada, and particularly of the Blackfoot tribes, he has published a large number of articles and books. His wife, Pauline, is a daughter of the famous Blackfoot chief James Gladstone, once a member of the Canadian Senate. Dempsey's numerous books include *Jerry Potts, Plainsman* (1966), *Crowfoot, Chief of the Blackfeet* (1972), *The Gentle Persuader: A Biography of James Gladstone, Indian Senator* (1986), *The Golden Age of the Canadian Cowboy: An Illustrated History* (1995), *Tom Three Persons: Legend of an Indian Cowboy* (1997), and *Indians of the Rocky Mountain Parks* (1999). His most recent book is *Firewater* (2002).

The Snake Man

1   On a lonely hill near the Belly Buttes lies the unmarked grave of a Blood chief who, upon his death in 1901, carried with him one of the strangest secrets of the Canadian West. The man was Calf Shirt, or *Onistahsisokasim*; his secret was a strange power which permitted him to talk to rattlesnakes.

2   Calf Shirt was a paradox, for in 57 years of life he played with equal dexterity
the roles of informer and tribal leader, police scout and criminal. But his power over
rattlesnakes was his strangest trait, a gift of his own religion. This power came to him
when he was 36 years old, just before the Bloods and their Blackfoot allies began to
experience the bitterness of life on a reserve and to hunger for the vanished buffalo.

3   Calf Shirt's career was filled with adventure. Even in the years before his strange
control over rattlesnakes, he had had an eventful life. Born in 1844, the son of The
Shoulder, he was a member of the Many Tumors band and earned a favourable reputation as a warrior. After one particular experience, he took the name of Calf Shirt
which had belonged to an uncle killed by whisky traders during the winter of
1873–4. Names were considered to be family possessions which could be claimed
after some particular achievement or event.

4   Calf Shirt did his best to live up to his name. He joined several war parties,
mostly against the Crows in Montana, and became so highly regarded that he was a
leader of revenge war parties. These were formed whenever the Bloods suffered
humiliating defeat at the hands of the enemy. He took part in a great battle between
the Crees and Blackfoot near the present city of Lethbridge in the fall of 1870. He had
been out hunting and, upon his return, was told by his father that the battle was in
progress. The young warrior let his father daub bright war paint on his face and, as a
gesture of scorn, promised that should he be struck by an enemy arrow, he would
leave it in his body for his father to remove.

5   Grasping a double-bladed knife from his religious Bear medicine bundle, Calf
Shirt arrived while the battle was in progress in time to see the Crees being trapped in
a long shallow coulee. Among those making a stand were two warriors, one tall and
the other wearing a calfskin robe. Armed only with his Bear knife and singing his war
song, Calf Shirt rushed the men, but took an arrow in the wrist before he reached
them. Heedless of the shaft protruding from his arm, the warrior grabbed the bow
with his wounded hand and struck the tall Cree a mortal blow with his knife. The calf-
skinned comrade, waiting for a clear shot, was stabbed to death in a similar manner.

6   After the fight, people offered to remove the enemy arrow, but Calf Shirt
reminded them of his promise and accompanied the victorious Bloods back to their
camp. On the way, his arm became greatly swollen until he could not travel unaided
but when he still refused to remove the arrow, he was lashed onto a travois and
dragged into camp where his father was waiting to take out the shaft.

7   According to elderly Bloods, Calf Shirt received his special rattlesnake powers
through a vision in the late 1870s. The event occurred shortly after Calf Shirt's father
had died and the young warrior had wandered away by himself to mourn. The Bloods
were camped in a rattlesnake-infested area east of the present Medicine Hat, at a place
called 'Where We Drowned'. Calf Shirt walked aimlessly in his sorrow until, at last,
he laid down exhausted on a sand hill and fell asleep. While there, he had a dream in
which a person appeared before him. 'I've heard you mourning the loss of your father
and have taken pity on you,' said the stranger. 'My father has sent me to you to say
that you'll be his son and we'll be brothers. All of our people who live here are his
children and you're now one of us. You'll become a leader of your people and we'll
watch over you. Always carry some sagebrush with you so that we'll know you and
so you can use it to treat those who are sick.'

8   In his dream, Calf Shirt could see the person but still did not recognize him. Realizing this, the figure explained, 'I'm from the Big Snake tribe; our people are rattlesnakes. When you die, you'll become one of us.'[1]

9   Returning to his home camp, Calf Shirt soon demonstrated his newly gained powers. Grasping a rattlesnake, he wrapped it around his waist, carried it before a   55
shocked group of Bloods, and played with it as though it were a child. At first his friends shunned him, for they feared the rattling serpents, but in time they learned that they had nothing to fear as the snakes were his brothers and did his bidding. If he whistled, they slithered through the grass to his feet; if he made a sign, they quietly slipped away.   60

10   By the time the Bloods settled on their reserve in 1881, Calf Shirt had become a prominent member of the tribe. He was not a chief, for the Many Tumors were then under the leadership of the aged Medicine Calf and a younger brother, Strangling Wolf. But Calf Shirt was an ambitious man and to gain the coveted role of chief, he chose to turn his back on his people and become an informer for the Indian agent.   65
He saw that enough support for a chieftainship would not likely come from his band, but was astute enough to realize the Indian agent needed chiefs who would co-operate in matters of farming and rationing, even if these wishes were not always in the best interest of the tribe.

11   Calf Shirt also knew that Medicine Calf would not live many more years and if   70
outside influence was not used, Strangling Wolf would become sole leader of the band.

12   The warrior's first move took place at the autumn treaty payments in 1884, at a time when Medicine Calf was on his death bed. The agent later explained to his superiors that 'Calf Shirt sat at the pay table with me and through his honesty I was in a position to refuse paying a number of South Peigans representing themselves to   75
be Bloods. Through services rendered, this Indian has got the ill will of all the Blood tribe. . . . I may state that of his own free will he reduced his family three souls.'[2]

13   This statement was based on the government's belief that Indians resorted to the wholesale padding of ration lists, claiming to have more persons in their families than was the fact. This, believed the Indian agent, often was accomplished by borrowing   80
friends' children and dressing them so they would not be recognized during treaty and ration payments.

14   After the death of Medicine Calf in October 1884, Calf Shirt vigorously pursued his plan of action. Three months later, he reported to the agent that white men were selling alcohol to the Bloods in the form of Jamaica ginger, essence and Pain Killer.   85
Then, during the 1885 Riel rebellion, he kept the agent informed of all activities, rumours and gossip among the Bloods, as well as intelligence of any runners or visitors from other tribes. This concentrated program of helping the Indian agent had the desired effect for, in the summer of 1885, Calf Shirt was made a minor chief to replace the deceased Medicine Calf.   90

15   Once appointed, Calf Shirt knew the agent would have a hard time deposing him, so the astute Blood promptly abandoned his policy of co-operation. He had used

---

1 Interview with Jim White Bull, Blood Reserve, 29 Dec. 1995. In author's possession.
2 Letter, Indian Agent William Pocklington to the Indian Commissioner, 30 Sept. 1884. Letter-book, RG-10, 1552: 56, Public Archives of Canada.

the Indian agent for his own advantage and now was prepared to resume a position of prestige among his people.

16   His first opportunity came late in 1886, when the Bloods learned that six of their men had been killed and scalped by Assiniboine Indians in Montana. These included three of Calf Shirt's close relatives. As a ripple of excitement swept through the camps, the once-peaceful Calf Shirt stirred the young people into action. He organized a revenge party of some two hundred warriors, just as he had in the buffalo days, and was prepared to lead them out against their enemy when an autumn snowstorm cut short his plan. Continued cold weather made the raid impractical and before the snows had melted in the spring, the Blood elders had made a peace treaty with their old enemies.

17   In the following winter of 1887–8, Calf Shirt displayed his disregard for the white man's law when he smuggled a supply of whisky onto the reserve from Montana. Then sitting placidly in his tepee, he bragged that the Mounted Police were afraid to arrest him. However, he was wrong and was sentenced to one month in Fort Macleod guardhouse.

18   During these years, Calf Shirt continued to live with his snakes and to turn his remarkable gift into a profitable enterprise. As early as 1881, he was a visitor to Fort Macleod where he collected money for performing tricks with a large snake. On one such visit a local newspaper man wrote that 'Calf Shirt is the snake charmer of the Blood branch and the great Blackfoot nation, and he handles the deadly rattlesnake with the most consummate indifference to the awful absolute death that is contained in its slender fangs. He keeps it coiled round his body next to the skin, inside the shirt, where it lovingly nestles, and anyone who is willing to pay for his curiosity can see him put his hand in and drag the living, writhing death out.

19   'Calf Shirt claims', continued the writer, 'to have some subtle power over snakes and to see him take his present specimen up, she measuring about three feet long, catch it by the neck and cram about eight inches of it, the deadliest reptile in America, head downwards down his throat, is calculated to make the marrow in any man's bones shiver. He also puts it out on the ground and playfully pats it on the back of the head with his fingers, till the snake rattles as if it was performing for the benefit of all the babies in Canada. It is not a pleasant sight for one with weak nerves and who understands what a rattlesnake is.'[3]

20   In 1888, Calf Shirt broke away from the Many Tumors band and, retaining his chieftainship, formed a new band called the Crooked Backs. He and about 40 followers left the main Blood camps on the Belly River and settled on the northern tip of the reserve, just across the river from Lethbridge. The location had two good features for the snake-loving chief, for it was close to the only supply of rattlers on the reserve and was almost on the outskirts of the coal mining town. Calf Shirt soon became friends of the shopkeepers and regularly earned money by performing with his venomous pets.

21   But the chief also had problems, for his camp, being so near the town, was a convenient focal point for prostitution. To discourage this demoralizing practice, the government had forbidden the Indians from entering any white settlements unless they

3 *The Macleod Gazette*, 2 Nov. 1894.

had passes. However, the location of Calf Shirt's camp made it easy for female members of the tribe to slip into town in the evening, or for whites to come out. The situation was observed by the Indian agent who said that 'the authorities in Lethbridge will not allow Indians to stay in town, consequently these Indians having good-looking squaws   140 want to get as near Lethbridge as possible so that they can run back and forth. . . .'⁴

22   To combat the problem, Calf Shirt was appointed a scout for the North-West Mounted Police. During the time he held this position, he fought to keep the undesirables out of his camp and succeeded to some extent in stamping out prostitution. As a scout he also mixed with white people more than any other Blood chief and his   145 facility for handling snakes was enough to grant him respectful attention from his non-Indian audience.

23   One day, when a circus featuring a lady snake charmer came to Lethbridge, Calf Shirt was urged by residents of the town to see the show. He watched the entertainer pick up her de-fanged reptiles then twist them around her body and over her head.   150 Calf Shirt was unimpressed. The townspeople, who crowded the tent to see the Indian's reaction, did not have long to wait, for as soon as the show was over, he nonchalantly pulled a venomous rattler, one of his biggest, out of his shirt and offered it to the charmer. The woman took one look at the beady-eyed reptile, screamed, and fled. Calf Shirt snickered, returned his pet to its resting place, and commented in   155 broken English, 'I gave that pretty white woman something to wear around her neck, but she nearly jumped out of her nice dress to get away from it.'⁵

24   On another occasion, a rancher brought a live rattler into Lethbridge to show the townspeople. The clerk at the Hudson's Bay Company store saw it as a unique attraction, so he bought the reptile and put it on display. But no sooner had the snake   160 been placed in the rudely constructed cage than it escaped and disappeared into a stock of dry goods.

25   Frightened, everyone fled from the store and the clerk did not know what to do until someone suggested Calf Shirt. The scout was summoned and, agreeing on a price for his services, he went into the store, poked around the counters, and finally   165 found the missing reptile curled up in some cotton goods. He picked up the frightened creature and played with it while carpenters hurriedly built a sturdier cage.

26   Calf Shirt's exploits became well known in western Canada, so when plans were made to hold a large Territorial Exhibition in Regina in 1895, the chief received an invitation to attend. Not only was he happy to make the long journey with his pets,   170 but he confided to his friends that the capital city was close to the Sand Hills, so he might have a chance to pick up some new snakes.

27   The exhibition was the biggest ever held in the West. There were two circus tents, agricultural exhibits, rodeo events, and examples of Indian life, past and present. Calf Shirt was depicted as part of the 'pagan' past and delightedly demonstrated   175 his great gift over his snakes.

28   Some people did not believe the performance was genuine and claimed that Calf Shirt's snakes had been defanged. They were convinced of this when they saw the Blood chief put a snake's head in his mouth.

---

4 Indian Agent William Pocklington, monthly report for March, 8 April 1888. Letter-book, RG-10, vol. 1555, Public Archives of Canada.
5 'Byegone Days of the Blackfeet Nation', by Joe Beebe. Manuscript in author's possession.

29   'Calf Shirt told one white man that, if he would give him a dollar he would   180
allow a snake to bite a dog which was standing near,' commented the *Regina Progress*.
'The white man put up the dollar and the Indian immediately made one of the snakes
bite the dog, which died in a few minutes.'[6]

30   Another experience with his snakes occurred at Calf Shirt's home camp when
his sister, the wife of Coming Singing, had a fight with her husband. He had collected   185
their treaty money but being an inveterate gambler, he had lost it and came home with
nothing. In anger, his wife deserted him and when she moved in with Calf Shirt, her
husband asked for her to be sent back. Calf Shirt commented that the woman was not
being forced to stay with him but added, 'if you really want your wife back, you do
as I say.'[7]   190

31   Calf Shirt pointed to a coulee and told the man to ride in that direction until
he found two rattlesnakes together, then to pick the biggest of them and bring it back.
Coming Singing went as directed and soon found the two snakes coiled and ready
to strike.

32   'Don't do that,' he told the reptiles. 'Calf Shirt has sent me to get you.' Coming   195
Singing chewed some sage brush, as he had been instructed, rubbed it on his hands
and as he walked close to the biggest snake he spat some of the mixture on its head.
The creature immediately uncoiled, allowing Coming Singing to pick it up and put it
inside his shirt. There the snake coiled tightly around the body of the frightened
Blood. Riding back to the camp, Coming Singing tried to trot but the jogging made   200
the snake tighten its grip, so he slowed to a walk. By the time he reached the camp,
he was shaking with fear and sweat was trickling down his brow.

33   The chief, gathered with others in front of his tepee, took the snake and praised
his brother-in-law for proving that he truly wanted his wife back. 'You gambled away
your $5.00 treaty money,' he said, 'but I'm a chief and get $15.00. I'll give you $5.00   205
for this deed and tell my sister to go back home with you.'[8]

34   During the latter years of his life, Calf Shirt lived in a small log cabin with his
wives Double Killer and Many Stars. Visitors observed, sometimes with anxiety, the
numerous snake holes under the cabin's log walls and the dusty trails across the
earthen floor. Sometimes, if he felt in a good mood, the chief might whistle to bring   210
one of the reptiles slithering across the room to be with his human brother.

35   After his death in 1901, Calf Shirt was buried on a lonely hill near his camp not
far from Snake Coulee. Soon after, travellers swore that a huge rattler had joined the
pack and liked to lie in the sun near Calf Shirt's grave, just as though he belonged
there. And perhaps he did.   215

1981

---

6 Cited in *The Macleod Gazette*, 23 Aug. 1895.
7 Interview with Jim White Bull, op. cit.
8 Ibid.

QUESTIONS
Reader and Purpose

1. Although Dempsey mentions Calf Shirt's strange power over rattlesnakes in each of the first three paragraphs, he doesn't explain the reasons for this power until paragraph 7. Why not?

2. In dealing at length with Calf Shirt as Indian warrior and leader, Dempsey is attempting to show that Calf Shirt was not a wild, eccentric, romantic young man given to passionate extravagances, but that he was, rather, a sensible and level-headed person who claimed to have had, only once, a vision, a vision that affected the rest of his life. But does Dempsey, in your opinion, provide too much background of this sort? Does it get in the way of the subject of his essay? On the other hand, would it be correct to say that Dempsey's topic is not just Calf Shirt's prowess at handling snakes, but, rather, his life as a whole, of which the snakes are just a small part?

3. What **tone** does Dempsey adopt towards his extraordinary subject? Is there any evidence to show that Dempsey believes in Calf Shirt's vision? that he disbelieves? Or does he simply retell the tale as it was told to him, without in any way indicating his attitude towards it?

4. In his footnotes Dempsey refers to several sources. How do references to such sources affect the reader's attitude towards this essay?

Organization

5. In the first paragraph the author briefly answers several questions: *where? who? when? what?* Do the next two paragraphs provide further answers to these questions, or do they answer other questions?

6. Paragraphs 7 and 8 recount Calf Shirt's vision, and paragraph 9 gives some examples of his power over snakes. However, neither the snakes nor his power over them are mentioned again until paragraph 18. Why not? What is Dempsey doing in paragraphs 10–17?

7. For the most part, this essay follows Calf Shirt's life chronologically, beginning, in the third paragraph, with his birth. However, there are places where the chronological order is either not followed, as in the opening paragraph, or where there is no clear indication of time. Find three or four occasions of this sort, and explain why references to time are unnecessary, or why the time sequence has been rearranged.

8. Could paragraphs 24 and 25 be joined into one paragraph? If they were joined, what would the effect be on the immediate context? on the entire essay?

9. How are the opening and closing paragraphs related? Is a **closing by return** involved here? If not, what would you call this sort of closing?

Sentences

10. Should there be a comma after 'essence' and after 'rumours' in paragraph 14? Or is the comma here optional? Should commas be placed around 'but' in the last sentence of paragraph 6?

11. Is the first sentence in paragraph 4 an **organizing sentence**? Why, or why not? What about the first sentence in paragraph 7? in paragraph 18?

12. In the fourth sentence of paragraph 16, should the comma after 'days' be replaced by a semicolon? Would either mark be correct?

13. Are the first two sentences in paragraph 17 examples of **inversion**? Do you think they are effective sentences? Try to explain your answer.
14. Should the quotation in paragraph 18 be introduced by a colon?
15. 'But' usually functions as a **coordinate conjunction**, a form of **connective**. Is that its function at the beginning of paragraph 21? If not, what other functions does it have?
16. Why is there a comma after 'however' in paragraph 21?

Diction

17. Look up: paradox (5), *trait* (7), *daub* (23), *scorn* (24), *coulee* (28), *travois* (37), *sagebrush* (49), *bidding* (58), *coveted* (64), *astute* (67), *consummate* (114), *inveterate* (186).
18. Why is the word *pagan* enclosed in quotation marks in paragraph 27? What does this say about the author's attitude towards his subject?
19. Identify the **figure of speech** in paragraph 10. Can you find any other places where Dempsey uses **figurative** language?
20. Phrase such as *mortal blow* (32), *ripple of excitement* (97), and *shaking with fear* (202) have, through overuse, become **clichés**. Can you find any others? Do they weaken Dempsey's essay?

POINTS TO LEARN

1. One effective way of introducing a topic is to answer briefly some, or all, of the questions *who? what? where? when? why?*
2. The chronological ordering of an event may be interrupted in order to provide background, to establish reasons, to clarify motives.

SUGGESTIONS FOR WRITING

Even if you have never known a person as unusual as Calf Shirt, you undoubtedly have encountered two or three people who, because of some character trait, struck you as extraordinary, or at least quite unusual.

In an essay of two or three pages (or even more, if you wish), describe this person. Your emphasis should be on what makes this person stand out, but you should not neglect such matters as family history, education, travels, unusual experiences, and so on.

IMPROVING YOUR STYLE

In your essay include

1. an introductory paragraph that briefly supplies some information about the character you have chosen;
2. at least three paragraphs that begin with **organizing sentences**.

Henry David Thoreau

Henry David Thoreau (1817–62), simultaneously both a mystic and a carefully observant 'natural philosopher' (a scientist, in our terms), is best known for *Walden, or Life in the Woods* (1854) and 'Civil Disobedience', a lecture (first published in 1849) in which he firmly voiced his opposition to the Mexican–American War, denouncing the Americans for their approval of slavery. This essay has inspired many activist politicians, from Gandhi to Martin Luther King, Jr.

Thoreau is often regarded as a writer about nature, and indeed there is much observation of the natural world in *Walden* and in such other books as *A Week on the Concord and Merrimack Rivers* (1849), *Cape Cod* (1865), and *A Yankee in Canada* (1866). But Thoreau's primary concern is not the details of nature, however finely he presents them. He is, essentially, a moralist, not a narrow giver of rules but a person for whom moral commitment is the essence of life. The following selection (from *Walden*) may not seem to be moralism. In its literal content it is not. Yet in a more subtle way 'Bubbles in the Ice' illustrates one of Thoreau's most fundamental commitments: to see things whole, to see them as they are, and to be precise and honest about what he sees.

Bubbles in the Ice

The pond had in the mean while skimmed over in the shadiest and shallowest coves, some days or even weeks before the general freezing. The first ice is especially interesting and perfect, being hard, dark, and transparent, and affords the best opportunity that ever offers for examining the bottom where it is shallow; for you can lie at your length on ice only an inch thick, like a skater insect on the surface of the water, 5 and study the bottom at your leisure, only two or three inches distant, like a picture behind a glass, and the water is necessarily always smooth then. There are many furrows in the sand where some creature has travelled about and doubled on its tracks; and, for wrecks, it is strewn with the cases of caddis worms made of minute grains of white quartz. Perhaps these have creased it, for you find some of their cases in the fur- 10 rows, though they are deep and broad for them to make. But the ice itself is the object of most interest, though you must improve the earliest opportunity to study it. If you examine it closely the morning after it freezes, you find that the greater part of the bubbles, which at first appeared to be within it, are against its under surface, and that more are continually rising from the bottom; while the ice is as yet comparatively 15 solid and dark, that is, you see the water through it. These bubbles are from an eightieth to an eighth of an inch in diameter, very clear and beautiful, and you see your face reflected in them through the ice. There may be thirty or forty of them to a square inch. There are also already within the ice narrow oblong perpendicular bubbles about half an inch long, sharp cones with the apex upward; or oftener, if the ice is 20 quite fresh, minute spherical bubbles one directly above another, like a string of beads. But these within the ice are not so numerous nor obvious as those beneath. I sometimes used to cast on stones to try the strength of the ice, and those which broke through carried in air with them, which formed very large and conspicuous white bubbles beneath. One day when I came to the same place forty-eight hours afterward, 25

I found that those large bubbles were still perfect, though an inch more of ice had formed, as I could see distinctly by the seam in the edge of a cake. But as the last two days had been very warm, like an Indian summer, the ice was not now transparent, showing the dark green colour of the water, and the bottom, but opaque and whitish or grey, and though twice as thick was hardly stronger than before, for the air bubbles 30 had greatly expanded under this heat and run together, and lost their regularity; they were no longer one directly over another, but often like silvery coins poured from a bag, one overlapping another, or in thin flakes, as if occupying slight cleavages. The beauty of the ice was gone, and it was too late to study the bottom. Being curious to know what position my great bubbles occupied with regard to the new ice, I broke 35 out a cake containing a middling sized one, and turned it bottom upward. The new ice had formed around and under the bubble, so that it was included between the two ices. It was wholly in the lower ice, but close against the upper, and was flattish, or perhaps slightly lenticular, with a rounded edge, a quarter of an inch deep by four inches in diameter; and I was surprised to find that directly under the bubble the ice 40 was melted with great regularity in the form of a saucer reversed, to the height of five-eighths of an inch in the middle, leaving a thin partition there between the water and the bubble, hardly an eighth of an inch thick; and in many places the small bubbles in this partition had burst out downward, and probably there was no ice at all under the largest bubbles, which were a foot in diameter. I inferred that the infinite number 45 of minute bubbles which I had first seen against the under surface of the ice were now frozen in likewise, and that each, in its degree, had operated like a burning glass on the ice beneath to melt and rot it. These are the little air-guns which contribute to make the ice crack and whoop.

1854

QUESTIONS
Reader and Purpose
1. Is Thoreau observing the ice with an objective, scientific detachment; or is he viewing it impressionistically, projecting his values and emotions into what he sees? Does he do more than passively observe—conduct experiments, say, or take specimens?
2. What assumptions does Thoreau appear to have made concerning his reader's attitude toward nature? What effect do you believe Thoreau wishes to have upon his reader? Does he succeed?

Organization
3. Which **clause** near the beginning of the paragraph serves as a **topic statement**?
4. Thoreau's paragraph is quite long (though this is not unusual; paragraphs tended to be longer in the literary prose of the nineteenth century). What is Thoreau primarily concerned with up to line 11? What shift in topic occurs at that point? There are at least two other places where similar minor turns of thought occur. Identify them.
5. Study the passage from lines 12 to 22 and discuss how Thoreau organizes his discussion of the bubbles.

Sentences

6. Read the two following sentences carefully and decide what principle Thoreau has observed in arranging the sequence of their phrases and clauses:

   (a) 'I sometimes used to cast on stones to try the strength of the ice, and those which broke through carried in air with them, which formed very large and conspicuous white bubbles beneath.' (22–5)

   (b) 'Being curious to know what position my great bubbles occupied with regard to the new ice, I broke out a cake containing a middling sized one, and turned it bottom upward.' (34–6)

7. Why is this revision less effective than Thoreau's sentence?

   Revision: You find that the greater part of the bubbles are against the under surface of the ice (though at first they appear to be within it), if you examine the ice closely the morning after it freezes, and that more are continually rising from the bottom. . . .

   Thoreau: 'If you examine it closely the morning after it freezes, you find that the greater part of the bubbles, which at first appeared to be within it, are against its under surface, and that more are continually rising from the bottom. . . .' (12–15)

8. In the clause in lines 19–20, to what is 'cones' **in apposition**?

Diction

9. Look up: *coves* (2), *quartz* (10), *Indian summer* (28), *opaque* (29), *cleavage* (33), *middling* (36), *lenticular* (39), *inferred* (45).
10. Find specimens of Thoreau's diction that suggest the exact scientific eye. Find others that suggest a more impressionistic, emotionally coloured vision.
11. In several places Thoreau uses **similes** and **metaphors**. Point these out and consider what purpose he probably intended them to serve and whether or not they succeed.

POINTS TO LEARN

1. Exactness of detail is vital to objective description.
2. When possible, organize sentences to reflect the order of perception or of thought.

SUGGESTIONS FOR WRITING

Look closely at some commonplace natural object and describe it as exactly as you can: a stalk of grass or grain, a mackerel, a pumpkin, an ear of corn, a gladiolus.

IMPROVING YOUR STYLE

In your description include

1. a sentence containing an **appositive**;
2. a long sentence (25–30 words minimum) in which the sequence of elements (that is, the words, phrases, clauses) exactly follows the order of events;
3. two metaphors and two similes.

PAUL HEMPHILL

Paul Hemphill (1936–) is a journalist whose methods, like those of John McPhee (see pp. 235–45), exemplify what is loosely called the 'New Journalism'. He has published articles in a number of magazines (*Cosmopolitan, Life, Sport, True*) and is the author of many books, among them *The Nashville Sound: Bright Lights and Country Music* (1970), *Long Gone: A Novel* (1979), *The Sixkiller Chronicles* (1985), *The Heart of the Game: The Education of a Minor-League Ballplayer* (1996), and *Wheels: A Season on NASCAR's Winston Cup Circuit* (1997). His most recent book is *Nobody's Hero* (2002).

    The Good Old Boys (1974), from which the following essay is taken, is a collection of pieces about interesting Southerners (Hemphill is from Alabama), some famous, some once-famous, and some relatively obscure. But all are variants of a type known in the South as 'the good old boy', a regionalism difficult to translate. Hemphill quotes a definition from Tom Wolfe's 'The Last American Hero' that describes the qualities of the good old boy: 'He has a good sense of humour and enjoys ironic jokes, is tolerant and easygoing enough to get along in long conversations at places like on the corner, and has a reasonable amount of physical courage. . . .' On the whole, Hemphill admires the good old boy, but not uncritically. In this portrait of an enterprising funeral director named H. Raymond Ligon Hemphill shows both the type and its manifestation in one individual. And notice that he shows, he does not tell; he lets his subject speak and act for himself.

Welcome to the Death Hilton

> *Show me the manner in which a nation or a community cares for*
> *its dead, and I will measure with mathematical exactness the tender*
> *sympathies of its people, their respect for the laws of the land, and*
> *their loyalty to high ideals.*
>
>   —Gladstone

1   'Wife found that quote somewhere, typed it up and gave it to me. Been carrying it around ever since. Believe in it. Ray Ligon's motto, don't you see.' Reverently rereading it to himself, H. Raymond Ligon smiles at the card through black horn-rimmed glasses, stuffs the bulging billfold back into his hip pocket, swings his dusty cowboy-booted feet onto the dishevelled desk, and sways back deeply in a swivel 5 chair. Everything is right on this soft summer morning at the Woodlawn Cross Mausoleum and Funeral Home, Inc., on the edge of downtown Nashville. Grieving families sit quietly in several of the ten 'repose rooms', waiting for services to begin. Sombre music drones through the carpeted hallways. Ligon's army of funeral directors and embalmers and secretaries and janitors goes about its business inside, while 10 outside two dozen labourers preen the grassy undulating 192 acres representing the final resting place for some 100,000 souls. But the true centre of activity is behind the main building, where dozens of hard-hatted construction workers swarm over a hulking square concrete-and-steel edifice, now rising five storeys out of the ground like one of the Pyramids, soon to be the third tallest building in Nashville. Ray Ligon's 15 dream. A twenty-storey mausoleum, cold storage for 129,500 bodies.

2   'Yes, sir,' he is saying, 'Ray Ligon is one of the most fortunate people in the funeral business, and I'll tell you why.' It is only nine o'clock, but already he has been at work for nearly three hours, and the construction on the mausoleum is going so well that he is in an ebullient mood, his bright yellow shirt and gaudy boots and dyed   20 black hair and leathery sunburned face belying his 70 years. 'Hard work, and treating people right. I remember one time this lady called and said she'd had a vision that her husband was buried at my place with his head downhill. Said she couldn't sleep for thinking about it. I told her to come on out, and I got two lawn chairs and we sat there under a tree while the workers dug. When they put a level on the coffin, the   25 bubble was straight up. She appreciated what Ray Ligon did for her, don't you see. Every human being is entitled to our love and respect, and to a decent farewell.'

3   Ligon's chief engineer on the mausoleum project opens the door to the cluttered panelled office. He is wearing a bright yellow hardhat, and holding a bill of lading in one hand. 'Got a load we need you to sign for, Mr Ligon.'   30

4   'What we got here?'

5   'One load of marble.'

6   'Stuff from Italy?'

7   'Yes, sir.'

8   'Fine. You know what to do with it.' Ligon scrawls his signature on the bill. 'Keep   35 'em rolling.'

9   That business done ('Sent my engineer all the way to Italy just to find the right marble for the crypts'), Ligon sways back again and races off on another monologue about himself and his plans. While he talks, a 76-year-old retired newspaperman named Sewall B. Jackson—reedy, chain-smoking, ruined voice, pencil-thin mustache,   40 mod high-heeled shoes and tacky checkered suit—takes shorthand notes for the book he will write on Ligon's life. 'If it's never been done before, I thrive,' Ligon is saying. 'Night funerals. Funeral home and cemetery combined. Mausoleum. Ray Ligon likes to do sensible things that've never been done before. I tell 'em everything else in this world has changed, why not the funeral business. Know what I'm thinking about   45 doing next?' Sewall Jackson's pen poises. He looks up at Ligon with an expectant conspiratorial grin. 'Helicopters. Here's a loved one at the airport. Died in Chicago, wanted to be buried here. Put the remains on a helicopter, fly over here and land on top of the mausoleum, bring him down on the elevator to the repose room. Save time, save money. I can get a helicopter for $18,000, as cheap as a fancy hearse. Got to keep   50 thinking all the time, don't you see. . . .'

———

10   For the time being, before he goes airborne, Raymond Ligon's latest scheme will suffice in solidifying his claim as the most innovative, if not controversial, funeral director in America. The largest mausoleum in the country had been one of four floors at California's Forest Lawn, but when Ligon announced his audacious design for the   55 Woodlawn Cross Mausoleum he left quite a target for any other entrepreneur who might care to shoot for the record. At a cost of $12 million, the mausoleum will provide, Ligon boasts, 'a burial as fine as the Taj Mahal'. The name Cross Mausoleum comes from the shape of the building, its four wings converging in the centre, the foundation and immediate grounds consuming only seven of the 300 acres held by   60

Ligon. Each floor will have bright carpet, air conditioning, elevators, piped music, cushy sofas, and seven tiers of crypts beginning at floor level with the most expensive (the 'Westminster' for couples buried side by side) and ending at the ceiling with the least expensive vault (the 'Heaven Level'). There will be nighttime funerals ('working folks can't make it in the daytime'), visiting at all hours, and lounging downstairs in 65 the Garden of Jesus: a natural underground spring spilling water into a corner rock pile, a clear fiberglass roof allowing natural sunlight to feed the flowers, and a 'tomb of Jesus' made of rocks brought over from Jerusalem.

11   The reaction to Ligon's plans ranged from utter disbelief to jollity. 'This is one time I'm sort of glad I can't see,' said a blind Nashville singer named Ronnie Milsap. Joked 70 Johnny Carson on his television talk show: 'How would you like to be the elevator operator on duty about three in the morning, and you're sitting on the sixth floor, and you hear somebody say, "*Down*"?' One magazine referred to it as 'the Death Hilton', and a Nashville newsman no longer surprised by anything Ligon does guessed that 'as soon as he finishes this one he'll go out and build a chain of the damned things across the 75 country.' Buyers of space in the mausoleum were hard to find at first, Southerners being more traditional about such matters as death and religion than most, but an aggressive sales campaign ('Keeping up with kings, queens, and presidents costs less than you think,' read one brochure) soon brought into the coffers some $2 million in 'Pre-need' sales—the backbone of the burial business—so Ligon could begin construction. When 80 the first five floors were topped out and put into service this fall (for the ribbon cutting, a state official landed atop the building in a helicopter), there remained some skeptics, one of them a disgruntled former Ligon business associate: 'I don't see any necessity for a 20-storey mausoleum, except that it'll get Raymond a lot of publicity. He contends that land in America is going to run out. I disagree. You can go three miles outside Nashville, 85 on an old farm, and find plenty of land for plenty of cemeteries.'

12   To Ligon, though, the availability and price of land in America today make the argument for mausoleum burial overpowering. 'We just can't afford to keep on burying folks on these shady little hillsides,' he says, pointing out that he will bury the same number in a mausoleum covering seven acres that he has buried on the 192 90 developed acres of his cemetery. 'I know what they say about the cemetery business, that you buy by the acre and sell by the inch, but you can't even make any money that way these days. Some of the land I paid $700 an acre for in the 1930s is worth $35,000 today, and some adjoining property just brought $55,000 an acre. We're sitting right next to the busiest intersection in Nashville now. I'm just not going to 95 develop another acre. It's mausoleums from now on. Ground burial is going to go out.' Armed with arguments, Ligon can go on and on about the desirability—for himself and for the client family—of mausoleum burial: it is dryer, less expensive (no need for a tombstone, vault, or elaborate coffin), offers lower maintenance costs (two people will be able to take care of the mausoleum, while 28 are required for the cemetery 100 grounds), and 'if there was a strike, why me and the preacher could get on the elevator and do the burying ourselves.' Ligon does not mention that 130,000 crypts sold at an average $2,000 would turn his $12 million investment into $260 million, and that air space comes free.

13   'Let's go across the road for a minute and see the old place, Mr Jackson.' Clapping 105
his own personal yellow hardhat on his head, Ligon strides through a maze of corridors until he bursts out into the bright morning sun, quickly slipping behind the wheel
of the luxury pickup truck he prefers to drive. Gliding over the smooth paved lane
leading to the main entrance, he points straight ahead across busy Thompson Lane to
a squat two-storey concrete building with the world MAUSOLEUM discreetly printed on 110
a green awning which shades the entrance. It was his first mausoleum—and probably
the first of any size in the South—and today, seven years later, its 3,500 crypts are just
about taken up. 'I told 'em I wanted it soft and beautiful like a living room, not harsh
and cold,' Ligon says as he steps into the air conditioning and waves a hand over the
bright carpeting and the deep sofas. A woman is vacuuming, her machine drowning 115
out the soft music, and Ligon asks her to stop when he sees that several people—most
of them old—are sitting around, apparently visiting family crypts.
14   'Mr Ligon.' Coming Ligon's way, his eyes red and bloated, is a retired Army
colonel who has lost his entire family during the past 18 months, the last a son killed
in a skyjacking. The man says, 'I just wanted to thank you.'   120
15   'What for, Colonel Giffe?'
16   'For this place you got here.'
17   'Everything's all right, then.'
18   'It's wonderful. Just wonderful. Well, you know what I mean. My wife, she sat
right there on that divan. She knew she was going. But she wasn't horrified by this 125
place. No, sir. Another thing, I can come visit with her even if it's snowing.'
19   Ligon nods to some of the others and makes a quick tour. 'Here's my first wife,'
he says, pointing to a crypt. The place is cool and quiet and eerie, in spite of the flashy
colours and deep carpet. Here and there against the walls are small tables adorned
with plastic flowers. On one of the tables is a stack of index cards and a note inviting 130
visitors to 'leave word so we can acknowledge your visit'. One card has already been
used. 'Dear Lela,' says a laborious scrawl. 'Ethel and Norma came by to see you. We
miss you so much.' Beside the note is a tiny framed picture of the dead woman.

———

20   The burial business has changed very little in the decade since the publication
of Jessica Mitford's scathing book *The American Way of Death*, still regarded as the 135
definitive work on the subject. (Who, for that matter, can forget the grotesqueries in
the movie made of Evelyn Waugh's *The Loved One*?) Mitford gets to the point on the
very second page of the opening chapter: 'Gradually, almost imperceptibly, over the
years the funeral men have constructed their own grotesque cloud-cuckooland where
the trappings of Gracious Living are transformed, as in a nightmare, into the trappings 140
of Gracious Dying.' About 1 per cent of America dies each year, leaving the disposal of
some 2 million bodies to 22,000 'funeral directors' (not 'undertakers', please) who do
a gross of $1.8 billion each year. The competition is mean and often bitchy, the object
of the hunt usually a grieving widow suddenly forced to make her first major financial
decision within hours, and this fall the Federal Trade Commission announced an 145
investigation into 76 District of Columbia funeral homes—tantamount to a national
study—following numerous complaints about inflated prices and the selling of
unneeded services. In the burial business today, as strongly as ever, 'cremation' is a

dirty word (35 per cent of the dead in England are cremated, only some 60,000 a year
in the United Sates). Indeed, semantics is important in the business: 'grief therapy' and   150
'memory pictures' and 'slumber room' are the ABCs of the burial salesman's language.
Talk about everything but death. A hole in the ground is a hole in the ground. *It's the
last chance you will have to do something for your loved one . . . Now here is a nice casket, fit
for a man of his stature . . . Oh, by all means, you'll want fresh flowers . . . For the memory
picture, I would suggest a dark wool suit and a bowtie . . . It's going to be a nice funeral, I'm*   155
sure of that . . .

21   Sales, then, is the most important aspect of the business. 'They say Ray Ligon
is a great salesman,' says Ligon, 'but he knows anybody can sell a couple if they love
each other.' The head of Woodlawn's 15-man sales force is Ligon's 34-year-old stepson, John Spivey, a handsome favourite at the Tennessee statehouse, who recently   160
received a six-year appointment to the state's Youth Advisory Commission. When he
dies, he says, somebody will simply pull out a file in the business office at Woodlawn
and it will all be there: choice of casket, names of pallbearers, number of the crypt in
the mausoleum, and so forth. 'I remember this young guy whose wife had died,' says
Spivey. 'Just before they closed the lid on her, he picked up his four-your-old daughter   165
and leaned her over and said, "Kiss your mother goodbye." A lot of people go hysterical at a funeral. You have all kinds. I don't see any reason why that should happen;
any reason why it should be a hot, agonizing ordeal. It should be planned, together,
in advance.'

22   This 'pre-need' selling is Spivey's responsibility, and he wraps his arguments   170
around the low-key, sensible, pragmatic trappings of, say, a life insurance agent. 'The
funeral director doesn't have to put pressure on a couple, the family does that,' he
says. 'A funeral is the third largest investment you make in your life, behind a car and
a house. You going to let your brother-in-law do it? It's all a process of education, like
my juvenile job. I just tell them the straight true story and put it in an honest, believ-   175
able, attractive package.' At Woodlawn, one price covers all: coffin, hearse, police
escort, flowers, 'open-and-close' grave charges, and so forth. The price can vary
greatly, depending on such choices as gravesite and coffin, but Spivey says an average
burial in the ground there runs around $2,500. In the new mausoleum, however, he
says he 'can do one' for $1,600. Woodlawn will also sell you the coffin, more than a   180
dozen styles of them being on display in a sales room at the funeral home, and for the
mausoleum there is a $495 Ligon-designed bier called the 'cross repose', which is the
cheapest way of all to go. 'We don't back the hearse up to the door,' says Spivey, 'we
just tell them the facts. Pre-need is the way you stop the high cost of dying.' Ray
Ligon, his stepson says with reverence, 'is the greatest teacher who ever lived.'   185

---

23   The funeral business is all Herschel Raymond Ligon has known since his birth
in 1903 to the owner of the local funeral home in Lebanon, one of those lovely little
middle Tennessee towns about 30 miles east of Nashville. When he graduated from
high school ('All I've got is that diploma and a Dale Carnegie course'), he became a
partner in Ligon & Sons Funeral Home, doing everything from embalming to direct-   190
ing services. 'The first service I ever held, I was 24 years old,' he recalls. 'A logger had
been killed on the job and was so poor they were having to bury him out back of the

house in the garden, don't you see. We fixed him up nice and took him over there, but there wasn't a preacher or any music. An old lady pulled me aside and said, "I'll sing a song if you'll read some scripture." The next day my father got a preacher to 195 teach me how to lead a service, and I was in business.'

24   Ligon was too adventurous to stick around Lebanon forever, and his chance at much bigger things came during the Depression when a large holding company in Nashville went into bankruptcy. In addition to insurance, real estate, and a false-teeth factory, the group held a 40-acre cemetery in Nashville. One of the attorneys repre- 200 senting the creditors had been a high school classmate of Ligon's, so Ligon was hired as a trustee at $35 a week ('That's when folks felt lucky to make a dollar a day') and charged with disposing of the cemetery to pay off a $110,000 tax bill. He soon became an expert on the cemetery business in America—visiting major ones like Forest Lawn in Hollywood on fact-finding excursions—and when it came time to put 205 the cemetery up on bids, Ligon decided he wanted it. His bid for $90,000 was the only one submitted, so he took over Memorial Park and prefixed Woodlawn to its name and began building an empire.

25   Accustomed to checking into the office at daylight, Ligon quickly became a national figure in the funeral industry and a financial power to be reckoned with in 210 Nashville. Bit by bit he bought up surrounding land, some of it for as little as $700 an acre, ultimately acquiring a package of 300 acres. Stressing 'pre-need' sales to a growing sales force, he was able to get his hands on money and put it to his own use long before it was needed to service his clients. With the funds he began acquiring other cemeteries in the Nashville area and claiming endless 'firsts' in the region: the 215 first crematorium, the first funeral home–and–cemetery operation under one roof, the first night funeral services, the first weddings in the funeral home chapel, the first previously all-white cemetery opened to blacks. That Ray Ligon knows how to come up with cash when necessary is never questioned around Nashville. 'One time I needed some capital,' he says, 'so I announced plans for a white 25-foot "Tower of 220 Memories" across the road. I got 450 people to put up $10 each in exchange for their name on a bronze plaque. Me and two Negroes built it in no time.' Finally, seven years ago, he raised his first mausoleum.

26   Today Ligon lives an active life. At one time or another in the past he has had his hands in many pies—a bronze works, a concrete vault factory, a half-dozen ceme- 225 teries, a finance company, a downtown office building—but has divested himself of most of these so he can concentrate on his dream mausoleum. His two sons are well-set now—one operates the Mount Olivet cemetery in Nashville, the other a bank in Lebanon and a tourist attraction in Gatlinburg called Christus Gardens—leaving Ligon and his second wife (a high-powered cemetery entrepreneur in her own right 230 before they married) alone in a roomy white brick ranch house, set on a wooded knoll across from the rising mausoleum, of a simplicity belying his estimated net worth of some $10 million. Except when he is on brief visits to central Florida, overseeing a real estate development there, he starts his day with a 6:30 a.m. meeting with con-struction engineers and spends the rest of it swinging deals or hanging around the 235 construction site. 'He comes up with the ideas,' says the current Mrs Ligon, 'and we what you call "implement" them.' Says Ligon of his standing in the community: 'You know who criticizes me? Other funeral directors. You think there might be a little jealousy there?'

27   The man on the street in Nashville may hold little more than passing awe for a 240 man audacious enough to build a skyscraper cemetery, but there is a tight corps of others whose emotions toward Ligon run from begrudging respect to outright hostility. 'He can easily differentiate between the person who needs the services of a pious Bible-quoter and the one who needs a drink,' says Nat Caldwell, a veteran reporter for the *Nashville Tennessean*. Says a young ex-banker who once wrote a 30-page report on 245 Ligon's financial empire: 'It was so complex, if there was any hanky-panky going on you couldn't find it.' Says an embittered former associate who claims he once lost $15,000 in a cemetery development scheme engineered by Ligon: 'Every time I get to thinking about the bastard, my angina starts acting up. I wouldn't speak to him if I saw him on the street.' Even his enemies, however, respect his drive. 'If Raymond 250 Ligon stayed straight', says one, 'he'd be the hottest thing in America.'

28   The nearest Ligon has been to serious trouble was in the early 1960s when he became involved in the National Cemetery Development Corporation, which eventually sued him and his sons for $240,000 in damages on the charge that 'transactions . . . resulted in diversion of funds to the Ligons'. NCDC was organized in 1958 255 by a dozen or so Nashville businessmen, with plans to develop cemeteries and allied businesses all over the nation. As soon as its formation was announced, Ligon offered his services as an expert in the field and was promptly named president. More than $1 million was raised in a public stock sale during the first four months, the major partners kicking in as much as $30,000 each, and in the beginning all was happiness 260 and light. 'People bought because of what they knew about Woodlawn, because Ligon was obviously successful,' says one of the original partners, Jim Bulleit, now a candy manufacturer in Nashville. 'We finally got around to going to Raymond Ligon to find out who he was.' Over the first three years the corporation lost some $300,000, bringing about Ligon's 'resignation' as president. Finally, in 1963, claiming that Ligon and 265 his sons were raking money off the top for themselves and doing little else for the corporation, the NCDC filed suit. The NCDC lies dormant today, the suit still tabled somewhere in court, and the embittered partners seem to have little heart to continue fighting. 'Hell,' says one, 'our attorney moved off to Florida and won't even return my calls.' The publicity did little for Ligon, for when he tried to give a farm to his Church 270 of Christ the church gave it right back on the grounds that it didn't want to get involved. 'But the man has good lawyers,' says reporter Caldwell, 'and he always protects his flanks.' Indeed, when the Securities Exchange Commission showed an interest in Ligon and the NCDC it was shut out of any investigation because Ligon had seen to it that only Tennesseans bought stock in the group. 275

---

29   Late in the afternoon, curious to see what sort of progress the engineers have made during the day, Ligon invites a visitor to ride with him to the top of the mausoleum and check out the work. The dark elevator groans and clangs as it rises from the wet and musty ground floor before finally bursting into the sparkling summer sunlight. Looking like one of the construction workers himself, hardhat and all, Ligon 280 waves a hand at the two dozen men and asks the foreman to call the men together. Off in the distance can be seen Ligon's rambling house, sitting serenely in the cluster of shade trees beyond the grassy acres of his cemetery. The spread is dotted with tiny oases Ligon calls his 'Biblical Gardens', each featuring a statue of a character from the Bible standing amid a garden of flowers. 'Boys,' Ligon is saying, flopping his hardhat 285 back and forth on his head, 'this gentleman here is writing a story on us. *New York Times*. About the biggest newspaper in the world. Wants to find out how excited you are about having a part in this, don't you see. Y'all talk to him, now.' It was an awkward moment. The young ones suppressed giggles. The foreman babbled something he thought Ligon wanted to hear. 'Let's go downstairs and relax,' says Ligon, getting 290 back onto the elevator and going down a couple of floors.

30   He also has a conference room, which he hopes to entice various civic and business groups to use for their meetings. 'Want to get 'em used to coming out to Woodlawn,' he says. On the walls are pictures of Ligon with beasts he once shot on safari, and one of a group of middle-aged women he once threw a party for on a whim. 295 'Bought every one of 'em, 15 of 'em, a $165 dress,' he is saying. 'Silly. But they had fun.'

31   'You hunt?' he is asked.

32   'Used to, all the time. Quit now. Got to where I didn't want to kill anything anymore.'

33   For several minutes, he rambled on about life and death and his own machi- 300 nations. You see one cremation, he says, you'll never believe in it ('Reminds you of Hitler and the Jews'). He may lease out the rest of his land, he says, and go mausoleum all the way ('Government's going to get 30 per cent of the price if I sell the land, anyway'). On the first floor of the mausoleum, he says, 'we are already burying beautifully.' People make jokes, he says, about funeral directors ('Call me the white Southern 305 planter'), but you have to laugh with them and forget it. What would he be, he is asked, if he had it to do over?

34   'Evangelist,' he says. 'I never got to be what you'd call religious until I was about 15 or 16. Just went to church and slept up until then. Now I give 10 per cent a year to the church. Believe in it now. But I got to thinking about these evangelists, and me. Got 310 the same things in common. Trying to console people, don't you see. *Help* people. And here I got this way with people, know how to talk 'em into things.' He bends over in his chair to knock some mud off his cowboy boots. 'Yes, sir, an evangelist is what I'd want to be. Instead of working with their bodies, work with their souls, don't you see.'

1974

QUESTIONS
Reader and Purpose

1. In journalism a distinction is made between fact and comment. Facts are the province of the reporter, commentary of the editorial writer or columnist. Is Hemphill acting primarily as a reporter in this essay or as a commentator?

2. Because a reporter sticks to facts and offers no overt comments on them does not mean, of course, that he makes no judgments or offers no angle of vision from which the facts may be interpreted. But he effects such judgments tacitly by the

careful selection and arrangement of details. For example, what details in the first paragraph influence our perceptions of and response to Ligon?

3. How do you think Hemphill feels about his subject? Does he succeed in communicating his feelings to you?

4. The essay begins with an epigraph from the liberal statesman William Gladstone, a prime minister of Great Britain in the late nineteenth century. It serves Ligon as a credo, justifying his life's work. Might it cast a different light upon Ligon's career?

5. Who is the 'visitor' referred to at the beginning of paragraph 29? What is the relationship of this visitor to the passive construction 'he is asked' in paragraphs 31 and 33? What, in short, is the author doing here, and why does he use this approach?

Organization

6. Hemphill divides his essay into seven sections. What shifts of subject do these involve? Give a brief title to each.

7. Like some short-story writers Hemphill moves back and forth between present and past. On the one hand, we follow Ligon through a day's activities. Which of the seven sections are primarily concerned with this? Identify within them the words or phrases establishing the chronological structure.

8. On the other hand, some sections are primarily (though not exclusively) concerned with what in fiction is called 'exposition', the background information we need in order to understand what is happening in the present. Identify these sections. How do they enhance our understanding of Ligon and the funeral business?

9. What detail brought to our attention in the opening paragraph is repeated in the closing? What value has such repetition as a means of ending an essay? In this case, does the detail also provide an implicit authorial comment?

10. What is the **topic sentence** of paragraph 11? How is it supported? What is the topic of paragraph 20? How is paragraph 9 tied to the material that precedes it?

Sentences

11. Hemphill is fond of the intrusive sentence, an independent construction that is simply inserted into the middle of another statement without being syntactically connected to it. Here is an example: 'That business done ("sent my engineer all the way to Italy just to find the right marble for the crypts"), Ligon sways back again and races off on another monologue about himself and his plans' (37–9). Hemphill prevents confusion by using parentheses or dashes to signal that the enclosed construction is absolute (not grammatically connected to the main statement). While such constructions are not syntactically integrated with the sentences that enclose them, they are, of course, related in idea. How does the parenthetical remark bear upon the writer's point? Find other examples of such intrusive sentences and explain their relevancy.

12. Does this technique of the intrusive sentence make Hemphill's style sound formal and literary, or relaxed and conversational? Do you think it would be appropriate for, say, a term paper in a history course?

13. Point out the **parallel** elements in the very first sentence of the essay and also in the sentence in lines 64–8.

Diction

14. Look up: *Taj Mahal* (58), *coffers* (79), *eerie* (128), *tantamount* (146), *pragmatic* (171), *bier* (182), *dormant* (267), *musty* (279), *entice* (292), *machinations* (300–1).
15. As fully as possible explain the meanings of the following phrases: *dishevelled desk* (5), *scathing book* (135), *the definitive work* (136), *grotesque cloud-cuckooland* (139), *the trappings of Gracious Living* (140), *wooded knoll* (231).
16. What are the **etymologies** of *mausoleum* (16), *crypts* (38), *brochure* (79), *divested* (226), *entrepreneur* (230), *audacious* (241), *evangelist* (308)?
17. Why are the following less effective than Hemphill's words: 'floats' for 'drones' (9), 'care' for 'preen' (11), 'hums' for 'groans and clangs' (278), 'muttered' for 'babbled' (289)?
18. Explain how these **pointers** prepare us for the writer's turn of thought: 'though' (87), 'then' (157), 'say' (171). Suppose that 'though' were replaced by 'however' or 'nevertheless': how would the **tone** alter?
19. In what sense is the title of this essay **ironic**?

POINTS TO LEARN

1. Reporters may 'stick to the facts' yet subtly impose an interpretation upon the facts.
2. The intrusive sentence gives a **colloquial** flavour to writing and is appropriate to relaxed, conversational style.

SUGGESTIONS FOR WRITING

'Welcome to the Death Hilton' may be read as a criticism of the funeral business. Write a commentary upon Hemphill's essay from this point of view, discussing the more important failings that he tacitly suggests funeral directors are guilty of and supporting your points by evidence from Hemphill's text.

IMPROVING YOUR STYLE

In your essay include

1. two examples of intrusive sentences—that is, independent statements related in idea but not in syntax to the sentence that encloses them. Punctuate the intrusive sentences with dashes or parentheses;
2. two cases of parallelism.
3. these **connective** words to link sentences to what precedes them: *though*, *then*, *say*.

DAVID BERGEN

David Bergen (1957–) is a high-school teacher who published his first book in 1993, *Sitting Opposite My Brother*, a collection of short stories. His novel *A Year of Lesser* (1996) was named by the *New York Times* as a Notable Book of 1997; this was followed by another novel, *See the Child* (1999). He has also contributed articles and stories to such publications as *Saturday Night*, *Prairie Fire*, and the *Journey Prize Anthology*, and he won the Canadian Literary Award for best short story in 2000. His work has been widely anthologized and broadcast on the CBC. He lives in Winnipeg with his family.

Lucy in the Sky

1 The graduation for the high school where I teach took place in Winnipeg on the last day of June at the Immanuel Pentecostal Church on Wilkes Avenue. There were 271 graduates. Lucy Young was the second-last to cross the stage. Her face was pale against her dark gown; the gold tassel of her mortarboard banged against her left eye. She shook it away and accepted her diploma. Slid off the stage.   5

2 When Lucy was in my English class, she wrote a piece called 'Why I am a Liar'. She said that lies were more interesting than the truth. She said that she was duplicitous, no doubt about that, not out of meanness but out of kindness: she was trying to save others pain. And she was trying to save herself. 'Besides, Mr Bergen,' she wrote, 'you don't want to know what I really think.'   10

3 And yet, Lucy went out of her way to tell me what she thought. She loved drugs. She had researched many different kinds: ecstasy and its nasty cousin, Special K; heroin, grass, acid, mushrooms. She knew their compositions, side effects, uses, dangers. Of course Lucy believed she was lucky and that for her, there was no danger. And so far she has been right. She has no interest in anything to do with needles. She has 15 read *Junky*, by William Burroughs, and every pamphlet put out by the Alcohol and Drug Addictions Foundation of Manitoba. She thinks she is safe.

4 One time, for an assignment on 'personal experiences', she wrote about a lazy afternoon when she and some friends called up Noah, who was known as a 'people's dealer' because he sold not only to the elite but to kids as well. They ended up at a 20 loading dock off Portage Avenue, along with fifty other kids. Some were boarding, some hacking. Lucy wanted pot but rumour had it the dealer only had acid. It was spring and, as Lucy wrote, 'there's nothing better than tripping outside under a blue sky.' Still, she wanted some pot so she leaned into the car's rear window and asked Noah if he could spare some of his personal stock and give her a five-bucker.   25

5 In her essay, Lucy continued: 'So he eyed a five-bucker for me. It struck me as really nice of him. Quietly we left the scene and Noah with it and we went and smoked our tiny pathetic five-bucker. The evening seemed quiet after that. Noah was on my mind. I wanted to go back and see him. Ask him what it was like. I wanted to know the guy who sat so peacefully in the back seat cutting up acid. To me he was 30 the greatest guy in world.'

6   Lucy met Noah a few more times. She adored his hands and his mouth and the way he smelled when he was high. He was sixteen and sexy. Lucy said Noah was like a clear smooth lake with lots happening under the surface.

7   I went to the school's graduation dinner and dance because I had had a partic- 35 ularly good group of students that year and I was reluctant to let them go. I saw Lucy between the dinner and the dance. She was sitting with her boyfriend, and after she'd introduced us she leaned towards me and confessed with a bright smile that she had dropped some acid on the way to the dance but that it wasn't working and so had taken another hit between the stuffed chicken and the Fantasy Torte and now she 40 couldn't wait to start dancing. She took a quick breath.

8   There was a hum of voices. Hundreds of girls tottered about on high heels, their bare backs dark and beautiful, hanging onto boys dressed like men, in tuxes, tight ties, patent-leather shoes. Lucy was wearing a black knee-length dress, black hose, black heels, black false eyelashes, and a platinum-blonde wig. With the wig and her 45 white face people told her she looked like Uma Thurman. She said she liked being Uma. When she threw back her head and laughed, her red lips opened to the yawning ceiling, she was Uma. The music started and smoke spread out over the dance floor. The DJ played Britney Spears and Tupac.

9   She didn't dance. Not yet. She rubbed one thigh with her left hand as if she 50 were itchy or concerned about something.

10   'Are you okay?' I asked her.

11   'I'm alert. Whatever. I'm on the cusp of cognizance. My mom's coming to pick me up later. You know, Safe Grad. I must behave.'

12   Lucy's mother is a doctor. Her father is a philosophy professor. Lucy can be 55 whatever she wants to be. She's smart. She can out-argue anybody. She's quick with her tongue and writes a good essay. She once did a piece called 'The Fetishes of J.D. Salinger'. *The Catcher in the Rye* is her favourite book. She hears how people speak, and she's skeptical, very skeptical for an 18-year-old. Her favourite Burroughs line is, 'I have never regretted my experience with drugs.' She thinks she will live a long time 60 and be married to one man all her life. She wants children, wants to live a good middle-class life.

13   I left the dance about 1 a.m., long before the end. I saw Lucy at the table alone with her boyfriend, leaning into him. Her white head was lying in that space between his shoulder and neck. Like a bowl made just for her.   65

1999

QUESTIONS
Reader and Purpose

1. What do you think is the author's purpose in this essay: to describe a high-school student physically and psychologically? to describe the high-school drug scene? to warn parents of the lying and hidden drug-taking of their apparently virtuous children? to describe how drug-taking by today's high-school students isn't the vicious habit it's so often made out to be? all of these? all of these and something else?

2. The essay's title, as well as playing on the title of the Beatles song supposed to be about taking LSD, is a reference to Lucy's comment in paragraph 4 that 'there's nothing better than tripping outside under a blue sky.' Does this title reflect the author's optimism about Lucy's situation? Or is the author being **ironic**?

3. The third paragraph, which describes some aspects of Lucy's drug habit, ends with the comment that 'She thinks she is safe.' Would this comment also apply to paragraph 12?

4. Does the final paragraph leave the reader feeling optimistic about Lucy, or pessimistic?

Organization

5. Why does the author end his introductory paragraph with such a brief sentence? Is it effective as the conclusion to the paragraph?

6. The key point of this essay, that Lucy 'loved drugs', isn't made until the second sentence of paragraph 3. What does the author do before this?

7. Is the conclusion to this essay the last paragraph, or the last two paragraphs?

Sentences

8. What is the function of the colon in the third sentence of paragraph 2? Would a dash work just as well?

9. In the last sentence of paragraph 2 could the expression 'she wrote' be placed anywhere else in the sentence without causing awkwardness? Apply this same question to the phrase 'of course' in the fifth sentence of paragraph 3.

10. Note the length of the four sentences in paragraph 7. In each sentence what is the relationship between the length of the sentence and the feelings and thoughts being expressed?

Diction

11. Look up: *duplicitous* (7–8), *elite* (20), *pathetic* (28), *cusp* (53), *cognizance* (53), *fetishes* (57), *skeptical* (59).

12. In the first sentence of paragraph 4 is the phrase 'people's dealer' spelled correctly, or should it be 'peoples' dealer'? Justify your answer.

13. Explain the verb tenses in the first sentence of paragraph 7. Why is one of these verbs in a different tense from the other two?

POINTS TO LEARN

1. A sentence consisting of several consecutive clauses joined by coordinate conjunctions can produce an effect of rushing, of breathlessness.

2. Irony is more effective when it is understated.

SUGGESTIONS FOR WRITING

Write a description of a person you know who has a drug habit, whether it be taking legal drugs (sleeping pills, pain killers, alcohol) or illegal ones. You may want to include physical description, but focus on the person's character, trying to show the nature of the habit and how it is affecting the person's thinking and acting.

IMPROVING YOUR STYLE

1. Use two or three quotations from the person you are describing.
2. Make at least one ironic comment.

CHARLES WILKINS

Born in Toronto, Charles Wilkins has lived in various towns throughout Ontario, as well as in the Bahamas and in Israel. In 1991 he moved to Thunder Bay as a writer-in-residence at the Thunder Bay Public Library; he has lived in that city ever since. Some of his books are *Hockey, the Illustrated History* (1985); *Old Mrs Schmatterbung and Other Friends*, a book for young people (1989); *Breakaway: Hockey and the Years Beyond* (1995); with James Duplacey, *Forever Rivals: Montreal Canadiens, Toronto Maple Leafs* (1996); and *The Circus at the End of the Earth: Travels with the Great Wallenda Circus* (1998). His latest book is *A Wilderness Called Home: Dispatches from the Wild Heart of Canada* (2001).

Above the Line

1   There is something crazily exhilarating about skimming across dense boreal forest, barely above the treetops, in the glass bubble of a helicopter, at close to 200 kilometres an hour. You dive over headlands, hover over waterfalls, track along the edge of cliffs. Or you just howl straight ahead, spilling perpetually into the next IMAX of jackpine and spruce.   5

2   I was a passenger on such a flight in mid-February, with a pilot named Bob Latimer, one of a handful of helicopter jockeys whose job it is to make regular inspections of the Trans-Canada Pipeline.

3   Unofficially, every flight Bob makes is also an alfresco inquiry into the stupendous variety of wildlife that wanders regularly into the 40-metre-wide clearing that is   10 maintained along the pipeline as it snakes through the forests of northwestern Ontario. Our own flight to Vermilion Bay, some 300 kilometres west of our starting point at Thunder Bay Airport, took in bobcats, foxes, rabbits, deer, porcupine, whisky-jacks, and hawks. Somewhere west of Dryden we witnessed a standoff between a ravaged old moose swinging a five-foot rack and a trio of rib-skinny wolves. Near Ignace, we saw   15 five or six ravens—'the bikers of the bird world', as they are sometimes called up here—noshing aggressively on what was left of a slaughtered deer.

4   It is a secret known only to half-a-dozen helicopter pilots that, for a couple of weeks in late winter, the pipeline is both the cause and the site of one of the most interesting ecological quirks in the Canadian wilderness. The gist of it is that pipeline   20 gas, which is warmed as it passes through pressure-boosting stations, radiates a constant low-level heat that creates a pathway of gently warmed soil running some 5,000 kilometres from Alberta's eastern border, across the prairies, Ontario, and part of Quebec, to the border of Vermont. In some places the line is just a single pipe; in others it can be as many as four pipes side by side.   25

5   At a point late in February or early March, when the landscape is still in the deep freeze but the climate has begun to soften, each pipe's heat is sufficient to melt a narrow snow-free corridor bordered by thick ice and snow and (seen from the air) running endlessly off in both directions. This metre-wide strip of false spring, with its winter-wasted plant life and mosses—and, quite quickly, its first new shoots— 30 becomes a lifeline for herbivores famished from their winter privations. They arrive by the thousands—mice and voles to tear at the roseships and cones, rabbit and deer to gobble mouldy salads of last year's broadleaves and grasses. Black bears—at least those with a local education—emerge dopey from hibernation and go immediately to the pipeline to reinvigorate their stomachs with old browse.   35

6   But on the pipeline, as elsewhere, a free lunch has its price. Inasmuch as the long thin table is a smorg for the rabbits and deer, so these animals quickly become a banquet for equally opportunistic predators.

7   The smallest prey disappear without a trace, in the beaks of owls and hawks, or bleeding into the jaws of foxes. The largest become feeding stations that draw a 40 succession of meat-eaters and onmivores, ranging from wolves, lynx, foxes, even bears, down to whisky-jacks and ravens, and in some cases, less likely diners such as martens, mink, and skunks. And, of course, maggots.

8   On our return journey, Bob speculated on the 'connectedness' of this intense axis of life and death stretching west toward the prairies, east and south into the hard- 45 wood forests and farmland. 'It certainly gives new meaning to the term food chain,' he said.

9   In the months to come, the animals will continue to visit the pipeline—not for the waterlogged leftovers they now crave, but for good long feeds on the grasses and berries that, by July, will be thick on the artificial edgelands. By that time, the remains 50 of the late-winter drama will be little more than a scattering of sun-dried bones and hair, and only the ravens will be interested.

10   On this day in February, however, when survival is less certain, a dozen such ravens, already at work, glance skyward, screaming warnings at the metallic bird that appears suddenly above their carrion grounds, thwacking its wings and raining 55 downwind on their conclave.

11   Only when it is clear that we are not about to intrude do they drop their beaks and bury their faces in the vivid red mess of what appears to be a hip of venison.

1999

QUESTIONS
Reader and Purpose

1. You have undoubtedly seen film footage, either in movies or in documentaries, taken from a low-flying helicopter. Would you agree that the experience is 'crazily exhilarating'? Or was it for you something else entirely?

2. This essay might have been included elsewhere in this book: in the *Narration* section or in the Illustration section of *Exposition*. Might it also have been included in the *Persuasion* section? Can a descriptive essay be thought of as persuasive?

ORGANIZATION

3. Of this essay's eleven paragraphs, three have only one sentence and three others have only two sentences—six short paragraphs out of eleven. What does this tell you about the author's method of organization? Or is there an entirely different reason for the short paragraphs?
4. How effective is the **organizing sentence** of the second paragraph?
5. Is the **topic sentence** of this essay the first sentence of paragraph 3? Explain why it is, or is not.
6. Is the **transition** between paragraphs 6 and 7 awkward, or too obvious? Should these two paragraphs really be one? Or was the author quite right in structuring these paragraphs as he did?
7. How does paragraph 6 act as a transition between paragraphs 4 and 5 and paragraphs 7–11?

Sentences

8. The second sentence of the first paragraph is an example of **asyndeton**. How else could you write this sentence?
9. In his description of the fight between the moose and the wolves in paragraph 3, does the writer reveal on which side his sympathies lie?
10. In paragraphs 4 and 5 does the author use any **balanced** sentences? Does he use any **periodic** ones?
11. Would it be correct to say that the author uses more **simple sentences** than any other kind, but that his simple sentences appear complex because he often uses modifying phrases and **interrupted movement**? Or does he in fact use both **compound** and **complex** sentences?

Diction

12. Look up: *exhilarating* (1), *boreal* (1), *alfresco* (9), *noshing* (17), *ecological* (20), *quirks* (20), *gist* (20), *herbivore* (31), *omnivore* (41), *carrion* (55), *conclave* (56).
13. What does the author mean by the phrase *spilling perpetually into the next IMAX of jackpine and spruce* (4–5)? Would the phrase be clearer if you substituted another word for 'perpetually'?
14. At the end of paragraph 3 the author describes the ravens as 'noshing aggressively' on the remains of a deer. Is 'noshing' appropriate in this context? If you feel that it is not, explain why and then find a better word.
15. One of the ways in which descriptive prose is different from other modes, such as exposition, or narration, or persuasion, is that **imagery** is normally more common to this mode than to the others. What images particularly struck you as memorable? Can you explain why?

POINTS TO LEARN

1. Good descriptive writing often rests on details that are perceived accurately and precisely.
2. Modifying phrases can add texture and depth to a sentence.

SUGGESTIONS FOR WRITING

Describe a vivid experience in nature that you have witnessed. If you have had an adventure as unusual as that of Charles Wilkins, fine, but you could also deal with a much more common experience, such as a fight between a magpie and a crow, a cat sneaking up on a robin, a dog trying to catch a gopher, a puppy running up to greet an old tomcat, a squirrel trying to take over a birdfeeder from the blue jays, etc. Narration will play a part here, certainly, but your essay (5–8 paragraphs) is to be mainly descriptive. Let your imagination have some fun with imagery, but at the same time you will have to keep it under control: you must convince your reader of your honesty as a writer of description.

IMPROVING YOUR STYLE

1. Use a short paragraph as the transition between several paragraphs before and after it.
2. Write at least two simple sentences to which you add—logically—several phrases.

SID MARTY

Sid Marty (1944–) is an Alberta writer and musician. His first narrative book, *Men for the Mountains* (1978), is an engrossing account of his adventures during the years he spent as a park warden in Banff, Yoho, and Jasper national parks. His latest book, *Switchbacks: True Stories from the Canadian Rockies* (1999), develops many of the same themes. He has published two other non-fiction books, *A Grand and Fabulous Notion* (1984) and *Leaning on the Wind* (1995), which describes his present life on a ranch in the mountains of southwestern Alberta. He has also published three books of poetry, including *Nobody Danced with Miss Rodeo* (1981), as well as numerous articles.

In the Eye of the Wind

1   Aspen Valley, Alta, is not a place on the map and if I had my way, it never would be. We came here 16 years ago, fleeing the developers who are still busily paving paradise around Banff and Canmore. Our place lies at the mountain foot, tucked in behind an apron of southwestern Alberta's montane foothills. It is a country ruled by the raunchy chinook, the famous warm wind of winter, the creator wind that made   5 the buffalo prairie. So winters are a potlatch of temperature extremes. In the course of 24 hours, it may switch from a subpolar cold to a chinook spring-in-January, followed by a bobsled run back down the thermometer, greased by an arctic front. The tenderfoot treads ice at dawn, mud at noon, and diamond ice again, with cutting teeth, by midnight. As a hillman, I winter on a slant of ice, and some days I cannot   10 stay on my feet without wearing corked boots.

2   On January 15 this year the ruling God of Chinook country wound my anemometer up to 150 kilometres per hour; it gusted to 209 kilometres per hour near the summit of the Crowsnest Pass. It boomed down the chimney like a stoned jug

band from hell. It hailed poplar boughs on Smudgepup, my little diesel truck. On the   15
highways leading to Pincher Creek and the Crowsnest Pass, it overturned semitrailer
trucks and scattered their cargo over the banks of the Crowsnest River. Chinook eats
the snow; the crystals that it blows up from the ground evaporate into the maw of the
wind when the temperature is warm enough.

3   I went trudging up the valley to see what other Chinook calling cards there   20
were. The valley is a u-shaped channel between 1,700-metre-high sandstone ridges;
it was carved out by a glacier's tongue during the last Ice Age. The ridges were spiked
more recently (in geological terms) with 500-year-old limber pine, called bullpine
hereabouts, while their coulees are graced with a species of massive Douglas fir, some
more than 300 years of age. The evergreen forest and groves of aspen are home to   25
deer, bobcats, and occasional bears, and also herds of Herefords and Charolais.

4   I know my valley in every undulation, so when I found a thick branch of
bullpine lying in a treeless meadow, I knew it had been torn from a tree on the skyline and hurled 500 metres laterally through the air. This is a tree that loves the rocky
ridgetops, and seems to savour the buffets of the chinook. But though it is an old res-   30
ident, it is a teenager compared to the chinook, a foehn-type wind conjured up by the
mountains themselves some 70 million years gone by.

5   The miracle is that more trees are not uprooted by the 'perfect hurricane' as
Alexander Mackenzie called the chinook on his famous passage to the Pacific in 1793.
More than anything, this five-needled pine, fiercely determined to draw sustenance   35
from solid stone and moving air, symbolizes for me the spirit of these foothills. On
the ridgetops, it adapts to the wind by becoming a krummholz, or dwarf tree, spreading its branches out in ground-hugging fans that trail out to the northeast with the
prevailing wind. Its gnarled limbs and generous cones will one day be as revered in
the public's eye as the famous bonsai of Japan, which it rivals, to my mind, in beauty.   40
When I picture it, I always glimpse through its breezy boughs a distant view of that
humble white house where we raised our sons, built long ago by a wise old rancher,
who found a pocket of calm where a family might flourish, even in the jealous eye of
the creator wind itself.

1996

QUESTIONS

Reader and Purpose

1. If, as Sid Marty says in his first paragraph, he doesn't want Aspen Valley, Alberta,
   ever to be on a map, why does he describe the nearby countryside in a magazine
   article? Wouldn't this be unwanted publicity?
2. After having lived near Aspen Valley (or is he actually in the village, or town, or
   merely in the general area?) for 16 years, the author clearly seems in no hurry to
   leave. Given the extremes of nature that he describes, why does he continue to live
   there? Does he clearly give reasons, or must the reader infer them?
3. *Men for the Mountains* is a fascinating collection of true stories from the years
   Marty spent as a warden in Jasper, Banff, and Yoho national parks. Do you find any
   evidence in this essay of Marty's past as an outdoorsman?

Organization

4. Where does the author first tell us what his subject is?
5. What method of development does Marty follow throughout: cause–effect? spatial? chronological? something else? Does he follow the same method in each paragraph?
6. What connection is there between Alexander Mackenzie and the chinook mentioned at the beginning of paragraph 5, and the points mentioned in the essay's final sentence?

Sentences

7. In the first sentence of paragraph 2 what is the function of the semicolon? Could it not just as well be replaced by 'and'? Could the same not be said of the semicolon in the last sentence of this paragraph? If you believe that the semicolons are stylistically preferable, explain why.
8. In the second paragraph 'it' occurs five times. In each case what is its grammatical function? What **parallel** use has the author made of it? How has he varied its use?
9. Can you find any examples of **interrupted movement**? of **periodic sentences**? of **balanced sentences**? As the result of your answers to these three questions, what conclusions can you draw about Marty's sentence structure?

Diction

10. Look up: *montane* (4), *potlatch* (6), *tenderfoot* (9), *anemometer* (13), *maw* (18), *coulees* (24), *undulation* (27), *laterally* (29), *savour* (30), *buffets* (30), *foehn* (31), *sustenance* (35), *gnarled* (39).
11. When Marty refers, in his second sentence, to 'paving paradise', what famous song of the 1960s is he referring to? If you can answer this, do you think that someone who can't answer is at a disadvantage in interpreting the essay? If you don't recognize the reference, how did the phrase strike you?
12. Explain the **imagery** in the second sentence of paragraph 2.
13. In the first sentence of paragraph 3 what other word could Marty have used instead of 'trudging'? Or is his choice the best one for that context?
14. Paragraph 3 contains the phrases *carved out by a glacier's tongue*, *ridges were spiked*, *coulees are graced*. How are these images appropriate for what the author is describing?
15. Choose any two or three images that you find especially striking or remarkable. Can you explain why they impress you?

POINTS TO LEARN

1. Creating vivid, effective imagery takes work and imagination.
2. In order to be able to describe well, you must be able to observe keenly.

SUGGESTIONS FOR WRITING

Living in Canada, you have certainly experienced some extremes of nature. Describe, in an essay of 4–6 paragraphs, one such event that you will remember for a long time. After you have decided on the experience you want to describe, consider the various methods of development you could choose and settle on the one best suited to the topic. For instance, a description of an extraordinary rainfall could be arranged mainly in a cause–effect manner, a description of a horrid blizzard could be developed chronologically, that of a drought by both chronology and cause–effect, etc.

IMPROVING YOUR STYLE

1. Use at least three images that are colourful and unusual.
2. Come to a conclusion about how the experience you went through affected you or those close to you.

NARRATION

At its simplest, narrative writing is much like descriptive. As description develops by analyzing a physical object or scene into its parts and arranging these in space, so narration develops by analyzing a story into the events that compose it and arranging these in time. In its more highly evolved forms, such as novels and short stories, narration obviously includes more than a mere reporting of events. The novelist will elaborate a finely drawn plot and pay as much attention to the psychology of the characters as to what they do. However, such literary refinements are beyond the usual needs of the composition student. Here we are concerned with a simpler type of narration that restricts itself to action and does not probe deeply into the motives of the characters. Such narrative writing is often adapted to the needs of exposition. Thus the historian must frequently relate stories, and the essayist depends on narration to develop illustrations and anecdotes.

For whatever it is used, the essence of good narration is organizing the story into beginning, middle, and end. Most often these parts are arranged in their natural order. On occasion they may be inverted, so that the story opens with the end and then turns back to the beginning and middle. A film that starts with its main character already on death row and then relates for ninety minutes the circumstances that brought him to such an unenviable position is an example of this kind of flashback technique. But the brief narrative used in exposition is best organized in the usual chronological order.

In how much detail these parts are developed will depend, of course, on the writer's intention and the space he has available. Long or short, however, all narration is highly selective. No reporter or historian can afford to tell us everything. He must choose only those details relevant to his purpose and reject those that are not. The criteria for selecting those details will be based on his reason for telling the story—the meaning he sees in it.

This meaning is what the writer tries to communicate to the reader. It is here that beginners most often fail. The inexperienced writer is likely to step forth before he knows where he is going, before he has determined in his own mind exactly what meaning the story has. It is hardly surprising, then, that his narrative turns out like a poorly mixed cake, lumpy with unrelated details and without the flavour of meaning. Even when he has understood its significance, the beginner is likely to commit another error: this is being afraid to let the story stand on its own legs. We have all suffered the would-be comedian who is so concerned with pointing out why his story is funny that he kills its humour. The meaning of a narrative, like the point of a joke, is best left to the reader, for a well-written narrative clearly implies its meaning. The writer's task, especially in brief narration, is to concentrate on the story itself. If he knows from the outset why the story is important, and if he has selected and arranged its details accordingly, he will communicate its meaning.

Margaret Atwood

Margaret Atwood (1939–), one of the most highly respected fiction writers of our time, was born in Ottawa and educated at the University of Toronto, Radcliffe College, and Harvard. Her novels include *The Edible Woman* (1969), *Surfacing* (1972), *Bodily Harm* (1981), *The Robber Bride* (1993) and *The Blind Assassin* (2000); her short stories are collected in several books, *Dancing Girls* (1977), *Bluebeard's Egg* (1983), and *Wilderness Tips* (1991), among others; and important collections of her poetry are *The Animals in that Country* (1968), *The Journals of Susanna Moodie* (1970) and *Morning in the Burned House* (1995). Atwood's literary criticism can be found in *Survival: A Thematic Guide to Canadian Literature* (1972), a book that has been both influential and controversial; *Second Words* (1982), in which the following essay is included; and *Strange Things: The Malevolent North in Canadian Literature* (1995). Her latest books are *Good Bones and Simple Murders* (2001), a collection of parables, fairy tales, monologues, etc., with her own illustrations; and *Negotiating With the Dead: A Writer on Writing* (2002), based on the Empson Lectures she delivered at Cambridge University in 2000.

Atwood won the Governor General's Award for her second collection of poetry, *The Circle Game* (1966), and also for her novel *The Handmaid's Tale* (1985). She later won the Booker Prize for her novel *The Blind Assassin* (2000). She has an international reputation solidly based on more than forty books, and she has won more than fifty national and international awards. In the essay below, which is both analytical and personal, readers should be alert for Atwood's characteristic irony and her sardonic humour.

True North

> *Land of the silver birch,*
> *Home of the beaver,*
> *Where still the mighty moose*
> *Wanders at will,*
> *Blue lake and rocky shore,*
> *I will return once more;*
> *Boom-diddy-boom-boom*
> *Boom-diddy-boom-boom*
> *Boo-OO-oo-oo-oom.*
>
> —Archaic Song

1   We sang this once, squatting around the papier-mâché Magic Mushroom in the Brownie pack, while pretending to be wolves in Cub Scouts, or while watching our marshmallows turn to melted Styrofoam on the ends of our sticks at some well-run, fairly safe summer camp in the wilds of Muskoka, Haliburton, or Algonquin Park. Then we grew up and found it corny. By that time we were into Jean-Paul Sartre and 5 the lure of the nauseous. Finally, having reached the age of nostalgia, we rediscovered it on a cassette in The Children's Book Store, in a haunting version that invested it with all the emotional resonance we once thought it possessed, and bought it, under the pretence of giving our children a little ethnic musical background.

2   It brought tears to our eyes, not for simple reasons. Whales get to us that way 10
too, and whooping cranes, and other things hovering on the verge of extinction but
still maintaining a tenuous foothold in the world of the actual. The beavers are doing
all right—we know this because they just decimated our poplars—but the mighty
moose is having a slimmer time of it. As for the blueness of the lakes, we worry about
it: too blue and you've got acid rain.   15

3   *Will* we return once more, or will we go to Portugal instead? It depends, we
have to admit, partly on the exchange rate, and this makes us feel disloyal. I am,
rather quixotically, in Alabama, teaching, even more quixotically, a course in Canadian
literature. Right now we're considering Marian Engel's novel *Bear*. Since everything in
Canada, outside Toronto, begins with geography, I've unfolded a large map of Ontario 20
and traced the heroine's route north; I've located the mythical house of the book
somewhere on the actual shore of Georgian Bay, northern edge. I've superimposed a
same-scale map of Alabama on this scheme, to give the students an idea of the distances. In the north, space is larger than you think, because the points of reference are
father apart.   25

4   'Are there any words you came across that puzzled you?' I ask.

5   *Blackfly* comes up. A large black fly is proposed. I explain blackflies, their
smallness, their multitude, their evil habits. It gives me a certain kick to do this: I'm
competing with the local water moccasins.

6   *Mackinaw.* A raincoat? Not quite. *Loon. Tamarack. Reindeer moss. Portage. Moose.* 30
Wendigo.

7   'Why does she make Lucy the old Indian woman talk so funny?' they ask. Lucy,
I pointed out, is not merely Indian but a *French-speaking* Indian. This, to them, is a
weird concept.

8   The north is another country. It's also another language. Or languages.   35

---

9   Where is the north, exactly? It's not only a place but a direction, and as such its
location is relative: to the Mexicans, the United States is the north, to Americans
Toronto is, even though its on roughly the same latitude as Boston.

10   Wherever it is for us, there's a lot of it. You stand in Windsor and imagine a line
going north, all the way to the pole. The same going south would end up in South 40
America. That's the sort of map we grew up with, at the front of the classroom in
Mercator projection, which made it look even bigger than it was, all that pink stretching on forever, with a few cities sprinkled along the bottom edge. It's not only geographical space, it's space related to body image. When we face south, as we often do,
our conscious mind may be directed down there, towards crowds, bright lights, some 45
Hollywood version of fame and fortune, but the north is at the back of our minds,
always. There's something, not someone, looking over our shoulders; there's a chill at
the nape of the neck.

11   The north focuses our anxieties. Turning to face north, face the north, we enter
our own unconscious. Always, in retrospect, the journey north has the quality 50
of dream.

---

12   Where does the north begin?

13   Every province, every city, has its own road north. From Toronto you go up the 400. Where you cross the border, from here to there, is a matter of opinion. Is it the Severn River, where the Shield granite appears suddenly out of the earth? Is it the sign 55 announcing that you're halfway between the equator and the North Pole? Is it the first gift shop shaped like a wigwam, the first town—there are several—that proclaims itself The Gateway to the North?

14   As we proceed, the farms become fewer, more desperate-looking, the trees change their ratios, coniferous moving in on deciduous. More lakes appear, their 60 shorelines scraggier. Our eyes narrow and we look at the clouds: the weather is important again.

15   One of us used to spend summers in a cottage in Muskoka, before the road went in, when you took the train, when there were big cruise ships there, and matronly motor launches, and tea dances at the hotels, and men in white flannels on 65 the lawns, which there may still be. This was not just a cottage but a Muskoka cottage, with boathouse and maid's quarters. Rich people went north in the summers then, away from cities and crowds; that was before the cure for polio, which has made a difference. In this sort of north, they tried to duplicate the south, or perhaps some dream of country life in England. In the living room there were armchairs, glass- 70 fronted bookcases, family photos in silver frames, stuffed birds under glass bells. The north, as I said, is relative.

16   For me, the north used to be completely in force by the Trout Creek planing mill. Those stacks of fresh-cut lumber were the true gateway to the north, and north of that was North Bay, which used to be, to be blunt, a bit of an armpit. It was beef- 75 sandwich-on-white-bread-with-gravy-and-canned-peas country. But no more. North Bay now has shopping malls, and baskets of flowers hanging from lampposts above paving-stone sidewalks downtown. It has a Granite Club. It has the new, swish, carpeted buildings of Laurentian University. It has gourmet restaurants. And in the airport, where southbound DC-9s dock side by side with northbound Twin Otters, 80 there's a book rack in the coffee shop that features Graham Greene and Kierkegaard, hardly standard airport fare.

17   The south is moving north.

18   We bypass North Bay, which now has a bypass, creeping southerliness, and do not go, this time, to the Dionne Quints Museum, where five little silhouettes in black 85 play forever beside an old log cabin, complete with the basket where they were packed in cotton wool, the oven where they were warmed, the five prams, the five Communion dresses.

19   Beyond North Bay there is a brief flurry of eccentricity—lawns populated with whole flocks of wooden-goose windmills—and then we go for miles and miles past 90 nothing but trees, meeting nothing but the occasional truck loaded with lumber. This area didn't used to be called anything. Now it's the Near North Travel Area. You can see signs telling you that. Near what, we wonder uneasily? We don't want to be near. We want to be far.

20   At last we see the Ottawa River, which is the border. There's a dam across it, two dams, and an island between them. If there were a customs house it would be here. A sign faces us saying *Bienvenue*; out the back window there's one saying *Welcome*. This was my first lesson in points of view.

21   And there, across the border in Quebec, in Témiscaming, is an image straight from my childhood: a huge mountain made of sawdust. I always wanted to slide down this sawdust mountain until I finally did, and discovered it was not like sand, dry and slippery, but damp and sticky and hard to get out of your clothes. This was my first lesson in the nature of illusion.

22   Continue past the sawdust mountain, past the baseball diamond, up the hill, and you're in the centre of town, which is remarkable for at least three things: a blocks-long public rock garden, still flourishing after more than 45 years; a pair of statues, one a fountain, that look as if they've come straight from Europe, which I think they did; and the excellent, amazingly low-priced hamburgers you can get at the Boulevard Restaurant, where the decor, featuring last year's cardboard Santa Claus and a stuffed 23-pound pike, is decidedly northern. Ask the owner about the pike and he'll tell you about one twice as big, 45 pounds in fact, that a fellow showed him strapped to the tailgate of his van, and that long, too.

23   You can have this conversation in either French or English: Témiscaming is a border town and a northern one, and the distinctions made here are as likely to be north–south as French–English. Up in these parts you'll hear as much grumbling, or more, about Quebec City as you will about Ottawa, which is, after all, closer. Spit in the river and it gets to Ottawa, eh?

24   For the north, Témiscaming is old, settled, tidy, even a little prosperous-looking. but it's had its crises. Témiscaming is the resource economy personified. Not long ago it was a company town, and when the company shut down the mill, which would have shut down the town too, the workers took the unprecedented step of trying to buy it. With some help they succeeded, and the result was Tembec, still going strong. But Témiscaming is still a one-industry town, like many northern towns, and its existence is thus precarious.

25   Not so long ago, logging was a different sort of business. The men went into the woods in winter, across the ice, using horse-drawn sledges, and set up camp. (You still come across these logging camps now and then in your travels through the lakes, abandoned, already looking as ancient as Roman aqueducts; more ancient, since there's been no upkeep.) They'd cut selectively, tree by tree, using axes and saws and the skills that were necessary to avoid being squashed or hacked. They'd skid the trees to the ice; in the spring, after the ice went out, there would be a run down the nearest fast river to the nearest sawmill.

26   Now it's done with bulldozers and trucks, and the result is too often a blitzed shambles; cut everything, leave a wreck of dead and, incidentally, easily flammable branches behind. Time is money. Don't touch the shoreline though, we need that for tourists. In some places, the forest is merely a scrim along the water. In behind it's been hollowed out.

27   Those who look on the positive side say it's good for the blueberries.

———

28   Sometimes we went the other way, across to Sudbury, the trees getting smaller and smaller and finally disappearing as you approached. Sudbury was another magic 140 place of my childhood. It was like interplanetary travel, which we liked to imagine, which was still just imagination in those days. With its heaps of slag and its barren shoulders of stone, it looked like the moon. Back then, we tell the children, before there were washer-dryers and you used something called a wringer washer and hung the sheets out on something called a clothesline, when there weren't even coloured 145 sheets but all sheets were white, when Rinso white and its happy little washday song were an item, and Whiter than White was a catch phrase and female status really did have something to do with your laundry, Sudbury was a housewife's nightmare. We knew people there; the windowsills in their houses were always grey.

29   Now the trees are beginning to come back because they built higher 150 smokestacks. But where is all that stuff going now?

———

30   The Acid Rain Dinner, in Toronto's Sheraton Centre, in 1985. The first of these fund-raising events was fairly small. But the movement has grown, and this dinner is huge. The leaders of all three provincial parties are here. So is the minister of the environment from the federal government. So are several labour leaders, and several high- 155 ranking capitalists, and representatives of numerous northerly chambers of commerce, summer residents' associations, tourist-camp runners, outfitters. Wishy-washy urban professionals who say 'frankly' a lot bend elbows with huntin', shootin', fishin', and cussin' burnt-necks who wouldn't be caught dead saying 'frankly'. This is not a good place to be overheard saying that actually acid rain isn't such a bad thing 160 because it gets rid of all that brown scum and leeches in the lake, or who cares because you can water-ski anyway. Teddy Kennedy, looking like a bulky sweater, is the guest speaker. Everyone wears a little gold pin in the shape of a rain drop. It looks like a tear.

31   Why has acid rain become the collective Canadian nightmare? Why is it—as a 165 good cause—bigger than baby-seal bashing? The reasons aren't just economic, although there are lots of those, as the fishing-camp people and foresters will tell you. It's more than that, and cognate with the outrage aroused by the uninvited voyage of the American icebreaker *Polar Sea* through the Northwest Passage, where almost none of us ever goes. It's territorial, partly; partly a felt violation of some area in us that we 170 hardly every think about unless it's invaded or tampered with. It's the neighbours throwing guck into our yard. It's our childhood dying.

32   On location, in summer and far from the glass and brass of the Sheraton Centre, we nervously check our lakes. Leeches still in place? Have the crayfish, among the first to go, gone yet? (We think in terms of 'yet'.) Are the loons reproducing, have you 175 seen any young? any minnows? How about the lichen on the rocks? These inventor-ies have now become routine, and that is why we're willing to fork out a hundred

dollars a plate to support our acid-rain lobbyists in Washington. A summer without loons is unthinkable, but how do you tell that to people who don't know it because they've never had any to begin with?

180

———

33   We're driving through Glencoe, in the Highlands of Scotland. It's imposing, as a landscape: bleak, large, bald, apparently empty. We can see why the Scots took so well to Canada. Yet we know that the glens and crags round about are crawling with at least a thousand campers, rock climbers, and other seekers after nature; we also know that, at one end of this glen, the Campbells butchered the MacDonalds in the   185 seventeenth century, thus propelling both of them into memorable history. Go walking here and you'll find things human: outlines of stone fences now overgrown, shards of abandoned crofts.

34   In Europe, every scrap of land has been claimed, owned, re-owned, fought over, captured, bled on. The roads are the only no-man's-land. In northern Canada,   190 the roads are civilization, owned by the collective human *we*. Off the road is *other*. Try walking in it, and you'll soon find out why all the early traffic here was by water. 'Impenetrable wilderness' is not just verbal.

35   And suppose you get off the road. Suppose you get lost. Getting lost, elsewhere and closer to town, is not knowing exactly where you are. You can always ask, even   195 in a foreign country. In the north, getting lost is not knowing how to get out.

36   You can get lost on a lake, of course, but getting lost in the forest is worse. It's tangly in there, and dim, and one tree does begin to look remarkably like another. The leaves and needles blot up sound, and you begin to feel watched: not by anyone, not by an animal even, or anything you can put a name to, just watched. You   200 begin to feel judged. It's as if something is keeping an eye on you just to see what you will do.

37   What will you do? Which side of the tree does moss grow on, and here, where there are ferns and the earth is damp, or where it's dry as tinder, it seems that moss grows everywhere, or does not grow at all. Snippets of Boy Scout lore or truisms   205 learned at summer camp come back to you, but scrambled. You tell yourself not to panic: you can always live off the land.

38   Easier said than done, you'd soon find. The Canadian Shield is a relatively foodless area, which is why even the Indians tended to pass through it, did not form large settlements except where there was arable land, and remained limited in numbers.   210 This is not the Mekong delta. If you had a gun you could shoot something, maybe, a red squirrel perhaps; but if you're lost you probably don't have a gun, or a fishing rod either. You could eat blueberries, or cattail stems, or crayfish, or other delicacies dimly remembered from stories about people who got lost in the woods and were found later in good health although somewhat thinner. You could cook some reindeer moss,   215 if you had matches.

39   Thus you pass on to fantasies about how to start a fire with a magnifying glass—you don't have one—or by rubbing two bits of stick together, a feat at which you suspect you would prove remarkably inept.

40   The fact is that not very many of us know how to survive in the north. Rumour   220 has it that only one German prisoner of war ever made it out, although many made it out of the actual prisoner-of-war camps. The best piece of northern survival advice is: *Don't get lost.*

---

41   One way of looking at a landscape is to consider the typical ways of dying in it. Given the worst, what's the worst it could do? Will it be delirium from drinking salty 225 water on the high seas, shrivelling in the desert, snakebite in the jungle, tidal waves on a Pacific isle, volcanic fumes? In the north, there are several hazards. Although you're probably a lot safer there than you are on the highway at rush hour, given the odds, you still have to be a little wary.

42   Like most lessons of this sort, those about the north are taught by precept and 230 example, but also, more enjoyably, by cautionary nasty tale. There is death by blackfly, the one about the fellow who didn't have his shirt cuffs tight enough in the spring and undressed at night only to find he was running with blood, the ones about the lost travellers who bloated up from too many bites and who, when found, were twice the size, unrecognizable, and dead. There is death from starvation, death by animal, death by 235 forest fire; there is death from something called 'exposure', which used to confuse me when I heard about men who exposed themselves: why would they intentionally do anything that fatal? There's death by thunderstorm, not to be sneered at: on the open lake, in one of the excessive northern midsummer thunderstorms, a canoe or a bush plane is a vulnerable target. The north is full of Struwwelpeter-like stories about peo- 240 ple who didn't do as they were told and got struck by lightning. Above all, there are death by freezing and death by drowning. Your body's heat-loss rate in the water is twenty times that in air, and northern lakes are cold. Even in a life jacket, even holding on to the tipped canoe, you're at risk. Every summer the numbers pile up.

43   Every culture has its exemplary dead people, its hagiography of landscape mar- 245 tyrs, those unfortunates who, by their bad ends, seem to sum up in one grisly episode what may be lurking behind the next rock for all of us, all of us who enter the territory they once claimed was theirs. I'd say that two of the top northern landscape martyrs are Tom Thomson, the painter who was found mysteriously drowned near his overturned canoe with no provable cause in sight, and the Mad Trapper of Rat River, 250 also mysterious, who became so thoroughly bushed that he killed a Mountie and shot two others during an amazing wintertime chase before being finally mowed down. In our retelling of these stories, mystery is a key element. So, strangely enough, is a presumed oneness with the landscape in question. The Mad Trapper knew his landscape so well he survived in it for weeks, living off the land and his own bootlaces, eluding 255 capture. One of the hidden motifs in these stories is a warning: maybe it's not so good to get *too* close to Nature.

44   I remember a documentary on Tom Thomson that ended, rather ominously, with the statement that the north had taken him to herself. This was, of course, pathetic fallacy gone to seed, but it was also a comment on our distrust of the natural 260 world, a distrust that remains despite our protests, our studies in the ethics of ecology, our elevation of 'the environment' to a numinous noun, our save-the-tree campaigns. The question is, would the trees save us, given the chance? Would the water, would the birds, would the rocks? In the north, we have our doubts.

---

45   A bunch of us are sitting around the table, at what is now a summer cottage in   265
Georgian Bay. Once it was a house, built by a local man for his family, which finally
totalled 11 children, after they'd outgrown this particular house and moved to
another. The original Findlay wood-burning cook stove is still in the house, but so
also are some electric lights and a propane cooker, which have come since the end of
the old days. In the old days, this man somehow managed to scrape a living from the   270
land: a little of this, a little of that, some fishing here, some lumbering there, some
hunting in the fall. That was back when you shot to eat. 'Scrape' is an appropriate
word: there's not much here between the topsoil and the rock.

46   We sit around the table and eat, fish among other things, caught by the children. Someone mentions the clams: there are still a lot of them, but who knows what's   275
in them any more? Mercury, lead, things like that. We pick at the fish. Someone tells
me not to drink the tap water. I already have. 'What will happen?' I ask. 'Probably
nothing,' they reply. 'Probably nothing' is a relatively recent phrase around here. In
the old days, you ate what looked edible.

47   We are talking about the old days, as people often do once they're outside the   280
cities. When exactly did the old days end? Because we know they did. The old days
ended when the youngest of us was ten, fifteen, or twenty; the old days ended when
the oldest of us was five, or twelve, or thirty. Plastic-hulled super-boats are not old
days, but ten-horse-power outboard motors, circa 1945, are. There's an icebox in the
back porch, unused now, a simple utilitarian model from Eaton's, ice chamber in the   285
top section, metal shelves in the bottom one. We all go and admire it. 'I remember
iceboxes,' I say, and indeed I can dimly remember them, I must have been five. What
bits of our daily junk—our toasters, our pocket computers—will soon become obsolete and therefore poignant? Who will stand around, peering at them and admiring
their design and the work that went into them, as we do with this icebox? 'So this was   290
a *toilet seat*,' we think, rehearsing the future. 'Ah! A *light bulb*,' the ancient syllables
thick in our mouths.

48   The kids have decided some time ago that all this chat is boring, and have asked
if they can go swimming off the dock. They can, though they have to watch it, as this
is a narrow place and speedboats tend to swoosh through, not always slowing down.   295
Waste of gas, in the old days. Nobody then went anywhere just for pleasure, it was
the war and gas was rationed.

49   'Oh, *that* old days,' says someone.

50   There goes a speedboat now, towing a man strapped in a kneeling position to
some kind of board, looking as if he's had a terrible accident, or is about to have one.   300
This must be some newfangled variety of water-skiing.

51   'Remember Klim?' I say. The children come through, trailing towels. 'What's
Klim?' one asks, caught by the space-age sound of the word.

52   'Klim was "milk" spelled backwards,' I say. 'It was powdered milk.'

53   'Yuk,' they say.   305

54   'Not the same as now,' I say. 'It was whole milk, not skim; it wasn't instant. You
had to beat it with an eggbeater.' And even then some of it wouldn't dissolve. One of
the treats of childhood was the little nodules of pure dry Klim that floated on top of
your milk.

55   'There was also Pream,' says someone. How revolutionary it seemed.   310

56   The children go down to take their chances in the risky motorized water. Maybe, much later, they will remember us sitting around the table, eating fish they themselves had caught, back when you could still (what? Catch a fish? See a tree? What desolations lie in store, beyond the plasticized hulls and the knee-skiers?). By then we will be the old days, for them. Almost we are already.   315

57   A different part of the north. We're sitting around the table, by lamplight—it's still the old days here, no electricity—talking about bad hunters. Bad hunters, bad fishers, everyone has a story. You come upon a campsite, way in the back of beyond, no roads into the lake, they must have come in by float plane, and there it is, garbage all over the place, beer cans, blobs of human poop flagged by melting toilet paper, and   320 22 fine pickerel left rotting on a rock. Business executives who get themselves flown in during hunting season with their high-powered rifles, shoot a buck, cut off the head, fill their quota, see another one with a bigger spread of antlers, drop the first head, cut off the second. The woods are littered with discarded heads, and who cares about the bodies?   325

58   New way to shoot polar bear: you have the natives on the ground finding them for you, then they radio the location in to the base camp, the base camp phones New York, fellow gets on the plane, gets himself flown in, they've got the rifle and the clothing all ready for him, fly him to the bear, he pulls the trigger from the plane, doesn't even get out of the g.d. *plane*, they fly him back, cut off the head, skin it, send   330 the lot down to New York.

59   These are the horror stories of the north, one brand. They've replaced the ones in which you got pounced upon by a wolverine or had your arm chewed off by a she-bear with cubs or got chased into the lake by a moose in rut, or even the ones in which your dog got porcupine quills or rolled in poison ivy and gave it to you. In the   335 new stories, the enemies and the victims of old have done a switch. Nature is no longer implacable, dangerous, ready to jump you; it is on the run, pursued by a number of unfair bullies with the latest technology.

60   One of the key nouns in these stories is 'float plane'. These outrages, this banditry, would not be possible without them, for the bad hunters are notoriously   340 weak-muscled and are deemed incapable of portaging a canoe, much less paddling one. Among their other badnesses, they are sissies. Another key motif is money. What money buys these days, among other things, is the privilege of no-risk slaughter.

61   As for us, the ones telling the stories, tsk-tsking by lamplight, we are the good hunters, or so we think. We've given up saying we only kill to eat; Kraft dinner and   345 freeze-dried food have put paid to that one. Really there's no excuse for us. However, we do have some virtues left. We can still cast a fly. We don't cut off heads and hang them stuffed on the wall. We would never buy an ocelot coat. We paddle our own canoes.

62   We're sitting on the dock at night, shivering despite our sweaters, in mid-August, watching the sky. There are a few shooting stars, as there always are at this time   350 in August, as the earth passes through the Perseids. We pride ourselves on knowing a few things like that, about the sky; we find the Dipper, the North Star, Cassiopeia's

Chair, and talk about consulting a star chart, which we know we won't actually do. But this is the only place you can really *see* the stars, we tell each other. Cities are hopeless.

63   Suddenly, an odd light appears, going very fast. It spirals around like a newly 355 dead firecracker, and then bursts, leaving a cloud of luminous dust, caught perhaps in the light from the sun, still up there somewhere. What could this be? Several days later we hear that it was part of an extinct Soviet satellite, or that's what they say. That's what they would say, wouldn't they? It strikes us that we don't really know very much about the night sky at all any more. There's all kinds of junk up there: spy planes, old satel- 360 lites, tin cans, man-made matter gone out of control. It also strikes us that we are totally dependent for knowledge of these things on a few people who don't tell us very much.

64   Once, we thought that if the balloon ever went up we'd head for the bush and hide out up there, living—we naively supposed—off the land. Now we know that if the two superpowers begin hurling things at each other through the sky, they're likely 365 to do it across the Arctic, with big bangs and fallout all over the north. The wind blows everywhere. Survival gear and knowing which moss you can eat is not going to be a large help. The north is no longer a refuge.

---

65   Driving back towards Toronto from the Near North, a small reprise runs through my head: 370

> Land of the septic tank,
> Home of the speedboat,
> Where still the four-wheel-drive
> Wanders at will,
> Blue lake and tacky shore,   375
> I will return once more:
> Vroom-diddy-vroom-vroom
> Vroom-diddy-vroom-vroom
> Vroo-OO-oo-oom.

Somehow, just as the drive north inspires saga and tragedy, the drive south inspires 380 parody. And here it comes: the gift shops shaped like teepees, the maple-syrup emporiums that get themselves up like olde-tyme sugaring-off huts; and, farther south, the restaurants that pretend to offer wholesome farm fare, the stores that pretend to be general stores, selling quilts, soap shaped like hearts, high-priced fancy conserves done up in filly cloth caps, the way Grandma (whoever she might be) was 385 fondly supposed to have made them.

66   And then come the housing developments, acres of prime farmland turning overnight into Quality All-Brick Family Homes; and then come the Industrial Parks; and there, in full anti-bloom, is the city itself, looming like a mirage or a chemical warfare zone on the horizon. A browny-grey scuzz hovers above it, and we think, as 390 we always do when facing re-entry, we're going into *that*? We're going to breathe *that*?

67   But we go forward, as we always do, into what is now to us the unknown. And once inside, we breathe the air, not much bad happens to us, we hardly notice. It's as if we've never been anywhere else. But that's what we think, too, when we're in the north.

1987

QUESTIONS

Reader and Purpose

1. The author begins her essay by quoting an old song, and the concluding section of the essay repeats the song, although only two of the original nine lines remain the same. She then comments that 'just as the drive north inspires saga and tragedy, the drive south inspires parody' (380–1). What does she mean?
2. In paragraph 15 what does the author mean when she says that the North 'is relative'? How is this relevant to her title?
3. In the final paragraph the author describes her return to Toronto, 'into what is now to us the unknown'. Why is Toronto 'the unknown'? And if this is so, has the North now become 'the known'?
4. This essay involves both analysis and narration. In a paragraph of about 20 lines, briefly summarize both the subject of Atwood's analysis and the story she tells.

Organization

5. Which paragraphs make up the introduction to this story: 1–8? 9–11? 10–14? In these three sections does the author make the same point, with variations, or is there a different kind of progression?
6. The **transition** between paragraphs 29 and 30 is not expressed by any one word or by any expression; it is, rather, a transition of ideas, of thought. What is the transitional thought here? Where is this idea first mentioned in the essay? Apply these same kinds of questions to the transitions between paragraphs 27 and 28, paragraphs 32 and 33, 40 and 41.
7. How is the section comprising paragraphs 41–44 a logical progression from the section involving paragraphs 33–40?
8. How is the last sentence of paragraph 44 related to the last sentence of paragraph 40?

Sentences

9. What examples of **asyndeton** and **polysyndeton** do you find in paragraph 15? in paragraph 58?
10. The fifth sentence of paragraph 28 is **periodic**. What emphasis is the author trying to achieve here?
11. In the first sentence of paragraph 62 what is the function of the colon?
12. What kind, or kinds, of sentences does Atwood prefer: **periodic**? **loose**? **cumulative**? **freight-train**? **balanced**? In order to answer this question, examine the sentences in paragraphs 30–32, or in paragraphs 33–40.

Diction

13. Look up: *resonance* (8), *tenuous* (12), *coniferous* (60), *deciduous* (60), *unprecedented* (121), *scrim* (136), *cognate* (168), *crofts* (188), *inept* (219), *cautionary* (231), *hagiography* (245), *poignant* (289), *luminous* (356), *saga* (380), *parody* (381), *emporium* (382).
14. What kind of person is the author describing in the third sentence of paragraph 16? Does she describe the same sort of person in the seventh sentence of paragraph 30, or a different sort?

15. In paragraph 44 what does the author mean by the following expressions: *pathetic fallacy gone to seed*; *ethics of ecology*; *numinous noun*?
16. What would be the best place to find out the meaning of *Struwwelpeter-like* (244): your desk dictionary? the reference section of your school library? the Internet? Try each of these to see which offers the most useful information. What are the advantages and disadvantages of each?
17. In paragraph 65 why is *olde-tyme* spelled as it is? Is the author being cynical with this spelling? If so, explain the cynicism. If not, why does she use this spelling?

POINTS TO LEARN
1. Analysis and narration can complement each other very effectively.
2. A good stylist uses a variety of sentence structures.
3. Transitions between paragraphs or between groups of paragraphs can be effected not only by words but by the development of an idea or by a contrast to a previous idea.

SUGGESTIONS FOR WRITING
What is 'True North' in your province?

Whether you have travelled or lived in the North, spent time camping or staying at a cottage in the 'Near North', or studied northern cultures in school, your essay (1,200–1,500 words) on this topic should deal with the North as you know it, not only geographically but culturally, historically, morally, and from any other point of view that you know something about. Like Atwood's, your essay should be an analysis using a narrative as foundation.

IMPROVING YOUR STYLE
1. Divide your essay into sections of 2–4 paragraphs each.
2. In your essay include

   (a) at least one long periodic sentence;
   (b) several short paragraphs of dialogue;
   (c) several long paragraphs of analysis.

ROBERT CARSE

Robert Carse (1902–71) combined two professions: those of seaman and writer. He published more than thirty books about seafaring life and exploration, including *The High Country: A History of the Exploration of Northwest America* (1966), *Ports of Call* (1967), *The River Men* (1969), *A Cold Corner of Hell: The Story of the Murmansk Convoys, 1941–45* (1969), and *Dunkirk, 1940: A History* (1970). He also wrote stories and articles for many periodicals, including *Redbook* and the *Saturday Evening Post*, in the 1930s and 1940s. Carse's narrative of the *Cospatrick*, an excerpt from his *The Twilight of Sailing Ships* (1965), is well constructed and well paced, much of its sense of realism and economy coming from his precise use of nautical terminology. Since some of these terms may not be familiar to you, we will briefly define them here. If you are a sailor you may skip on to Carse's narrative, but if you are not you will find the following discussion helpful.

On a ship *forward* (pronounced 'for'ard') and *fore* mean 'toward the bow' or front of the vessel; *aft* means 'toward the stern' or rear. *Aloft* refers to any place in the masts, yards, or rigging, and *below* to any place under the main deck. The *focsle* (a shortening of *forecastle*) is the crew's compartment and on sailing ships was usually forward of the first mast, and the *poop* is a small raised deck near the stern. On three-masted vessels the mast nearest the bow is the *foremast*, the next is the *mainmast*, and the third is the *mizzenmast*.

Rigging designates all the ropes, wires, and chains used to steady the masts; *shrouds* run from the sides of the vessel to the masts and help them withstand forces at right angles to the ship, and *stays* run fore and aft and resist forces from ahead or astern. *Running rigging*, or *running gear*, includes all the ropes and chains that lead from the *yards* (heavy round lengths of wood attached at right angles to the masts from which the sails are hung) and sails to the deck. *Ratlines*, *sheets*, *braces*, *clewlines*, and *halyards* are various kinds of running rigging.

A ship's captain is known among seamen as her *master*; the officers under him are the *first*, *second*, and *third mates*. The *bosun* (from *boatswain*) is a petty officer responsible for keeping the ship seaworthy, particularly its boats, rigging, sails, paint, and so on. The crew in nineteenth-century ships were divided into two work gangs called *watches*; the watches alternated working the ship in four-hour stints, with the six watches making up the twenty-four-hour day.

The Loss of the *Cospatrick*

1   Fire at sea aboard a wooden vessel that carried highly inflammable sails and tarred hemp rigging had always been one of the greatest concerns of any shipmaster. With crude and slow, hand-operated pumps, and no other fire-fighting equipment except axes and buckets, a ship might easily be consumed, and many were.

2   The loss of the splendidly built teakwood frigate *Cospatrick* stayed in the minds   5
of shipowners on both sides of the Atlantic for a long time after the event. Her tragic circumstances represented an extreme case, yet showed what could take place at any time aboard another vessel.

3   *Cospatrick* had been built in India in 1856, and was still in first-class condition in 1874 when she sailed for Auckland, New Zealand, from London with general   10
cargo, 429 emigrants, and a crew of 44 men. She was under the command of Captain John Elmslie, a veteran master, who had his wife aboard with him. *Cospatrick* had made a good run to the southward and was standing around Cape Horn in fair weather on November 17 when fire was reported.

4   This was at night, in the middle watch. The wind was light, Northwest, and on   15
the quarter. 'Fire!' had been cried from forward. The watch below came piling out of the focsle in their drawers and shirt tails. They were followed by the emigrants. Smoke plucked by the breeze billowed up from the fore-peak hatch. Captain Elmslie, quickly on deck, realized that the fire was in the fore-peak, and serious. The bosun

kept the usual ship's stores there, which under the circumstances formed an almost 20
explosive combination—shellack, varnish, turpentine, paint, oakum, and rope.

5   The fire hose was connected at the main pump and led forward. *Cospatrick* was
sailed off the wind. When pumping began and the fore part of the vessel was flooded,
it seemed that she might be saved. But there was no fire-proof hatch that could be
shut, no bulkheads that could contain the fire only to the fore-peak. Flame leaped 25
high and streaked in the darkness along the sheets and running gear of the foremast.
That finished the ship; she veered head-up into the wind.

6   The men handling the fire hose were driven aft by the thick, acrid masses of
smoke. They were cut off from each other, and as the deck planks groaned and crack-
led under them with heat, the foresail caught fire. Emigrants panicked, the women 30
screamed. Sailors could no longer hear the orders from their officers. Work was interrupted at the pump.

7   The fire gained furiously below. It sprang into the 'tween-decks, and then aloft
through every hatchway, port-hole and ventilator shaft. Flame spiralled the rigging,
raced swiftly along the tarred ratlines and shrouds. Then it widened out onto the 35
yards. Sheets, braces, halyards and clewlines were next, and before they burned
through and fell in charred tangles, they ignited the sails. The sails burned with wild,
incandescent bursts of light; released from the gear, they dropped in great gouts of
sparks upon the people crowding the main deck.

8   Discipline was gone. *Cospatrick*'s people were seized by panic. Aflame fore and 40
aft, there was no chance of saving her. It had taken a little over an hour for the fire to
make her condition hopeless. Captain Elmslie gave the order to abandon ship.

9   The starboard quarter boat was lowered away and put in the water. But then,
frantic with fear, emigrants piled aboard her and she was capsized. Flames licked forth
at the longboat strakes when that craft was lowered from the ship, and she became 45
useless. There were at last only two boats that got clear of the ship. They were the port
and starboard lifeboats, one with 42 persons, the other with 39 aboard.

10   The starboard lifeboat was under the command of Henry MacDonald, the second mate. He told both boats to lie off until the ship sank. It was a slow and terrible
process. *Cospatrick* took 36 hours to go. 50

11   Flame spread steadily aft towards the remaining people, crowded together on
the poop. The foremast fell blazing, and the main, and the mizzen. When the mizzen
dropped, a number of passengers on the poop were crushed to death. The rest never
stopped shrieking. They gestured to Mr MacDonald and the others in the boats—
pleading for their lives. 55

12   But nothing could be done. Rescue was impossible with the boats overcrowded by weak, half-crazed men and women who sat in their night clothing, without food or water for a day and a night. Both boats lacked masts and sails, and
aboard Mr MacDonald's boat there was only one oar. He kept the craft at a safe distance from *Cospatrick*. 60

13   Her quarter galleries gave during the second day, let go with a fierce gust of heat-
compressed air, a belch of smoke and flame. The people left aboard her jumped.
Captain Elmslie was the last. He tossed his wife down into the sea, then leaped after her.

14   They drowned. The lifeboat people, unable to help them, could only sit and
watch as the screaming victims begged for help. *Cospatrick* burned almost to the 65

waterline before she sank. When she slipped beneath the waves, Mr MacDonald gave the order, and slowly the boats moved away on the course he had reckoned.

15   The boats stayed together until the night of November 21, when the weather became heavy. MacDonald's survived. The other boat was never again seen. MacDonald rigged a sea-anchor with the painter and the oar, but lost it. Then, two 70 days later, with pieces of wood ripped from the thwarts and floorboards, a second sea-anchor was made.

16   It held, eased the strain on the boat, and kept her up to the wind, although she was half-filled with water. During the night of November 26 just before daylight, a ship passed within fifty yards of them. They cried out with all their strength, but it 75 was not enough, and they were not heard.

17   This was very hard for the survivors to take. Mr MacDonald later testified at the inquiry that by November 27 'there were but five left—two able seamen, one ordinary, myself and one passenger. The passenger was out of his mind. All had drunk salt water. We were all dozing when the madman bit my foot and I woke up. We then saw 80 a ship bearing down on us. She proved to be the *British Sceptre*, from Calcutta to Dundee. We were then taken on board and treated very kindly. I got very bad on board of her. I was very nigh at death's door. We were not recovered when we got to St Helena.'

18   While aboard *British Sceptre*, both the ordinary seaman and the passenger died. 85 Mr MacDonald and the two able-bodied sailors were the sole survivors out of the company of 473 persons which had left London in *Cospatrick*.

1965

QUESTIONS

Reader and Purpose

1. In a paragraph of no more than 10 lines explain what you think Carse is attempting to do in this passage. Is he successful? Why, or why not?
2. Does Carse assume that his readers are familiar with the sea and ships?

Organization

3. In reality, an event such as a fire at sea does not divide neatly into acts and scenes like a play. The writer must impose an organization on the continuous happening he or she describes and analyze it into parts. Paragraphs 1 and 2 compose the first part of Carse's narrative. What is their function?
4. The remaining 16 paragraphs can be divided into three groups. Identify these three sections and give a title to each.
5. Events exist in time, and while the flow of time is more significant in some stories than in others, the writer of any narrative must establish temporal reference points. Does Carse? Can you make an outline fixing the dates and times of various events in his narrative?
6. Why does Carse make paragraph 5 a separate paragraph? paragraphs 6 and 7?
7. What word links paragraph 4 to 3? Paragraph 12 to 11? 14 to 13? 16 to 15? 17 to 16? These links are quick and light. Are they adequate for the writer's purpose?

Sentences

8. There is a change in sentence style after the third paragraph. Paragraph 1 has 51 words in two sentences, an average of 25.5 words per sentence. The averages in paragraphs 2 and 3 are about the same: 23.5 and 27.3. In the fourth paragraph, however, the average drops to 11.5, even with the long final sentence; and in the eighth to 8.8 Why does Carse write shorter, simpler sentences in these places? What generalization might you make about the value of such a style in narrative?

9. What is the average number of words in the sentences of paragraph 6? Do these sentences sound too much the same, or are they varied enough to avoid monotony? If you think they are, explain how the variations are achieved.

10. Do these revisions improve Carse's sentences? Why, or why not.

   (a) ***Revision:*** Flame spiralled all through the rigging, and then it raced swiftly along the tarred ratlines and the shrouds.
   Carse: 'Flame spiralled the rigging, raced swiftly along the tarred ratlines and shrouds.' (34–5)

   (b) ***Revision:*** Because the ship was aflame fore and aft, there was no chance of saving her.
   Carse: 'Aflame fore and aft, there was no chance of saving her.' (40–1)

   (c) ***Revision:*** Flame spread steadily aft towards the remaining people, who were crowded together on the poop.
   Carse: 'Flame spread steadily aft towards the remaining people, crowded together on the poop.' (51–2)

11. The sentence in lines **75–6** is an example of a **tricolon**: one sentence composed of three independent clauses of roughly equal length and construction. Here the tricolon varies the simple style, linking three brief statements instead of expressing them separately. It also creates a pleasing rhythm by repeating the same pattern three times. On what word does the major emphasis come in each clause?

Diction

12. Look up: *emigrant* (11), *oakum* (21), *acrid* (21), *incandescent* (38), *capsized* (44), *strakes* (45), *painter* (70), *thwarts* (71), *nigh* (83).

13. Why are these alternates less effective than Carse's words: 'unfortunate' for 'tragic' (6), 'shouting' for 'shrieking' (54), 'burst' for 'belch' (62)?

14. In paragraph 6 which words appeal to our sense of hearing? In paragraph 7 which words appeal to our sense of sight? In grammatical terms, what type of word is predominant?

POINTS TO LEARN

1. Narrative renders an event in words, showing what happened, when and where and how or why.
2. Vivid active verbs create a sense of movement, vital to good narrative.
3. Temporal reference points are important in narrative, enabling readers to trace the flow of events.

4. Short **simple sentences** beginning with the subject and verb and without interruption express dramatic action.

5. Technical diction, while it makes demands on the reader, is precise and economic.

SUGGESTIONS FOR WRITING

In an essay of 8–12 paragraphs narrate a dramatic event you have witnessed or taken part in: an automobile accident, an avalanche, a bar fight, an elderly person collapsing on the sidewalk, a house fire, a robbery in a convenience store, a canoe tipping over in a strong current, a panhandler aggressively confronting a pedestrian, a confrontation between protestors and police at a political demonstration, etc.

Think carefully about the order of events and organize your narrative so that readers can grasp the pattern and time flow. Try, however, to do this subtly; avoid such mechanical formulae as 'The first thing that happened was . . . The second thing was . . .'

IMPROVING YOUR STYLE

1. In your narrative use as many short, strong sentences as you can to render the action. But vary this style occasionally so that it does not sound like a third-grade reader.
2. Include at least one tricolon.
3. Experiment with different verbs, choosing ones that convey a dramatic movement.

JAMES THURBER

The American writer James Thurber (1894–1961) was one of the finest humorists and satirists of his time. He wrote essays, sketches, stories, and books for children, and collaborated with Elliott Nugent on a successful stage comedy, *The Male Animal* (1940). Thurber was also an idiosyncratic but effective cartoonist, and his drawings are an essential part of his many works. Thurber and E.B. White co-authored *Is Sex Necessary?* (1929), a satirical (and hilarious) treatment of the 'scientific' sex manuals of the time. Thurber's best-known short story, 'The Secret Life of Walter Mitty' (1939), first appeared—as so much of his work did—in *The New Yorker*. Thurber later wrote a personal history of the magazine and its greatest editor, Harold W. Ross, *The Years with Ross* (1959).

The following piece is from *Fables for Our Time* (1940). A fable is, strictly speaking, a short tale in which birds or animals talk and act like human beings and which illustrates a simple moral truth, often literally stated in a closing tag or 'moral'. More loosely, the term *fable* applies to any short, illustrative tale even if the characters are human, as they are here. But even then the genre allows the use of fabulous elements, such as the unicorn. 'The Unicorn in the Garden' is about one of Thurber's most constant themes: the struggle between men and women for dominance. It features two stock characters: the domineering wife, and the mild, little husband—patient and long-suffering—a character common in Thurber's writing. Thurber's mild little men, however, often reveal another trait: they will be pushed just so far and then they get even. It is funny, but beneath the humour—as so often in Thurber—the matter is serious.

The Unicorn in the Garden

1   Once upon a sunny morning a man who sat in a breakfast nook looked up from his scrambled eggs to see a white unicorn with a gold horn quietly cropping the roses in the garden. The man went up to the bedroom where his wife was still asleep and woke her. 'There's a unicorn in the garden,' he said. 'Eating roses.' She opened one unfriendly eye and looked at him. 'The unicorn is a mythical beast,' she said, and 5 turned her back on him. The man walked slowly downstairs and out into the garden. The unicorn was still there; he was now browsing among the tulips. 'Here, unicorn,' said the man, and he pulled up a lily and gave it to him. The unicorn ate it gravely. With a high heart, because there was a unicorn in his garden, the man went upstairs and roused his wife again. 'The unicorn', he said, 'ate a lily.' His wife sat up in bed and 10 looked at him, coldly. 'You are a booby,' she said, 'and I am going to have you put in the booby-hatch.' The man, who had never liked the words 'booby' and 'booby-hatch', and who liked them even less on a shining morning when there was a unicorn in the garden, thought for a moment. 'We'll see about that,' he said. He walked over to the door. 'He has a golden horn in the middle of his forehead,' he told her. Then 15 he went back to the garden to watch the unicorn; but the unicorn had gone away. The man sat down among the roses and went to sleep.

2   As soon as the husband had gone out of the house, the wife got up and dressed as fast as she could. She was very excited and there was a gloat in her eye. She telephoned the police and she telephoned a psychiatrist; she told them to hurry to her 20 house and bring a strait-jacket. When the police and the psychiatrist arrived they sat down in chairs and looked at her, with great interest. 'My husband', she said, 'saw a unicorn this morning.' The police looked at the psychiatrist and the psychiatrist looked at the police. 'He told me it ate a lily,' she said. The psychiatrist looked at the police and the police looked at the psychiatrist. 'He told me it had a golden horn in 25 the middle of its forehead,' she said. At a solemn signal from the psychiatrist, the police leaped from their chairs and seized the wife. They had a hard time subduing her, for she put up a terrific struggle, but they finally subdued her. Just as they got her into the strait-jacket, the husband came back into the house.

3   'Did you tell your wife you saw a unicorn?' asked the police. 'Of course not,' 30 said the husband. 'The unicorn is a mythical beast.' 'That's all I wanted to know,' said the psychiatrist. 'Take her away. I'm sorry, sir, but your wife is as crazy as a jay bird.' So they took her away, cursing and screaming, and shut her up in an institution. The husband lived happily ever after.

4   *Moral: Don't count your boobies until they are hatched.*   35

1940

QUESTIONS
Reader and Purpose

1. The essential elements of narrative are characters and action. Such things as setting, **symbols**, and **imagery** may be made more, or less, important, but ultimately a story stands or falls on action and character. This important fact is illustrated by

Thurber's brief, but perhaps not so simple, fable. Consider his treatment of character. Deftly and quickly he creates the protagonist and the antagonist, but he does this without hanging signs around their necks; he renders his characters dramatically, that is, in terms of what they say and do. We must infer what kind of people these are; the author does not tell us explicitly. The wife is plainly unlikeable. What does she do that makes her so? The husband, although he is the protagonist, is no saint. Do you think that Thurber intends us to like this husband? At what point does he begin to turn on his wife and try to get even?

2. Why do you suppose it is a unicorn that the man sees instead of, say, a pink elephant? Are we supposed to accept the unicorn of the story as real? It is clear that the wife, the police, and the psychiatrist do not. But has Thurber given us any reason to doubt that the unicorn the man sees is a real unicorn, really browsing among the tulips and eating a lily? (Read the opening sentence carefully if you are unsure about how to answer this question.)

3. Assuming that he intends us to generalize from this couple, what is Thurber suggesting about marriage? about the different values by which men and women live? What in addition to marital relations does he poke fun at? Do the psychiatrist and the police arouse our admiration? Are they any less literal-minded than the wife?

4. How do you interpret the moral of this story? How does the pun contained in the moral affect your interpretation?

Organization

5. A story is composed of bits of action called episodes, which are dramatically rendered in scenes. A scene is a unit of action defined by time, place, and characters; when any of these elements changes significantly a new scene begins. Thus, in paragraph 1 the first scene depicts the man in the nook eating his breakfast and seeing the unicorn. When he goes upstairs to his wife's bedroom we have scene 2. This paragraph consists of five such scenes; identify the remaining three. Make a similar scenic analysis of paragraphs 2 and 3.

6. In a well-constructed story each scene must be informative; that is, it must relate something new about the characters, prepare for future action, clarify the theme in some way, or do all of these. What new bits of information are conveyed by each scene in paragraph 1?

7. In many stories the action is of the special kind called plot. Briefly, a plot has these characteristics: (1) at least one character is working toward a specific goal; (2) this effort brings him or her into conflict with one or more of the other characters; (3) the conflict is ultimately resolved; (4) only episodes that bear upon either the goal or the conflict are included; and (5) all episodes are tied together in a tight chain of cause and effect. Show that the action of Thurber's story may properly be called a plot. In a well-made plot the action is brought to a logically satisfactory conclusion. Do you feel that such is the case here?

8. Plots begin with what we call a *datum*—an initial event, often implying a question or problem, out of which the goal and the conflict develop. What is the datum in Thurber's tale? Even more important than the datum is the climax, the scene in which the conflict is finally resolved; in a cowboy movie, for instance, the climax is the shoot-out between the white hat and the black. Which scene in Thurber's story

constitutes the climax? For one character or another the climax of a plot usually involves a reversal—the black hat, for example, expects to win, not to be shot down in the dust. What is the reversal in 'The Unicorn in the Garden'?

9. The plot generally carries an important part of the meaning of a story. Often in tragic drama, for instance, the plot demonstrates that the hero's destruction is the logically necessary consequence of a moral lapse; had Macbeth not murdered Duncan, he would not in turn have been killed by Macduff. What meaning is conveyed by Thurber's plot?

10. There is an important difference, however, between a play like *Macbeth* and a fable. *Macbeth* presumably reflects the real world, however it may simplify that world; what happens to Macbeth is a sign of what will happen to similar men in real life. In fables and fairy tales, on the other hand, the point may be that the universe of the story does not reflect the world as we experience it. Do you think that such is the case in 'The Unicorn in the Garden'?

11. The final element in a plot is often called the denouement. It logically follows the climax, wrapping up any loose threads and bringing the story to a close. What is the denouement of Thurber's fable?

Sentences

12. A narrative writer must solve the problem of fitting the bits and pieces of action into appropriate compositional units. In a novel, such units would include groups of paragraphs, chapters, and even whole books. Thurber's units, however, are paragraphs and sentences. Study the sentence structure of the first paragraph and be able to discuss how Thurber has used his sentences effectively to analyze the action.

13. Comment upon these revisions of Thurber's sentences:

   (a) **Revision:** His wife sat up in bed and coldly looked at him.
   Thurber: 'His wife sat up in bed and looked at him, coldly.' (10–11)

   (b) **Revision:** The wife got up and dressed as fast as she could, as soon as the husband had gone out of the house.
   Thurber: 'As soon as the husband had gone out of the house, the wife got up and dressed as fast as she could.' (18–19)

Diction

14. Look up: unicorn (2), *cropping* (2), *mythical* (5).

15. In line 19 Thurber writes of the wife that 'there was a gloat in her eye'. 'Gleam' would be more idiomatic here, but 'gloat' is better. Why? And why is 'shining' better in line 13 than 'bright' would be?

16. What words in the first paragraph establish the wife's reaction to her husband? the husband's reaction to his wife? What words characterize the unicorn? Is it a nice unicorn? Is there any significance in the fact that the setting is a *'sunny* morning'?

POINTS TO LEARN

1. Character and action are the essence of narrative.
2. The action of a story must be organized and must be presented as a series of scenes.

3. Plot is a common way of organizing action. A plot begins with a datum, develops a conflict, which it resolves in the climax, and concludes with a denouement.
4. Narrative action, whether or not it is plotted, must be fitted into compositional units appropriate to the length of the story; these units include clauses, sentences, sentence groups, paragraphs, paragraph groups, and chapters.

SUGGESTIONS FOR WRITING

It is far easier to analyze a fable than to write one. Indeed, because they must be stripped down to the essentials of narrative action, fables are much more difficult to write well than you may think. Listed below are several suggestions, but you should feel free to invent your own situation if none of these appeals to you. Before you begin to write decide what your theme is, and as you write control your characters and action to demonstrate that theme. Do not, however, deliver the message in person. Simply tell the story and let your readers infer its point for themselves.

>the alligator in the phone booth
>the horse in the bathtub
>the yellow pussy cat who thought she was boss
>the Great Dane who felt superior

IMPROVING YOUR STYLE

Before you begin to write, make

1. a list of the characters and a synopsis of the plot;
2. a rough outline of the scenes through which the plot will develop. Indicate briefly what you want to accomplish in each scene.

WILLIAM FRANCIS BUTLER

William Francis Butler (1838–1910) was born in Ireland; he first came to Canada in the year of Confederation as an officer in the British Army. He subsequently returned to Ireland where, in 1869, he learned of the Red River resistance led by Louis Riel. Butler was never a man to pass up a chance for action and adventure, and, hastily returning to Canada, he served as an intelligence officer for Colonel Wolseley, the commander of the force sent to put down the resistance. In 1870 he was dispatched by the lieutenant-governor of Manitoba to report on the conditions at the Hudson's Bay Company's posts on the Saskatchewan River, and to carry medicines to the Indians in the region, who were suffering the ravages of a smallpox epidemic. Butler was by nature an enthusiastic traveller and explorer, and gladly took up this assignment. In 1872 he published an account of his six-month journey of 1870–1, which took him 2,700 miles up the Saskatchewan as far as the Rocky Mountains. This book, *The Great Lone Land*, was widely read in Butler's time, and it remains a vivid and perceptive narrative by a writer acutely aware of details and able to record them in clear, vigorous prose.

From *The Great Lone Land*

1   I remained only long enough at Fort Ellice to complete a few changes in costume which the rapidly increasing cold rendered necessary. Boots and hat were finally discarded, the stirrup-irons were rolled in strips of buffalo skin, the large moose-skin 'mittaines' taken into wear, and immense moccasins got ready. These precautions were necessary, for before us there now lay a great open region with treeless expanses that were sixty miles across them—a vast tract of rolling hill and plain over which, for three hundred miles, there lay no fort or house of any kind.

2   Bidding adieu to my host, a young Scotch gentleman, at Fort Ellice, my little party turned once more towards the North-west and, fording the Qu'Appelle five miles above its confluence with the Assineboine, struck out into a lovely country. It was the last day of October and almost the last of the Indian summer. Clear and distinct lay the blue sky upon the quiet sun-lit prairie. The horses trotted briskly on under the charge of an English half-breed named Daniel. Pierre Diome had returned to Red River, and Daniel was to bear me company as far as Carlton on the North Saskatchewan. My five horses were now beginning to show the effect of their incessant work, but it was only in appearance, and the distance travelled each day was increased instead of diminished as we journeyed on. I could not have believed it possible that horses could travel the daily distance which mine did without breaking down altogether under it, still less would it have appeared possible upon the food which they had to eat. We had neither hay nor oats to give them; there was nothing but the dry grass of the prairie, and no time to eat that but the cold frosty hours of the night. Still we seldom travelled less than fifty miles a-day, stopping only for one hour at midday, and going on again until night began to wrap her mantle around the shivering prairie. My horse was a wonderful animal; day after day would I fear that his game little limbs were growing weary, and that soon he must give out; but no, not a bit of it; his black coat roughened and his flanks grew a little leaner, but still he went on as gamely and as pluckily as ever. Often during the long day I would dismount and walk along leading him by the bridle, while the other two men and the six horses jogged on far in advance; when they had disappeared altogether behind some distant ridge of the prairie my little horse would commence to look anxiously around, whinnying and trying to get along after his comrades; and then how gamely he trotted on when I remounted, watching out for the first sign of his friends again, far-away little specks on the great wilds before us. When the camping place would be reached at nightfall the first care went to the horse. To remove saddle, bridle, and saddle-cloth, to untie the strip of soft buffalo leather from his neck and twist it well around his forelegs, for the purpose of hobbling, was the work of only a few minutes, and then poor Blackie hobbled away to find over the darkening expanse his night's provender. Before our own supper of pemmican, half-baked bread, and tea had been discussed, we always drove the band of horses down to some frozen lake hard by, and Daniel cut with the axe little drinking holes in the ever-thickening ice; then up would bubble the water and down went the head of the thirsty horses for a long pull at the too-often bitter spring, for in this region between the Assineboine and the South Saskatchewan fully half the lakes and pools that lie scattered about in vast variety are harsh with salt and alkalis. Three horses always ran loose while the other three worked in harness.

These loose horses, one might imagine, would be prone to gallop away when they 45
found themselves at liberty to do so: but nothing seems farther from their thoughts;
they trot along by the sides of their harnessed comrades apparently as though they
knew all about it; now and again they stop behind, to crop a bit of grass or tempting
stalk of wild pea or vetches, but on they come again until the party has been reached,
then, with ears thrown back, the jog-trot is resumed, and the whole band sweeps on 50
over hill and plain. To halt and change horses is only the work of two minutes—out
comes one horse, the other is standing close by and never stirs while the hot harness
is being put upon him; in he goes into the rough shafts, and, with a crack of the half-
breed's whip across his flanks, away we start again.

3   But my little Blackie seldom got a respite from the saddle; he seemed so well up 55
to his work, so much stronger and better than any of the others, that day after day I
rode him, thinking each day, 'Well, to-morrow I will let him run loose'; but when tomorrow came he used to look so fresh and well, carrying his little head as high as
ever, that again I put the saddle on his back, and another day's talk and companionship would still further cement our friendship, for I grew to like that horse as one only 60
can like the poor dumb beast that serves us. I know not how it is, but horse and dog
have worn themselves into my heart as few men have ever done in life; and now, as
day by day went by in one long scene of true companionship, I came to feel for little
Blackie a friendship not the less sincere because all the service was upon his side, and
I was powerless to make his supper a better one, or give him a more cosy lodging for 65
the night. He fed and lodged himself and he carried me—all he asked in return was
a water-hole in the frozen lake, and that I cut for him. Sometimes the night came
down upon us still in the midst of a great open treeless plain, without shelter, water,
or grass, and then we would continue on in the inky darkness as though our march
was to last eternally, and poor Blackie would step out as if his natural state was one 70
of perpetual motion. On the 4th November we rode over sixty miles; and when at
length the camp was made in the lea of a little clump of bare willows, the snow was
lying cold upon the prairies, and Blackie and his comrades went out to shiver through
their supper in the bleakest scene my eyes had ever looked upon.

4   About midway between Fort Ellice and Carlton a sudden and well-defined 75
change occurs in the character of the country; the light soil disappears, and its place
is succeeded by a rich dark loam covered deep in grass and vetches. Beautiful hills
swell in slopes more or less abrupt on all sides, while lakes fringed with thickets and
clumps of good-sized poplar balsam lie lapped in their fertile hollows.

5   This region bears the name of the Touchwood Hills. Around it, far into endless 80
space, stretch immense plains of bare and scanty vegetation, plains seared with the
tracks of countless buffalo which, until a few years ago, were wont to roam in vast
herds between the Assineboine and the Saskatchewan. Upon whatever side the eye
turns when crossing these great expanses, the same wrecks of the monarch of the
prairie lie thickly strewn over the surface. Hundreds of thousands of skeletons dot the 85
short scant grass; and when fire has laid barer still the level surface, the bleached ribs
and skulls of long-killed bison whiten far and near the dark burnt prairie. There is
something unspeakably melancholy in the aspect of this portion of the North-west.
From one of the westward jutting spurs of the Touchwood Hills the eye sees far away
over an immense plain; the sun goes down, and as he sinks upon the earth the straight 90

line of the horizon becomes visible for a moment across his blood-red disc, but so distant, so far away, that it seems dreamlike in its immensity. There is not a sound in the air or on the earth; on every side lie spread relics of the great fight waged by man against the brute creation; all is silent and deserted—the Indian and the buffalo gone, the settler not yet come. You turn quickly to the right or left; over a hill-top, close by, 95 a solitary wolf steals away. Quickly the vast prairie begins to grow dim, and darkness forsakes the skies because they light their stars, coming down to seek in the utter solitude of the blackened plains a kindred spirit for the night.

6   On the night of the 4th November we made our camp long after dark in a little clump of willows far out in the plain which lies west of the Touchwood Hills. We had 100 missed the only lake that was known to lie in this part of the plain, and after journeying far in the darkness halted at length, determined to go supperless, or next to supperless, to bed, for pemmican without that cup which nowhere tastes more delicious than the wilds of the North-west would prove but sorry comfort, and the supper without tea would be only a delusion. The fire was made, the frying-pan taken out, the bag 105 of dried buffalo meat and the block of pemmican got ready, but we said little in the presence of such a loss as the steaming kettle and the hot, delicious, fragrant tea. Why not have provided against this evil hour by bringing on from the last frozen lake some blocks of ice? Alas! why not? Moodily we sat down round the blazing willows. Meantime Daniel commenced to unroll the oilcloth cart cover—and lo, in the ruddy 110 glare of the fire, out rolled three or four large pieces of thick, heavy ice, sufficient to fill our kettle three times over with delicious tea. Oh, what a joy it was! and how we relished that cup! for remember, cynical friend who be inclined to hold such happiness cheap and light, that this wild life of ours is a curious leveller of civilized habits— a cup of water to a thirsty man can be more valuable than a cup of diamonds, and the 115 value of one article over the other is only the question of a few hours' privation. When the morning of the 5th dawned we were covered deep in snow, a storm had burst in the night, and all around was hidden in a dense sheet of driving snow-flakes; not a vestige of our horses was to be seen, their tracks were obliterated by the fast-falling snow, and the surrounding objects close at hand showed dim and indistinct through the 120 white cloud. After a fruitless search, Daniel returned to camp with the tidings that the horses were nowhere to be found; so, when breakfast had been finished, all three set out in separate directions to look again for the missing steeds. Keeping the snow-storm on my left shoulder, I went along through little clumps of stunted bushes which frequently deceived me by their resemblance through the driving snow to horses grouped 125 together. After awhile I bent round towards the wind and, making a long sweep in that direction, bent again so as to bring the drift upon my right shoulder. No horses, no tracks any where—nothing but a waste of white drifting flake and feathery snow-spray. At last I turned away from the wind, and soon struck full on our little camp; neither of the others had returned. I cut down some willows and made a blaze. After a 130 while I got on to the top of the cart, and looked out again into the waste. Presently I heard a distant shout; replying vigorously to it, several indistinct forms came into view, and Daniel soon emerged from the mist, driving before him the hobbled wanderers; they had been hidden under the lea of a thicket some distance off, all clustered together for shelter and warmth. Our only difficulty was now the absence of my friend 135 the Hudson Bay officer. We waited some time, and at length, putting the saddle on

Blackie, I started out in the direction he had taken. Soon I heard a faint far-away shout; riding quickly in the direction from whence it proceeded, I heard the calls getting louder and louder, and soon came up with a figure heading right away into the immense plain, going altogether in a direction opposite to where our camp lay. I   140
shouted, and back came my friend no little pleased to find his road again, for a snow-storm is no easy thing to steer through, and at times it will even fall out that not the Indian with all his craft and instinct for direction will be able to find his way through its blinding maze. Woe betide the wretched man who at such a time finds himself alone upon the prairie, without fire or the means of making it; not even the ship-   145
wrecked sailor clinging to the floating mast is in a more pitiable strait. During the greater portion of this day it snowed hard, but our track was distinctly marked across the plains, and we held on all day. I still rode Blackie; the little fellow had to keep his wits at work to avoid tumbling into the badger holes which the snow soon rendered invisible. These badger holes in this portion of the plains were very numerous; it is not   150
always easy to avoid them when the ground is clear of snow, but riding becomes extremely difficult when once the winter has set in. The badger burrows straight down for two or three feet, and if a horse be travelling at any pace his fall is so sudden and violent that a broken leg is too often the result. Once or twice Blackie went in nearly to the shoulder, but he invariably scrambled up again all right—poor fellow, he was   155
reserved for a worse fate, and his long journey was near its end! A clear cold day fol-lowed the day of snow, and for the first time the thermometer fell below zero.

7   Day dawned upon us on the 6th November camped in a little thicket of poplars some seventy miles from the South Saskatchewan; the thermometer stood 3° below zero, and as I drew the girths tight on poor Blackie's ribs that morning, I felt happy in   160
the thought that I had slept for the first time under stars with 35° of frost lying on the blanket outside. Another long day's ride, and the last great treeless plain was crossed and evening found us camped near the Minitchinass, or Solitary Hill, some sixteen miles south-east of the South Saskatchewan. The grass again grew long and thick, the clumps of willow, poplar, and birch had reappeared, and the soil, when we scraped   165
the snow away to make our sleeping place, turned up black and rich-looking under the blows of the axe. About midday on the 7th November, in a driving storm of snow, we suddenly emerged upon a high plateau. Before us, at a little distance, a great gap or valley seemed to open suddenly out, and farther off the white sides of hills and dark tree-tops rose into view. Riding to the edge of this steep valley I beheld a mag-   170
nificent river flowing between great banks of ice and snow 800 feet below the level on which we stood. Upon each side masses of ice stretched out far into the river, but in the centre, between these banks of ice, ran a swift, black-looking current, the sight of which for a moment filled us with dismay. We had counted upon the Saskatchewan being firmly locked in ice, and here was the river rolling along between its icy banks   175
forbidding all passage. Descending to the low valley of the river, we halted for dinner, determined to try some method by which to cross this formidable barrier. An exami-nation of the river and its banks soon revealed the difficulties before us. The ice, as it approached the open portion, was unsafe, rendering it impossible to get within reach of the running water. An interval of some ten yards separated the sound ice from the   180
current, while nearly 100 yards of solid ice lay between the true bank of the river and the dangerous portion; thus our first labour was to make a solid footing for ourselves

from which to launch any raft or make-shift boat which we might construct. After a great deal of trouble and labour, we got the waggon-box roughly fashioned into a raft, covered over with one of our large oil-cloths, and lashed together with buffalo leather. 185 This most primitive looking craft we carried down over the ice to where the danger-ous portion commenced; then Daniel, wielding the axe with powerful dexterity, began to hew away at the ice until space enough was opened out to float our raft upon. Into this we slipped the waggon-box, and into the waggon-box we put the half-breed Daniel. It floated admirably, and on went the axe-man, hewing, as before, with might 190 and main. It was cold, wet work, and, in spite of every thing, the water began to ooze through the oil-cloth into the waggon-box. We had to haul it up, empty it, and launch again; thus for some hours we kept on, cold, wet, and miserable, until night forced us to desist and make our camp on the tree-lined shore. So we hauled in the waggon and retired, baffled, but not beaten, to begin again next morning. There were many 195 reasons to make this delay feel vexatious and disappointing; we had travelled a dis-tance of 560 miles in twelve days; travelled only to find ourselves stopped by this par-tially frozen river at a point twenty miles distant from Carlton, the first great station on my journey. Our stock of provisions, too, was not such as would admit of much delay; pemmican and dried meat we had none, and flour, tea, and grease were all that 200 remained to us. However, Daniel declared that he knew a most excellent method of making a combination of flour and fat which would allay all disappointment—and I must conscientiously admit that a more hunger-satiating mixture than he produced out of the frying-pan it had never before been my lot to taste. A little of it went such a long way, that it would be impossible to find a parallel for it in portability; in fact, 205 it went such a long way, that the person who dined off it found himself, by common reciprocity of feeling, bound to go a long way in return before he again partook of it; but Daniel was not of that opinion, for he ate the greater portion of our united shares, and slept peacefully when it was all gone. I would particularly recommend this mix-ture to the consideration of the guardians of the poor throughout the United 210 Kingdom, as I know of nothing which would so readily conduce to the satisfaction of the hungry element in our society. Had such a combination been known to Bumble and his Board, the hunger of Twist would even have been satisfied by a single help-ing; but, perhaps, it might be injudicious to introduce into the sister island any condi-ment so antidotal in its nature to the removal of the Celt across the Atlantic—that 215 'consummation so devoutly wished for' by the 'leading journal'.

8   Fortified by Daniel's delicacy, we set to work early next morning at raft-making and ice-cutting; but we made the attempt to cross at a portion of the river where the open water was narrower and the bordering ice sounded more firm to the testing blows of the axe. One part of the river had now closed in, but the ice over it was 220 unsafe. We succeeded in getting the craft into the running water and, having strung together all the available line and rope we possessed, prepared for the venture. It was found that the waggon-boat would only carry one passenger, and accordingly I took my place in it, and with a make-shift paddle put out into the quick-running stream. The current had great power over the ill-shaped craft, and it was no easy matter to 225 keep her head at all against stream.

9   I had not got five yards out when the whole thing commenced to fill rapidly with water, and I had just time to get back again to ice before she was quite full. We

hauled her out once more, and found the oil-cloth had been cut by the jagged ice, so
there was nothing for it but to remove it altogether and put on another. This was   230
done, and soon our waggon-box was once again afloat. This time I reached in safety
the farther side; but there a difficulty arose which we had not foreseen. Along this farther edge of ice the current ran with great force, and as the leather line which was
attached to the back of the boat sank deeper and deeper into the water, the drag upon
it caused the boat to drift quicker and quicker downstream; thus, when I touched the   235
opposite ice, I found the drift was so rapid that my axe failed to catch a hold in the
yielding edge, which broke away at every stroke. After several ineffectual attempts to
stay the rush of the boat, and I was being borne rapidly into a mass of rushing water
and huge blocks of ice, I saw it was all up, and shouted to the others to rope in the
line; but this was no easy matter, because the rope had got foul of the running ice,   240
and was caught underneath. At last, by careful handling, it was freed, and I stood once
more on the spot from whence I had started, having crossed the River Saskatchewan
to no purpose. Daniel now essayed the task, and reached the opposite shore, taking
the precaution to work up the nearer side before crossing; once over, his vigorous use
of the axe told on the ice, and he succeeded in fixing the boat against the edge. Then   245
he quickly clove his way into the frozen mass, and, by repeated blows, finally reached
a spot from which he got on shore.

10   This success of our long labour and exertion was announced to the solitude by
three ringing cheers, which we gave from our side; for, be it remembered, that it was
now our intention to use the waggon-boat to convey across all our baggage, towing the   250
boat from one side to the other by means of our line; after which, we would force the
horses to swim the river, and then cross ourselves in the boat. But all our plans were
defeated by an unlooked-for accident; the line lay deep in the water, as before, and to
raise it required no small amount of force. We hauled and hauled, until snap went the
long rope somewhere underneath the water, and all was over. With no little difficulty   255
Daniel got the boat across again to our side, and we all went back to camp wet, tired,
and dispirited by so much labour and so many misfortunes. It froze hard that night,
and in the morning the great river had its waters altogether hidden opposite our camp
by a covering of ice. Would it bear? that was the question. We went on it early, testing
with axe and sharp-pointed poles. In places it was very thin, but in other parts it rang   260
hard and solid to the blows. The dangerous spot was in the very centre of the river,
where the water had shown through in round holes on the previous day, but we hoped
to avoid those bad places by taking a slanting course across the channel. After walking backwards and forwards several times, we determined to try a light horse. He was
led out with a long piece of rope attached to his neck. In the centre of the stream the   265
ice seemed to bend slightly as he passed over, but no break occurred, and in safety we
reached the opposite side. Now came Blackie's turn. Somehow or other I felt uncomfortable about it and remarked that the horse ought to have his shoes removed before
the attempt was made. My companion, however, demurred, and his experiences in
these matters had extended over so many years, that I was foolishly induced to allow   270
him to proceed as he thought fit, even against my better judgment. Blackie was taken
out, led as before, tied by a long line. I followed close behind him, to drive him if necessary. He did not need much driving, but took the ice quite readily. We had got to the
centre of the river, when the surface suddenly bent downwards, and, to my horror, the

poor horse plunged deep into black, quick-running water! He was not three yards in 275
front of me when the ice broke. I recoiled involuntarily from the black, seething
chasm; the horse, though he plunged suddenly down, never let his head under water,
but kept swimming manfully round and round the narrow hole, trying all he could to
get upon the ice. All his efforts were useless; a cruel wall of sharp ice struck his knees
as he tried to lift them on the surface, and the current, running with immense veloc- 280
ity, repeatedly carried him back underneath. As soon as the horse had broken through,
the man who held the rope let it go, and the leather line flew back about poor Blackie's
head. I got up almost to the edge of the hole, and stretching out took hold of the line
again; but that could do no good nor give him any assistance in his struggles. I shall
never forget the way the poor brute looked at me—even now, as I write these lines, the 285
whole scene comes back in memory with all the vividness of a picture, and I feel again
the horrible sensation of being utterly unable, though almost within touching distance, to give him help in his dire extremity—and if ever dumb animal spoke with
unutterable eloquence, that horse called to me in his agony; he turned to me as to one
from whom he had a right to expect assistance. I could not stand the scene any longer. 290

11   'Is there no help for him?' I cried to the other men.

12   'None whatever,' was the reply; 'the ice is dangerous all around.'

13   Then I rushed back to the shore and up to the camp where my rifle lay, then
back again to the fatal spot where the poor beast still struggled against his fate. As I
raised the rifle he looked at me so imploringly that my hand shook and trembled. 295
Another instant, and the deadly bullet crashed through his head, and, with one look
never to be forgotten, he went down under the cold, unpitying ice!

14   It may have been very foolish, perhaps, for poor Blackie was only a horse, but
for all that I went back to camp, and, sitting down in the snow, cried like a child. With
my own hand I had taken my poor friend's life; but if there should exist somewhere 300
in the regions of space that happy Indian paradise where horses are never hungry and
never tired, Blackie, at least, will forgive the hand that sent him there, if he can but
see the heart that long regretted him.

15   Leaving Daniel in charge of the remaining horses, we crossed on foot the fatal
river, and with a single horse set out for Carlton. From the high north bank I took one 305
last look back at the South Saskatchewan—it lay in its broad deep valley glittering in
one great band of purest snow; but I loathed the sight of it, while the small round
open hole, dwarfed to a speck by distance, marked the spot where my poor horse had
found his grave, after having carried me so faithfully through the long lonely wilds.
We had travelled about six miles when a figure appeared in sight, coming towards us 310
upon the same track. The new-comer proved to be a Cree Indian travelling to Fort
Pelly. He bore the name of the Starving Bull. Starving Bull and his boy at once turned
back with us towards Carlton. In a little while a party of horsemen hove in sight: they
had come out from the fort to visit the South Branch, and amongst them was the
Hudson Bay officer in charge of the station. Our first question had reference to the 315
plague. Like a fire, it had burned itself out. There was no case then in the fort; but out
of the little garrison of some sixty souls no fewer than thirty-two had perished! Four
only had recovered of the thirty-six who had taken the terrible infection.

16   We halted for dinner by the edge of the Duck Lake, midway between the North
and South Branches of the Saskatchewan. It was a rich, beautiful country, although 320

the snow lay some inches deep. Clumps of trees dotted the undulating surface, and lakelets glittering in the bright sunshine spread out in sheets of dazzling whiteness. The Starving Bull set himself busily to work preparing our dinner. What it would have been under ordinary circumstances, I cannot state; but, unfortunately for its success on the present occasion, its preparation was attended with unusual draw- 325 backs. Starving Bull had succeeded in killing a skunk during his journey. This per- formance, while highly creditable to his energy as a hunter, was by no means conducive to his success as a cook. Bitterly did that skunk revenge himself upon us who had borne no part in his destruction. Pemmican is at no time a delicacy; but pemmican flavoured with skunk was more than I could attempt. However, Starving 330 Bull proved himself worthy of his name, and the frying-pan was soon scraped clean under his hungry manipulations.

17   Another hour's ride brought us to a high bank, at the base of which lay the North Saskatchewan. In the low ground adjoining the river stood Carlton House, a large square enclosure, the wooden walls of which were more than twenty feet in 335 height. Within these palisades some dozen or more houses stood crowded together. Close by, to the right, many snow-covered mounds with a few rough wooden crosses above them marked the spot where, only four weeks before, the last victim of the epidemic had been laid. On the very spot where I stood looking at this scene, a Blackfoot Indian, three years earlier, had stolen out from a thicket, fired at, and 340 grievously wounded the Hudson Bay officer belonging to the fort, and now close to the same spot a small cross marked that officer's last resting-place. Strange fate! he had escaped the Blackfoot's bullet only to be the first to succumb to the deadly epi- demic. I cannot say that Carlton was at all a lively place of sojourn. Its natural gloom was considerably deepened by the events of the last few months, and the whole place 345 seemed to have received the stamp of death upon it. To add to the general depres- sion, provisions were by no means abundant, the few Indians that had come in from the plains brought the same tidings of unsuccessful chase—for the buffalo were 'far out' on the great prairie, and that phrase 'far out', applied to buffalo, means starva- tion in the North-west.   350

1872

QUESTIONS
Reader and Purpose

1. Butler's narrative describes his journey, in the late fall of 1872, through what is today southwestern Saskatchewan and southeastern Alberta. In his first three para- graphs how does he give us a sense of the extraordinary journey he is about to undertake?

2. Does the author seem to have any purpose other than to tell the story of his jour- ney? That is, could you say that his essay is partly descriptive? or persuasive? expository? argumentative?

3. Why does the author not mention the death of Blackie in his conclusion? Does this omission reveal something about Butler, or about his purpose in writing his book?

Organization

4. Does the first sentence of paragraph 5 logically belong at the end of paragraph 4? Explain why, or why not.
5. Butler's paragraph structure is typical of much nineteenth-century writing in that the paragraphs are far longer than we today are accustomed to or feel comfortable with. The sixth paragraph, for instance, runs to more than a full page, yet there are two points in this paragraph where another paragraph could logically have begun. Identify these two points, explaining why they would be suitable places to begin a new paragraph. At what points, and why, could paragraph 7 also be divided?
6. The **topic sentence** of paragraph 5 is the fifth sentence. Is this an effective place for it? Would Butler's feeling of melancholy have been more or less convincing to the reader if it had been expressed in the first sentence of the paragraph in place of the sentence now there? Could it have been omitted altogether?
7. Should paragraph 15 be divided into two paragraphs? If so, where would you place the dividing point, and why? Or is the paragraph so well unified that it should not be divided?

Sentences

8. The third sentence of paragraph 2 is an example of **inversion**. Do you find any other examples of inverted word order in this paragraph?
9. In sentences 2, 3, and 4 of paragraph 5, Butler makes use of repetition to emphasize what particular aspects of the prairie? Give some examples of words and phrases that are either repeated directly or with slight variation. Are these effective in making the reader share Butler's general impression as stated in sentence five?
10. Although most of Butler's sentences are long and complicated, they are nevertheless varied in structure. With regard to paragraphs 16 and 17, how many sentences does he begin with **prepositional phrases**? With the subject–verb nucleus? How often does he use **interrupting phrases**? **coordinate clauses**? differently positioned **subordinate clauses**?

Diction

11. Look up: *tract* (6), *adieu* (8), *incessant* (15–16), *provender* (37), *respite* (55), *lea* (72), *kindred* (98), *vestige* (118–19), *betide* (144), *strait* (146), *dexterity* (187), *hew* (188), *vexatious* (196), *allay* (202).
12. How do their **etymologies** help you to understand the following words in paragraph 10: *exertion* (248), *solitude* (248), *demurred* (269), *chasm* (277)?
13. Identify the following **figures of speech** in paragraph 13: *the fatal spot* (294), *the deadly bullet* (296), *the cold, unpitying ice* (297). Are any of these expressions **clichés**? Explain.

POINTS TO LEARN

1. A good narrative needs no elaboration; let the story speak for itself.
2. A tightly constructed paragraph cannot be arbitrarily divided.
3. Even though an author's sentences are generally quite long, there are numerous ways to vary sentence structure and thus avoid monotony.

SUGGESTIONS FOR WRITING

1. Tell the story of the disappearance and/or death of a cherished pet, an animal that you and your family had come to know well and have considerable affection for. Set the stage carefully by showing why the animal was important to you and how it had become a part of your life. Then tell your story simply, letting the events speak for themselves rather than deliberately trying to draw the reader's sympathy.
2. Have you ever experienced the feeling of being completely by yourself, or even lost, on the prairie, or in the mountains, or in a forest or swamp? Describe this feeling as part of the story of how you came to be in this situation.

IMPROVING YOUR STYLE

In your essay include

1. an inverted sentence in each of two different paragraphs;
2. three consecutive sentences in which you emphasize a specific point or two by using synonyms, repetitions, or repetitions with variations.

ANNIE DILLARD

Poet, essayist, and novelist Annie Dillard (1945–) was awarded a Pulitzer Prize for her first work of non-fiction, *Pilgrim at Tinker Creek* (1974), a mystical meditation on nature. Among her other much-praised books are *Holy the Firm* (1977) and *Teaching a Stone to Talk* (1982), from which the essay below is taken—both books being accounts of her observations of the natural world; *An American Childhood* (1987), a memoir; *The Living* (1992), a novel set in the nineteenth-century American Northwest; and *Living by Fiction* (1982), a collection of essays on the art of writing and on various writers. In her foreword to this book, Dillard dedicates it to those people who, 'if you told them the world would end in ten minutes, would try to decide—quickly—what to read.' Her most recent books are *Mornings Like This: Found Poems* (1995), and *For the Time Being* (1999).

On a Hill Far Away

1   In Virginia, late one January afternoon while I had a leg of lamb in the oven, I took a short walk. The idea was to exercise my limbs and rest my mind, but these things rarely work out as I plan.
2   It was sunset by the time I crossed Tinker Creek by hopping from stone to stone and inching up a fallen tree trunk to the bank. On the far side of the creek I followed   5
a barbed-wire fence through steers' pasture and up to a high grassy hill. I'd never been there before. From the hill the distant creek looked still and loaded with sky.
3   On the hilltop, just across the barbed-wire fence, were three outbuildings: a fenced horse barn, around which a dun mare and a new foal were nervously clattering; a cyclone-fenced dog pen with a barking shepherd and a barking bird dog; and a frame   10
toolshed under whose weedy eaves a little boy was pretending to write with a stone.

4   The little boy didn't see me. He looked to be about eight, thin, wearing a brown corduroy jacket with darker brown pile on the collar and a matching beaked corduroy cap with big earflaps. He alternated between pretending to write big letters on the toolshed wall and fooling with the dogs from outside their pen. The dogs were going 15 crazy at their fence because of me, and I wondered why the boy didn't turn around; he must be too little to know much about dogs. When he did see me, by accident, his eyebrows shot up. I smiled and hollered and he came over to the barbed wire.

5   We watched the horses. 'How old's the foal?' I asked him. The golden foal looked like a test model in a patent office—jerky, its eyes not set quite right, a mar- 20 vel, it ran to keep from falling.

6   'That one is just one. You'd have to say he was *one*. . . .'

7   Boy, I thought. I sure don't know anything about horses.

8   '. . . he was just *born* six days ago.'

9   The foal wanted to approach. Every time it looked at us, the mare ran inter- 25 ference and edged the foal away.

10   The boy and I talked over the barbed wire. The dogs' names were Barney and Duke. 'Luke?' I said. The boy was shocked. 'Duke,' he said. He was formal and articulate; he spoke in whole sentences, choosing his words. 'I haven't yet settled on a name for the foal, although Father says he is mine.' When he spoke this way, he gazed 30 up at me through meeting eyebrows. His dark lips made a projecting circle. He looked like a nineteenth-century cartoon of an Earnest Child. This kid is a fraud, I thought. Who calls his father 'Father'? But at other times his face would loosen; I could see then that the accustomed gesture of his lips resembled that of a person trying not to cry. Or he would smile, or look away shyly, like now: 'Actually, I've been considering the 35 name Marky Sparky.'

11   'Marky Sparky,' I repeated, with as much warmth as I could muster. The sun was down. What was I doing chatting with a little kid? Wasn't there something I should be reading?

12   Then he paused. He looked miserably at his shoetops, and I looked at his 40 brown corduroy cap. Suddenly the cap lifted, and the little face said in a rush, 'Do you know the Lord as your personal saviour?'

13   'Not only that,' I said, 'I know your mother.'

14   It all came together. She had asked me the same question.

———

15   Until then I had not connected this land, these horses, and this little boy with 45 the woman in the big house at the top of the hill, the house I'd approached from the other direction, to ask permission to walk the land. That was about a year ago. There had been a very long driveway from the highway on the other side of the hill. The driveway made a circle in front of the house, and in the circle stood an eight-foot aluminum cross with a sign underneath it reading CHRIST THE LORD IS OUR SALVATION. 50 Spotlights in the circle's honeysuckle were trained up at the cross and the sign. I rang the bell.

16   The woman was very nervous. She was dark, pretty, hard, with the same trembling lashes as the boy. She wore a black dress and one brush roller in the front of her hair. She did not ask me in.
                                                                                              55

17   My explanation of myself confused her, but she gave permission. Yes, I could walk their property. (She did not add, as others have, 'But I don't want no kids in here roughhousing.') She did not let me go; she was worried about something else. She worked her hands. I waited on the other side of the screen door until she came out with it: 60

18   'Do you know the Lord as your personal saviour?'

19   My heart went out to her. No wonder she had been so nervous. She must have to ask this of everyone, absolutely everyone, she meets. That is Christian witness. It makes sense, given its premises. I wanted to make her as happy as possible, reward her courage, and run.   65

20   She was stunned that I knew the Lord, and clearly uncertain whether we were referring to the same third party. But she had done her bit, bumped over the hump, and now she could relax. She told me about her church, her face brightening. She was part of the Reverend Jerry Falwell's congregation. He is the powerful evangelist in Lynchburg, Virginia, who has recently taken to politics. She drove, I inferred, 120   70 miles round trip to go to church. While I waited behind the screen door she fetched pamphlets, each a different colour. I thanked her kindly; I read them later. The one on the Holy Spirit I thought was good.

———

21   So this was her son. She had done a good job. He was a nice little kid. He was glad now his required speech was over; he was glad that I was talking easily, telling   75 about meeting his mother. That I had met her seemed to authenticate me to him and dissolve some wariness.

22   The wind that follows sunset was blowing from the western ridge, across our hill and down. There had been ice in the creek. The boy moved closer to the barbed-wire fence; he jammed his fists in his pockets. Whenever I smiled or laughed he   80 looked at me disbelieving, and lifted his eyes from beneath his cap's bill again and again to my face.

23   He never played at the creek, he said. Because he might be down there, and Father might come home not knowing he was there, and let all the horses out, and the horses would trample him. I had noticed that he quailed whenever the mare in   85 her pen jerked his way.

24   Also there were snakes down there—water moccasins, he said. He seemed tired, old even, weary with longings, solemn. Caution passes for wisdom around here, and this kid knew all the pitfalls. In fact, there are no water moccasins this far north, except out on the coast, but there are some copperheads; I let it go. 'They   90 won't hurt you,' I said. 'I play at the creek,' I said. 'Lots.' How old are you? Eight? Nine? How could you not play at the creek? Or: Why am I trying to force this child to play at the creek? What do I do there alone that he'd want to do? What do I do there at all?

25   The distant creek looked like ice from the hill, lightless and unmoving. The   95 bare branches of sycamores on its banks met soundlessly. When was spring coming? The sky was purpling. Why would anyone in his right mind play at the creek?

26   'You're cold,' I said to the boy. His lips were blue. He tried to keep his corduroy shoulders against his bare neck. He pretended not to hear. 'I have to go,' I said.

27   'Do you know how to catch a fish when you haven't got a rod, or a line, or a   100
hook?' He was smiling, warming up for a little dialect, being a kid in a book. He must
read a lot. 'First, you get you a *stick. . . .*' He explained what sort of stick. 'Then you
pull you a thread of honeysuckle . . . and if you need you a *hook . . .*'
28   We talked about fishing. 'I've got a roast in the oven,' I said. 'I've got to go.' He
had to go too; Father would be home, and the boy had to set the table for dinner. His   105
mother was fasting. I said so long, so long, and turned. He called, 'One more thing!'
I looked back; he hesitated a second and began loudly, 'Did you ever step on a big
old snake?'
29   All right, then. I thanked God for the sisters and friends I had had when I was
little; I have not been lonely yet, but it could come at any time. I pulled my jacket col-   110
lar up as high as I could.
30   He described stepping on the snake; he rolled his eyes and tried to stir me. 'I
felt it just . . . *move* under my foot. It was so . . . *slimy. . . .*' I bided my time. His teeth
were chattering. 'We were walking through the field beneath the cemetery. I called,
"Wait, Father, wait!" I couldn't lift my foot.' I wondered what they let him read; he   115
spoke in prose, like *le bourgeois gentilhomme*.
31   'Gee,' I kept saying, 'you must have been scared.'
32   'Well, I was *about* knee-deep in honeysuckle.'
33   Oh! That was different. Probably he really *had* stepped on a snake. I would have
been plenty scared myself, knee-deep in honeysuckle, but there was no way now to   120
respond to his story all over again, identically but sincerely. Still, it was time to go. It
was dark. The mare had nosed her golden foal into the barn. The creek below held a
frail colour still, the memory of a light that hadn't yet been snuffed.
34   We parted sadly, over the barbed-wire fence. The boy lowered his enormous,
lighted eyes, lifted his shoulders, and went into a classic trudge. He had tried again to   125
keep me there. But I simply had to go. It was dark, it was cold, and I had a roast in
the oven, lamb, and I don't like it too well done.

1982

QUESTIONS
Reader and Purpose

1. Although Annie Dillard's introductory paragraph is quite short, it nevertheless refers
   to six points: the place and time, the leg of lamb, the short walk, the purpose of
   the walk, and a hint about the results. What do these points tell us about the
   author? What do they tell us about her essay?

2. In narrating her encounter with the fundamentalist mother and son (and, in the
   background, the father), Dillard is faced with a difficult situation: on the one hand
   she is sympathetic to mother and son; but, on the other hand, she is skeptical,
   even, perhaps, a bit condemnatory. How does she approach this problem? What
   evidence do you find of both attitudes? Is one stronger than the other?

3. In paragraph 7 the author confesses her ignorance about horses. Is she correct?
   Where else does she state her ignorance? What do such professions of ignorance
   reveal about the author?

4. Is paragraph 9 just an interesting observation on how the mare protects its colt, or is it also a comment on the relationship among the mother and son and the stranger? Consider also the final sentence of paragraph 23 and the second-last sentence of paragraph 33. What conclusion can you come to about the nature of this family?

5. In Christian theology the Holy Spirit, the third person of the Trinity, is often associated with knowledge and enlightenment. Keeping this in mind, do you find the final sentence of paragraph 20 open to more than one interpretation?

6. Are the questions in the last sentence of paragraph 24 and of paragraph 25 **rhetorical** ones? If so, what dramatic effect is intended? If not, what is the author getting at?

7. Is the final **independent clause** of this essay—'I don't like it too well done'—merely a statement of the author's preference about how she likes lamb, or is she being subtly ironic? If you believe that there is a touch of **irony** here, what is she being ironic about?

8. What kind of person is the father of this family? How does Dillard give us the information by which we get to know something about him?

Organization

9. Why does the author insert a symbol between paragraphs 14 and 15? between paragraphs 20 and 21? Do these breaks mark a change in topic? a change in **point of view**? a change in **tone**? something else entirely?

10. A good narrative has a beginning, a middle, and an end. Which paragraphs constitute each of these parts of Dillard's essay?

11. What words or expressions does the author use to mark the passage of time throughout her narrative?

12. Throughout her essay Dillard uses quite short paragraphs. Does this approach to paragraph structure help her narrative, or would the story flow better if the paragraphs were longer—if, for example, paragraphs 9 and 10 were joined? paragraphs 16 and 17? 22 and 23? 24 and 25?

Sentences

13. Why has the author used a colon in the first sentence of paragraph 3? Would it be more effective to replace the colon by a dash, or by such an expression as 'including' or 'such as'?

14. Would the final sentence of paragraph 20 be improved by setting off 'I thought' by commas?

15. In the last paragraph of this essay the sentence 'But I simply had to go' is set off by itself. Should it not, rather, be part of the preceding sentence?

Diction

16. Look up: *foal* (19), *patent* (20), *articulate* (28–9), *inferred* (70), *authenticate* (76), *wariness* (77), *quailed* (85), *bided* (113).

17. How effective are these phrases: *loaded with sky* (7), *nervously clattering* (9), *weedy eaves* (11), *meeting eyebrows* (31), *projecting circle* (31)?

18. In paragraph 10 why is the boy shocked at the author's misinterpretation of the name of one of the dogs? How is this misinterpretation related to the rest of the essay?

19. Explain the **imagery** that the author has used in describing the foal in paragraph 5.
20. In the second sentence of paragraph 29 why does the author write 'I had had' instead of "I had"?

POINTS TO LEARN

1. A sincere profession of ignorance and a sympathetic attitude when dealing with an awkward subject will both tend to attract the reader.
2. A well-constructed introductory paragraph, even if it is quite short, can still provide considerable information.

SUGGESTIONS FOR WRITING

What story can you tell about an encounter with a strange or unusual person whom you somehow felt attracted to?

Centre your narrative on this one person, although you may deal briefly with others for background or explanation. Don't hesitate to be critical about this person's beliefs, attitudes, characteristics, clothing, personal habits, or anything else that strikes you; keep in mind, however, that you are writing a narrative, not just a character sketch.

Thus, your emphasis should be on story, although description will be a necessary part of your essay.

IMPROVING YOUR STYLE

1. Write an introductory paragraph that is short but provides necessary information about time, place, purpose, etc.
2. On one or two occasions (no more) confess your ignorance about something which the person you are describing considers important.
3. On several occasions use short passages of dialogue.

HARRY J. BOYLE

Harry J. Boyle (1915–) has had a varied career. Born in Ontario, he became a journalist and broadcaster, and eventually program director of the trans-Canada network for the CBC. He was appointed vice-chairman of the Canadian Radio-Television Commission in 1968, and later became its chairman. In 1979 he was inducted into the Canadian News Hall of Fame for his contributions to journalism in Canada. Boyle has written extensively and in a variety of forms: numerous articles in periodicals such as the *Financial Post* and *Maclean's*; radio and stage plays; books of essays and memoirs—one of which, *Homebrew and Patches*, won the Stephen Leacock Medal for humour in 1963; novels, including *The Great Canadian Novel* (1972) and *The Luck of the Irish* (1975), which also won a Leacock Medal; and collections of short stories and reminiscences, such as *With a Pinch of Sin* (1966), from which the following selection is taken.

Tobogganing

1   The year I made up my mind Santa Claus was only going to give me useful presents of mittens and scarves and a small treat like a book or a jackknife, he completely surprised me.

2   On Christmas morning, in place of the small wooden sleigh I had seen Grandfather working on, there was a toboggan.   5

3   Snow was lean that year and the Big Hill, being sandy and exposed to the sun had scarcely any sliding surface.

4   I went to bed each night after scanning the skies for any sign of snow and praying for a real blizzard. Perversely, the elements would sprinkle a little snow and then blow it into fence drifts or the hollows of the fields.   10

5   It was beginning to look hopeless. I could sit in the kitchen and look out to where the toboggan leaned against the house in the lee of the veranda. It was varnished and new-looking. Pushing it around the yard was frustrating. This long, sleek affair was made for the big slopes and long runs.

6   It looked as if I might have to go back to school after the New Year without 15
having had a real outing on the toboggan. Then, on the Saturday before the New Year, the morning was overcast. The world seemed poised and waiting for something. Big snowflakes ruptured from the clouds and floated down to earth. They were melting as fast as they arrived, but the tempo increased and the bare spots soon had a thin coating of white. Mother had a time restraining me from pushing out to the hill.   20

7   The world was a creation of cotton batting by next morning. The teams on the sleigh made a convoy on the way to church. Everyone was sharing in that hearty friendliness that comes when nature has a transformation. Church was secondary in my thoughts to the anticipation of tobogganing, and when we got home I had to be almost forcibly restrained from going to the hill without anything to eat.   25

8   I was swallowing cake as I wallowed through the deep snow to the top of the hill. The toboggan was a delight. On the first run the snow flared out on each side with a great white spume effect. A touch of morning breeze had blown snow off the pond so that when we hit the ice the momentum carried the toboggan part way up the low hill opposite.   30

9   Snap, my old collie, was suspicious of getting on the toboggan at first, but he soon tired of romping through the deep snow and then having to wade back to the top. First time down he jumped halfway and landed head over heels in the snowbank. Next time he crouched and made the journey.

10   It had seemed all week that if the snow came my wildest dreams of play and 35
happiness would come true. Yet, somehow I grew tired of being alone.

11   Grandfather was the first to wander over to the hill. He stamped around a bit and hedged about going down the hill for ride. Sensing my mood, he got on, neglecting to take the pipe out of his mouth. He made a wild swipe for it about halfway down and left a foot dragging that sent both of us sprawling into the snow, while the con- 40
veyance went wildly to the bottom.

12   Father, at the stable door, yelled for us to stay where we were. He retrieved the toboggan and climbed the hill. 'Takes some knack to handle one of these things,' he suggested to Grandfather.

13 'You think you're so smart . . . then try it,' retorted the older man. 45
14 'Well, I don't know what you're crowing about.'
15 'Go on . . . just try it.'
16 Father got on, adjusted his hands to the ropes, and nodded for a push. He sailed down gracefully, getting an extra boost where the hill bulged a bit, and flashed down to the pond. Lifting both hands in triumph as it came to the ice he flipped off 50 as the toboggan went sideways and hit a clump of grass frozen and protruding above the surface.
17 Grandfather laughed so hard Mother looked out from the kitchen. Soon, in fact before Father had trudged up the hill, she came out to investigate, wearing his overcoat and an old stocking cap. 'Are you children having a good time?' 55
18 Father lurched to grab her. 'Come on, see for yourself what it's like.'
19 Grandfather gave them both a push, and they lost their balance and went sprawling on the toboggan. Down the hill they went but when they reached the bump, both rolled into the snow.
20 By the time Mother and Father came up, our neighbours Ed Higgins and his 60 wife, driving along the concession in a horse and cutter, swung in the laneway.
21 'Do you see what you've done,' exclaimed Mother in mock anger. 'They thought you were killing me.'
22 It developed they were just curious about the toboggan, and it took practically no coaxing to get both of them on the ride. I half expected to go along, but Mother 65 shook her head. Then Father dared Ed to go down the hill standing up, and he did, keeping his balance almost to the pond.
23 After that Father tried it and flipped at the bump. Mother and Mrs Higgins got on and went down, taking ages to bring the toboggan back.
24 I finally got a chance to go down by myself, but when I looked up they had all 70 gone. I trudged back up the hill, half hoping someone might come back to play with me. No one appeared, and when I went to the house Grandfather was asleep on the sofa in the kitchen, Mother was on the couch in the front room, and Father had gone up to bed for a rest.
25 I kept looking at the models of toboggans in the catalogue until I fell asleep in 75 the old chair. Mother woke me up with the noise as she started to get supper.
26 'Didn't you have a wonderful time with your toboggan?' she said.
27 I didn't answer her, and she was so busy she didn't notice. What was there to say?

1966

QUESTIONS
Reader and Purpose

1. How old do you think the narrator is on the occasion he describes here? What difference does it make to the reader whether the narrator is six or sixteen?
2. What do you think Boyle's purpose is in this essay: is he simply describing a part of his youth? Is he trying to make a moral point? Is he analyzing child–parent relationships? All of these? Something else?
3. There is in this essay a feeling of joy mingled with innocence that envelops all: the narrator, his dog, his parents and grandfather, the neighbours. How does Boyle

achieve this feeling? Is it realistic? How is it related (if at all) to the narrator as young boy?

4. At the time this essay was written (1966) many readers would have found a statement such as 'church was secondary in my thoughts' (23–4) somewhat objectionable. Yet in the context of this essay it would probably not have been quite so repellent. Why? What does this expression tell us about the kind of person the narrator is?

Organization

5. Since there are some 21 paragraphs in this fairly short essay (each one averaging about five lines), and since the first four paragraphs contain only five sentences in all, Boyle is clearly not developing his paragraphs in the usual way. Instead of being self-contained units, each with a topic sentence that is substantiated, or explained, Boyle's paragraphs are often no more than single thoughts or feelings, recorded as the narrator experiences them. How do you explain, or justify, this sort of structure?

6. In the first sentence the narrator mentions his complete surprise at the gift of the toboggan; in the last sentence he says that he had no reply to his mother's question. Is there any relation between these two comments? Does the last sentence constitute a form of **closing by return**?

7. Is this essay organized as a narrative, i.e. with a beginning, middle, and end? Explain how it is, or isn't.

8. The ordering principle of this narrative is obviously chronological: events are recounted in the order in which they occurred. But what other method is at work here? Why, for example, does the dog enter the story before the grandfather? Why does the father come after the grandfather and before the mother? Why does the mother's comment in line 77 occur there instead of after line 69?

9. There are a number of sentences that are both dividing points and **transitions**, such as that in line 36. Find the others, and then describe briefly what is contained in each section of this essay.

Sentences

10. Analyze the structure of the first four sentences. Are they **simple**? **complex**? **compound**? Now do the same for the sentences in paragraph 8 and for the last five sentences of the essay. What pattern (if any) do you find?

11. Do you see any relation between the nature of Boyle's subject and his sentence structures? For example, can you say that Boyle's subject is an incident from simple, ordinary farm life that is expressed in simple sentences? Or that Boyle's subject is the complex child–parent relationship that is expressed in complex sentences? Can you see any other relationships between subject and style?

12. Is the last sentence a **rhetorical question**? If so, why? If not, what sort of answer might the narrator provide?

13. Should there be a comma after 'sun' (6)? Why, or why not?

14. Explain how the first sentence is a **periodic sentence**. Then rewrite this sentence to make it a **loose** one, and explain the difference between the two.

Diction

15. Look up: *perversely* (9), *elements* (9), *lee* (12), *tempo* (19), *spume* (28), *momentum* (29), *conveyance* (40–1), *knack* (43), *crowing* (46), *cutter* (61).
16. Boyle does not often use **figures of speech**, but he does use some, such as *snowflakes ruptured* (18) and *a creation of cotton batting* (21). Does he use any others? What effect is achieved by using figures of speech only occasionally?
17. How does one 'push' a toboggan? Do you think Boyle meant the sentence in line 13 to be taken literally or **figuratively**?
18. How can a toboggan be called 'sleek' (13)? What specific word mentioned previously prepares the reader for this description of the toboggan as 'sleek'?
19. To what is the narrator referring when he says that 'the tempo increased' (19)? Explain why 'tempo' is or is not an appropriate word here, and, if it is not, supply a better one.

POINTS TO LEARN

1. In writing of a very personal nature, the normal development of paragraphs may sometimes be neglected in favour of brief expressions of feelings or ideas.
2. There may be two methods of organization at work in a narrative at the same time.
3. A transitional sentence can also act as the indicator of a major division in a narrative.

SUGGESTIONS FOR WRITING

Writing in the first person, describe, in 500–700 words, a memorable experience from your youth: the crisis at your tenth birthday party, your first swim in a lake, the time you got lost in the woods during a family picnic, your encounter with a strange old woman while you delivered newspapers, learning to ride a bike, your first schoolyard fight, the boy you had a crush on in grade five. Organize your narrative chronologically, use figures of speech occasionally, and ensure that your narrative has a beginning, middle, and end.

IMPROVING YOUR STYLE

In your narrative include

1. a few subtle indications of your approximate age;
2. a number of brief paragraphs, of only one or two sentences, each containing only one idea or feeling;
3. a number of sentences that act as both transitions and indicators of the major divisions of your narrative;
4. a closing by return.

STEPHEN LEACOCK

Stephen Leacock (1869–1944), Canada's most famous humorist, was born in England and emigrated to this country with his family in 1876. He was educated at Upper Canada College and the University of Toronto, and did post-graduate work at the University of Chicago. Leacock spent most of his professional life teaching political economy and serving as chairman of his department at McGill University. A dauntingly prolific writer, Leacock published more than thirty books dealing with economics, politics—his *Elements of Political Science* (1906, with later revised editions) was a standard text in North America for more than a generation—history, literature, and social criticism. Today he is best known for his humorous books, of which he wrote more than twenty, and through them gained an international reputation as the finest and most popular comic writer in English of his time. Leacock's most successful works of humour include *Nonsense Novels* (1911), *Sunshine Sketches of a Little Town* (1912), *Arcadian Adventures with the Idle Rich* (1914), *Moonbeams from the Larger Lunacy* (1915), and *My Discovery of England* (1922). The story that follows, one of his most popular, is from *Literary Lapses* (1910).

A, B, and C

1   The student of arithmetic who has mastered the first four rules of his art, and successfully striven with money sums and fractions, finds himself confronted by an unbroken expanse of questions known as problems. These are short stories of adventure and industry with the end omitted, and though betraying a strong family resemblance, are not without a certain element of romance.   5

2   The characters in the plot of a problem are three people called A, B, and C. The form of the question is generally of this sort:

'A, B, and C do a certain piece of work. A can do as much work in one hour as B in two, or C in four. Find how long they work at it.'

3   Or thus: 10

'A, B, and C are employed to dig a ditch. A can dig as much in one hour as B can dig in two, and B can dig twice as fast as C. Find how long, etc. etc.'

4   Or after this wise:

'A lays a wager that he can walk faster than B or C. A can walk half as fast again as B, and C is only an indifferent walker. Find how far, and so forth.'   15

5   The occupations of A, B, and C are many and varied. In the older arithmetics they contented themselves with doing 'a certain piece of work'. This statement of the case, however, was found too sly and mysterious, or possibly lacking in romantic charm. It became the fashion to define the job more clearly and to set them at walking matches, ditch-digging, regattas, and piling cord wood. At times, they became 20 commercial and entered into partnership, having with their old mystery a 'certain' capital. Above all they revel in motion. When they tire of walking-matches—A rides

on horseback, or borrows a bicycle and competes with his weaker-minded associates on foot. Now they race on locomotives; now they row; or again they become historical and engage stage-coaches; or at times they are aquatic and swim. If their occu-   25
pation is actual work they prefer to pump water into cisterns, two of which leak through holes in the bottom and one of which is watertight. A, of course, has the good one; he also takes the bicycle, and the best locomotive, and the right of swimming with the current. Whatever they do they put money on it, being all three sports. A always wins.   30

6   In the early chapters of the arithmetic, their identity is concealed under the names John, William, and Henry, and they wrangle over the division of marbles. In algebra they are often called X, Y, Z. But these are only their Christian names, and they are really the same people.

7   Now to one who has followed the history of these men through countless   35 pages of problems, watched them in their leisure hours dallying with cord wood, and seen their panting sides heave in the full frenzy of filling a cistern with a leak in it, they become something more than mere symbols. They appear as creatures of flesh and blood, living men with their own passions, ambitions, and aspirations like the rest of us. Let us view them in turn. A is a full-blooded blustering fellow, of energetic   40 temperament, hot-headed and strong-willed. It is he who proposes everything, challenges B to work, makes the bets, and bends the others to his will. He is a man of great physical strength and phenomenal endurance. He has been known to walk forty-eight hours at a stretch, and to pump ninety-six. His life is arduous and full of peril. A mistake in the working of a sum may keep him digging a fortnight without   45 sleep. A repeating decimal in the answer might kill him.

8   B is a quiet, easy-going fellow, afraid of A and bullied by him, but very gentle and brotherly to little C, the weakling. He is quite in A's power, having lost all his money in bets.

9   Poor C is an undersized, frail man, with a plaintive face. Constant walking, dig-   50 ging, and pumping has broken his health and ruined his nervous system. His joyless life has driven him to drink and smoke more than is good for him, and his hand often shakes as he digs ditches. He has not the strength to work as the others can, in fact, as Hamlin Smith has said, 'A can do more work in one hour than C in four.'

10   The first time ever I saw these men was one evening after a regatta. They had   55 all been rowing in it, and it had transpired that A could row as much in one hour as B in two, or C in four. B and C had come in dead fagged and C was coughing badly. 'Never mind, old fellow,' I heard B say, 'I'll fix you up on the sofa and get you some hot tea.' Just then A came blustering in and shouted, 'I say, you fellows, Hamlin Smith has shown me three cisterns in his garden and he says we can pump them until to-   60 morrow night. I bet I can beat you both. Come on. You can pump in your rowing things, you know. Your cistern leaks a little, I think, C.' I heard B growl that it was a dirty shame and that C was used up now, but they went, and presently I could tell from the sound of the water that A was pumping four times as fast as C.

11   For years after that I used to see them constantly about town and always busy.   65 I never heard of any of them eating or sleeping. Then owing to a long absence from home, I lost sight of them. On my return I was surprised to no longer find A, B, and C at their accustomed tasks; on inquiry I heard that work in this line was now done by N, M, and O, and that some people were employing for algebraical jobs four foreigners called Alpha, Beta, Gamma, and Delta.   70

12   Now it chanced one day that I stumbled upon old D, in the little garden in front of his cottage, hoeing in the sun. D is an aged labouring man who used occasionally to be called in to help A, B, and C. 'Did I know 'em, sir?' he answered, 'why, I knowed 'em ever since they was little fellows in brackets. Master A, he were a fine lad, sir, though I always said, give me Master B for kind-heartedness-like. Many's the job as we've been   75 on together, sir, though I never did no racing nor aught of that, but just the plain labour, as you might say. I'm getting a bit too old and stiff for it nowadays, sir—just scratch about in the garden here and grow a bit of a logarithm, or raise a common denominator or two. But Mr Euclid he use me still for them propositions, he do.'

13   From the garrulous old man I learned the melancholy end of my former   80 acquaintances. Soon after I left town, he told me, C had been taken ill. It seems that A and B had been rowing on the river for a wager, and C had been running on the bank and then sat in a draught. Of course the bank had refused the draught and C was taken ill. A and B came home and found C lying helpless in bed. A shook him roughly and said, 'Get up, C, we're going to pile wood.' C looked so worn and pitiful that B said,   85 'Look here, A, I won't stand this, he isn't fit to pile wood to-night.' C smiled feebly and said, 'Perhaps I might pile a little if I sat up in bed.' Then B, thoroughly alarmed, said, 'See here, A, I'm going to fetch a doctor; he's dying.' A flared up and answered, 'You've no money to fetch a doctor.' 'I'll reduce him to his lowest terms,' B said firmly, 'that'll fetch him.' C's life might even then have been saved but they made a mistake about the   90 medicine. It stood at the head of the bed on a bracket, and the nurse accidentally removed it from the bracket without changing the sign. After the fatal blunder C seems to have sunk rapidly. On the evening of the next day, as the shadows deepened in the little room, it was clear to all that the end was near. I think that even A was affected at the last as he stood with bowed head, aimlessly offering to bet with the doctor on C's   95 laboured breathing. 'A,' whispered C, 'I think I'm going fast.' 'How fast do you think you'll go, old man?' murmured A. 'I don't know,' said C, 'but I'm going at any rate.'— The end came soon after that. C rallied for a moment and asked for a certain piece of work that he had left downstairs. A put it in his arms and he expired. As his soul sped heavenward A watched its flight with melancholy admiration. B burst into a passion- 100 ate flood of tears and sobbed, 'Put away his little cistern and the rowing clothes he used to wear, I feel as if I could hardly ever dig again.'—The funeral was plain and un-ostentatious. It differed in nothing from the ordinary, except that out of deference to sporting men and mathematicians, A engaged two hearses. Both vehicles started at the same time, B driving the one which bore the sable parallelepiped containing the last   105 remains of his ill-fated friend. A on the box of the empty hearse generously consented to a handicap of a hundred yards, but arrived first at the cemetery by driving four times as fast as B. (Find the distance to the cemetery.) As the sarcophagus was lowered, the grave was surrounded by the broken figures of the first book of Euclid.—It was noticed that after the death of C, A became a changed man. He lost interest in racing with B,   110 and dug but languidly. He finally gave up his work and settled down to live on the interest of his bets.—B never recovered from the shock of C's death; his grief preyed upon his intellect and it became deranged. He grew moody and spoke only in mono-syllables. His disease became rapidly aggravated, and he presently spoke only in words

whose spelling was regular and which presented no difficulty to the beginner. Realizing   115
his precarious condition he voluntarily submitted to be incarcerated in an asylum,
where he abjured mathematics and devoted himself to writing the History of the Swiss
Family Robinson in words of one syllable.

1910

QUESTIONS
Reader and Purpose
1. What does the title tell you about this essay, not just with regard to subject matter but, especially, about the author's attitude? Is the title of the book—*Literary Lapses*—from which this selection is taken also relevant here?
2. The phrase 'the student of' is usually applied to the advanced study of a difficult topic; thus one reads of 'the student of physics', 'the student of Aristotle', 'the student of Renaissance literature'. How, then, does Leacock's 'the student of arithmetic' strike you? Note that he does not use the words 'mathematics' or 'algebra'. What **connotations** is Leacock working with that he expects his readers to grasp fully?

Organization
3. The **tone** of Leacock's essay is established at the beginning, when we find out, in paragraph 1, that, although his topic is the very ordinary (even dull) one of problems in arithmetic, yet these problems are really 'short stories of adventure and industry' (3–4) that contain 'a certain element of romance' (5). How would you describe this tone? What other means of establishing tone does Leacock use in the first seven paragraphs? In attempting to answer this important question, look closely at, among other things, the implications of the two quotations above.
4. In paragraph 8 we see Leacock not only dealing with the elements of a mathematical problem as living characters, but exaggerating the characterization to the point of the ridiculous. How does this affect the tone he has established in the first seven paragraphs of the essay? Is he being consistent?
5. What is the function of paragraph 12? Do you think that it accomplishes its purpose effectively, or not?
6. The last two paragraphs are introduced by the expression 'Now it chanced one day' (71). What does this expression mean? Comment on the effectiveness of this introduction, in view of what is dealt with in these final paragraphs.
7. Is the last sentence of this essay an effective conclusion? Why, or why not? Would you have omitted the last two lines of this sentence (after 'asylum')?

Sentences
8. Paragraph 5 begins with two **periodic sentences**. Do these appear normal, or do they strike you as slightly artificial? Find the other periodic sentences (if there are any) in the first five paragraphs, and comment on their effectiveness, or lack of it.
9. 'Let us view them in turn' (40). Comment on this as an **organizing sentence**.
10. Analyze the sentence structure of paragraphs 1, 8, and 13 (from line 102). Deal with such questions as these: are the sentences **simple, compound, complex**, or

compound-complex? Do they begin with the subject–verb nucleus, with a **subordinate clause**, or with a **phrase**? Are they **loose, balanced, cumulative, freight-train, parallel**, or periodic? Does the writer use dashes and parentheses? Does he use **interrupted movement, antithesis, appositives**, or emphasis by isolation of words or phrases? Finally, compare the sentence structures of these paragraphs, and draw what conclusions seem to you both justified and appropriate.

Diction

11. Look up: *striven* (2), *expanse* (3), *wager* (14), *indifferent* (15), *sly* (18), *revel* (22), *cistern* (26), *blustering* (40), *fortnight* (45), *plaintive* (50), *fagged* (57), *parallelepiped* (105), *incarcerated* (116), *abjured* (117).
12. Why is there no comma after 'full-blooded' (40) and after 'hot-headed' (41)? How would these sentences be affected by inserting commas after these words?
13. On a number of occasions Leacock uses puns and plays on words, as, for example, in lines 73–4, 77–9, 83–4, and 97. Do you think such word games detract from the overall effect of the essay? Or are they consistent with the tone?

POINTS TO LEARN

1. The various connotations of specific words, puns, and plays on words are effective tools for writing good comedy.
2. Even the most dull and prosaic of subjects can be dealt with in a humorous manner.

SUGGESTIONS FOR WRITING

1. Rewrite the first six paragraphs of this essay in a straightforward and factual manner, removing all traces of humour. Then comment on the differences between your version and the original, and try to show how Leacock achieves his comic effects.
2. In four or five paragraphs, try to write an imitation of Leacock. Use a different subject, however, such as one of these: the geography of the Atlantic provinces; the economics of the supermarket; the importance of the various Canadian political parties; the cultural diversity of the local convenience store; the difficulties of learning the irregular verbs in French; the apparatus of the apprentice chemist; the hazards of walking the family dog; etc.

IMPROVING YOUR STYLE

If you decide to write on the second topic, above, remember that the most successful comedy achieves its results not by exaggeration but by understatement—that is, don't underestimate the role played by the reader's imagination.

ANNE U. FORER

Born in New York City, Anne Forer (1945–) was educated at Antioch College, at the City College of New York, and at the New School. She has published short stories in a variety of magazines, as well as several books, among which are *Stories and Letters of Anne and Basha* (1977), *Vague* (1980), *Stories from the East Village* (1983), and *Trouble in Paradise* (1986). The essay below was first published in the August 1984 issue of *Room of One's Own*.

Overeating in College

I got the idea to go to Dr Cantor after they played a tape recording for freshmen at Antioch, where he sort of defined a happy person, or a normal person, or the way to be, as a person who can sit quietly under a tree and say to themselves 'I am a fine wonderful person.' Now I was 17 years old, and away from home for the first time, at a liberal progressive college. I wonder if anyone could have been as unhappy 5 as I was. I was living on chocolate cake and chocolate fudge. Away from home for the first time, I stayed up as late as I possibly could. Forget sleep! I was best friends with the girls I wholeheartedly admired the most, so I could learn to be like them, and I only got crushes on boys who seemed very cool and sophisticated and who didn't like me back. I gained so much weight it wasn't funny, and all I cared about in life was 10 being thin. In short, life was an agony, a total agony, on every level. And I stole chocolate candies from the other girls in the dorm. Now there was no way in the world, when I heard Dr Cantor's tape, that I could have sat under a tree by myself and thought 'all's well with the world and I'm the wellest part of it.' Or maybe the way he said it was 'I have my faults and my assets but by and large I like myself.' Like myself! 15 I hated myself. Not only that, I knew that in my whole entire life I had never sat under a tree by myself just to enjoy the beauty of the day and have a lovely quiet talk with myself. It seemed totally admirable to be that kind of person, I hated myself that I wasn't, it seemed self-composed and poetic and self-sufficient. But at 17 it wasn't my idea of fun. I liked to walk in the woods with a girlfriend, and we would talk about 20 who we would marry, and whether we would live on a farm. You know, have fantasies together. Or I liked to talk to my new friend Sue about intellectual topics—we both liked Einstein. Love, sex or Einstein, or movies, were the only topics that interested me. And what could I talk about with myself? So I knew I was screwed. I couldn't sit under a tree by myself for an afternoon without getting bored, and I could never 25 decide that after all I liked myself, because I was in such suffering. So when my mother sent that letter (explaining how therapy can be so helpful) I went to see the man who did the tape recording, so he could turn me into that kind of person. Well, he made me feel worse. So I never went back.

1984

QUESTIONS
Reader and Purpose

1. In this short autobiographical narrative the author (who is either Anne Forer herself or a character created by her) describes her attitude towards life when she was a 17-year-old girl during her first year as a college student. In telling her story the author uses the fictional technique known as stream-of-consciousness. This technique tries to reproduce, as accurately as possible, the thought processes and language of the speaker as they flow through the speaker's mind—with, as in real life, the hesitations, the stops and starts, the illogicalities, the lack of transitions, etc., that one finds in one's own common train of thought. The result is an intense, detailed look into the mind of the speaker or author.

   What kind of person is this author? Is she a naive young girl who exaggerates her situation, or is she completely accurate when she states that 'life was an agony' (11)? When she tells us that 'Love, sex or Einstein, or movies, were the only topics that interested me' (23–4), what does this tell us about the sort of person she is, about her attitude towards life? Is she realistic in her expectation that Dr Cantor 'could turn me into that kind of person' (28), or is she suffering from romantic delusions?

Organization

2. What is the chronological progression in this essay?
3. Does this essay have a beginning, a middle, and an end? If so, identify each of these parts. If not, explain which part, or parts, are missing.
4. If you were to divide this short essay into two paragraphs, which sentence would make an effective conclusion to the first paragraph? Which sentence would make a good introduction to the second paragraph?
5. What is the relationship between the opening sentence and the sentence in lines 26–8?
6. Is the concluding sentence of this essay logically appropriate? stylistically appropriate?

Sentences

7. Stream-of-consciousness writing is usually quite informal. Is the sentence structure in this essay limited to the **simple sentence**, or is there the occasional **compound sentence**. Does the narrator also use **complex sentences**?
8. Is the sentence in lines 6–7 a **periodic sentence**? Why, or why not?
9. Why is 'Like myself!' (15) followed by an exclamation mark rather than a question mark?
10. Why is the sentence in lines 18–19 punctuated only with commas? Is this correct? If not, is it nevertheless stylistically effective?

Diction

11. In line 6 is the repetition of 'I was' awkward? If so, what rewriting would you do? If not, how can you justify it?
12. An expression typical of today's speech is 'You know' (21). Does the author use any other such **colloquialisms**? Do you believe that they are out of place in this essay, or are they in keeping with the context?

POINTS TO LEARN

1. Even a short, informal essay benefits from a tight structure.
2. A prose style that approaches that of speech can be both lively and entertaining.

SUGGESTIONS FOR WRITING

Using Anne Forer's essay as an example, write your own one-paragraph narrative about a personal problem you once had to suffer through. (If, for whatever reason, you would prefer not to write about yourself, you are free to invent at will). Use a style that is close to that of everyday speech, but without the clumsiness, awkwardness, and repetitions. Structure your paragraph carefully, making sure that there is a definite chronological progression in the events you narrate.

IMPROVING YOUR STYLE

1. Use several compound and complex sentences.
2. Include one sentence that has two or three **comma faults**.

E.B. WHITE

Elwyn Brooks White (1899–1985) was one of several talented writers who joined the staff of *The New Yorker* soon after its foundation in 1925. From 1938 to 1943 he also wrote a regular column for *Harper's Magazine*. White's humorously critical comments on American culture can be found in such works as *Is Sex Necessary?* (1929), a collaboration with James Thurber (see pp 380–4); *One Man's Meat* (1942); *The Wild Flag* (1946); and *The Points of My Compass* (1962). White also published poetry and short stories, as well as two classic works of children's literature: *Stuart Little* (1945) and *Charlotte's Web* (1952). In 1959 White revised a short book by one of his teachers at Cornell University, William Strunk, Jr; *The Elements of Style* has been a bestseller ever since.

'Once More to the Lake' is a carefully crafted narrative that well repays the reader's attention. Like all good narratives, however, it is much more than a recounting of events. The observational, analytical, and personal elements that the narrative conveys show why it is an often-reprinted classic. Students may find a comparison with Thoreau (p. 340–2) most useful.

Once More to the Lake

1   One summer, along about 1904, my father rented a camp on a lake in Maine and took us all there for the month of August. We all got ringworm from some kittens and had to rub Pond's Extract on our arms and legs night and morning, and my father rolled over in a canoe with all his clothes on; but outside of that the vacation was a success and from then on none of us ever thought there was any place in the world like 5 that lake in Maine. We returned summer after summer—always on August 1st for one month. I have since become a salt-water man, but sometimes in summer there are days

when the restlessness of the tides and the fearful cold of the sea water and the incessant wind which blows across the afternoon and into the evening make me wish for the placidity of a lake in the woods. A few weeks ago this feeling got so strong I bought 10
myself a couple of bass hooks and a spinner and returned to the lake where we used to go, for a week's fishing and to revisit old haunts.

2   I took along my son, who had never had any fresh water up his nose and who had seen lily pads only from train windows. On the journey over to the lake I began to wonder what it would be like. I wondered how time would have marred this 15
unique, this holy spot—the coves and streams, the hills that the sun set behind, the camps and the paths behind the camps. I was sure that the tarred road would have found it out and I wondered in what other ways it would be desolated. It is strange how much you can remember about places like that once you allow your mind to return into the grooves which lead back. You remember one thing, and that suddenly 20
reminds you of another thing. I guess I remembered clearest of all the early mornings, when the lake was cool and motionless, remembered how the bedroom smelled of the lumber it was made of and of the wet woods whose scent entered through the screen. The partitions in the camp were thin and did not extend clear to the top of the rooms, and as I was always the first up I would dress softly so as not wake the others, and 25
sneak out into the sweet outdoors and start out in the canoe, keeping close along the shore in the long shadows of the pines. I remembered being very careful never to rub my paddle against the gunwale for fear of disturbing the stillness of the cathedral.

3   The lake had never been what you would call a wild lake. There were cottages sprinkled around the shores, and it was farming country although the shores of the 30
lake were quite heavily wooded. Some of the cottages were owned by nearby farmers, and you would live at the shore and eat your meals at the farmhouse. That's what our family did. But although it wasn't wild, it was a fairly large and undisturbed lake and there were places in it which, to a child at least, seemed infinitely remote and primeval.

4   I was right about the tar: it led to within half a mile of the shore. But when I 35
got there, with my boy, and we settled into a camp near a farmhouse and into the kind of summertime I had known, I could tell that it was going to be pretty much the same as it had been before—I knew it, lying in bed the first morning, smelling the bedroom, and hearing the boy sneak quietly out and go off along the shore in a boat. I began to sustain the illusion that he was I, and therefore, by simple transposition, that 40
I was my father. This sensation persisted, kept cropping up all the time we were there. It was not an entirely new feeling, but in this setting it grew much stronger. I seemed to be living a dual existence. I would be in the middle of some simple act, I would be picking up a bait box or laying down a table fork, or I would be saying something, and suddenly it would be not I but my father who was saying the words or making 45
the gesture. It gave me a creepy sensation.

5   We went fishing the first morning. I felt the same damp moss covering the worms in the bait can, and saw the dragonfly alight on the tip of my rod as it hovered a few inches from the surface of the water. It was the arrival of this fly that convinced me beyond any doubt that everything was as it always had been, that the years were 50
a mirage and there had been no years. The small waves were the same, chucking the rowboat under the chin as we fished at anchor, and the boat was the same boat, the same colour green and the ribs broken in the same places, and under the floorboards

the same fresh-water leavings and debris—the dead helgramite, the wisps of moss, the
rusty discarded fish-hook, the dried blood from yesterday's catch. We stared silently 55
at the tips of our rods, at the dragonflies that came and went. I lowered the tip of mine
into the water, tentatively, pensively dislodging the fly, which darted two feet away,
poised, darted two feet back, and came to rest again a little farther up the rod. There
had been no years between the ducking of this dragonfly and the other one—the one
that was part of memory. I looked at the boy, who was silently watching his fly, and it 60
was my hands that held his rod, my eyes watching. I felt dizzy and didn't know which
rod I was at the end of.

6   We caught two bass, hauling them in briskly as though they were mackerel,
pulling them over the side of the boat in a businesslike manner without any landing
net, and stunning them with a blow on the back of the head. When we got back for 65
a swim before lunch, the lake was exactly where we had left it, the same number of
inches from the dock, and there was only the merest suggestion of a breeze. This
seemed an utterly enchanted sea, this lake you could leave to its own devices for a few
hours and come back to, and find that it had not stirred, this constant and trustworthy body of water. In the shallows, the dark, water-soaked sticks and twigs, 70
smooth and old, were undulating in clusters on the bottom against the clean ribbed
sand, and the track of the mussel was plain. A school of minnows swam by, each min-
now with its small individual shadow, doubling the attendance, so clear and sharp in
the sunlight. Some of the other campers were in swimming, along the shore, one of
them with a cake of soap, and the water felt thin and clear and unsubstantial. Over 75
the years there had been this person with the cake of soap, this cultist, and here he
was. There had been no years.

7   Up to the farmhouse to dinner through the teeming, dusty field, the road under
our sneakers was only a two-track road. The middle track was missing, the one with
the marks of the hooves and the splotches of dried, flaky manure. There had always 80
been three tracks to choose from in choosing which track to walk in; now the choice
was narrowed down to two. For a moment I missed terribly the middle alternative.
But the way led past the tennis court, and something about the way it lay there in the
sun reassured me; the tape had loosened along the backline, the alleys were green with
plantains and other weeds, and the net (installed in June and removed in September) 85
sagged in the dry noon, and the whole place steamed with midday heat and hunger
and emptiness. There was a choice of pie for dessert, and one was blueberry and one
was apple, and the waitresses were the same country girls, there having been no passage of time, only the illusion of it as in a dropped curtain—the waitresses were still
fifteen; their hair had been washed, that was the only difference—they had been to the 90
movies and seen the pretty girls with the clean hair.

8   Summertime, oh summertime, pattern of life indelible, the fade-proof lake, the
woods unshatterable, the pasture with the sweetfern and the juniper forever and ever,
summer without end; this was the background, and the life along the shore was the
design, the cottages with their innocent and tranquil design, their tiny docks with the 95
flagpole and the American flag floating against the white clouds in the blue sky, the
little paths over the roots of the trees leading from camp to camp and the paths leading back to the outhouses and the can of lime for sprinkling, and at the souvenir
counters at the store the miniature birch-bark canoes and the postcards that showed

things looking a little better than they looked. This was the American family at play, 100
escaping the city heat, wondering whether the newcomers in the camp at the head of
the cove were 'common' or 'nice', wondering whether it was true that the people who
drove up for Sunday dinner at the farmhouse were turned away because there wasn't
enough chicken.

9   It seemed to me, as I kept remembering all this, that those times and those 105
summers had been infinitely precious and worth saving. There had been jollity and
peace and goodness. The arriving (at the beginning of August) had been so big a
business in itself, at the railway station the farm wagon drawn up, the first smell of
the pine-laden air, the first glimpse of the smiling farmer, and the great importance
of the trunks and your father's enormous authority in such matters, and the feel of 110
the wagon under you for the long ten-mile haul, and at the top of the last long hill
catching the first view of the lake after eleven months of not seeing this cherished
body of water. The shouts and cries of the other campers when they saw you, and
the trunks to be unpacked, to give up their rich burden. (Arriving was less exciting
nowadays, when you sneaked up in your car and parked it under a tree near the 115
camp and took out the bags and in five minutes it was all over, no fuss, no loud wonderful fuss about trunks.)

10   Peace and goodness and jollity. The only thing that was wrong now, really, was
the sound of the place, an unfamiliar nervous sound of the outboard motors. This
was the note that jarred, the one thing that would sometimes break the illusion and 120
set the years moving. In those other summertimes all motors were inboard; and when
they were at a little distance, the noise they made was a sedative, an ingredient of
summer sleep. They were one-cylinder and two-cylinder engines, and some were
make-and-break and some were jump-spark, but they all made a sleepy sound across
the lake. The one-lungers throbbed and fluttered, and the twin-cylinder ones purred 125
and purred, and that was a quiet sound too. But now the campers all had outboards.
In the daytime, in the hot mornings, these motors made a petulant, irritable sound;
at night, in the still evenings when the afterglow lit the water, they whined about
one's ears like mosquitoes. My boy loved our rented outboard, and his great desire
was to achieve singlehanded mastery over it, and authority, and he soon learned the 130
trick of choking it a little (but not too much), and the adjustment of the needle valve.
Watching him I would remember the things you could do with the old one-cylinder
engine with the heavy flywheel, how you could have it eating out of your hand if you
got really close to it spiritually. Motor boats in those days didn't have clutches, and
you would make a landing shutting off the motor at the proper time and coasting in 135
with a dead rudder. But there was a way of reversing them, if you learned the trick,
by cutting the switch and putting it on again exactly on the final dying revolution of
the flywheel, so that it would kick back against compression and begin reversing.
Approaching a dock in a strong following breeze, it was difficult to slow up sufficiently by the ordinary coasting method, and if a boy felt he had complete mastery 140
over his motor, he was tempted to keep it running beyond its time and then reverse
it a few feet from the dock. It took a cool nerve, because if you threw the switch a
twentieth of a second too soon you would catch the flywheel when it still had speed
enough to go up past centre, and the boat would leap ahead, charging bull-fashion
at the dock. 145

11   We had a good week at the camp. The bass were biting well and the sun shone endlessly, day after day. We would be tired at night and lie down in the accumulated heat of the little bedrooms after the long hot day and the breeze would stir almost imperceptibly outside and the smell of the swamp drift in through the rusty screens. Sleep would come easily and in the morning the red squirrel would be on the roof, tapping out his gay routine. I kept remembering everything, lying in bed in the mornings—the small steamboat that had a long rounded stern like the lip of a Ubangi, and how quietly she ran on the moonlight sails, when the older boys played their mandolins and the girls sang and we ate doughnuts dipped in sugar, and how sweet the music was on the water in the shining night, and what it had felt like to think about girls then. After breakfast we would go up to the store and the things were in the same place—the minnows in a bottle, the plugs and spinners disarranged and pawed over by the youngsters from the boys' camp, the fig newtons and the Beeman's gum. Outside, the road was tarred and cars stood in front of the store. Inside, all was just as it had always been, except there was more Coca Cola and not so much Moxie and root beer and birch beer and sarsaparilla. We would walk out with a bottle of pop apiece and sometimes the pop would backfire up our noses and hurt. We explored the streams, quietly, where the turtles slid off the sunny logs and dug their way into the soft bottom; and we lay on the town wharf and fed worms to the tame bass. Everywhere we went I had trouble making out which was I, the one walking at my side, the one walking in my pants.

12   One afternoon while we were there at the lake a thunderstorm came up. It was like the revival of an old melodrama that I had seen long ago with childish awe. The second-act climax of the drama of the electrical disturbance over a lake in America had not changed in any important respect. This was the big scene, still the big scene. The whole thing was so familiar, the first feeling of oppression and heat and a general air around camp of not wanting to go very far away. In midafternoon (it was all the same) a curious darkening of the sky, and a lull in everything that had made life tick; and then the way the boats suddenly swung the other way at their moorings with the coming of a breeze out of the new quarter, and the premonitory rumble. Then the kettle drum, then the snare, then the bass drum and cymbals, then crackling light against the dark, and the gods grinning and licking their chops in the hills. Afterward the calm, the rain steadily rustling in the calm lake, the return of light and hope and spirits, and the campers running out in joy and relief to go swimming in the rain, their bright cries perpetuating the deathless joke about how they were getting simply drenched, and the children screaming with delight at the new sensation of bathing in the rain, and the joke about getting drenched linking the generations in a strong indestructible chain. And the comedian who waded in carrying an umbrella.

13   When the others went swimming my son said he was going in too. He pulled his dripping trunks from the line where they had hung all through the shower, and wrung them out. Languidly, and with no thought of going in, I watched him, his hard little body, skinny and bare, saw him wince slightly as he pulled up around his vitals the small, soggy, icy garment. As he buckled the swollen belt suddenly my groin felt the chill of death.

1941

QUESTIONS

Reader and Purpose

1. 'Once More to the Lake' appeals to almost everyone. Yet the degree of appeal probably varies. Describe the reader to whom it would appeal the most; the reader to whom it might appeal the least.

2. Which of the following do you think best expresses the theme of 'Once More to the Lake'? Why?

   (a) The first years of the twentieth century were more innocent, more idyllic than those of our violent, destructive, contaminated time.

   (b) Nothing ever really changes.

   (c) Summertime is the happiest season.

   (d) Expecting to find the lake changed and the past unrecapturable, the writer suddenly realizes that the real victim of time is not the lake, but himself.

Organization

3. What does each of the first three paragraphs contribute to the beginning of the essay?

4. Among other things, a beginning often establishes the writer's **tone**. What is E.B. White's feeling about the lake? about his son?

5. The middle portion of the essay (beginning with paragraph 4) is an analysis of the summer ritual. Paragraph 4 might be entitled 'Settling In'; paragraphs 5 and 6, 'Fishing the First Morning'; paragraph 7, 'Returning to the Farmhouse for Dinner'. Give a title to the remaining paragraphs of the middle section.

6. Each paragraph in the body of the essay deals with sameness, change, or a mixture of the two. Which predominates overall—change or sameness? Which appears to be the more unsettling to the writer? Underline those passages in which the author expresses his deepest feelings about sameness and change.

7. What rather unusual method of development is used in paragraph 12?

8. The final paragraph is constructed so that it leads up to and ends on the word death. Is this term (or rather the idea it denotes) central to White's essay? Do you think this paragraph makes an effective conclusion to the essay? Why, or why not.

Sentences

9. The fourth sentence of paragraph 5 ('The small waves . . .') is a detailed expansion of what key word near its beginning? Show how White similarly spins out the first sentence of paragraph 8 by expanding a key term. Such expansion is not padding. What would have been lost had White simply written 'The small boat was the same' and let it go at that?

10. Point to places where White relieves long, complicated sentences like those referred to in the preceding question with short, direct ones.

Diction

11. Look up: *incessant* (8–9), *placidity* (10), *spinner* (11), *gunwale* (28), *primeval* (34), *helgramite* (54), *undulating* (71), *mussel* (72), *cultist* (76), *teeming* (78), *plantains*

(85), *indelible* (92), *juniper* (93), *petulant* (127), *Ubangi* (152), *Moxie* (160), *sarsaparilla* (161), *melodrama* (168), *premonitory* (175).

12. (For the mechanically minded.) What do these expressions mean: *make-and-break* (124), *jump-spark* (124), *one-lungers* (125), *twin-cylinder ones* (125), *needle valve* (131), *flywheel* (133)?

13. This essay is remarkable for its **concrete**, specific, and sensuous diction. Make a list of the various sounds, smells, tastes, and tactile sensations in 'Once More to the Lake'.

14. Compare the two revisions below with the sentence E.B. White wrote and explain why his diction is far better:

> **White:** 'In the shallows, the dark, water-soaked sticks and twigs, smooth and old, were undulating in clusters on the bottom against the clean ribbed sand, and the track of the mussel was plain.' (70–2)

> **Revision 1:** Where the water was shallow you saw the usual trash on the bottom.

> **Revision 2:** Smooth twigs and sticks bobbed near the bank, but the sand was clean. You could see the tracks made by some creature in the sand.

15. List four or five **colloquial** words or phrases in this essay. The following words, on the other hand, are relatively formal: *placidity* (10), *primeval* (34), *imperceptibly* (149), *premonitory* (175). Which kind of diction is more common in this selection—formal or informal?

16. In paragraph 9 White says, 'There had been jollity and peace and goodness' (106–7). How would the emphasis and rhythm have changed had he written instead 'jollity, peace, and goodness'?

17. Point out all the **similes** and **metaphors** you can find in this selection. Which two or three did you like the most?

POINTS TO LEARN

1. Almost any kind of personal experience can be turned into enduring literature if one has the eye, the ear, and the sensibility.

2. Turning an **abstract**, general statement into a series of particulars is an effective way to develop a sentence or paragraph.

3. 'Once More to the Lake' succeeds in part because the writer knows the names of things. His diction is concrete and specific. At the same time, E.B. White can use Latinate diction when precision of thought or feeling is required. Colloquial diction gives the illusion of a speaking voice and reminds us that we are listening to an individual human being, to his longings, fears, joys, biases, and insights.

SUGGESTIONS FOR WRITING

Write your own version of 'Once More to the Lake', telling the story of your return to a place you once enjoyed. The setting, your reactions, and your interpretation will be different, of course, but your purpose will be the same as White's: to tell the story of a place, and perhaps of an event, that profoundly affected you.

IMPROVING YOUR STYLE

Include in your composition

1. a long sentence, like White's in lines 51–5, in which a general image (in his case the boat) is expanded into a series of particulars;
2. two or three short emphatic sentences;
3. several metaphors and several similes.

SUSAN JUBY

Susan Juby's first novel, *Alice, I Think* (2000), is the subject of her essay below. The story is about a teenage girl growing up in the small town of Smithers, BC. The book was shortlisted for the Amazon/Books in Canada First Novel Award and nominated for the Canadian Library Young Adult Novel Award. The former managing editor of Hartley & Marks Publishers and currently a graduate student at Simon Fraser University, Juby (1969–) has already signed a large contract for her next novel, *Miss Smithers*, as well as for a third novel, so far untitled.

A Tale of a Canadian Book up against the System

1   I was once naive enough to think that getting my book published would be the biggest challenge that I would face as a new writer. I have since discovered that getting Canada's Largest Bookstore to fill orders or stock the book is a herculean task, best suited to writers without any outstanding self-esteem issues about personal or artistic worthiness and endowed with a healthy ability to focus aggression.   5

2   It was one of the greatest days in my life when a reputable Canadian literary press agreed to publish my book. It wasn't the biggest publishing company around, and the promotional budget for my little book was decent but modest. So I was realistic. I knew my book would not be available on the shelves of convenience stores and big box bookstores across the land. Still, I was certain that my local warehouse book- 10 store would carry at least one copy and that people would be able to order my book from stores in the chain. After all, the chain supports Canadian authors. The size of their banners declaring the fact hints at actual devotion.

3   When neither my publishing company nor my distributor were able to get a response from anyone at the store regarding stocking my book, at least in my local 15 store, I decided to help. With freshly minted book in hand and keen to be a tireless (but not annoying) self-promoter (a good thing according to my Author's Handbook), I sent a jovial message introducing myself and my book to the Sales Manager at my neighbourhood chapter of the behemoth bookstore. She was reputed to have a strong commitment to local authors.   20

4   She didn't answer. Perhaps the joking tone of the first message had been a mistake. I sent her another message, this one more decorous. 'Dear Ms XXXX, I would be very grateful if . . .' No answer. Had her fondness for local authors been overstated? Or was it just me? Self-doubts began to creep in. Who was I to publish a book? Who asked

me to write the damned thing anyway? I fought back my misgivings, just as I had when   25
my first rejection slip arrived, and kept trying.

5   Finally, I phoned and got through. Although she offered no explanation, I was
sure the Sales Manager had been too busy supporting other Canadian authors to
respond to my variously styled introductions earlier. When she suggested I drop off
some signed copies of my book at the store, no one could have been more thrilled. I   30
rushed several copies to the store, where the Sales Manager attached cheery red stick-
ers proclaiming, 'Signed by the Author!' Heart pounding, I could barely suppress tears
of pride as she placed my books on the Signed by the Author table. I was an author.
My book was available in a major bookstore. Now this was author support! No
Olympic gold medallist could have been more proud.   35

6   Feeling as though I had *arrived* in some fundamental, available-at-warehouse-
bookstores way, I was breezy when people asked where they could get my book. When
the same potential readers reported back that the staff at that store had never heard of
my book, I quickly deflated. 'It's right there on the Signed by the Author table.' I
caught myself adding, 'But it has a sticker . . .' with a pathetic hopeful note in my voice.   40

7   I lost no time contacting the supportive Sales Manager, who responded that it
takes time to get books into the inventory system. Aha! So that was it. I'd read newspaper stories about the plan for 'improved inventory management' at the chain. This
must be part of the new initiative. Of course the mix-up had nothing to do with my
book's worthiness.   45

8   A week later, after several more people reported their failure to locate my book
at the store, I decided to look into the situation for myself. Well, almost myself. I felt
acutely self-conscious about my apparent non-entity author status (if your book was
any good it would be available at this chain, wouldn't it?), so I camouflaged my hair
and donned a salesclerk-style jean shirt. Ready to blend in, I recruited the services   50
of a supportive friend and sent her on a reconnaissance mission to the order desk.

9   'Excuse me. Do you carry *Alice, I Think*?'

10   'You don't know the title?'

11   'No, that is the title. Alice, comma, I Think.'

12   The clerk rolled her eyes.   55

13   'Did you look it up on the system?'

14   'Yes. It says you don't have it.'

15   'Then we don't have it.'

16   'Are you sure?'

17   She checked.   60

18   'Nope. We don't carry that one.'

19   What kind of Improved Inventory Management was this? Quickly abandoning
any notions of covertness, I pushed in front of my friend.

20   'You do so have that book! It's right over there on the special Author table!'

21   The clerk looked at me warily.   65

22   'Do you work here or something?'

23   'No. No I don't. But I do know you carry that book!'

24   I strode the four steps to the Author table, grabbed a copy, and flourished it in
front of me.

25   The clerk shrugged.   70

26   'Well, it's not in the system.'

27   Oh.

28   Defeated, I trailed my friend at a short distance as she went to buy the book. The actual purchase took at least ten minutes, and involved a lot of gesturing, staring blankly at the screen, and several staff members in vigorous consultation. My atten-   75
tion was diverted several times when customers asked me for directions to the coffee shop and floor managers tried to get me to work. The outfit was obviously a mis-calculation. When I returned my attention to the transaction, I heard my friend loudly demand to buy the book while rejecting the claim that she had actually smug-gled it into the store. Eventually the sales team agreed to sell it as a miscellaneous   80
item. They probably rang it up as a candle. When the nightmarish transaction was complete, I slunk out behind my friend, hoping I wouldn't be reprimanded for not signing out, and realizing too late that the unknown shouldn't go anywhere incog-nito—it's too demoralizing.

29   Obviously, this was a serious situation. The chain owns the majority of book-   85
stores in urban areas, and supplies many of those they don't own. For most readers, if a book is not available at this store, it is not available at all. Refusing to let my feelings of unworthiness send me straight into hiding, I comforted myself with the fact that at least people could buy my book online. I knew from surfing the bookstore's website that they have an Extremely Wide Selection, including Hard-To-Find Canadian titles.   90
Of course, my book has a well-known Canadian publisher, and an established dis-tributor, so it couldn't really be classed as hard to find. Still, it was good to know that the online store took a democratic approach to supplying books.

30   Then reports began to pour in that it had been nine weeks and no readers had received their online orders. Nor had their special orders arrived! The website has   95
the largest selection of books in Canada—how could they be missing mine? Independent bookstores, including those in very small towns, were able to get the book for customers. Indigo Books in Toronto and even the US-based Amazon.com were able to fill orders in a reasonable amount of time. What the hell was the prob-lem with Canada's largest bookstore and its online distributor? I was being shut out   100
by the largest bookstore in the country! Paranoia mixed with my feelings of inad-equacy. Whose idea was it to become a writer anyway? Fraud.

31   After the agony of giving birth to my twisted teen comedy, I couldn't let it die without a fight. I went back to the store to check on my signed copies. They had dis-appeared from the Signed by the Author table. Gone! Sold out! Surely now the chain,   105
with its Demonstrated Commitment to customers, would reorder this at least some-what popular item. I approached the clerk and asked about my book.

32   'No, we don't have that one.'

33   'Don't you mean you're sold out?'

34   'No, I don't think we've ever had that one.'   110

35   The clerk checked another computer screen.

36   'It says here that it won't be published until next fall.'

37   More or less hysterical with thwarted ambition and self-help mantras turned wrong (I'm good enough, I'm smart enough, why won't they fill orders for my book?), I became defiant. I hand-delivered more signed books and told the clerk it was my   115
stated intention to assist the store in their Commitment to Customer Convenience.

The clerk wouldn't take them. I insisted. She called her manager. I thrust my books on the pair, refusing to take no for an answer. Eventually they allowed me to leave the books and assured me they would go out on the shelf.

38   I checked back a week later to discover that my unwanted books had vanished.   120
Sold? Stolen? No one knew. There was no record of them. A kindly young clerk took me around the store and showed me all the sections where my book was not. I told him my sad story and he broke into a conspiratorial whisper, 'I know, man. There's a reason people say we're evil.'

39   Impotent authorial rage washed over me. Should I sneak a book onto the shelf?   125
I was afraid the Sales Manager might call security. I was so distraught I tripped and fell, knocking over the Young Adult display, where I had been lurking, waiting to recommend my book to passing customers. I limped out of the store, having been nailed on the foot with the complete works of Judy Blume. Posters declaring the store's passion for Canadian authors watched my ignoble retreat.   130

40   The missing signed copies eventually surfaced and now, almost half a year after the order was placed, one of my readers has received his online book order.

41   So what are the conclusions to be drawn from this? Do only writers with established reputations, large promotional budgets, and huge publishing companies deserve to have their work available to readers who shop at warehouse bookstores?   135
Maybe. Personally, I have worked through my issues. In fact, I've developed a whole new mantra: my book is good enough, it's funny enough, and it is available through independent booksellers.

2000

QUESTIONS

Reader and Purpose

1. In her opening paragraph Susan Juby describes the challenges she faced as a new writer, first, to get her book published, and then to have her book accepted by a bookstore. Thus she has, in only two sentences, told us what her essay will be about. How does she entice the reader to keep reading?

2. Juby never describes her book, but are there any hints or passing references about its nature?

3. Do you believe that the conclusions the author reaches in her final paragraph are reasonable? Are there any other conclusions you would have liked to see her reach?

4. The author often pokes fun at herself. Does this occasionally make her appear a bit silly, or does it always attract the reader's sympathy?

5. The bookstore clerks don't come off very well in Juby's narrative. Is she being unfair?

6. Does this narrative essay have a crisis, or climax, as a short story normally does? If so, where is it? If not, why not?

Organization

7. Is the first sentence of paragraph 2 an **organizing sentence**? Or does it have some other function?

8. What **transitions** join paragraphs 3 and 4? paragraphs 4 and 5? 5 and 6?

9. What is the significance of paragraph 12?

10. The author proceeds chronologically, for the most part, as indicated by such expressions as 'When' (paragraph 3), 'Finally' (paragraph 5), 'A week later' (paragraph 8). But does she signal any other method of development?

Sentences

11. Is the second paragraph constructed of anything but **simple sentences**?
12. Identify the **complex sentences** in paragraph 5.
13. Identify the series in the second sentence of paragraph 28. What verb governs this series?
14. The first two sentences in paragraph 6 are constructed in the same manner: a fairly long **subordinate clause** followed by the **main clause**. Are there any such sentences in paragraphs 29 and 30?
15. In the first sentence of paragraph 37, why has the author used a parenthetical expression around certain points rather than put those ideas into a separate sentence?

Diction

16. Look up: *herculean* (3), *endowed* (5), *minted* (16), *behemoth* (19), *decorous* (22), *misgivings* (25), *acutely* (48), *reconnaissance* (51), *covertness* (63), *transaction* (78), *incognito* (83–4), *paranoia* (101), *mantra* (113), *impotent* (125), *distraught* (126).
17. Although good writers rarely use italics for emphasis, is Juby justified in using italics in the first sentence of paragraph 6?
18. *available-at-warehouse-bookstores way* (36–7) Is this expression awkward? Or is it acceptable on the grounds that it expresses briefly an idea that otherwise would be quite long? Or is it acceptable for some other reason?
19. What effect is the author trying to achieve when she capitalizes words that are not normally capitalized, as in paragraphs 29, 31, and 37?
20. What is the effect of the **irony** in paragraph 39?

POINTS TO LEARN

1. A writer who uses irony at her own expense will very likely attract the reader's sympathy.
2. A narrative tells a story, but in a more restricted manner than a short story.

SUGGESTIONS FOR WRITING

All of us, at one time or another, have had our high hopes, our great expectations, ruined, dashed down, by a variety of unhappy circumstances, or perhaps by one horrid event. In a narrative essay of 5–8 paragraphs, tell this story. Before you start writing decide what it is that you want to convey about your experience, and then select details and organize action accordingly. Use irony if you wish, but without exaggerating.

IMPROVING YOUR STYLE

1. Try to think of an imaginative title for your essay.
2. In one sentence use a three-part series that is governed by one verb.
3. Use a few lines of dialogue.

The essays contained in the final section of this book deal with writing about writing, with writing as a topic that can be defined, described, analyzed; as a topic that can be made the subject of argument and about which one can attempt to persuade others.

The tradition of writing about rhetoric, or, in today's terms, the art of written composition, is one that can be traced back at least as far as Aristotle in the fourth century BC. And, although the tradition has flourished at some times and waned at others, in the modern age—and particularly during the second half of the twentieth century—there has been an extraordinary amount of writing about writing. Books and articles about the nature of writing and how to write have appeared by the thousands; there has been a proliferation of scholarly periodicals devoted to the advanced study of writing and of popular magazines advising how to write articles and stories; even daily newspapers carry articles about writing, and publish letters to the editor complaining about poor writing by their own reporters and about sloppy speaking and writing by politicians and other public figures. The tradition continues, and perhaps stronger than ever.

In spite of the almost infinite possibilities the topic of writing opens up, the eight essays that follow do cover a certain range, if only most briefly and incompletely. Thus, Sanders and Ozick deal with the nature and characteristics of the essay; Lucas and Zinsser emphasize variously the importance of clear writing; Thomas and Rushin focus on punctuation and on clichés, two of the undergraduate writer's most vexing problems; and Branden and Taylor discuss, respectively, poor imagery and the problems faced by Native writers in Canada.

'The essay renews language and clears trash from the springs of thought' (Sanders, p. 426); 'The social purpose of language is communication—to inform, misinform, or otherwise influence our fellows' (Lucas, p. 434); 'To write clear English you must examine every word you put on paper' (Zinsser, p. 437); 'A genuine essay is made out of language and character and mood and temperament and pluck and chance' (Ozick, p. 454). However one-sided or incomplete these statements strike you, they each contain some truth about the writer's craft; they are representative of the attitude towards writing of experienced writers who care fervently about their work.

SCOTT RUSSELL SANDERS

A professor of English and creative writing at Indiana University, Scott Russell Sanders (1945–) has published more than a dozen books, on subjects as diverse as the fiction of D.H. Lawrence, American folksongs, the settlement of America, and the writings of Audubon. He has also published science fiction, children's stories, and historical novels, and he has made numerous contributions to both literary journals and popular magazines, such as *Harper's*, the *New York Times Book Review*, *Carolina Quarterly*, and the *Magazine of Fantasy and Science Fiction*. He has won many awards for his writing, including fellowships from the Guggenheim Foundation and the National Endowment for the Arts. His most recent works are *A Place Called Freedom* (1997) and *Crawdad Creek* (1999).

The Singular First Person

1   The first soapbox orator I ever saw was haranguing a crowd beside the Greyhound station in Providence about the evils of fluoridated water. What the man stood on was actually an upturned milk crate, all the genuine soapboxes presumably having been snapped up by antique dealers. He wore an orange plaid sports coat and a matching bow tie and held aloft a bottle filled with mossy green liquid. I have for- 5
gotten the details of his spiel except his warning that fluoride was an invention of the Communists designed to weaken our bones and thereby make us pushovers for a Red invasion. What amazed me, as a tongue-tied kid of 17 newly arrived in the city from the boondocks, was not his message but his courage in delivering it to a mob of strangers. It would have been easier for me to jump straight over the Greyhound 10
station than to stand there on that milk crate and utter my thoughts.

2   To this day, when I read or when I compose one of those curious monologues we call the personal essay, I often recall that soapbox orator. Nobody had asked him for his two cents' worth, but there he was, declaring it with all the eloquence he could muster. The essay, although enacted in private, is no less arrogant a performance. 15
Unlike novelists and playwrights, who lurk behind the scenes while distracting our attention with the puppet show of imaginary characters—and unlike scholars and journalists, who quote the opinions of others and take cover behind the hedges of neutrality—the essayist has nowhere to hide. While the poet can lean back on a sev-
eral-thousand-year-old legacy of ecstatic speech, the essayist inherits a much briefer 20
and skimpier tradition. The poet is allowed to quit in less than a page, but the essayist must generally hold forth over several thousand words. It is an arrogant and fool-
hardy form, this one-man or one-woman circus, which relies on the tricks of anecdote, memory, conjecture, and wit to hold our attention.

3   It seems all the more brazen or preposterous to address a monologue to the 25
world when you consider what a tiny fraction of the human chorus any single voice is. At the Boston Museum of Science an electronic meter records with flashing lights the population of the United States. Figuring in the rate of births, deaths, emigrants leaving the country, and immigrants arriving, the meter calculates that we add one fellow citizen every 21 seconds. When I looked at it recently, the count stood at 242,958,483. 30

As I wrote the figure in my notebook, the final number jumped from 3 to 4. Another mouth, another set of ears and eyes, another brain. A counter for the earth's population would stand somewhere past 5 billion at the moment and would be rising in a blur of digits. Amid this avalanche of selves, it is a wonder that anyone finds the gumption to sit down and write one of those naked, lonely, quixotic letters to the world.   35

4   A surprising number do find the gumption. In fact, I have the impression that there are more essayists at work in America today, and more gifted ones, than at any other time in recent decades. Whom do I have in mind? Here is a sampler: Edward Abbey, James Baldwin, Wendell Berry, Carol Bly, Joan Didion, Annie Dillard, Stephen Jay Gould, Elizabeth Hardwick, Edward Hoagland, Barry Lopez, Peter Matthiessen, 40 John McPhee, Cynthia Ozick, Paul Theroux, Lewis Thomas, and Tom Wolfe. No doubt you could make up a list of your own—with a greater ethnic range, say, or fewer nature enthusiasts—and one that would provide even more convincing support for my view that we are blessed right now with an abundance of essayists. We have no one to rival Emerson or Thoreau, but in sheer quantity of first-rate work our time stands compar- 45 ison with any period since the heyday of the form in the mid-nineteenth century.

5   In the manner of a soapbox orator, I now turn my hunch into a fact and state boldly that in America these days the personal essay is flourishing. Why are so many writers taking up this risky form, and why are so many readers—to judge by the statistics of book and magazine publication—seeking it out?   50

6   In this era of prepackaged thought, the essay is the closest thing we have, on paper, to a record of the individual mind at work and at play. It is an amateur's raid in a world of specialists. Feeling overwhelmed by data, random information, and the flotsam and jetsam of mass culture, we relish the spectacle of a single consciousness making sense of a portion of the chaos. We are grateful to Lewis Thomas for shining 55 his light into the dark corners of biology, to John McPhee for laying bare the geology beneath our landscape, to Annie Dillard for showing us the universal fire blazing in the branches of a cedar, to Peter Matthiessen for chasing after snow leopards and mystical insights in the Himalayas. No matter if they are sketchy, these maps of meaning are still welcome. As Joan Didion observes in her own collection of essays, 60 *The White Album*, 'We live entirely, especially if we are writers, by the imposition of a narrative line upon disparate images, by the "ideas" with which we have learned to freeze the shifting phantasmagoria which is our actual experience' (Didion, 11). Dizzy from a dance that seems to accelerate hour by hour, we cling to the narrative line, even though it may be as pure an invention as the shapes drawn by Greeks to 65 identify the constellations.

7   The essay is a haven for the private, idiosyncratic voice in an era of anonymous babble. Like the blandburgers served in their millions along our highways, most language served up in public these days is textureless, tasteless mush. On television, over the phone, in the newspaper, wherever humans bandy words about, we encounter 70 more and more abstractions, more empty formulas. Think of the pablum ladled out by politicians. Think of the fluffy white bread of advertising. Think, Lord help us, of committee reports. In contrast, the essay remains stubbornly concrete and particular: it confronts you with an oil-smeared toilet at the Sunoco station, a red vinyl purse shaped like a valentine heart, a bow-legged dentist hunting deer with an elephant 75 gun. As Orwell forcefully argued, and as dictators seem to agree, such a bypassing of abstractions, such an insistence on the concrete, is a politically subversive act. Clinging to this door, that child, this grief, following the zigzag motions of an inquisitive mind, the essay renews language and clears trash from the springs of thought. A century and a half ago, Emerson called on a new generation of writers to cast off the hand-me-down rhetoric of the day, to 'pierce this rotten diction and fasten words again to visible things' (Emerson, 30). The essayist aspires to do just that.

8   As if all these virtues were not enough to account for a renaissance of the protean genre, the essay has also taken over some of the territory abdicated by contemporary fiction. Pared down to the brittle bones of plot, camouflaged with irony, muttering in brief sentences and grade-school vocabulary, today's fashionable fiction avoids disclosing where the author stands on anything. Most of the trends in the novel and short story over the past twenty years have led away from candour—toward satire, artsy jokes, close-lipped coyness, metafictional hocus-pocus, anything but a direct statement of what the author thinks and feels. If you hide behind enough screens, no one will ever hold you to an opinion or demand from you a coherent vision or take you for a charlatan.

9   The essay is not fenced round by these literary inhibitions. You may speak without disguise of what moves and worries and excites you. In fact, you had better speak from a region pretty close to the heart, or the reader will detect the wind of phoniness whistling through your hollow phrases. In the essay you may be caught with your pants down, your ignorance and sentimentality showing, while you trot recklessly about on one of your hobbyhorses. You cannot stand back from the action, as Joyce instructed us to do, and pare your fingernails. You cannot palm off your cockamamie notions on some hapless character. If the words you put down are foolish, everyone knows precisely who the fool is.

10   To our list of the essay's contemporary attractions we should add the perennial ones of verbal play, mental adventure, and sheer anarchic high spirits. The writing of an essay is like finding one's way through a forest without being quite sure what game you are chasing, what landmark you are seeking. You sniff down one path until some heady smell tugs you in a new direction, and then off you go, dodging and circling, lured on by the songs of unfamiliar birds, puzzled by the tracks of strange beasts, leaping from stone to stone across rivers, barking up one tree after another. Much of the pleasure in writing an essay—and, when the writing is any good, the pleasure in reading it—comes from this dodging and leaping, this movement of the mind. It must not be idle movement, however, if the essay is to hold up; it must be driven by deep concerns. The surface of a river is alive with lights and reflections, the breaking of foam over rocks, but beneath that dazzle it is going somewhere. We should expect as much from an essay: the shimmer and play of mind on the surface and in the depths a strong current.

11   To see how the capricious mind can be led astray, consider the foregoing paragraph, in which the making of essays is likened first to the romping of a dog and then to the surge of a river. That is bad enough, but it could have been worse. For example, I began to draft a sentence in that paragraph with the following words: 'More than once, in sitting down to beaver away at a narrative, felling trees of memory and dragging brush to build a dam that might slow down the waters of time . . .' I had set out to make some innocent remark, and here I was gnawing down trees and building dams, all because I had let that 'beaver' slip in. On this occasion I had the good sense to throw out the unruly word.

12　I might as well drag in another metaphor—and another unoffending animal— by saying that each doggy sentence, as it noses forward into the underbrush of thought, scatters a bunch of rabbits that rush off in all directions. The essayist can afford to chase more of those rabbits than the fiction writer can but fewer than the poet. If you refuse to chase any of them, and keep plodding along in a straight line, you and your reader will have a dull outing. If you chase too many, you will soon wind up lost in a thicket of confusion with your tongue hanging out.

13　The pursuit of mental rabbits was strictly forbidden by the teachers who instructed me in English composition. For that matter, nearly all the qualities of the personal essay, as I have been sketching them, violate the rules that many of us were taught in school. You recall that we were supposed to begin with an outline and stick by it faithfully, like a train riding the rails, avoiding sidetracks. Each paragraph was to have a topic sentence pasted near the front, and these orderly paragraphs were to be coupled end to end like so many boxcars. Every item in those boxcars was to bear the stamp of some external authority, preferably a footnote referring to a thick book, although appeals to magazines and newspapers would do in a pinch. Our diction was to be formal and dignified, shunning the vernacular. Polysyllabic words derived from Latin were preferable to the blunt lingo of the streets. Metaphors were to be used only in emergencies, and no two of them were to be mixed. And even in emergencies we could not speak in the first person singular.

14　Already as a schoolboy, I chafed against those rules. Now I break them shamelessly, in particular the taboo against using the lonely capital *I*. My speculations about the state of the essay arise from my own practice as reader and writer, and they reflect my own tastes, no matter how I may pretend to gaze dispassionately down on the question from a hot-air balloon. As Thoreau declares in his brash manner on the opening page of *Walden*: 'In most books the *I*, or first person, is omitted; in this it will be retained; that, in respect to egotism, is the main difference. We commonly do not remember that it is, after all, always the first person that is speaking. I should not talk so much about myself if there were anybody else whom I knew as well' (Thoreau, 3). True for the personal essay, it is doubly true for an essay about the essay: one speaks always and inescapably in the first person singular.

15　We could sort out essays along a spectrum, according to the degree to which the writer's ego is on display—with John McPhee, perhaps, at the extreme of self-effacement and Norman Mailer at the opposite extreme of self-dramatization. Brassy or shy, stage centre or hanging back in the wings, the author's persona commands our attention. For the length of an essay, or a book of essays, we respond to that persona as we would to a friend caught up in a rapturous monologue. When the monologue is finished, we may not be able to say precisely what it was about, any more than we can draw conclusions from a piece of music. 'Essays don't usually boil down to a summary, as articles do,' notes Edward Hoagland, one of the least summarizable of companions, 'and the style of the writer has a "nap" to it, a combination of personality and originality and energetic loose ends that stand up like the nap of a piece of wool and can't be brushed flat' (Hoagland, 25–6). We make assumptions about that speaking voice, assumptions that we cannot validly make about the narrators in fiction. Only a sophomore is permitted to ask how many children had Huckleberry Finn. But even literary sophisticates wonder in print about Thoreau's love life, Montaigne's domestic arrangements, De Quincey's opium habit, Virginia Woolf's depression.

16   Montaigne, who not only invented the form but perfected it as well, announced from the start that his true subject was himself. In his note 'To the Reader', he slyly proclaimed: 'I want to be seen here in my simple, natural, ordinary fashion, without straining or artifice; for it is myself that I portray. My defects will here be read to the life, and also my natural form, as far as respect for the public has allowed. Had I been placed among those nations which are said to live still in the sweet freedom of nature's first laws, I assure you I should very gladly have portrayed myself here entire and wholly naked' (Montaigne, 6). A few pages after this disarming introduction, we are told of the Emperor Maximilien, who was so prudish about displaying his private parts that he would not let a servant dress him or see him in the bath. The emperor went so far as to give orders that he be buried in his underdrawers. Having let us in on this intimacy about Maximilien, Montaigne then confessed that he himself, although 'bold-mouthed', was equally prudish, and that 'except under great stress of necessity or voluptuousness', he never allowed anyone to see him naked (11). Such modesty, he feared, was unbecoming in a soldier. But such honesty is quite becoming in an essayist. The very confession of his prudery is a far more revealing gesture than any doffing of clothes.

17   Every English major knows that the word 'essay', as adapted by Montaigne, means a trial or attempt. The Latin root carries the more vivid sense of a weighing out. In the days when that root was alive and green, merchants discovered the value of goods and alchemists discovered the composition of unknown metals by the use of scales. Just so the essay, as Montaigne was the first to show, is a weighing out, an inquiry into the value, meaning, and true nature of experience; it is a private experiment carried out in public. In each of three successive editions, Montaigne inserted new material into his essays without revising the old material. Often the new statements contradicted the original ones, but Montaigne let them stand, since he believed that the only consistent fact about human beings is their inconsistency. Lewis Thomas has remarked of him that 'he [was] fond of his mind, and affectionately entertained by everything in his head' (Thomas, 148). Whatever Montaigne wrote about, and he wrote about everything under the sun—fears, smells, growing old, the pleasures of scratching—he weighed on the scales of his own character.

18   It is the *singularity* of the first person—its warts and crotchets and turn of voice—that lures many of us into reading essays and that lingers with us after we finish. Consider the lonely, melancholy persona of Loren Eiseley, forever wandering, forever brooding on our dim and bestial past, his lips frosty with the chill of the Ice Age. Consider the volatile, Dionysian persona of D.H. Lawrence, with his incandescent gaze, his habit of turning peasants into gods and trees into flames, his quick hatred and quicker love. Consider that philosophical farmer, Wendell Berry, who speaks with a countryman's knowledge and a deacon's severity. Consider E.B. White, with his cheery affection for brown eggs and dachshunds and his unflappable way of herding geese while the radio warns of an approaching hurricane.

19   E.B. White, that engaging master of the genre, a champion of idiosyncrasy, introduced one of his own collections by admitting the danger of narcissism:

I think some people find the essay the last resort of the egoist, a much too self- 215
conscious and self-serving form for their taste; they feel that it is presumptuous
of a writer to assume that his little excursions or his small observations will
interest the reader. There is some justice in their complaint. I have always been
aware that I am by nature self-absorbed and egotistical; to write of myself to the
extent I have done indicates a too great attention to my own life, not enough to 220
the lives of others. [White, viii]

Yet the self-absorbed Mr White was in fact a delighted observer of the world and shared
his delight with us. Thus, after describing memorably how a circus girl practised her
bareback riding in the leisure moments between shows ('The Ring of Time'), he confessed: 'As a writing man, or secretary, I have always felt charged with the safekeeping 225
of all unexpected items of worldly or unworldly enchantment, as though I might be
held personally responsible if even a small one were to be lost' (White, 153). That statement may still be presumptuous, but the presumption is turned outward on the world.
20   Such looking outward on the world helps distinguish the essay from pure autobiography, which dwells more complacently on the self. Mass murderers, movie stars, 230
sports heroes, Wall Street crooks, and defrocked politicians may blather on about
whatever high jinks or low jinks made them temporarily famous and may chronicle
their exploits, their diets, and their hobbies in perfect confidence that the public is
eager to gobble up every last gossipy scrap. And the public, according to sales figures,
generally is. On the other hand, I assume that the public does not give a hoot about 235
my private life (an assumption also borne out by sales figures). If I write of hiking up
a mountain, with my one-year-old boy riding like a papoose on my back, and of what
he babbled to me while we gazed down from the summit onto the scudding clouds,
I do so not because I am deluded into believing that my baby, like the offspring of
Prince Charles, matters to the great world. I do so because I know that the great world 240
produces babies of its own and watches them change cloud-fast before its doting eyes.
To make that climb up the mountain vividly present for readers is harder work than
the climb itself. I choose to write about my experience not because it is mine but
because it seems to me a door through which others might pass.
21   On that cocky first page of *Walden*, Thoreau justified his own seeming self- 245
absorption by saying that he wrote the book for the sake of his fellow citizens, who
kept asking him to account for his peculiar experiment by the pond. There is at least
a sliver of truth to this, since Thoreau, a town character, had been invited more than
once to speak his mind at the public lectern. Most of us, however, cannot honestly
say that the townspeople have been clamouring for our words. I suspect that all writ- 250
ers of the essay, even Norman Mailer and Gore Vidal, must occasionally wonder
whether they are egomaniacs. For the essayist, in other words, the problem of authority is inescapable. By what right does one speak? Why should anyone listen? The traditional sources of authority no longer serve. You cannot justify your words by
appealing to the Bible or some other holy text; you cannot merely stitch together a 255
patchwork of quotations from classical authors; you cannot lean on a podium at the
Atheneum and deliver your wisdom to a rapt audience.
22   In searching for your own soapbox, a sturdy platform from which to deliver
your opinionated monologues, it helps if you have already distinguished yourself at

some other, less fishy form. When Yeats describes his longing for Maud Gonne or 260
muses on Ireland's misty lore, his words are charged with the prior strength of his
poetry. When Virginia Woolf, in *A Room of One's Own*, reflects on the status of women
and the conditions necessary for making art, she speaks as the author of *Mrs Dalloway*
and *To the Lighthouse*. The essayist may also lay claim to our attention by having lived
through events or travelled through terrains that already bear a richness of meaning. 265
When James Baldwin writes his *Notes of a Native Son*, he does not have to convince us
that racism is a troubling reality. When Barry Lopez takes us on a meditative tour of
the Far North in *Arctic Dreams*, he can rely on our curiosity about that fabled and forbidding place. When Paul Theroux climbs aboard a train and invites us on a journey
to some exotic destination, he can count on the romance of railroads and the allure of 270
remote cities to bear us along.

23   Most essayists, however, cannot draw on any source of authority from beyond
the page to lend force to the page itself. They can only use language to put themselves
on display and to gesture at the world. When Annie Dillard tells us in the opening
lines of *Pilgrim at Tinker Creek* about the tomcat with bloody paws who jumps through 275
the window onto her chest, why should we listen? Well, because of the voice that goes
on to say: 'And some mornings I'd wake in daylight to find my body covered with paw
prints in blood; I looked as though I'd been painted with roses' (Dillard, 1). Listen to
her explaining a few pages later what she is about in this book, this broody, zestful
record of her stay in the Roanoke Valley: 'I propose to keep here what Thoreau called 280
"a meteorological journal of the mind", telling some tales and describing some of the
sights of this rather tamed valley, and exploring, in fear and trembling, some of the
unmapped dim reaches and unholy fastnesses to which those tales and sights so
dizzyingly lead' (Dillard, 11). The sentence not only describes the method of her literary search but also displays the breathless, often giddy, always eloquent and spiri- 285
tually hungry soul who will do the searching. If you enjoy her company, you will
relish Annie Dillard's essays; otherwise you will not.

24   Listen to another voice which readers tend to find either captivating or insuf-
ferable:

> That summer I began to see, however dimly, that one of my ambitions, perhaps 290
> my governing ambition, was to belong fully to this place, to belong as the
> thrushes and the herons and the muskrats belonged, to be altogether at home
> here. That is still my ambition. But now I have come to see that it proposes an
> enormous labour. It is a spiritual ambition, like goodness. The wild creatures
> belong to the place by nature, but as a man I can belong to it only by under- 295
> standing and by virtue. It is an ambition I cannot hope to succeed in wholly,
> but I have come to believe that it is the most worthy of all. [Berry, 52]

The speaker is Wendell Berry writing about his patch of Kentucky. Once you have
heard that stately, moralizing, cherishing voice, laced with references to the land, you
will not mistake it for anyone else's. Berry's themes are profound and arresting ones. 300
But it is his voice, more than anything he speaks about, that either seizes us or drives
us away.

25   Even so distinct a persona as Wendell Berry's or Annie Dillard's is still only a literary fabrication, of course. The first person singular is too narrow a gate for the

whole writer to pass through. What we meet on the page is not the flesh-and-blood 305
author but a simulacrum, a character who wears the label *I*. Introducing the lectures
that became *A Room of One's Own*, Virginia Woolf reminded her listeners that ' "I" is
only a convenient term for somebody who has no real being. Lies will flow from my
lips, but there may perhaps be some truth mixed up with them; it is for you to seek
out this truth and to decide whether any part of it is worth keeping' (Woolf, 4). Here 310
is a part I consider worth keeping: 'Women have served all these centuries as looking-
glasses possessing the magic and delicious power of reflecting the figure of man at
twice its natural size' (Woolf, 35). It is from such elegant, revelatory sentences that we
build up our notion of the 'I' who speaks to us under the name of Virginia Woolf.

26   What the essay tells us may not be true in any sense that would satisfy a court 315
of law. As an example, think of Orwell's brief narrative, 'A Hanging', which describes
an execution in Burma. Anyone who has read it remembers how the condemned man
as he walked to the gallows stepped aside to avoid a puddle. Only an eyewitness
should be able to report such a haunting detail. Alas, biographers, those zealous
debunkers, have recently claimed that Orwell never saw such a hanging; that he 320
reconstructed it from hearsay. What then do we make of his essay? Or has it become
the sort of barefaced lie that we prefer to call a story?

27   Frankly, I do not much care what label we put on 'A Hanging'—fiction or non-
fiction, it is a powerful statement either way—but Orwell might have cared a great
deal. I say so because not long ago I found one of my own essays treated in a schol- 325
arly article as a work of fiction. When I recovered from the shock of finding any reference to my work at all, I was outraged. Here was my earnest report about growing
up on a military base, my heartfelt rendering of indelible memories, being confused
with the airy figments of novelists! To be sure, in writing the piece I had used dialogue, scenes, settings, character descriptions, the whole fictional bag of tricks; I had 330
picked and chosen among a thousand beckoning details; and I had downplayed some
facts and highlighted others. But I was writing about the actual, not the invented. I
shaped the matter, but I did not make it up.

28   To explain my outrage, I must break another taboo, which is to speak of the
author's intention. My teachers warned me strenuously to avoid the intentional fallacy. 335
They told me to regard poems and plays and stories as objects washed up on the page
from some unknown and unknowable shores. Now that I am on the other side of the
page, so to speak, I think quite recklessly of intention all the time. I believe that, if we
allow the question of intent in the case of murder, we should allow it in literature. The
essay is distinguished from the short story, not by the presence or absence of literary 340
devices, not by tone or theme or subject, but by the writer's stance toward the material. In composing an essay about what it was like to grow up on that military base,
I *meant* something quite different from what I mean when I concoct a story. I meant
to preserve and record and help give voice to a reality that existed independently of
me. I meant to pay my respects to a minor passage of history in an out-of-the-way 345
place. I felt responsible to the truth as known by other people. I wanted to speak
directly out of my own life into the lives of others.

29   You can see I am teetering on the brink of metaphysics. One step farther and I
will plunge into the void, wondering as I fall how to prove there is any external truth
for the essayist to pay homage to. I draw back from the brink and simply declare that 350

I believe one writes, in essays, with a regard for the actual world, with a respect for the shared substance of history, the autonomy of other lives, the being of nature, and the mystery and majesty of a creation we have not made.

30   When it comes to speculating about the creation, I feel more at ease with physics than with metaphysics. According to certain bold and lyrical cosmologists,   355 there is at the centre of black holes a geometrical point, the tiniest conceivable speck, where all the matter of a collapsed star has been concentrated and where everyday notions of time, space, and force break down. That point is called a singularity. The boldest and most poetic theories suggest that anything sucked into a singularity might be flung back out again, utterly changed, somewhere else in the universe. The   360 lonely first person, the essayist's microcosmic 'I', may be thought of as a verbal singularity at the centre of the mind's black hole. The raw matter of experience, torn away from the axes of time and space, falls in constantly from all sides, undergoes the mind's inscrutable alchemy, and reemerges in the quirky, unprecedented shape of an essay.   365

31   Now it is time for me to step down, before another metaphor seizes hold of me, before you notice that I am standing, not on a soapbox, but on the purest air.

1989

Works Cited

Berry, Wendell. *Recollected Essays, 1965–1980*. San Francisco: North Point, 1981.

Didion, Joan. *The White Album*. New York: Simon and Schuster, 1979.

Dillard, Annie. *Pilgrim at Tinker Creek*. New York: Harper's Magazine Press, 1974.

Emerson, Ralph Waldo. Nature. Vol. I of *The Complete Works of Ralph Waldo Emerson*. Boston: Houghton Mifflin, 1903.

Hoagland, Edward. *The Tugman's Passage*. New York: Random House, 1982.

Montaigne, Michel de. *Essays*. Trans. Donald Frame. Stanford: Stanford University Press, 1958.

Thomas, Lewis. *The Medusa and the Snail*. New York: Viking, 1979.

Thoreau, Henry David. *Walden*. Ed. J. Lyndon Shanley. Princeton: Princeton University Press, 1973.

White, E.B. *Essays of E.B. White*. New York: Harper, 1977.

Woolf, Virginia. *A Room of One's Own*. New York: Harcourt, Brace and World, 1957.

QUESTIONS

Reader and Purpose

1. Why does Sanders title his essay 'The Singular First Person' rather than 'The First Person Singular'? What difference is there between these two expressions? What emphasis is there in his title that is not present in the other expression? Note what he says at the end of paragraph 14, as well as his comments in paragraph 30.

2. In paragraph 2 to what extent is Sanders expressing your own views or attitude when you write an essay?

3. Which of the essayists mentioned in paragraph 4 have you read? Are any of them among your favourite writers? Which of them would you like to read more of?

4. Paragraph 5 has several functions: it is the **transition** between the first four paragraphs and paragraphs 6–12, it makes a statement of belief, and it asks two questions that the paragraphs following will try to answer.

   Identify two other transitional paragraphs in this essay and describe the functions of each.

5. In two different sentences in paragraph 7 the author gives several specific (and quite
unusual) examples of how the essay, as he puts it, 'remains stubbornly concrete and
particular'. What unusual examples do you remember from your own reading?

6. How are paragraphs 7–10 linked thematically? What expressions are used as transitions? Apply these same questions to paragraphs 20–22.

7. In discussing his use of **metaphors** in paragraphs 11 and 12, what is the author's
tone? What effect does this **tone** have on you?

8. Is the last sentence of paragraph 12 a fitting conclusion to paragraphs 10–12?
Explain why, or why not.

9. How is paragraph 13 related to paragraph 12? paragraph 14 to paragraph 13? 15
to 14?

10. Is the first sentence of paragraph 15 an **organizing sentence**? If so, what does it
organize? If not, what function does it have?

11. How is the final sentence of paragraph 16 a logical conclusion to the paragraph?

12. What does Sanders mean when he says, in his final paragraph, that he is 'standing, not on a soapbox, but on the purest air'?

13. The book in which Sanders' essay appeared is titled *Essays on the Essay: Re-
defining the Genre*. How has this essay redefined the genre for you? How—if at
all—will it affect the way in which you read essays? Can you say that it will change
the way in which you approach the writing of an essay?

SUGGESTIONS FOR WRITING

1. 'The essay, as Montaigne was the first to show, is a weighing out, an inquiry into
the value, meaning, and true nature of experience; it is a private experiment carried
out in public' (193–5).

   To what extent is this description of the nature of the essay accurate as a
description of the writing you have done so far in your secondary or post-secondary
education?

2. On the basis of all the writing you have done in junior and senior high school, in college or university, or outside of school, describe yourself as an essayist.

   Although this might seem like a difficult topic, you should already have considerable information to use as the basis for your essay, information that would answer
such questions as the following:

   • What kinds of writing do I prefer doing: persuasive? narrative? descriptive?
     argumentative? expository?
   • What kinds of writing do I prefer reading?
   • What are my strengths as a writer: sentence structure? imagery? vocabu-
     lary? paragraph structure? What are my weaknesses: punctuation? gram-
     matical functions? verbosity?
   • What sorts of topics attract me? Which repel me?

- What **tone** do I prefer?
- What kind of reader do I like to address myself to?
- What kinds of subjects do I not like to write about?
- How do I prepare an essay: by outlining in detail? by outlining in general? by writing first and then reorganizing? by writing small bits and then amalgamating them? etc., etc.

F.L. LUCAS

F.L. Lucas (1894–1967), British essayist and critic, was a fellow of King's College, Cambridge, and a university lecturer in English. His critical works reflect his interest in the personalities of writers and their moral values. Typical of his best criticism is *The Search for Good Sense*; *Four Eighteenth-Century Characters: Johnson, Chesterfield, Boswell, Goldsmith* (1958), a model of lively, urbane prose. Lucas was thoroughly grounded in the classics and widely acquainted with European literature. His familiarity with the finest prose in several languages accounts for the success of his book *Style* (1955), from which the following selection comes.

Courtesy to Readers—Clarity

> *One should not aim at being possible to understand, but at being impossible to misunderstand.*
>
> —Quintilian

> *Obscurité . . . vicieuse affectation.*
>
> —Montaigne

1   Character, I have suggested, is the first thing to think about in style. The next step is to consider what characteristics can win a hearer's or a reader's sympathy. For example, it is bad manners to give them needless trouble. Therefore clarity. It is bad manners to waste their time. Therefore brevity.

2   There clings in my memory a story once told me by Professor Sisson. A   5 Frenchman said to him: 'In France it is the writer that takes the trouble; in Germany, the reader; in England it is betwixt and between.' The generalization is over-simple; perhaps even libellous; but not without truth. It gives, I think, another reason why the level of French prose has remained so high. And this may in turn be partly because French culture has been based more than ours on conversation and the salon. In most   10 conversation, if he is muddled, wordy, or tedious, a man is soon made, unless he is a hippopotamus, to feel it. Further, the salon has been particularly influenced by women; who, as a rule, are less tolerant of tedium and clumsiness than men.

3   First, then, clarity. The social purpose of language is communication—to inform, misinform, or otherwise influence our fellows. True, we also use words in soli-   15 tude to think our own thoughts, and to express our feelings to ourselves. But writing is concerned rather with communication than with self-communing; though some writers, especially poets, may talk to themselves in public. Yet, as I have said, even these, though in a sense overheard rather than heard, have generally tried to reach an audience. No doubt in some modern literature there has appeared a tendency to 20 replace communication by a private maundering to oneself which shall inspire one's audience to maunder privately to themselves—rather as if the author handed round a box of drugged cigarettes of his concoction to stimulate each guest to his own solitary dreams. But I have yet to be convinced that such activities are very valuable; or that one's own dreams and meditations are much heightened by the stimulus of some other 25 voice soliloquizing in Chinese. The irrational, now in politics, now in poetics, has been the sinister opium of our tormented and demented century.

4   For most prose, at all events, there is a good deal in Defoe's view of what style should be: 'I would answer, that in which a man speaking to five hundred people, of all common and various capacities, idiots or lunatics excepted, should be understood 30 by them all.' This is, indeed, very like the verdict of Anatole France on the three most important qualities of French style: 'd'abord la clarté, puis encore la clarté, enfin la clarté.' Poetry, and poetic prose, may sometimes gain by a looming mystery like that of a mountain-cloud or thunderstorm; but ordinary prose, I think, is happiest when it is clear as the air of a spring day in Attica.   35

5   True, obscurity cannot always be avoided. It is impossible to make easy the ideas of an Einstein, or the psychology of a Proust. But even abstruse subjects are often made needlessly difficult; for instance, by the type of philosopher who, sometimes from a sound instinct of self-preservation, consistently refuses to illustrate his meaning by examples; or by the type of scientific writer who goes decked out with technical jargon 40 as an Indian brave with feathers. Most obscurity is an unmixed, and unnecessary, evil.

6   It may be caused by incoherence; by inconsiderateness; by overcrowding of ideas; by pomp and circumstance; by sheer charlatanism; and doubtless by other things I have not thought of.

7   And how is clarity to be acquired? Mainly by taking trouble; and by writing to 45 serve people rather than to impress them. Most obscurity, I suspect, comes not so much from incompetence as from ambition—the ambition to be admired for depth of sense, or pomp of sound, or wealth of ornament. It is for the writer to think and rethink his ideas till they are clear; to put them in a clear order; to prefer (other things equal, and subject to the law of variety) short words, sentences, and paragraphs to 50 long; not to try to say too many things at once; to eschew irrelevancies; and, above all, to put himself with imaginative sympathy in his reader's place. Everyone knows of Molière reading his plays to his cook; eight centuries before him, in distant China, Po Chu-i had done the like; and Swift's Dublin publisher, Faulkner, would similarly read Swift's proofs aloud to him and two of his men-servants—'which, if they did not com- 55 prehend, he would alter and amend, until they understood it perfectly well.' In short, it is usually the pretentious and the egotistic who are obscure, especially in prose; those who write with wider sympathy, to serve some purpose beyond themselves, must usually be muddy-minded creatures if they cannot, or will not, be clear.

1955

QUESTIONS

1. At the beginning of his essay Lucas makes the rather unusual statement that lack of clarity in writing has to do with one's character. What does he mean? How is this statement related to the title of his essay?

2. In paragraph 6 the author mentions that there are five reasons for obscurity in writing, as well as 'other things I have not thought of'. What do you believe are some of these other reasons?

3. When the author states, at the beginning of paragraph 7, that clarity is to be acquired 'Mainly by taking trouble', is he oversimplifying a complex problem? Is your own principal difficulty in writing that of not taking sufficient trouble? If not, what is it about writing that gives you the most difficulty?

4. Most of Lucas's words are simple, and polysyllabic words do not occur as often as words of one and two syllables. Yet he sometimes uses rare or unusual words that help to give his prose interest, variety, and emphasis—'maundering' (21), for example. How many others can you identify?

5. Frequent **allusions** and quotations are characteristic of Lucas's style. Point out several. Do these contribute to, or detract from, the clarity of his writing? Explain.

6. Several times Lucas uses **metaphors** and **similes**. Identify each one and explain its purpose. Rewrite each sentence containing one of these figures in order to express the same idea in non-figurative language. Describe the difference in effect in each instance.

7. Does Lucas win his reader's sympathy in this selection? If so, how? If not, why not?

8. Describe as fully as you can the personality behind this prose. What are Lucas's assumptions about writing, about literature, about what we vaguely call a philosophy of life? What does he like and dislike? How does he regard his reader? What kind of reader might be hostile to this writer?

9. Although the author does not specifically mention grace, or elegance, as one attribute of a good prose style, what do you think he would say of it?

10. Does Lucas succeed in following his own advice? Your answer to this question should be as specific as possible.

SUGGESTIONS FOR WRITING

1. Imitating Lucas's style generally, but not slavishly, write an essay on the virtue of either economy or simplicity in prose.

2. Choosing your best essay, compare and contrast your own prose with that of F.L. Lucas. Try also to improve the clarity and grace of one of your less successful essays by applying Lucas's advice.

WILLIAM ZINSSER

A newspaperman who spent 13 years as a writer and editor for the *New York Herald Tribune*, William Zinsser has also frequently contributed to such publications as *The New Yorker* and *Life*. He taught writing courses at Yale in non-fiction and humour, and was general editor of the Book-of-the-Month Club. Among his many books are *Writing with a Word Processor* (1983) and *Writing To Learn* (1988). He has also edited a wide variety of books, among them *Extraordinary Lives: The Art and Craft of American Biography* (1986), *Inventing the Truth: The Art and Craft of Memoir* (1987), and *Worlds of Childhood: The Art and Craft of Writing for Children* (1990). His latest book is *Easy To Remember: The Great American Songwriters and Their Songs* (2000). *On Writing Well: An Informal Guide to Writing Nonfiction*, from which the essay below is taken, was first published in 1976 and is now in its sixth edition.

Clutter

1   Fighting clutter is like fighting weeds—the writer is always slightly behind. New varieties sprout overnight, and by noon they are part of American speech. Consider what President Nixon's aide John Dean accomplished in just one day of testimony on TV during the Watergate hearings. The next day everyone in America was saying 'at this point in time' instead of 'now'.   5

2   Consider all the prepositions that are draped onto verbs that don't need any help. We no longer head committees. We head them up. We don't face problems anymore. We face up to them when we can free up a few minutes. A small detail, you may say—not worth bothering about. It *is* worth bothering about. Writing improves in direct ratio to the number of things we can keep out of it that shouldn't be there. 'Up' 10 in 'free up' shouldn't be there. To write clean English you must examine every word you put on paper. You'll find a surprising number that don't serve any purpose.

3   Take the adjective 'personal', as in 'a personal friend of mine', 'his personal feeling', or 'her personal physician'. It's typical of hundreds of words that can be eliminated. The personal friend has come into the language to distinguish him or her from 15 the business friend, thereby debasing both language and friendship. Someone's feeling is that person's personal feeling—that's what 'his' and 'her' mean. As for the personal physician, that's the man or woman summoned to the dressing room of a stricken actress so she won't have to be treated by the impersonal physician assigned to the theatre. Someday I'd like to see that person identified as 'her doctor'. Physicians are 20 physicians, friends are friends. The rest is clutter.

4   Clutter is the laborious phrase that has pushed out the short word that means the same thing. Even before John Dean, people and businesses had stopped saying 'now'. They were saying 'currently' ('all our operators are currently busy'), or 'at the present time', or 'presently' (which means 'soon'). Yet the idea can always be 25 expressed by 'now' to mean the immediate moment ('Now I can see him'), or by 'today' to mean the historical present ('Today prices are high'), or simply by the verb 'to be' ('It is raining'). There's no need to say, 'At the present time we are experiencing precipitation.'

5   'Experiencing' is one of the ultimate clutterers. Even your dentist will ask if you 30
are experiencing any pain. If he had his own kid in the chair he would say, 'Does it
hurt?' He would, in short, be himself. By using a more pompous phrase in his professional role, he not only sounds more important; he blunts the painful edge of truth.
It's the language of the flight attendant demonstrating the oxygen mask that will drop
down if the plane should run out of air. 'In the unlikely possibility that the aircraft 35
should experience such an eventuality', she begins—a phrase so oxygen-depriving in
itself that we are prepared for any disaster.

6   Clutter is the ponderous euphemism that turns a slum into a depressed socio-
economic area, a salesman into a marketing representative, garbage collectors into
waste-disposal personnel, and the town dump into the volume reduction unit. I think 40
of Bill Mauldin's cartoon of two hoboes riding a freight car. One of them says, 'I started
as a simple bum, but now I'm hard-core unemployed.' Clutter is political correctness
gone amok. I saw an ad for a boys' camp designed to provide 'individual attention for
the minimally exceptional'.

7   Clutter is the official language used by corporations to hide their mistakes. 45
When the Digital Equipment Corporation eliminated 3,000 jobs, its statement didn't
mention layoffs; those were 'involuntary methodologies'. When an Air Force missile
crashed, it 'impacted with the ground prematurely'. When General Motors had a plant
shutdown, that was a 'volume-related production-schedule adjustment'. Companies
that go belly-up have 'a negative cash-flow position'. 50

8   Clutter is the language of the Pentagon calling an invasion a 'reinforced protective reaction strike' and by justifying its vast budgets on the need for 'counterforce
deterrence'. As George Orwell pointed out in 'Politics and the English Language', an
essay written in 1946 but often cited during the Vietnam and Cambodia years of
Presidents Johnson and Nixon, 'political speech and writing are largely the defence of 55
the indefensible. . . . Thus political language has to consist largely of euphemism,
question-begging, and sheer cloudy vagueness.' Orwell's warning that clutter is not
just a nuisance but a deadly tool has become true in the recent decades of American
military adventurism in Southeast Asia, and other parts of the world.

9   Verbal camouflage reached new heights during General Alexander Haig's tenure 60
as President Reagan's secretary of state. Before Haig, nobody had thought of saying 'at
this juncture of maturization' to mean 'now'. He told the American people that he saw
'improved pluralization' in El Salvador, that terrorism could be fought with 'meaningful sanctionary teeth', and that intermediate nuclear missiles were 'at the vortex of
cruciality'. As for any worries the public might harbour, his message was 'leave it to 65
Al,' though what he actually said was: 'We must push this to a lower decibel of public fixation. I don't think there's much of a learning curve to be achieved in this area
of content.'

10   I could go on quoting examples from various fields—every profession has its
growing arsenal of jargon to throw dust in the eyes of the populace. But the list would 70
be tedious. The point of raising it now is to serve notice that clutter is the enemy.
Beware, then, of the long word that's no better than the short word: 'assistance' (help),
'numerous' (many), 'facilitate' (ease), 'individual' (man or woman), 'remainder' (rest),
'initial' (first), 'implement' (do), 'sufficient' (enough), 'attempt' (try), 'referred to as'
(called), and hundreds more. Beware of all the slippery new fad words: paradigm and 75

parameter, prioritize and potentialize. They are all weeds that will smother what you write. Don't dialogue with someone you can talk to. Don't interface with anybody.

11   Just as insidious are the little word clusters with which we explain how we propose to go about our explaining: 'I might add', 'It should be pointed out', 'It is interesting to note'. If you might add, add it. If it should be pointed out, point it out. If it is   80 interesting to note, *make* it interesting; are we not all stupefied by what follows when someone says, 'This will interest you'? Don't inflate what needs no inflating: 'with the possible exception of' (except), 'due to the fact that' (because), 'he totally lacked the ability to' (he couldn't), 'until such time as' (until), 'for the purpose of' (for).

12   Is there any way to recognize clutter at a glance? Here's a device my students at   85 Yale found helpful. I would put brackets around any component in a piece of writing that wasn't doing useful work. Often just one word got bracketed: the unnecessary preposition appended to a verb ('order up'), or the adverb that carries the same meaning as the verb ('smile happily'), or the adjective that states a known fact ('tall skyscraper'). Often my brackets surrounded the little qualifiers that weaken any sen-   90 tence they inhabit ('a bit', 'sort of'), or phrases like 'in a sense', which don't mean anything. Sometimes my brackets surrounded an entire sentence—the one that essentially repeats what the previous sentence said, or that says something readers don't need to know or can figure out for themselves. Most first drafts can be cut by 50 per cent without losing any information or losing the author's voice.   95

13   My reason for bracketing the students' superfluous words, instead of crossing them out, was to avoid violating their sacred prose. I wanted to leave the sentence intact for them to analyze. I was saying, 'I may be wrong, but I think this can be deleted and the meaning won't be affected. But *you* decide. Read the sentence without the bracketed material and see if it works.' In the early weeks of the term I handed   100 back papers that were festooned with brackets. Entire paragraphs were bracketed. But soon the students learned to put mental brackets around their own clutter, and by the end of the term their papers were almost clean. Today many of those students are professional writers, and they tell me, 'I still see your brackets—they're following me through life.'   105

14   You can develop the same eye. Look for the clutter in your writing and prune it ruthlessly. Be grateful for everything you can throw away. Re-examine each sentence you put on paper. Is every word doing new work? Can any thought be expressed with more economy? Is anything pompous or pretentious or faddish? Are you hanging on to something useless just because you think it's beautiful?   110

15   Simplify, simplify.

1976

QUESTIONS

1. Which is the key sentence of the first two paragraphs? Explain why it is the key sentence and why it is positioned where it is.
2. 'Clutter is the enemy' (71). Is this sentence the conclusion to the first 10 paragraphs? If so, how? If not, why not? To what extent does the position of this sentence in the paragraph affect your answer?
3. In paragraph 10 why has Zinsser used quotation marks around specific words in

the first half of the paragraph but not around other words in the second half? Would his point have been clearer if he had used quotation marks in the second half?

4. What is the author doing in the last two sentences of paragraph 10?

5. Outline the **parallel structure** of paragraph 14.

6. How does the author define clutter? Why does he define it in various ways and at different points in his essay?

7. Which of the examples of clutter mentioned in the first four paragraphs have you used? Has Zinsser convinced you that you should no longer use them? Or will you continue to use them—out of habit? because so many others do? because you think Zinsser is too strict in his condemnation?

8. Later on in the essay Zinsser condemns a number of words and phrases that you are certainly accustomed to hearing and reading, and that you have yourself used. Choose two or three of these phrases and defend your continued use of them.

9. Is there any sentence in the last two paragraphs that could be taken as the concluding idea of the whole essay? Justify your answer in detail.

SUGGESTIONS FOR WRITING

1. What has been your experience with verbal clutter?

    In order to write an essay on this broad topic, you will have to restrict it. You could, for instance, listen to a number of weather forecasts on radio and television, make a list of examples, perhaps arrange them in categories, and draw conclusions or make generalizations based on the examples. Your essay then would deal with your generalizations, with the best examples brought in to support them. You could use the same approach for broadcasts of football or hockey games, interviews, national or local news programs, etc.

2. 'Every profession has its growing arsenal of jargon to throw dust in the eyes of the populace' (69–70).

    In which profession have you encountered the blinding dust of jargon? Consider your relationship—verbal and/or written—with an architect, a medical doctor, a social worker, a professor, a lawyer, a high-school teacher, a dentist, a clergyman or priest, a politician, a newspaper reporter, etc. You might then deal with such questions as these: what was the nature of the jargon? what effect(s) was it intended to produce? was it a legitimate part of the profession? was the user aware of the jargon? was it intended to deceive? etc.

3. Carefully examine any three or four essays you have written for any of your university or high-school courses and apply to them the questions the author asks in his fourteenth paragraph. The essay you write will describe the results of your examination.

LEWIS THOMAS

A physician and scientist, Lewis Thomas (1913–93) was one of the most important essay-ists of our time on scientific subjects. In addition to his medical research, he wrote on a wide variety of topics—personal, sensitive, meditative essays about the conditions of modern life. He taught at a number of medical schools, including the universities of Minnesota, New York, and Yale. He was also president, and later chancellor, of the Memorial Sloan-Kettering Cancer Center in New York. Among the many awards he received were those from the American Association of Pathologists, the New York Academy of Medicine, and the American Society for Experimental Biology. His books include *The Lives of a Cell: Notes of a Biology Watcher* (1974), for which he won the National Book Award; *The Medusa and the Snail: More Notes of a Biology Watch*er (1979); *Late Night Thoughts on Listening to Mahler's Ninth Symphony* (1983); and *The Fragile Species* (1992). The essay below is taken from *Et Cetera, Et Cetera: Notes of a Word-Watcher* (1990).

Notes on Punctuation

1   There are no precise rules about punctuation (Fowler lays out some general advice (as best he can under the complex circumstances of English prose (he points out, for example, that we possess only four stops (the comma, the semicolon, the colon and the period (the question mark and exclamation point are not, strictly speaking, stops; they are indicators of tone (oddly enough, the Greeks employed the semicolon 5 for their question mark (it produces a strange sensation to read a Greek sentence which is a straightforward question: Why weepest thou; (instead of Why weepest thou? (and, of course, there are parentheses (which are surely a kind of punctuation making this whole matter much more complicated by having to count up the left-handed paren-theses in order to be sure of closing with the right number (but if the parentheses were 10 left out, with nothing to work with but the stops, we would have considerably more flexibility in the deploying of layers of meaning than if we tried to separate all the clauses by physical barriers (and in the latter case, while we might have more precision and exactitude for our meaning, we would lose the essential flavour of language, which is its wonderful ambiguity)))))))))))))).   15
2   The commas are the most useful and usable of all the stops. It is highly impor-tant to put them in place as you go along. If you try to come back after doing a para-graph and stick them in the various spots that tempt you you will discover that they tend to swarm like minnows into all sorts of crevices whose existence you hadn't real-ized and before you know it the whole long sentence becomes immobilized and 20 lashed up squirming in commas. Better to use them sparingly, and with affection, pre-cisely when the need for each one arises, nicely, by itself.
3   I have grown fond of semicolons in recent years. The semicolon tells you that there is still some question about the preceding full sentence; something needs to be added; it reminds you sometimes of the Greek usage. It is almost always a greater plea- 25 sure to come across a semicolon than a period. The period tells you that that is that; if you didn't get all the meaning you wanted or expected, anyway you got all the writer intended to parcel out and now you have to move along. But with the semicolon there

you get a pleasant little feeling of expectancy; there is more to come; read on; it will
get clearer.   30

4   Colons are a lot less attractive, for several reasons: firstly, they give you the feeling of being rather ordered around, of at least having your nose pointed in a direction
you might not be inclined to take if left to yourself, and, secondly, you suspect you're
in for one of those sentences that will be labelling the points to be made: firstly, secondly, and so forth, with the implication that you haven't sense enough to keep track   35
of a sequence of notions without having them numbered. Also, many writers use this
system loosely and incompletely, starting out with number one and number two as
though counting off on your fingers but then going on and on without the succession
of labels you've been led to expect, leaving you floundering about searching for the
ninethly or seventeenthly that ought to be there but isn't.   40

5   Exclamation points are the most irritating of all. Look! they say, look at what I just
said! How amazing is my thought! It is like being forced to watch someone else's small
child jumping up and down crazily in the centre of the living room shouting to attract
attention. If a sentence really has something of importance to say, something quite
remarkable, it doesn't need a mark to point it out. And if it is really, after all, a banal sen- 45
tence needing more zing, the exclamation point simply emphasizes its banality!

6   Quotation marks should be used honestly and sparingly, when there is a genuine quotation at hand, and it is necessary to be very rigorous about the words
enclosed by the marks. If something is to be quoted, the *exact* words must be used. If
part of it must be left out because of space limitations, it is good manners to insert   50
three dots to indicate the omission, but it is unethical to do this if it means connecting two thoughts which the original author did not intend to have tied together.
Above all, quotation marks should not be used for ideas that you'd like to disown,
things in the air so to speak. Nor should they be put in place around clichés; if you
want to use a cliché you must take full responsibility for it yourself and not try to fob   55
it off on anon., or on society. The most objectionable misuse of quotation marks, but
one which illustrates the dangers of misuse in ordinary prose, is seen in advertising,
especially in advertisements for small restaurants, for example 'just around the corner', or 'a good place to eat'. No single, identifiable, citable person ever really said, for
the record, 'just around the corner', much less 'a good place to eat', least likely of all   60
for restaurants of the type that use this type of prose.

7   The dash is a handy device, informal and essentially playful, telling you that
you're about to take off on a different tack but still in some way connected with the
present course—only you have to remember that the dash is there, and either put a
second dash at the end of the notion to let the reader know that he's back on course,   65
or else end the sentence, as here, with a period.

8   The greatest danger in punctuation is for poetry. Here it is necessary to be as economical and parsimonious with commas and periods as with the words themselves,
and any marks that seem to carry their own subtle meanings, like dashes and little rows
of periods, even semicolons and question marks, should be left out altogether rather   70
than inserted to clog up the thing with ambiguity. A single exclamation point in a
poem, no matter what else the poem has to say, is enough to destroy the whole work.

9   The things I like best in T.S. Eliot's poetry, especially in the *Four Quartets*, are
the semicolons. You cannot hear them, but they are there, laying out the connections

between the images and the ideas. Sometimes you get a glimpse of a semicolon com- 75
ing, a few lines farther on, and it is like climbing a steep path through woods and seeing a wooden bench just at a bend in the road ahead, a place where you can expect
to sit for moment, catching your breath.

10   Commas can't do this sort of thing; they can only tell you how different parts
of a complicated thought are to be fitted together, but you can't sit, not even take a 80
breath, just because of a comma,

1979

QUESTIONS

1. The **tone** of Thomas's essay is rather informal, even playful—as witnessed from the outset by the 12 parenthetical expressions in the opening paragraph. Is his title also to be taken as playful—that is, is this piece really just a collection of 'notes', or is it a well-structured essay, with a beginning, middle, and end?
2. Another characteristic of this essay is the author's use of gentle **irony**, as in his discussion of parentheses. How is he being ironic in this first paragraph?
3. In the fourth sentence of paragraph 2 Thomas tells us that commas should be used 'sparingly'. Has he done that in this sentence? in the preceding one? What is he getting at?
4. Has the author's discussion of the semicolon, in paragraph 3, helped you to better understand this punctuation mark? If not, how else might he have clarified it for you?
5. What has the author done in the last sentence of paragraph 5? How is this similar to what he does in the last sentence of paragraph 2?
6. In view of what the author says in paragraph 5, do you feel that you have overused exclamation marks? Have you ever used capital letters, italics, or underlining for emphasis? If so, what do you think Thomas would say about this?
7. In paragraphs 8 and 9 has the author contradicted himself with regard to what he says about semicolons? If not, how is he being consistent?
8. Why does this essay end with a comma? Is this ending in keeping with the tone of the rest of the essay, or is it too startling and thus stylistically inappropriate?

SUGGESTIONS FOR WRITING

1. After you have reread Pico Iyer's 'In Praise of the Humble Comma' (pp. 86–8) and Thomas's 'Notes on Punctuation', write your own essay on some aspect of punctuation. Give full play to your imagination here, as Iyer and Thomas have obviously done. They have also used a rather playful, humorous tone, which you could also adopt, although there are other tones you might use: serious, haughty, condescending, self-deprecating, irritated, disdainful, spiteful, vituperative, etc.
2. What have you learned from reading, and thinking about, the Iyer and Thomas essays? Your essay on this topic should deal not only with what you have learned but with points these authors have not touched upon but, in your opinion, might have. You should consider as well how your study of these essays has affected your general approach, or attitude, towards punctuation; or, if they have not had any effect on you, why that is so.

STEVE RUSHIN

A senior writer for *Sports Illustrated*, Steve Rushin has published dozens of articles on a wide variety of sports topics. His column 'Air and Space', which appears weekly in the magazine, occasionally deals with the language used, and misused, by sportswriters, fans, and athletes, as in the selection below. He is the author of two books: *Pool Cool* (1990), about the game of pool and the characters who play it; and *Road Swing* (1998), an account of the year Rushin spent touring American sports shrines. What he wanted to do in this book neatly encapsulates his attitude towards sports: 'I wanted to put my finger on the pulse of American sports, and I wanted that finger to be one of those giant, foam-rubber index fingers worn by pinhead fans across the land.'

Clichés Aren't Everything

1   Men, if we play our game, bring our A game, take it one game at a time, stick to the game plan, stay within ourselves, dictate the tempo, impose our will, give 110 per cent, take it to another level, take the crowd out of the game, make something happen, show some athleticism, stop the penetration, step up our intensity, execute, focus, convert, and leave it all on the floor, it's anybody's ball game.   5

2   But there's no tomorrow, our backs are against the wall, it's crunch time, gut-check time, do or die. To click, to gel, to fire on all cylinders, we'll need good chemistry, and you can't teach that.

3   So I'm juggling the lineup, making wholesale changes, trying to light a fire under you, put a fire in your belly, fire you up, because those other guys won't roll   10 over, they won't lay down, they can flat-out play, they're on fire, they're peaking at the right time, they've got ice water in their veins, my hat's off to them, you gotta hand it to them, they thrive in the clutch, they feed off the pressure, they own us, they're hungry, they'll take you to school, they'll eat your lunch, they'll make you pay, I'd pay to see them play, even though they put their pants on one leg at a time, same as we do.   15

4   But their go-to guy, we gotta contain him, that kid's something special, he makes it look easy, he comes to play every day, he makes everyone around him better, he's got something to prove, he's got game, he's got skills, he's got our number, he's got a very bright future in this league.

5   Although some of you couldn't play dead, couldn't play a radio, couldn't hit   20 sand if you fell off a camel, we've been here before, we match up well, we know how to win, we're not happy just to be here, our goal is a championship, and defence wins championships, and we're in it to win it, and we're all in this together, 'cause there's no *I* in team, so let's just go out there and have some fun, let's dance with the one that brung us, let's see what happens, and if the ball bounces our way, we'll control our   25 own destiny, and that's what it's all about.

6   Because we have nothing to lose, the pressure's on them, nobody expected us to be here, nobody thought we could do it, nobody gave us a chance, everyone counted us out, the naysayers all doubted us, and that was the turning point, the key factor, the shift in momentum, so let's silence the critics, let's send 'em a message, let's   30 make a statement, let's shock the world, let's get that monkey off our backs.

7   Because at the end of the day, on any given Sunday, when you step between the lines and answer the bell, down in the trenches, you can throw out the record books, 'cause anything can happen. But hey, they don't play these games on paper, so let's tee it up, let's get it on, let's get ready to rumble.   35

8   We're not protecting the ball, we're not capitalizing on their mistakes, turnovers are costing us, we need to regroup, we need to dig deep, we need to show some poise, one big play and we're right back in it, but we gotta generate some offence, we gotta put some points on the board, we gotta get everybody on the same page, or that's all she wrote, we'll have a long flight home, we'll have a long cold winter to think about 40 it. Still, it ain't over till it's over, it ain't over till the fat lady sings.

9   It's all over but the shoutin'. Turn out the lights, the party's over. Give them credit, they flat-out beat us, they just plain outhustled us, they wanted it more, they showed a lotta class, but we need to look in the mirror, this was a real wake-up call, it just wasn't our day, but I'm proud of our guys, I take full responsibility, coaches are 45 hired to be fired, it's been a great ride.

10   I look forward to spending more time with my family.

2000

QUESTIONS

1. Although at first reading Rushin's piece might seem to be little more than an enumeration of trite expressions, it really is an essay, that is, it does have a definite structure—a beginning, a middle, and an end. Summarize what each of these three steps consists of.

2. The opening paragraph, which consists of only one sentence, is constructed as follows: the anticipatory subject, 'Men'; a subordinate conjunction, 'if', which governs eighteen **subordinate clauses** (in three of which only the verb is expressed); followed by the **principal clause**. Analyze the structure of paragraphs 4 and 6 in this same manner.

3. In this long collection of **clichés**, **parallelism** plays a major role. Analyze the parallel structure in any two paragraphs. Can you decide which paragraph is the more effective because of its structure? If you are unable to decide, what does this tell you about the author's style?

4. Although this essay gathers clichés found especially in sports, a good number of these expressions are frequently found in contexts that have nothing to do with sports. Identify several such clichés and the context in which you are accustomed to seeing or hearing them.

5. Can you identify which sport these clichés are associated with? Does it matter, or are most of these expressions applicable to just about any team sport?

6. In addition to the progression in the essay as a whole—the beginning, middle, and end—there is also a progression within paragraphs. Show what this progression consists of in any three paragraphs.

7. How is paragraph 10 an **ironic** comment on the coaching profession?

8. Clichés are to be avoided because they are tired expressions that have been worn out by constant use over an extended time. Occasionally, however, they are useful because they describe a situation accurately and briefly. Choose any three or four

clichés in Rushin's essay which you might use in your own writing and defend
your choices.

SUGGESTIONS FOR WRITING

1. You are a radio announcer who is broadcasting a game (choose the team sport that
   you know best). Narrate what happens during the last ten or fifteen minutes, using
   any style you wish, from the most sober and proper to the most informal and wild.
   You must not, however, use any clichés. Your essay will consist of the transcription
   of your broadcast.
2. Assume that you are the coach of a team involved in an important game, a game
   that your team must win. During the intermission you will first tell your players about
   technical matters: what your team must do or must not do to win the game. After
   that, however, what will you say to them that will lift their spirits, that will give them
   the will to win? You have only five minutes, and you want your speech to be not just
   inspiring but fresh, so you are determined not to use the kind of language that
   coaches normally use in this kind of situation. What will you tell them?

VICTORIA BRANDEN

The career of Victoria Branden has included raising a family, working in journalism and
publishing, teaching in high schools and colleges in Ontario, and writing several books—
including two novels, *Mrs Job* (1979) and *Flitterin' Judas* (1985)—and numerous short
stories. She has also written several non-fiction works, such as *Understanding Ghosts*
(1980), *In Defence of Plain English: The Decline and Fall of Literacy in Canada* (1991),
The New Illiteracy (1992), and *The Canadian Book of Snobs* (1998). She has published
extensively in such magazines as *Chatelaine*, *Saturday Night*, *Catholic Digest*, and
Canadian Forum, and is the author of dozens of radio and television scripts for the CBC.
The following essay, from *In Defence of Plain English*, shows her sense of humour and
her forthright critical judgment.

Mad Metaphors

1   A dubious practice among teachers of English is that of forcing children to
decorate their writing with figures of speech. They are required to write stories and
essays which incorporate a number of metaphors and similes—an agonizing exercise,
which produces some of the worst writing, with the least spontaneous images in the
history of language. It should be forbidden by law, with severe penalties.   5

2   This sadistic activity arises from a misunderstanding of the creative process. It
isn't developed by practice. Images should flash upon one, in a kind of revelation; and
they will, too, if you become a good observer of the world about you, and if you read
work in which metaphor is used successfully, so that you see how it's done.

3   I don't believe, for example, that T.S. Eliot slogged away practising similes, so   10
that when he looked at a twilight sky one day, he was perversely reminded, not of a

beautiful sunset, but of 'a patient etherized upon a table'. Raymond Chandler is an excellent exponent of vigorous imagery. At one point, his detective, Marlowe, finding himself in flossy and pretentious surroundings, feels as welcome 'as a louse on a wedding cake'. Carnally watching a pretty girl, he lost interest when '. . . she opened a mouth like a fire bucket and laughed. . . . the hole in her face when she unzippered her teeth was all I needed.' Another of his unforgettable images was his description of a blonde (Chandler and Marlowe loved/hated blondes obsessively): '. . . a blonde. A blonde to make a bishop kick a hole in a stained-glass window.' Now that's a blonde, and that's an image you remember. I can't remember which book it comes from, and someone has borrowed/stolen all my Chandler, so I can't check. But the line and the beautiful image of the kicking bishop has stayed ineradicably in my mind.

4   You can't teach that kind of thing by practice exercises. All you can do is encourage your students to read good metaphor-makers, and learn to look at the world. If you try to teach it by rule and rote, you fall into the Miss Groby trap. Remember James Thurber's Miss Groby, prototype of the teacher who tries to reduce English to a formula, and who produces generations of literature-haters? I would quote you an illustrative passage, but all my Thurber has disappeared: poltergeists? Never mind. Everyone should read 'Here Lies Miss Groby' for themselves. In passing, a warning: never lend books, and always search your guests' luggage before you let them out of the house.

5   Peter de Vries had a lot of fun mocking literary devices. Attending, against his will, a jolly sleigh-ride, he moodily watches the moon rise—first like a rotten orange, then like a bloody cliché.

6   These are the professionals. Most of the time, unfortunately, the use of metaphor detracts from the desired effect, rather than adding to it. For instance, CBC interviewer Christopher Thomas described a place as being 'steeped in ghosts'. Now come on, Christopher. To steep means to soak in water. So that just won't wash, huh?

7   A great favourite, currently, is 'to coin an old phrase' and its alternate, 'to coin the old cliché'. This arises from a misunderstanding of the meaning of both *coin* and *cliché,* which do NOT mean to use, or to repeat. To coin is to manufacture money by stamping metal. If you coin something, it must by definition be new—you've just stamped it out, this minute. You can't coin an old coin, an old phrase, an old anything. Metaphorically, to coin is 'to invent or fabricate (esp. a new word or phrase)'. You cannot, I repeat, invent or fabricate something that's already old.

8   Stipulation: the phrase can be used ironically, with a deprecating smile. You catch yourself using some weary old cliché—'he's as strong as an ox'—and so you add, facetiously, 'to coin a phrase'. Classy speakers should not attempt mild jests of this type, for they are sure to screw them up.

9   Again, it is impossible to coin a cliché. Wrong metaphor. You have to know what words mean to use metaphors successfully. A cliché was originally a metal casting of stereotype or electrotype. Once cast, there was no changing it. Thus it takes on the metaphorical meaning of something locked in, unchangeable, unoriginal, hackneyed. *Not coined.*

10   Carol Verdun, of *The Independent*, provided me with a nice instance of metaphor-madness, from an Atlanta newspaper:

'I hope I can help Dan,' Campbell said. 'I'm going to work my tail off for him. We've got to get in the pits now, put our nose to the jugular vein and go after it.'

11   Campbell's gift is for mixing metaphors. 'Going for the jugular vein' usually 60
means attacking with lethal intent: with a knife, if the agent is human, with teeth if
it's an animal, or possibly a vampire. The nose is usually applied to the grindstone,
implying not slaughter but dedication and hard work.

12   Another category badly in need of correction is what might be labelled 'phoney
imagery'. That is, it pretends to be a simile or metaphor, but is really just padding. 65
Consider this by Leonard Cohen:

> Like a bird on a wire
> Like a drunk in a midnight choir
> I have tried, in my way, to be free.

13   What has a bird on a wire in common with a drunk in a choir, and why are they 70
made parallel? Is the bird sitting on a telephone wire, like a starling, or a swallow
preparatory to migration? Because they *are* free, and have no need to 'try'. In what other
circumstances do birds sit on wires? Perches in cages are not made of wire. It doesn't
make sense.

14   Now—about that drunk. What is he doing in a midnight choir, if he's drunk? 75
Was he dragged there against his will? If he's there voluntarily, he's free, and doesn't
have to try for something he already has achieved. Why would anyone drag a drunk
into a choir, if he doesn't want to be there? Drunks are not desirable additions to
choirs and most choir-leaders would prefer that they stay away.

15   In short, these phrases mean exactly nothing, and one is forced to the embar- 80
rassing realization that Mr Cohen stuck them in to get a rhyme, because he was too
lazy to work on a valid image. He was once a promising young poet, but he sold out
long ago to the song-writing biz, since when he's written some ineffably bad stuff,
though I dare say he's made a lot of more money than he would have in the poetry
biz, which is notoriously ill-paid.   85

16   That first verse is the best—correction: the least rotten—in the song. Later, Mr
Cohen rhymes *free* with *thee*. 'I will try to make it up to thee.' How could anyone with
even vestigial rags of artistic conscience perpetrate a rhyme like that? And it doesn't
scan—he has to squeeze the words into the beat. Nor is this poetic offence compen-
sated by lovely sound: in another song, Mr Cohen refers to his 'golden voice', which 90
in reality resembles the creaking on its rusty hinges of a badly corroded farm gate. In
spite of which, CBC tirelessly inflicts these atrocities upon us, and pretends they're Art,
although if an unknown person tried to sell songs as feeble as Cohen's, he would be
laughed out of the business. Another example of the Canadian infatuation with Big
Names as a substitute for art.   95

17   I digress; perhaps this belongs in the chapter on popular songs (Words and
Music). But Mr Cohen's recent *oeuvre* is bad in so many ways that one simply doesn't
know where to put him.

18   Back to metaphors, then. My finest example of metaphor-madness occurred in
a review in the *Hamilton Spectator* of a stage production of 'Murder on the Nile'. The 100
criticism was extremely negative, although the review itself—as will be seen—could

be used as an object lesson in bad writing. It nevertheless carried an unmistakeable aura of self-congratulation. Really Classy!

19 'The play struggles to maintain credulity in the face of some virtuoso subterfuge.' Surely the struggle was to maintain *credibility*: why would anyone want to maintain *gullibility, readiness to believe on weak or insufficient grounds*? Our critic's problem is that he doesn't know what credulity means. What in the world 'virtuoso subterfuge' may be I simply can't imagine. (I know what the words mean, taken separately, but together they make no sense: *special knowledge or skill in technique of evading censorship by deception*. Huh? Sound and fury, signifying nothing. As Polonius would have said, 'It is an ill phrase, a vile phrase.') 105 110

20 'Not even Dame Agatha can sustain the warren of convolutions that threaten to sink this feeble effort.'

21 I'll bet Dame Agatha wouldn't mix her metaphors like that. Rabbits live in warrens, but convolutions don't. (They're twists, coils, or sensuous folds.) And how can you sustain this dubious warren, especially if it's (presumably) on a ship, since it's threatened with sinking? Warrens are underground rabbit towns. 115

22 'The action chugs at a yawning pace that is positively lethal.' Yawning may be a sign of boredom but it is rarely lethal. I submit that 'chugs' is an unsuitable word— if something is chugging along, it's usually making steady progress. It's when it drags that one feels like yawning. An inexcusably bad sentence. 120

23 'There are some unconscionably bad performances that verge on the edge of hysteria.' If they're verging, they're already on the edge. 'Canon Pennefather's throat was constricting with indignation.' It may have been constrict*ed* with indignation, but it couldn't be constrict*ing* unless it had wound itself around something and was choking it—a good trick, for an old gentleman's throat. 125

24 'Stephen Russell is so garbled as to be unintelligible.' His speech may have been garbled, but Mr Russell himself could not easily have been, or his state would have been far worse than unintelligible. 'Garble: To mutilate with a view to misrepresentation.' 130

25 Finally, 'Genevieve Caslin is amusing as a hustling lackey . . .' A lackey is by definition a man-servant. What on earth was Miss Caslin up to?

26 Sad stuff. It's odd that a man who writes as badly as this has the gall to criticize another's work. I didn't see the play, but it's difficult to believe that it could be as bad as the review. No doubt he believed his efforts at metaphor made it vivid, or even Classy. But metaphors don't work unless you think of their meaning, so that the review becomes a kind of exemplar of How Not To Use a Metaphor. It's the work of someone who really never thinks about the meaning of the words he uses, who doesn't seem even to realize that words to have definite meanings. If he ever thought about what a warren was, he couldn't have written that silly stuff about it sinking. He's just picked up words promiscuously, and stuck them in without thinking of making sense. How can anyone who writes as incompetently as this hold a job on a newspaper—or get one in the first place? 135 140

27 A note in passing on 'promiscuously'. I found that my use of the word sent some of my auditors into fits of laughter, an unexpected response. The hilarity derived, I discovered, from the fact that the word is frequently used in the phrase 'sexual promiscuity.' They believed this was its exclusive meaning. Sorry to disappoint 145 you, guys, but there are other varieties of promiscuity. Promiscuous means 'making no distinctions; undiscriminating; carelessly irregular; casual.'

28   See how it works? If you look up a word in the dictionary, you have a lot 150
more flexibility in its use. You can talk about promiscuity without being stuck with loose morals.

29   If you would like an example of a really effective metaphor at work, see Dylan Thomas's 'Fern Hill'. The whole poem is structured around the image of time, along with brilliant metaphorical use of colours.   155

30   Before I conclude this chapter, an apology to all guests whom I may have slandered, above. The Chandler image (blonde, bishop kicking hole in stained-glass window) is from *Farewell, My Lovely*, p. 78. Thurber is still missing.

1992

QUESTIONS

1. How effective are the title and the first sentence in introducing the author's topic?
2. What does the last sentence of the introductory paragraph tell us about Branden's **tone**?
3. In paragraph 3 Branden says that her books by Raymond Chandler are missing, and in the next paragraph she says the same about her books by James Thurber. What do these points suggest about her attitude towards her subject? Then consider her concluding paragraph.
4. 'I digress,' the author begins paragraph 17. What does the digression consist of? Is it really a digression, or is it a rhetorical strategy? If it is a strategy, why does she use it?
5. Paragraphs 1 and 2 comment on the teaching of **figures of speech**, and paragraph 3 mentions several examples of how excellent writers have used them. How do paragraphs 4, 5, and 6 function?
6. Branden uses more short paragraphs than do most writers. Can you justify this approach to paragraph structure, given her subject matter and tone?
7. Explain the effectiveness, or lack of it, of the **transitions** at the beginnings of paragraphs 8, 9, 14, 17, 18, and 26.
8. Did you share the reaction of Branden's 'auditors' to her use of *promiscuously* in paragraph 26? Why do you think she defends her use of this word? Would it not have been easier simply to choose another word to use? Or is she trying to make an important point?
9. Both Branden and William Zinsser (pp. 437–9) criticize the writing of others. What tone does each writer use? Can one writer criticize another writer without being condescending? Which of the two is more condescending? What does either one do to sound less condescending?

SUGGESTIONS FOR WRITING

1. In criticizing the poetry of Leonard Cohen, Branden uses both humour and sarcasm. Write your own criticism of this poem, 'Bird on a Wire', but use a serious tone, without either sarcasm or humour (you may use a different Cohen poem, if you wish).

2. Using as your sample one or two columns from the sports page or from the society and fashion pages from your local newspaper, write a critique of the writing used in these columns. You may wish to deal with several aspects of the writing, or you could concentrate on, for instance, the writer's use of imagery, or paragraph structure, or active and passive verbs, punctuation, transitions, sentence length and variety, etc.

Drew Hayden Taylor

An award-winning writer of documentaries, television scripts, and magazine and newspaper articles, Drew Hayden Taylor (1962–) is best known for his plays, including *The Bootlegger Blues* (1991), *Someday* (1993), *Funny, You Don't Look Like One: Observations from a Blue-Eyed Ojibway* (1996), *Only Drunks and Children Tell the Truth* (1998), and *Fearless Warriors* (1998). He also co-edited, with Linda Jaine, *Voices: Being Native in Canada* (1992). Much of his writing, both fiction and non-fiction, explores identity; as half-Caucasian, half Ojibway, he has jokingly described himself as an 'Occasion'. His latest works, all plays, are *AlterNatives* and *The Boy in the Treehouse/Girl Who Loved Her Horses*, both published in 2000, and *Buz'Gem Blues*, published in 2002.

Native Themes 101

1   I remember reading once that the great Canadian author Margaret Atwood described Canadian literature as being strongly influenced by our unique environment (or environments). The rivers, the land, and the climate have left their fingerprints all over the books stocked in the Can Lit row of your local bookstore. To be a literate Canadian is to appreciate the essence of the book *Who Has Seen the Wind* (and perhaps understand the title).

2   But for those who write stories in a more Aboriginal context, it seems different influences tickle the creative spirit of the writer. In the world of Native theatre, the primary themes explored dramatically repeatedly consist of the three B's—bingo, beer, and brutality.

3   In the fifteen or so years during which contemporary Native theatre has come into its own, the average patron of theatre could expect to see a Native character in a Native play dealing with the fickleness of bingo, the effects of beer and other alcohol on body and soul, and perhaps most pervasive, there was always a female character who suffered some form of sexual or physical abuse. Often, all three were combined in various and unique fashions.

4   In the macrocosm of film and television, yet again a different set of themes and characteristics pours forth from the computers of Aboriginal writers. Recently, the Banff Centre for the Arts hosted a Native Scriptwriter's Workshop where eight talented writers (of various other mediums) from across Canada were brought together to try their hands at storytelling for that beast known as the boob tube.

5   Scriptwriter Jordan Wheeler, filmmaker Carol Geddes, and myself were brought in as instructors and mentors in the two-week writing experiment. Each writer was to come with a complete first draft script. These scripts varied from a dozen pages all the way up to full-length movie scripts, all of varying levels of complexity. But what caught our eyes were the recurring themes represented in the stories.

6   Keep in mind, the participants shared no common traits, other than the simple fact that they were Native (though a variety of different Nations) and wanted to write. They came from locales ranging from BC to Ontario, an even split of male and female, from different walks of life: actor, university professor, poets, etcetera. Yet, the same three concepts kept reappearing in their work, as if beacons for Native identity on the television.

7   All eight stories, in various combinations, explored the following three notions of Aboriginal existence: Residential schools—past, present, and future. At least half of the stories dealt in some way with the effects of this misguided government policy. Residential school stories are evidently the new industry for Native writers.

8   Second was the past as salvation or a method of redemption. Many of the stories had their central characters find their true path or happy ending by either participating in a mystical visit to the past (i.e. wandering into an ancient Native village before contact), or by having a representation from the past enter their contemporary reality (i.e. they meet an ancestor or somebody similar who is there to provide guidance). A surprisingly common theme. I myself dabbled in this ten years ago for a play called *Toronto at Dreamer's Rock*.

9   And finally, it was obvious in most of the scripts that practically all White people are racists. Overt racists at that. Most scripts had White individuals, mostly minor characters, make an appearance, and their only function was to sling epithets and racial slurs at the Native characters. Enter White character. 'You fuckin' Indian!' Exit White Character.

10   Now these remarks are in no way meant as comment on these writers' talents. Writing for television is a particular and difficult talent that takes a fair amount of time and practice to master. These eight brave souls were parachuted in with little background or training and were expected to run as fast as they could without knowing what kind of shoes to wear, the shape of the track, or if they were in a sprint or long distance race. Once the shock of learning that there is no such thing as a good writer—only a good rewriter—sunk in, they did their best to reshape their scripts.

11   But I personally found this to be a fascinating experience in discovering what is on the minds of Native scriptwriter-wannabes today, and perhaps writers in general. Residential schools. Trips to and from the past. Racist White people. And from playwrights . . . Beer. Bingo. Brutality. The literary world seems kind of bleak when you take all of these factors into consideration. And redemption can only be achieved through either bingo or time travel.

12   But repetition is an age-old Hollywood tradition, one these young writers seem to have embraced. I remember when the two volcano movies were released within months of each other. Same with the meteor/asteroid films. One trip to Mars film was released last year with another one flooding the screens later this year. Why should we be any different? Though one cannot help noting the obvious difference in reality levels between the films about asteroids, volcanoes, or trips to Mars, and Residential

Schools, racist White people, and redemption from the past. Perhaps that best explains the difference between the two cultures.

13   But thank Heaven for small literary miracles. The one theme I was expecting to 70 permeate the scripts did not raise its over-hyped head. The one over-riding factor in the majority of Native literature, as perceived by non-Native academics, has to be the definite, ever-so-positive, belief that in every Aboriginal story ever written, there has to be a Trickster character somewhere buried deep in the prose.

14   I cannot tell you how many times I have been asked, and have answered, ques- 75 tions about Trickster influences in my works (very little) and those of other Native writers (it varies). And I can safely say that in these eight stories, there was not one single Trickster image, element, or appearance made. It seems the future bodes much sadness for non-Native academics.

15   Oddly enough, one other minor observation came from those two weeks in 80 Banff: Carol Geddes, a filmmaker who works frequently with the National Film Board, told me of a jury she was on. She and several other people had spent hours screening films, and they made a pact, however unenforceable, that the NFB should not be allowed to finance any more films having the word *spirit* in the title or that has that ubiquitous flute music on the soundtrack.   85

16   No Trickster but lots of flute and spirit. Add to that the beer, bingo, and some brutality towards some racist White people and you've got the makings of a great weekend. And a snapshot of what appears to be the Aboriginal creative mind at work. At least I now know what to write in my next book.

2000

QUESTIONS

1. What is Drew Taylor's purpose in his essay: is he criticizing Native writers for having so long dealt with the same topics? is he suggesting other subjects they should deal with? is he trying to educate non-Natives about the disturbing themes preoccupying Native writers? all of these? something else?
2. As an aspiring Native writer, would you, or do you, find this essay discouraging? encouraging? Explain your reasons.
3. Taylor implies that there are some differences between Native and non-Native culture. What are some of these differences? How does he imply them?
4. How is paragraph 11 a summary of paragraphs 1–10?
5. In paragraph 14 what new point does the author add to what he has already noted in paragraphs 2 and 7–9?
6. Explain the **parallel structure** of the first sentence in paragraph 3, showing how Taylor has varied the normal parallelism. Is this variation successful?
7. The sixth sentence of paragraph 12 ends with a three-part series. How has the author changed the ordering of the three parts as they occur earlier? Why might he have done this?
8. How is the point the author makes in paragraph 15 related to the rest of the essay?
9. Explain the **irony** in the last sentence of paragraph 14 and the final sentence of this essay. What is the purpose of the irony? Is it successful?

SUGGESTIONS FOR WRITING

What would you tell an aspiring young writer who has asked you for advice about writing?

This topic doesn't ask you to give advice about how to write novels or plays. Rather, as someone who has already done a fair amount of writing in both high school and college or university, and perhaps also at work, you should be able to tell this student something about how to approach the writing of a formal or informal essay, a report of a survey, a description of an accident, a letter of complaint to a businessperson, a request for an important favour from an older person, etc. How do you approach the job of writing?

Cynthia Ozick

Playwright, essayist, novelist, and short-story writer Cynthia Ozick's works have won numerous awards, including the Strauss Living Award from the American Academy of Arts and Letters, the Rea Award for the Short Story, and the O. Henry Prize for short fiction, which she has won four times. Ozick (1928–) has also received a Guggenheim Fellowship and several honorary doctorates. Among her books are *The Cannibal Galaxy* (1983), *Levitations, Five Fictions* (1983), *The Messiah of Stockholm* (1987), *The Shawl* (1989), *Fame & Folly: Essays* (1996), *The Puttermesser Papers* (1997), and *Quarrel and Quandary: Essays* (2000). The selection included here is her introduction to the 1998 edition of *The Best American Essays*, which she guest-edited.

Portrait of the Essay as a Warm Body

1   An essay is a thing of the imagination. If there is information in an essay, it is by-the-by, and if there is an opinion in it, you need not trust it for the long run. A genuine essay has no educational, polemical, or sociopolitical use; it is the movement of a free mind at play. Though it is written in prose, it is closer in kind to poetry than to any other form. Like a poem, a genuine essay is made out of language and charac-   5
ter and mood and temperament and pluck and chance.

2   And if I speak of a genuine essay, it is because fakes abound. Here the old-fashioned term poetaster may apply, if only obliquely. As the poetaster is to the poet—a lesser aspirant—so the article is to the essay: a look-alike knockoff guaranteed not to wear well. An article is gossip. An essay is reflection and insight. An article has the   10
temporary advantage of social heat—what's hot out there right now. An essay's heat is interior. An article is timely, topical, engaged in the issues and personalities of the moment; it is likely to be stale within the month. In five years it will have acquired the quaint aura of a rotary phone. An article is Siamese-twinned to its date of birth. An essay defies its date of birth, and ours too.   15

3   A small historical experiment. Who are the classical essayists who come at once to mind? Montaigne, obviously. Among the nineteenth-century English masters, the long row of Hazlitt, Lamb, De Quincey, Stevenson, Carlyle, Ruskin, Newman, Martineau, Arnold. Of the Americans, Emerson. It may be argued that nowadays

these are read only by specialists and literature majors, and by the latter only when   20
they are compelled to. However accurate the claim, it is irrelevant to the experiment,
which has to do with beginnings and their disclosures. Here, then, are some introductory passages:

> One of the pleasantest things in the world is going on a journey; but I like to go
> by myself. I can enjoy society in a room; but out of doors, nature is company   25
> enough for me. I am then never less alone than when alone.
> —William Hazlitt, 'On Going a Journey'

> To go into solitude, a man needs to retire as much from his chamber as from
> society. I am not solitary whilst I read and write, though nobody is with me. But
> if a man would be alone, let him look at the stars.   30
> —Ralph Waldo Emerson, 'Nature'

> I have often been asked how I first came to be a regular opium eater; and have
> suffered, very unjustly, in the opinion of my acquaintance, from being reputed
> to have brought upon myself all the sufferings which I shall have to record, by
> a long course of indulgence in this practice purely for the sake of creating an   35
> artificial state of pleasurable excitement. This, however, is a misrepresentation
> of my case.
> —Thomas De Quincey, 'Confessions of an
> English Opium Eater'

> The human species, according to the best theory I can form of it, is composed   40
> of two distinct races, the men who borrow, and the men who lend.
> —Charles Lamb, 'The Two Races of Men'

> I saw two hareems in the East; and it would be wrong to pass them over in an
> account of my travels; though the subject is as little agreeable as any I can have
> to treat. I cannot now think of the two mornings thus employed without a   45
> heaviness of heart greater than I have ever brought away from Deaf and Dumb
> Schools, Lunatic Asylums, or even Prisons.
> —Harriet Martineau, 'From Eastern Life'

> The future of poetry is immense, because in poetry, where it is worthy of its
> high destinies, our race, as time goes on, will find an ever and surer stay. There   50
> is not a creed which is not shaken, not an accredited dogma which is not
> shown to be questionable, not a received tradition which does not threaten to
> dissolve. . . . But for poetry the idea is everything; the rest is a world of illusion,
> of divine illusion.
> —Matthew Arnold, 'The Study of Poetry'   55

> The changes wrought by death are in themselves so sharp and final, and so ter-
> rible and melancholy in their consequences, that the thing stands alone in man's
> experience, and has no parallel upon earth. It outdoes all other accidents

because it is the last of them. Sometimes it leaps suddenly upon its victims, like a Thug; sometimes it lays a regular siege and creeps upon their citadel during a 60 score of years. And when the business is done, there is a sore havoc made in other people's lives, and a pin knocked out by which many subsidiary friend-ships hung together.

—Robert Louis Stevenson, 'Aes Triplex'

It is recorded of some people, as of Alexander the Great, that their sweat, in 65 consequence of some rare and extraordinary constitution, emitted a sweet odour, the cause of which Plutarch and others investigated. But the nature of most bodies is the opposite, and at their best they are free from smell. Even the purest breath has nothing more excellent than to be without offensive odour, like that of very healthy children. 70

—Michel de Montaigne, 'Of Smells'

4   What might such a little anthology of opening sentences reveal? First, that lan-guage differs from one era to the next: there are touches of archaism here, if only in punctuation and cadence. Second, that splendid minds may contradict each other (outdoors, Hazlitt never feels alone; Emerson urges the opposite). Third, that the 75 theme of an essay can be anything under the sun, however trivial (the smell of sweat) or crushing (the thought that we must die). Fourth, that the essay is a consistently recognizable and venerable—or call it ancient—form. In English: Addison and Steele in the eighteenth century, Bacon and Browne in the seventeenth, Lyly in the sixteenth, Bede in the seventh. And what of the biblical Koheleth—Ecclesiastes—who may be 80 the oldest essayist reflecting on one of the oldest subjects: world-weariness?

5   So the essay is ancient and various: but this is a commonplace. There is some-thing else, and it is more striking yet—the essay's power. By 'power' I mean precisely the capacity to do what force always does: coerce assent. Never mind that the shape and intent of any essay is against coercion or suasion, or that the essay neither 85 proposes nor purposes to get you to think like its author. A genuine essay is not a doctrinaire tract or a propaganda effort or a broadside. Thomas Paine's 'Common Sense' and Émile Zola's 'J'Accuse' are heroic landmark writings; but to call them essays, though they may resemble the form, is to misunderstand. The essay is not meant for the barricades; it is a stroll through someone's mazy mind. All the same, 90 the essay turns out to be a force for agreement. It co-opts agreement; it courts agree-ment; it seduces agreement. For the brief hour we give to it, we are sure to fall into surrender and conviction. And this will occur even if we are intrinsically roused to resistance.

6   To illustrate: I may not be persuaded to Emersonianism as an ideology, but 95 Emerson—his voice, his language, his music—persuades me. When we look for superlatives, not for nothing do we speak of 'commanding' or 'compelling' prose. If I am a skeptical rationalist or an advanced biochemist, I may regard (or discard) the idea of the soul as not better than a puff of warm vapour. But here is Emerson on the soul: 'when it breathes through [man's] intellect, it is genius; when it breathes through 100 his will, it is virtue; when it flows through his affection, it is love.' And then—well, I am in thrall, I am possessed; I believe.

7   The novel has its own claims on surrender. It suspends our participation in the society we ordinarily live in, so that—for the time we are reading—we forget it utterly. But the essay does not allow us to forget our usual sensations and opinions; it does something even more potent: it makes us deny them. The authority of a masterly essayist—the authority of sublime language and intimate observation—is absolute. When I am with Hazlitt, I know no greater companion than nature. When I am with Emerson, I know no greater solitude than nature.

8   And what is most odd about the essay's power to lure us into its lair is how it goes about this work. We feel it when a political journalist comes after us with a point of view—we feel it the way the cat is wary of the dog. A polemic is a herald, complete with feathered hat and trumpet. A tract can be a trap. A magazine article generally has the scent of so-much-per-word. What is certain is that all of these are more or less in the position of a lepidopterist with his net: they mean to catch and skewer. They are focused on prey—i.e., us. The genuine essay, by contrast, never thinks of us; the genuine essay may be the most self-centred (the politer word would be subjective) arena for human thought ever devised.

9   Or else, though still not having you and me in mind (unless as an exemplum of common folly), it is not self-centred at all. When I was a child, I discovered in the public library a book that enchanted me then, and the idea of which has enchanted me for life. I have no recollection either of the title or of the writer—and anyhow very young readers rarely take note of authors; stories are simply and magically there. The characters included, as I remember them, three or four children and a delightful relation who is a storyteller, and the scheme was this: each child calls out a story element—most often an object—and the storyteller gathers up whatever is supplied (blue boots, a river, a fairy, a pencil box) and makes out of these random, unlikely, and disparate offerings a tale both logical and surprising. An essay, it seems to me, may be similarly constructed—if so deliberate a term applies. The essayist, let us say, unexpectedly stumbles over a pair of old blue boots in a corner of the garage, and this reminds her of when she last wore them—twenty years ago, on a trip to Paris, where on the banks of the Seine she stopped to watch an old fellow sketching, with a box of coloured pencils at his side. The pencil wiggling over his sheet is a greyish pink, which reflects the threads of sunset pulling westward in the sky, like the reins of a fairy cart . . . and so on. The mind meanders, slipping from one impression to another, from reality to memory to dreamscape and back again.

10   In the same way Montaigne, in our sample, when contemplating the unpleasantness of sweat, ends with the pure breath of children. Or Stevenson, starting out with mortality, speaks first of ambush, then of war, and finally of a displaced pin. No one is freer than the essayist—free to leap out in any direction, to hop from thought to thought, to begin with the finish and finish with the middle, or to eschew beginning and end and keep only a middle. The marvel of it is that out of this apparent causelessness, out of this scattering of idiosyncratic seeing and telling, a coherent world is made. It is coherent because, after all, an essayist must be an artist, and every artist, whatever the means, arrives at a sound and singular imaginative frame—or call it, on a minor scale, a cosmogony.

11   And it is into this frame, this work of art, that we tumble like tar babies, and are held fast. What holds us there? The authority of a voice, yes; the pleasure—sometimes the anxiety—of a new idea, an untried angle, a snatch of reminiscence, bliss displayed or shock conveyed. An essay can be the product of intellect or memory, lighthearted- 150 ness or gloom, well-being or disgruntlement. But always there is a certain quietude, on occasion a kind of detachment. Rage and revenge, I think, belong to fiction. The essay is cooler than that. Because it so often engages in acts of memory, and despite its gladder or more antic incarnations, the essay is by and large a serene or melancholic form. It mimics that low electric hum, sometimes rising to resemble actual speech, that 155 all human beings carry inside their heads—a vibration, garrulous if somewhat indistinct, that never leaves us while we wake. It is the hum of perpetual noticing: the configuration of someone's eyelid or tooth, the veins on a hand, a wisp of string caught on a twig, some words your fourth-grade teacher said, so long ago, about the rain, the look of an awning, a sidewalk, a bit of cheese left on a plate. All day long this 160 inescapable hum drums on, recalling one thing and another, and pointing out this and this and this. Legend has it that Titus, emperor of Rome, went mad because of the buzzing of a gnat that made its home in his ear; and presumably the gnat, flying out into the great world and then returning to her nest, whispered what she had seen and felt and learned there. But an essayist is more resourceful than an emperor, and can be 165 relieved of this interior noise, if only for the time it takes to record its murmurings. To seize the hum and set it down for others to hear is the essayist's genius.

12   It is a genius bound to leisure, and even to luxury, if luxury is measured in hours. The essay's limits can be found in its own reflective nature. Poems have been wrested from the inferno of catastrophe or war, and battlefield letters too: these are the 170 spontaneous bursts and burnings that danger excites. But the meditative temperateness of an essay requires a desk and a chair, a musing and a mooning, a connection to a civilized surround; even when the subject itself is a wilderness of lions and tigers, mulling is the way of it. An essay is a fireside thing, not a conflagration or a safari.

13   This may be why, when we ask who the essayists are, it turns out—though nov- 175 elists may now and then write essays—that true essayists rarely write novels. Essayists are a species of metaphysician: they are inquisitive—also analytic—about the least grain of being. Novelists go about the strenuous business of marrying and burying their people, or else they send them to sea, or to Africa, or (at the least) out of town. Essayists in their stillness ponder love and death. It is probably an illusion that men 180 are essayists more often then women (especially since women's essays have in the past frequently assumed the form of unpublished correspondence). And here I should, I suppose, add a note about maleness and femaleness as a literary issue—what is popularly termed 'gender', as if men and women were French or German tables and sofas. I *should* add such a note; it is the fashion, or, rather, the current expectation or obli- 185 gation—but there is nothing to say about any of it. Essays are written by men. Essays are written by women. That is the long and short of it. John Updike, in a genially confident discourse on maleness ('The Disposable Rocket'), takes the view—though he admits to admixture—that the 'male sense of space must differ from that of the female, who has such an interesting, active, and significant inner space. The space that 190 interests men is outer.' Except, let it be observed, when men write essays: since it is only inner space—interesting, active, significant—that can conceive and nourish the contemplative essay. The 'ideal female body', Updike adds, 'curves around the centres of repose,' and no phrase could better describe the shape of the ideal essay—yet

women are no fitter as essayists than men. In promoting the felt salience of sex,   195
Updike nevertheless drives home an essayist's point. Essays, unlike novels, emerge
from the sensations of the self. Fiction creeps into foreign bodies; the novelist can
inhabit not only a sex not his own, but also beetles and noses and hunger artists and
nomads and beasts; while the essay is, as we say, personal.

14   And here is an irony. Though I have been intent on distinguishing the marrow   200
of the essay from the marrow of fiction, I confess I have been trying all along, in a sub-
liminal way, to speak of the essay as if it—or she—were a character in a novel or a
play: moody, fickle, given on a whim to changing her clothes, or the subject; sometimes obstinate, with a mind of her own; or hazy and light; never predictable. I mean
for her to be dressed—and addressed—as we would Becky Sharp, or Ophelia, or   205
Elizabeth Bennet, or Mrs Ramsay, or Mrs Wilcox, or even Hester Prynne. Put it that it
is pointless to say (as I have done repeatedly, disliking it every moment) 'the essay', 'an
essay'. The essay—an essay—is not an abstraction; she may have recognizable con-
tours, but she is highly coloured and individuated; she is not a type. She is too fluid,
too elusive, to be a category. She may be bold, she may be diffident, she may rely on   210
beauty, or on cleverness, on eros or exotica. Whatever her story, she is the protagonist,
the secret self's personification. When we knock on her door, she opens to us, she is
a presence in the doorway, she leads us from room to room; then why should we not
call her 'she'? She may be privately indifferent to us, but she is anything but unwel-
coming. Above all, she is not a hidden principle or a thesis or a construct: she is *there*,   215
a living voice. She takes us in.

1998

QUESTIONS

1. Cynthia Ozick's essay was written as the introduction to a book titled *The Best American Essays 1998*, a volume in an annual series. Admittedly, an introduction is no substitute for the essays themselves, and this book might contain works by some of your favourite writers. But, assuming that you have read only the intro- duction, what is there about the author's **tone**, about her attitude towards her sub- ject, that might make you want to read on? Conversely, is there anything in what she says, or in her approach to the nature of the essay, that would make you reject the book?

2. Is the contrast between article and essay in paragraph 2 convincing? Do you have a favourite article that has survived the 'five years' mentioned by the author? Or do you agree with her that an article 'is likely to be stale within the month'? A visit to the library to look at a few of last year's magazines might be appropriate here.

3. Rewrite the **fragment** at the beginning of paragraph 3 in several different ways, each one a complete sentence. Is any one of your sentences more effective than the author's fragment?

4. In the fourth point of paragraph 4, Ozick mentions several English essayists from various centuries. None of them, however, is the author of any of the eight intro- ductory passages she has just quoted. Would her point be more convincing had she referred to these eight authors instead?

5. Note how Ozick begins paragraphs 5–10: 'So the essay is ancient and various'; 'To illlustrate'; 'The novel has its own claims'; 'And what is most odd'; 'Or else;' 'In the same way'. What conclusions can you draw about these beginnings?

6. When Ozick says, in paragraph 10, that 'No one is freer than the essayist—free to leap out in any direction, to hop from thought to thought,' is she arguing for lack of structure in the essay? If so, how does she justify this unusual position? If not, then just what is she saying?

7. Furthermore, does Ozick herself 'hop from thought to thought'? Or does her essay have a definite structure? Can an author do both? Has Ozick ?

8. 'The essay is by and large a serene or melancholic form' (154–5). Judging from the essays you have read over the past few years in books, newspapers, and magazines, would you tend to agree with Ozick? Or has your reading experience been a bit different? very much different?

9. The author's final paragraph, complex and full of ideas, deserves a close look. In trying to get its full meaning you might consider some of the following questions (and you will likely come up with a few of your own): What is the **irony** she refers to in her first sentence? What does she mean by 'the marrow of the essay'? How effective is the **metaphor** she introduces in the second sentence? Who are the women mentioned in the third sentence (you will probably already have identified Ophelia as a character from *Hamlet*)? What metaphor governs the final eight sentences? How does the expression 'When we knock on her door' (sentence 9) introduce the conclusion of this paragraph and the conclusion to the essay? What is the meaning of the final sentence?

SUGGESTIONS FOR WRITING

'The essay is not meant for the barricades; it is a stroll through someone's mazy mind.' (89–90)

'A genuine essay has no educational, polemical, or sociopolitical use; it is the movement of a free mind at play.' (2–4)

There will obviously be exceptions to these generalizations, but, on the whole (and restricting yourself to either one), do you agree with Ozick? Your discussion here will be based on your reading, over the past few years, of a wide variety of essays—in books of all kinds, in an assortment of magazines, and in newspapers.

ACKNOWLEDGEMENTS

Since the copyright page cannot accommodate all the copyright notices, pages 461–4 constitute an extension of the copyright page.

FREDERICK ALLEN. 'Unreasonable Facsimile' from *Atlantic Monthly*, August 1994. Reprinted by permission of the author.

ALLAN ANDERSON. 'Scouts' from *Roughnecks & Wildcatters* (Toronto: Macmillan, 1981).

MARGARET ATWOOD. 'True North' from *Saturday Night*, January 1987.

JACQUES BARZUN. 'What If—? English versus German and French' from *A Word or Two Before You Go . . .* , copyright © 1986 by Jacques Barzun. Reprinted by permission of Wesleyan University Press.

MARTHA BAYLES. 'The Shock-Art Fallacy' from *Atlantic Monthly*, February 1994. Reprinted by permission of the author.

DAVID BERGEN. 'Lucy in the Sky' by David Bergen, copyright © 1999 by David Bergen. First published in Canada in *Saturday Night*, October 1999.

PIERRE BERTON. 'Hard Times in the Old West' from *Canadian Heritage*, 11, 1 (February/March 1985). Reprinted by permission of the author.

HARRY BOYLE. 'Tobogganing' from *With a Pinch of Sin* by Harry Boyle, copyright © 1966 by Harry J. Boyle. Used by permission of Doubleday, a division of Random House, Inc.

VICTORIA BRANDON. 'Mad Metaphors' from *In Defence of Plain English* (Willowdale: Hounslow Press, 1992). Reprinted by permission of Dundurn Press Ltd.

CHRISTOPHER BUCKLEY. 'How I Learned to (Almost) Love the Sin Lobbyists' from *Wry Martinis* (New York: Random House, 1997).

STEVE BURGESS. 'Blazing Skies' from *Western Living*, June 2001. Reprinted by permission of the author.

ROBERT CARSE. 'The Loss of the Cospatrick' from *The Twilight of Sailing Ships* by Robert Carse, copyright © 1965 by Robert Carse. Used by permission of Grosset & Dunlap, Inc., a division of Penguin Putnam Inc.

WINSTON COLLINS. 'The Belly of Ontario' from *Equinox*, January/February 1987. Reprinted by permission of the author.

J.A. DAVIDSON. 'Talking "Funny" ' from *The Beaver*, June/July 1993. Reprinted by permission of the author.

HUGH DEMPSEY. 'The Snake Man' from *Alberta History*, 29, 4 (Autumn 1981). Reprinted by permission of the author.

JOAN DIDION. Excerpt from 'Los Angeles Notebook' from *Slouching Towards Bethlehem* by Joan Didion, copyright © 1966, 1968, renewed 1996 by Joan Didion. Reprinted by permission of Farrar, Straus and Giroux, LLC.

ANNIE DILLARD. 'On a Hill Far Away' from *Teaching a Stone to Talk: Expeditions and Encounters* by Annie Dillard, copyright © 1982 by Annie Dillard. Reprinted by permission of HarperCollins Publishers Inc.

DALE EISLER. 'Cultural genocide stalks Dene trapped in white man's world' from *The StarPhoenix*, 30 January 1994. Reprinted by permission of The StarPhoenix, Saskatoon, SK.

NORA EPHRON. 'The New Porn' from *Scribble, Scribble: Notes on the Media* (New York: Alfred A. Knopf, 1978).

HENRY FAIRLIE. 'The Fact of Sin'. Reprinted by permission of The New Republic, copyright © 1977, The New Republic, Inc.

E.M. FORSTER. 'Plot' from *Aspects of the Novel* (New York: Harcourt, Brace and Company, 1927, 1954). Reprinted by permission of The Provost and Scholars of King's College, Cambridge, and the Society of Authors as the Literary Representatives of the EM Forster Estate.

RODERICK HAIG-BROWN. 'Conservation Defined' from *The Living Land* by Roderick Haig-Brown, copyright © Roderick Haig-Brown 1961. Reprinted by permission of Valerie Haig-Brown.

HARRY F. HARLOW. 'Of Love in Infants' from Ants, *Indians and Little Dinosaurs*, ed. Alan P. Ternes, copyright © 1975 by The American Museum of Natural History. Reprinted with the permission of Scribner, an imprint of Simon & Schuster Adult Publishing Group.

WILLIAM FAULKNER. 'On Receiving the Nobel Prize' from *The Faulkner Reader* (New York: Random House, 1954).

ANNE U. FORER. 'Overeating in College' from *A Room of One's Own*, August 1984.

ADRIAN FORSYTH. 'Flights of Fancy' from *Equinox*, January/February 1986.

NORTHROP FRYE. 'The Motive for Metaphor' from *The Educated Imagination* (Toronto: CBC, 1963). Reprinted with permission of Victoria University in the University of Toronto.

CHARLES GORDON. 'Bungee jumping over Victoria Falls' from *Maclean's*, 29 March 1999. 'The Threat to Canada's Beauty' from *Maclean's*, 27 June 1994.

WAYNE GRADY. 'The Haunting Power of God's Dog' from *Equinox*, January/February 1995, copyright © 1995 by Wayne Grady. Reproduced by permission of the author. 'The Metric System (Sort Of)' from *Saturday Night*, March 1999.

GERALD HANNON. 'Romancing the Stones' from *Report on Business*, February 2001. Reprinted by permission of the author.

RALPH HEINTZMAN. 'Liberalism and Censorship' from *Journal of Canadian Studies*, 13, 4 (Winter 1978–9).

PAUL HEMPHILL. 'Welcome to the Death Hilton' from *The Good Old Boys* by Paul Hemphill, copyright © 1974 by Paul Hemphill. Reprinted with permission of Simon & Schuster Adult Publishing Group

PICO IYER. 'In Praise of the Humble Comma' from *Time*, 13 June 1988, copyright © 1988 Time Inc. Reprinted by permission.

JANE JACOBS. 'Streets That Work' from *Canadian Heritage*, 13, 2 (May/June 1987).

WAYNE JOHNSTON. 'A Whale of a Time' from *Saturday Night*, May 1995.

SUSAN JUBY. 'A Tale of a Canadian Book Up Against the System' from *NewWest Review*, 25, 4 (2000), copyright © Susan Juby. Reprinted by permission of the author.

JOANNE KATES. 'The Chicken Farm' from *The Taste of Things* (Toronto: Oxford University Press, 1987).

ELIZABETH KELLY. 'Untamed World' from *Canadian Geographic*, May/June 2002. Reprinted by permission of the author.

CHARLES K. LONG. 'Out of the Shadow of the Bay' from *Equinox*, 1, 1 (January 1982).

ALEXANDRA LOPEZ-PACHECO. 'That &*?#@ Machine' from *Report on Business*, October 2001. Reprinted by permission of the author.

DONNA LOPIANO. 'Purse Snatching' from *Ms.* Magazine, October/November 1999. Reprinted by permission of Ms. Magazine, copyright © 1999.

F.L. LUCAS. 'Courtesy to Readers—Clarity' from *Style*.

JAMES MCCOOK. 'Man's Best Friend?' from *The Beaver*, 310, 3 (Winter 1979). Reprinted by permission.

JOHN MCPHEE. 'The Search for Marvin Gardens' from *Pieces of the Frame* by John McPhee. Published in Canada by Macfarlane Walter & Ross, Toronto.

SID MARTY. 'In the Eye of the Wind' from *Canadian Geographic*, May/June 1996. Reprinted by permission of the author.

NANNETTE VONNEGUT MENGEL. 'The Dissertation and the Mine' from 'Coming of Age the Long Way Around' from *Working It Out*, ed. Sara Ruddick and Pamela Daniels. Used by permission of Pantheon Books, a division of Random House, Inc.

RUTH MORRIS. 'Women in Prison' from *Canadian Dimension*, 20, 8 (February 1987).

L.M. MYERS. Excerpt from *The Roots of Modern English* (Boston: Little, Brown and Company, 1966).

PETER C. NEWMAN. 'Igniting the Entrepreneurial Spark' from *Royal Bank Letter*, October 2001. Reprinted by permission of the author.

P.J. O'ROURKE. 'Fiddling While Africa Starves' from *Give War a Chance: Eyewitness Accounts of Mankind's Struggle Against Tyranny, Injustice and Alcohol-Free Beer*, copyright © 1992 by P.J. O'Rourke. Used by permission of Grove/Atlantic, Inc.

CYNTHIA OZICK. 'Portrait of the Essay as a Warm Body' by Cynthia Ozick, from *The Best American Essays* 1998, copyright © 1998 by Cynthia Ozick. Reprinted by permission of Houghton Mifflin Company. All rights reserved.

KEVIN PATTERSON. 'The Right Call' from *Saturday Night*, March 1999. © Kevin Patterson. Reprinted with permission of Carlisle and Co.

LESTER B. PEARSON. 'The Implications of a Free Society' from *Words and Occasions* by Lester Pearson (Toronto: University of Toronto Press, 1970). Reprinted by permission of University of Toronto Press.

JOHN HENRY RALEIGH. Excerpt from 'Victorian Morals and the Victorian Novel' from *Time, Place, and Idea: Essays on the Novel* by John Henry Raleigh, copyright © 1968 by Southern Illinois University Press. Reprinted by permission of the publisher.

HUGH RAWSON. 'Toilet' from *A Dictionary of Euphemisms & Other Doubletalk*. © 1981 by Hugh Rawson. Reprinted with permission of the author.

ALAN RAYBURN. 'Hot and Bothered by "Disgusting" Names' from *Naming Canada: Stories about Place Names from 'Canadian Geographic'* by Alan Rayburn (Toronto: University of Toronto press, 1994). Reprinted by permission of University of Toronto Press.

ROGER REVELLE. Excerpt from *The Metropolitan Enigma*, ed. James Q. Wilson (Cambridge, MA: Harvard University Press, 1967).

BART ROBINSON. 'Cold Fury, White Death' from *Equinox*, January/February 1987. Reprinted by permission of the author.

STEVE RUSHIN. 'Cliches Aren't Everything' from *Sports Illustrated*, 16 October 2000.

CARL SAGAN. 'Night Walkers and Mystery Mongers: Sense and Nonsense at the Edge of Science' © 1979 by the estate of Carl Sagan. Originally printed in *Broca's Brain: Reflections on the Romance of Science* by Random House. Reprinted with permission from the estate of Carl Sagan.

SCOTT RUSSELL SANDERS. 'The Singular First Person', copyright © 1988 by Scott Russell Sanders. First appeared in *Sewanee Review*. Reprinted by permission of the author.

DAN SCHNEIDER. 'Biter's Banquet' from *Canadian Geographic*, May/June 1995. Reprinted by permission of the author.

CHARLES SIEBERT. 'Call of the Wild' from *Saturday Night*, November 1999.

CHRISTINA HOFF SOMMERS. 'Indignation, Resentment, and Collective Guilt' from *Who Stole Feminism?* by Christina Hoff Sommers, copyright © 1994 by Christina Sommers. Reprinted with the permission of Simon & Schuster Adult Publishing Group.

DREW HAYDEN TAYLOR. 'Native Themes 101' from *NewWest Review*, 25, 4 (2000).

PETER SHAWN TAYLOR. 'Be Fruitful, Or Else' from *Saturday Night*, 7 July 2001. Reprinted by permission of the author.

LEWIS THOMAS. 'Notes on Punctuation', copyright © 1979 by Lewis Thomas, from *The Medusa and the Snail* by Lewis Thomas. Used by permission of Viking Penguin, a division of Penguin Putnam Inc.

JAMES THURBER. 'The Unicorn in the Garden' from the book *My Life and Hard Times*, copyright © 1933, 1961 by James Thurber. Reprinted by arrangement with Rosemary A. Thurber and The Barbara Hogenson Agency, Inc. All rights reserved.

JAMES S. TREFIL. 'The Golf Ball on the Grass' from 'Odds Are Against Your Breaking That Law of Averages', *Smithsonian*, September 1984. Reprinted by permission of the author.

BARBARA TUCHMAN. Excerpt from 'The Missing Element: Moral Courage' from *In Search of Leaders: Current Issues in Higher Education*, ed. G. Kerry Smith (Washington, DC: National Education Association, 1967).

JOHN UPDIKE. 'Thirteen Ways of Looking at the Masters' from *Hugging the Shore: Essays and Criticism* by John Updike, copyright © 1983 by John Updike. Used by permission of Alfred A. Knopf, a division of Random House, Inc.

ROY VONTOBEL. Excerpt from 'Reluctant Villain' by Roy Vontobel from *Nature Canada*, 8, 1(1979). Reprinted by permission of the author.

GERALD WEISSMANN. 'Titanic and *Leviathan*' from *The Doctor with Two Heads and Other Essays* by Gerald Weissmann, copyright © 1988 by Gerald Weissmann. Used by permission of Alfred A. Knopf, a division of Random House, Inc.

E.B. WHITE. 'Once More to the Lake' from *One Man's Meat*, text copyright © 1941 by E.B. White. Copyright renewed. Reprinted by permission of Tilbury House, publishers, Gardiner, Maine.

CHARLES WILKINS. 'Above the Line' from *Saturday Night*, March 1999.

GEORGE WOODCOCK. Excerpt from *Gabriel Dumont: The Métis Chief and His Lost World* (Edmonton: Hurtig, 1976).

WILLIAM ZINSSER. 'Clutter' from *On Writing Well: An Informal Guide to Writing Nonfiction*, 6th edn (New York: HarperCollins, 1998), copyright © 1976, 1980, 1985, 1988, 1990, 1994, 1998 by William K. Zinsser. Reprinted by permission of the author.

Every effort has been made to contact copyright owners. In the case of any omissions, the publisher will be pleased to make suitable acknowledgement in future editions.

GLOSSARY

This glossary offers brief definitions of those grammatical and rhetorical terms that are used in the questions. The first time such a term appears in any group of questions, it is set in bold, a signal that it appears in the Glossary.

ABSTRACT, ABSTRACTED, ABSTRACTION. A word or phrase that refers to theoretical concepts, ideas, or generalities is abstract: e.g. *truth, justice, democracy, realism, interdependent*. Unlike **concrete** words, which name specific things, abstractions make little or no appeal to the senses; they are qualities, characteristics, or essences shared by a large class of things. Not all abstractions, however, are equally general in meaning. The word *man*, for example, is more specific than *organism*. But *man* seems quite abstract when set beside 'a sturdy, corpulent old man with a baseball cap, paint-stained overalls, and a tattered shirt'. The more general the meaning of any given word the more abstract it tends to be.

   Abstractions must be used with caution. They tempt the writer to speak in hazy generalities, to forget that good writing is specific. It is impossible to avoid abstract words, especially in exposition, but the writer should anchor his thoughts as firmly as possible in concrete reality. The number of abstract words in any composition will, of course, depend upon the writer's subject and purpose: the philosopher discussing the nature of being will use more abstract words than a traveller describing a trip to Iqaluit. Wherever possible abstract words should be avoided. When the key words in any essay are abstractions, they should be defined and illustrated at the beginning. See **concrete**.

ADJECTIVE PHRASE (or ADJECTIVE CLAUSE). A group of words that functions as an adjective, modifying a noun or pronoun, is an adjective phrase: e.g. 'I was walking the dog *that belongs to my brother*'; 'Some people *who buy contemporary paintings* have no interest in art'; 'It was a glorious day *when everything went right*.'

ADVERB PHRASE (or ADVERB CLAUSE). A group of words that functions as an adverb, modifying a verb, adjective, or adverb, is an adverb phrase: e.g. 'The dog ran *with great speed*'; 'He lived in Alberta for many years but returned to Montreal *when he lost his job*'; '*After the rain delay*, the game continued for another two hours.'

ALLITERATION. The repetition in successive words of the same initial consonant sound, or of any vowel sound, is alliteration. Most often the sound in the first syllable is repeated: 'The majestic, the magnificent Mississippi'; 'In a summer season, when soft was the sun' (Fowler); 'the soft, lilting lyric of love'. Alliteration should be used only when the writer makes a strong emotional response to his subject; it is usually out of place in matter-of-fact exposition. But even in emotive writing alliteration just be used rarely with extreme caution. Excessive alliteration is offensive.

ALLUSION. An allusion is a reference to a generally familiar person, place, or thing, whether real or legendary: Queen Elizabeth, the Dalai Lama, Cleopatra, Apollo, Gabriel Dumont, Tom Sawyer, Peggys Cove, the Garden of Eden, the Plains of Abraham, the Great Pyramid of Cheops, the shield of Achilles. Most allusions are drawn from history, geography, religion, mythology, and literature. One value of allusions is their economy: they allow the writer to evoke in one or two words an atmosphere, a whole story, a whole period of history.

AMBIGUITY, AMBIGUOUS. When a word or passage can be understood in more than one way, it is ambiguous. Unintentional ambiguity is usually a fault, as in, 'He forgot his book on the piano,' where it is not clear whether the book was about the piano or was left lying on top of the piano. Sometimes, however, ambiguity is a deliberate strategy, either as a kind of humour or irony or as a way of suggesting the complexities and uncertainties of experience.

ANALOGY. An analogy is a form of comparison in which two things, often quite different, are compared in order to suggest that what is true of one applies to the other. Some common analogies are a human heart compared to a pump, a government compared to a ship, a university compared to a business, a large city compared to an anthill. A writer may use an analogy to show how things that resemble each other in some respects will resemble each other in other respects as well. For example, after establishing that a heart and a pump have similar functions, one might conclude that just as a pump needs regular maintenance to ensure that it functions properly, so a heart needs regular exercise to keep it in good working order.

An analogy can help us to visualize ideas, to see relationships more clearly; it can help clarify or emphasize an idea because of its strong appeal to the emotions; it can help outline perspectives and proportions.

On the other hand, however, the danger of using an analogy is that it must not be taken as proof. A university may certainly resemble a business in that both institutions take in money, but in many essential respects they are quite different—for instance, they both have widely differing purposes in society, the university being dedicated to teaching and research and the business being dedicated to making a profit.

ANAPHORA. The repetition of a word, or group of words, at the beginning of successive **clauses**, sentences, or lines of poetry is anaphora. Like most forms of deliberate repetition it is emphatic; it has the secondary effect of aiding the writer's coherence or flow. In the following passage, Loren Eiseley is scolding modern humans for their resistance to fact in political and social thinking:

> '*We are always more willing* to accept mechanical changes in an automobile than to revise, or even to examine our racial prejudices, to use one painful example. *We are more willing* to swallow a pill that we hope will relax our tensions than to make the sustained conscious effort necessary to alter our daily living habits.' [our italics]

ANTECEDENT. The noun for which a pronoun stands is its antecedent: e.g. *cats* in 'Cats are happiest when *they* are sleeping'; *George* in 'In spite of *his* long prison record, *George* made no effort to rehabilitate himself.'

ANTITHESIS, ANTITHETICAL. Antithesis is the balancing of two opposite or contrasting words, **phrases**, **clauses**, paragraphs, or even larger units of writing. Antithesis refers most often, however, to the balancing of opposites in independent clauses within a sentence or in two adjacent sentences. Sir William Osler, for example, writes: 'The quest for righteousness is Oriental, the quest for knowledge, Occidental.' Frequently, as here, the second clause is elliptical: the verb appears only in the first clause and is omitted and represented by a comma in the second. Mark Twain makes two clauses antithetical: 'Good breeding consists in concealing how much we think of ourselves and how little we think of the other person.' Samuel Butler creates antithesis in two short sentences: 'God is Love, I dare say. But what a mischievous devil Love is.' Antitheses are emphatic, often witty, and usually memorable. If not overused, they are effective in development by contrast.

APPOSITIVE, (IN) APPOSITION. A noun or **noun phrase** that repeats and further identifies a preceding noun is an appositive: 'Francis Bacon, *the youngest son of Sir Nicholas*, was born at York House, *his father's residence in the Strand*, on the twenty-second of January 1561.' Here 'the youngest son of Sir Nicholas' renames and further identifies 'Francis Bacon' just as 'his father's residence in Strand' renames and further identifies 'York House'. In each instance the second noun is said to be in apposition to (or, in apposition with) the first. The appositive is in effect an abbreviated clause in place of 'who was the youngest son of Sir Nicholas' and 'which was his father's residence in the Strand'. See **non-restrictive modifier**, **restrictive modifier**.

ASSONANCE. The repetition of internal vowel sounds in closely following words is called assonance: 'a deep green stream'; 'She moaned in pain, and with a low groan went into violent convulsions.' The same warnings that apply to alliteration also apply to assonance. See **alliteration**.

ASYNDETON. Asyndeton is the use of commas to separate members of a compound construction, most often a series of words. Rather than 'A, B, and C' ('He hurriedly threw into the suitcase a variety of *balls, bats,* and *gloves*') asyndeton employs 'A, B, C' without the conjunction *and* ('*Balls, bats, gloves* were hurriedly thrown into the suitcase'), which gives equal emphasis to each item in the series instead of placing slightly more stress on the last item. Asyndeton speeds up the sentence: '*Drays, carts, men, boys,* all go hurrying to a common centre, the wharf' (Mark Twain). See **polysyndeton**.

BALANCE, BALANCED SENTENCE (or BALANCED CONSTRUCTION). A balanced sentence or construction contains two distinct halves or parts, each of about the same length and importance. Similar constructions appear in the same place in each half and balance one another: 'Our heritage of Greek literature and art is priceless; the example of Greek life possesses for us not the slightest value'; 'There's never time to do it right, but there's always time to do it over.'

CLAUSE. A clause is a grammatically related group of words containing a subject and a **predicate**. The two principal kinds are *independent* (or *main*) and *dependent* (or *subordinate*). An *independent clause* (if taken out of the sentence in which it is found) can stand by itself as a complete sentence: 'From the beginnings of civilization until very recently, *women in most societies were literally the property of their husbands and fathers*' (Ellen Willis). The italicized independent clause here could be used by itself as a whole sentence.

A *dependent clause* (if taken out of the sentence in which it is found) cannot stand alone as a complete sentence: '*When the Liberal government of Premier Ross Thatcher cut off all welfare for "employables"*, the economy of the town collapsed' (Charles Long). The italicized dependent clause here cannot act by itself as a whole sentence; it needs a main clause to complete its meaning. Note that dependent clauses are introduced by words that make them subordinate. Thus, omitting 'when' (the subordinating word) from the example would leave 'The Liberal government of Premier Ross Thatcher cut off all welfare for "employables"'—now an independent clause.

Dependent clauses are of three kinds: **noun clauses**, which have the same functions in a sentence as nouns (subjects, objects, complements); **adjective clauses**, which modify nouns, pronouns, or groups of words acting as nouns or pronouns; and **adverb clauses**, which modify verbs, adjectives, adverbs, clauses, or even entire sentences.

For more detailed information, students should consult a standard writing handbook.

CLICHÉ. 'White as snow', 'strong as an ox', 'cold as ice', 'smart as a whip', 'quick as a cat', 'red as a rose'. These are all clichés, overused **figures of speech** that are so common that the listener or reader can usually finish them before the speaker or writer does: 'heavy as _____', 'big as a _____', 'clumsy as a bull in a _____', 'as pure as the driven _____', 'as pretty as a _____', 'from the bottom of my _____', 'easier said than _____'. Clichés are not entirely avoidable; some of them express an idea or a feeling in a manner that is both complete and admirably brief, as in the expressions 'There's no tomorrow', or 'It's been a great ride'. Both these clichés encompass a considerable range of meaning; trying to say the same thing in different words, and as briefly, would be very difficult. Nevertheless, clichés should be avoided as much as possible, since their use is a sign that the writer is not willing to make the effort to find different, and fresher, language.

CLOSING BY RETURN. To end a long paragraph or one section of an essay or an entire composition, the writer sometimes returns to an image, an idea, or a statement that occurs in the beginning. This completed cycle, or closing by return, signals to the reader that the unit of writing is done. See, for instance, the first and last sentences in the introductory paragraph of Lester Pearson's 'The Implications of a Free Society' (p. 273), or the first and last paragraphs of Wayne Johnston's 'A Whale of a Time' (pp. 31–4).

COLLOQUIAL, COLLOQUIALISM. A colloquial expression (or colloquialism) is one that occurs more often in speech than in writing. It is informal, conversational language. Although not necessarily vulgar or bad, it is the kind of language that would not be accepted as good usage in formal speech or writing. Thus, in the sentence, 'He revered the dignity of her face and the quiet beauty of her smile; in sum, he thought that she was pretty cute,' the last clause is colloquial, because it is obviously inappropriate for this context. The same sort of error occurs here: 'After having committed a succession of grisly murders, he was thrown in the slammer for life.'

Colloquialisms can give writing something of the flavour of talk, making it more informal and more entertaining. They must, however, be appropriate to the context.

COMMA SPLICE (or COMMA FAULT). A comma splice occurs when two independent (or main) **clauses** are joined by a comma only: 'The two men hurriedly jumped aboard the truck, they then looked at the map.' The correct punctuation here is either a semicolon, or a comma followed by a **coordinate conjunction**. See **run-on sentence**.

COMPLEX SENTENCE. A sentence containing one independent (or main) **clause** and one or more dependent (or subordinate) clauses is complex: '*Although she missed playing first base*, she was willing to give third base a try for the first part of the season.' The italicized part of this sentence is the dependent clause, and the rest is the independent clause. The following complex sentence begins with an independent clause and is followed by two dependent ones: 'She tried very hard to make a decent life for herself, although her children constantly rebelled because their father had mistreated them.'

COMPOUND-COMPLEX SENTENCE. A sentence is called compound-complex if it contains two or more independent (or main) **clauses** and one or more dependent (or subordinate) clauses: '*When the fog lifted*, I saw the accident and I reported it.' The italicized part of this sentence is the dependent clause, which is followed by two independent ones. The following compound-complex sentence begins with an independent clause followed by a dependent clause and a second independent clause: 'They took some time off while we worked, but we could not finish the job.'

COMPOUND SENTENCE. A compound sentence contains two or more independent (or main) **clauses** joined by one or more **coordinate conjunctions**: 'She was never allowed to go to a dance alone, but she had been given permission to come home after midnight and she could have a few beers.' Here three independent clauses are joined by two coordinate conjunctions, whereas in the following sentence there are two independent clauses joined by one coordinate conjunction: 'General Custer could fight all right, but there was a great deal of question about his competence as a commander' (Ralph K. Andrist).

CONCRETE. Words or phrases that name specific things as opposed to generalities are concrete: 'coarse sandpaper', 'a rotten orange', 'a blue silk gown with four flounces', 'dirty snow', 'the buzzing of yellow bees'. It is not quite accurate to say that concrete words make a direct appeal to one or more of the five senses and **abstractions** do not. Some words, like *chair*, are at once both concrete and abstract. The word *chair* is a general term that names a large class of objects; yet *chair* brings to mind a clearer mental image than *furniture*, and it is more specific. However, chair is not as concrete as 'the battered old Windsor chair in my grandmother's attic', which identifies a single object that really exists. Words move toward the concrete as they re-create actual, specific things. For most purposes, we can define concrete words as those that make us touch, smell, taste, hear, and see. Since, like good writing, concrete words are definite and specific, they are usually preferable to abstractions. See abstract.

CONJUNCTION. A conjunction is a word used to link words, **phrases**, or **clauses**. A *coordinate conjunction* (e.g. *and*, *or*, *but*, *for*, *yet*) links two independent clauses.

Independent clauses can also by joined by a **conjunctive adverb** (e.g. *thus, however, consequently, therefore, also, hence, nevertheless*). A *subordinate conjunction*, placed at the beginning of a dependent clause, shows the logical dependence of that clause on an independent clause: '*Although* I am poor, I am happy'; '*While* others slept, he studied.' *Correlative conjunctions* are pairs of coordinate conjunctions: *either/or; neither/nor; not only/but.*

CONJUNCTIVE ADVERB. A conjunctive adverb functions as both adverb and **conjunction**. As adverb, it answers the questions *in what manner?*, *under what conditions?*; it signifies the logical relationships such as addition, contrast or contradiction, cause and effect. As conjunction, it joins two independent **clauses**. It is almost always preceded by a semicolon. English is particularly rich in conjunctive adverbs, among the most common being *therefore, consequently, however, nevertheless, moreover, furthermore, hence, still, thus*: 'The law was passed after a debate that had lasted well past midnight; *thus*, its final form would likely need a good deal of rewording and polishing'; 'This has been an extremely dry winter; *consequently* we can expect some difficulties with crops.'

CONNECTIVE, CONNECTING. Any word or phrase that signifies a relationship between two words, **phrases**, **clauses**, sentences, or paragraphs can be called a connective, or connecting word. Thus, the term encompasses parts of speech like **prepositions**, pronouns, **conjunctions**, and **conjunctive adverbs** in addition to connective phrases like *of course, for example, in addition, to be sure*. Most beginning writers need to build their active vocabulary of connective words and phrases, for although it is possible to overuse them, the student writer seldom uses them enough. Connectives express, among others, such ideas as

- addition (*and, moreover, furthermore, in addition*)
- contrast or contradiction (*but, yet, in contrast, however*)
- cause and effect (*so, therefore, for this reason*)
- disjunction and division (*either . . . or, some . . . others*)
- conclusion (*finally, at last, ultimately*)

These are only a few of the great number of connectives and only a few of the logical notions they can express. Connectives deserve the student's closest attention.

CONNOTATION. The connotation of a word is not the thing or idea the word stands for, but the attitudes, feelings, and emotions aroused by the word. Connotations tend to be favourable or unfavourable. Thus *village* and *hick town* both refer to a small settlement. Village is favourable, or at least neutral, in its connotations, but *hick town* suggests the writer's scorn or contempt.

The *denotation* of a word refers only to the thing the word represents, stripped of any emotional associations the word might carry. The denotation of both *village* and *hick town* is the same; both identify a small community.

CONSONANCE. In verse, consonance is a kind of rhyme in which the same consonant follows different vowel sounds: for example, the rhyme of <u>late</u> and <u>light</u>. In prose, the term generally refers to a harmonious repetition of internal consonant sounds as in the phrase 'a pa<u>l</u>e go<u>l</u>d c<u>l</u>oud'. However, the term has also been used to refer to the correspondence of both the initial and the final consonant sounds, as in such words as <u>red</u> and <u>read</u>, <u>moon</u> and <u>mine</u>, <u>blew</u> and <u>blow</u>.

COORDINATE CLAUSES. Two independent **clauses** of grammatically equal importance (and of whatever length) joined together are said to be coordinate. They are linked either by a semicolon or by one of the **coordinate conjunctions**—*and*, *but*, *or*, *nor*, *for*, *so*, *yet*: 'The children's game, which at first had been quiet and orderly, had degenerated into a mad rush to pile on to each other, but they all came out of it with no crying and not so much as a scratch'; 'Margaret and her sister Rose are always being invited to the most luxurious and expensive parties, yet they still haven't managed to gain the confidence of any of the parents.' See **dependent clause**.

COORDINATE CONJUNCTION. See **conjunction**.

CORRELATIVE CONJUNCTION. See **conjunction**.

CUMULATIVE SENTENCE. A cumulative sentence is an extended variety of the **loose sentence**. Often used in description, the cumulative sentence begins with a general statement, which it then expands in a series of particulars, as in this description of a ward in a state mental hospital:

> 'The geriatric section is always the most unattractive, poorly lighted, no brightness, no pictures, no laughter. Just long green corridors, lined by doors; white-gowned nurses moving silently, expressionless; large wards with beds filling the room, allowing no space for anything'. (Sharon R. Curtin)

Some further examples:

> 'The small waves were the same, chucking the small rowboat under the chin as we fished at anchor, and the boat was the same boat, the same colour green and the ribs broken in the same places, and under the floorboards the same fresh-water leavings and debris—the dead helgramite, the wisps of moss, the rusty discarded fish-hook, the dried blood from yesterday's catch.' (White, pp. 412–13)

> She had made up her mind, in spite of her financial difficulties, and aware that her boyfriend would strongly disagree.

> The high-school band played enthusiastically, the occasional mistakes of the clarinets and trombones smoothed over by the thundering drums.

DANGLING MODIFIER. A modifying word or **phrase** (often including a **participle**) that is not grammatically connected to any part of the sentence is said to be dangling. In the following example, the italicized phrase is not grammatically connected to the subject of the sentence (*street*): '*Walking to school*, the street was slippery.' Some further examples: '*Being made of thin plastic*, Robert handled the picture frame carefully'; '*In taking these pictures* the mountain was often featured prominently.'

DENOTATION. See **connotation**.

DEPENDENT CLAUSE (or SUBORDINATE CLAUSE). A **clause** functioning within a sentence as an adjective, adverb, or noun is said to be dependent (or subordinate). Since it is grammatically less important than the main clause, a subordinate clause should express ideas of lesser importance. See **clause**.

ELLIPTICAL CONSTRUCTION. This is the omission of words necessary to the syntax of a sentence but not to its sense, as in 'He is taller than I,' where the words 'am tall' are understood but not expressed. Similar constructions are 'My car is small, hers [is] big'; and 'Surround yourself with good people, preferably [ones who are] smarter than you [are].'

ETYMOLOGY. The derivation or origin of a word, whatever its source—a person, a place, a thing, a word from another language—is called its etymology:

> telescope . . . [NL. *telescopium* from Gr. *teleskopos*, viewing afar, farseeing, from *tele*, far, far off + *skopos*, a watcher.]

Some dictionaries list etymologies in brackets just before or at the end of the definition, and the abbreviations and signs used in the etymologies are explained at the front of the dictionary. Etymologies often help the writer to understand the first or root meaning of a word, from which any further meanings have been derived. Knowing an etymology helps the writer to remember a word and to use it accurately.

EUPHEMISM. A euphemism is a word or phrase used to avoid some other word or phrase that might be considered offensive or too harsh: 'pass away' for *die*, 'mortal remains' for *corpse*; 'intoxicated' for *drunk*; 'negative growth' for *decline*; 'at the present time' for *now*.

EXPLETIVE. A word or **phrase** used to fill out a sentence without adding to the sense is an expletive. The most common expletives are *it* and *there*, which often take the place of the subject: 'It is likely that they would have perished had help not arrived so soon.' In this case, the sentence could easily be rewritten to avoid the expletive: 'They likely would have perished had help not arrived so soon.' Expletives can help the writer achieve emphasis, but they can also make sentences wordy and can often be avoided.

FIGURE OF SPEECH, FIGURATIVE, FIGURATIVELY. Any use of language for stylistic effect other than the plain, normal, straightforward manner of writing or speaking is called figurative. Some of the common figures are **alliteration**, **assonance**, **irony**, **metaphor**, **metonymy**, **personification**, **simile**.

FLOW. The term flow refers to the continuity, or coherence, among the sentences of a paragraph. Flow is created (1) by repeating a key word or its synonym in successive sentences; (2) by using logical **connectives**; (3) by using a pronoun whose antecedent is in the preceding sentence; (4) by using identical or similar grammatical constructions at the beginning of successive sentences. The following illustrates all of these techniques:

> 'One never forgets Masefield's face. It is not the face of a young man, for it is lined and grave. And yet it is not the face of an old man, for youth is still in the bright eyes. Its dominant quality is humility.' (Beverley Nichols)

FRAGMENT. Conventionally defined, a sentence is a grammatically independent statement containing a subject and a finite verb. Any construction punctuated as a sentence but not conforming to this definition is a fragment: e.g. 'People who live in Vancouver.' 'People living in Vancouver.' 'When we visited Vancouver.' Generally fragments are a serious fault; wisely employed, they may prove more emphatic or realistic than grammatically complete sentences: e.g. 'I have another Sicilian memory that will not soon fade. *The waiter.*' It is worth noting, however, that a fragment such as this is a deliberate effect of style, not, as is often the case in student essays, the accident of carelessness or ignorance. Even such successful fragments quickly become an awkward mannerism if used very often. Students are well advised to use them sparingly.

FRAMING WORDS. To separate clearly and to introduce several divisions of a subject or thought, the writer often uses framing words: *First, Second, Third*; *First, Next, Last*; *The most significant effect, A less important effect*; and so on. These usually occur in a paragraph introduced by an **organizing sentence**. Although framing words are effective because they are so clear, they are also rather mechanical and thus should be used sparingly. See **organizing sentence**.

FREIGHT-TRAIN SENTENCE. A freight-train sentence consists of three or more independent **clauses**, usually relatively short and joined either by **coordinate conjunctions** (commonly *and*) or by semicolons without conjunctions: 'It was a hot day and the sky was very bright and blue and the road was white and dusty' (Ernest Hemingway). 'She cooked the dinner furiously; slamming cupboard doors and banging drawers; slapping the ingredients into pots; occasionally looking at him with hatred.' Although the occasional freight-train sentence can be an effective stylistic device, it must be used carefully; there is little that separates an effective freight-train sentence from a rambling **run-on sentence**.

GERUND. See **participle**.

IMAGE, IMAGERY. At its simplest an image is a picture made with words, although images may also appeal to the senses of touch, smell, hearing, taste, and movement. In this sense, 'imagery' refers to an author's use of specific images. But 'imagery' is also often used in a much broader sense to refer to the use an author makes of **figures of speech** of any kind, especially images, **symbols**, **similes**, **metaphors**, and **metonymy**. Description and narration make frequent use of images, but imagery appears in exposition and persuasion as well, and it can also be used in argument. See **concrete**.

INDEPENDENT CLAUSE. See **clause**.

INTERRUPTED MOVEMENT, INTERRUPTING PHRASE. The normal word order of the English sentence is subject–verb–object (or complement). Normally, short modifiers like adjectives, adverbs, or **prepositional phrases** may stand between subject and verb or between a verb and its object. Such normal word order may be called *straightforward movement*. But to introduce a **clause** or a **phrase** between subject and verb or between a verb (or verbal) and its object creates interrupted movement: 'The Renaissance, as we have seen, has not yet reached Northern Europe.' Here the clause 'as we have seen' interrupts the normal order. Interrupted movement is an important variation of normal sentence structure, but it is more at home in a relatively formal style than in informal writing.

INVERSION. Any variation of the normal order of subject–verb–object (or complement) is inversion. In some sentences the object stands first: 'That story I did not believe.' Occasionally a verb appears before the subject: 'In the far corner of the room sat a very old man.' Such inversions are emphatic, but like all variations of the normal, their emphasis depends upon their rarity.

IRONY, IRONIC, IRONICALLY. When the writer uses words to mean something different from what they seem to say on the surface, she is being ironic. The simplest form of irony means the reverse of what it says. Thus a terrible stench may be called a perfume, a stupid man a genius. Yet irony may range from a complete reversal of meaning to a subtle qualification of the surface meaning. Irony surprises and makes its point with the greatest emphasis because it forces us to contemplate two incongruous things. Most often a device of satire and persuasion, irony appears in all kinds of prose except the driest kind of exposition.

JARGON. Jargon is technical or specialized terms used unnecessarily or in inappropriate places: e.g., 'peer-group interaction' for friendship; 'perambulate' for walk; 'monetary remuneration' for pay.

LOOSE SENTENCE. The loose sentence begins with the main idea, which is then followed by explanation, details, and modifiers: 'The mountain climber must use her head first, and only then her rope, ice-axe, and pitons.' The word 'loose' has no bad connotations here but simply refers to a more or less 'natural' sentence order, as opposed to the **periodic sentence**, in which elements are reversed. See **cumulative sentence, periodic sentence**.

MAIN CLAUSE. See **clause**.

METAPHOR. A metaphor is an implied comparison between two things seemingly quite different: 'All the world's a stage, / And all the men and women merely players' (Shakespeare). Here the poet, by describing the world as a stage, implies a comparison between these two things. If the poet had made the comparison more explicit by saying that the world is like a stage, and men and women like players, this would be a **simile** rather than a metaphor. The following are some examples of metaphor in prose: 'Man's imagination is limited by the horizon of his experience'; 'The large deck she had to repair, which spread over much of the back yard, was a small forest of rotting wood'; 'The hikers had now been lost for hours, ghosts wandering shakily in a world of icy mist.' Since one term of the metaphor is usually commonplace and concrete, the metaphor not only makes writing more vivid, it may help the writer to make her point clearly. Metaphors make the abstract, concrete; the elusive, definite; the unfamiliar, familiar.

METONYMY. The figure of speech called metonymy substitutes something closely associated with a thing for the thing itself. We may speak of 'Shakespeare' to mean his works; we speak of seeing three 'sails' on the horizon to mean three ships, of 'the Crown' to mean the British monarch.

MISPLACED MODIFIER. A misplaced modifier is a word or group of words that can cause confusion because it is not placed next to the element it should modify. In the following examples, the modifying words or phrases in italics are misplaced: 'We returned to North Bay after a month's holiday *on Friday*'; 'Near Elk Island Park, *grazing peacefully like cattle*, we saw a herd of buffalo'; 'I *only* ate the pie.'

MODIFIER. A word or group of words that describes or limits or makes more exact or in some way qualifies another element in the sentence is a modifier.

NON-RESTRICTIVE MODIFIER (or NON-RESTRICTIVE ELEMENT). See **restrictive modifier**.

NOUN PHRASE (or NOUN CLAUSE). A noun phrase is a group of words that functions like a noun as a subject, an object, or a subject complement. In the following three examples, the italicized noun phrases act, respectively, as subject, prepositional object, and subject complement: (1) '*Whatever you decide* is fine with me.' (2) 'I'll agree to *whatever you decide*.' (3) 'The trouble is *that you cannot decide*.'

ORGANIZING SENTENCE. Standing at the beginning of a paragraph or of a major section of an essay or at the beginning of the composition, an organizing sentence indicates the subject to be treated, how it is to be divided, into how many parts the division falls, or any variation of these: 'There were four underlying causes of the recession of 1984'; 'The camp of a Roman legion presented the appearance of a fortified city' (Gibbon); 'The structure of a large university is fairly complex: faculties, divisions, schools, institutes, departments, and a variety of other, less common divisions.'

PARALLEL, PARALLEL CONSTRUCTION (or PARALLEL STRUCTURE). Constructions are parallel when two or more words, **phrases**, or **clauses** of the same grammatical rank are related in the same way to the same word or words. Thus two or more subjects of the same verb are parallel; two or more verbs with the same subject are parallel; two or more **adverb clauses** modifying the same verb are parallel; and so on. In the following sentence Rachel Carson is describing the face of the sea:

'Crossed by colours, lights, and moving shadows, sparkling mysterious in the sun, in the twilight, its aspects and its moods vary hour by hour.'

Here the writer uses three parallel adjectives (*crossed, sparkling, mysterious*) to modify the same parallel subjects, *aspects* and *moods*. Each adjective is modified by a **prepositional phrase**, the first with three parallel objects (*colours, lights, moving shadows*).

In the eighteenth century many writers often strove for a more involved parallelism combined with balance. In the following example, Samuel Johnson balances a series of parallel independent clauses in the first half of the sentence against parallel dependent clauses in the second half. This already complex pattern he further complicates by parallel constructions within the dependent clauses:

'. . . much of my life has been lost under the pressures of disease; much has been trifled away; and much has always been spent in provision for the day that was passing over me; useless but I shall not think my employment useless or ignoble if by my assistance foreign nations, and distant ages, gain access to the propagators of knowledge, and understand the teachers of truth; if my labours afford light to the repositories of science, and add celebrity to Bacon, to Hooker, to Milton, and to Boyle.'

This elaborate architecture has all but disappeared from even the most formal writing. Yet parallelism of a much simpler kind appears often in both formal and informal writing. In skilful hands it is an interesting variation of the normal sentence pattern, allowing the writer to compress many ideas into a small space. Parallelism may be used to sustain a mood or to suggest rapid action, as it does in this description of a boxing match by A.J. Liebling:

'Instead of flicking, moving around, and so piling up enough unhurting points to goad Johnson into some possible late activity, he was reconnoitring in close, looking the challenge over as if he had never seen him before.'

Nanette Vonnegut Mengel uses this form of parallelism to describe action:

'As his act began, Kanar, alone on the stage, playfully bounced an imaginary basketball, tossed it in the air, and dribbled rhythmically at varying speeds.'

PARTICIPLE, PARTICIPIAL, PARTICIPIAL PHRASE. See **verbal**.

PERIODIC SENTENCE. A sentence that delays the expression of a complete thought until the end, or until near the end, is called periodic. The following is an example from an essay by Virginia Woolf:

'If behind the erratic gunfire of the press the author felt that there was another kind of criticism, the opinion of people reading for the love of reading, slowly and unprofessionally, and judging with great sympathy and yet with great severity, might not this improve the quality of his work?'

One must read this entire sentence before a complete thought emerges. In contrast, most sentences exhibit what is called **loose** structure, as does this sentence from the same essay by Virginia Woolf:

'Thus the desire grows upon us to have done with half-statements and approximations; to cease from searching out the minute shades of human character, to enjoy the greater abstractness, the purer truth of fiction.'

This sentence can be terminated at several points before the end and still make sense. The periodic sentence, because it is rare and because it demands closer attention from the reader than does the loose sentence, is one means of achieving emphasis through sentence structure. Although it appears in all kinds of writing, the periodic sentence, especially when long, is more suited to the formal than to the informal level of usage. If overused, the periodic sentence becomes an irritating mannerism, but it is extremely useful for variation and emphasis.

PERSONIFICATION. In the **figure of speech** called personification, ideas, animals, or things are given human attributes. Justice, for example, is often personified as a blindfolded woman of heroic proportions holding a pair of scales, cowardice is personified by the rat, aggression by the snarling tiger.

PHRASE. A phrase is a group of related words that normally appears in a sentence. A phrase has three characteristics: it has neither subject nor verb, it cannot stand alone, and it functions as a single part of speech. There is a wide variety of phrases: **prepositional**, **verbal**, infinitive, **participial**, **restrictive** and **non-restrictive**, disjunctive, absolute. Distinguishing phrases from **clauses** should not be difficult if the student keeps in mind the three characteristics mentioned above. Some examples:

> He was just in *from a small logging town* [prepositional phrase modifying the verb 'was in'] *on the BC coast* [prepositional phrase modifying the noun 'town'].

> *Running the race* [gerund phrase used as subject] *in several phases* [prepositional phrase modifying the subject] *was her only plan* [predicate].

> *Announcing a time-out* [introductory verbal phrase], the plate umpire consulted with the first-base umpire.

> *To accomplish the reorganization* [infinitive phrase used as subject] was the only objective.

POINTER. A pointer is a word (usually called a conjunctive, or transitional, adverb) or phrase that stands at or near the beginning of a sentence or of an independent **clause** and prepares the reader for a turn of thought. Thus the word *however* points to an approaching contradiction; *for instance* to an oncoming illustration; *therefore* to a logical conclusion. It is possible to overuse pointers, but more often students tend to use too few of them. See **conjunctive adverb**, **connective**.

POINT OF VIEW. In the study of prose, point of view can mean two things. It can, first, refer to the writer's attitudes or values, her way of looking at things in general, her viewpoint. The range of possibilities here is almost endless. It can perhaps be exemplified by the story of a house fire: the wife, who knows that her husband is trapped in the burning attic, is intensely involved in the situation; the fireman, who has faced this sort of thing before, is more dispassionate.

More precisely, however, point of view refers to the grammatical person of the writer's composition. She may use *I*, the first-person point of view, explaining what happened to her, what she thought, or what she saw happen to others. This is the point of view of autobiography, of much narrative, and often of the familiar essay. On the other hand, the third-person point of view detaches the writer from any personal relationship with her material. In place of *I*, the writer uses a noun or third-person pronoun—not 'I like to travel,' but 'Travelling is the best of educations.'

POLYSYNDETON. Polysyndeton is the use of *and* to separate each member of a compound construction, especially the members of a series. Instead of 'A, B, and C,' poysyndeton uses 'A *and* B *and* C.' Mark Twain, describing a steamboat, writes: 'And the boat is rather a handsome sight, too. She is long and sharp and trim and pretty.' Had he used **asyndeton** in the last sentence, it would read 'She is long, sharp, trim, pretty.' Polysyndeton stresses equally each member of the series; it is slower and more emphatic than asyndeton. See **asyndeton**.

PREDICATE. The predicate is the part of a sentence or **clause** that contains a verb and all words related to it and states something about the subject. In the sentence 'John went home,' the predicate is 'went home'; In the sentence 'Inevitably the rights of the protesters will be acknowledged,' the predicate is 'will be acknowledged'.

PREPOSITION, PREPOSITIONAL PHRASE. A preposition is a word that shows the relationship (often spatial) between a noun and another word in the sentence: e.g. *under, at, before, in, of, through*. A preposition and its object form a *prepositional phrase*. In the following examples, the prepositional phrases are italicized: 'He came *from a small village in the Eastern Townships of Quebec*'; 'He dodged *through the traffic*, leaping *from side to side*.'

PRINCIPLE CLAUSE. Another word for *main clause*. See **clause**.

QUALIFICATION, QUALIFIER. Usually a sweeping statement must be slightly altered or modified in the interest of truth. This modification or adjustment we call qualification, and a word or phrase that achieves this modification a qualifier. Thus, George Orwell writing of Dickens might have said, 'One cannot point to a single one of his central characters who is primarily interested in his job.' But what he does say in order to be accurate is this: 'With the doubtful exception of David Copperfield (merely Dickens himself), one cannot point to a single one of his central characters who is primarily interested in his job.' Qualifiers are often necessary, but they must not overshadow the statements they qualify.

RELATIVE CLAUSE, RELATIVE PRONOUN. A relative clause is a **dependent clause** introduced by a *relative pronoun*. The relative pronouns are *who, whom, whose, which, what, that*, and their compounds (*whoever, whatever*, etc.). In the sentence 'The man *who came to dinner* is my uncle,' the relative clause, in italics, is introduced by the relative pronoun 'who'.

RESTRICTIVE MODIFIER (or RESTRICTIVE ELEMENT). A phrase or clause that identifies or is essential to the meaning of a term is a restrictive modifier. In the sentence, 'The book *that my aunt gave me* is missing,' the restrictive modifier, in italics, identifies the missing book. It should not be set off by commas. A *non-restrictive modifier* is not needed to identify the term and is usually set off by commas, as in the following example: 'This book, *which my aunt gave me*, is one of my favourites.' A non-restrictive modifier can be omitted from the sentence without changing its essential meaning; a restrictive modifier cannot.

RHETORICAL QUESTION. A rhetorical question is a question asked for dramatic effect: 'What student of politics has not heard of Karl Marx or Thomas Jefferson?' It does not normally require an answer. In prose, rhetorical questions often serve an organizing purpose, setting up the point the writer wishes to develop: 'Who has not heard of this man's outstanding qualities?'

RUN-ON SENTENCE (or FUSED SENTENCE). A run-on sentence is a sentence in which two independent **clauses** are joined without either punctuation or **coordinate conjunction**: 'She missed the bus through no fault of her own the night before her brother had promised to wake her.' A **comma splice** occurs when two independent clauses are joined by a comma only: 'Alfred had gone to the movies all day, he had said that he wanted to get away from everyone.'

SENTENCE. See **complex sentence**, **compound-complex sentence**, **compound sentence**, **simple sentence**.

SENTENCE FRAGMENT. See **fragment**.

SIGNPOST. A signpost is any word, **phrase**, **clause**, or sentence that tells us what the writer plans to do next, is currently doing, has already done, or will not do at all. Examples of signposts are: 'Next we must consider . . .'; 'This is a point we shall treat more fully in the following chapter; here we must concentrate upon . . .'; 'As was noted in the preceding section, . . .'; 'This is a matter, which, interesting though it is, cannot be discussed in this essay.' Like **pointers**, signposts can be overused as well as used too little.

SIMILE. Using *like* or *as*, a simile makes a brief comparison between things seemingly unlike: 'The air seemed blindingly clear and cold, like arctic summer' (Orwell, p. 319). 'When all is done,' writes Sir William Temple, 'human life is, at the greatest and best, but like a forward child that must be played with and humoured a little to keep it quiet till it falls asleep, and then the care is done.' At times the simile can be rather extended:

> 'Anybody, like a schoolmaster, a stage director or an orchestral conductor, whose business it is to teach others to do something, knows that, on occasion, the quickest—perhaps the only—way to get those under him to do their best is to make them angry.' (W.H. Auden)

The purpose of simile is the same as that of **metaphor**.

SIMPLE SENTENCE. A simple sentence contains one subject–verb nucleus: 'The *boys rowed* across the lake.' It is possible for a sentence to have multiple subjects and verbs, yet to remain simple so long as these form only one nucleus: 'The *boys and girls rowed* across the lake, *had* a picnic on the other side, *enjoyed* a brief swim, and then *came* home.'

SPLIT INFINITIVE. A split infinitive is a construction in which a word is placed between *to* and the base verb: '*to* completely *finish*'. Many still object to this kind of construction, but splitting infinitives is sometimes necessary when the alternatives are awkward or ambiguous. Be aware, however, that splitting infinitives can also result in awkward sentences, as in the following example: 'She would try *to*, as often as she possibly could, *pay* her taxes on time.'

SQUINTING MODIFIER. A squinting modifier is a **misplaced modifier** that could be connected to elements on either side, making the meaning ambiguous: 'When he wrote the letter *finally* his boss thanked him'; 'The prime minister said *after* the election he would not raise taxes.'

STRAIGHTFORWARD MOVEMENT. See **interrupted movement**.

SUBORDINATE CLAUSE. Another word for *dependent clause*. See **clause**, **dependent clause**.

SUBORDINATE CONJUNCTION. See **conjunction**.

SYMBOL. A symbol is a person, place, or thing that both exists in its own right as something real and tangible and also stands for something else—an attitude, a belief, a quality, a value. Thus, a rose is a beautiful flower that also is symbolic of love. More broadly speaking, however, the word *symbol* is applied to an object whose only function is to stand for something other than itself. Thus, the Canadian flag is a piece of coloured cloth which is also a symbol of Canada.

TONE. A writer's tone results from (1) his attitude toward the subject and (2) his attitude toward the reader. A writer may love his subject, despise it, revere it, laugh at it, or seem detached from it. He may wish to shock his reader, outrage him, charm him, play upon his prejudices, amuse him, or merely inform him in the briefest and most efficient way possible. A writer conveys his tone largely through diction, through the connotations of the words he uses. But tone may be carried by sentence structure as well.

TOPIC SENTENCE (or TOPIC STATEMENT). The topic sentence is the controlling idea, or key point, or central idea of a paragraph. Most often it stands as the first sentence in a paragraph or occurs near the beginning. However, some paragraphs are constructed so that details are first given, and these lead to the main point in the last sentence of the paragraph. Another form, much less common, is the paragraph in which the topic sentence is implied. Becoming more frequent today is the topic sentence that occurs at the beginning of one paragraph and is the main idea not only of that paragraph but of the two or three (or even more) following paragraphs, all of which explain, or substantiate, the topic sentence at the beginning of the first paragraph.

TRANSITION, TRANSITIONAL. See **connective**.

TRICOLON. A tricolon is a sentence consisting of three clearly defined parts of roughly equal length and weight. Usually the three parts are independent **clauses**: 'Her showmanship was superb; her timing matchless; her dramatic instinct uncanny' (Carey McWilliams).

VERBAL. The present participle, the past participle, and the gerund are all forms of the verb called verbals. A verbal cannot make a statement by itself, but it is derived from a verb and can take an object or be modified by an adverb. The key point to remember about verbals is that they look like verbs but they are not verbs because they do not function as verbs do.

The present participle ends in *–ing* (*running, thinking, believing, hearing, trying*). The past participle either ends in *–d, –ed, –t, –n, –en* (*heard, believed, heard, tried, taken*) or changes its vowel (*ran, sung, begun*). Although participles look like verbs, in fact they function as adjectives (the *running* dog, the *thinking* journalist, the *believing* policeman, an *exciting* trip to Paris).

Participial phrases are word groups built around participles; as modifiers they are an efficient way of working additional information into a sentence.

The *gerund* is really a participle, but it functions as a noun rather than as an adjective. Usually it is the present participle that is used in this way: '*Jogging* is good exercise'; '*Meditating*, as a form of relaxation, has many benefits'; *Hitting* is essential for anyone who wants to play in the NHL.'

VOICE. Generally in composition courses, voice means whether the action designated by the verb originates in the subject (the active voice) or is received by the subject (the passive voice). Here, however, voice means the illusion—common in good prose—of a unique personality speaking to the reader.

THEMATIC INDEX

AUTHOR-TITLE INDEX

50